Society in India

Society in India

David G. Mandelbaum

Popular Prakashan
www.popularprakashan.com

Published by
Asmita Mohite for
POPULAR PRAKASHAN PVT. LTD.
301, Mahalaxmi Chambers
22, Bhulabhai Desai Road
Mumbai - 400 026
info@popularprakashan.com

First Indian Edition 1972
Reprint in 1984
Reprint in 1989
Reprint in 1990
Reprint in 2008
Reprint in 2010
Reprint in 2016
Reprint in 2021
Reprint in 2025

(3061)
ISBN: 978-81-7154-013-6

PRINTED IN INDIA
by Trinity Academy For Corporate Training Ltd.
Pune

To
Ruth

Contents

Volume Two: Change and Continuity

PART V: VILLAGE, REGION, CIVILIZATION

PART VI: RECURRENT CHANGE THROUGH SOCIAL MOBILITY

Preface

The idea of this work began soon after I started my first field research in India in 1937. Like other students of the people of India, I was struck by the great diversity among them and yet I could sense the common qualities of society and civilization which they shared. These shared qualities have been noted by many earlier writers, but their observations lacked the detailed information available in modern field studies and were not guided by the concepts developed in recent years in cultural-social anthropology and in other social sciences. It seemed to me that a new general frame for understanding the Indian people and their society was possible; such a frame was clearly needed in order to understand particular groups and to grasp the trends of social change.

My military service in India, Ceylon, and Burma in 1943–45 brought me to a wide variety of places and considerably enlarged my knowledge of South Asian peoples. A period of field work in India in 1949–50 again stimulated me to thinking about the common ground of Indian social relations. In 1957–58 a fellowship at the Center for Advanced Study in the Behavioral Sciences enabled me to begin writing a general account of Indian society. A brief stay in India in 1958–59 gave me additional data for the analysis I had under way. The draft manuscripts of this phase of the work were read by several colleagues and friends; Cora DuBois' comments were particularly useful. These appraisals were encouraging but convinced me that in certain matters I needed to develop a different approach and a new set of concepts. For several years I turned to other projects and meanwhile tried to work out ideas that would help bring together in an orderly way the large body of data on Indian society, data that were rapidly being increased and immeasurably improved by the generation of fine anthropologists, both Indian and non-Indian, who began their field studies in India after national independence.

In 1963–64 I was Senior Fellow in New Delhi of the American School of Indian Studies and was able then to give more attention to this project. This work has taken a long time to complete not only because of the size of the task and because of personal vicissitudes, but also because some of the key concepts were developed as the work progressed. As these new ideas took shape, some parts of what had already been written had to be recast.

Many of my colleagues at Berkeley have been helpful, particularly Murray B. Emeneau (companion in my first field experience in India) and Gerald D. Berreman. I have mulled over the nature of Indian society with anthropologists of several academic generations when they were students; among those from whose knowledge I have continued to benefit are Alan Beals, Henry Orenstein, and Surajit Sinha. Fellow anthropologists in India have been helpful over many years. I owe special thanks to M. N. Srinivas, N. K. Bose, and Mrs. Irawati Karve.

Support for the present work has come from several sources, including the Guggenheim Foundation, the Center for Advanced Study in the Behavioral Sciences, the American Institute of Indian Studies, the Committee on Research and the Center for South Asian Studies of the University of California, Berkeley. To them I express my grateful appreciation. Among the administrative officers whose efficient skills facilitated my work, I am especially obliged to D. D. Karve and

P. R. Mehendiratta of the American Institute of Indian Studies and to Ralph Tyler and Preston Cutler of the Center for Advanced Study in the Behavioral Sciences. I am indebted to Mrs. Anne Brower, editor for the Department of Anthropology at Berkeley, for her editorial aid, her fine perception and patience. Hundreds of villagers have helped me toward some understanding of the people of India. Two who were among my first guides and friends were the late K. Sulli of Kollimalai village and M. N. Thesingh of Horanelli village, both in the Nilgiris district. To my family go the deepest thanks of all.

Berkeley, California **David G. Mandelbaum**

VOLUME ONE

CONTINUITY AND CHANGE

PART I

INTRODUCTION

CHAPTER 1

Task, Concepts, and Scope

There was an observant Greek ambassador in India about 300 B.C., Megasthenes, whose account of the country and its people gives us our first general view of India as seen by a visitor. Megasthenes took note of the special way in which Indian society was organized. He observed that the people divided themselves into a number of occupationally specialized groups, that a person could marry only within his own group, and that no one could change affiliation from one group to another (McCrindle 1877, pp. 85, 212, 1901, p. 55; R. C. Majumdar 1960, pp. 224–226, 236–238, 263–268).

Many other voyagers to India after Megasthenes remarked upon this distinctive social order. It regulated a large part of public and private behavior; it was a most important concern of the people of the land. It seemed both familiar and quite unfamiliar to a visitor. It was familiar in that like tended to marry like elsewhere; sons commonly followed their father's occupation in the voyager's homeland; a hierarchy of society and privileges of rank were not strange to anyone. What did strike observers as unfamiliar was the rigor of these social divisions, the bases on which the divisions were made, and the thoroughgoing way in which they were applied to all aspects of life.

Because this kind of social order has been a central interest for a great civilization and a huge population, much has been written about Indian society. Both Indian and non-Indian writers have used the term "caste," originally from the Portuguese, for the prevalent social order in India as well as the component groups within that order. The very bulk of the literature has discouraged a good many readers who have sought a general understanding of Indian society. Some have been confused by the large tomes packed with details but devoid of clarifying concepts. Those writings that are more lucid and cogent generally cover only a limited part of the subject without making much attempt to trace how the various parts are fitted together. A good many readers, plunged into detailed descriptions of caste practices, come away with the feeling that Indian society is complex and inchoate beyond the hope of comprehension.

Indian society is indeed complex, but not necessarily beyond reasonable understanding, provided that the fundamental uniformities of caste behavior are grasped. Nor is it inchoate. Villagers use and manipulate their social organization in regular ways. They generally have no great difficulty in understanding the social arrangements of villages other than their own. One way of getting at the basic regularities in Indian society is to look at that society, and at its various components, as a system. Such a view directs attention to the whole social organization within which each component group functions. Emphasis on the whole helps to clarify the nature of the component groups because the function and definition of any group depends in large part on the relations of its members with members of other groups. Each person acts in more than one social role; he can take a number of different positions within his social system. The roles he is taught to assume and how he fulfills them often involve choice, strain, conflict, decision. The regular outcome of recurrent conflict and decision is also integral to the social system.

In taking this perspective, the student of society does more than observe the actors as though through the invisible fourth wall of a stage set. He must understand their actions in their own terms and incorporate the importance of their outlook and feelings into his larger view of their social system. In that larger view, it is possible to distinguish between the repetitive dynamic that is inherent in any social system and those changes that alter the nature of a whole system.

The Concepts of Social System and of Caste Order

A social system consists of a set of groups whose members together perform certain functions that they do not accomplish as separate groups. The groups are thus interdependent, and they are interdependent in a particular arrangement. That is to say, the participants in each group act in regular, anticipated ways toward members of the other groups and toward the external environment. When some participants do not carry out the kind of *interchange* that others in the system anticipate, the others respond in regular ways of *counterchange* to restore some systemic regularity to their relations.

The boundaries of a social system are therefore defined by the limits of interchange and counterchange among participant members and groups. The participants' awareness that they are interacting in regular ways is usually an important factor in the maintenance of any social system, but the description and analysis of a social system is primarily the analyst's formulation of the regularities in the participants' actions.

The members of a single family and their relations with each other can be viewed as comprising a system of social relations in themselves. However, the social scientist's focus is on a wider scale and so we have tried to formulate not only those systemic regularities that occur within and among the families of a particular place and social level, but also those that we can discern among most village families in India.

In addition to family systems, Indian villagers typically maintain lineages, the endogamous groups called *jatis*, and village communities, all of which may usefully be described and analyzed as systems. When a system of lineage organization is discussed, the component families are treated as subsystems of a lineage. Lineages can, in turn, be viewed as subsystems of a jati. People of different jatis commonly work together (and sometimes compete) in their village; in this sense, jatis may be seen as component groups of the system of village-community relations. For certain purposes we can treat villages as component parts of regions or of administrative units, which in turn can be taken as subsystems within the whole society of the people of India.

However, no living society, certainly not a vast and complex one, actually works as smoothly and rationally as an abstracted flow chart might imply. An individual fulfills many roles in various systems. There are myriad interrelations among the roles and systems in which any one person takes part. What is attempted here is to sort out several of the principal institutions of Indian society—notably family, jati, and village—to understand them both as systems and as subsystems of the larger society, to indicate some regularities among a person's roles in various subsystems, and to formulate the social changes that people in India have made and are now making.

This conception of social system is an underlying premise of the analysis, but each part of the analysis is not closely structured after the definition of system. In each part component groups (or individuals) are noted, as are common patterns of interchange and characteristic ways of counterchange, but not necessarily in that order or in any complete way, mainly because adequate data on each subject are not yet available for such regular procedures.

There is a further examination of the concept of social system in Appendix I, together with a discussion of the concept of social stratification as it pertains to an understanding of caste organization in India.

The kind of social system that is called a caste system involves a special quality in the order of interdependence. It is a quality of pervasive inequality among the component groups. Inequality in privilege and reward, in dominance and subordination, is in one sense a universal characteristic of human society. Adults are not the equals of children. Each sex has its own spheres of privilege and dominance, even in societies where males are said to be all dominant. In most societies, whole groups have different degrees of dominance and privilege as against other groups; that is, most societies are stratified to some degree, either in the ranking of functioning groups or in class attributions. The term "stratification" emphasizes this hierarchical arrangement.

Human societies can be placed along a continuum of stratification. Some are very little stratified. For example, two tribal groups mentioned later, the Chenchu and the Paliyan, live by hunting and gathering; the people in these groups are so scattered and their social organization is so simple that there is little possibility for stratification. More stratified are those societies in which people sort themselves into classes, groupings differentiated in privilege but relatively open to recruits. Beyond such societies, at the other extreme of the stratification range, are those societies in which people group themselves into more sharply defined, more rigid and pervasive divisions with strongly regulated relations among the divisions. These are caste orders.

Though Indian caste society has often been depicted as a static social order, in reality the people of India have kept adjusting their social systems and at times have made fundamental changes in them. All social systems are used with some flexibility, if only because people have to cope with the dynamics of the seasonal round and of the life cycle. The biological stages of the human life cycle induce a cycle of family development, and the cyclical pattern of family growth, division, and reconstitution in India will be discussed in the chapters on family relations.

Another kind of repetitive change involves shifts in rank positions. Such shifts typically begin when lower groups become strong enough to challenge their superiors. They meet opposition and some are quelled, but others succeed in raising their rank. In so doing, they revise the previous order of precedence, though not the structure of the local order. Yet another recurrent process in India has typically been started when the followers of a religious leader form a sect; at first they deny certain features of the existing social system, but in time they become reabsorbed into that system. Tribal groups also have frequently been absorbed into caste orders.

In addition to these recurrent changes, there have also been systemic changes. The earliest literary sources in India, the Vedas, reflect a system of relatively open classes in which people carried on a culture and society that were basically different from those of later times, though the later forms were developed out of the earlier ones. G. S. Ghurye outlines four periods of social development. The Vedic period, which in his estimate ended about 600 B.C., was succeeded by a period in which the trend toward a thoroughgoing caste structure had begun. (Megasthenes observed Indian society in this second period.) During the third period a number of features of "classic" caste society became crystallized. Then, about the tenth or eleventh century, the system was developed that remained in operation with considerable consistency for about a thousand years (Ghurye 1961, pp. 42–111).

Within the past century the people of India have been strongly affected by the worldwide tides of change. The extent to which the technological and social-political innovations are bringing about systemic changes are noted throughout much of the following discussion and are reviewed in the final chapter.

The Nature of the Evidence

Social change, whether on a grand systemic scale or within a recurrent local cycle, flows from the choices, decisions, and dilemmas faced by individual men and women. Our study tries to include the individual's perspective, his understandings and motivations. To attempt to do this for so large a part of the world's population and for so complex a civilization, some writers have remarked, is to undertake a task of doubtful feasibility. Denzil Ibbetson began his extensive account of Punjab groups for the 1881 census with the statement that the only thing he knew about caste groups was that he knew nothing and he was not quite sure of that (1916, p. 1). In the opening passages of his book *Social Change in Modern India*, Professor Srinivas writes, "I am acutely aware of the difficulties and hazards involved in making statements claiming to hold good for Hindus all over India" (1966, p. 2).

Still, it is a task worth trying and one that has been made more feasible by the advances in research data and ideas during recent decades. Yet despite the notable improvement in research information, there remains the question of how adequate that information is as a basis for the generalizations that are drawn from it here. One answer is that though only a relatively few of more than half a million Indian villages have been studied or even surveyed, there are studies and surveys from all the major parts of the country, and the evidence so far seems to be consistent with the principles of social action that are formulated here. Moreover, the villagers among whom anthropologists and other social scientists have lived and from whom they have learned are aware of similarities and differences within their society; they can tell about those they see, and their generalizations can be tested against wider evidence. The generalizations presented here will be tested and undoubtedly revised as more data become available and sharper concepts are developed. But, obviously, no generalization can be proved, disproved, or modified before it is formulated. The formulations given in this study are offered more as working hypotheses to help grasp the nature of Indian society than as final facts about its total composition. A biologist once used the folklore motif of the magic well to describe the study of bees. It is also apt for the study of the people of India—the more one draws up, the more there is to draw.

Greater use is made of recent works by trained observers, both Indian and non-Indian, than of the older writings by scholars in the classic tradition or by officials and travelers. Much of the older thought and evidence has been absorbed into the newer studies, and although some of the older accounts are still useful for social as well as historical analyses, the newer studies are generally much better based. Yet good as the modern observers often are, they have observed certain aspects of Indian life relatively little. There are few studies of social relations in towns and cities. The emphasis here is on villagers, not only because the bulk of India's people are villagers, but also because we have so few good studies of town and city life. Although the roots of adult behavior and of personality lie in the common experiences of childhood, there are as yet only a handful of studies of childhood and child rearing in India that are based on close observation and informed research design.

In addition, there is a paucity of usable statistical data on significant matters. Outlines of behavior patterns can be drawn, but most questions of variation within a range and of distribution and deviation await more and better quantitative data. The present state of the evidence permits statements that something "often" or "characteristically" occurs when the present state of our inquiry requires additional information about how often and under what circumstances. Some good statistical data are available and have been used; but other published figures are difficult to use because it is not clear what was counted, in what manner, and for what purpose. So the case examples given here illustrate general conditions and concepts. They exemplify some part of the general range of behavior that is outlined; they do not necessarily indicate a mean or mode within that range.

The Scope, the Time, the Focus

Village society is the principal subject of this study. More than four-fifths of India's people are counted as villagers. Traditional urban society in India seems to have been basically similar to village society, insofar as we can tell from the studies that are available, though in recent decades educated city people have been in the forefront of social change. Because the village is the characteristic locale for the social relations discussed here, the term "villagers" is often used for the people whose activities are discussed. Much of what is said, however, applies as well to many town and city residents.

The geographic scope of this work includes mainly the people of present-day India. Examples from Pakistan villages are given for particular purposes, especially in the discussion of social organization among Muslims. But the civilization of India was developed over the whole subcontinent; every major linguistic region and major religion contributed to it.

The time is the present. The main period of observation is roughly the middle third of the twentieth century. Before that period considerable social change was under way, but during it the people of India have undergone especially marked changes. Some groups have been in the vanguard; they have changed far more than most of their countrymen. Others, not many, have been little affected. Most villagers try to hold firmly to some of the traditional ways while reaching for the benefits of modern ways.

This sketch of Indian social organization, then, does not apply in equal detail to all social groups or to all aspects of life at all times. It is intended as a general survey of basic social principles and patterns followed by most of the people of India. It is more a grammar of social relations than a dictionary of caste practices or a glossary of names. A sketch cannot show everything that is important at once. We begin with a discussion of the general nature of Indian society and of the customary relations among members of different groups. Then the chief components—family, jati, and village—are examined. The dynamic functions of these components are next considered as they have been adaptively used in the overall system of Indian society and as they are being evolved at the present time.

The focus is on the principal groups of village society and on the patterns of interchange and counterchange among them. An emphasis on religion, or economics, or politics would entail a different treatment. This societal emphasis is one that is made by many of the people themselves; the local social order is commonly a paramount concern of village life. The impact of other forces—economic, religious, political, demographic, psychological—is taken into account, but these forces are not the center of our inquiry.

The inquiry is meant for several kinds of inquirers. A reader seeking a general introduction to Indian society may find this work useful. Such readers will encounter a relatively limited number of technical and indigenous terms. The transcription of indigenous terms follows general usage rather than attempting strict phonological accuracy. Efforts toward such accuracy may become confusing or spurious, partly because there is no standard pronunciation throughout India for widely used terms and the pronunciation of a term usually varies within a linguistic region as well as among regions. It seemed better for our purposes to dispense with most diacritical marks and special typography. The term "caste" itself has often been used confusingly to denote the whole system as well as several of its components; here it is used mainly as an adjective, as in "caste system," rather than as a noun.

Some of the common geographic terms are not precisely defined in many of the works on India. What is meant by "South India" is relatively clear; the term refers to the regions in which the principal Dravidian languages are spoken, chiefly the states of Andhra Pradesh, Mysore, Madras, and Kerala. The term "southern India" refers to the same regions; "western India" is usually taken to mean most of the present states of Maharashtra and Gujarat. But "northern India" and "North India" are usually less well defined. "North India" is here used for the Hindi-speaking region centered in the state of Uttar Pradesh. The term "northern India" refers to a vast territory, the area from Bengal to Rajasthan, indeed almost all of India except for those regions included in southern and western India.

Specialists in the study of Indian society will find much here that they already know, though they may also find familiar ideas and data in unfamiliar contexts. Whatever may be usefully new to them has resulted in large part from the attempt to bring together the rich results of their research.

Those whose home is in India may find that the general description does not correspond at all points with their personal experiences. They may also feel a lack of those enlivening details and variations that make an abstracted view very different from the substance of reality. Analytical truth is rarely a good mirror for emotional truth, and the subject of caste relations in India is a matter of profound personal feeling for many.

In the opening sentence of a perceptive article on caste patterns, Surajit Sinha writes, "Social reformers and political leaders in India tend to regard the caste system as a major stumbling block to national integration, economic development and the moral regeneration of the nation" (1967, p. 92). Sinha does not contest the moral issues involved, but takes his first task to be that of showing the principles of interaction among caste groups. This is a commendable approach both for those who study Indian society and for those who want to improve it. It is most useful to have a clear understanding of what caste relations really entail in order to have a firm basis for evaluations and for programs of reform.

That understanding has been notably advanced in recent years by the work of both Indian and non-Indian scholars. Professor M. N. Srinivas has discussed the advantages and disadvantages of studying one's own society (1966, pp. 147–163). There are comparable benefits and drawbacks in studying a society other than one's own. In the study of Indian society there has happily been fruitful cooperation between both kinds of research workers. All students of Indian society have gained from the earlier work of scholars of various countries, among them J. N. Bhattacharya, L. K. Anantakrishna Iyer (Ayyar), and G. S. Ghurye of India; C. Bouglé and Emile Senart of France; Max Weber of Germany; L. S. S. O'Malley and J. H. Hutton of England. Each of these men has contributed to our knowledge from his particular perspective. Taken together, their works and those of similarly able observers have enabled us to view the Indian social scene from our present point of vantage.

CHAPTER 2

The Basic Groups and Groupings

At the beginning of a study of Indian society, two of its general characteristics should be noted. One is that certain basic ideas about society were, and are, shared by most people in the land. Yet social relations have been regulated locally, by the residents of a village or of a limited vicinity. The macro-themes for social behavior have been realized largely through micro-organizations.

Another characteristic lies in the difference between the common theory about social organization that villagers usually express and the ways in which they actually organize their social relations. A prime element in this discrepancy is their concept of *varna*. It is the popular theory, based on Hindu scripture, that society is composed of people in four ranked categories called varnas. In reality, not all Hindus are subsumed in those categories, and frequently there are differences of opinion in a village about who belongs to which category. Though insufficient as a sociological theory, this concept nonetheless is a significant factor in villagers' social perceptions and actions. They use it as a handy gross classification of others in their society, making much finer classifications for those within their own social groups. The jati is such a social group—a unit of great importance to the villager, and a basic component of the social system.

JATI

The answer a villager gives to the question, "Who are you?" depends, as it does everywhere in the world, on who is asking and on what the villager thinks the questioner wants or should know (cf. Mandelbaum 1956). Yet villagers throughout India are likely to include in their answer the information that they are members of the particular group to which both their parents and all their kin belong. To further questions they explain that each person is a member of this group by virtue of his birth into it; he may marry only within it; his (or her) children will also belong to that group.

The people of each endogamous group follow certain characteristic patterns of behavior and have certain assigned attributes—among them a specialized occupation—according to which the group is ranked in the local hierarchy. The criteria for ranking have to do, village respondents declare, with the ritual pollution and purity that are inherent in the group's practices. These ritual criteria are usually mentioned first. More closely questioned on this matter, a villager is likely to allow that considerations of power and wealth also enter into the ranking. Every member of the endogamous group shares in the rank position of the group and this affects his relations with members of other groups.

A villager from a low-ranked group may hasten to add that the defiling practices attributed to his group are imposed or inadvertent or nonexistent or unimportant. He will point out some groups in the locality that, in his opinion, should be ranked below his own and some supposedly superior groups to whom his own people are, at least, equal. Most villagers, however, assume that there should be a ranked hierarchy of groups, even though they may disagree about the particulars of the ranking. They also agree that members of their own group must keep themselves separate from those of other, especially lower, groups, not only in marriage but also in domestic intimacies such as eating together, and must observe a host of other prescribed distances.

The term *jati* is used here for this endogamous group. The word is common to a number of the languages of northern India, being derived from the Sanskrit root meaning "to be born." This word and equivalent terms in other Indian languages carry the connotation of one's social birthright as well as one's inherited group (cf. Karve 1965, p. 139; Ghurye 1961, pp. 48, 64).

Explanations of jati by villagers can be summarized in this definition. A jati is an endogamous, hereditary social group that has a name and a combination of attributes. All members of a jati are expected to act according to their jati attributes, and each member shares his jati's status in the social hierarchy of a village locality in India. Like all capsule definitions of fundamental social relations, this one begs many questions. If it did not, there would be little more to say on the subject.

The term "jati-group" refers to the members of a jati who live in the same village. They are likely to have more frequent communication with each other than with jati fellows in other villages. An Indian village typically holds several jati-groups, from two to more than thirty, each with its traditional rights and duties, its privileges and restraints, its special contribution in services or manufactures to the total functioning of the community. A complement of jati-groups may include landowning cultivators; tenants; priests; artisans such as carpenters, blacksmiths, and potters; service groups such as barbers and launderers; and menial workers such as sweepers and laborers. The people of each group in the village maintain marriage and kinship ties with their compeers in other villages. The endogamous group, the jati, includes members spread across a number of villages.

Every person is thus a member of his village and of his jati. The village, or a set of neighboring villages, forms a localized community of specialized, interdependent groups. The members of a jati, in their respective villages, form a set of actual or potential kin. A man depends on the village community for his livelihood and for services necessary to maintain his jati's style of life, but the position and the practices of his jati mold his career, define the range of his kinsmen and his closest companions, and affect a large part of his social relations.

Within a man's jati are those with whom he may have close and unquestioned relations. He may form a friendship with a man of different jati, but it is not usually as durable and unconstricted as a friendship within the jati. He may deal with others daily, but his closest links, those of marriage and kinship, are only with his jati fellows. His life and aspirations are intertwined with theirs. So a person's jati affects the nature of his relations with many other people. His family typically commands his most intense loyalties and efforts and his village encompasses much of his life, but his jati provides him with his circle of kin; it is usually a source of social support, and contributes much of his identity in village affairs.

Flexibilities in Jati Relations and Roles

Although considerations of jati are important, there are some activities in which the jati affiliations of the actors are not highly relevant. In work situations, men of widely different jatis may work side by side without keeping their usual physical and social distance. In play also, jati considerations are muted; two wrestlers, for example, may be from jatis whose men otherwise keep considerably farther apart. In some situations of devotional worship, devotees from different jatis may mingle in a closeness that is not allowed in other contexts.

Villagers commonly speak of a jati as though its members concentrated on one occupation and maintained rigid jati boundaries. The facts reveal more flexibility. A jati's traditional occupation does not necessarily restrict all members of the jati to that calling. A villager of a priestly jati often manages land or grows crops. Some in a carpenter jati are carpenters, but others may be farmers, or soldiers, or, nowadays, teachers or government officials. What the traditional calling did was to limit the possible range of a villager's occupations; for example, a man of priestly jati was not permitted by his jati fellows to engage in defiling work such as handling hides or leather.

Conversely, a leatherworker was not permitted by the higher jatis to enter the precincts of the high gods, much less to act as a priest in their worship. A leatherworker, however, may be a farmer, since agriculture is open to all. In one village of Kanpur district, U.P., men of the leatherworker jati now engage in seven occupations, including farming and masonry as well as leather work. There is no bar in this locality to their being cart drivers or tradesmen, but they do not have the capital for such enterprises (Sharma 1956a, pp. 122–123). The range of occupations open to men of any jati is now wider than it was at the beginning of the twentieth century, but many still follow their jati's traditional work, and many keep within the range of occupations open to those of their jati.

Marriage is the relation that demarcates each jati most clearly. All marriages are supposed to be between a bride and groom of the same jati; no marriage may be made outside it. Yet there is some degree of flexibility even in this. A wealthy man may not find a suitably prestigious bridegroom for his daughter among the families known to be of the same endogamous circle. In his search he may discover in a more distant village a desirable groom of a family of jati name and status position similar to his own. His task then is to uncover some previous marriage between the familial forebears of the couple. Given mutual desire and diligent ransacking of real or supposed connections, such historical precedent may be found and the marriage arranged. (Other means of reinterpreting jati boundaries will be noted later.) Most marriages do indeed take place within a limited cohort, from a few hundred to several thousand families in a given territory, but a villager tends to view his jati as a more firmly bounded, more clearly demarcated unit than it may actually be.

Groups and Groupings within the Jati

Each person belongs to certain groups within his jati. One such group is the family. Related families commonly act together as a lineage. The jati-group is another unit within a jati. In addition, some jatis have clan groupings. In some jatis families also are ranked in prestige groupings.

The best kind of family, in the common belief, is the joint family, a family in which two or more married men who are closely related—as father and son, or as brothers—live together in one household with their wives, sons, and unmarried daughters. All share a common kitchen and a common purse. This ideal form is actually realized, even if only for a short period, in the development of most Indian families, but at any one time there are also many nuclear families, consisting of one married couple, their unmarried children, and perhaps one or two other dependents.

A family usually cooperates with closely related families in a localized lineage. A lineage is a set of families whose men are related in patrilineal descent—perhaps as sons and grandsons of a set of brothers—whose households are commonly near each other in the village, and whose members exchange many kinds of mutual support. The tie that binds the men of a lineage is their descent from the same, known, patrilineal ancestor. (Some jatis of Kerala observed matrilineal descent, but as will be noted later, their jati organization followed the same broad principles used by patrilineal peoples.)

A larger grouping consists of those who trace their patrilineal descent from a remote and usually legendary ancestor. The members of such a grouping, here called a "clan," are dispersed among a great many villages and share in few or no joint functions. A clan is usually more of an attributive grouping than it is a corporate group. The most common function of the clan is to distinguish eligible from ineligible spouses. It is an exogamous unit within the endogamous jati; a man may not marry a woman of his clan just as he may not marry one of his family or lineage.

The members of a jati-group, those of one jati who live in the same village, unite in action on occasion, especially in defense of their joint rights in the village. They usually consider themselves to be sharply distinctive in the village. Even when two or more jati-groups in a village are culturally very close and are treated alike by others, they may keep themselves socially separate. For example, there are two jati-groups of carpenters in Dewara village (Adilabad district of Andhra Pradesh). The members of one speak Marathi and the members of the other Telugu. Dube notes that "the two may not intermarry; language, dress, customs, and beliefs separate them still further" (1955a, p. 182).[1] Two jati-groups in a village may use the same language, have the same traditional occupation, and follow much the same jati customs, yet the members of each will cherish some unique traits that distinguish them from other groups. Others in the village may lump the two jati-groups together; usually the members of the two do not.

A different kind of distinction is commonly made within a jati. Some families are recognized as being more prestigious than others, either because of wealth, education, ancestral honor, or for other reasons. These classlike distinctions are not necessarily formalized, although as we will discuss

[1] There are a few jatis that include, in one endogamous unit, families from two different linguistic regions. Thus the Deshastha Rigvedi Brahmins include some families that speak Marathi and some that speak Kannada. A majority of the marriages within this jati are arranged between families of the same language, but there are some in which one spouse is from a Marathi-speaking family and the other from a Kannada-speaking family (Karve 1958b, p. 137). Such jatis, however, are exceptional and are usually groups that have been located along a linguistic boundary for centuries. is far more common for all jati fellows to speak one mother tongue.

later, such distinctions have sometimes led to the establishment of formal sections within the jati and occasionally to the formation of new jatis when the higher families split off from the rest.

In sum, a villager's interchange with others of his jati is largely through his roles as member of his family, lineage, and jati-group. But in his dealings with people of other jatis, a villager uses other social categories, such as jati-cluster, to define the roles and rules for interaction.

Jati-Cluster

A principal category used for dealing with people of other jatis is the jati-cluster. This is a set of separate jatis, classed together under one name, whose members are treated by others as having the same general status. It is easier to deal with many people, as one must in a complex society, by using jati-cluster categories rather than by regulating one's own behavior to each individual in terms of such narrower social distinctions as those of family or lineage or jati. The finer distinctions are necessary within the jati, not cutside it.

The jatis that are classed together are usually similar in traditional occupation, jati practices, and relative rank. When people of different jatis classed together in a cluster live in the same village, the members of each generally hold themselves socially apart from other jati-groups of the same jati-cluster, though all members of the cluster may be considered very much alike by other villagers.

Some jati-clusters include only a few jatis and several thousand people; others cover dozens of jatis and millions of people. In a smaller cluster, especially within a confined territory, the members of the component jatis know about each other and do act together on occasion. The fact that they all are treated in like manner by others paves the way for some joint action, especially defensive action. In a larger cluster, few may know the full spread of the cluster and concerted action does not occur (cf. Karve 1961, pp. 11–12). Under modern conditions of widening communication the people of a jati-cluster, who may not previously have acted together or have known of each other's existence, can now form associations.

An example of a small jati-cluster is that of the Badagas of the Nilgiri Hills in South India, who now number more than ninety thousand and are mainly cultivators. They are divided into several endogamous groups, each self-consciously different from the others, though all speak the distinctive Badaga language. A Badaga villager refers to himself, in his conversations and dealings with other Badagas, by the name of his group, such as Wodeya. This division within Badaga society is his main unit of self-identification among the people collectively known to outsiders as the Badagas. It is a unit of paramount importance to him, not only for marriage purposes, but also because much of his daily life is carried on with his jati fellows rather than with any others who may be Badagas in name and culture. There are some occasions, mainly ceremonial, in which any Badaga irrespective of jati may participate, but in other social contexts the various jatis remain as separate groups.

On the other hand, their neighbors, including the lower-ranked Kotas whom I have studied, are little concerned with these distinctions among Badagas; they tend to view all Badagas as much of a piece and refer to them as one. Kotas are indeed sensitive to individual differences, especially of wealth, among the Badagas with whom they have dealings, but the ritual gradations among Badaga jatis are of little concern to Kotas.

A much larger cluster consists of the many jatis of Maharashtra known as Kunbis. These jatis have some cultural characteristics in common. Villagers of this name work on the land and speak

Marathi. A jati called Kunbi is generally ranked below the farmer-military jatis called Maratha. Beyond these similarities there are wide differences among Kunbis in such matters as kinship arrangements, dress, and economic functions. Kunbis live in different parts of the Marathi-speaking region, and those of one group may not know of the existence of most of the others (Karve 1958b, pp. 126–127).

Two of the main jati-clusters in Gujarat are the Patidars and the Barias. Both are cultivators by traditional occupation, but the former are ranked higher than the latter. The Patidars tend to ignore differences in status among the Barias. In one village, as David Pocock reports, certain Baria families are superior in their ritual practices to some Patidar families. But this does not perturb the Patidar villagers who "*include* the higher levels of the Bāriā with the lower level of the Bāriā and so exclude them from any claim to equality." Several of the Baria families are more strictly vegetarian than are some Patidars, but their Patidar neighbors "refer to them simply as Baria and include them in the general statement 'The Bāriā eat meat'" (Pocock 1957b, p. 28).

This gross, oversimplified classification is useful; dealing with people of other jatis is simplified. One does not have to calculate and adjust to all the actual gradations of ritual practice among members of large and varied groups. All are Baria or Badaga (or some other inclusive term) and are so treated.

A villager follows the common human tendency to make finer social distinctions among those who are socially more intimate with him than among those with whom he has more distant relations. A farmer of a village in Gujarat, for example, knows that a local shopkeeper is likely to belong to one of the jatis collectively known as Bania and that Banias belong to the third of the four scriptural categories. He can deal with the shopkeeper on the basis of this gross classification. If the farmer were fully informed about the social position of the shopkeeper, he would know such details as that the shopkeeper was of the Sarta jati, of the Visa subdivision of that variety of Banias who originated in Desawal (Toothi 1935, p. 125). Further, he would know the status of the shopkeeper's family and lineage within the jati. It is unnecessary for the farmer to know all this; indeed it would be impossible for him to adjust his relations with all others on the basis of such extensive knowledge.

However, for the shopkeeper himself, detailed information about his jati is supremely important. He maintains his bonds of kinship on the basis of such information and he is likely to recruit his business assistants and associates from among his closer kinsmen. Many of his religious duties are bound up with family and jati obligations. He uses these fine perceptions to guide his intimate relations, and in doing so he helps maintain his jati as a firm unit in the local social order. The shopkeeper, in turn, is quite uninterested in the precise social position of his farmer customer. All he needs to know is the general category of the customer's jati because it will not do to serve a menial sweeper as though he were a member of a high jati and, still less, to speak to one of the highborn as though he were a sweeper.

In his study of Ramkheri village, Adrian Mayer has discussed these classifications from the perspective of social function (1960, pp. 270–275). When a man performs services for others in his village, Mayer comments, he is classed by them in a broad category. When he interacts with jati fellows in other villages as a kinsman, he is classed by them as belonging to narrower groups and groupings.

The social vantage of the perceiver is another factor in social perspective. A landowner of high rank is not much concerned about the divisions among the lowest in his village. He lumps them all as untouchables or, to use the term that Gandhi preferred, *Harijans*, "children of God." Conversely, those of the lowest groups are usually not much interested in the detailed social differences among the highest in the village. These powerful people are all overlords to them and have to be so treated.

Such differences in social perception are necessary in all complex societies. The finer perceptions about one's social intimates make for firm, viable social units; the grosser perceptions enable people of different units to carry on effective social relations. The more detailed distinctions made by Indian villagers have mainly to do with their groups of close interaction—family and lineage, jati-group and alliance within the village. The broader groupings are mainly those of jati-cluster and varna, both are taxonomic groupings more than they are corporate groups, attributed categories rather than interactional units (cf. Marriott 1959b).

Varna: Villagers' Theory and Theorists' Fallacy

The most widely known social categories are the four varnas, the principal parts of society as given by the sage Manu in the law code of perhaps the second century A.D. (cf. Ghurye 1961, pp. 87–97; Dutt 1931, pp. 4–23). Most villagers accept the varna categories as the primordial makeup of their society. Into that scheme local jatis and jati-clusters are fitted.

The origin story, first noted in a hymn of the earliest scripture, the Rig-Veda, has it that the four varnas came into being from the body of the primeval man. From his mouth issued the Brahmins, who became priests and scholars. From his arms came the Kshatriyas, warriors and rulers; from his thighs came the Vaishyas, tradesmen, and from his feet rose the Shudras, cultivators (Basham 1954, pp. 240–241). Traditionally, those in the Brahmin category are supposed to manage the culture through their control of religion, Kshatriyas to manage the society through their control of armed might, Vaishyas to manage the distributive economy through their control of trade, and Shudras to produce the economic wherewithal for the whole society.

Similar versions of the proper division of labor and the assignment of rank in a society have come out of other civilizations. Plato, for one, propounded a comparable plan. In the Manu version, high as well as low lived in the villages; the high ranks were not concentrated at urban or court centers. Hence all four varnas could be represented in a village, although the actual village hierarchy did not necessarily follow the four-ply model.

There were, and are, considerable discrepancies between the scriptural plan and the real social order. The scheme omits from Hindu society the many jatis of so-called untouchables whose services are essential for a traditional village order. Further, all four categories were not everywhere represented. In much of South India, there seem to have been few indigenous Kshatriyas or Vaishyas, the martial and the mercantile categories. Historically, the varnas of the early texts were more like open classes than like fixed social strata (Bouglé 1908, pp. 28–29; Dutt 1931, pp. 58 ff.; Prabhu 1954, pp. 290–342).

Moreover, the scriptural scheme is highly oversimplified in some ways and quite misleading in others. M. N. Srinivas has noted the main distortions implicit in it (1966, pp. 2–12). One is that there is a single all-India hierarchy without any variations between one region and another. The many variations in ranking will be discussed below; sometimes the same jati will be ranked higher in one village than in another not many miles away.

Another mistaken notion is that the varna divisions are the functioning groups of the social order. The principal groups of social interaction are families, lineages, jati-groups, jatis, village communities, and other groups, but not the varna categories.

A third distortion is that the hierarchal order stands as clear and accepted by all, when in fact vagueness and disputes about ranking are common. Ambiguities and conflicts about precise rankings are indeed regular features of the system. Finally, the varna plan has been interpreted to mean that the groups and order of Indian society are immutably fixed. Historical evidence shows that there has been a good deal of social change.

To an Indian villager, however, these gaps in the folk theory are of far less consequence than the uses of that theory. With it he can sort out the principal parts of society and can readily place an unfamiliar jati within the general scheme. It provides a summary evaluation of jati rank. Rising groups take one of the higher categories as model and target for their mobility efforts. And the fourfold division offers a simple, hierarchical plan of society for villagers who assume that society is hierarchically arranged.

The varna scheme corresponds well enough to most villagers' social experience so that it can be used for preliminary sorting. A villager typically knows that Brahmins were decreed as the highest of four social layers as far as ritual affairs are concerned. That usually fits with what he finds in his own village; jatis of the Brahmin category are commonly in the topmost bracket of the ritual hierarchy, even though men of a local Brahmin jati may be neither scholars nor priests. It does not worry him that a jati claiming to be Kshatriya may seem to be more farmer than warrior or that a jati claiming to be Vaishya holds dubious credentials for such classification.

People of the three higher varnas, Brahmins, Kshatriyas, and Vaishyas, are supposed to conduct themselves in close accord with scriptural rules for purity. The three categories are collectively called the "twice-born" varnas from the initiation ceremony undergone by males of the jatis classed in these varnas. In that rite, a boy is invested with the symbol of the sacred thread. Each initiate is thenceforth and forever supposed to wear the thread over his left shoulder. The rite is deemed a second birth; those who wear the sacred thread are *dvija*, twice-born, in contrast to all others who do not undergo a ritual second birth. This rite is no longer so meticulously performed among "twice-born" jatis as it traditionally was, and some of their men no longer bother to wear the sacred thread. Nevertheless, the varna scheme still applies, in that jatis classed in the higher varnas are commonly the most respectable and powerful in a village. Their members, for reasons discussed later, usually do observe purity rules more rigorously than do other villagers.

Another use of the varna scheme is in providing a simple, handy approximation of complex evaluations of jati rank. In Ramkheri village (Dewas district of Madhya Pradesh) the varna classification can "be seen as the best assessment of a caste's various rankings" (Mayer 1956, p. 138). There, as in other villages, the varna divisions do not quite fit the facts of the social organization. Mayer lists the village jatis in rank order and appends this note: "The Vaisya *varna* has been placed below the Kshatriya in the traditional manner. In Ramkheri, however, the vegetarianism of the former is said by many to make the Vaisya equal to, if not superior to, the Kshatriya" (Mayer 1956, pp. 138, 141). But such discrepancies are not taken by villagers as serious objections to the four-part classification.

The varna outline also offers a convenient way of assessing jatis of different geographic and linguistic regions. When a villager encounters people of unfamiliar jati, he can make a quick appraisal of them by asking about their position in the scale of four. Most jatis can be fitted into the procrustean frame of varna.

The three higher varnas also are taken as reference categories, that is as models for conduct, by aspiring people of lower jatis. Each model is also a target in the sense that a rising group tries to become accepted as legitimately belonging to one of the higher varnas. When its people become so accepted, they have achieved a principal aim of their mobility efforts.

Finally, the varnas provided a neat outline of social relations, which villagers like to think of a trimly hierarchical but which characteristically involve ambiguous positions, disputed rank, and overlapping jurisdictions. The precise rank of a jati-group in its village may be nebulous, and jati rankings are often differently given by different residents of the same village. But the varna outline assures villagers that there really is a changeless, India-wide hierarchy. "More important, perhaps," Mayer comments, "it helps to distinguish the hierarchy in the area of greatest obscurity, the middle reaches, where statements about varna membership are almost the only verbalizations of general status" (1956, p. 143).

The classical varna plan is a series of binary divisions (Leach 1967, pp. 10–11). Human beings are either within Hindu society or outside it. If they are within that society, Edmund Leach observes, they are either "twice-born" or ordinary persons. If they are twice-born, they are either religious or secular specialists; if they are secular, they are either warrior-rulers or merchants. If they are ordinary persons (Shudras), they are either "clean" or "unclean," depending on whether people of the "twice-born" varnas can accept water from their hands or have similar interchange with them.[2]

A society, like music, exists in time; it develops, changing yet formed, through time. Indian music flows with great spontaneity, but against the formed background of the tonic notes of the drone, the *thanpura*. Indian society has been full of changes and improvisations, but also against a background frame, the tonic themes of varna hierarchy. As the drone is an essential element in Indian music, so has the varna idea been essential in Indian society. Srinivas has commented that it is a matter for wonder that, in spite of the distortions of reality implicit in the varna model, it has continued to survive (1966, p. 4). Perhaps it has been used for so long just because of its distortions. People in complex societies tend to use some simple—indeed oversimple—theory of their society. The varna scheme has been such a theory, one that reflected and reinforced the basic attitude about social relations.

Students of society are familiar with theorists who, often unwittingly, shape their reports of a people's behavior to fit their theory. In this case, the people have provided the theoretical conception and have not been abashed by the lack of fit between fact and theory. That theory, we should note, has served its purposes for a long time.

Varna is frequently mentioned in Sanskrit scripture—jati less often. Emile Senart warned that the two terms are confused in the literary tradition, which, he wrote, "is less concerned with the faithful record of facts than with their arrangement in systems conforming to the tendencies of a strongly biased group" (1930, p. x). K. M. Panikkar has similarly noted (the emphasis is his) that "this four-fold division *is only ideological* and is not in any manner based on the facts of the social system. It is what Hindu sociologists wanted their society to be—a theory of caste-idealism unrelated to actual practice" (1956, p. 7).

Panikkar, a historian-statesman who successfully engaged in practical political affairs, underestimated the influence a popular theory can exert. The varna scheme may not have been well based on social facts but its long reign has certainly influenced the facts of Indian society.

---

[2] Anthony Wallace has observed that folk taxonomies require about four binary discriminations, perhaps the minimal level of cognitive capacity required to sort out such complex arrangements as kinship terminologies or military rank (1961, pp. 146–147). The varna scheme, with its four categories and with the distinction between clean and unclean Shudras, requires four binary discriminations.

Component Groups and Social Concepts

The main social locale is the village. Each family depends on families of other jatis in the village and its vicinity for certain essential goods and services. High-ranking landowners must have the services of the menial sweepers. If any one of the landowners' jati should take pay to perform menial services for others, the status of the whole jati would be jeopardized. The families of sweepers depend on the patrons for their livelihood, for emergency help, and for aid in their ceremonies. The mutual dependence is woven of many strands.

More will be said later about the nature of the village community or village locality. A village is usually a clear social and territorial entity, not only in the records and accounts of governmental administration, but also in the view of its inhabitants. But the people who take part in the community activities of a village, that is in the joint functions carried on within the village, are not so clearly bounded. A village family typically uses goods and services provided by people from a number of surrounding villages. Its washerman may live in one, its carpenter in another, and the family itself may provide services or goods to others in a circuit of villages. Its kinship relations will extend to jati fellows in a number of villages. So the actual village settlement is more the center of the community functions of its residents than a neat package for these functions.

Villagers have maintained important ties with people at urban centers since the beginnings of the civilization. At these centers they have carried on trade, religious acts, governmental contacts. A village is not, and never was, an isolated entity. Characteristically, its people have many ties with other villages in the locality and with specialists at centers.

Other components of village society have become increasingly important in recent times. Government agencies used to carry on police and tax-collecting functions principally; they had little direct effect on social relations among villagers. Voluntary associations were few in number and limited in purpose, consisting largely of gatherings for religious devotion. But with modern developments, governmental programs have had some impact on village relations. Voluntary associations, whether for political purposes or to promote civic welfare, have grown in number and influence. Nonetheless, the traditional social components discussed in this chapter are still the fundamental social realities in a villager's life.

The terms that villagers use for these groups and categories have sometimes seemed confusing to observers. The meaning of a term may vary depending on the social position of the speaker, or the context of use, or the functions that are being emphasized. Indeed, the field of societal analysis in India is strewn with pitfalls of terminology. A villager's style of expression can seem literally self-contradictory to an overliteral listener or reader.[3] Further, some of the common terms used by professional students of Indian society are not unambiguous.

---

[3] G. M. Carstairs discusses such seemingly contradictory statements, which he heard in the course of his study in a town of Rajasthan. He comments that his respondents were not at all disconcerted by the juxtaposition of opposites and indicates that this is different from Western modes of thought. But the difference may well exist more in conventions of expression than in canons of logic. One man told Carstairs emphatically "I never see ghosts, I'm not that kind of man." Almost in the same breath he went on to tell how he had seen a ghost in the jungle quite recently (1957, pp. 52–53). This apparently contradictory statement may instead have been meant to convey emphasis rather than logic. Perhaps this man should be understood as telling Carstairs that he is not at all the kind of person who looks for ghosts around every corner, but in this episode he *did* see a ghost.

In the U.P. village of Kishan Garhi, for example, the people of the high jatis use the classical term, *gotra* or *got*, for their exogamous clans and the same word is used to mean the endogamous jati by villagers of the lower ranks (cf. Karve 1965, p. 124). In Ramkheri village all villagers use the same word, *kutumb*, to mean either lineage or clan. The meaning conveyed depends on the context of use, as we shall note in the discussion of these groups (Mayer 1960, pp. 167–168).

When Mayer asked in this village about jati relations, many of the replies indicated "there is no caste left" (1960, p. 48). This is obviously not so, as Mayer's study, drawn from some of the same respondents, clearly shows. But the purport of such answers is to say, in an emphatic if hyperbolic way, that there are now state laws against discrimination (not necessarily strictly enforced), or that the former condition of jati relations has changed.

As for the ambiguities in observers' terms, we have mentioned the varying usages of the word "caste." The inadequacy of this term as it is often used in the literature is put succinctly by H. N. L. Stevenson, "It is difficult to pin the term caste to any sociological reality" (1954, p. 49). It has been pinned to too many social entities—endogamous group, a category of such groups, a system of social organization. It seems best to use the term, apart from direct quotations, as an adjective that refers to the highly stratified social system. The term "subcaste" has been used by some writers to refer to the endogamous group, the jati, but the definition of this word tends to be blurred if "caste" is concurrently used in several different senses.

The phrase, "the caste system of India" is best taken to refer to that set of ideas about society that many people of India share and that they use systematically in governing their social relations. Salient among these ideas is the view, implicitly held and sometimes explicitly expressed, that most social relations should be hierarchically arranged (cf. Dumont 1966).[4]

Hence villagers tend to establish rankings among the families of a lineage, among the lineages of a jati, among the jatis of a locality. The commonly held criteria for ranking will be discussed in later chapters, as will the behavioral consequences of these criteria. The shared ideas include some about the makeup of society that are not, as we have noted, objectively accurate, but are nonetheless subjectively powerful. All these central understandings form an important part of the overarching frame of Indian civilization.

The India-wide precepts were enacted in a multitude of village localities with little or no supervening control. Because government agencies now have increasing influence on village society, social controls and regulations are not as completely in local hands as before. But a large part of villagers' interchange and counterchange still takes place among the people of a locality as they act in the component groups of the local system. Our survey of these groups begins with the most intimate, the family.

[4] Louis Dumont's able and detailed exposition of this concept appeared after the present volume was well along and so the analysis in that work was not incorporated in this.

PART II

FAMILY AND KINSHIP RELATIONS

CHAPTER 3

Family

As the jati is fundamental to village society, so is kinship fundamental to the jati. All of a person's kin by descent and marriage, both actual and potential, are within his jati; none are outside it. The boundaries of his jati are continually revalidated through marriage; his closest interactions are typically with his kinsmen. A man's responsibilities to his kin are important considerations in the social enterprises he undertakes. So we must understand how villagers act as kinsmen in order to understand how this social system works.

Kinship begins with the family. In one sense the whole society begins with the family because a society is a living entity that must continually be replenished. The system of a whole society cannot be stopped and started again like a mechanical device. If replenishment is halted, the society ceases to exist. This imperative of replenishment for every society is met by its smallest social component, the family.

Everyone is born, not of a collectivity or into a full-fledged social system, but of parents into a family. In societies of all types, the family is the fundamental multipurpose organization for many of the principal life functions of the individual and of society. Moreover, as Eric Wolf has written, the family is the bearer of virtue and of public reputation; a man's reputation is linked with that of his family and with his own relations to his family. Although the standards used for social ranking vary widely, Wolf notes, the rankings in each society define whom one can trust and whom one may marry. "Invariably, they refer back to ways in which people handle their domestic affairs" (1966, p. 8). Domestic patterns establish the nature of the relations between the sexes and among the generations. They teach the fundamental lessons of who "we" are and who "they" are; how we may link with others; whom we may marry and whom we must not marry. Such patterns instill motivation in the young so that, in time, they will bring up their own young to seek similar life goals and follow similar cultural patterns.

These common functions of families across the world are carried out through a great variety of family forms, that is, of particular definitions and alignments of family roles. Yet each form of family structure is grounded in the biological constants—in the relation of parent and child, of husband and wife, of sibling and sibling. Another constant feature is a recurrent cycle of family development, in which a family is formed through marriage and mating, expands with the arrival of children, disperses as the children marry and eventually separate to establish new households, and sooner or later is totally replaced after the parents die (cf. Fortes 1958, pp. 4–5; Collver 1963, pp. 86–87).

Among village families in India these general features bear a characteristic Indian stamp, partly because of the widely shared ideal model for family relations and partly because of the common perspective of hierarchy. There are, to be sure, many differences in family organization according to jati, regional, and economic variations. Yet underlying the variety there is also a notable degree of similarity in family relations.

Ideal Model and Actual Form

The common ideal is that of filial and fraternal solidarity, which prescribes that brothers should remain together in the parental household after they marry, sharing equally in one purse and in common property, helping each other according to need and each giving according to his best abilities. Brothers should not only cleave to one another, but, even more important, they should remain with their parents and be steadfast to them. This ideal has has strongest sway while the father is alive and influential, and fades after both parents are dead and the brothers' children marry (cf. Gore 1965, pp. 211–213). It has more influence among those who are higher and wealthier than among the low and landless. It applies to the men of a family but is a central concern for women also. In most jatis, high and low alike, daughters customarily leave their natal family on marriage. A bride goes to live where her husband lives (which is with his father) and does not share in her own father's and brothers' property. Women, especially as mothers, uphold the ideal at least as vigorously as men do, but they themselves are not implicated in it in the same way.

Indian village society is patrilineal and virilocal except for a few matrilineal groups, notably the Nayars of Kerala who are discussed below. The patrilineal principle defines those men who are expected to cooperate most closely in a family and lineage group. The family ideal governs the relations between close male kin. It is a motif that holds constant interest; villagers hear it told over and again in tales from the *Mahabharata* and other classical sources. It is celebrated in popular song and is a common background of village gossip.

This ideal of filial-fraternal solidarity has been reinforced by being built into the chief textbook of Hindu law, the *Mitakshara* of the twelfth century. Under this code each male is entitled to an equal share of the family property from the moment of his birth; hence all brothers are coparceners, each entitled to the same share his father and brothers have. Joint ownership is assumed by law, and the assumption usually implies, though it does not require, joint residence and joint social and economic activities (cf. Desai 1955, p. 110; Mandelbaum 1948). Women, whether in the status of daughter, wife, or widow, are entitled to maintenance by their male kin, but under the ancient law they had no other vested rights in the family property.

No voluntary act is required to establish a close life partnership among brothers that binds them together in a firm legal entity. But the act of legal separation of family property does require voluntary action. When brothers or brothers' sons separate their households and property, as eventually they feel forced to do, they must petition to some formal authority in order to divide the joint property. This family law for Hindus was enforced during the British regime.[1] Though post-independence legislation has changed the inheritance laws, there is still a strong inclination among villagers, lagers, men and women alike, to follow the ancient mode of property rights and inheritance. There were regional variations in legal tradition, notably the *Dayabhaga* code of Bengal, but essentially all the regional codes and local customs postulate that it desirable for married sons to live, work, and share property with their parents and to remain together after their parents have died.

This kind of family cannot go on indefinitely; there are both physical and social limitations to its continuance. If sons and sons' sons keep adding their wives and children, there is a physical limit to the number that can be fed and housed in one household. Brothers' sons are not under the same obligation to stay together as are true brothers. The fission of the larger family is an inevitable step in the cycle of domestic development.

Taking that step results in the hiving off of smaller family groups, usually nuclear families, each consisting of a married couple and their children. When the sons grow up and a new bride is brought in, the family becomes what is known as a joint family, one that includes two or more married couples. The distinction between nuclear and joint families is one that is made by outside observers and census officers rather than by the villagers themselves. Family members do not consider that they have merged disparate nuclear families when there are two married couples in a family rather than just one; they regard this change as a natural and much desired growth of the original family. Nor do they use different terms for a single-couple and a multicouple family; there is usually only a single basic term for both. Each son is expected to bring his wife into his natal household. All eat from the same kitchen, live in the same house or compound, and share income. The males pool all property, support each other closely in the village and advance each other's cause in the world—and even into the afterworld.

The inducements to maintain close filial-fraternal relations are considerable. To begin with, most newly wed couples are barely into adulthood and have neither the material nor psychological resources to start a household of their own. Later in their married life, when they have more resources, they may still stay on in the household because the disadvantages of separating are greater than the annoyances of living together. Brothers are expected to help each other whether they live together or not. I knew two brothers in a village who became bitter enemies, yet when one grew so deranged mentally that no one would care for him, his estranged brother took him into his own house and nursed him until he was well enough to earn his living again. Then the mutual enmity was promptly resumed. Though brothers who live separately may still feel mutual obligations, living together in a joint household makes these obligations more automatic and compulsive.

In the joint family there is immediate aid to tide a member over illness; there is the increased efficiency of pooled labor and the economies of a single kitchen and household; and there is greater strength to ward off encroachments from others. Domestic rites and celebrations can be staged more elegantly by a large family, and the resulting prestige enhances all within the family. Each person is seen by others in the village in the light of his family's reputation. When he comes to a major life transition such as marriage, the reputation of the family weighs heavily in the decisions that are

---

[1] The administration of Hindu family law by British courts, according to K. M. Kapadia and others, undermined the traditional family organization because it made rigid and inflexible a law that had been dynamic and adaptable. (See Kapadia 1958, pp. 250–251; Cohn 1965, pp. 111–113; Derrett 1961, pp. 251–252.)

made. He is much advantaged if his family is large, harmonious, and joint, thus demonstrating that its members are reliable, worthy people.

Despite these advantages, centrifugal forces inevitably build up so that every family sooner or later breaches the ideal. Among the very poor the breach typically comes not long after the new bride is brought into the family. Early separation also occurs among families at the other end of the economic scale, those with men in the modern professions. Those families who own and cultivate their land are likely to keep up the ideal pattern longer. The ideal is acknowledged by almost all villagers and this tends to prolong fraternal cohesion. Cohesion and cooperation are not completely severed when a family splits into smaller households. Though the partition may have taken place in bitterness, family ties are often repaired and some degree of mutual support resumed.

Hierarchy in Family Roles

Hicrarchical authority within a family rests on the biological facts. Parents have to exert authority to socialize their children and human offspring must remain dependent on their parents for years. Human males, if only because they are larger and stronger than females, possess a certain, if limited, authority in their families. Indian villagers tend to place special emphasis on hierarchy within the family as part of their general presumption that interaction takes place, unless otherwise defined, between a superior and a subordinate.

Age and sex are the main ordering principles in family hierarchy. "The men have the more decisive authority in the traditional Indian family as compared with women," M. S. Gore notes, "and elders have greater authority as compared with young persons" (1965, p. 216). He adds that difference of a year or two in age is sufficient to establish firmly who is the formal superior. As between the authority of an elder woman and a younger man, sex is the more important determinant. Men have the formal property rights, and so the formal authority of a younger man—not necessarily his actual influence—is higher than that of his older sister, though he is expected to respect and cherish her.

The spheres of men's and women's activities tend to be sharply separated, especially among those in North India who observe *purdah*, the custom of keeping the women of a family close to the household. Women secluded in this way can have only very limited visits and contacts outside the kinship circle. Only a small proportion of Indian families ever wanted or could afford to practice purdah, but the principle of restricting women much more narrowly than men has been common.

A husband is expected to be his wife's superior and to receive symbolic and actual deference from her. There is no great expectation that the couple should share thoughts and tastes. This is not to say that conjugal love and devotion are any less than in other societies. Indeed the devotion of the Indian wife, both in legend and in fact, is one of the proud values of family life. It is to say that the roles of man and woman are markedly segregate. A woman moves about within her household and perhaps in those fields and households where she may work, not often going beyond these limits. A man has a much wider ambit in space and among people.

A married couple may not meet often in the course of the daily round. At meals the women customarily serve all the men first and eat only after the men have finished and risen. A wife, in all her relations with her husband, should adhere to the scriptural ideal of being a *Pativrata*, one who follows her husband's will and authority in all respects (Karve 1953, p. 78). And while many villagers know very little about scripture and less about this particular term, the ideal exemplified, at least in formal ways, at all social levels. Thus a wife customarily follows behind her husband when the two happen to walk together; she scrupulously avoids uttering his personal name lest this be taken as a disrespectful liberty; she greets him ritually with gestures of respect and deference.

A woman is deferent as wife, but not as mother. Children owe permanent deference to both parents. Parental authority is unceasing as an ideal and is sustained in fact, though the actual duration and degree of this authority are affected by economic circumstance and jati tradition. Within a household a son or daughter must not flout a parent's will, especially not the father's. If grown sons do not wish to follow a parental mandate, they usually find ways to circumvent rather than to contradict it. A widowed mother may wield considerable influence on her son and his family, as one educated woman of an eminent family has testified: "When I was growing up, Father was the chief authority in the house on all official and financial matters. He was a district commissioner and practically ruled the district like a king, and yet he would always go to his mother, who was nearly illiterate, for her final decision in any important family matters. Grandmother was the authority too in all household matters and Father left everything to her. In such matters as settling weddings Father and Mother did the preliminary choosing, then Father would ask Grandmother for her final approval" (Ross 1961, p. 96). The ideal of deference to parents is rarely questioned, and in practice it endows the elders with an authority that is not lightly ignored by their children.

Among brothers, authority rests with the elder. Some of the same respectful compliance that a son gives to his father, a younger brother should give, in formal terms at least, to his elder brother. When an eldest brother succeeds as head of the joint family, his younger brothers, and their wives and children, are supposed to give him the kind of allegiance and obedience that the father commanded. Within the realm of women's activities, a woman's authority usually depends on the position of her husband in the household. The wife of the senior man is the paramount authority in women's affairs subject only to the presence in the household of his mother, who must be heard out patiently and respectfully (Ross pp. 55, 132).

As in any human relationship, the weight of influence in a family may be wielded by a forceful personality, say a youngest brother, even though he does not have an acknowledged position of power in the family structure (cf. Sarma 1951, p. 52); however, the formal hierarchy is clear and influential. All understand that a man should have authority over his wife and children, that a woman should exert control over her unmarried daughters and her daughters-in-law, that a senior brother has legitimate authority over his younger siblings in the family. Each person's dominance yields to the presence of higher family authority. The eldest brother should give ear to the wishes of the mother; the mother should defer to the wishes of the father; the father should give way in family affairs if he is overruled by his father or by the senior male of the joint family. People do not always behave in this way; personal inclination and particular circumstance may induce them to act against these expectations, but the hierarchical norms are usually powerful influences on family conduct.

With family authority goes responsibility. The superior is also obliged to look after the welfare of his charges so that they will not suffer, either by their own misjudgment or because of untoward circumstances. The general ideal, as related by a villager of Poona district, is that a man should respect and obey his elder brother as he would his father and should treat his elder brother's wife as an elder sister. "The oldest male of the highest generation is supposed to receive the most respect and obedience, the female at the opposite pole, the most protection and care" (Orensteir 1965, pp. 47–48).

One quality of family life among villagers has been particularly noticed by some observers. Thus T. N. Madan writes of the Pandit Brahmins of a Kashmir village, "What strikes the observer is the extreme restraint which characterizes relations between adult men and women in Pandit society" (1965, p. 76). Adrian Mayer (1960, p. 214) makes a similar comment about a village in Madhya Pradesh: "The dominant note in the formal pattern of relations in the household is that of restraint. There is restraint between people of different age and restraint between those of opposite sex." Mayer adds that while his characterization may make the household appear (to one from a different tradition of family life) as a place full of restrictions and autocratic authority, "Yet, in a happy household this is patently not the case. Authority on the one hand, and respect on the other mix in an easy carrying out of duties, and the reticence of the women is one of modesty, not fear." Restraint and hierarchy, it should be noted, are also characteristic of relations among people of different jatis as well as within the family.

FAMILY FUNCTIONS

A family in India, as elsewhere, is a corporate group whose members act together to meet their common purposes. Typically they live in the same house and eat food prepared in the same kitchen; they work together, pool their income, expenditures, and property and perform religious rituals as a family.

These functions are scarcely distinctive; similar functions are performed by family groups through much of the world. But in village India a great many of a person's activities are carried out with his family throughout his lifetime. In the larger joint families, in which several adult men and women and their children live and work in closest proximity, lines of authority must be made plain lest disagreements about them escalate. In such joint families, the nature of the family as a system, with its regular, expected interchange and redressive counterchange, becomes more readily apparent.

Each person learns the fundamentals of his culture and society from his family; he experiences his main satisfactions and shares his personal achievements with other family members. In his jati-group he primarily identified as a member of his family, and he assumes the reputation of his family in the village. His whole life experience is embedded in his family relations. The main transitions of the life cycle are family celebrations, and the grand occasions of a person's life are mainly those that occur in the context of the family (cf. Kapadia 1958).

In a village, the family is the principal unit of economic production as well as of consumption. Land is owned and worked by families. The exchange of goods and services in the traditional manner is largely between families of different jatis. Property is traditionally held in common by the men of the family and it was not until the Hindu Gains of Learning Act of 1930 that a man could legally lay claim to the economic returns of his own skill and enterprise.

A family is a unit before the gods. In almost every house there is a special place for the holy things that help guard all in the household. That place may be no more than a lithograph tacked to a wall or it may be an elaborate shrine in a separate room; in either case all in the family come under its protection. Religious observances entail much participation by family groups. In Senapur village of U.P., for example, Opler found some forty calendrical rites being observed, twenty-five of which revolved mainly around family needs and purposes. He concluded that "a large part of the religious system is an elaborate apparatus for putting family members and family interests under the protection of benign supernaturals, and for defending the family from unfriendly supernatural attacks" (1959a, p. 273).

Priests do not usually have much to do with these rituals, which are planned, directed, and carried out mainly by members of a family for the family's welfare. The women of the family have the greatest responsibility for this sphere of religion (cf. Minturn and Hitchcock 1966, pp. 67–68). Life cycle observances are mainly family affairs, each of them marking an occasion when the family, helped by its other kin, delivers up to society a person in successive stages of social completion, from newborn baby to ancestral soul. It is in the name of his family and on their behalf as well as his own that a man pays ritual homage to the ancestors, thus linking each person with the remembered and with the infinite past.

Rites for the family's ancestors are particularly important in families of the higher varnas and in these families the father acts on behalf of all. If he gone and the grown brothers live together, only the eldest need perform the memorial rites. Among Kashmiri Brahmins, if the family has separated the eldest brother still must conduct these rites for all, but among Brahmins in Tanjore district each household head must separately carry out this ritual duty (Madan 1962b, p. 14; Gough 1956, p. 839). The crises of death and birth affect all who live together in a family; all must observe proper seclusion and cleansing to rid themselves of their common defilement. The whole ritual purity and pollution of the jati rests largely on conduct in the family context as in eating, in mating, in ritual observance.

A family is not only a reproductive unit and a socializing agency; it also provides each person with his main link to the wider society. Kinship ties are generally taken to be the most durable, reliable, worthy, and moral of all social relations (cf. Madan 1965, p. 222). Kinship begins with the family and is extended through the family. The family is also a principal unit in village organization. When labor or money or participation is needed for a village purpose, one man or one amount is levied from each family household. When gifts are given as part of the stringent competition for family status, they are given and received as from one family to another, even though the immediate recipient may be a bride or new initiate.

All these functions are met by people acting in family groups, whether the group is large or small. The number of people in a family varies according to the phase of the developmental cycle, being greater when there are coresident sons, their wives and children, and smaller when the couples split to set up separate households. A good part of the discussion of family life in India has assumed that there is a basic discontinuity between the single-couple family, called the nuclear or elementary family, and the larger family of more than the one couple and their children, called the joint or extended family. Some commentators have further assumed that a joint family is a merger of nuclear families. Neither assumption is valid, as we have noted, from the villagers' point of view. Nor was a distinction made between nuclear and joint families in the *Mitakshara* or in the more recent interpretations of Hindu law. Only for modern income-tax purposes is the distinction legally recognized (Shah 1964a, pp. 11, 18, 32; Madan 1962b, pp. 13–14).

Yet the number of people in a household and the nature of their family roles do make a difference in the way in which a family functions. When the first bride joins a previously single-couple family, only one person is added but several new role relations are established. She is not only a new wife for the son, she is also daughter-in-law to the father, daughter-in-law to the mother, and perhaps also sister-in-law to a younger son and to a younger daughter. The relations between parents and children are affected if the children's grandparents live in the same household because the younger couple must be more restrained toward their own children in the presence of elders. A couple with one child considers the family incomplete if that child is a girl, but if it is a boy, they are likely to see their family as unduly small yet in an important way complete (Shah 1964a, pp. 7, 33). The number of men in a family is economically significant because the pooled labor and wealth of several men may give them advantages over a smaller family.

Many classifications of family form are logically possible because there are hundreds of combinations of kin roles, including widowed mothers or father's sisters, resident sons-in-law, and orphans who may be related quite distantly. Although detailed classifications by role composition have been made, it is not always clear what useful purposes such typologies serve. The joint family has been defined in different ways, depending on which of the common features is selected as essential.

Some scholars have followed the traditional legal definition, which takes the joint ownership of property as an indispensable feature of the joint family (Madan 1962b, p. 13; Bailey 1960a, p. 347). But a man and his infant son are coparceners in the traditional legal sense, and a household group that contains only one couple and one child is scarcely a joint family. Moreover, under modern land tenure legislation, it has become profitable in some places for fathers and sons to separate their property legally while continuing to share residence, kitchen, and the rest of joint family living. The legal definitions are necessary for legal purposes, but they seem less useful for understanding actual behavior.

The Census of India procedure has been to take the household as a principal unit of enumeration, defined as a group whose members take food from a common kitchen (Gopalaswami 1953, pp. 48–50). That definition, however, is not suited for general analyses because a set of married brothers may set up separate kitchens to avoid domestic ruckus while they continue to share the same house, property, and work (cf. Mayer 1960, pp. 177–182).

While fine classifications of family forms in India have not so far been very fruitful, some useful distinctions have been indicated. The differences between a family that is felt to be incomplete and one that is more nearly complete have been noted by A. M. Shah (1964a, pp. 3–4); family striving and family goals are probably quite different in the two types. A distinction has been made by T. N. Madan between patrilineal and paternal extended families, the former consisting of the parental couple and an only son and his wife, the latter including parents and two or more married sons. In the former there will be no partition of family property accompanied by the usual tensions; in the latter, partition and domestic friction are quite probable (1962b, p. 14). One difficulty in some discussions of family forms is that the term "family" is used too loosely, including a wide range of lineal kin or kindred as well as the coresidential, tightly knit, and closely related domestic group (cf. Dumont and Pocock 1957c, pp. 48–49).

Any cogent analysis of Indian family life must include the concepts shared by most Indian villagers—of patrilineal ties and virilocal residence, of proper relations between father and son, between brother and brother. The family members are expected to form one solidarity, living in one household as long as possible, supporting each other in the round of their days and in the cycle of their lives. A family may be physically separated, even legally split, yet the brothers may continue to act as a functioning family. This happens, not infrequently, when a brother from a village family moves to a city with his wife and children. He and his dependents return to the village home as often as they can; he contributes to the income of the village family; he rallies to their help and they to his whenever there is emergency need or ceremonial occasion. Before arranging a marriage or taking any decisive measures affecting their careers or fortunes, the members consult with each other, giving due deference to the views of the elders among them. This traditional spirit of the family is frequently upheld in both village and city (cf. Agarwala 1955, pp. 141–142; Desai 1955, p. 103; 1956, pp. 147–148; Kapadia 1959, pp. 74–75; Ross 1961, pp. 9, 39).

Within these general characteristics of Indian families, there are three broad types of variation—within a family over time, within a village and region, and among regions.

Changes in Relations within a Family

Within a family the constellation of relations changes in the course of the family cycle. Within a village and region there are differences in family relations according to wealth, occupation, and jati rank. Finally, there are differences among the linguistic-cultural regions.

The way in which any family role is carried out changes over time even though the same persons are involved. A girl of fifteen, newly arrived in a family as a bride, owes and gives deference to her mother-in-law. Twenty years later, as the mother of sons, she still is a daughter-in-law and still owes deference to her husband's mother. But the quality and the mode of deference alter a good deal over the years. Her relations with the wives of her husband's brothers, as Madan has observed in a Kashmir village, shift from friendliness or indifference to a competitive attitude (1965, pp. 132–135).

A woman's change of role behavior can be quite great. Mrs. Karve writes that "it is not rare to see women who were nothing but meek nonentities blossom into positive personalities in their middle-aged widowhood, or boss over the weak old husband in the latter part of the married life" (1965, p. 136).[2] And the wife who urges her husband to separate from the joint family, Desai comments, is commonly the same person who later, as mother and mother-in-law, is most unwilling to see her joint family split (1955, p. 104).

The relations between father and son normally change as a boy grows into adolescence. A father is expected to act more sternly toward his adolescent son than he did when the boy was a young child. Later still the relations shift again, as is illustrated in Mayer's account of Ramkheri village in Madhya Pradesh. A boy there begins to be held responsible for his actions at about the age of ten. From this age through adolescence his father is expected to be more of a disciplinarian than at any other stage. After the son marries, and certainly when he begets a son of his own, he can become somewhat more independent, though he must always observe great respect for his father. Some men of the village carry this respect to the point where they will not even smoke in front of their fathers. Should the father become infirm, another shift in the son's role behavior takes place. He continues to give formal respect to his father but takes over actual authority and the direction of the household (Mayer 1960, pp. 214–219).

The context of behavior also affects family conduct. In the context of public behavior a wife should not challenge her husband's formal precedence and authority. But inside the house, as Mrs. Karve has

---

[2] Occasionally an aberrant person will violate the proprieties and nothing much will be done about it, perhaps because only extreme measures are needed and are not easily taken. Thus D. N. Majumdar tells of one village family in which the daughter-in-law, who ought to have conducted herself with the most circumspect bearing toward her father-in-law, fell into a quarrel with him and beat him over the head with a piece of iron (1958a, p. 217).

indicated, domineering women are not unknown. For young married couples, public behavior is that carried on in the presence of *any* third adult. Alone they may chat, laugh, tease, but as soon as one other adult can see or hear them, they must lapse into quiescence. In the presence of the husband's father or mother they must be exceedingly restrained in their communications with each other to the point of seeming to ignore each other, and they must refrain from paying much attention to their own children. It is this contextual factor in particular that makes relations within a three-generation family different from those in a two-generation family. The presence of the husband's parents in the joint family intervenes between husband and wife and their children.

Economic Factors in Family Form

Within a village, there are differences in family relations according to jati rank, occupation, and wealth. These are well illustrated in the studies of Kumbapettai village in South India (Gough 1956) and of Senapur village near Banaras in North India (Cohn 1961a). Kumbapettai, in the Tanjore district of Madras, had been dominated by Brahmin landowners since it was founded in the 1780s.

During 1951–1953, when Dr. Gough studied the village, the Brahmins were still paramount. At the bottom of the village order there are three jatis of landless laborers, who are now called Adi Dravidas, "original" Dravidians. Among the Brahmins a father's authority is strong and enduring. Among the Adi Dravidas a son becomes a wage earner shortly after puberty, usually moves into a separate house a few years after marriage, and as an adult is expected to work independently with his siblings and peers rather than to be submissively dependent on his father. Adi Dravida women are much more independent, economically and socially, than are Brahmin women. They may divorce easily and frequently; widows can remarry; these women are not so isolated from their natal families as are Brahmin women, and they can earn wages as field workers.

Economic factors bolster the differences in family roles. The Brahmins are landowners and farm managers who do no manual labor. Since their whole economic resource is land, and the land is owned jointly, a young man can scarcely afford to leave his paternal family after marriage. Joint ownership and common management require a structure of authority; the head of a Brahmin joint household can effectively be the manager of the lands and can thus wield decisive authority in his family until he is quite old. Their women own no land in their own right and make no contribution to the household income. Adi Dravida women, by contrast, are quite self-sufficient economically and can therefore be more independent in family matters. The son of an Adi Dravida family quickly comes to earn as much as his father does and thus a father has no economic hold over the young man. Hence paternal authority does not last long as compared with the authority of a Brahmin father.[3]

The Adi Dravidas do not believe, as do the Brahmins, that the fate of a woman's soul depends on lifelong union with and service to one husband. An Adi Dravida father does not have to bind his son closely to him, since he does not consider, as does a Brahmin father, that his own fate in the hereafter depends on the son's performing memorial rites for him. Despite these differences, both

[3] In commenting on Gough's account, Louis Dumont states that, at least on the basis of his experience with South Indian villagers, the disparities are not so great as Gough depicts them. He does agree that there are certainly differences in familial relations as between the two social levels (Dumont 1961b, p. 83).

groups share the same family ideal. The Adi Dravidas do not disparage Brahmin values in secluding women or in prohibiting the remarriage of widows. Families of lower rank who become prosperous and can afford to keep their women out of the fields often try to adopt the kind of family relations they see maintained by the local Brahmins (Gough 1956, p. 827).

In Senapur village the Chamars, traditionally leatherworkers and mostly landless laborers, share the ideal of family relations held by the dominant landowners, the Thakurs. Chamars would like to follow the same model as do Thakurs, having three generations living in one house and eating from the same *chula* (hearth). "Those who take food from one *chula* form the commensal group, which means to a Chamar the sharing of property and rights, a common pocketbook, a common larder, common debts, common labor force, and usually one recognized head" (Cohn 1961a, p. 1052). A good many of the Chamars do succeed in maintaining joint families for a time; in 1953 there were 42 joint families out of 122 Chamar households in the village. But the Chamars' poverty militates against long-lasting joint families. One consequence of poverty is the short life span. Only a few Chamar males live long enough to be the head of a three-generation household. At the time of the study only about 6 percent of the Chamar males in the village were more than fifty years old. When the father dies before his sons have children, a binding influence on the joint family is eliminated.

Moreover, every year most of these Chamars must live through two to four months in which they have little food and are frequently hungry. In eight of twelve instances of family partition among Senapur Chamars, quarrels over distribution of food and income caused the split. "A brother with one small child does not see why he should share his meager earnings with a brother who has three small children and hence gets a larger share of the household food supply" (Cohn, p. 1053). Such quarrels are not readily suppressed by the father's authority, even if he is alive, in part because he has little economic power. A man's earnings as a laborer decline sharply after age thirty-five and a grown son may earn more than his father does. Among the Thakur landowners, older men retain their economic influence because they can, like the Brahmin elders of Kumbapettai, wield managerial functions into old age. Brothers among the artisans and middle-rank farmers of Senapur may keep together because of the greater efficiency of pooled labor. Since Chamars have little land or joint enterprise, they cannot gain much from such economies.

Nor do the Chamar wives contribute to fraternal and filial solidarity. Women's explosions in a Thakur household can usually be controlled short of fission, but a Chamar woman is neither as submissive nor as secluded. She earns almost as much as a man does and earns it for a longer period. If she decides to leave her husband's family and goes back to her father's house, she is welcomed there because she brings food and money into whatever household she chooses to join. If she does not want to live with a mother-in-law, she does not have to do so. A young Thakur wife has no such choice.

Chamars are not rooted to a particular locality, as Thakurs are, and readily leave their parental families to go where economic opportunity may be found. When a Chamar man goes to the city to work, his wife and children usually remain with his family. This brings advantages of added income for the joint family. Each of the three Chamar schoolteachers in the village grew up in a joint family. Only through the combined resources of a multicouple family can Chamars generally afford to let a child acquire some education.

All Chamar families in which there are sons become joint families for at least a few years. A young man brings his bride into the household when he is between the ages of fifteen and seventeen and usually does not set up a household of his own until he is over twenty (Cohn, p. 1052). To maintain joint living for a longer period requires both higher income and higher aspirations. Income alone is not enough; some of the richer Chamars do not choose to live in joint families, but those Chamars who have some education usually aspire to the family standards of the higher jatis. Here, as in the South Indian example, those who want to raise themselves socially emulate the prestigious family model.

Family occupation affects family form throughout the land. Village surveys from different regions show that families who own and cultivate their own land tend to remain together longer as multicouple families than do noncultivating landowners and still longer than do landless laborers of the same locality. Hence at any one time owner-cultivators tend to have a higher proportion of joint families. In a survey of four villages of West Bengal, Sarma found some correlation between higher jati status and a higher proportion of joint families but found a more marked relationship between occupation and family form. In a sample of 111 families of owner-cultivators, 35 percent were nuclear and 65 percent were joint families. In a sample of 126 families of agricultural laborers, 75 percent were nuclear and 25 percent were joint families. Sharecroppers and noncultivating landowners came between, with nuclear families making up 45 percent of a sample of 148 and 58 percent of a sample of 53 families respectively (Sarma 1964, pp. 198–201; 1959, pp. 104–105; other tabulations from this survey in Burdwan district in 1953–1954 are in L. K. Sen 1965).

Similar differentiation by occupation is indicated in other surveys, although the results are not directly comparable because the several authors do not use the same categories or definitions. In Senapur, for example, among the families of the landowning Thakurs 19 percent are nuclear but among the largely landless Chamars 59 percent are nuclear. In Rampur near Delhi, the families of the Jats, who are the main landowners, are 70 percent joint, of the Chamars 19 percent are joint. In a sample of high school students in Baroda, 65 percent of those from Patidar jatis, who are mainly owner-cultivators, lived in joint families, while 37 percent of those from Bania jatis, traditionally tradesmen, lived in joint families (Kolenda 1968, pp. 363, 368; Shahani 1961). The lower proportion of joint families among tradesmen indicates a shift in their family form. Merchants commonly have a relatively high proportion of joint families, in the economic and legal if not in the residential sense. There are considerable economic benefits from having joint family ownership and management of a string of shops even though the separate households may come together only for family convocations (Desai 1964, pp. 177, 186, 189, 194, 208, 212; Agarwala 1955, pp. 140–144). But the Bania families represented in the Baroda sample were giving up trade and their men were seeking professional and government occupations. Among them, the occupational rationale for keeping joint families intact over a long period was no longer so important as it had been (Shahani 1961, p. 1827).

Owner-cultivators are likely to maintain joint families longer than do others in the same village, but different jatis of owner-cultivators vary in this regard. In Ramkheri village, for example, both Rajputs and farmers (Khati) are owner-cultivators, but the joint families of farmers continue longer on the whole than do those of Rajputs. This is the case, Mayer explains, because the farmers are true husbandmen and are much concerned with the greater efficiency of farming by a joint family, whereas the Rajputs are more interested in land as a means to wealth and status (1960, p. 181).

Another variable that affects family form has been discerned by Pauline Kolenda in her comparative study of families in six places (Senapur, Khalapur, and Sirkanda in U.P.; Rampur in Delhi State; Ramkheri in Madhya Pradesh; and the Pramalai Kallar in Madras). This variable depends on the contribution that a woman and her natal family make to her husband's livelihood. When the husband and his family provide much social and economic support and when the wife and her family offer little, then married couples stay longer in the joint family. Conversely, when the wife is an important earner and her natal family contributes to her conjugal family, then the agnatic joint family tends to be of shorter duration. Kolenda finds that the key difference between the three communities in her sample with many joint families, on the one hand, and the three with few, on the other, is that in the former "the *husband* does not develop important economic bonds or continuous social bonds with his wife's kin" (1967, pp. 173, 211).

Agricultural technology also can affect family form. In a survey of fifty-nine villages of Poona district, Orenstein found that there were proportionately fewer joint families in those villages that had the most acreage per family under irrigation. Families with more irrigated land, he suggests, get more of their income in cash. Their members are likely to separate more quickly because the disposition of money income leads to arguments, and both the cash and the irrigated lands are readily divisible. Perhaps also the managerial function and the authority of the family head is lessened under small-scale irrigation farming (Orenstein 1960, pp. 318–319).

Yet the presumed general decline of the joint family in India, the subject of much discussion, both popular and scholarly, is not apparent from census returns. To take one possible indicator, the average number of people in a household has not changed markedly since the Census of 1891 (Gait 1913, pp. 46–47; Goode 1963, pp. 239–240; Sengupta 1958, pp. 387–388). A close study of the census data for eleven states between 1911 and 1951 shows a net increase rather than a decrease in average household size. But this may be a result of increased population and insufficient housing rather than indication of a rise in joint family living (Orenstein 1961; Lambert 1962, pp. 126–127).

The passing of joint families is supposed to be particularly marked in cities, but the evidence so far available shows no great rejection of joint family living among urban people. A study of 201 families in Calcutta, 100 from an old and poorer area and 101 from a new, wealthier section, showed that 80 percent of the families in the wealthier part and 57 percent in the poorer neighborhood were joint. An over-all sampling of Calcutta families showed 42 percent to be joint (J. Sarma 1964, pp. 201–205). A survey of Poona in 1937 showed 28 percent joint families; a resurvey of 1954–55 showed 32 percent. In a narrower sampling in Poona, of 182 fathers with married, employed sons, 66 percent had sons living with them. Two-thirds of those in the sample who could do so, actually fulfilled the ideal for multi-couple residence (Sovani and others 1956, pp. 95, 450; Sovani 1961, p. 207; Dandekar and Dandekar 1953, pp. 127–129).

As this survey shows, it is useful to find the ratio of multi-couple families to *possible* joint families. Couples who have only daughters or are childless cannot readily develop into joint families. Such a calculation was made in a 1958 survey of 2314 couples of Nagpur district. Of the total sample, 30 percent lived in multi-couple families. But when the proportion was calculated of those who had "eligible primary kin," that is, those who had some choice in the matter, the percentage of joint families was 41.8 percent. Among those who had such a choice 49.6 percent of the village couples, 39.5 percent of the town couples, and 32.2 percent of the city couples were living in joint families (Driver 1963, pp. 41–44). The main purpose of this study was to assess fertility; no significant differences were found in fertility as between single and multi-couple families. Other studies have also shown no greater fertility in multi-couple families (*ibid.*, p. 82; Bebarta 1966).

Surveys of two towns in Gujarat reveal that joint family living there also is far from defunct. In Mahuva, a town in South Gujarat, 21 percent of a sample of 423 families were joint in the full traditional sense, and 95 percent maintained some kind of family cooperation with related families

(Desai 1964, p. 69). In the town of Navsari 56.5 percent of a sample of 246 families were joint by the author's definition; they included 66.6 percent of the population in the sample. A survey of families in 15 villages in the same area showed 49.7 percent joint families (Kapadia 1956, pp. 112–115).

One student of family organization has concluded that the changes in India are not yet great but that the direction of change is clear (Goode 1963, p. 247). But from the evidence he summarizes, it seems that such directional change, even as reflected in attitude and opinion surveys, is also not great or at least not yet very great. The filial-paternal ideal is still strongly respected in cities as well as in villages and is quite often observed in practice, though insufficient housing has probably forced added joint-family living. The conditions of urban life may ultimately make for a decreasing proportion of joint families, but so far we must agree with the conclusion reached by N. V. Sovani, that urban living must have some effects on family relations but what they are has not so far been made clear (Sovani 1961, pp. 206–207).

In sum, people tend to remain in joint families longer when economic factors favor such families. The poorest and the lowest groups tend to have fewest joint families, but even at these social levels, most families become joint for at least a time after a son marries. When families of low jati acquire enough economic substance to be able to aspire to the higher model and enough education to want to do so, they are apt to take on the more esteemed family patterns including longer duration of the joint family. Joint ownership of land and close dependence on the land help keep joint families together. Among merchants and artisans the economies of scale of a large household are reasons for upholding joint families. When land income is mainly in cash, or when newer occupations bring in money earnings, the economic basis for a joint family is weakened and the family tends to exist for a shorter duration. But, as the urban figures show, the joint family is not by any means totally eliminated nor is the ideal of filial-fraternal solidarity abruptly abandoned.

Differences among Regions

A third kind of variation in family style is by region. Although the available studies of this kind of variation are quite preliminary, certain differences among linguistic-cultural regions can be noted. Thus the recruitment of wives differs between Hindus of the Hindi and adjacent regions, on the one hand, and, on the other, Hindus of South India, who speak Tamil, Telugu, and Kannada (cf. Marriott 1960, pp. 40–42). In the northern parts, wives are usually taken from beyond the village and beyond the closer kin. In the south, a man is expected to marry a girl from among his closer kin. In some southern jatis there is preference for marriage to a mother's brother's daughter or an elder sister's daughter. We shall consider this difference later in our discussion of marriage rules and kinship practices.

The most divergent region of all in matters of family and kinship was—and to some degree still is—Kerala. The Nayars and some of the other jatis of this region were matrilineal; they counted the tie between mother and daughter to be the durable relationship. Nayar women stayed in their natal household—their mother's house—after marriage. Inheritance was from mother to daughter, from brother to sister's children, rather than from father to son. Men also continued to live with their natal, matrilineal families; a Nayar man was a visitor in the household where his wife and children lived. Yet despite this reversal of patterns followed elsewhere in India, Nayar families were quite like the patrilineal families in other respects. Their kinship terminology follows the basic

Dravidian pattern used by the patrilineal societies of South India (Yalman 1967, pp. 359–372). The joint family of several married sisters, their children, their mother and her sisters, occasionally their sojourning husbands, was the ideal type and seems to have been the common type. The permanent bonds were between mother and daughter, among sisters, and between brother and sister. A Nayar man in his role as father had no legal rights or authority over his own children. He would play with them, give them gifts, offer friendly counsel. As the male head of a family, his authority was over his sisters' children.

Father-son relations were more complicated if the boy was the child of a union of a Nambudiri Brahmin man and a Nayar woman. Only the eldest son of a Nambudiri family was permitted to marry. A younger son would have an alliance with a Nayar woman in a union that was regular and approved, but was not full marriage. Colonel Unni Nayar (who was born in 1911) has described his boyhood in a Nayar joint family and his Nambudiri father whom he greatly admired. Neither he nor his mother would eat with his father or even watch him eat. He could not touch his father during the day, between the father's morning bath and until the time after his dinner when he was in a more relaxed state of personal purity. Here also the context of behavior influenced the nature of permitted relations. "If I touched Father during the day, he had to bathe afresh and change his clothes. In point of fact, Father, although undemonstrative, did not object to being touched when he was by himself. If others were present he had to observe the decorums, and we got thrashed, not for polluting a Brahmin, but for being tactless" (1952, p. 56). It was not so much the children's violation of propriety that mattered, but the fact that they did so in the presence of others, in the context of the public view.

Whether the father was a Nambudiri or a Nayar, his relations with his children were quite like those which, in much of India, a boy has with his mother's brother. Among the Nayar the mother's brother, especially if he were the head of the family, was expected to carry authority and enforce discipline over his nephew. A Nayar boy had to give the same deference and instant obedience to the head of his mother's family that the patriarchal elder receives in families of patrilineal jatis.

Though roles were reversed, a Nayar family resembled the usual patrilineal joint family in that it was the basic unit of economic activity; its members were coparceners; its male head managed the external family affairs while the senior woman managed the home economy. The family members united in the ritual of the household deities. Just as brothers of a patrilineal family are exhorted to stand fast together and to rise above the divisive influence of their wives, so in a Nayar household the sisters and their brothers were expected to remain united and impervious to divisive arguments from spouses and children. In recent decades special external pressures, legal, economic, and social, have made the traditional matrilineal family rare among the Nayars, but matriliny is still a force among them. The Nayar family is a kind of mirror image of the usual Indian joint family. It provides an important example of one extreme of human family organization, in which the social role of father is minimal. It also demonstrates that so radical a variation as matriliny could be accommodated within the general Indian family and jati framework (cf. Gough 1961c, pp. 298–370; Unni 1956, pp. 45–46; Karve 1965, pp. 291–308; Kapadia 1958, pp. 273–280; Dumont 1961a, pp. 32–33; Dumont 1964a, pp. 85–86; Mencher 1965).

That framework of assumptions and expectations about family life includes the ideal of filial-fraternal solidarity, the emphasis on hierarchy, the pervasive scope of family functions, and the tight identification of person with family. How these assumptions and expectations are actually carried out depends on how individuals act in their family roles.

CHAPTER 4

Family Roles: Boy and Man

Certain characteristics of family roles are common to families throughout the land. Some common features, to be sure, are biologically given. As in other human societies, the major roles are those of husband and wife who are also father and mother, of son and daughter who are siblings to each other. And as in other societies, people use broad stereotypes of proper family behavior to guide and judge family conduct. These formulas mask as well as explain; they gloss over some recurrent tensions and ignore other regularities of family life. In the following descriptions of family roles the popular stereotypes must be taken into account, but the descriptions themselves are to be taken not as revised stereotypes but rather as broad outlines of actual behavior within which much variation occurs. Some major variations are those noted in the preceding chapter, by family wealth and ritual rank and by region.

The family roles to be considered are first those of a boy and man, then those of a girl and woman. Not every family has a full complement of members and roles but there is a strong tendency to fill in a missing major role. If a child's father dies, one of the father's brothers, his own elder brother, or another man suitably related, able and willing to do so, acts as father to him. When a girl has several brothers, there is often one in particular (perhaps the one closest to her in age) with whom she shares the essential brother-sister relation and who later is foremost in the important role of mother's brother to her children.

As Son: Filial Respect and its Consequences

Some of the main features of the family roles of a male have already been mentioned. As boy and man he should treat both parents with great respect. Respect entails obedience and the avoidance of any behavior that might indicate a contrary will or wayward desires not under firm parental control. In the ideal depictions, a son devotes himself completely to the welfare as well as to the will of his parents. This ideal graphically presented in Mahatma Gandhi's autobiography when he tells how, as a boy, he was deeply affected by a drama about a son's self-sacrificing devotion to his parents. A picture of that devoted son carrying his blind parents on a pilgrimage by means of slings fitted to his shoulders left an indelible impression on Gandhi's mind. He goes on to tell of his marriage at age thirteen and of his great preoccupation with his wife. But nothing in his role as husband could be allowed to conflict openly with his devotion as son. "I dared not meet her in the presence of the elders, much less talk to her" (1940, pp. 11, 17).

At the moment of his father's death, Gandhi was with his wife rather than devotedly caring for his sick father, as he thought he should have been. This marked a crucial point in his career; the experience turned him more firmly toward asceticism. He said that the unfilial deed remained "a blot I have never been able to efface or forget…." (S. H. Rudolph 1965, pp. 86–89).

Not every young man has such an experience or responds so sensitively; Gandhi was then of an age, from a jati, and in a region where filial respect was required in utmost degree. Yet similar deference to parents is seen in parts of India far from Gandhi's birthplace and at the lower as well as the higher reaches of a local hierarchy (e.g., Sarma 1951, p. 55; Dumont 1957b, pp. 212–214).

Parents also owe a certain respect to their children; they should not behave in ways that make it difficult for their children to respect them. This is even more important when a son is grown and his parents are, or may soon be, dependent upon him. In Dr. K. Gnanambal's account of a village in northern Mysore, she tells of old men who would be "gabbing away gaily about their old days, but shutting up like clams when their sons appeared on the scene." A woman of this village, of a cultivator jati, often amused the other women with song and dance imitations of actors. One day while she was doing a lively step her son passed by and happened to see her. Seeing him, she stopped and left abruptly. When Dr. Gnanambal later asked her why she had fled, she said, "Now that my son is married, he is my protector. My husband is alive; but who knows at what time I may have to depend on my son for a cup of gruel?" (1960, p. 58). Her blithe deportment was unseemly for a grown man's mother and could diminish the son's social stature in the village.

Between father and son, relations are supposed to be formal and restrained and are often so in reality. Each may have great affection for the other, but after the boy becomes adolescent there should be little familiarity, intimacy, or demonstrativeness between them. This holds especially true among landowners of high ritual rank. Thus among the Brahmins of a Tanjore village, a father gives a good deal of attention to his sons in their early childhood, being particularly concerned with giving them food. Later, when a boy is eight or nine, he comes under stricter training; he and his father must keep physically more distant from each other. The boy does not touch either parent and he should prostrate himself in obeisance before each of them daily. After the son's marriage he may be given some economic responsibilities but while his father is alive and while the son is in the same village as his father, he does not attain to the full responsibility of an adult. "I am only a young boy, madam!" one man of thirty-five, a husband and father, replied to Kathleen Gough's questions about his responsibilities. "My father is alive—what is my responsibility?" (1956, pp. 835–838).

Such long dependence of son on father is reversed after the father's death, when the fate of his soul depends on his son's ritual observances. The imperative need for sons and the long dependence of son on father is sanctioned and sanctified in scriptures. The father-son relation and duties constitute the essential legal bond of the classic Hindu family (Kapadia 1947, pp. 83–92; Derrett 1960. p. 311).

In families of lower jatis, as has been noted, a son's dependence is not typically so intense or protracted, yet even among them a father is expected to maintain an aloof authority toward his son. Thus among the Pramalai Kallar, a cultivator jati of the Tamil area, a father is generally indulgent with a young child. But as his child grows up, Dumont observes, the father becomes a more distant person, isolated in his authority. The son takes orders from his father but scarcely dares to discuss anything with him, even to clarify important matters on which the father has given orders. The father's authority is so great yet so sensitive of challenge that the two have very little direct communication (1957b, pp. 212–213). A similar relationship is noted in the account of the Balahis, a Harijan jati of Madhya Pradesh. Firm and formal authority is exercised by the father of a Balahi family; he is expected to keep a considerable social distance between himself and his adolescent and grown sons (Fuchs 1950, p. 21). In other jatis and regions as well, an adolescent boy is usually subjected to much stricter authority than he felt as a child; his father is supposed to become more reserved and distant.

The father-son relation is not without personal strain even among those who extol the ideal. In one Rajasthan town the men of the high jatis insisted to the inquirer that it was unthinkable to disregard a father's command, but they also gave him reason to think that the tension between father and son was very strong (Carstairs 1957, pp. 68–69). A grown man may resent his father's strong authority, but open defiance is rare.

Whenever such defiance does erupt, the son can stand on his legal rights and demand partition and his equal share of the family property. One such case was still talked about in a Maharashtrian village years after the event. Among Brahmin landowners of a Kashmir village this occurs only in rare circumstances; normally a son behaves as if his father were the sole owner of the estate. So is it also in a Mysore village, save that there the possibility of a demand for partition is said to soften the father's stern control (Orenstein 1965, p. 57; Madan 1965, pp. 63, 168; Harper 1963, pp. 169–170).

A questionnaire on family relations was given in Bangalore to 157 men and women, mainly educated and of high jati origin. There were many more spontaneous mentions of affection between sons and fathers than of dislike and hostility. Only 16 mentioned antagonism as against 74 references to affection. Yet this was the highest incidence of hostility mentioned for any family relationship. Several respondents noted that there was a marked drawing apart of the two when the son was a young man but was not yet independent. In the words of one respondent, "The father is always a little like a stranger to the son and the mother acts as intermediary between them" (Ross 1961, pp. 101, 137, 144).

The mediating function of the mother is depicted as a central factor in family organization among the Pramalai Kallar, where the social distance and incipient rivalry between father and son make mediation necessary. This circumstance, Dumont comments, helps explain the extremely strong position of the mother of a family in the Tamil country. If she is competent she can manipulate the affairs of the family into which she originally came as a lowly stranger. She can wield decisive influence, if not formal authority, through her sons (1957b, pp. 212–213; see also Orenstein 1965, pp. 56–59).

Between mother and son there is everywhere in India a strong, tender, unchanging, dependable bond. The bond is celebrated in sacred writing, romanticized in popular tale, upheld in the actuality of family life. A mother is respected; motherhood is revered. Sons give abundantly of both the tokens and the substance of esteem. She is not the aloof person a father is supposed to be. She is everlastingly loving and caring, certainly in ideal, often in reality. This is particularly true of a woman in a wealthy family who has little more to do than to care for her children. In that care lies her greatest fulfillment as a person.

Her authority over her son's domestic life continues after he brings home a bride, and sometimes includes the regulation of his sexual relations with his wife (Karve 1965, p. 12; Gough 1956, p. 838). In his autobiography, Rajendra Prasad, first President of India, tells of his visits to his village home in Bihar while he was a student. His was a landowning family of a Kayasth jati and the women, including his young wife, were kept in the strictest kind of purdah seclusion. He met his wife only during his school holidays and then he had to sleep apart from her. "In the middle of the night, my mother would send a maid-servant to wake me up and she would take me to my wife's room." He had to be back in his own bed before others woke in the morning. Later in his life he saw to it that some of the more extreme family practices were changed in his own joint family and he pressed for similar reforms in wider circles (1957, pp. 22–23, 238–239).

Women of the middle and lower jatis who work outside the home are not usually as totally centered on their children. Their control over their sons is not as ubiquitous and prolonged, but in all jatis the mother-son relation is a pivotal one. The principal strain on it commonly comes when the son's wife feels securely enough established in the household to assert some independence, if only by a gesture. As quarrels burst forth, a man is apt to feel himself torn between irreconcilable adversaries—between his mother whom he cannot cross and the mother of his sons whom he really does not want to make unhappy (cf. Dube 1955b, p. 143).

A test of these opposing pulls was made in a questionnaire given in the Delhi area to 590 Aggarwal men and women. Their traditional jati occupation is that of merchants and shopkeepers. Each man was asked whether he was closer to his mother or to his wife or equally close to both. A majority of the men, 56 percent, replied that they were closer to their mothers; only 20 percent said that they were closer to their wives; 19 percent replied that they were equally close; and 5 percent gave other replies. However, only 17 percent of the wives of these men thought that their husbands were closer to their mothers; 57 percent said that their husbands were closer to them. The author comments, "It seems obvious that men's own experience of their relationship to mother and wife is different from the image the women have of these relationships" (Gore 1961, p. 102). The majority of the men in this sample followed the traditional pattern, in the questionnaire reply at least, of holding the maternal bond above the marital one.

As Brother to Brother: Partners and Sometimes Rivals

Among brothers the ideal of unity, solidarity and mutual support is better realized when brothers are under the firm authority of their father or when they rally against a threat from outsiders. But when paternal authority is weak or absent and when they are not defensively united, grown brothers often rub each other the wrong way and find reasons for argument. However, if one brother is considerably older than another, say by ten years or more, their relationship is less likely to become strained. Then the elder more easily assumes some of the responsibility and respect that the father commands, and if the father dies while the younger is still a boy the elder brother usually fulfills the duties of a father.[1]

[1] This happened in Jawaharlal Nehru's family. His father, Motilal Nehru, was a posthumous child who had two brothers much older than he was. One of them raised Motilal. Nehru writes that the relation between his father and his uncle was a strange mixture of the brotherly, the paternal and the filial (1041, p. 17).

All agnatic relations tend to be formal, Mayer says of Ramkheri villagers, and this holds widely true (1960, p. 219). A major ambiguity and common cause of strain in the fraternal relation is that brothers are equals and yet are not equal. They are all equal in property rights, all equally representative of the family, all equally bound in with the family's social status and fortunes. Yet an elder brother is also vested with some authority over a younger and the younger should, in some degree, be submissive to his elder brothers. But sooner or later the question arises of the degree and nature of deference. The uncertainty as to when equality should be paramount and when inequality should prevail tends to rile their relations.

Men of lower jatis are more likely to emphasize the equality of brothers—the peer rather than the unequal relationship. The Kotas of the Nilgiri Hills were formerly a low-ranking tribal group, traditionally artisans and musicians. Their traditional occupations fostered the peer relationship, since a man could not work a smithy alone or be a one-man band. A man had to have the cooperation of other Kotas in making a living, and the cooperation was best accomplished by a band of brothers, if not real brothers then classificatory ones. Fraternal equivalence is assumed in Kota ritual. One brother can substitute for another in such rituals as that of divorce; if a man does not want to face his wife's father, before whom he must formally divorce his wife, he can send his brother to stand in for him at the rite. Just as brothers shared equally in work, property, and ritual so they shared rights in each other's wives. Each brother had the right of sexual access to another brother's wife (Mandelbaum 1938).[2]

In contrast to this Kota example, people of most jatis in northern India (and of the higher in the south), give formal expression to inequality among brothers. An elder brother must avoid direct communication with his younger brother's wife; when he approaches she must veil her head and face. A younger brother, on the contrary, may have familiar and easy relations with an elder brother's wife (cf. Karve 1965, pp. 19–20, 136; Sarma 1951, pp. 66–68; Lewis 1958, pp. 191–192; Mayer 1960, pp. 220–221). In some groups an elder brother must proclaim, through ritual act at the younger brother's wedding, that thenceforth he will not so much as touch the garment of the bride (cf. Planalp 1956, pp. 507–508; Freed and Freed 1964, p. 153). Should he do so, even accidentally, the woman will resent it and is likely to make her resentment known.

So different is the relation of a younger brother to his elder brother's wife that the two joke with each other, even tease each other on sexual matters.[3] She may discuss his future wife with him. Gandhi wrote of his nuptials, "My brother's wife had thoroughly coached me about my behaviour on the first night" (1940, pp. 14–15).

Among some of the cultivator jatis near Delhi this joking relationship was customarily allowed to extend to sexual relations as well, although those with some education in the jati have learned that such practices are uncouth by both Sanskritic and modern standards. The case of a young wife,

---

[2] Similar rights used to be held by brothers among Nayars of Travancore (Gough 1965, pp. 9–11). This pattern of fraternal equality is still followed by some of the hill people at the Himalayan edge of India. It is the basis for tacit wife sharing in some groups as well as of institutionalized polyandry among others in this region (Berreman 1962c). Another practice that involves the substitutability of brothers is the levirate under which a widow is expected to become the wife of her deceased husband's brother (Srinivas 1965, p. 41; Karve 1965, pp. 19–20, 224). This obviously cannot occur among those who prohibit widow remarriage, but it is a custom of some middle-ranking jatis.

[3] This difference between the roles of elder and younger brother is generally more marked in the north, but some south Indian jatis also maintain similar patterns, particularly in the permissive relations between a man and his elder brother's wife (cf. Dube 1955b, pp. 153–156; Reddy 1952, p. 232).

sorely troubled on this account, is told by K. D. Gangrade (1964). She had recently been married to a man considerably older and less educated than herself. Her husband was employed in the city and in his absence her husband's younger brother began to claim his fraternal rights. When she realized that his joking had become pointedly serious she took her troubles (her fifth-standard education was probably a factor in this) to a social worker. The welfare worker advised her to put the matter tactfully to her husband and to her mother-in-law. Both the client and the social worker (who was of a Brahmin jati) were taken aback when the other members of the family indicated to the young wife that she had no cause for complaint and that she should do her proper duty as wife and sister-in-law.

The mother-in-law plainly said that, "after all the children belong to the household" and that sexual relations with a husband's younger brother are not tabooed (*ibid*., p. 252). The account of this case ends happily for wife and welfare worker; they convinced the mother-in-law that following the traditional practice now leads to the break-up of a joint family. What transpired in this family later, the published record does not reveal. Though the people of this jati gave unequal privileges to brothers, an elder being vested with more authority, a younger endowed with sexual rights not held reciprocally by his elder brother, they nonetheless share the characteristic concern for fraternal unity and condemnation of fraternal discord.

The bond between brothers is taken ideally as a durable and cohesive relationship for cooperative action, second only to the tie between father and son. In actuality the fraternal bond tends to become unstable in time. Brothers of a poor family of low jati may have little to quarrel about. If they are all laborers or heavily dependent on an overlord, they have little cooperative enterprise of their own. But those brothers who together manage and work the land or jointly provide goods and services are likely sooner or later to fall out.

Such estrangement among adult brothers is noted as a salient feature of the family system in a Kashmir village (Madan 1965, p. 169). Similarly, an account of a village of Poona district mentions that brothers commonly quarrel after their father has died, each viewing the others as rivals. Their quarrels sometimes become bitterly vindictive (Orenstein 1965, pp. 45, 48). The same fraternal conflict is reported from a village near Bangalore in Mysore. There the incidence of brothers' quarrels is not a large proportion of all village conflicts but "it is the most shocking kind of conflict and the most contrary to traditional values" (Beals and Siegel 1966, pp. 130–131). In most places and jatis, brothers are expected to be allies; they are so exhorted by parents, kin, and neighbors. But as they become husbands and fathers they tend to become rivals within the one household and they may be abetted in this by their wives. They usually want to be friendly and mutually supportive, yet the younger may find himself irked by the elder's arrogation of undue authority, and the elder by the younger's flaunting of unwonted independence.

As Brother to Sister: Durable Bond

No such uneasiness mars the usual relations of brother and sister, which are typically more stable, durable, and affectionate. A man can be giving and protective to his sister, open-handed and openhearted, without formal reserve or inward calculation. He gives more to her than he receives from her and feels rewarded just to do so. He keeps up the relation after his sister has married and has left her original home. This entails special responsibility toward her husband and particularly to her children, and the relationship is of major importance for the individual and for the jati. So in acting as brother to his sister a man also assumes the duties of brother-in-law and of mother's brother. In discussion of the one role, it is well to consider the extensions of that role as well.

Rivalry figures little in the brother-sister bond, nor is there rivalry between mother and daughter for the affection of son and brother. Because the daughter must soon leave her natal home, her mother is eager that the girl's brother be fond of her. Then the family will be able to keep closely informed about the girl's fate among those people in whose household she must live. A girl's brother is often the mother's emissary to her. Should she need help and protection in that house, he tries as best he can to give it (Karve 1965, p. 131; Dumont 1957b, pp. 206–207; Carstairs 1957, p. 70; Sarma 1951, p. 54; Mayer 1960, pp. 219–223; Ross 1961, pp. 110, 163–165; Rowe 1960, p. 304).

The moment when a bride leaves her natal home is commonly a poignant one in the wedding ceremony. Then the brothers of the bride (often it is a particular brother) are apt to demonstrate great grief and not only because the occasion demands it. Srinivas tells that he has seen a Coorg man, from one of the proudest warrior traditions in South India, break down with grief at that moment (1952a, p. 147).

A boy's elder sister may be his special childhood companion. Though just barely older, she may care for the boy child, lugging him about on her hip and treating him as her playmate as well as her main chore. If all others in the household are too busy or too constrained to look after him with continual loving care, at least she is neither distracted nor inhibited from treating him as a real person rather than as a container of urgent biological needs or a carrier of future social status. A younger sister does not tend him in the same way but she may also be more companionable and relaxed with him than a preoccupied adult is apt to be.[4]

Though a study of child care among the Rajputs of Khalapur village north of Delhi indicates that girls do not usually take care of younger children, this may be exceptional (Minturn and Lambert 1964, p. 234). Certainly it is common in villages to see small girls taking care of even smaller tots. Carstairs makes the point, on the basis of his observations in a Rajasthan town, that a growing child experiences a continuity of physical and emotional contact with his sisters of a kind that is denied to him by his parents. Even his mother is constrained with the child when the mother-in-law is about and she also is engaged in other work. A sister's care is not diminished for these reasons (Carstairs 1957, p. 71).

There is ritual recognition of the special bond between brother and sister in an annual rite observed in northern and western India. The sister gives her brother a charm, often a thread which she ties around his wrist, as symbol of her solicitude for him. He gives her a gift in return, token of his role as benefactor. On this day (called *Raksha Bandhan* or some variant thereof) a man may receive charms from several donors, from his wife, from a Brahmin with whom he has dealings, or from others who can give him ritual protection. But usually the principal charm is that given by his sister, and the occasion is one when sister and brother should meet. If they cannot meet, a man's

[4] Nehru's recollection of the birth of his next younger sister when he was eleven years old illustrates how people outside the family can help set the scene for relations between siblings. "One of the doctors came and told me of it and added, presumably as a joke, that I must be glad that it was not a boy, who would have taken a share in my patrimony" (1941, p. 26). Nehru remembered that he had been bitter and angry at the thought that anyone should imagine that he would harbor so vile a notion. The implications of the doctor's little joke, that brothers were rivals and one should be glad at the birth of a sister because she was not a brother, were angrily rejected in this instance but would hardly be lost on other boys in like circumstance.

sister may send him the charm through the mail. In South India this affirmation occurs as part of other rites. In the region of Dharwar in Mysore, brothers and sisters are expected to meet in the festival of Naga Panchami and Deepavali. The brothers give gifts in kind, the sisters mainly in blessings (Gupte 1919, p. 178; Lall 1933, p. 147; Underhill 1921, p. 134; Marriott 1955b, p. 198; Orenstein 1965, p. 59; Lewis 1958, p. 208; Ishwaran 1965, p. 84).

When a man's sister marries, he too takes on a new and different set of relations. Over much of northern India he becomes inferior to his sister's new family. To her he remains one of the closest of the dearly beloved in her childhood home. To her new family he becomes one who, by definition, is to be taken lightly. As she is subordinate to her husband, so is her whole natal family in some degree subordinate to that of her husband. A family that takes in a girl as bride considers itself superior to the family that gives her in marriage. Her family acknowledges this, though sometimes only grudgingly.

In South India this kind of rank differential is not built into marriage alliances. In some Tamil groups the bride's family is thought inferior to the groom's but, as Dumont comments, the difference in rank at the marriage ceremony fades away in time, "so that there is no suggestion of the wife coming from a lower-ranking lineage." The superiority of one family line over the other is continued only if matrilateral cross-cousin marriages are consistently made between the two (Dumont 1961b, p. 84; see also Dumont 1953; 1957a, pp. 33–37).

No inferiority at all attaches to the bride's family in other parts of South India. In the Kannada-speaking village of Gopalpur, for example, a woman's new family receives her brother as an equal and her father as an honored guest because he has conferred on them the boon of a bride (Beals 1962, p. 27).

Yet whatever formal status may be applied to each family, a brother throughout most of India is expected to keep giving gifts and ritual services to his married sister, perhaps also to her husband and certainly to her children. His benefactions are not requited in any equal measure. There is little calculation of reciprocity; the giving is supposed to be its own reward. Moreover, in the process of being benefactor he gets little glory. Since he is a chief link between his family and his sister's conjugal household, he bears the brunt of their superior airs. In North India and Bengal, the very word for wife's brother is a common term of abuse which a man flings at a cursed ox, which he uses for a shoddy tool, and by which he refers to the affinal kinsman who periodically appears bearing gifts (cf. Nicholas 1965, p. 33). For all that, a brother does not usually flinch from going to visit his sister if he thinks she needs to see him. And, of course, he gives the same kind of treatment to his own wife's brothers and to all the brothers of his brothers' wives. Receiving such treatment does not sap a man's regard for his sister nor does it block a real, as well as ritual, devotion to her children.

In many South Indian jatis, brother and sister are important figures in the marriage arrangements for each other's children and even, in some groups, for their own marriages. Thus in some of the southern jatis an elder sister is expected to urge her younger brother to marry her own daughter.[5] In one Mysore village about 7 percent of 518 marriages studied were between actual maternal uncle and niece, about 3 percent more between classificatory uncle and niece (McCormack 1958b, p. 39). A university professor who came from one of the cultivator jatis of Tamil Nadu once recounted to me how fortunate his marriage had been. The children of his elder sisters had not been well

[5] Marriage to a younger sister's daughter is commonly forbidden in the north and west. But it is permitted in one jati of Marathi-speaking Brahmins, who have apparently taken up the southern custom (Karve 1953, p. 233).

educated but luckily for him only the boys survived to adolescence, so he was not under pressure to "preserve the family" by marrying an elder sister's daughter and was able to marry an unrelated, educated girl of his jati. The marriage of a man to his elder sister's daughter, Yalman points out, is one variation on the main theme of South Indian kinship, that brother and sister have close relations (1967, pp. 351–352).

Much more common in the south is the preference for marriage between cross-cousins, that is, the children of a brother and sister. It is a preference rather than a firm prescription; most matches are actually contracted outside this preferred range of kin. Thus the percentage of marriages made outside this range is 60.4 percent in one Mysore village, 70 percent and 80 percent for the dominant cultivator jatis in two other Mysore villages. 82 percent in an Andhra Pradesh village, and 88 percent among the Brahmins of a village in Tanjore district, Madras (McCormack 1958b, p. 36; Epstein 1962, pp. 168, 297; Dube 1955b, p. 119; Gough 1956, p. 844).

Nevertheless, a sister in these villages is generally expected to have the right of first refusal for her child in selecting a spouse for her brother's child. A brother has a similar right, which in some jatis is formalized in ritual. Thus among the Nadar of the Tinne-velly district in Madras there is a special rite before a wedding in which the mother's brothers of a bride publicly disavow their claims to her if she is not marrying either a mother's brother or his son (Raj 1959, pp. 104–105). Similarly at weddings in Morsralli village in Mysore the bridegroom's sister is especially honored with gifts and she is later honored again at the weddings of his children as a token of her rights in him and in his children. In Morsralli, McCormack observes, the brother-sister relation is the main basis for cordial relationship among relatives (1958b, pp. 44–46).

As Mother's Brother: Supportive Kinsman

A man is expected to take his sister's children as his special charge and in almost every jati and region, he does so. He takes particular interest in her sons. In the northern regions he is not, as he is in much of the south, a potential father-in-law; but in all regions his attitude toward a sister's son is one of benevolent concern. Toward this boy he can be both happily attached and conveniently detached. He can have the satisfaction of giving freely of his bounty to a beloved youngster without also having the duty of molding him into a proper member of society. That responsibility is upon the father and the agnatic relatives of the patriline. The people of the mother's natal family (and later of the wife's) are more sympathetic and supportive of him as an individual, as will be noted again below, and among them, the mother's brother is a main source of support (cf. Dumont 1957a, p. 36; 1961b, pp. 86–87). A child typically looks forward to the exciting, happy visits to his mother's first home. There both mother and son are welcome guests, and her brothers are chief among those who welcome and cherish them.

The mother's brother is an important figure in life cycle ceremonies from birth to marriage. Thus at the initiation ceremony of a Pandit Brahmin boy in a Kashmir village, one of his mother's brothers performs rites designed to help and protect him, while his father's siblings remind him of his new duties and responsibilities. In this region a busybody who takes undue interest in the welfare of others is sarcastically called a mother's brother, but the image of the truly benevolent and affectionate mother's brother is a repeated theme of song and folktale (Madan 1965, pp. 213–215). At the other end of the social scale and of the subcontinent from this highest jati of the northernmost region, are the Nayadis, traditionally beggars and the most polluting of jatis in Kerala. Among them also, special ritual services are performed by the brother of the mother at a child's life-cycle rites. In turn, the nephews take a special part in his funeral rites (Aiyappan 1937, pp. 62, 68–70).

Though the precise ritual varies by jati and region and the reality of the relationship varies by personality and domestic circumstance, yet a man commonly does perform special ritual services for the children of his sister and generally gives them help and care as well. If several brothers are eligible to perform the rites, the senior or most suitable among them does so. The marriage of a sister's child usually calls forth the brothers' best efforts and they may then cooperate willingly even if otherwise they are cool to each other.

This is not to say that there is no strain in relations between any brother and sister or that the ideal is regularly enacted to the full.[6] In his account of Shamirpet village near Hyderabad for example, Dube notes that "family histories recorded for the purpose of this study do not reveal any permanent tender emotional ties between brothers and sisters." And in Gamras (Kanpur district) Sharma found that the cordial and intimate relations between brother and sister tend to change after the brother's marriage, when his wife begins to intervene. But in both places a mother's brother is still the giver of gifts and ritual services whenever his sister's child is the subject of ritual observance (Dube 1955b, pp. 157–159; Sharma 1956a, pp. 282–284).

The more common sentiment is illustrated in a proverb heard in Ramkheri village. "One hundred Brahmins, one sister's son." That is, one gains more spiritual merit when he helps his nephew than when he gives lavishly to Brahmins. The brother-sister relation and its extensions in this village are like those in many jatis and villages. Mayer notes that the one-sided giving by the mother's brother to his nephews and nieces is really an extension of a brother's protective, beneficent relation to his sister. A man takes more interest in the nephew while the sister is alive. "The primary interest thus lies in the sister rather than the people of her conjugal household" (1960, p. 223). A sister, in turn, performs important ritual services for her brothers' children. But she does not have as firm an attachment to her brother's children as he has to hers, perhaps because she is more recipient than donor and, being less mobile and independent, she is less able to give either of goods or services.

The relation of a boy to his father's brother, Mayer continues, is an extension of the relation to his father and of that between brothers which is "correct" and restrained as often as it is warm and cooperative. Since the mother's brother lives in another place, he need not be concerned with daily affairs or rivalries; he appears only as a gift-giver and helper. "His is either a positive or a neutral, but not a negative role; and distance enables him to cast a cloud of excuses over his actions if they contradict the ideal pattern" (1960, p. 224). A boy's father's brother is usually a kind of secondary father, perhaps less aloof and more approachable than his own father, but nevertheless a figure of similar authority. One's mother's sister may be sentimentally close, but she is physically remote in her own married home, less free to visit and to give to her sister's children than is their mother's brother.

---

[6] Among the Nayars of Kerala, the brother-sister relationship was different from that in patrilineal India because both lived in the same household throughout their lives. Yet this, also, was a strong and supportive relationship. This was not so among the Nambudiri Brahmins, the neighbors and ritual superiors of the Nayars. Only the eldest son in a Nambudiri family could marry a Nambudiri girl. There were many spinsters, and since they were kept in seclusion, they contributed little to the family. "Relations between brother and sister were never close; indeed there was a tendency to regard sisters, both elder and younger, as simply a drain on the family resources" (Mencher and Goldberg 1967, pp. 95, 101). The patrilineal Nambudiris, in this regard, diverged more from the Indian norm than did the matrilineal Nayars.

The ancient literature attests to the protection a man gives to his sister's children; the mother's brother is the one to whom a character turns when he is in dire straits (Kapadia 1958, p. 219). So is it today; when a boy or man feels oppressed by home pressures, he is apt to turn to his mother's people for refuge and help. Later in life, when the mother's brothers are dead or declining, he may similarly turn to his wife's brothers.

The social consequences of these ties with feminal kinsmen will be discussed later. The solidarity of a jati across villages is continually reinforced by the brother-sister relation and its ramifications. Children come to know quite early in life that there are kinsmen and jati fellows in other villages who are friends and protectors. When a man's sister marries into another village, he is obligated to maintain good relations with his jati fellows in that village for his sister's sake, just as his wife's brothers keep up relations with him and his family. Cohesion within the jati is thus strengthened because of the loyalty and affection which men have for their sisters and the sister's children.

As Husband: Social and Personal Gains

In his role as husband, a man should always be the superior, the initiator, the receiver of deference from his wife. A village wife rarely flouts these expectations openly. Commonly she renders the expected gestures freely, spontaneously, and in full, as part of her womanhood, not out of feelings of duress. The man is expected to make clear demonstration of his husbandly authority at the beginning of a marriage and never to relinquish it, at least not publicly. Moreover, a young husband's personal, conjugal interest in his wife should in no way interfere with his duties to his parents, his siblings, or to other elders of his household.

A marriage begins with the newlyweds as the most junior couple in a multi-couple household. In private, alone together, the new husband may be playful, passionate, argumentative, affectionate. The physical arrangements are usually such that privacy can be attained only briefly, hurriedly, and in darkness. In fine weather, the fields offer some haven. But in the presence of other persons, especially elders of the household, the two must keep their distance and the husband's aloof precedence must prevail (cf. Dube 1955b, p. 142; Mayer 1960, p. 220; Sharma 1956a, p. 272). In later life they need not ignore each other quite so studiously in public, but a husband's formal superiority must always be duly acknowledged by his wife.

This prescription of the husband's role is held at almost all social levels and regions. A husband's authority is more durably imperative among the higher and wealthier jatis than among the lower and poorer, where women can earn on their own and therefore are less totally dependent. Yet it is also upheld among the lowest jatis, as Fuchs' account of an untouchable jati, the Balahis of Nimar district of Madhya Pradesh indicates. A Balahi husband, Fuchs writes, takes no notice of his wife in the presence of strangers, and does not talk to her unless they are alone or with near relatives or neighbors. But after some years, the two become easier with each other, and a clever woman learns how to lead her husband without his becoming aware of it. Her range of influence is limited, but she can exert some influence; and her husband is restrained from mistreating her beyond the conventionally acceptable limit lest she be taken back by her natal family (Fuchs 1950, pp. 165–167).

Husband-wife relations, as described for the highest jati of Kashmir, are broadly similar. One informant illustrated them by describing the return of a Pandit Brahmin traveler to his home. The men, women, and children of his household flock around him. Men and women embrace him, kiss his forehead. The women weep with joy, the children run about and shout. Even the neighbors, Muslims as well as Brahmins, join in the joyous welcome. But there is one woman who does not join in, who continues to do whatever she was doing before the commotion began. She may go into the kitchen, ostensibly to work there. In any event she will take no overt notice of the returned man or he of her. She is his wife.

One reason for this formal aloofness, Madan explains, is that any display of special interest between the two is taken as a sign of a bond that may disrupt the man's filial and fraternal duties and so is highly disfavored. For this reason a young wife may not prepare any food especially for her husband. If she wants to do some household task for him, she must do it for the whole family. Another reason for the display of indifference is the elders' view that a young couple should have only one interest of their own apart from the rest of the family—in sexual relations and those only in order to beget children. "Consequently there is a sense of shame which surrounds the wife-husband relationship for many years after marriage when sexual drive is held to be the main interest which a man and his wife have in one another" (Madan 1965, pp. 134–135).

Such shame is generally much less strong in middle and lower jatis. Although a young wife among them is supposed to be exceedingly shy and demure and the couple may have to make clandestine arrangements to have sexual relations, others in the family do not necessarily decry their sexual interest in each other. In all jatis the formal superiority of the husband must be diligently manifested, and in all it may covertly be directed by his wife. So among the Balahis, "the formal domination of husbands over wives, though true, conceals the fact that women are able to exert a far greater influence over their husbands than even they care to admit" (Fuchs 1950, p. 136).

When a youth becomes a husband, not much in his daily life seems altered. He lives in the same household, does the same work, acts in much the same family roles. But the marriage does typically make a difference in his social potential and in his concept of himself. He now has a woman of his own whose whole being is directed to him even if she must not show it openly. He knows that he is receiving an intensity of attention from her that he may not have experienced since infancy. His social potential has been enhanced; an unmarried man in most groups is not considered to be a complete person, and in some he does not even rate a full funeral ceremony when he dies.

The personal impact of the marriage on the young man is dramatically begun with the wedding ceremony. He becomes a king for those days, a being so exalted that even his elders give deference to him. That lofty feeling, usually coming at a time of adolescent restiveness, is made possible by the girl as bride and is reawakened daily by her covert ministrations as his wife. Her presence thus assures him that he truly is a superior individual, no matter what his jati rank or personal capacity may be.

This is sensitively shown in the Wisers' account of Karimpur village in Mainpuri district of Uttar Pradesh. The authors observe that no matter how humble a man's position in the village, he becomes a personage when he enters his own courtyard. His wife is ready to do his bidding with head bowed and voice subdued and so are other women junior to him. A young husband finds this most pleasant. He has been dependent on others, now he has a human being under his control. Mrs. Wiser tells how she and some of the village women were sitting together one day when a young man, not long out of boyhood, appeared delivering a storm of abuse. She was momentarily puzzled and then noticed that the girl at her side was smiling under her scarf. It was the young man's new wife whom he was ordering about. She hurried to do what he ordered and returned, all smiles. He had shown that he was a proper husband, she that she was a proper wife; both were satisfied (1963, pp. 79–81).

Later in a marriage, there may well be quarrels in which the wife gives as well as receives. In the Andhra village of Shamirpet, Dube observes, almost everyone will verbalize the ideal of husband-wife relations in similar words, but the reality of family life is not quite as the ideal formula would have it. "The husband is, without doubt, superior and has, in most families, the upper hand; but practically nowhere do we find him a completely dominant, authoritarian, and patriarchial figure" (1955b, p. 142).

A woman then is not without certain powers. For one thing, she is in charge of domestic ritual purity. If she feels vexed and vengeful, she may be careless about the purity of food or of her own person. She need not go to the length of traffic with other men, she need only be a bit lax about her own menstrual seclusion. Furthermore, a wife is readily seen by her husband's family as an active temptress. A man is supposed to have only a limited amount of life-giving fluids and rapid loss is believed to weaken a man drastically. Women are not so debilitated by frequent intercourse (Beals and Siegel, 1966, pp. 43–46; Berreman 1963, p. 170; Carstairs 1957, pp. 83–88).[7]

The rhetoric of marital quarrels in a Mysore village has been noted by Alan Beals. Certain actions, such as "salutary beatings" lead to reconciliation, others quite surely to divorce (Beals MS. 1965). There are probably similar patterns of domestic discord in other villages and regions. Generally the elders who are most closely related to the quarreling pair try to prevent a serious break. Each marriage bond is permanent among those higher jatis in which divorce and the remarriage of widows are forbidden. A woman of these jatis, once married, is linked to her husband with the finality of birth and death. As we have previously noted, divorce and widow remarriage are permitted in many of the other jatis, but even where divorce is very common, as it is among the Kotas of the Nilgiri Hills, the parents of each spouse typically hope for a durable marriage for their child. Marriage among the Kotas is a simple matter, quickly arranged and consummated. It is often a brittle arrangement for young people. Divorce is readily contrived and frequently accomplished. Most men and women have a history of a number of marriages and divorces. After a couple has a child or two, their marriage is more likely to settle into the lasting relationship that their elders urge them to have (Mandelbaum 1938).

Divergent as these Kota marriage practices are from those of the high jatis, the Kotas hold quite similar notions about the desirability of a stable marriage and of the formal superiority of the husband in such a union. At all social levels, a man may take additional wives, especially if the first produces no children. This right has been curtailed by recent legislation but in any event polygyny was not common. A particularly wealthy or powerful man might take more than one wife. A widower could always remarry. In some jatis the sororate is preferred or mandatory; that is a sister of the wife is taken as additional or substitute wife. Where widows can remarry, the levirate is commonly preferred; a brother of the deceased husband becomes the next husband or at least he has the right of first refusal. Generally a second marriage, whether for a man or a woman, is marked with a much simpler wedding than was the first and is not as prestigious an arrangement as the first might be (Srinivas 1965, pp. 40–41; Dumont 1960; Karve 1965, p. 134).

[7] The common men's notion that women make aggressive sexual demands is attested in the account of the Balahis. This account also mentions the women's view, which is rarely noted. Many Balahi men complain, the author tells, that their wives would run away if they omitted intercourse for three consecutive nights. "Balahi women maintain that the nights with their husbands are their only pleasures in a hard and dreary life, for, so they say, a woman has nothing else to think of, while a man may have many other interests and distractions" (Fuchs 1950, p. 165).

Other Roles and Social Consequences

When a man marries he acquires not only a wife but also a new set of relatives, his wife's close kin. To them, as was mentioned earlier in this chapter, he is a respected person, the recipient of their good will and gifts. Among the Pandit Brahmins "his affines are his well-wishers and sympathizers." In the early years of a Pandit Brahmin's marriage his relations with his wife's kin are not close, but when his children are growing up they induce closer ties. A man's affines typically support him both in word and in substance. Their gifts are for his entire household as well as for him personally, given partly for their daughter's benefit, to help better her lot in her husband's family, and also as a means of building and maintaining their own family's status in the jati. The families rated highest are those who are most lavish in their gifts to their daughters' marital families (Madan 1965, pp. 137–140). Similar relationships between a man and his affines have been noted in a wide spread of jatis and regions (e.g., Mayer 1960, pp. 225–227; Harper 1963, pp. 171–173).

Another aspect of the husband's role in the Kashmir village may also be of common occurrence, though wider evidence is not as yet on record. Madan notes that a man with adult children is rather a lonely person in his household. His sons must keep a respectful distance from him and their wives even more so. A woman in her old age can more easily shift her interests to others in the household, but the older a man grows the more dependent he is on his wife since he cannot readily be on familiar terms with the younger people in the household (1965, p. 137). Apparently the pivotal, mediating role a mother often takes between her husband and her sons when they are adolescents, continues when they are mature men with children of their own.

To those children their father's father is part of the paternal authority and the agnatic discipline. Even more than their own father, he must be respected. While they are in his presence, levity, horseplay, demonstrations of parental affection are unsuitable. Relatively few poor men survive long enough to be grandfathers for any considerable length of time. Those who do are often in separate households from their grandchildren and, in any case, they may be enfeebled or senile.[8]

In the joint families of high-ranking landowners, however, the paternal grandfather is often a figure of some consequence to his grandchildren. He is expected to exert his authority in instructing and disciplining the children and so should be strict with them. Hence among the Pandit Brahmins he does not favor frequent visits by them to their mother's natal family and frowns on the loving attention they are likely to get from the mother's parents and brothers there. "They complain that children get spoiled during such visits and by the time they return they usually become undisciplined" (Madan 1965, p. 212). But the same man who may make such complaint about his son's children may well act as the benevolent admirer of his daughter's children when they come to visit.

A Pandit child's attitude toward each of his grandmothers is similarly divided. He may sense some of the characteristic strain between his mother and his father's mother. But his mother's mother welcomes him most fondly as the darling son (or daughter) of her beloved and sorely missed daughter. A Pandit Brahmin's ties to his mother's first family are most important to him when he is young. After he marries and especially after his mother dies, his principal home of affection is with

[8] The retirement of an elder from paramount influence in a household occurs at all social levels. In Driver's sample of 2314 multi-couple families in Nagpur district, the elder couple occupied a subordinate position in 26.3 percent (Driver 1963, p. 41).

his wife's rather than his mother's natal family (Madan 1965, pp. 210–213; see also Sarma 1951, pp. 62–65; Mayer 1960, p. 220; Ross 1961, pp. 92–98).

This Pandit example illustrates general themes in the family roles of a man at most social levels and regions. He works with the other men of the household, as their assigned life partner, to achieve many vital purposes—food, shelter, socialization, defense. With them his roles are cast largely as a member of a cooperating group. Cooperation among the men is continuous in daily tasks and grand events but there is commonly also an element of rivalry or strain in these relations.

A man's relatives through his mother and wife do not contribute much to the daily maintenance and cohesion of the family group, but they are a fundamental resource for him as a person. Our later discussion of feminal kin will note that men who are related through women need not deal with each other as responsible members of a group but more as persons worthy of support. A man gets respect, affection, and sympathy from his mother's and wife's natal family and he gives of the same supportive currency to his sister's and daughter's conjugal family. In his roles as an agnate, a man supports the residential household group and the local lineage, but in his relations through the women of his family he also contributes to identification and cooperation within the jati. Hence these individual, affectionate, affective aspects of a man's family roles do much to foster the cohesion of the larger social group, the jati.

CHAPTER 5

Family Roles: Girl and Woman

The break between being a daughter and sister in one family and becoming a wife and daughter-in-law in another is sharp and, as many women recall, sorely difficult. Their recollection of the sweet joy of girlhood is not merely a construct of nostalgia; girls are commonly under less stern discipline than are boys, especially as their puberty and time of departure approaches.

As Daughter: The Brief Sojourn

Formally and manifestly the birth of a daughter is a much less auspicious event than the birth of a son. When a choice must be made between the needs of a young son and a young daughter, a son is far more likely to get the better food, clothes and care. This is eminently so in the Kashmir village that Madan describes, and yet the girls themselves do not seem resentful of any discrimination. Their parents admit and justify discrimination but also insist that they do not love their daughters less than their sons (Madan 1965, p. 78). Similar favoring of sons is common elsewhere in India, as is a similar lack of strong resentment by daughters, either as children or in their later recollection.

One clue to the reason for this response is offered in the study of child-rearing among Rajputs of Khalapur village in Uttar Pradesh. Rajput mothers of this village, as observed and as questioned, are less warm and more hostile to their sons than to their daughters. "This hostility to boys is particularly interesting in view of the fact that these Rajputs, like most Indians, want to have sons rather than daughters" (Minturn and Lambert 1964, p. 232). A possible explanation offered by Leigh Minturn is that women prefer daughters on emotional grounds, partly because a daughter must soon leave her mother, partly because a woman must never directly express hostility or resentment of her husband. These emotions, Dr. Minturn suggests, are expressed in the coldness with which these women treat their sons (Minturn and Lambert 1964, pp. 232–233; Minturn and Hitchcock 1966, p. 97).

These Rajputs may be exceptional among Indian villagers in this and, as was mentioned in the previous chapter, their girls are given less work and responsibility for domestic chores than are those in many other jatis and regions. Nevertheless, it is quite typical that a girl's place in her original family involves less restraint and permits more open affection than she enjoys after her marriage. Her father usually sees no great need to assert strong authority over her. Among the Havik Brahmins of a Mysore village, a girl is said to be "like a flower," which needs to be cherished and cared for because she will soon marry and come under the stern discipline of another family (Harper 1963, pp. 171–172). Similar sentiments are expressed in families from a wide array of levels and places (e.g., Madan 1965, p. 77; Gore 1965, p. 227).

A girl, especially one who is a younger child, may have a particularly affectionate relation with her father. Such a relationship is described by Mrs. Ranade in her autobiography. When her elder siblings were young, their father's mother was still in the house. Her father could not talk to his children in the presence of his mother, and she was always present: "But Grandmother died the year before I was born, and so, for the first time, my father was free to follow his own desire. He made much of the baby daughter.... I dared take liberties and be familiar with him in a way that quite scandalized my older brothers and sisters" (1938, p. 3). This was in a Brahmin family of Maharashtra toward the end of the nineteenth century; similar affection between father and daughter is noted in more recent accounts (e.g., McCormack 1958b, p. 44).

Such fond relations cannot well be carried on after the daughter goes to her new house. A father, especially in North India, rarely visits his daughter in her married home. His position in that household is an ambivalent one. As an elder he should be respected and given food, but as one who has given a girl to the other family, he must not take anything from them, not even a cup of tea. The donor of a bride must not receive anything at all from those who have taken his daughter (Karve 1953, p. 130; Dumont 1961b, pp. 84 ff.). Despite such ambivalence or disadvantage, a father may greatly benefit from a daughter's marriage. One important way in which a prospering man can demonstrate his power and enhance his family's status is through arranging a prestigious marriage for his daughter. She thus helps translate his secular gains into the more durable and desirable gain of higher status within his jati.

The responsibility for rearing a daughter, for molding her into a proper social person, rests with her mother. Her father may pamper her or remain aloof, but her mother must train and discipline her. That training is mainly aimed at turning her into a good daughter-in-law, obedient, skillful, demure. The girl's chances of a fine marriage are much improved if she gives evidence of these qualities (even more are her chances damaged if she displays contrary inclinations); the family's prestige is enhanced if she demonstrates these virtues after she is married, and her own happiness hinges on making the best of her roles as daughter-in-law and as wife. As a daughter approaches puberty her mother tends to draw closer to her and to remember poignantly that this child of hers will soon be cast beyond her mother's help. This thought softens discipline and leavens training with maternal compassion (cf. Srinivas 1942, p. 195; Ross 1961, pp. 61, 104, 150).

As Young Wife: Great Transition and Critical Role

The nuptial rites mark the great divide in a girl's life. She is physically transferred from the familiar intimacy of her childhood home to a strange place and new people, some of whom are, by reason of their roles, either distant or disciplinary. The transition is not easy and the bride has been prepared to find that it is not easy. Describing the lot of a bride in Senapur village, Opler writes that "In story, proverb, and song, the society has from her earliest years reminded her of the sharpness of the transition at marriage, and of the possible hostility of the mother-in-law and sisters-in-law" (1958, p. 561).

The sad parting scene, when the bride is taken away from her parents' home, touches onlookers' hearts when it is enacted in reality as it does when described over and again in drama and story. The modern relevance of one classic version of this scene has been remarked by Mrs. Karve. It occurs in the fourth act of Kalidasa's drama, *Shakuntala*, of about the fifth century A.D. Mrs. Karve comments that this act well portrays "the situation in every Hindu household." The parents are happy about the match, yet apprehensive about their daughter's future. The girl is eager to join her husband, but tremulous about leaving her beloved family and friends. The father gives advice to the girl on how she should behave in her new home. Mrs. Karve writes that this situation has been depicted in song and drama, in religious poetry and in proverbs, in almost all languages of India as far back as literary records exist; "and a study of these illumines the present situation as it is enacted before our eyes" (1953, p. 20).

In the parting scene, Shakuntala's father advises her to obey her elders, to be very kind to her rivals, and not to be perversely blind and angry with her husband even though he should prove less faithful than a man might be. He adds that when she brings forth a son, she will not any longer miss her father (Kalidasa, 1959 edition, pp. 48–49). In this advice there is the assumption that she will encounter personal rivals in her husband's household and that the husband may not actually behave like the revered figure she must take him to be. Still, she must keep her emotions in check, for "self-willed women are the curse of life." And there can be a redeeming event, the birth of a son.

Some fourteen centuries later, a Brahmin woman of western India, Mrs. Ranade, recalled her father's advice when she was about to leave her home as a bride. He told her to endure silently whatever trouble might come. She was not to talk back even to a servant and should control herself even if something seemed utterly unendurable. He warned her that he expected her behavior to enhance his family's name and that if it did not he would never allow her to visit her mother's house. "Already I was beginning to sense that the discipline in this new home would soon make my carefree life in my mother's home seem like heaven itself" (Ranade 1938, pp. 20–21).

Her forebodings were soon realized. She found herself separated from her mother for the first time in her life and surrounded by a chattering, inquisitive group of women of her new home, who let her hear their cool, unflattering appraisals of her appearance and prospects. This was in nineteenth century Poona. Writing in mid-twentieth century, Mrs. Karve depicts a similar atmosphere in which a contemporary bride of North India finds herself. When her affinal kin take their first look at her face, she must keep her glance demurely lowered or her eyes entirely shut. After marriage she must be self-effacing, neither seen nor heard too much. Whatever misfortunes come to the household within a year or so of her arrival may well be attributed to her inauspicious qualities (1965, pp. 135–136).

A young wife, of any jati and region, usually has lowest status in the family and is given the more onerous chores. Whatever goes awry, she is apt to be called the culprit. Whenever the finger of blame is pointed, it somehow swings toward her. A common saying is that a pot was golden if a daughter-in-law has broken it, only earthen if the mother-in-law broke it. The Pramalai Kallar have a version of this saying. They put a new daughter-in-law in a similar position, even though their women are relatively independent and a new couple usually lives with the parents for only a brief time (Dumont 1957b, p. 207).

The young woman must keep out of the way of the male elders. Communication with her husband's father and elder brothers is minimal; in some jatis it is entirely prohibited. These men may give warning coughs when they come into a room where she is, but the responsibility for avoidance behavior, whether it is covering her head or leaving the room, is hers (cf. Sarma 1951, pp. 57, 67; Karve 1953, p. 134; Dube 1955b, p. 155; Fukutake *et al*. 1964, pp. 43–44).

Her greatest responsibility is to bear a child, preferably a son. Barrenness is a fear, a curse, an unending reproach. Among Kannada-speaking women, not only is the word for barrenness, *banje*, forbidden, but the word for the root of a certain plant, *baje*, is also taboo because it sounds like that fearsome term (Srinivas 1942, p. 171). Everywhere in the land a newly married wife can hardly escape constant reminders of this ominous possibility. An unfortunate who must at last conclude that she will bear no child may well urge her husband to adopt a son or to take another wife so that there may be a child to his name. In any event, the biological facts are such that relatively few young women become pregnant in the first months after the start of their marital life. For those who join their husbands immediately after first menstruation there is an even longer average interval before conception takes place than among those who begin married life a few years after menarche (Mandelbaum 1954a). So a great many young wives undergo harrowing months or years before they know that they are pregnant and feel blessed.

During this period of stringent responsibility, a young wife is also more isolated than ever before or again. Her mother-in-law is supposed to be more of a disciplinarian than a comforter. The other women in the household are not allies. The male elders must keep their distance; the husband's younger brother, who is eligible to be her friend, may not yet have established really easy relations with her. And her husband, her life's mainstay and the whole reason for her presence in the house, cannot appear to take an interest in her. She, in turn, should not show special interest in him though all know that she must perforce pin her hopes and fasten her thoughts on him alone. She does not address him directly and never uses his name. Only his seniors and close friends may do that, not his wife (cf. Bharati MS. 1966).

Where village exogamy is the rule, a young wife is physically isolated from her childhood home and companions. But even in those places where she can see her mother every day, she must be careful to show that she is under the hegemony of her mother-in-law. An incident told by Gerald Berreman illustrates this. A young wife who lived near her parents in Sirkanda village had stopped to talk with her mother when Berreman came by. The two women asked him to take a photograph of them sometime, but when he offered to do so then and there, the younger woman quickly declined. She had been sent by her mother-in-law to gather fodder and the mother-in-law would not like it if she dallied to be photographed. The women suggested that he approach the mother-in-law and offer to take the photograph without mentioning their conversation (1962a, p. 282). Reflected in this small incident is a major precept of Indian family structure, that on marriage a woman comes under the authority of the husband's family, that the authority is mainly exerted by her mother-in-law, and that nothing, neither her relations with her husband nor those with her parents, should impair that legitimate authority or her willing submission.

The situation of a young wife can easily be depicted in more somber tones than is the common reality. She is relatively isolated within the family structure, but she is not in solitary confinement. She can maintain a joking relation with some in the family; perhaps with her husband's younger sister, as well as with his younger brother, or with another brother's wife (cf. Sarma 1951, pp. 67–68). This banter may well be, as joking relations often are in human society, an expression of ambivalence about the true nature of the relation, yet it also relieves the strained tautness of her conduct. She is usually quite a young girl and has the resilience of girlhood. A chore such as getting water from the well can be used as a refreshing relief from the presence of the elders; in the new home there is the excitement of new sights, new people, and the discovery of the person and personality of her husband. She may get to visit her parents' home even before she is pregnant.

But the real relief comes when she becomes pregnant. Her mother-in-law can afford to relax a bit in her role as taskmistress; her husband is pleased; the men of the household are glad; there is an awakened interest in seeing that she eats well and rests easily. This first burgeoning also marks her first upward move in the family status hierarchy.

Before the birth of her first child a woman in some regions returns to her parents' home.[1] Even where birth takes place in the husband's household, as it often does in Hindi-speaking regions, she goes to her parents for a lengthy visit after the childbirth (cf. Karve 1953, pp. 154, 163; Mullick 1882, p. 112; Lewis 1958, p. 49). There in her familiar home she is a favored, freer person. She is a daughter of the house and a daughter of the village, the very terms have a benign ring. She is apt to use quite a different mode of conduct when she visits her old home—less restrained, more outgoing—and in a few places she may even assume different standards of personal morality (Karve 1953, p. 129; Majumdar 1944, p. 163).

As Matron: Increasing Influence

On her return with the child, the young wife's status begins to change. She is no longer the lowly probationer she was at first. If the child is a son, she has proved herself in the most important way of all and her confidence is the more secure. The son is her social redeemer and thenceforth her importance in the family tends gradually to increase. In Ramkheri village the change in her position is symbolized in the eating pattern. When she first arrives in the household, she eats last of all, after the other women. Later she eats at the same time, but turned away from the other women as a sign of respect and of her diffidence before them. Finally, when she feels quite secure, she will face the other women, even those of the elder generation, while eating or eat side by side with them, a sign of equality inside the house as it is at public feasts (Mayer 1960, p. 220).

A young wife, once past the initial stage of her marriage, can enjoy the advantages of her wifely role. She is now a full person, capable of joining as a needed ritual partner in her husband's domestic rites, having certain jural rights in her married home and contingent rights in her original family. Now that she lives away from her girlhood home, she is free of the strains of everyday living together there and may be emotionally closer to her natal family than she was before (cf. Yalman 1967, p. 350; Madan 1965, pp. 79, 124–125, 224).

In some domestic matters she can have her own way. For example, a woman's ritual stringency is largely her own affair. She may be, and often is, more stringent about domestic purity than is her husband. Among the Rajputs of Khalapur, men commonly eat meat but their wives will not. The men must cook their own meat on separate hearths because the women will not touch it or have their

[1] For one Indian woman who was to give birth to her third child, this required a trip from New York to Moscow. Her husband was an official of the United Nations, her father was India's Ambassador to Moscow (Bacon 1956, pp. 257–258).

kitchens defiled by it (Minturn and Hitchcock 1966, p. 44). In South India I have known of women of vegetarian sections of the Badaga of the Nilgiri Hills who were married to men of non-vegetarian sections. Although among the Badagas as among most other Indian villagers a bride is socially assimilated into her husband's household, these brides do not give up their purer diet. And when such a bride becomes first lady of the house, no meat is ever cooked in her kitchen. If her husband and sons want to eat meat, they must cook it themselves, outside.

In South India generally, a woman's activities are not so closely restricted as they are in the Hindi-speaking North. "A woman in the South," Mrs. Karve observes, "lives and moves freely in her father-in-law's house" (1965, p. 242). She does not usually have to cover her face in the presence of elder males as she does in the Hindi region, nor is she so cut off from her natal family. Yet women of the highest jatis in the south are also quite restricted. In Kumbapettai village of Tanjore district, women of the lowest groups, the Adi Dravidas, remain in close touch with their mothers after marriage; young women of the Brahmin jatis are far more isolated both spatially and socially from their mothers. Sisters of the Adi Dravidas usually are in more frequent and close relations with each other after they are married than Brahmin sisters of this village can possibly be[2].

One feature that is consistent across jatis and regions is the great concern of the husband's family about the conduct of the young wife. Should she deviate from the prescribed obedient, complaisant conduct, the corrective forces are, as it were, already poised, and the family elders are quick to bring redressive pressures. Counterchange is on a hair trigger in respect to the behavior of a newly married woman.

The Women of a Family: Expected Friction and Central Importance

Another constant feature is the disciplinary role of the mother-in-law and the gradual resistance of the daughter-in-law. As the younger woman comes to feel more self-assured, as she grows more mature physically and psychologically, she becomes less complaisant and less automatically yielding to the directives of her mother-in-law. Quarrels tend to erupt with increasing frequency and with escalating acrimony.[3] Women do not feel as constrained in venting hostility against other women as do the men in a family and their quarrels are not taken as seriously as are struggles among the men. The degree of verbal hostility varies by jati practice as well as temperament. Among Kumbapettai Brahmins little open hostility can be shown within the family and within the jati. Among the Kotas of the Nilgiri Hills differences of opinion can quickly blossom into loud, vituperative argument. But

[2] Because sisters are likely to be separated after their marriage, with little opportunity for visiting each other, relations between sisters are not central to family structure. Yet the errant behavior of one can affect the whole life status of the other. An educated woman in Bangalore told that when she was studying for the M.A. degree her family arranged a marriage for her to which she objected so violently (and ultimately successfully) that she was about to commit suicide in the traditional way by jumping into a well. "My mother found out and stopped me at the last minute. She told me I had no right to commit suicide, for it would interfere with my sister's marriage, for people would think I had an affaire with someone" (Ross 1961, p. 272).

[3] A young wife, pushed to desperation, may take extreme measures. In Senapur village near Banaras she may become possessed by an evil spirit (Opler 1958, pp. 560–566). Among the Havik Brahmins of Mysore she may similarly fall prey to malevolent intrusion, or she may starve herself or attempt suicide (Harper 1963, p. 173). Throughout village India, instances are graphically told of women who drowned themselves in wells.

whatever the permitted level may be, the women's quarrels in the household generally exceed those of the men both in frequency and volume.

The women of the family are not expected to get along well. As a Kannada proverb puts it, a thousand moustaches can live together, but not four breasts. The hostility between mother-in-law and daughter-in-law is both proverbial and a frequently observed fact. Thus among one of the very lowest of low jatis, the Nayadis of Kerala, the stereotype appears in their expression for crocodile tears, "like a daughter-in-law weeping for her dead mother-in-law"; and the reality is summarized by Dr. Aiyappan's statement that there is always considerable friction between a mother-in-law and her daughter-in-law (1937, p. 37).

The Wisers tell of loud quarrels in Karimpur village and add that to intrude in affairs between husband and wife is futile, but to interfere in a quarrel between mother-in-law and daughter-in-law is to invite the verbal obliteration of one's self, one's forebears, and one's descendants (1963, p. 83). Such quarrels may flare up on almost any pretext but the root causes are generally the same everywhere. The daughter-in-law wants to strengthen the interests of her husband and children; the mother-in-law looks to the interests of the household. The elder woman finds that the younger is disrupting unity among the brothers; the younger finds the elder to be intolerably demanding and domineering (cf. Nicholas 1961, p. 1059; Madan 1965, p. 132).

This opposition between mother-in-law and daughter-in-law is graphically shown in an account of a Mysore village in which uncle-niece marriages occur. When a girl marries her mother's brother, her maternal grandmother then becomes her mother-in-law also. Her maternal grandfather, who would not otherwise have much to do with her marriage arrangements, assumes some authority in his capacity as prospective father-in-law. "The same amount of suppressed hostility and ill feeling seems to exist between a grandmother and granddaughter when their relationship becomes one of mother-in-law and daughter-in-law" (Gnanambal 1960, pp. 54–55).

Nor are relations among women of the same generation more amicable in the family. One example is given in Sarma's depiction of family life in Bengal. She notes that a young wife can have very friendly relations with the girls, her husband's sisters, in her new home. She is anxious to please and they are quite pleased to accept her. But when they marry and leave the family, the relation alters. Each of them becomes more and more cut off from their father's household, and each can hardly help being envious of her brother's wife, who is, or will be, mistress of her former happy home. The wife of the brother, on her part, is not overjoyed by her husband's aid and gifts to his sister. Even while the sisters are unmarried and on close, friendly terms with their brother's wife, they can be her severest critics if they think that she is not behaving properly. In folk songs of many regions the two, a man's wife and his sister, are characterized as natural enemies (Sarma 1951, pp. 68–69; Karve 1965, pp. 129–130; Madan 1965, pp. 132, 171; Srinivas 1942, p. 193).

The women who have married into the family, the wives of the brothers, must live in very close proximity. A description of their relations as observed in Shamirpet village tells of the common situation. Dube writes that the brothers' wives have rivalry, jealousy, and suspicion for one another. "There is always considerable backbiting and telling of tales. Alliances are formed and broken periodically.... The intrigues and jealousies among the womenfolk in a joint family are the despair of men" (1955b, p. 155).[4] No doubt there are some families in this village as in other villages whose womenfolk live

[4] Traditional family life in China was characterized by quite similar relations among women. Maurice Freedman thus summarizes the usual situation in traditional China: "Mother-in-law, daughters-in-law, and unmarried daughters

together in smooth harmony. But whatever tensions are built up, and some tensions inevitably arise in all family life, they tend to be readily expressed in women's intrigues and jealousies. These often lead to the dissolution of the joint family but they support the people's notion that men are inclined to live in amicable partnership but are riven apart by their women (cf. Srinivas 1952b, p. 30). This notion is well worth protecting because the men should continue to cooperate as members of the lineage and jati-group even after they separate the household. So attributing the split to the women helps the men break an uncomfortable solidarity and then to resume cooperative relations.

The popular stereotypes omit important aspects of a woman's family roles. Though boys are indeed favored over girls within a family, yet girls generally seem to suffer little emotional deprivation on that account. And after a girl's marriage the favoring among siblings is reversed. Then her brothers give in to her; she gets much more from them than she is ever expected to give Furthermore, a young woman is expected to feel the chock of transfer from daughter to daughter-in-law and typically she does feel it keenly. Her low status as young wife is part of the systemic separation between agnatic and affinal bonds. But though the young wife is taken to be a person of little consequence in the family, her role is one of great importance. Few family roles are subject to such close scrutiny or so liable to such quick redressive action.

The formal subordination of women in the household does not bar an elder woman from dominating her domestic scene nor does it hamper a younger woman from competitive struggle with other women of the house. Though a young woman may have the lowliest place in her conjugal family she nevertheless may be a main vehicle for a rise in status of her natal family. And although a marriage must be between two who are ritual equals in the local jati system, the two may be from families that are unequally endowed within the jati. A principal lever in the competition for family status is the prestigious marriage of a daughter.

Villagers fulfill their family roles in a cycle of family development that is vital for all of village society and economy, as well as for the maintenance of the jati.

formed a battlefield on which any one daughter-in-law must fight for herself and, later, for her children." As in India, there was a difference between the higher and lower social-economic levels. "In a family of low status and simple structure … each brother stood close to his wife, so that while a wife might be made miserable by poverty and hard work, at the lower levels of society she had greater strength as an individual." Freedman indicates that solidarity among brothers in families of higher status was strengthened by their mutual opposition to the powerful father who controlled their economic fate and social relations (1962, pp. 328–329). In India, brothers in a family of higher rank are not so united by mutual opposition to their father.

CHAPTER 6

Family Cycle: Formation and Maintenance

The characteristic stages of the family cycle in village India are less clearly demarcated than they generally are in urbanized, industrialized, societies. In a demographic comparison of family cycle in India and in the United States, Andrew Collver points out that the stages in America are quite distinct. The American cycle begins with two relatively short phases, one from marriage to first birth and the second comprising the childbearing period. Then follows a longer period, mainly of child-rearing, and a shorter one during which the children marry and leave the parental home. Next is a long period in which the parents live alone, often followed by several years of widowhood.

Among Indian families, as we have seen, there is much greater overlap of successive stages. The marriage of a couple and the period to first birth typically take place as part of the growth phase of the husband's natal family. Often the childbearing years occur in the same milieu; sometimes, although it is not approved, a woman may still be bearing children after she has become a grandmother. The phase after the childbearing years tends to be brief or absent because of the short life expectancy. Collver notes that more than half of all marriages in India end before the wife reaches age forty-five because of the death of one of the pair (1963, pp. 86–87).

Nonetheless, family development throughout village India does occur in several stages, distinguishable to the observer and demarcated by the villagers. Marriages, deaths, and formal partition are the main marking events. The marriages of the children are the grand events of a family's career. The new union is only potentially a new family. The potentiality may be realized in short order, as among the lowly poor and the professional elite, or the pair may remain an incipient new family for many years. The stage during which children are born to a couple may cover much the same years as those of child-rearing. The subsequent marriage of sons is seen as part of the family's growth rather than as the harbinger of dispersal. The actual dispersal, through death or partition or both may take a long time in coming to pass, but it finally comes, sometimes with traumatic tension.

Each incipient new family begins through the efforts of an old family to maintain itself. Family members feel obligated to assure the input of new members and to cope with the output of former members. The inflow is of infants and of brides; the outflow is of departing girls and departed souls.

The Recruitment of Males and Females

Males come into the family at birth and remain until separated by death or partition. If husband and wife find themselves unable to bring forth a son biologically, or if no son survives childhood, they may bring one into the family socially through adoption. The need for adopting a child is indicated in one survey in which over a fifth of the older couples in the sample had no living son. Out of a sample of 626 married women over 50 years of age in Banaras district, 22 percent had no son. About 30 percent had one son alive; less than half enjoyed the security of two or more living sons (Collver 1963, pp. 95–96).

Adoption is firmly rooted in formal law and customary practice. An adopting father takes a boy from his own jati, preferably one who is from his lineage. Among the Pandit Brahmins of Kashmir a man may adopt a boy of his wife's kin if no suitable child of his agnatic line is available (Madan 1965, pp. 82–86).

The incidence of adoptions can be stimulated by economics. In one Mysore village where irrigation has made land far more remunerative than before, the orderly transmittal of an estate is of high importance. Among the landowners, 10 percent of all the males had been adopted. But in a nearby village, where the lands are not irrigated and economic opportunities are not so bound in with the land, only 2 percent of the men of the same jati had been adopted (Epstein 1962, pp. 179, 306). But whatever may be the rate of adoption, it is everywhere in India an approved method of maintaining family development when parturition does not do so.

Another alternative, less commonly taken because of considerations of cost and temperament, is that the husband take another wife, or several, in order to beget a son. Still another alternative is open to a prosperous landowner who has a daughter but not a son. He can arrange a marriage for his daughter to a man who will join his family. The son-in-law helps work the family lands which eventually pass to the daughter's children. This is an inferior kind of marriage for a man, to go to live on the bounty of his father-in-law. Yet there are some such marriages in most places, since an impoverished young man will reckon that the attractions of the estate make up for whatever stigma for him may be involved in the marriage (cf. Klass 1966, p. 960; Madan 1965, pp. 62, 127–128; Fukutake *et al.* 1964, p. 139).

Whatever means are used to assure the inflow of males, the family members do not usually have to ponder difficult choices or manipulate touchy social considerations. They have only to celebrate a birth with proper ritual or, being convinced that a birth is not forthcoming, to secure a suitable alternative with main dispatch and little fuss.

Marriage, the transfer of a female from one family to another, is commonly a matter of transcendent concern and much activity in both families. It is an inescapable choice point and usually brings into the balance every aspect of the family's status, resources, and social relations. It cannot be avoided, because the person of a pubescent daughter in a household, unwed and unclaimed, is uncomfortable, even ritually dangerous for the other members of the family. It is uncomfortable, because her continuing presence betokens either neglect of duty on their part or grave personal defect on hers. It can be dangerous because her untethered sexuality may bring social disgrace, perhaps supernatural retribution, on the whole family unless she is promptly bound in marriage (cf. Kapadia 1958, p. 140).

The need for marrying off a grown son is not quite so urgently felt as that of marrying a daughter. This is in part because there is not the same spur of fear about his unbespoken sexuality and in part because his status and the reputation of his family do not suffer so much if he remains unmarried. Still, his family should do their duty by him and do justice to him by getting him married. Marriage is a sacrament, ordained and imperative, which every normal man and woman should undergo.

A marriage mobilizes the family's social resources. Through marriage the members renew their kin ties or establish new bonds of kinship. Celebrating a marriage requires that all who can be genuinely counted as kin or allies participate through giving gifts, performing services, or just being present for the occasion. The closest kin must take part in all these ways. Other related families should send at least one representative if only to keep alive the kinship bond. The family's jajmani associates contribute their goods and services: the barber often acts as go-between and ceremonial assistant, the potter, washerman, and other clients fulfill their roles in the ritual and receive gifts in return. In a village near Lucknow, for example, client families of ten different jatis must perform ceremonial roles in the marriage of a landowner's child. In a village of Mysore, clients of seven jatis assist in marrying off their patron's child (Majumdar 1958a, pp. 43–49; Epstein 1960, p. 230). A patron family, in its turn, need not attend the wedding of a child of their sweeper's family, but that wedding elicits some gifts from every patron of the sweeper family.

Marriage as a Test of Status

On all social levels, a marriage is a test of a family's status. Then more than at any other time a family's alliances stand forth proven and personified by gifts and attendance; its status hinges on its strength in allies and clients. Hence a marriage provides the prime opportunity for demonstrating and validating family status. A family, like other social units in this society, is hierarchically appraised, judged by jati fellows and by fellow villagers as superior or inferior to other families.

Such judgments frequently differ on specific rankings but usually agree on the general position of a family, whether of landowners or of sweepers, as being among the more eminent or among the more negligible in its sector of the community. There are some villagers who may not be particularly concerned, in the ordinary round, with their family's status, but they can scarcely avoid some such concern when a marriage is to be arranged. A comparative weighing of status factors is built into the process. Even when a marriage takes place within the close circle of kin, as when a man in South India marries his sister's daughter, the family elders must consider the relative advantage of strengthening the family by inner reinforcement as against bolstering its status by external connection.

In the marriage negotiations, the achievements of each family's forebears are weighed, as are the current assets, such as the wealth and power of its members and the personal charm of the principals. Temporal assets do not automatically bestow higher status. They must be used in ways that confer status, and one of the main avenues is through establishing a marriage alliance with a family of unquestioned higher standing. The alliance does not at once make the lower family the absolute equal of the higher, certainly not in those parts of North India where inequality is stipulated through the formal inferiority of every bride's family to that of her groom.

What an advantageous marriage accomplishes for a status-ambitious family is to put its members into the same bracket of rank as the higher family. If previously that higher family had not deigned to take brides from the lower family because it was too poor or undistinguished—though since both were of the same jati they could have done so—the marriage demonstrates for all to see that the lowlier family has risen far enough for the higher to accept one of its daughters. The higher family, in North India, gains by this match through the lavish gifts that the lower gives to its daughter in her married home. The bride's family, in a Muslim village of Punjab where this gift flow has been closely studied, gives about ten times as much in gifts to the groom's family as they receive from them (Eglar 1960, pp. 108–115; Marriott 1962, p. 265).

In some other parts of India, no such formal disparity is required and the two families are expected to be of about the same status. Even in such places there is close examination of the respective status of each to assure that they are really on equal footing. Thus in Ramkheri village of Madhya Pradesh, marriages are arranged between families that are about equal in reputation and wealth. Gift-giving is not heavily one-sided; the groom's family has somewhat greater expenses at the wedding although after the marriage it receives more from the bride's kin. Here, also, a wedding involves great expenditure, much gift-giving, and large attendance by kin and allies of the two families (Mayer 1960, pp. 227–235). Each of the families must be able to contribute an amount appropriate to their mutual, equal status.

A family's status is tested whenever one of its children is married, whether the regional pattern is one of relative equality or of built-in inequality between the contracting families. Status mobility, for a family as for a jati, requires a solid economic base. Wealth is not a sufficient condition for attaining a higher rating, but it is usually a necessary precondition. A very poor family cannot begin to indulge in fancies about raising its status; its members can only marry off a child as best they can.

Under some conditions, economic considerations are given more importance than direct status gain. This has been so in Dalena, the Mysore village whose lands are not irrigated but those of surrounding villages are. Dalena men have nevertheless prospered through the purchase of irrigated lands and through work in a nearby town. They have also increased their marriage alliances with nearby irrigated villages. "As Dalena farmers bought wet lands in neighbouring villages they wanted to strengthen their foothold in these villages by marriage ties" (Epstein 1962, p. 296). Dalena girls, in turn, are sought as wives because families of these other villages like to establish affinal ties with the entrepreneurs and town workers of Dalena.

Experience in the town has become an asset for a prospective groom. This was demonstrated when the daughter of a wealthy traditionalist of Dalena was married to a man of an inferior lineage and from a very poor household of that lineage. The man is a factory worker and is familiar with town ways. When the girl's father appeared uncertain about the match, the suitor got his town friends to convince the father of the suitability of the marriage. For the young man it meant a marked rise in status. His work in the factory enabled him to achieve higher prestige in the traditional social system of the village (Epstein 1962, pp. 296–301; 1960, p. 199). Town and factory affiliations are becoming recognized here as economic assets along with the more traditional economic holdings.

The advantages for the two principals as well as for the two families are not ignored. A family will hesitate to give its daughter in marriage into a village in which there is much conflict or into a family in which the work will be extraordinarily hard. But the girl and the boy are not expected to take much part in the family deliberations because their youthful fancies are not very relevant to the serious, long-range considerations that have to be kept paramount in negotiating a marriage alliance.

Explicit Rules for Marriage Alliances

Two kinds of rules are followed in marriage negotiations, explicit structural rules such as those of endogamy and exogamy, and the implicit rules of the game of maneuvering for family advantage. The structural rules require that the couple belong to the same endogamous group, the jati, and also that each spouse come from a different exogamous category within the jati. Each jati defines these categories in its own way and there are myriad elaborations on these rules, but in fundamental outline they are quite similar throughout the land.

Exogamy means that husband and wife may not be related to each other before marriage in ways that are prohibited, quite as incest is prohibited. The tabooed relationships are those of kin position, of kin grouping, and, in some of the northern regions, of locality. Two people in certain specific kin positions are forbidden to marry, as, for example, a man and his mother's sister. Prohibited also are unions within kin groupings, such as between two who are patrilineally descended from the same real or mythical ancestors. In jatis which follow Sanskritic usage, the prohibited kin positions are collectively known as the *Sapinda* relations and are traced through both father and mother. The kin grouping of Sanskrit scripture called *gotra* will be discussed later, as well as similar groupings noted here under the generic term clan. People of all jatis observe some exogamy by kin position and, in many jatis, by clan groupings also (cf. Srinivas 1942, pp. 32–49, 57–65; 1965, pp. 42–46).

Exogamy by locality as well as by kinship is observed in some regions. Over a large part of northern India, husband and wife must not come from the same village or cluster of villages. This local exogamy is found from Bihar to eastern Punjab, in Rajasthan, Gujarat, and into Madhya Pradesh. It does not hold for some of the Himalayan hill people (Berreman 1962d) and its southward limit is reached about the Malwa region of Madhya Pradesh, where marriage within the village is allowed but is uncommon and not very well regarded. An argument sometimes given against intravillage marriages is that children who were reared in the same village may have called each other brother and sister as children and are, in a vague way, related. But the more cogent reason is that such marriages conflict with the proper relationship between spouses and between affinally related families.

The practical reasons for village exogamy are shown in Morton Klass' account of marriage in a West Bengal village. Marriage alliances within the village are permitted there but most marriages are made between families from different villages. The father of a girl knows that she will want to come back for visits as often as possible after her marriage. If she can easily carry her complaints back to her original family and if they can readily attempt to intervene, there may be more tension between the two families than would otherwise occur and more than will be good for the newly married couple and the two affiliated families. Hence a father is reluctant to make a match within the village. "For a number of reasons, which he assesses quite correctly, such conflicts are more likely between families of the same village and less likely between families of different villages" (Klass 1966, p. 966).

The same arguments against intravillage matches are given by the Brahmins of a Kashmir village, even though some 20 percent of their marriages are of this kind. Not only is the assimilation of a bride to her husband's family impeded if her natal family is in the same village but also the proper superiority of her conjugal over her natal family is awkwardly disarranged if the two are fellow villagers (Madan 1965, pp. III–112). So also in a hill village of Orissa where village exogamy is not mandatory but is usually practiced. Marriage there "almost always is outside the political community" (Bailey 1960b, p. 168).

Where village exogamy is strictly mandatory, the men who live and work together as agnates are quite insulated from any influence from their respective affines. Harold Gould has noted this in villages of Lucknow district, where only a woman's brother will customarily come to visit her in her conjugal home, and where she must meet him in an outbuilding or in some other place that is separate from the family's main house. These villagers hold that an affine should not make even an occasional intrusion into the place of agnatic solidarity. "The wife ceremonially wails on her brother's shoulder when he comes, an act which announces the continuation of affective ties between a woman and her natal family, and I have observed the considerable strain that crosses the faces of the husband and his agnates on such occasions" (Gould 1961a, p. 298; see also Gould 1960b).

Village exogamy seems to be an outcome not only of a special need for filial-fraternal solidarity, but also of special fear for the fragility of those bonds. The wives in a family and their natal kinsmen are apparently perceived as potential sources of family disruption. Hence the wives should be isolated from their original kin, which also means that their husbands, in their roles as brothers, are equally isolated from their own beloved sisters.

That isolation is additionally marked in those parts of North India where another rule (noted later in the discussion of hypergamy) is added to village exogamy. There, if *any* family of Village A has taken a bride from Village B, a girl of Village A, of *any* jati, must never be given in marriage to Village B. As between any two villages, all in one must be the marital superiors to their respective jati fellows in the other (Karve 1965, p. 125). I have seen an old woman of a village in Delhi State, senior enough not to have to veil her face before men, do so nevertheless when a young man of another village came in, because he had married a daughter of her village. All in her village were obliged to show respect to one who had married a village daughter. Another kind of village exogamy is that exemplified in Rampur village also near Delhi, where a bride may not be taken from any contiguous village or from those in which the bridegroom's clan is well represented (Lewis 1958, p. 161; Karve 1965, pp. 119–120).

Where marriage within the village is permitted, the villagers are not necessarily less concerned with filial-fraternal solidarity but, rather, more influenced by other factors. In the Himalayan village of Sirkanda, as Berreman explains, in-village marriage seems to be preferred because a woman is an economic asset and relatively independent, and marriageable women are quite scarce. A young wife can readily leave her husband and return to her natal family if she does not like her marital home, a possibility not usually open to village women in the Hindi-speaking area. A woman of this hill region is more apt to stay with her husband if her own parents are nearby. Hence marriage within the village helps a family keep a young wife (Berreman 1962d).

In South India also, marriages within a village are permitted, possibly because of the importance of strengthening existing kinship ties. This will be noted in the later discussion of the extensions of kinship. The differences in exogamy and other kinship patterns between North and South have been described by Mrs. Karve who postulates four zones, each characterized by certain family and kinship usages. In addition to a northern and southern zone, she delineates a central zone culturally and geographically intermediate between the two, and also an eastern zone, mainly of tribal groups (Karve 1953; revised edition 1965). Mrs. Karve's pioneering work has opened the way for further studies of kinship and marriage practices in India.

Jati endogamy is the other part of the explicit rules for marriage, on which, as has been noted, the whole system is seen to rest by those who maintain it. We need only repeat here that a village couple must stem from two families that have historically belonged, because of their common attributes, to the same set of intermarrying families. That historical nexus is usually accounted for in myth, bolstered by ritual, manifest in daily practice, and maintained by forces within and outside the jati. Yet there are ways of reinterpreting the history and of readjusting the boundaries of the endogamous group. Those boundaries are more inviolate in the villager's notion of their society than is sometimes the case in actuality.

Implicit Rules and General Procedures

Rules for exogamy and endogamy are quite explicitly expressed, other rules for marriage are usually less explicitly stated. Within each jati's code of exogamy and endogamy, marriage negotiations follow a complex series of stylized maneuvers and spontaneous manipulations. Among very poor families the preliminaries are brief, the matter quickly settled. But with families of any jati who have something to bargain about, who can afford to aspire to better place, or who strive to maintain their traditional position, the negotiations are typically intricate. They follow an unwritten game theory that is well understood by the participants, certainly by the adept marriage brokers and go-betweens. Each family attempts to maximize its gain through the marriage and to minimize any loss, either in status, wealth, or the welfare of its child. Each brings to bear whatever resources it has; if it is deficient in one kind of resource it plays up its other strengths. A family with a dim-witted, torpid son uses its wealth and influence to secure a passable bride for him. A family whose son has a research degree and a foot in the higher civil service can arrange a match that bejewels the family with dowry, prestige, and the comely person of the bride.

The negotiations are usually initiated by the family of a girl. This is in accord with traditional prescription and with the fact that a girl's family feels under pressure of time as a boy's family does not. A girl has only a short period during which she is properly eligible for marriage. After that, as has been noted, her unmarried state raises questions and dark suspicions. In the quest, the searchers look for a boy with suitable family and personal attributes. His family should be of somewhat higher status within the jati (or certainly not lower), of the proper exogamous group, and a family that is not likely to inflict undue hardship on a young wife. In his person the boy should be active, healthy, somewhat older than the girl, not unusually disfavored in appearance, and of a suitable level of education. The family of the boy looks for counterpart attributes in the girl; her demeanor, health, and diligence are politely but firmly ascertained. Fairness of skin is a decided boon as is also her general attractiveness of appearance.

The wealth of the bride's family is particularly important among northern jatis, because her natal family must be perpetual donors. Among many of the jatis of the South, there is some notion that the groom's family should be the wealthier, but this is mitigated by the concurrent idea that the bride should be from a closely related family and that her family should be the principal givers after the wedding (Beals and Siegel 1966, pp. 43–46; Klass 1966, pp. 960–962; Orenstein 1965a, pp. 48–50; Lewis 1958, pp. 159–195; Madan 1965, pp. 112–113).

These are some of the premises for negotiation; all are in some degree negotiable. Each side is alert to its own advantage and the family's long-run gain, but this does not mean that one side must lose in the transaction. The mutually desired outcome is that both sides should feel that they have gained. To advance this end there are ritual devices by which, once the collective bargaining is over and agreement reached, the two sides ritually signify their present and future amity (cf. Epstein 1960, p. 204).

Ordinarily both sides do gain, though not the same things. When a family has wealth but low status in the jati, its members will usually try to make an alliance with a family that needs the wealth and can impart better status. The drive for social mobility, which animates the social system and which, as will be discussed later, has made for recurrent change in it, is typically expressed by villagers when they act as members of their smallest social unit, the family, as well as when they act as participants in larger groups and groupings. A family's status, like the ritual purity of its members and the ranking of its jati, requires continual revalidation. Family prestige can, in some degree, be transmitted through a marriage alliance, unlike ritual purity and jati rank, which cannot be imparted across families. Families that have no great imbalance between resources and respectability, tend to seek alliances with families that are about equal, or, under hypergamy, as nearly equal as the hypergamic rules permit.

A marriage alliance always entails some redistribution of wealth as well as of persons. The rules for that redistribution vary among regions. In a good many jatis of South India, the family of the groom pays bride wealth at marriage to the family of the bride (Karve 1965, p. 180; Srinivas 1942, pp. 14–21). After marriage, however, the woman's family continue to give gifts to her and her children. In most of North India it is the family of the bride that gives a dowry to the groom and his family, with little or no return from them. In all regions, the negotiators must reach agreement on the exact amounts of gifts in money and kind that are to be given before, during, and after the wedding. The principal payments, whether dowry or bride wealth, are intended to stabilize the marriage, to benefit the girl, and, if magnanimous, to enhance the prestige of the donors.

Dowries are usually given by those who maintain marked status differentials within their jati and who assume the bridegroom's family to be superior to the bride's family (cf. Yalman 1967, pp. 172–177, 352). Bride wealth rather than dowry is given where women are strong economic assets to a family, where they are relatively independent, and where they are relatively scarce. Thus among some of the Pahari-speaking people of the Himalayas a bride price is paid at marriage and the transaction is initiated by the groom's family. Women there are more independent socially, more valuable economically, and proportionally fewer than they are in the plains below the Pahari villages (Berreman 1962d, p. 57).

The type of marriage payment which is customarily given may vary among the jatis of a village. In Gaon village of Poona district, the higher jatis pay dowries, while bride price is customary among the Harijan jatis. But even in the higher jatis of Gaon the family of a man may pay bride wealth if their son has personal defects and if the maiden is especially attractive (Orenstein 1965a, p. 50).

Arranging for the marriage of children is a critical responsibility for the head of a family, and many men come to find themselves under severe pressure on that account both from inside and outside the family. An example of a particularly difficult series of choices occurs in a study of a village near the city of Baroda in Gujarat. The landowners are of the Leva jati of Patidars. Each Patidar jati-group belongs to one of the ranked, hypergamous sections of its jati. The Patidars of this village, though landowners, belong to one of the low sections. Their girls can marry into a higher section but their boys can only marry a girl of an equally low Patidar level. As a result there is a shortage of girls for the Patidar boys of this village to marry because many of their girls have married into higher sections. The shortage is aggravated by the higher ratio of males to females and by the fact that widowers—though not widows—may remarry, and some of these take young girls (Poffenberger and Pandya, MS. n.d.; see also Fukutake *et al*. 1964, p. 60.

Consequently a Patidar father of this village must give a dowry in order to get his daughter suitably married into a higher section and must pay a bride price in order to get a Patidar girl for his son at all. A few men remain unmarried, more marry girls of lower, non-Patidar jatis. When this occurs the family tries to convince the other villagers that she is a Patidar and their neighbors are willing to go along with that fiction publicly. But they well know which of the village wives were born Patidars and which were not. Of twenty-seven Patidar couples mentioned in the study, two-thirds of the wives had been taken from a lower jati.

In one family with three sons and two daughters, the father steadfastly refused to sacrifice his daughter's marriage prospects for those of his sons. He tried to arrange for a Patidar bride for his eldest son but the bride price needed was more than he could muster and he finally had to get a bride of lower, carpenter, jati for his first-born son. He could have secured a large sum by marrying his daughter to a family of low section but refused to do so since that would have been a greater blow to his family status than was arranging an inferior match for his eldest son. So he married his elder daughter into a higher village and had to give a large dowry. This drain meant that there was no capital available for the marriage of his second son who, at age thirty-four, was still unmarried and kept protesting until he reached the point of refusing to work the family lands.

The youngest son, interestingly, gave his father no trouble in the matter of marriage. He is both physically handsome and able enough to have done a year of college work and to have secured a post as a teacher. He was a good enough match to marry into a Patidar family of equal status, and after his first wife's death, to marry again and even to obtain a token dowry. This case illustrates several factors in marriage negotiations: the different circumstances under which dowry or bride wealth may be given, the covert transgression of jati endogamy under dire necessity, the weight of personal attractiveness, and particularly the greater importance for a family's reputation that is often attached to the proper marriages of its daughters than to the marriages of its sons.

The education of his daughter may present a knotty problem to a father. If she can read and write there may be no difficulty and some advantage on that score in getting a daughter married. But if she has gone through secondary school, it may be hard to find a groom for her whose family will be willing to take in an educated girl. They may fear that she will not make a proper, dutiful wife because of her schooling. If there are a good many educated men in her jati, education can be an asset to a marriageable girl, but if there are few she may have been educated beyond her marriage bracket.

The situation in some village families is all the more difficult for college-educated girls. The village father who encourages his daughter to take a college degree when there are few male college graduates in the jati may be accused of sacrificing his daughter's chances in life to a mistaken whim intended to glorify his own name. Moreover, a family whose sons and daughters are educated beyond the usual level of their jati and village may be thought to be presumptuous. Unless they are skillful in mollifying their kinsmen and neighbors, they may become a target for opposition.

Yet education is now seen by villagers as a generally desirable asset, for the sake of one's child as well as for the good of a family. Educated boys and their families increasingly, as we shall note again later, insist on a bride with an education suitable to the education of the groom. Thus, as more boys receive high school or college education, the incentive to educate girls also increases.

Providing a suitable dowry for a marriageable daughter is a common problem for families. It is often a difficult, burdensome matter, but it is an imperative of the system of family and jati. To skimp on the dowry is not only to put one's own child at a disadvantage but also to demean the whole family. So although social reformers have long opposed the payment of large dowries and legislators have tried to limit dowry size, a father faced with the problem rarely has the heart to heed the reformers' arguments (with which he may agree) rather than to promote his daughter's welfare. Nor does he usually have the fortitude to follow the law rather than his wife's urging. And the payment of the dowry is only one part of the total expense of a marriage.

The redistribution of wealth affects many more people than just the members of the two principal families. A wedding can be used to activate a network of gift-giving involving families of different jatis as well as kin. A newly prosperous villager can give generous gifts at a wedding to people with whom he could not previously have afforded to exchange gifts or favors. Establishing a wider range of gift-giving brings returns in power as well as in prestige to a magnanimous donor because, as we shall discuss below, the recipients are more apt to support the gift-givers in the perennial contentions of village life. The distribution of wealth, like the alliance itself, entails both explicit and implicit rules. Which family gives more, what kinds of gifts are given and to whom, are explicitly stipulated by village and jati consensus. The amounts to be given to jajmani associates are sometimes stipulated in a written code (cf. Lewis 1958, p. 163). But just how much is given, in what proportions and under what circumstances, is finally determined only after playing the serious game of negotiating a match.

Precautions: Astrology and Prepuberty Marriage

So momentous is the occasion of marriage that several kinds of precautions may be taken to minimize the uncertainties involved in the decision. Astrology is one such means; arranging prepuberty marriages is another.

All marriage plans must reckon with the supernatural forces that affect the course of every critical venture—auspicious and inauspicious days, favorable and unfavorable omens, the horoscopes of the couple and their astrological congruence. Through astrology man's uncertainty about his personal fate is made more tolerable. One's fate is seen as linked in a grand mechanism of astral spheres, which move in preordained and predictable cycles across the firmament of time. The fortunes of persons and societies move in conformity with the celestial cycles. Each person—better, each soul—becomes geared into the cosmic movement at the moment of birth. The nature of his entrainment is forever determined at that moment when his personal fate latches into the grand apparatus. One's horoscope reveals how his life fits into the celestial progression to which all life attaches. The fate so ordained for one person may be forecast as being utterly incompatible with that of another; if the two join their lives in marriage only disaster for them can ensue, and so any plans for their union must be abandoned.

Yet astrology is a flexible art, not entirely impervious to manipulation. It is always possible for determined matchmakers to seek another, more favorable reading from a different astrologer. Conversely, should one side want to withdraw tactfully from a proposal, it is sometimes possible to locate an astrologer whose examination of the two horoscopes will find an insuperable bar to the match.

Astrology, as part of the Sanskrit tradition, is used for planning marriages by those who guide their rituals according to Sanskrit scripture. A person's horoscope among such families is consulted at every juncture of his career, sometimes with far-reaching results.[1] In the middle and lower jatis, especially in South India, there are many who make no use of astrology. But peoples of all jatis believe in auspicious and inauspicious days and in favorable and unfavorable omens. These beliefs postulate a similar, though simpler, view of grand, impersonal mechanisms, which affect each life and through which each person must thread his fate.

There is a certain parallel between these beliefs and the people's theory of a caste society. In both instances the universal structure, of fate and of society, is seen as absolutely decreed and, in the large, immutable. Yet within both these fixed frames men try hard to better their position and that of their kin.

Another way of reducing the uncertainties of a complex marriage negotiation is to make a definite agreement before the prospective bride reaches puberty. Then all can proceed according to a clear schedule without pressure of the problem of the girl's sexuality. She begins full marital life soon after menarche. In some jatis the exact interval is prescribed, thus for certain Brahmins the nuptial rites that mark the start of sexual relations traditionally took place sixteen days after the onset of first menstruation. This firm calendar is not the only advantage of celebrating the formal wedding before the bride's—or even the groom's—puberty. Another advantage that each family can immediately benefit by whatever advantages it has achieved through the alliance. This status capital can then be used to push its ranking still higher in other negotiations.

Prepuberty marriages have been forbidden in a series of legislative acts of both the British regime and the independent government of India. But there is still great pressure on the head of a family to make suitable arrangements for a girl's marriage as soon as it is feasible to do so. Though the median age of marriage for girls in India has been rising in recent decades and has gone up dramatically in some places, it is still relatively low. The system of village family life militates against any general rise in age at marriage substantial enough to affect the fertility rate significantly (Srinivas 1965, pp. 38–40; Goode 1963, pp. 232–236; Karve 1965, pp. 73–74, 126–127; Mandelbaum 1954a).

Marriage Links and Communication among Villages

A family with both ambition and means is likely to search as far afield for a prospective spouse as it can, because a wider radius of search produces more alternatives from which to select the best alliance. Families of the higher and wealthier jatis usually bring in brides from a wider territory than do lower groups. Thus the average distance of the bride's village is 37.5 miles in the highest bloc

[1] A former Chief Justice of India, Mehr Chand Mahajan, tells in his autobiography that immediately after his birth the family astrologers declared that the moment had been so disastrously inauspicious that the infant's father would surely die if he saw the face of his son. So the infant was taken away to be raised in an isolated hamlet by a family of a different jati. After seven years his father succeeded in getting a new reading from a council of astrologers, that the boy had been born under a very lucky conjunction and that he would become a great man, a judge or a minister (Prime Minister of princely Kashmir as it turned out, as well as Chief Justice of republican India). His mother and grandmother took him back, but it was not until five years later that his father mustered enough courage, amid lavish ritual precautions, to look at the face of his son (Mahajan 1963, pp. 3–7).

of jatis of a village in Faizabad District (U.P.) while the average distance for the next lower blocs is 6.4 and 7.5 miles (Gould 1960b, p. 486).

A similar spread can occur within a jati, as it does among the Noniyas (earthworkers by traditional occupation) of Senapur in U.P. In that village, the average distance of Noniya marriage alliances is 12 miles, the nearest affinal link being 3 miles and the farthest 55 miles. But among the educated people of the jati who live in towns as professional men or government officials, there is a different marriage network, mainly with similarly wealthy and elite families. This net has a much broader range, extending for a few families to as far as three hundred miles. But for families whose wedding parties and visitors must come by oxcart or local bus, no such extensive and expensive range is possible; the bulk of their marriage alliances are made within a quite compact territory. The shape of that territory is defined as much by the main travel routes and by the existence of previous alliances as it is by physical distance alone (Rowe 1960, pp. 301, 307; Gould 1960b, pp. 481–482; Miller 1954).

Other influences on the radius of matrimonial alliance are geographic distribution and jati power. Thus in Rampur, near Delhi, two of the lower groups have a much greater average distance for matrimonial alliance than do the two highest jatis. The dominant Jats and the Brahmins bring brides from an average of about 12.5 miles while the low Chamars average 20 miles and the Nais, barbers, average about 24 miles. The Nais have only a few families in any one village and so must sometimes reach far to find an eligible bride or groom. The Chamars have long struggled against the overlord Jats and have recently found good jobs away from the village. With more resources and rekindled hope they are probably seeking a broader base of power beyond the close neighborhood of their village (Lewis 1958, p. 161).

The outer limits of search for a spouse are set by the boundaries of the linguistic region. Very rarely is a village girl married into a family which uses a language different from her own. Within the linguistic bounds, each jati-group of a village has its own usual range of intermarriage. Their jati fellows within this range are known to them, relationships with their families are easily traced, ancestry and familial characteristics can be ascertained, marriage customs are mutually shared and understood.[2]

These families and jati-groups, as Klass notes of a West Bengal village, constitute the villagers' effective jati. A family does not like to marry its daughter beyond that circle because visits will then be infrequent and expensive, so most marriages in this village are arranged within a radius of from five to ten miles (Klass 1966, pp. 960–966). Here also a wealthy, ambitious family can afford the greater expense of a more distant marriage and may seek such a match for the prestige it will bring.

Within a jati's geographic spread, some areas may be more prestigious than others. Among Rajputs, for example, the more westerly or northerly are the higher and there is a general tendency

---

[2] Calculations of average marriage distance are available for a few villages. Thus in Haripura in Mysore, 21 percent of 397 marriages of villagers are within the village, 57 percent within a radius of five miles, and the rest mainly within 15 miles (Dhillon 1955, pp. 75–76). In Wangala, also in Mysore, 50 percent of existing marriages are within 4 miles, 82 percent within 10 miles, and 9 percent outside a radius of 20 miles (Epstein 1962, p. 169). A much wider range is given for Shamirpet in Andhra Pradesh. Of 380 marriages, 68 percent are within a radius of 35 miles, 30 percent were farther, up to 60 miles, and 2 percent even more distant that that (Dube 1955b, p. 54).

In Ramkheri in Madhya Pradesh, the average distance village girls go is 12.8 miles for Rajputs and 12.5 miles for Farmers. Brides are brought in for these two jati-groups at an average distance of 17 and 11.8 miles respectively. Cotton-carders go a bit farther afield, 18.6 and 19.7 miles (Mayer 1960, p. 210).

to marry daughters to the west and take brides from the east. This is the way it is often put, though the phrasing more consistent with Rajput practice is that girls are married into families that live in the direction of upstream on the main rivers, and girls are taken from the downstream direction (Karve 1965, p. 125; Mayer 1960, pp. 211–212).

One important outcome of this seeking for family and jati advantage in marriage is that every person is tied into a network of social relations extending across many villages, and each person's network is linked to innumerable other networks. For all the social avoidance and segregation inherent in a local caste system, there is no sharp break in communications and relations among the local systems of Indian culture and society. "This small village of 150 households," Lewis says of Rampur, "may therefore be seen as forming the locus of affinal kinship ties with over four hundred other villages.... This rural cosmopolitanism provides a striking contrast with the characteristic village isolation found in rural Mexico" (1958, pp. 161–162).

It is a salient fact of Indian society that the people of one village are in touch with kin in scores, often hundreds, of other villages. An analysis of 446 marriages in Ramkheri showed affinal relations with 219 villages (Mayer 1960, p. 208; see also Rowe 1960, p. 299; Mayer 1962; Cohn and Marriott 1958). The multiple interlacing of villages is primarily a function, not of polity or economy, but of jati and of family. In their totality these lively networks profoundly influence the whole culture and society, but each link is fashioned with an eye to the welfare of a little domestic group, its status, its economic advantage, and, by no means the least, the future well-being of its child.

This is true even where marriages within a village are permitted, as they are in Wangala in Mysore. There 85 percent of the couples studied come from different villages; the couples were of the dominant peasant jati, traced over four generations.[3] A village is far from being an isolated and insulated community; each has been continually affected by influences from beyond the village bounds. Not the least of these outside influences is brought in by the wives.

The Wedding

After the negotiations are completed, the wedding is solemnized and enjoyed. A wedding not only confirms a particular couple's union and the alliance of families, it also affirms the centrality of marital union in the universe of man and God (cf. Hsu 1963, pp. 31, 185–186). It proclaims the alliance so that all people in each family's social orbit may know of it. The immense importance attached to weddings throughout village India is reflected in the example of wedding expenditures in two Mysore villages where these costs have been studied.

[3] In recent years there has been an increase in marriages within this village because of a special economic influence. The whole range of the villagers' social relations has been narrowed because their energies are concentrated on growing sugar cane and under the quite exceptional local conditions of sugar production, in which a state-owned factory takes care of marketing and managerial functions, they do not need wide social contacts. Hence when only the currently existing marriages are tabulated, 42 percent are within the village and 58 percent between villages.

A different trend has occurred in the nearby village of Dalena. As noted above, their lands did not get irrigation as did the villages all about them and Dalena people had to enlarge their social relations if they were to benefit from the prosperity of the region. Hence the proportion of intervillage marriages rose from 44 percent in the four-generation record to 69 percent in existing marriages (Epstein 1962, pp. 167–169, 296–297).

A wedding is the largest single expense that most families have to bear. Weddings in Wangala, Mrs. Epstein notes, provide a principal step in the struggle for status. The groom's family in this region bears most of the wedding costs. A family of the very poorest level spends (in 1955 prices) about Rupees 272 to marry a son, a relatively poor farmer family Rs. 1,218, a richer farmer Rs. 2,110, and one of the very richest, "magnate" families Rs. 2,866. The very poorest family, with exceedingly little to spare, still manages to pour out three or four months' income on the marriage rites. The relatively rich families devote close to a year's total income to marry each son.[4]

When the total cash expenditures, those made by everyone in Wangala during 1955, were calculated, it was found that 4 percent of that total was spent on weddings. Savings in this prospering village came to 16 percent of the average monthly budget. "Most of the savings are spent on weddings when economic differentiation displays itself in lavish feasts" (Epstein 1962, pp. 101, 108, 110). That is, when family wealth is translated into family prestige.

In the contrasting village of Dalena, where people have been impelled to turn outward while the Wangala villagers were turning inward, the struggle for prestige among middle-farmers is differently expressed. They think it more important to have a bicycle or a watch and similar possessions than to give a lavish wedding feast. Such personal possessions bring prestige both in town and village, while wedding expenditures impress mainly one's fellow villagers. Hence weddings are less expensive in Dalena than in Wangala and are one-day affairs rather than three-day celebrations as is normal in Wangala. For all that, Dalena people still spend a very sizable sum on weddings. A typical wedding expenditure budget for one of the poorest families is Rs. 225, for a poor farmer Rs. 712, for a rich farmer Rs. 895, and for a "magnate" Rs. 2,402. Despite the partial eclipse of weddings as occasions for prestige gain, the chief lender of money in Dalena attempted to improve his social status by staging a very costly wedding for his son. And Dalena farmers whether of the richer or the poorer class, still lay out a good part of a year's income on the wedding of a son (Epstein 1962, pp. 263–266).

As will be noted again in discussing social mobility, marriage remains a chief means of social rise for a family within its jati and a costly wedding is a main feature of a prestigious alliance. This holds through all social levels. Magnates and maharajahs have been known to impoverish their fortunes by grand marriages for their children. At the other pole, the Harijans may keep themselves in economic servitude, as they do in one Mysore village, mainly because of their passion for expensive marriage celebrations (Harper 1965).

Among the vast majority of India's people, a wedding is at once a culmination and a beginning, a demonstration and a test, a stage and a theater, an affirmation and a consolidation. It is the climax of the negotiations and the formal beginning of the new relationship. It is the grand occasion demonstrating the family's social worth through the participation of kin, jati fellows, village neighbors, and prestigious friends. Certain measures of their esteem are quite precise, as when the size of each gift and the name of its donor are loudly announced to the assembled guests.

---

[4] Mrs. Epstein estimates the average monthly income per consumption unit in Wangala at Rs. 33. Men older than fourteen are counted as one consumption unit, women and children at given fractions of a consumption unit. The poorest households have a monthly expenditure per consumption unit of Rs. 10 to 15 (1962, p. 342). I have based the estimated proportion of income devoted to weddings on rough extrapolations from these figures. A similar estimate, that between six months' to more than a year's income is spent on a wedding, is given for weddings in Ramkheri in Madhya Pradesh (Mayer 1960, p. 227).

It is both a demonstration and a test of status. Here, best of all, a family's claim to eminence can be gauged by the wealth, power, and purity that its members mobilize for the event. Also tested and demonstrated in the festivities are the relative standings of the guests: Who is accorded precedence by the hosts, who sits near whom, what courtesies are extended to which guests? All these proclaim relative rank among individuals within a jati as they do also among jatis. For this reason a wedding may be shot through with factional bickering and may become a scene of high tension.

For the principal actors the wedding provides the stage for a supreme pageant. It is an exalted occasion for the bride and groom; both are temporarily transfigured into a regal or divine pair and "the aura which shines around them also touches the members of their families" (Dumont 1959, p. 519). It is a theater for aesthetic enjoyment of many kinds—of the quality of the musicians, of the munificence of the bride's jewels and costumes, even of the elegance of the groom's equipage. A counterpoint of humor often sparkles through the solemnities, as in the chorus of bawdy songs sung by neighbor women and in the more private but equally ribald jokes made by the guests.

All major rites affirm, in a kind of metalanguage, a people's leading values: as principal nodes of social life in India, weddings are used to affirm a number of values. Some of these affirmations are in the ritual itself, others in what appears as byplay. There are certain ritual patterns by which the hopes and expectations for the marriage are expressed. Typically these include symbolic expressions of the couple's unity (as in taking steps together), some ritual action to show their new relation to each other and to their respective families, and ritual acts done together before the deities to invoke divine blessings and at the same time to proclaim the new social fact before society (cf. Lewis 1958, pp. 162–195; Madan 1965, pp. 117–121; Srinivas 1965, pp. 47–50).

In addition to such formal avowals, unscheduled assertions may crop up at a wedding. Just as tensions about disputed rank or village factions often intrude into the occasion, so also may the tensions between the newly allied families. Thus Mrs. Tilak in describing her wedding in a Maharashtra village about 1880 notes that "On those occasions the bridegroom is encouraged to have a fit of the sulks." Her bridegroom was instructed to ask for the gift of a ring and to sulk until he was promised it. But he tired of the tactic quickly, joined the wedding party and so forced his family to come along with him to the wedding feast. "There was none of the usual quarrelling and ill-feeling from beginning to end" (1950. p. 12). Such trials of strength between the two families at the time of marriage are still common. Where the two families are about equal, members of each want to make sure that the other does not arrogate undue superiority. In those regions where one is formally inferior to the other, its members want to show that there is a limit to the inferiority they will accept. A main theme of village drama, as Beals notes for Gopalpur village, concerns this tension (1962, p. 24).

Yet a wedding is a force for social consolidation. The alliance is formed; despite bickerings and other signs of tension, the bond is sealed. Each family, in rallying its kin and supporters, revitalizes its ties with other families of jati and village. It also keeps going, through the wedding and all the rest of the marriage complex, the endless cycle of family life and thus of society itself.

CHAPTER 7

Family Cycle: Growth and Completion

The advent of brides and the birth and rearing of their children constitute the growth phase of the family cycle. A common turning point occurs with the death of the family head. If several married brothers then remain in the household, there usually follows a period in which divisive strains mount. In time these strains lead to formal partition. The brothers separate into nuclear families and then as their children reach marriageable age, the cycle returns to the growth stage. Though daughters leave the household, sons" wives and sons" children come into the family. These cyclical phases, described by Gould for North India, occur in families of the other regions as well (Gould 1965a, pp. 39–41; 1965c, pp. 182–184).

The Growth Phase: The Rearing of Children

The bride settles in and in time brings forth her child, the family's child. Within the family circle the child learns the fundamentals of his culture and society; he is taught to become the kind of person who will, in his turn, fulfill the appropriate roles of family and society. This process is shown in a study of child rearing in Khalapur village, some ninety miles north of Delhi. The authors of this study observed family life in a sample of families from the dominant Rajput jati of the village (Minturn and Hitchcock 1963; paperbound edition 1966). These Rajputs take great pride in their warrior tradition and many of the men still uphold the traditional mode of family relations.

Among them, as elsewhere in village India, the way in which childbirth is managed foreshadows the expectations that the family has for the newly arrived member and the fundamental cultural lesson that the child will later be taught (cf. Gideon 1962). The notion of pollution is inherent in these practices. The newborn infant arrives in a highly polluting state and must be carefully and gradually brought into a safer ritual and social condition. Physiological processes have produced the baby, but it is only after the family performs the proper ritual that the infant becomes a member of society. Society, not nature, has the decisive word in adding a new person to its number.

The sharp difference between the status of male and female, a difference that runs through all social relations, is presaged by the kind of welcome given to a newborn son—with drumming, singing, and proud public announcements—in contrast to that accorded to a new daughter, whose advent is more quietly observed. The formal inferiority of girls to boys seems mitigated in this village, as was noted before, by the mothers" attitudes; in any event girls show little suffering on that score. But one result of this differential interest is that fewer girl babies survive, not because they are deliberately neglected but rather because much greater medical efforts are usually made to cure a sick baby boy than a sick infant girl. The infant mortality rate for boys in one Khalapur sample was 25 percent, for girls 41 percent (Minturn and Hitchcock 1963, p. 284). A similar mortality differential has been noted in successive reports of the Census of India and the same reasons, the relative favoring of boys rather than any deliberate neglect of girls, have been adduced for it (Gait 1913, p. 218; Blunt 1939, p. 70; Goode 1963, pp. 235–236).

As a Rajput child in this village begins to speak and can be trained, the most common form of punishment is scolding. A usual form of scolding is to call the child by a "derogatory but not obscene name"; that is, by the name of either of the two lowest jatis, the leatherworkers or the sweepers (Minturn 1963, p. 327). What he must not touch and who he should not be are inculcated as soon as the child can understand anything. The training repeatedly reinforces the idea that there is a hierarchy of relations, inside and outside the family, and that a proper child carefully observes the proprieties of subordinate and superior roles.

The domestic arrangements drive home this lesson. In Khalapur, as in many North Indian villages, men and women have virtually separate quarters; the women of the family usually do not enter onto the platform where the men spend most of their leisure time, asleep and awake. The men typically come into the women's quarters for some specific purpose, and, having accomplished that purpose, leave. Young children scoot fairly freely between the two, and they early become aware of the women's quick covering of the face when an elder man of the family enters and of his warning cough before he comes into the women's area. Social distance, respect avoidance, and hierarchical calibration of action are daily made manifest to the child in his own home.

The child, as junior in the household, must soon be taught deference and obedience. The virtues that Rajput parents in Khalapur most emphasized in interviews were obedience, politeness, peaceableness. But Rajputs pride themselves also as being a martial, dominant people, so while obedience in the family is emphasized, dominance over social inferiors is tacitly encouraged. Perhaps because of these conflicting injunctions, that the child must be quite deferent to some and quite imperious toward others, the Khalapur children did not seem to the observers to be particularly well trained. They were not quick to obey their mothers, nor were they closely attentive to the orders of their fathers (Minturn 1963, pp. 338–340).

The ways in which adults discipline and reward children in Khalapur, as everywhere, vary among individuals, between men and women, and according to kinship roles. But all agreed on one principle of child training: a child should not be praised to his face lest this make him disobedient. One Khalapur man summed it up in these words: "If we prake, the child will think that we love him too much and then he will not be under our control" (*ibid*., p. 325). This explanation can be interpreted to mean that control of the child is of paramount importance. He must be trained to be properly deferent, suitably observant of the hierarchy of family relations. Yet his deference and his adherence to the hierarchy cannot be taken for granted; they are jeopardized if the child hears himself praised, "loved too much," and so gets an overweening sense of his own importance. And a child, or anyone, who comes to feel so important will not easily accept subordinate status and the deferent demeanor that must go with it.

These men tend to blame the women for disregarding this principle. Although the observers "almost never heard a woman praise a child, the men complained that women lost control of children because of too much praise" (Minturn and Lambert 1964, p. 232). A child is indeed praised sometimes and held up as a model for other children, but not in his presence. Nor should parents praise their own children in any company lest the evil eye be attracted. Excellence, immoderately flaunted, draws envy if not malevolence.

Similar testimony about not praising children comes from a study by Joan Mencher of child rearing among the Nayars of Angadi village in Calicut district. (Khalapur is within sight of the Himalayas; Angadi is on the tropical coastal strip of Kerala.) In both places the views on this fundamental aspect of child rearing are alike. In Angadi all praise is suspect. It is taken either as untrue or if true as dangerous. The danger lies partly in encouraging the praised one to "take advantage." The latter explanation was given by everyone who was interviewed on this question. As one Angadi villager commented about praising children, "We won't say anything nice to them, feeling that if we say it out like that they will take advantage. So praise and affection will be in our mind only…." All through a villager's life in Angadi this attitude prevails. People have a natural desire to be praised and also a fear of praising. It is almost impossible to accept praise easily as being well deserved (Mencher 1963, p. 62).[1]

There are other parallels in child rearing between these two villages at opposite ends of the subcontinent. In the southern village as in the northern, a child "should, above all, be obedient and respectful to elders." The Nayar child in Angadi is not encouraged to assert himself, not rewarded for being self-reliant or innovative; much the same is true for the Rajput child in Khalapur (Mencher 1963, P 57; Minturn 1963, p. 359).

The pressures on these Rajput boys change as they begin to spend more time in the men's area. As early as six years of age and no later than twelve or fourteen, they move out of the women's quarters entirely. They are then under stricter discipline and are exposed to masculine values, particularly in respect to aggression and quarrels. Women do not try to pass on their personal quarrels to their children; a woman will usually allow her child to play with children of a mother with whom she is at odds or whose family is antagonistic to her own. But the men take care to instill their posture of loyalty or hatred. They warn their boys not to play with boys who belong to a hostile lineage. They are equally careful to point out the family's allies and the neutrals as well as the opponents. Men feel that they cannot afford to be passive about antagonisms. Each family has enemies in the

---

[1] The taboo on praising children is not equally observed everywhere in India (cf. Kennedy 1954, p. 168; Cormack 1961, p. 62). Urban, educated mothers, possibly because of acquaintance with Western child-rearing practices, do not observe it as do mothers in the two villages that have been cited. And yet in interviews with eighteen such women, mothers of children in the Baroda University nursery school, five said that a child should not be praised to his face because it would make the child "too proud," two that a child should not be praised at all, and two that a child should not be praised when others are present (Poffenberger 1964).

village; any one of them may in a fit of temper, drink, or zeal, decide to settle a grievance with a "conversation of sticks." A youth must be ready to defend himself and his family in physical combat (Minturn 1963, p. 332).

There is a marked change in what is expected of these boys and girls as they grow into adolescence. The shift is more gradual for the boys and takes place within the roles they have had all their lives, as sons, nephews, brothers. But the girls, in Khalapur as in other villages, must change more abruptly from one set of roles to another, from being daughter and sister to becoming daughter-in-law and wife. Both changes bring on a sharp stiffening of discipline after a relatively permissive childhood.

A Cross-Cultural Study of Child Rearing

The study of these Rajput families is part of a comparative study of child rearing in six societies. The data from Khalapur have been compared with similar data from villages in Mexico, the Philippines, Okinawa, Kenya, and from an American town in New England (Whiting 1963, pp. 1–13). Among the six, the sample from Khalapur village was low in training for self-reliance; it was also low in training for responsibility in domestic and farm tasks. The latter is congruent with the actual social situation of the Rajputs of this village; their associates and servants are responsible to them for providing goods and services. Their pride is in their warrior virtues and overlord position rather than in the skills and purposes of cultivators.

Another comparative analysis was made in respect to training about aggression. The Rajput mothers are unusual among the groups studied in the degree to which they allow their children to aggress against them. As boys join the men's groups they learn to extol fighting in defense of honor. Yet there are countervailing pressures against aggression. Mothers discourage fighting among the children, older men discourage fighting within the kin and jati-group. More than in the other five societies, aggression is allowed and prized by these Rajputs in certain contexts and vigorously disapproved in others (Minturn and Lambert 1964, pp. 230–239).

In a further comparison of the six case studies, Beatrice Whiting has noted that the Khalapur people engage in more physical assault, more litigation, more violent in-group quarrels, than do the people of the other societies, except possibly those of the Kenya sample. She suggests one of the reasons for this may be that Rajput males have to make a difficult transition in identity when they move during childhood from the female sphere to the separate, segregate world of the men. Among the six societies the two in which there is greatest violence are also the two in which there is greatest separation between the men and the women.

A Rajput woman of this village, during the years when her children are young, is mainly confined to the household and to the women's locale within it. With few exceptions, she never sleeps or eats with her husband. Their sexual relations are surreptitious and hasty. A very young child rarely sees his father and mother interacting at all. One man from a jati of similar tradition said that he grew up without ever hearing his father and mother talk to each other (Whiting 1965, pp. 128–135).

When a Rajput boy in Khalapur moves from the one realm to the other, he learns that his earlier home among the women is most inferior. It is then, Beatrice Whiting suggests, that conflict about sex identity may occur. He has previously identified mainly with women, now he must make a sharp change in identity and characteristically feels impelled to make a brave show of the masculine virtues. There seems to be a circle of causation. "The separation of the sexes leads to a conflict of identity in the boy children, to unconscious fear of being feminine, which leads to "protest masculinity," exaggeration of the difference between men and women, antagonism against and fear of women, male solidarity, and hence to isolation of women and very young children" (Whiting 1965, p. 137).

This is a tentative interpretation based on a sample of families in one jati-group. It provides an idea to be tested, not a conclusion to be accepted. As in any large population, there is a broad range of personality characteristics among Indian villagers.[2] Anthropologists and others who have known Indian villagers well know many who are outgoing, independent, enterprising persons, even though the prevailing emphasis for young children seems to be more on passivity, dependence, defense. The reciprocal relationship between child rearing and social organization among Indian villagers has yet to be clearly formulated and tested, but these first approximations open a wide range of interesting questions.

The Dispersal Phase

The whole constellation of family relations shifts in a characteristic way, as we have noted, as the children grow up. There comes the time when the daughter must be married and sent off, when the son must receive a wife. The necessary growth through incoming brides also guarantees eventual dispersal, because there follows a time when the household becomes too cramped, psychologically and socially if not physically, to hold the brothers, their wives and children. Even if the brothers manage to stay together as one joint family through their lives, their sons almost certainly grow restive when they, in turn, become fathers, and then they separate to establish families of their own.

Herein lies an inherent contradiction and continuing strain in family life. The partitioning of the joint family, typically the separation of brothers, is in fact inevitable. But the ideal belief is held through most of the society that fraternal solidarity should not be breached and when it is, someone is at fault and should be blamed. Hence family separation is frequently perpetrated in quarrel and accusation. Amicable separations do occur, and, in any event, kinsmen and village elders usually try to restore friendly relations among brothers after a stormy parting (cf. Kapadia 1956, pp. 125–126). But quite often long echoes of recrimination leave a legacy of bitterness into another generation. Thus in a Kashmir village most of the landowners complain that they failed to receive their just share of the joint estates because of the dishonesty of their former coparceners. Even voting behavior, as studied in a Sikh village near Ludhiana, is largely influenced to the third generation by the enmities generated through family partition (Madan 1965, p. 162; Izmirlian 1964, pp. 34–36, 122–125).

The more property there is to divide, the more protracted are apt to be the throes of parting; the more touchy each brother's honor, whether from jati tradition or personal bent, the more bitter the aftermath. Those whose education or job sends them forth from the household are often spared this fraternal fracas; an only son is also exempt. Among the poorer families of lower rank, as was noted, the divisive quarrel tends to come earlier, usually between father and son. The son and his wife leave quickly; whatever rancor flares then, soon dissipates.

---

[2] To cite just one example, a study of achievement orientation among trainees from one Orissa village showed a considerable differentiation in this personality trait. A similar study of Orissa school children showed that those whose fathers were in "entrepreneurial" activities (the sale and production of oil and of milk) had higher achievement orientation than children from jatis of weavers and cultivators (McClelland 1961, pp. 271–273, 380–381).

But among families of some substance, of the middle and higher echelons of local rank, the division does not usually take place all at once, in a clean decisive break. The strains mount, but at every stage there are countervailing forces and people urging continued cohesion. The first step in the process of family fission is usually that of establishing separate hearths within the household; all no longer eat from the same kitchen, food stores are divided, cooking and eating are done separately (cf. Bailey 1957, pp. 88–89; Sengupta 1958, p. 384; Minturn and Hitchcock 1963, p. 232). New walls may next be built inside the house as a physical partition foreshadowing the economic and legal partition to follow. The brothers may then separate their farming or craft activities and thereafter formalize the split in a legal act of joint family partition.

At any of these stages, the presence of the father tends to slow the process; the death of the father, and even more of both parents, tends to hasten the legal division. An examination of fifty instances of family partition in a Kashmir village showed that forty were among brothers, only four among fathers and sons. The rest were among relatives of different degrees of relationship. Similarly, a survey of married brothers in a village of Poona district showed 65 percent living together while their father was alive (a number had moved away from the village for economic reasons), but only 16 percent continued to live together after their father had died (Madan 1965, p. 165; Orenstein 1965a, p. 39; Fukutake *et al*. 1964, p. 50).

Frequently, married brothers act as if their father were the sole owner of the family property. Under the traditional code of Bengal, a married son was in fact not ordinarily entitled to claim his separate share until after the death of his father. Among the wealthier families in Bengal, Sarma notes, the possession of a substantial house delays family partition. It is awkward and expensive to separate living units within the home, and though the building could be sold and the proceeds divided, this is an unpalatable solution because of the pride and prestige in having an ancestral dwelling. In time, however, this pride is usually relinquished and the house is sold (Sarma 1964 pp. 194–198).

The causes of family strain, as has been noted before, are commonly said to be quarrels among the women. And commonly women do quarrel; theirs is a kind of accepted quarreling relation as other dyadic relations are accepted as joking or as solidary relations. Whatever may be the reasons for any particular argument, there are some general predisposing factors. Most village women spend a great deal of their lives within a narrow courtyard. The space is cramped and opportunities for friction abound. A woman, after she is a mother and a secure matron, does not hesitate to defend her rights in the household vigorously and loudly. She has come from another family, often from another village; she harbors no special loyalty or affection for her sister-in-law who is usually from yet another village and family.

This also holds true in South India, where there is preference for arranging marriages closer to home. It is so in Namhalli village, near Bangalore, in which about one third of the wives are from the village. In another village of Mysore, Ishwaran studied the break-up of joint families. "I was invariably told by my respondents that the arrival of the new wives was the main cause for it." They said that the women from unrelated families brought in new values and interests which led to conflict and the separation of the family. Hence they were convinced that brides should not be brought in from distant families, even though bringing them from closer areas did not seem to guarantee family cohesion (Ishwaran 1965, p. 86; Beals and Siegel 1966, p. 43).

Money in the common purse, whatever a family's rank or region, is usually in short supply for each woman's needs. Food in the common larder runs low in the lean seasons and doling out food to the children of the family can easily become a daily source of tension. As each wife pours out her trouble to her husband when he comes home, he is apt to remember how one of his brothers or another has not done his proper share in getting the family's livelihood or has shirked a clear responsibility. A younger brother is then likely to find the elder more insufferably overbearing than before, the elder finds the younger more incorrigibly impertinent than ever. The brothers seek and usually find support in different directions, from their respective wives" relations. Both brothers find the idea of separation attractive, all the more so if a man's mother and his wife are constantly at each other, placing him in the uncomfortable and hopeless middle (cf. Karve 1953, p. 79; Srinivas 1952b, pp. 29–31; Mayer 1960, pp. 178–179; Minturn and Hitchcock 1963, p. 261; Nicholas 1961, p. 1059).

"As long as the brothers stay united, the social personalities of the younger brothers do not attain completion," Srinivas writes of Rampura, in Mysore (1952b, p. 30); younger brothers elsewhere in India as well, find this a constant irritant as they come into manhood. Each brother has an equal right, as legal coparcener, to change this state of inequality by demanding the formal assignment of his share of the family's property. If the father is alive, vigorous, and forthright, he brooks no nonsense about family separation. He can only lose by it, in power, comfort, prestige, and wealth. The mother, who may have helped set off the outburst now tries to calm it; she scolds, reasons, weeps, bemoans her cruel fate and ungrateful sons.[3]

The elders and leaders of the family's lineage and jati-group counsel patience and unity. They too can only lose if their kinsmen and community come to be known as quarrelsome, irascible people. Parents will think twice before betrothing their daughters to a fractious lot. A council of the lineage or even of the jati may be assembled to hear out the case. In it the elders point out to the brothers what they already know, that each will lose by the division.

They will lose economically by the immediate expenses of setting up a separate household and in the long run by the dispersal of their land and labor. And there is the danger—for which ample precedents are quoted—of long lawsuits, which sap energy and drain away resources.

They will lose socially. The name of each one in the family may be diminished by their separation. The brothers hear eloquent arguments against separation. One elder in a Gujrat town, defending joint living, said that the five fingers are not of equal length, but the loss of any one makes the hand ugly and defective, so each member must allow for the shortcomings of the others for the good of all. Moreover, "even if the family is very poor, if all live jointly and there is unity among them, you will receive offers of marriage for your children as soon as they are born" (Desai 1964, p. 170).

Even more, no man can hope to stand alone and defend himself singly in the village. Each will go down before enemies, for enemies are immanent, unless they can unite in strength of arms, of wealth, of patrons, and of clients. Each will lose as an individual. Who will look after the children, if the foodwinner falls sick? Indeed, who will look after the livelihood of the sick man himself? The

[3] In a broad comparison of family life in India and China, Francis Hsu concludes that a main difference is that the father-son relationship is central in Chinese families while in Hindu families the mother-son bond is the central, satisfying relationship. Hence social cohesion and cooperation are greater in China because the core relationship of trust between men is a continuous one. In India there is not the same continuity or trust. The mother-son relationship is not a link in a continuous mother-son line because, as Hsu puts it, no mother is a son and no son is a mother. The father-son relationship, moreover, is one of mutual dependence and so lays the basis for cooperation within a group while the mother-son relationship is one of unilateral dependence. It does not enhance group solidarity because it is primarily a dyadic relationship (Hsu 1963, pp. 48–52). Compare, however, a different view noted in footnote 4, pp. 61–62 above.

elders may suggest various healing moves. Perhaps one brother may go off to find work in a city. Among some groups a younger brother is encouraged to find personal freedom in the army (Ross 1961, p. 47; Gould 1961c).

Brothers who cultivate their own land together, whose pride, strength, and security lie in their land, are usually ready to see the disadvantages of dispersing the ownership. Brothers whose income is in cash or who can raise cash crops as well apart as together are less likely to delay the parting (Bailey 1957, p. 92; Desai 1964, p. 103; Epstein 1962, pp. 176, 306). Yet whatever their economic circumstances may be, there is usually some delay in separating after the first restless signs because the parting goes against the grain of the ideal and is contrary to the pattern of domestic authority in which they have been reared. This keeps the restive ones quiescent for a time.

But only for a time. The smoothing measures repair cleavages only temporarily. Before long other cracks in family solidarity appear and the pacifying devices only paper them over until finally no devices can hide or stop the split. The limits of this kind of counterchange are reached. The old family can no longer be maintained and new ones are established to succeed it.

The Family as Module and as Model

Relations within a family are in certain important ways similar to relations within a jati and in a community. We should scarcely expect it to be otherwise; no society can long endure a clashing incongruence between its smaller and its larger social groupings. But in India there is a particularly close nexus between family and jati, and it is necessary to understand family life well in order to grasp the nature of jatis.

What a person does in his role as family member underlies his behavior as jati member. His family serves both as model and as module for his jati relations. It provides the matrix for the beginnings of his conduct and contains the ends, the purposes, of his social striving. It is his fundamental corporate group, the locale of much of his social action, and it is also a main unit of attribution, from which expectations about his behavior are projected and judgments of his activities are made.

The family is a module, a regular structural segment of the jati, just as the jati is a module of the community. Every person is born both into a family and into a jati, and not into one only. He cannot readily opt out of either family or jati. As his jati is the field of actual and potential kin, so the family is the actual field of closest kin. All in a jati are taken as ritual equals by the community primarily because they are considered to interact as equals in their family capacities.

The village family is also the fundamental module of production and of reproduction. Most economic activities—cultivation, crafts, services—are performed by people operating in family groups or acting as representatives of their families. The interchange of goods and services according to jati specialization is, as has been seen, an interchange between families of different jatis. And the interchange among families of a jati in marriage is the basis of jati integration, of much of the cultural communication, and of a good deal of the economic distribution.

As a reproductive, socializing group, the family provides the primary model of social relations for the child. He first learns the expectation of hierarchical order in society through the hierarchy of the family. Respect, deference, avoidance, are all inculcated as part of family roles (cf. Dumont 1957b, pp. 7, 11; Carstairs 1957, pp. 63–76; Sarma 1951, p. 53). Inside the family, deference to elders is essential in family relations. Among families, each must strive to keep up and, if possible, to improve its prestige among other families of its jati.

A child learns about pollution and purity in the daily round of household tasks, in the preparation of food, in the various degrees of purity of the separate precincts of the house, in the daily avoidances brought on by one's biological functions, and in the periodic avoidance brought on by his mother's menstrual cycle. The touch taboos observed between family members because of temporary pollution set the style for keeping permanent distance between members of different jatis. The household is the scene of stricter purity observance than is the village outside, the women are the most careful guardians of domestic purity, hence the child's earliest experiences are with the more rigorous observances of the purity-pollution theme (cf. Mayer 1960, pp. 51–52).

The importance of matching conduct to context, of switching role behavior as the social situation changes, is daily illustrated to the child in the household. Thus he feels the restraint that descends upon his relations with his mother or father, who may have been playing gaily with him a moment before, when his grandfather enters the room. He sees his mother joking with his younger uncle, withdrawing demurely from the presence of his elder uncle. Even in their quarrels, members of a family are likely to affirm the ideal of family solidarity, each charging the other with dereliction of family duty and loyalty. Such quarrelers implicitly agree—through their vehement disagreement—that loyalty to family ought to be put above all other personal and social considerations.

The basic patterns of social control, of systemic counterchange, are learned and are used in family relations. In Gopalpur village of Mysore, for example, the giving or withholding of food is a main means of control. "The individual is brought to feel that the major securities and satisfactions of life are to be found in the acquisition of a large number of friends and supporters and in the control of them through the use of food. The most important supporters of the individual are the members of his family" (Beals 1962, p. 22).

In much of his day-to-day activity a villager acts in the capacity of family member and is so perceived to act by others. In extraordinary situations of stress, a person's first loyalty inclines to his family, above all other considerations (cf. Cohn 1961a, p. 1055). It is scarcely possible to single out and deal with one person in a village. As one man is called forth, his family comes forth with him. Often enough this is physically so; typically it is symbolically and figuratively true.

Yet in the expansion of the family, cleavages regularly appear. It is part of the process of family growth, part of a family's natural, inevitable, yet disapproved development. The pattern of family fission, with each couple setting up a social space of its own, resembles the pattern of jati fission, which will be considered later.

A family can usefully be seen as a structure of roles and as a system of structure maintenance. So viewed, the similarities and recurrent crises of family life throughout a vast population can be formulated. But family life in any real family is much more than role structure and counterchange, just as a house is much more than the set of blueprints and a home infinitely more than a dossier of behavior patterns. In an actual family there are decisions, choice points, exigencies, rewards, sorrows. A villager's emotions, motivations, conflicts, achievements are chiefly played out within his family and with other families. The central themes of traditional drama and story have to do with family affairs. The scenes from the *Ramayana* that are dramatized in the annual pageant of Ram Lila in northern India, are mainly concerned with family problems. They show, for example, how a woman caused great difficulty by seeking to promote the interests of her own son above those of the others in the joint family. They depict the grief of a mother when her son is exiled, the devotion and virtue of a wife, the loyalty of a younger brother (Opler 1959, p. 28a).

Scenes from the other epic, the *Mahabharata*, are also staged, told, and retold in villages of every part of the land. In Mrs. Karve's words, "It is simply the story of a huge, big joint patri-family and illustrates the interrelations, the personality development, the feuds, the strength, the weakness, the ethos of the joint families" (1953, p. 21; see also Sarma 1964, p. 198).

Family battles there are in plenty, but their very intensity and the interest they elicit testifies to the importance of family to the individual and to society. For the family is at the core of a man's allegiance, of his loyalty, his identification. It is his own gauge of his success in life, it is a main standard used by others to measure his earthly achievement. All the more is it so for a woman. A man may have outside interests and achievements, a village woman cradles them all in her family.

However, caste society is not just the family writ large, nor is a family only a jati in miniature. There are other groupings, other bonds, other traditions within a jati and among jatis that together make up village society.

CHAPTER 8

The Wider Ties of Kinship

Beyond his family, a villager carries on much of his life with other kinsmen. A good part of his daily round, most of his visiting, all domestic ritual are typically done with relatives. A village family reaches out for help from its related families in an emergency, on ritual occasions, in the work of the field or the struggle of the feud. And those families turn to them for help when sudden necessity or regular occasions require.

A man relates to several classes of kinsmen beyond his immediate family. His most frequent interchange is usually with those families closest to him in patrilineal descent and in residence, a group that may be called a localized lineage. The men are brothers who have set up separate households or the sons of brothers or patrilateral cousins. All in these households, including wives, adopted children, and resident sons-in-law, are considered part of the group even though they are of different patrilineal descent from the related men. There may be as few as two families in such a localized lineage or as many as from twenty to thirty. The families belonging to one lineage usually perform formal ritual functions together, especially in mourning observance, and such joint observance helps to define the boundaries of the group. They also cooperate in many other activities. The lineage is regarded as an extension of the family and so it is an exogamous unit. There can no more be a marriage between a boy and a girl of the same lineage than of the same family.

A larger exogamous category is known in many jatis, though not in all. For our purposes it may be called simply the clan. It is usually a grouping rather than a group, a taxonomic category rather than the basis for joint action. Each person inherits the clan of his father, and marriage within the clan is forbidden because all in it are considered to be descended from the same progenitor. The common ancestor of lineage members is usually an actual, remembered person, but the common progenitor of fellow clansmen is typically a legendary, supernatural character. The members of a clan tend to be too dispersed and their kin ties too remote for them to share much in the way of common interests or joint action. Occasionally the clan does provide a basis for cooperative activity, as in the worship of a clan deity, but the clan grouping is mainly used to classify jati fellows into eligible and ineligible spouses.

Another class of kinsmen does provide a basis for some joint action. In this class are the families of the jati-group, those of the same jati who live in one village. They are kinsmen in the sense that all are either actual or potential relatives with the added bond of village residence. They may observe rituals together, they may aid each other economically, they normally come to the defense of any jati fellow whose welfare and status may be threatened by others. This group will be discussed in the following chapter, in the context of jati organization.

Another class of kin includes those related to a man through the women of his family, particularly through his mother and his wife. These kinsmen are concerned about him as a person rather than as the representative of his family or of any other corporate group. They are expected to sustain and protect him and commonly do so. He, in turn, does the same for the husband and the children of his sister and, later in life, for those of his daughter. The term "feminal kin" is used here for this class of relatives. A woman's feminal kin are mainly those through her mother, that is her mother's brothers and others of her mother's natal family.

A man shares the same lineage, clan, and jati-group with a good many other men. But only rarely do two men share the same feminal kindred. Even brothers have different relatives through their respective wives, unless they marry sisters. Further, a man belongs to only one lineage, one clan, one jati-group, but he may have a wide array of feminal kin who may not have any particular relationship with each other aside from their common jati.

Finally, there is the class of fictive kin. Because villagers consider kinship bonds to be the best basis for reciprocity and allegiance, people who are not actually related by descent or marriage can establish fictional bonds of kinship with each other. In that way a person can secure for himself the benefits of a wider circle of kin than biology can provide for him. These relatives, like all kinship relations, can be deployed in a man's quest for power and status or, as he might prefer to put it, in his striving for the security of his family.

The Lineage

A man's lineage fellows are literally and figuratively close to him for they are, after all, the brothers who have separated their fields and hearths but who continue to sustain their fraternal allegiance. Once the trauma of parting is past, they tend to honor the brotherly bond. Their sons and grandsons carry on the relationship with some of the fidelity that the fraternal ideal requires, and also with some of the friction that fraternal relationships often involve.

That ambivalence is the greater because the ideal of lineage solidarity is not so strongly proclaimed as is the fraternal ideal, and moreover it is not always clear who should be counted as a full lineage member. Lineage ties lapse after several generations, but the number of obligated generations is not usually specified clearly. A father's brother's son who moves to a distant village is a full lineage member for ritual purposes but he can hardly be a full participant in corporate activity (cf. Mayer 1960, pp. 182–183).

Hostility sometimes encroaches on lineage unity. This is recognized clearly in a village of Poona district, where one man commented that just as brothers always fight, so do their sons and grandsons (Orenstein 1965a, pp. 85–87). In a Kashmir village, lineage fellows help each other, and yet conflict among them is a prominent feature of kinship relations. "The sibling rivalry which leads to partition of the household is later revealed in more intense form in the relationship between cousins" (Madan 1965, p. 201).

Nevertheless, lineage fellows do commonly cooperate in ritual, in economic enterprise and in general rights and procedures. Thus they often participate together in life-cycle rites even when they are at odds on other matters. Lineage members who share jural rights may put up a common front in order to keep the rights but may also quarrel about who is to get greater advantage from them. As close neighbors they usually exchange economic aid, from fire for a cold hearth to the labor pool at harvest. In dispute settlement, the court of first appeal in domestic quarrels is commonly an assembly of the men of the lineage. They usually try to settle such an affair quickly and smoothly, lest the reputation and status of the whole lineage suffer. When a man gets into a quarrel with a villager of another lineage or a different jati, he generally finds immediate defenders and close allies among his lineage mates. His other kinsmen are mainly in other villages; his agnates are right there with him (cf. Mayer 1960, p. 239).

Such cooperation is continually reinforced because lineage families commonly live close together, in the same village street or in the same ward or hamlet. They are near each other because brothers set up their new households not far from the old one. This is in part because they must—their lands and homesites are there—in part because it is well to have close relatives nearby. So when one falls ill, the others cannot easily ignore his need; when there is a death in one house, the others will not plead ignorance; when emergency help is required by one family, the others cannot well be elsewhere (cf. Lewis 1958, pp. 22–23; Minturn and Hitchcock 1963, p. 237; Berreman 1963, p. 176; Epstein 1962, p. 174; Nicholas 1962, p. 174).

The strand that binds the lineage is that of patrilineal descent but the actual cooperation includes all those who reside with the related families. Notably this includes the wives, each of whom was born into another lineage, and also the adopted children and the occasional man who has come to live with his wife's relatives. When a bride joins her husband's family, she becomes a member of his lineage for most purposes, ritual, economic, and legal, but she also retains some affiliation with her original lineage and some rights in it. Only rarely is a woman totally cut off from her natal lineage.

Lineage Ties and Ritual Functions

A main link among the families of a lineage is the joint performance of ritual functions. They observe pollution seclusion together and participate together in each other's life-cycle observances. In some places they worship the same lineage deities; all the families of the lineage share the tutelary spirit who watched over the founding family and all think of themselves not only as wards of the same deity but also as descendants of the same ancestor.

In Totagadde village of western Mysore, for example, offerings are made to lineage deities who are believed to live near the house and to protect its people and animals from the depredations of other supernaturals. Vegetarian food is placed for the household deities of Brahmins, blood offerings for the guardians of lower ranking households.

The Havik Brahmins of this village observe lineage pollution to an exceptional extent (Harper 1964, pp. 161–167). After the death of a Havik Brahmin, every man and woman of the deceased's lineage must remain in seclusion for eleven days. During that period they may perform no rituals nor may they approach closely to other Brahmins. They are then like untouchables to the others of their jati. The touch of a Brahmin in mourning defiles another Brahmin. Moreover, their lineages are of unusually great depth, including all men who are patrilineally descended from a common ancestor up to the seventh ascending generation. Haviks say that even beyond that degree of kinship some mourning seclusion, though of progressively diminishing length, should be observed among men even more distantly related, up to the twenty-first ascending generation.

Women keep the full mourning period of their natal lineage so long as they live in one of its households. When they marry and move to another house, their seclusion on the death of a person of their original lineage is much curtailed, but they undergo full seclusion for a death in their husband's lineage.

These Brahmins also observe the happier restrictions because of a birth in the lineage. When a child is born to one of the lineage families, all men and women in it may not attain the highest state of ritual purity nor participate fully in ceremonies until the mother emerges from her eleven days of deepest avoidance (Harper 1964, pp. 167–169).

There are not many jatis whose people maintain such strict seclusion for all in a lineage nor who trace lineage connections back so far, but very commonly lineage relatives do share death pollution and contribute to the funeral expenses. They contribute also in money, goods, and by their presence to all the life-cycle observances of their lineage fellows (cf. Mathur 1964, pp. 43–44; Orenstein 1965a, pp. 75–79, 84–85; Madan 1965, p. 198)

Some of the limits to such reciprocal aid are illustrated in the account of Bisipara, a village of highland Orissa. Lineage fellows within each of the several jatis do help each other, especially with ritual and for a ritual emergency. But if one of them suffers a personal misfortune, as when his oxen die, he looks more for help to his relatives through his mother and his wife than to his supposedly closer agnatic kinsmen. The reason for this, Bailey writes, is perhaps indicated in the local proverb which says that the brother is the enemy. There is potential hostility among brothers, in Bisipara as in other parts of the land, at least when the family estate is to be divided. This does not mean that brothers hate each other. They often cooperate in the fields and aid each other in sickness or in ritual crises, but they may not be so responsive to a personal economic crisis. It is as though partition sets the pattern for their future relationship. "In sickness, or against outsiders, the brother is an ally and a friend. But if he mismanages his part of the estate, let him look after himself" (Bailey 1957, pp. 83–84).

Here as elsewhere the men of a lineage may fall out in a factional dispute and their factional enmity may reduce or even wipe out any effort at mutual assistance. However, lineage fellows do generally side with each other in village encounters, even though all do not necessarily become involved in each other's personal quarrels unless the name and fame of the lineage is involved. Among the Pramalai Kallar, for example, a man may act as a substitute in ritual for a lineage fellow when his lineage relative has had a quarrel with someone else involved in the ritual exchange (Dumont 1957b, p. 176).

Lineage Ties in Economic and Jural Affairs

Lineage fellows also cooperate for economic and jural purposes. For example, in Gaon village particular jatis render services for the whole village. This public service work is allocated according to lineage and lineage segment within each jati of the scavengers, Brahmins, temple priests, potters, leather workers, and rope makers (Orenstein 1965a, pp. 64–90). Such service to the village rather than to patron families is common in this part of Maharashtra.

Though the localized lineage is an important unit in Gaon, the villagers do not set precise, formal boundaries to it nor do they have a single word for it. A common term is *bhāuki*, which is used to refer both to those who are descended from a known patrilineal ancestor, wherever they may live, or to the cooperating, related families, who usually live in neighboring houses within a village. In most jati-groups of Gaon there is only a single lineage or one is highly dominant. Some of them keep no genealogical records and the families who hold themselves to be of one lineage may not really know which patrilineal ancestor they have in common; they assume that there has been at least one. Contiguity of residence is a more potent cause for collaboration than is exact genealogical history. For this reason and also because the group includes wives and others, Orenstein believes that these localized groups are not quite lineages in a technical sense of the term. For our present purposes they can be termed localized lineages, despite some lapses of genealogical record.

Two of the twenty-four jatis of Gaon do not have any lineage groups. One is the basket weaver jati, which is divided into exogamous moieties rather than into lineages. The other is the goldsmith jati. Orenstein points out that there are typically only one or two families of goldsmiths in a village, and kinsmen so dispersed cannot well cooperate in corporate lineage groups (1965a, pp. 62–65). Within the localized lineages in Gaon, a set of two to four households is taken as a segment which is "formed out of or inherits brothers' tensions and brothers' ties" (*ibid*. p. 84). A still larger segment of a lineage is the unit for rotating village work. Among the scavengers, for example, each such segment cleans the village for its allotted part of the year.

Since the boundaries of the lineage are not rigidly specified, questions arise as to whether, for example, a brother's son who has moved to the city should be considered a member of the lineage group. The test is whether he is invited to marriage and funeral ceremonies and participates fully in them. On occasions when lineage members foregather, decisions on lineage affairs and adjudication of lineage quarrels usually take place and lineage membership is then demonstrated (*ibid*., pp. 70–71, 85).

Among some groups, major economic functions are assigned to the lineage. This is so among the Jats of Meerut and other districts around Delhi. The men of a lineage have sole rights to a certain portion of the village lands and none of that portion can be transferred out of the lineage. This customary law of the jati has been recognized and enforced by the government courts. For these Jats and other landowners of the region it is continued as a main principle of social organization (Pradhan 1965). Such unity of land and descent is a common feature among tribal peoples in India, as will be noted later.

The great emphasis on the patrilineal line in North India made the jatis of genealogists very important. Their services were especially crucial among Rajputs, Jats, and similar groups whose lineages were wedded to land and where power could hinge on fine calculations of inheritance rights. As Shah and Shroff note for Gujarat, "a Rajput's status in society depends on his position in the genealogy of his lineage," and that position can only be validated by the genealogists' records (1958, p. 263). The genealogist does more than keep the pedigrees of lineage and clan. He is commonly also a bard who extols the feats of the patriline, tells of the glorious accomplishments of the ancestors, and not only links the living members to the shining past but also traces their descent from the deities themselves. Those whose patriline was thus kept fresh in memory and green in glory, have been inclined to form their action groups with their patrilineal kinsmen more commonly than in South India. There are few professional genealogists in the South while in North India some of the artisans, merchants, and even leatherworkers have acquired professional genealogists (Shah and Shroff 1958; Mayer 1960, pp. 194–201; Baines 1912, pp. 85–89).

In earlier centuries the nexus of land and lineage was the basis of state as well as of village organization in many parts of India. In the late eighteenth century, Bernard Cohn notes, dominant lineages in what is now eastern Uttar Pradesh acted as rulers of little kingdoms. A lineage of overlords was responsible for the payment of land revenue and for the provision of troops to the suzerain power. These lineages were far larger than they are now, sometimes comprising more than a thousand families, because men is who could maintain lineagelike solidarity for a larger number were stronger economically and politically (Cohn 1959a, pp. 79–80, 1961c, pp. 616–619; Srinivas 1966, pp. 33–35).

When the British first took control, they too made the lineage or its headman answerable for land revenue and for the maintenance of order. In 1789 the British began to change the system of land tenure and revenue in this region and impaired the power of the ruling lineages, but it was not until the settlement of 1880–1882 that the little kingdoms of the ruling lineages were drastically altered.

The political functions of lineages are now mainly confined to village alliances and factions; land rights in few jatis are still vested in the lineages, but it is still common for lineage elders to act in the settlement of disputes among the families of their lineage. In eastern Uttar Pradesh this is so not only among the descendants of the former rulers but also among the Chamars, the traditional leatherworkers and laborers. In Senapur village, disputes within a Chamar household that cannot be quelled by the family head are taken to the leader of the lineage. Since he lives in the same part of the Chamar hamlet he knows about the quarrel from its beginning and can usually suggest some solution. When the quarrel is between two families of the lineage, the lineage headman similarly tries to smooth over the eruption. If he cannot do so he calls a council of the Chamar hamlet, at which all the lineage leaders should be present together with other family heads in the hamlet.

The same kind of council is brought together to settle disputes between whole lineages with the addition of eminent Chamars from outside the hamlet. Quarrels between lineages can be serious affairs, which may even lead to the penalty of outcasting if they involve major defections of social obligations or irregularities in marriage or occupation.

The failure of a family to invite all its lineage relations to a wedding can precipitate a turmoil. All adult males from both lineages should attend a wedding and also at least one adult male from every other household in the Chamar hamlet. If one of the households is not invited, whether by error or intent, the insult will be resented and formal redress through the hamlet council will be demanded. And when one family suffers an insult from another Chamar family, its whole lineage may rise in wrath (Cohn 1959a, pp. 82–84; 1960, pp. 422–424).

Rights and privileges within a jati are often held by a lineage rather than by a particular family. The office of headman of a jati-group or of council elder may be in the keeping of particular lineages (cf. Reddy 1952, p. 243; Epstein 1962, pp. 127–128). Where lineages are shallow in depth and limited in function, there is usually not much difference in rank among them. But where important functions are assigned to the lineage as a unit, there are likely to be marked status gradations within and among lineages. Thus in one Gujarat village, a Rajput's status is commensurate with the rank of his lineage and also with the seniority of his branch within the lineage and of his family within the branch (Steed 1955, p. 127).

In general, then, a villager's next larger group for cooperation, beyond his family, is the set of families who are close in both descent and residence (cf. Dumont 1964b, pp. 75–76). Descent provides the rationale for cooperation, propinquity the opportunity. Coresidents of other descent lines participate with the men who stem from the same patrilineal ancestor. But identification with one's natal descent line can never be abandoned in matters of marriage and sexual intercourse. No man may have sexual relations, in or out of marriage, with a daughter of his own patriline on pain of the penalties of incest. No matter where she has lived, no matter how long she has been away from her childhood home, she remains until death a part of her natal line in this respect.

An example of the distinction between the ties of descent and of residence is given in the account of Ramkheri village in Madhya Pradesh. Three different words (*kutumb, bhaibandh, khandan*) may be used for lineage by these villagers. Each of them can also refer to yet another kind of grouping, the intended reference depends on the context of use. Thus the term *bhaibandh* means either lineage or clan. When a man is asked to which *bhaibandh* he belongs, he will give the name of his clan because he understands the question as referring to his patrilineal category. But if he is asked where his *bhaibandh* is living, he will reply with reference to his lineage, because that is his group of common residence as well as of common descent.

Close residence favors the continuation of the closer ties of lineage, distance makes for forgetting them. One man in this village said that he had *bhaibandh*, here referring to lineage fellows, in two nearby villages and while he was not sure of his exact relationship with them, he still invited them to his ceremonies. But he also had lineage relatives in a village some thirty miles away with whom he did not keep up the reciprocal exchange. Lineage connections with people in a village as distant as that are dropped after five or six generations. "Then the lineage passes into the clan (*bhaibandh gotra men jata hai*), and the people become clan mates (*gotra bhai*) only" (Mayer 1960, pp. 167–168).

THE CLAN

The lineage passes into the clan. This comment indicates a recurrent process in kin relations. A lineage, like its component families, develops through a cycle of growth and separation (cf. Madan 1965, pp. 225–227). But the separation of a lineage is usually a gradual process and comes about through the slow, piecemeal relinquishing of mutual exchanges—sometimes under protest, sometimes mutually accepted—rather than in an abrupt, explosive break. Just as a family, after partition, passes into the lineage, so does the lineage in time separate into the clan.

The exogamous principle is never relinquished. People who have abandoned lineage cooperation with each other still inherit affiliation in the same clan. They and their patrilineal descendants through all of time presumably remain in the same exogamous category. Lineage relations are limited in time and space; the clan endures through time and across space.

In that sense the clan is an affirmation that the incest taboos of patrilineal exogamy are immutable and eternal. The members of a clan usually have an origin story linking all of them to the same supernatural source. In Ramkheri there is a clan goddess for each clan of a jati; worship of the same goddess is the main test and affirmation of belonging to a particular clan. If a stranger comes to a village and claims to be of a certain clan, he is not allowed to worship with the other members until they have been assured of his claim by finding mutual, known kin or through the guarantee of someone whom they can trust (Mayer 1960, p. 184).

Cooperation within a clan depends in good measure on demographic and economic factors. Where the families of a jati are scattered and only one or two exist in a village, as among the goldsmiths of Gaon and in some of the Ramkheri jatis, there may be too few families to form a lineage cohort in any one locality. In that case, each family may establish close, supportive relations with families of its clan as well as of its lineage (Mayer 1960, pp. 168–169).

There are some jatis, mainly the lower and poorer, among whom lineage is little elaborated and clan ties are vestigial or absent. The potters of western Maharashtra, for example, do not have clans nor do the earthworkers of eastern U.P. (Karve 1958b, p. 131; Rowe 1960, p. 300). But in most regions the general pattern of lineage and clan relations that we have sketched is known, though the terms used by both villagers and anthropologists vary considerably. Thus in the Himalayan village of Sirkanda, related families group themselves as a lineage (Berreman uses the term clan for this unit) because of their common patrilineal descent and residential propinquity. A clan ("sib" is the term used by Berreman) has ritual functions in Sirkanda as it does in Ramkheri. Clan fellows in Sirkanda feel a certain allegiance to each other, so that there are few factional disputes in which men of the same clan are pitted against each other (Berreman 1963, pp. 176–187).

In Totagadde in the south, as we have seen, the Havik Brahmins maintain lineage connections among people linked to a quite remote ancestor. In actual practice the more distant kin ties are often sloughed off by being conveniently forgotten. But even in the long kinship reckoning of the Haviks, the descendants of a common ancestor are no longer lineage mates after a number of generations but only *sagotra*, members of the same clan or *gotra* (Harper, 1964, p. 163).

Gotra and Other Terms for Kinship Groupings

The Sanskrit term "gotra" is very widely used. A Brahmin must specify his gotra affiliation in his daily devotions when he makes an exact identification of himself before the gods. But this word refers to different kinds of grouping in different jatis and it is used by jatis at all social levels. Even in the Vedas there seem to be different meanings attached to it and there has been a lively difference of opinion among Indologists as to its central or original meaning (Madan 1962c, pp. 60–63; Kapadia 1958, pp. 124–130).

Gotra is most commonly used to mean what we have called a clan, that is an exogamous category within a jati. Its principal use, often the only one, is to regulate marriage matches. All members of a gotra are presumed to be descended from or associated with the same supernatural source. People of different jatis may carry the same gotra name and claim descent from the same legendary sage or deity. But this implies no special connection between them. Gotra names have been taken over by many who were adapting their ways to the Sanskritic norms and so the Sanskrit labels appear in jatis of various sorts (Hutton 1961, p. 55; Dumont and Pocock 1957c, p. 52; Madan 1962c, pp. 72–73; Mathur 1964, pp. 47–49).

The functions attached to the grouping called gotra vary by jati and region. The usage in Sirkanda is quite exceptional because the gotra category is used there only for ritual identification in the marriage rite and is not an exogamous unit. The Pandit Brahmins of Kashmir use the gotra category in more typical scriptural fashion for both exogamy and ritual identification but, less typically, they allow some marriages within a gotra to be arranged through the use of a legal fiction or by the performance of expiatory rites. In a West Bengal village, by contrast, gotra exogamy is said never to have been violated. In Ramkheri, as we have noted, the clans or gotras not only are exogamous but also have common deities and rites (Berreman 1963, pp. 187–191; Madan 1965, pp. 103–105; Klass 1966, pp. 957–958; Mayer 1960, pp. 184–188. See also Hutton 1961, p. 56; Karve 1965, p. 118; Karandikar 1929, p. 76).

In earlier times a band of Rajput warriors who conquered a territory and founded a state were sometimes related as clan brothers. In some of these princely states, even under British rule, there was a constant struggle between the prince and his clansmen, the nobles. He wanted to keep them in their subordinate place as his vassals; they claimed higher privileges as his clan brothers (Cole 1932, p. 135; Shah and Shroff 1958, p. 260).

A particular clan of a dominant jati sometimes wields leading influence in a set of villages. Thus in Rampura, near Delhi, one of the clans gives its name to a unit of some twenty villages because these villages accept the leadership of the members of that clan even though other clans are represented among them (Lewis 1958, pp. 29–30). Generally, however, clan functions are now minimal, and those villagers who do maintain clan divisions do so, whether under the term gotra or some other, mainly as categories for exogamy.

Exogamy may be extended beyond one's own clan. Some, especially in the higher jatis of north India, prohibit marriage into four gotras, namely: one's own, that of the mother, the father's mother, and the mother's mother. This is called the "four-gotra rule"; if strictly observed it forbids the marriage of a prospective bride and groom if they share any two of their combined eight gotra links (Karve 1965, pp. 115–125; Mayer 1960, pp. 202–203). Other North Indian jatis extend the prohibition less widely—only to one's mother's clan or to those of mother and of father's mother.

Clan exogamy may also be extended by clustering several clans into an exogamous bloc, called a phratry in kinship analysis. Among the Marathas, each clan has a totemic symbol, a javelin, or a kind of grass, or the leaves of certain trees. At the time of a marriage each family worships the clan symbol, but at other times it plays little part in family ritual. Several different clans have the same symbol and there may be no marriage between two persons who share a clan symbol. The clans of the Marathas are also ranked in a hierarchical order for purposes of marriage alliance. Mrs. Karve depicts the hierarchy as capped by the "five-clan" division and descending in five layers to the division of the "ninety-six clans" (Karve 1965, 176–179; Orenstein 1965a, pp. 62–63, 124–126).

One of the most complex clan arrangements of all is that of the Rajputs, who are widespread across northern India. Rajputs agree that an order of clan rank exists, but often disagree as to the ranking of a particular clan. Each Rajput clan is part of a larger grouping, the branch. Several branches make up one of the main lines and all in one line consider themselves descended from the same primordial progenitors such as the sun, the moon, serpents, or fire (Karve 1965, pp. 165–171; Mayer 1960, pp. 164–165).

In sorting out the groups and categories of kin at any level or region, it is especially important to recognize what was previously noted, that local terms can be misleading. A student who concentrates on the particular terms rather than on social structure and social function soon finds himself bogged down in a hopeless morass of seemingly conflicting usage. Villagers, like those in Ramkheri and elsewhere apply the same term to quite different groups, distinguishing one meaning from the other by the context of use. Further, a term that in one context may refer to a group may mean a kind of kin linkage in another context. In discussing an account of a Punjab village, Marriott notes that "the term '*biradari*' refers not to just one concrete structural unit at the village level, but rather to patrilineal connection, real, putative, or fictional, at any level of segmentation" (1962, p. 264; also see Honigmann 1960b, p. 836).

The same unit may bear different labels. In Sirkanda, for example, the exogamous grouping is called either jati or *biradari* (Berreman 1963, pp. 149, 182). But jati is also used by some Sirkanda people in the usual sense of the endogamous rather than the exogamous group. Nor, as has also been mentioned before, are the technical terms in the anthropological literature on India well standardized. The term "lineage" is used here instead of Murdock's "compromise kin group" for the group that combines unilineal descent with residential unity (Murdock 1949, pp. 65–78). There really is no "compromise" in the formation of such a group; rather the group shows the complementary effects of patrilineal descent and local propinquity.

In village practice, each of the larger social categories, the jati and clan, is usually known by a distinctive name to distinguish it from the others of its kind. But the smaller interactional groups, the family and lineage, do not have separate labels and are referred to usually by the name of a prominent member. These smaller kin groups operate mainly within a village community, while other kinship relations tie together people of different villages.

FEMINAL KIN

One important linkage across villages is that between a man and the relatives for whom we use the term feminal kinsmen. They are related to him through his mother, his married sisters, his wife, and his married daughters. A continuous flow of gifts goes on between a man and his feminal kin, as well as periodic visiting, regular communication, mutual bolstering of status, and reciprocal support in personal emergencies. A man gives to his married sisters and daughters and to their conjugal families; in turn, he receives from his wife's and mother's natal families. Central to these relationships are the perduring ties between parents and daughter, and especially between brother and sister. It has been noted that the mother's brother is an especially supportive kinsman because he cares deeply for the child of his sister. As a brother, a man characteristically wants to help his sister in her married house in every way that he can, by aiding her husband, by backing his family, by giving gifts and favors to her children. A father also seeks to help his married daughter in the same ways, but he usually leaves the direct participation to his sons.

In his family and lineage a man has to cope with the daily tasks of livelihood, with maintaining the kin group, defending its status and extending its power. His feminal kinsmen, through his mother and wife, are more concerned with him as a person than as a member of a group, with the special occasions of his life and of their lives rather than with the daily round, with support in personal exigencies rather than with the regular maintenance of a group. They live elsewhere than in his village—by reason of village exogamy in the North, by common occurrence in the South—and so they are not part of any local rivalry among brothers or power contest between families. Dumont describes how a Kallar of Madura district feels when he visits one of these kinsmen in their home. A change in his attitude is soon noticed, "there is no more etiquette, fun and jokes immediately appear: he feels released; it is a pleasure to go, even for some work, to such a place" (1950, p. 13). The same sentiment is expressed in a Muslim village of Gujrat district in West Pakistan. A man cherishes his mother's natal family throughout life. As a young child he learns that visits to them surround him with affection and return him with fine gifts (Eglar 1960, p. 80; also see Madan 1965, pp. 209–217). Women in all parts of the land also feel freer when they visit their father's house or their mother's brother's house, but women do not go about as readily and so these relations are more actively carried on by the men.

These feminal relationships, as has been noted, help to integrate each villager and each village into a social network of villages that affect many aspects of village life. One incidental effect is that a man's economic standing can be made known through these channels. Beals gives the example of a villager of Gopalpur who needs to be vouched for in order to do some business in a village in which he is a stranger; if a daughter of Gopalpur is married there, she can attest to his reputation. "The existence of marital ties facilitates all economic transactions, both on a village and on an individual level" (Beals 1962, p. 28).

The importance of affinal ties is documented in William Rowe's study of marriage networks among the Noniyas, who were traditionally the earthworkers of Senapur village near Banaras. In a sample count of visits by Noniyas from different villages, 86 percent were between households that were affinally related. Few of these visits were from jati fellows in the villages closest to Senapur because the Noniyas of these villages belong to the same exogamic locality as do the Senapur Noniyas and so they do not carry on the more intensive interchange that goes on among affines. It is intensive because a family must invite as many affinal relatives as possible to share with it in all its celebrations. Moreover, families related by marriage help each other in many ways. They exchange labor; they borrow farm equipment, animals, and cash from each other. When a Noniya wants to consult a shaman secretly, he goes to an affinal village. When he gets in trouble in his home village, especially if it is with the dominant landowners, he flees for refuge to his mother's brother or to his wife's brother (Rowe 1960).

The Chamars of this village cherish these ties in the same way. Their visits to feminal kinsmen are frequent and may be long. A Chamar child may spend two or three years with his mother's natal family. A Chamar, like a Noniya, flees to his mother's or his wife's people if he gets into trouble with one of the landowners in his own place. This is one reason why a number of men of the lower jatis in a village (15 percent in the case of Senapur Chamars) have come in from other villages. Some are attracted as resident sons-in-law, but others find haven or livelihood with relatives (Cohn 1955, pp. 57–58).

Men of higher as well as lower jatis turn first to a mother's brother or wife's brother for shelter. When it became known that a young Rajput of Khalapur village had become attached to a girl of lower jati, such great pressure was brought to bear that he could no longer remain in his village; he fled to his mother's brother. Among these dominant Rajputs, as among subordinate groups, a man's relations with his feminal kinsmen are quite different from his relations with his agnates, being "comradely and without strain" (Minturn and Hitchcock 1963, p. 239). These easy, comradely relations may be extended even to the fellow villagers of one's feminal kinsmen.

Such extension is evident in Bisipara in Orissa. There is hardly a man in Bisipara, Bailey writes, who cannot trace an effective kinship link with at least one household in every other Oriya village of Kondmals subdivision. Some of these links are agnatic, more often they are affinal or uterine—that is, through the mother's brother. And they are extended to all in the related village, even across caste lines. Thus a herdsman of Bisipara had visitors from his wife's natal village from time to time. Some were untouchables. "The welcome they received depended on their importance and the closeness of the tie, but at least they would be allowed to sleep in the courtyard" (Bailey 1957, p. 248).

Fictive Kinship

The range both of feminal kin connections and of agnatic bonds can be extended in some regions through establishing fictional ties of kinship. In Shanti Nagar, near Delhi, every villager customarily uses a kinship term for another resident of his village, irrespective of caste lines. The common terminology does not confuse villagers at all; they know quite well that a man of another jati whom they call father's brother is not in a relationship identical with that of the real father's brother. Nevertheless, the use of the term connotes some of the flavor of the real relationship (Freed 1963a, pp. 86–87; see also Marriott 1955b, pp. 177–178).

The link of fictive kinship between any two villagers is usually established first through two prominent men of their respective jatis. If these two call each other brother on the basis of generation and reciprocal aid, this provides a bridge for extending kinship terms across caste lines for others. Each person can trace the links between his family and the prominent man of his own jati. He then traces kinship affiliation to all in the other jati as though through a brother of that prominent man. Freed tested this and found that 81 percent of the total of 1543 terms he elicited were correct according to this procedure. Most of the other replies had been adjusted to minimize great incongruity between the fictive kinship term and the actual generational or status positions (1963a, pp. 97–102).

When kinship terms are similarly extrapolated to the fellow villagers of a mother's brother, the number of people who are subsumed within a person's kinship terminology is vastly expanded. There is a great difference between actual cooperation and the mere use of kin terms, but the terms do provide a potential beginning for the building of profitable reciprocity if a man chooses and is able to do so.

The Uses of Kinship

There is considerable scope for choice in kinship relations. In the sharp competition for status and livelihood, a man and his family must have kin as allies. A villager's staunchest supporters are his kinsmen, or, better stated, the most dependable allies are those linked by some kind of kinship bond. An ambitious man, seeking power and the status lift that power can bring, must enlarge and strengthen the circle of his kin. Any man who is anxious to protect his family's social position must constantly see to consolidating his defenses of kinship.

To be sure, not all persons feel the same pressure or have the same latitude of choice in establishing kinship relations. A child has no option about the close environs of kin into which he is born. A woman has little choice until she gains some influence in the household and then her influence in the wider spheres of kinship is exerted mainly through the men of her family. But a man, especially the head of a family, does have some freedom of choice. "The choices are presented so insistently and the need for decisions is so demanding that to many the option seems more a slavery to obligation than freedom of choice. How much to give at the birth of a second sister's third son? How many guests to invite, from how distant villages, to the eldest daughter's wedding? What to do for a deceased brother's importunate son?

Certain obligations permit little leeway. A man's responsibilities to his father and mother cannot be accepted or rejected at will, nor do most men consciously want to reject these duties any more than they want to avoid responsibility for their own children. As brother, a man characteristically wants to help and protect his sister, although he may have to decide which of his sisters to help more and how much to help any. As brother to his brothers, he feels compelled, inwardly and outwardly, to come to their aid when dangers to life or name threaten, but beyond that a man may fulfill fraternal obligations either formally and frugally or lovingly and lavishly. A Gujarati saying has it that "a useless brother is a stranger," thus combining the ideas that even the brother bond is subject to differing interpretation and that a kinship relation is valid only to the extent to which it is activated.

The more kinship ties a man activates with others, the more gifts he invests in each relationship, the more the others are likely to reciprocate with whatever they have to give—with allegiance even more than with goods—and the more his power grows. The scope and the limitations of that growth are sketched by Beals for Gopalpur in Mysore (1962, p. 32) and the description holds true over much of India. The Gopalpur man who extends his chain of relationships is able to arrange marriages for others even of different jatis, because he is known through the region and has relatives in many villages. A man who has made a great name constantly feeds and entertains his many relatives and for this he must have wealth. Once he has established a wide circle of kin, their help and influence enable him to keep and increase his wealth. But in acquiring wealth he competes with other men of Gopalpur, for their land if for nothing else, and he also competes with eminent men of his jati and locality for prestige and influence. He must somehow mollify or overshadow them or else they may unite to stem his advance. His success depends a great deal on his ability to recruit unwavering supporters from among his kinsmen.

A villager has scope for such recruitment because he can usually trace some kinship connection with many more of his jati-fellows than those with whom he actually keeps up kinship exchanges. This is the difference between the kinsmen of recognition and the kinsmen of cooperation, as Mayer calls them in his study of Ramkheri in Madhya Pradesh. There as elsewhere in village India a rich man invites many more relatives to a wedding, for example, than does a poor man. "Thus kinship largely depends on wealth and ability to invite and 'keep kin from growing cold' as the Ramkheri people say" (1960, p. 249).

In general, however, it is only the wider extension of kinship that depends on wealth because even a poor man must entertain his close relatives at the main life-cycle rites in his family. Also, even quite close relatives may not take great offense if they are not invited to the festivities of a poor man, but if they feel they have been snubbed by a man of wealth and prestige they must object vigorously or their own status and self-esteem will be by so much diminished.

Yet, as Mayer reports, kinship ties do lapse. In all classes of relationship there are instances in which the interchange has "grown colder," mainly by mutual abandonment. One man does less and then the potential partner in the reciprocity does less also. It was noted above that lineage bonds in Ramkheri are loosened with the passage of generations and with physical dispersal. The linkage, if not the precise ancestral links, tends to be remembered long after the interchange has lapsed. In Ramkheri the lineage of recognition is remembered about ten generations from the founder. The lineage of cooperation tends to last at the most for five or six generations. Among feminal kindred there is a similar difference between the cooperating kindred and those who are kindred of recognition only. Hence a rich man of Ramkheri is likely to include his wife's mother's brother among his kindred of cooperation and invite him to a wedding in the family, but a poor man is likely to omit such an invitation (Mayer 1960, pp. 169–172).

The villagers themselves, Mayer relates, make a clear distinction between those kin ties that exist only in theory and those that are maintained by coactivity. Many of them consider that kinship is defined more by social interchange than by remembered connections through descent or marriage. The ideal is to maintain as wide a kinship circle as wealth and energy will permit, and a successful family is one that keeps up a wide network of kin relations, that extends its kinship of cooperation as far as possible into the kinship of recognition. At the level of lineage and especially through the more expansible feminal kindred there is room for extension of relations. The feminal kindred provide a large field for maneuver; lineage mates are limited to the descendants of a founding ancestor, but the marriages of the several women of his family enable a man to establish bonds with a good many people of different families, kindreds, and lineages.

Among a man's fictive kin, also, there is a difference between those merely of recognition and those with whom he maintains close, friendly, supportive interchange. An ambitious man can create levers of power by transforming potential allies among his fictive kin into actual associates, just as he changes formal lineage kinsmen into close allies.

There is quite a different kind of fictive kinship that must be distinguished from the type just described. A man may establish an individual bond with another man as brother or with a woman as sister. Sometimes the pair may be of different jatis and usually the tie is created when the two take the same guru, the same mentor, and so become "guru" brothers and "guru" sisters (cf. Orenstein 1965a, p. 164). In the account of Ramkheri, these are called "ritual kin" and the other type of fictive bond is called "village kinship." The ritual tie provides a means of bridging differences of jati and neighborhood but little joint activity is entailed. Ritual kin treat each other as friends but not usually as close allies or working partners (Mayer 1960, pp. 139–146). Ritual kinship seems less motivated by considerations of power gain than by personal friendship and its effects are generally limited to the dyadic relationship.

The fact that kinship and power are often closely connected in village affairs should not lead us to view kinship as just a means to power. Quite apart from the other uses of kinship that we have noted—in the socialization of children and in the economic and religious spheres, for example—the chief environment in which a villager lives as an individual, in which he is cared for and cherished as a person, is the environment of kin. Such fundamental experiences in human relations as the private joys of husband and wife, the rearing of a child, the pride in children, the frolicking interplay among young brothers, the deep affection between brother and sister, the joyous welcome given to a sister's son, the happy visit of a mother's brother, the lively sojourn of a father's sister, the pleasure in grandchildren and the comfort of having grandparents—these and much else in kinship are apart from questions of power and are, in their way, as important for individual and society. But in the round of village life questions of power characteristically keep coming up, partly because social hierarchy is assumed yet the specific order is often contested and becomes an issue in a power struggle.

There are some men and families, even whole villages—who are relatively aloof from power struggles. Very many are not; they feel that they dare not be lest they sink shamefully to the lowest depths of their society. A villager's road to power is typically cleared first by mobilizing kin allies and by deploying them effectively. Nor can a villager shed his kin after he achieves a position of eminence. Thus, in the account of Khalapur, it is noted that a prominent man cannot afford to ignore his own kinsmen and friends. If he does to any marked degree, he is no longer a prominent man, no longer considered strong in village affairs (Minturn and Hitchcock 1963, p. 257). A powerful man, by definition, is one who sees to the welfare of many kinsmen. If he does not, whatever his resources of wealth may be and whatever connections he may have with higher sources of influence, villagers reckon that he cannot be a really powerful person.

To be respected, a man should accrue and support a wide range of kin; the pursuit of this ideal helps to explain and to rationalize his quest for power. A wealthy man can approach the ideal far better than can a poor man, and those jatis whose families are the wealthier in a community are better able to do so than are the poorer jatis. Any useful social relation among villagers is likely to be couched in the idiom of kinship because kinship relations are presumed to be more durable, stable, unconditional, and pervasive. Contractual and other kinds of relations are more limited in time, more constricted and conditional in use, fluctuating by occasion and context.

Kinship Bonds in North and in South India

Marriage alliances are the principal means by which new kinship bonds can be forged and, as has been noted in discussing family roles and maintenance, there is a fundamental difference in this regard between North and South India. Broadly put, in the South a family tries to strengthen existing kin ties through marriage, while in the North a family tends to affiliate with a separate set of people to whom it is not already linked.

The system of kinship terms used by most Dravidian-speaking people of South India is congruent with closer marriage. It dichotomizes all descent lines into those with whom one may marry and those with whom one may not. The terminology provides that in a man's own generation males are either brothers to him or brothers-in-law, and females are either sisters or potential spouses. Morgan long ago noticed that the Dravidian terminology is beautifully consistent and symmetrical (1871, p. 394). Its structure can be derived from a few postulates, a principal one being that the children of brother and sister should marry. The term used for cross-cousin of the opposite sex (a man's mother's brother's daughter and usually also his father's sister's daughter) has the connotation of prospective or possible spouse. By extension all potential mates are called cross-cousin. The kin of cooperation are periodically reconsolidated by marriages within that circle (cf. Dumont 1953; 1957a; Dumont and Pocock 1957c, pp. 58–64; Karve 1965, pp. 243–252).

In his analysis of South Indian kinship, Nur Yalman concludes that there is always emphasis on the connections and reciprocal rights between brother and sister. "Brother and sister must be separated, but their offspring must also be united." Yalman states that the preference that husband and wife should also be the children of a brother and sister is a close expression of the principal of jati endogamy (1967, pp. 374–375).

Ties of fictive kinship may be established in this pattern. Two jati fellows who are not actual kinsmen may arrange to become as of one kindred. Yalman cites an example of two newly rich men in a village in Ceylon (similar cases occur in South India) who found it expedient to join forces. One of them began to call the other mother's brother, and after the proper reciprocal terminology had been taken up by all in their respective families, he then married the other man's daughter. She had now become his cross-cousin and was a suitable spouse in Dravidian terminology (Yalman 1962, p. 554). Yalman also points out that the Dravidian-Kariera type of kinship terminology is used by the Sinhalese, by Ceylon Muslims of the East Coast who are matrilineal and matrilocal, and in South India by such very diverse peoples as the Todas, Coorgs, Pramalai Kallar, among many others. In his view, these varied societies share more than the system of terminology. They have in common a tendency to form close, intermarrying kindreds that are also centers of power (1962, pp. 567–569).

In most of North India, by contrast, there is a centrifugal rather than a centripetal tendency in making marriage alliances. A prospective match is seen more as an opportunity to ally two different sets of kin than as a way of strengthening an existing set. Each spouse is taken, in terminology and in practice, as a representative of his set, while the Dravidian terminology and practice is focused more on the person as an individual. In northern India, unilineal kin are often linked to a particular locality, either in fact or by implication, so that village exogamy is common. In the southern usage, the emphasis is more on bilateral connections, and there is little or no territorial exogamy. Affines in the south may cooperate and are involved in each other's affairs in a way that is not tolerated in northern jatis (cf. Karve 1965, pp. 104–138; Marriott 1960, pp. 40–43, 52–53; Yalman 1967, p. 348).

Résumé

The several echelons of kinship begin with the family as the primary multipurpose group. Family members provide for each other's biological needs and social care. The family is the main unit for reproduction and socialization, for consumption and production; it is a principal focus of interaction and attribution. Families develop through a cycle, with the major variations that we have noted.

In time, a family typically disperses into the local lineage, the next echelon of kinship cooperation. This consort of families, close both in agnatic descent and in residence, is usually close also in cooperation within the village. As a group, these related families form a unit for attribution as well as interaction within the jati. The clan, the larger kinship category, is used mainly to sort out potential spouses as possible or impossible. Another class of relatives, a person's feminal kin, interact importantly with him and he with them, but in a personal, dyadic way rather than as a corporate group.

A person's jati encompasses all his kin; its limits are the limits of his kinship relations both actual and potential. Kinship ties thus characterize and bound the jati. Relations among people of different jatis are fundamental in each local social system. These relations are examined in the next part of our inquiry.

PART III

RELATIONS AMONG PEOPLE OF DIFFERENT JATIS

CHAPTER 9

The Interdependence of Families and Jatis

To Carry on any civilization, men must specialize their work in complex ways and exchange their products and services in a regular manner. That is, they are interdependent and they follow a characteristic order of interdependence. This is scarcely a new revelation, but in studying the peoples of India it is especially important to clarify the actual as well as the purported interdependence.

The traditional specialization of a villager, as we have noted, follows the specialization assigned to his jati, which covers preferred, permitted and forbidden occupations. The traditional modes of exchange are the counterparts of this specialization; in village society they entail both contract and status relations, as Maine first used these terms (1861).[1] That is, they involve a range of relationships along a scale from purely contractual, individual, impersonal, temporary, limited transactions at one end to broadly supportive, group-oriented, long-term, multiple bonds at the other.

Contractual and Jajmani Relations

The broader, more durable relations are essentially those between a food-producing family and the families that supply them with goods and services. These are called "jajmani" relations, the Hindi

[1] Students of Indian society can benefit, not only by Sir Henry Maine's still useful writings, but also by the example of his life. In 1856 he was offered an appointment in India as legal member in council. His doctors told him then that if he went to India "his life would not be worth three months' purchase." But after a few years' delay he accepted the appointment and went to Calcutta. He stayed for seven years and returned "a much stronger man than he had been at his departure" (Stephen 1921).

word for them as used in William Wiser's study of the subject (1936). While contractual exchanges have become increasingly important in almost all villages, usually displacing some of the jajmani arrangements, commercial transactions have been part of the traditional economy for many centuries. Villagers in the region of Totagadde in western Mysore, for example, have been engaged in the production and export of a commercial crop, areca nuts, for at least six centuries (Harper 1959b, p. 776). Local, regional, even overseas markets have existed throughout the course of Indian civilization (cf. Thapar 1966, pp. 109–135); markets of a traditional kind are still important, as we shall note in a later chapter, for village economy and society.

Moreover, certain traditional occupations were, in many places, on a contractual rather than a jajmani basis. The weaver, Baines observed, "is not entitled to a customary share of the harvest, but is paid for what he makes and sells" (1912, p. 62). Finally, even in jajmani relations there are some products or services that have to be contracted and paid for separately. Thus in a village of Poona district, the ropemakers supply the farmers, under jajmani arrangements, with all necessary rope manufactures except for well ropes, which are specially long and thick and for which special payment must be made (Orenstein 1962, p. 304). I have known village barbers who provided their services in the traditional jajmani ways, except when a young man wanted a haircut in the city style. That had to be paid for in cash (cf. Sharma 1956a, pp. 128–130).

Cash or barter transactions have long been integral elements of village economy. Yet the traditional jajmani relations are more conspicuous in village life because they entail ritual matters and social support as well as economic exchanges. The whole of a local social order, the people and their paramount values, are involved in such jajmani links.

These links are between families rather than between jatis. Thus a family of farmers gets its metal tools from a particular family of the blacksmith jati and in return the blacksmith family gets a share of the farmer's crop at harvest. The relationship is supposed to be—and often is—durable, exclusive and multiple. It is durable in that the link may be inherited on both sides. A blacksmith serves the same farmer family that his father and grandfather served, and the farmer family gets its tools and repairs from the descendants of the blacksmith family whose men made tools for their forefathers. If one of the associated families dies out, another of its lineage may take its place in the relationship. If a blacksmith family has more sons than its clientele can support, some seek other associates in places where there is a shortage of smiths. Some take up other employment, often in farming, since men of any jati may work on the land.

Jajmani relations are exclusive in that the farmer family is supposed to carry on such relations with only one blacksmith family, and those blacksmiths should make tools only for their own farmer families. They may make some things for sale at a market as well, but they may not poach jajmani associates from other blacksmiths. Jajmani ties are multiple in that more than economic exchange is involved. There is much more to the association than just the exchange of shaves for rice or sickles for wheat.

The families of village officials or village servants, the watchman for example, maintain jajmani relations with the whole village rather than with particular families. Each watchman family gets a contribution at harvest time from every farmer family's crop. The village officials and servants may also have the tax-free use of village land. In some parts, especially in the Maharashtra region, the artisan and service families maintain jajmani relations with a segment of the village rather than with individual families. Such families there have rights to serve all who live in a particular section of the village, or who cultivate a certain section of land (Orenstein 1962, pp. 310–314;Baines 1912, p. 28).

In all jajmani relations, the right to provide goods or services to particular associates is vested in the family, inherited through the family or lineage, and enforced by the jati. If one blacksmith family attempts to take over the farmer associates of another, then the injured blacksmiths appeal to the council of their jati to call off the intruders. And if the blacksmiths of a village believe that the farmers are unfair to them, they may try to have all blacksmiths of the locality boycott the farmers until they give up their unfair practices.

The term "jajman" originally referred to the client for whom a Brahmin priest performed rituals, but it is generally used to refer to the patron or recipient of specialized services and the term "jajmani" refers to the whole relationship. The provider of goods or services is called by a variety of terms, "kamin," "parjan," "pardhan." "Balutedar" is the Marathi word (cf. Beidelman 1959, pp. 6–7).

Specialized Jatis and Multiple Functions

A patron family must carry on jajmani relations with those whose services are required for ritual purposes, especially concerning the family's pollution, and also with those whose services and products are materially useful (Pocock 1962, pp. 82–87). A family requires the services of a priest, often of a Brahmin jati, to maintain or restore the state of ritual purity suitable for its members. Even more, it must have the services of specialists of lower jatis to perform those necessary tasks that pollute those who do them—the washing of dirty clothes, the cutting of hair, the delivery of the newborn, the sweeping away of excreta, and similar defiling chores. All such tasks fall within the basic notion of pollution; all are ritually required in the traditional order.

The ritual specialists do not work for everyone in the village. Although washermen and barbers are not ranked among the higher jatis because their jati occupation involves work polluting to those who do it professionally, they will not ordinarily wash the clothes or cut the hair of the lowest villagers. Even they would be defiled and their jati status degraded by doing so.[2]

This is also true of a Brahmin jati of priests, whose services villagers see as on an entirely different plane from those rendered by the ritual specialists who absorb pollution (M. S. A. Rao 1961). They will not usually minister to families of the lowest jatis. Hence most Harijan families cannot get the services of these ritual specialists and so some of them perform these tasks for their jati fellows. When low-ranking families prosper, however, and are able to discard defiling practices, they try to get ritual specialists to serve them and, as we shall see later, they often succeed.

The other kind of jajmani workers are the artisans and the unskilled laborers. Artisans generally exchange their products with anyone in the village (cf. Harper 1959b, p. 772). They tend to be more independent of the patrons than are the laborers, because a laborer family usually has its jajmani relations with a single family of landowners or cultivators, while artisans deal with a number of patron families and so are not totally bound to any one of them (cf. Bailey 1960b, p. 169).

---

[2] In some places, there are different jatis of washermen to serve different blocs of the local hierarchy. In the south of Kerala, there is a special jati of barbers who serve Harijans (1931 Census, Vol. 28, Part 1, p. 382). Among the lowest of Kerala jatis are the Nayadis whose jati occupation is begging. The right to beg within a certain territory is held by a Nayadi family which can mortgage or sell this right to another Nayadi family (Aiyappan 1937, p. 29).

Economic exchange is only one facet of jajmani relations. A landowner family may have only occasional transactions with some of its associates, as with a goldsmith family in another village, but with others there is more frequent and many-sided interchange. A family of cultivators expects help on its ceremonial occasions from most of the associated families. There is also an expectation of mutual personal support in family emergencies or factional quarrels. Sometimes the specialist families are pressured to support the jati of their patrons when that whole jati is embattled.

Such reciprocal services are often formally stipulated, especially for life-cycle rites. In a village of Lucknow district, for example, a marriage in a family of Thakurs, the dominant landowners, involves the formal participation of families from ten of the fourteen jatis represented in the village (Majumdar *et al*. 1955. pp. 197–204; Majumdar 1958a, pp. 43–49).

A principal ceremonial role is taken by the associated family of the barber jati. The barber's wife cleans and refurbishes the house; she massages the bride, helps her bathe and dress. She joins in the wedding songs and in the stylized derisions with which the groom's party is met. The barber himself accompanies the marriage party in the ceremonial round, doing for the members of the wedding whatever tasks need to be done. He is present through all the ritual, helping the priest, performing such bits as the formal tying of the groom's shirt to the corner of the bride's dress. In return, the barber and his wife are given a sum of money and tips of a rupee or two when they perform some special service in the course of the rite.

At the birth of a Thakur child, the associated families also help. The household priest prepares the child's horoscope to guide in auspicious planning for its development. A woman of one of the low jatis helps with the delivery, cuts the cord, cleans and attends the mother for several days after the birth. Then the barber's wife takes over as attendant, bathes and massages the mother, cleanses the room, helps with the household tasks.

A man of the barber's family hurries about, delivers invitations to the birth feast, helps with the chores at the feast. The household servants of the Pasi jati also carry the good news to friends and relations. Iron bangles for the baby and other metal requisites are provided by the blacksmith family. The washerman family launders the clothes of mother and infant, a special task because these have to be cleansed of the extraordinary defilement of childbirth (Majumdar *et al.* 1955, pp. 193–195). All who help receive gifts in return—of food, of money, of clothes. The amount given is partly set by custom and partly by considerations of the donor's affluence and the recipient's entreaty.

Jajmani associates are expected to be, and some are, broadly supportive of each other, with the quality of ready help that close kinsmen are expected to show. Villagers tend to be nostalgic about such supposed support in the past. One farmer of Shamirpet village near Hyderabad reminisced about his family's relations with their barber family. As Dube translates his comment, "In many cases they were just like members of our family, and although both parties maintained the traditional caste distance, we could always take each other into confidence even on matters of a delicate nature" (1955b, p. 61).

Barbers often do have a privileged relationship, for one reason because they frequently are used for reconnaissance and to make preliminary feelers in arranging a marriage. They are commonly the stage managers and technical assistants at ceremonies. Their women act as midwives. Because their nonbarbering functions are so useful, there are even jatis of Sikh barbers in Sikh villages where the cutting of hair is forbidden but where the traditional managerial, midwifery, and communications functions of a barber jati are needed (Patnaik 1960b; I. P. Singh 1958, p. 481).

Even when a patron's jati is at odds with a client's jati, personal relations between the two families may well remain friendly, even covertly supportive, despite the antagonism between their groups (cf. Bailey 1960b, p. 138). In personal emergencies, as when a farmer needs help quickly to save his crop, he is likely to call on his jajmani associates for help. And when a worker is in dire need, he expects his patron to do something to help him, whether by loans or by supporting him before government officials or in the village council (Wiser 1936, pp. 112–116).

In factional contests each side usually tries to rally its jajmani associates. This occurred in Senapur, a village not far from Banaras, in 1957. The Noniyas, traditionally low-ranking earth workers, had prospered enough by then to build a primary school in their hamlet. The dominant landowners, the Thakurs, viewed this as a threat to their dominant position. When the Noniyas tried to get the village carpenters, tile-makers (potters), and bamboo workers to help in constructing the school, they failed because the Thakur patrons put pressure on these jati-groups. The Noniyas next tried to hire such workers from other villages and again they failed, because the Thakurs of Senapur had enlisted the support of the Thakurs in these other villages. In the end, the Noniyas did succeed in building the school by buying construction materials from a place adjacent to Banaras city and hiring carpenters from a distant village (Rowe 1963, p. 44).

Jajmani Payments and Obligations

The relation usually involves multiple kinds of payment and obligations as well as multiple functions. This is illustrated in a study of an artisan jati, the Lohars, of the same village of Senapur in Jaunpur district of eastern U.P. (Reddy 1955). The traditional work of the Lohars is with iron as blacksmiths. In Senapur they also work in wood, because there are no carpenters in the village. They make and repair agricultural implements for the landowner-farmers, the Thakurs.

This work is apportioned among the Lohars according to hereditary shares. Each family has an exclusive and inalienable right over its share of work, which is not encroached upon by others. The Thakurs too are bound by the same fixed tenure. "When a Lohar family multiplies and divides the work, each share comes to compass the work of fewer agriculturists unless they also multiply at the same rate" (Reddy 1955, p. 130).

A Lohar family's right to a certain set of clients is treated as a property right; at the father's death, his clients are divided among his sons or his-sons-in-law. Should one family have more clients than it can handle, its men may—after proper consultation with other Lohars and with the patrons—transfer some of their clientele to another family. As in other kinds of property, there is uneven distribution among Lohar families. One may have a larger, more lucrative practice than does another.

Lohars cooperate to maintain adequate service for all patrons. When one of the Lohars fell ill during a busy season, another took on the sick man's work in addition to his own. He asked for no recompense for the extra work, either from his jati-fellow or from the Thakurs. In the 1950s, there had been no encroachment within living memory by one Lohar on another's jajmani rights. When there was such a case in a nearby village, the jati council "came down with a heavy hand and fixed the offender in his former place" (Reddy 1955, p. 138).

The amount of work a Lohar family is expected to perform for an associated Thakur family is reckoned according to the amount of cultivated land. A standard measure is called a yoke of cultivation, the land which can be cultivated with one pair of bullocks. This is about fifteen *bighas*, some ten acres. For a Thakur family of one yoke cultivation, the Lohar family puts in about sixty to seventy man-hours of work each year and receives about 40 *seers* (about 80 pounds) of grain.

Certain kinds of work, as on new types of agricultural implements, are not clearly included in the customary arrangements. Some patrons own mechanical chaff-cutters and sugarcane presses. Minor repairs on these are treated as part of the jajmani work, but a patron who adds extra payment for these jobs is apt to get better service (Reddy 1955, pp. 138–139).

Lohars also make ritual accessories for their clients—bridal seats for weddings, tables for household worship, litters for funerals—and receive suitable gifts in return. When minor repairs are needed in a patron's house, his Lohar makes them—without charge if it takes a matter of minutes, paid with extra foodstuff if he must spend a few hours at it.

Here end the obligations of jajmani relations; work of other kinds is a matter of daily hire and wage competition. When a Lohar works at building a new house, or making a cart, or on major repair of a sugarcane press, he works for an agreed daily wage or at a piece rate. Some Lohars are known for special skills. Two brothers of Senapur are good at press repair; another Lohar specializes in making carts. A Lohar who takes on a large job shares the work with his jati-fellows. They share capital equipment too. "It is also a day-to-day occurrence that the few Lohars who have installed bellow furnaces freely offer their equipment to be made use of by other Lohars" (Reddy 1955, p. 138).

The distinction made by these Lohars between work in the jajmani relation and that in a more contractual context is often made in village economy. It is the difference between regular services in the traditional round and work on occasional jobs or on new varieties of equipment and service. Sometimes, as has occurred in Senapur, work on new equipment begins to merge into the regular jajmani account.

The traditional method of payment, in all regions, is made dramatically at harvest time when each farmer family hands over some newly cut sheaves to its jajmani families, or measures out a pile of grain on the threshing floor for each of them (Wiser 1936, pp. 65–67; Srinivas 1955b, pp. 14–15; Neale 1962, pp. 20–27). These harvest payments are only part of what the worker family receives. Where the cultivators own most or all the land of the village, all sorts of rights are under their control. An artisan or service family may be dependent on a landowning family for their house site, for places where their animals may graze, for wood and cow-dung fuel, for the loan of tools and draft animals, even for a plot to use for funeral pyres. In addition, the patron family gives them clothing and other gifts on ceremonial occasions, gives small tips for special service, and may help with loans of money in emergencies and with protection against predatory neighbors (cf. Wiser 1936, pp. 10–11).

Supply, Demand, and Flexible Payments

In some areas, the administrative land records for the village, through the British period, stipulated the precise obligations and payments that were to be met under jajmani arrangements. Even the gifts each associated family was entitled to receive at a wedding in the patron's family were specified (Wiser 1936, pp. 14–15; Lewis 1958, pp. 60–61, 163). But whether there were such officially recorded codes or not, the actual exchange varied with the bounty of the harvest, the respective claims of the associates, and conditions of supply and demand.

This still obtains where jajmani relations are kept up. During a lean year a farmer simply cannot share out as much as he normally does, but when the sheaves are heavy and the granaries full he does not begrudge some extra measures to those who have given good service. But even in the best of years, a farmer is not likely to parcel out more than the minimum amount to, say, a carpenter who has repeatedly put off doing the farmer's repairs or to a washerman who has lost and torn clothes beyond ordinary endurance.

Similarly, a worker family adjusts the measure of its service according to the payment and treatment its members receive. In Rampura in Mysore, for example, those who pay in grain are favored over those who pay only in money; grain payments imply enduring, reliable relationships. "The quality of the service rendered by the Smith, Potter, Washerman, and Barber depends on whether the customer pays annually in grain or not, on the quantity of grain paid, and on the customer's general social position" (Srinivas 1955b, pp. 11, 13).

There seem to be villages where jajmani payments are made quietly, without demur or harangue by any party. But in my own observation, at least some of those who pay feel themselves bedeviled by their importunate workers and they proclaim so loudly. And some of those who are paid argue vigorously against the miserable, miserly amounts that they say are offered; they may not feel strong enough to voice their complaints loudly, but they do so frequently, as though to accept the patron's payments too meekly and silently might invite a smaller payment next time.

Payments also fluctuate according to the available supply of skills and labor and the demand for them. If there is a shortage of blacksmiths, the farmer who is most liberal with extra gifts is likely to get the best service from a blacksmith family. Specialists are imported into a locality where there is need for them. Brahmins have been enticed to settle in places where previously there were no Brahmins, when some of the residents had become prosperous and ambitious enough to require their services. Leading villagers of Totagadde in Mysore recruited a barber from another village when their village barber died and left no successor (Harper 1959b, p. 770). In another Mysore village, all the local sweepers had taken other employment at the time I visited the village. The village leaders brought in a family of a Harijan jati from another linguistic region to do the sweeper's menial work.

Another means of alleviating a local shortage in a particular craft is to have men of another, similar jati do it in addition to their traditional profession. The Lohar blacksmiths of Senapur do carpentry because there is no family of a carpenter jati in the village. Conversely, when there are too many men in a jati-group for employment in their traditional occupations, some of them have to migrate or turn to work on the land. Agricultural labor is open to all, insofar as such work is available.

Supply-and-demand adjustments in traditional jajmani relations are, to be sure, less flexible than those provided through contractual and market transactions. A jajmani patron cannot abruptly discharge a superfluous or inefficient worker or quickly hire new workers, but there was and is a considerable degree of economic adjustability even in the traditional arrangements (Beidelman 1959, pp. 53–56; Orenstein 1962, p. 313; Pocock 1962, p. 91; Kolenda 1963, p. 22; Bose and Jodha 1965, p. 117).

The actual amounts paid to each participating family in a jajmani relation can vary according to differences in size of clientele. In a village of Poona district, the largest amounts are received by carpenters, blacksmiths, and menial workers of the untouchable jatis. A family of Brahmin priests gets lesser amounts from each patron (Orenstein 1962, p. 305). But though a Brahmin priest may get less from any one family, he may collect from more families and may have other sources of income.

In some Mysore villages that Alan Beals has studied, men of the lowest jatis are employed as village servants, as watchmen and irrigators. This gives them a more assured income than that enjoyed by families of several other jatis which rank higher in the local hierarchies. But overall, men of the higher jatis generally receive a higher rate of pay for their services than workers of the lower groups. Unskilled workers are most dependent on the good graces of patron families and are usually least able to exert leverage to better their condition. In Gould's tabulation of actual jajmani payments in Sherurpur village (Faizabad district, U.P.) "the washermen received the lowest average remuneration, the barbers next lowest, and the carpenters and blacksmiths the highest—an order of precedence which accords perfectly with their relative traditional statuses" (1964, p. 20).

Those who provide specialized skills and services themselves need the goods and services of others. A carpenter family requires a barber, a shopkeeper family needs its washermen and other service workers. In Senapur, the landowner family tended to manage the whole set of their workers; the carpenter, barber, and washerman families who served them also served the Noniyas who were their tenants, and each of these provided services for the others (Rowe 1963, pp. 42–43). But landowners in most other places did not manage their associated families so tightly; each specialist family made its own jajmani arrangements, either through direct exchange of labor or by paying in cash or kind (cf. Gould 1964, pp. 33–34).

Few villages hold a complete array of specialist families. The people of Sherurpur, for example, use the services of thirty-five households of specialists who live in a number of the nearby villages. Each of these villages has its own network of jajmani affiliates. Thus jajmani ties establish a web of relationships among villages across the land in which there are few complete breaks. Gould comments on jajmani affiliations radiating from Sherurpur, "Taken to its logical conclusion, therefore, such a network as this ultimately reaches to the borders of a linguistic region and perhaps to some extent even beyond" (1964, p. 34).

Enforcement of Jajmani Relations: Coercion and Consensus

Jajmani interchange is between families of a locality; jajmani counterchange, however, devolves on the jatis. The enforcing of jajmani rules rests with the jatis that are involved in an issue about them. These rules can be flexibly interpreted in various ways but certain minimum standards are maintained at any given time in each jajmani relation. Thus a shift in service arrangements between a blacksmith and a landowner family in Senapur village could not be done only by the families involved, but had to be approved by the elders of each jati-group. And when a blacksmith usurped clients from another blacksmith family, their jati council punished the offender.

If the dominant landowners of a village become convinced that one of their service or artisan groups is derelict in its obligations or threatens the power and status of the landowners, the patron families are likely to bring collective pressure on them by withholding payment, by beating their men, or through any number of other means of harassment. The attacked jati-group may retaliate through a boycott, refusing to provide their services until the landowners retract or compromise.

Such clashes are apt to spread from one village to others in the locality where jati-fellows of the opposed groups live. Both sides have the general village audience to their quarrel very much in mind because what is often at stake is not merely a demand for higher pay or fewer duties, but the insignia and prerogatives of higher rank within the whole local order.

Collective action by either side has to overcome loyalties to jajmani associates in favor of the interests of the jati (cf. Gough 1960, p. 27; Orenstein 1962, p. 710). Yet when jati fellows really become convinced that their jati status is in danger, jati solidarity prevails. Then the united strength of the landowners is usually greater than that which any artisan or service jati can muster. Historically, however, some artisans have maintained their stand quite well. We shall note later that a loose confederation of five artisan jatis pressed their claims for higher status over much of South India for several centuries until the present time. They did not overcome the resistance of higher jatis, but by the same token they were not beaten down. Landowners could not dispense with their services nor shatter their general unity.

But jatis whose men are mainly landless laborers have no such resources and can wage no such struggle. The vast differential in power between the richest and highest in a village and the lowest and poorest has been taken by some authors as the central element in jajmani relations. It is the main reason for their scathing critiques of jajmani relations (Beidelman 1959; Lewis and Barnouw 1956). These authors excoriate jajmani arrangements as the means by which the rich and powerful exploit the poor and coerce the workers into sustaining the power of those who have the upper hand and the higher rank.

Other students of Indian village life have replied to these critiques, saying that there is consensus as well as coercion in jajmani relations, that jajmani exchanges bring solidarity and mutual benefits as well as conflict and exploitation. These observers note that, in their own observations of jajmani interchange, artisans and service workers are not totally helpless against the landowners; all jatis seek to maximize their gains, all wield as much power as they can, all villagers want to avoid pollution insofar as they can, and some coercion and exploitation are inevitable in all societies. They argue that to condemn jajmani arrangements as brutally exploitative is too sweeping and obfuscating a generalization (Rao 1961; Orenstein 1962; Berreman 1962b, p. 393; Kolenda 1963, pp. 21–29; Gould 1964, pp. 29–39).

This exchange among anthropologists parallels the controversies among sociologists about stratification in which some writers stress the conflicts and disruptions that are involved in a stratified order and others emphasize the integration and effective action that orderly stratification makes possible.

Clearly, however, all these forces and elements are involved. At one stage in the development of a society conflict and disruption may be in the ascendant and at another period internal concord and unity will be more characteristic. Those who now decry jajmani arrangements as exploitative may be justified in doing so in order to arouse remedial action. But objective understanding of a traditional relationship is not much advanced through the use of polemical terms.

Change and Continuity in Jajmani Relations

The jajmani relationship has by now been largely supplanted in many villages, although in relatively few has it completely disappeared. It has been supplanted mainly because more money is now used in village economy and because modern transport makes market transactions more feasible. Cash crops are usually not included in jajmani arrangements. A worker or artisan who is paid with a load of sugarcane can only try to sell it, and he prefers to get the money in the first place. Where food grains are raised for sale, as in irrigated villages in Maharashtra, the cultivators who have money may prefer to pay for their shaves and pots with cash at a market center. Many artisans and specialists have moved to market centers and towns and do their work there (Orenstein 1962, pp. 313, 316; Karve and Damle 1963, p. 37).

Moreover, the power of a local dominant jati has been reduced in many places because their village dependents can move away more easily than was formerly possible, can get some income from outside the village, and can better summon political help for their complaints. With less isolation and reduced concentration of political power, the coercive element in jajmani relations has also been reduced (cf. Orans 1967).

Yet the advantages of jajmani for economic stability and security are still sufficiently great that many villagers want to continue with at least some such arrangements. The cultivator gains from them in that he gets better credit and a more certain labor supply than he usually can through cash transactions. Artisans and service families work for him through the year without much pay and then are given a large payment at the time when the farmer can best afford to do so, at harvest. At times of peak demand for labor, a farmer is more likely to get help from jajmani associates than from those who can charge whatever the market will then bear. The workers, in their turn, get more assured employment, and a variety of gifts and concessions, which together may amount to more than money wages could buy in the village. In recent decades, when grain has regularly been scarce and the value of the rupee whimsical, payment in grain is often preferred.

In a questionnaire survey in five Maharashtrian villages, over two-thirds of the respondents (222 of 326) answered that they thought the *balutdari* (jajmani) arrangements were convenient, mainly because of the credit facility. Only some 10 percent of the respondents thought that these arrangements were unprofitable. Others approved of them either because they were traditional or because of the general security they provided (Karve and Damle 1963, pp. 28, 151–152).

In addition to the economic benefits, the ritual services that jajmani associates provide are still in demand. Some landowners in villages of Poona district keep up jajmani relations mainly so that they may have ritual services readily available, as when a washerman must cleanse polluted clothing after a death, or when a messenger of low jati must be sent around to relatives with the news of a death, or when a goldsmith must purify the household deities (Orenstein 1962, p. 312). Presumably all such services can be obtained for hire but hired persons may not readily be available when needed nor can they be trusted to do their ritual work thoroughly if they do not have long-standing ties with the family served. Further, in villages where factional struggles are common, a landowner likes to have dependable support from at least some in other jatis, and worker families like to have a patron's protection.

This is not to say that jajmani relations are on the increase, but rather that this mode of traditional interdependence still has its uses as is shown in three villages where jajmani relations have been studied, one in Mysore, one in Rajasthan, and one in Uttar Pradesh.

Totagadde, in Shimoga district of northwestern Mysore, is the village in which the growing of a cash crop, areca nuts, has been the main productive enterprise for centuries. The relations between a landowner-horticulturalist and those who work for him are more limited, temporary, and contractual than are traditional jajmani relations where subsistence agriculture is the mainstay. Yet even in this village many persistent relationships exist between cultivators and workers. Some service workers serve for a year; some artisans keep the same customers for many years; many workers and artisans are under obligation to a landowner for the kinds of favors that are in his gift, such as lending money without interest, helping in litigation, lending tools, giving building materials and garden produce. In this village "the concept of obligation gives a greater measure of stability and permanency to economic relationships than otherwise might exist" (Harper 1959b, p. 773).

Jati separation is as sharp in this village as it is elsewhere in the region. The commercial economy did not undermine jati organization or the ranking of jatis. It did affect the nature of interdependence, but did not cancel out the inclination toward relationships more durable than monetary market dealings alone.

In a village of Barmer district in western Rajasthan, there have been notable changes, but when Bose and Jodha studied the villagers in 1963, many of them still maintained some jajmani relations. This is a village where subsistence agriculture is carried on under semi-arid conditions. Before independence, it was part of a princely state and the demesne of a feudal overlord. His departure opened the village to new influences and in their train jajmani relations have become more voluntary. Families that prefer to do so may contract for services, and some service families no longer perform their traditional occupations. But many keep up certain jajmani relations. Of a sample of 129 households out of a total of some four hundred, about 75 percent maintained jajmani ties with families of the low leatherworker jati. About 60 percent maintained such ties with carpenter families (Bose and Jodha 1965, p. 111).

Leatherworkers do the ritually polluting work of preparing hides and making leather goods; they also do such defiling chores as removing dead animals from the fields and such menial tasks as collecting fuel and carrying messages. Because the jati council of these leatherworkers had ruled against such degrading work, thirteen of the seventeen households of this jati in the village had stopped doing it. But four families have ignored the council's ruling and gain most of their income from carrying on their jati's traditional service. Of the fourteen carpenter families in the village, eight participate in jajmani relations but get only about half their income in that way. Both the blacksmith families maintain jajmani arrangements but get less than half their income from them (Bose and Jodha 19, p. 117).

Not much of the village economy is now carried on through jajmani arrangements; however, we do not know whether very much more was so managed in earlier years. Some ritual services are still carried on within jajmani arrangements, especially in matters concerning death pollution. Many express favorable opinions about jajmani. Of 129 patrons questioned in this study, 126 replied that jajmani relations were useful in providing cheap and dependable labor and 111 agreed that another benefit was in cheap and assured ritual services. Only 24 agreed that social support was one of the benefits of jajmani relations.

Among those who provide jajmani services, 12 of the 14 questioned replied that assured income was one benefit and 10 agreed that gifts and concessions were important. Payments are made in both cash and kind but most patrons (76 percent) replied that payment in kind gave better returns to the workers (Bose and Jodha 1965, pp. 118–123).

The situation in this village is repeated in many others. Villagers are generally favorable toward the real and supposed benefits of jajmani, but relatively few carry on complete jajmani relations. Those who provide services are now reluctant to accept any overall stigma of inferiority, those who receive services hesitate to take on multiple obligations. But many carry on some jajmani relations and even more give a jajmani-like quality to their economic and ritual exchanges with people of other jatis, gaining some stability of relations without the full roster of jajmani obligations.

Similar conclusions emerge from Gould's close study of contemporary jajmani relations in Sherurpur-Naktipur, adjoining hamlets in a densely populated area south of Faizabad city in U.P. Families of six specialist jatis maintain regular jajmani relations with the cultivators and other villagers. Washermen have the largest proportion of their clientele, 77 percent, on a fixed grain-payment basis. Here also it is the ritual, pollution-absorbing aspect of the service that is important.

Carpenters and blacksmiths are next highest in jajmani clientele with 69 percent and 67 percent respectively of their custom in such arrangements. This is not only because of the importance to a cultivator of having secure relations with these artisans but also because "the capacity to retain traditional ties with carpenters and blacksmiths marks a household as socially important" (Gould 1964, p. 18). The barbers in the village have 62 percent of their clientele on a jajmani basis; despite the easy availability of commercial barbering and its lucrativeness for barbers, this jajmani arrangement tends to be maintained because of the ritual importance of the barber. Two other specialist jatis, potters and plowmen, have only minor jajmani ties.

Among patrons of Sherurpur, the two highest jati-groups, Thakurs and Brahmins, have the highest proportion (70 percent) of jajmani relations. These families maintain "no relationships that do not retain at least some traditional flavor" (Gould 1964, p. 19). Even the families of "menial-impure" jatis carry on a considerable proportion (43 percent) of their dealings with the service jatis through jajmani arrangements. Among all jatis, families with the greatest proportion of cash income tend to rely least on jajmani arrangements while those who have grain but little cash use jajmani services most (Gould 1964, pp. 19, 35).

Though jajmani relations are clearly important in the eyes of these villagers, they are of minor consequence in the village economy. The most valuable and productive crop is sugarcane and this cash crop does not enter into jajmani. The harvest of grain and peas in 1960 for the 70 households that engage in jajmani relations came to 221 tons. Of this production, a little over three tons was disbursed as fixed payments to jajmani specialists. Only about 1.5 percent of the relevant harvest was distributed in the jajmani pattern (Gould 1964, pp. 30–31).

This figure does not include the many exchanges that are not fully on a jajmani basis but that are also not completely contractual or commercial. Thus the people who do the polluting tasks of removing dead animals, of working in leather, of assisting at childbirth are here paid in both cash and kind, with both wages and gifts, for a single job and over an extended period. But even if these payments were taken into account, they would add up to only a small part of total village production.

In the past, a greater part of village economy in this region was probably carried on through jajmani arrangements, but it is not at all clear that a major part of production and distribution was so channeled. What is clear, however, is that jajmani relations were and, to a degree, still are important for the ritual and social order. The jajmani pattern, Gould concludes, "arises from a religious dichotomy between pure and impure whose implications work themselves out as a complex system of religious and economic relationships embracing, and indeed in large part defining the dimensions of a locality" (1965, pp. 17, 38–39). Jajmani interchange, in this and many other villages, still provides a measure of economic credit and stability; even more, it helps to define the local social order by defining those who can secure ample ritual services.

SOLUTIONS TO THE PROBLEMS OF INTERDEPENDENCE

All peoples who maintain a civilization must establish effective interdependence among specialist groups. Such relations should be reliable, enduring, and trustworthy, but they should also be flexible, manipulable, and adaptable. The two kinds of qualities militate against each other. If a relationship is easily begun and readily terminated, it is not likely to be enduringly reliable. If it is endowed with an aura of durability, it cannot readily be adapted to changing circumstances.

Indian villagers have traditionally included both kinds of interdependence in their societal repertoire. Some relationships have been contractual, limited, and flexible through the use of money, barter, and markets. The other relationships have been broad and durable. Villagers define kinship relations as more broadly supportive and enduring than are most others and see jati as a unit whose members are or could be kinsmen. Jajmani relations provide for nonkinship interdependence in ways that nevertheless have some of the same qualities of reliability and perdurance. These relations are guided and enforced by villagers acting in their capacities as jati members, but the actual exchanges are made between villagers acting as members of their respective families.

We shall note later that tribal peoples in India remained in smaller, less productive groups because, for one reason, they did not have as effective ways of relating to nonkinsmen. The solution that was developed in Indian civilization remained in use for many centuries, until the impact of modern influences became felt. One response to these influences was to shift more exchanges to contractual relations and so to amplify that traditional side of economic activities. But villagers have been inclined to continue with at least some jajmani-like relations for the broader, more personal and supportive bonds that many villagers want to keep.

Villagers, moreover, tend to see social relations as hierarchically ordered. In those jajmani relations that involve ritual services, underlying ideas about hierarchical relations are symbolized. These ideas provide a rationale for the order of village society; they indicate who should be higher and who lower, and why it should be that way. We next examine the criteria that villagers use in explaining and calibrating their social order.

CHAPTER 10

Criteria for the Ranking of Jatis

Interdependence among families and jatis is more than an order of precedence for particular transactions: it is taken as an order of life. In each person's dealings with his neighbors of other jatis, their rank relative to his prohibits some kinds of interchange and sets limits on others.

The social order is made manifest in a thousand and one details of daily life. For the most part, these details are so commonplace that a villager is hardly aware of them. Thus, when men gather to talk, whether in gossip session or serious council meeting, they generally seat themselves with consideration to jati rank. A cot is often used as a bench; some sit on it, others sit on the ground. The upper part of the cot, the part where a sleeper puts his head, is reserved for those of higher rank in the assemblage. The seating order described for a village of Kanpur District is this: Brahmins must precede all others on the upper cot, Thakurs precede all but Brahmins. Those of next higher rank sit at the foot of the cot, those of quite inferior status sit on the ground. When only men from the lowest jatis are present, say Chamar leatherworkers and Dhanuk pigkeepers, men of the two jatis may sit on the same cot, but a Chamar will allow a Dhanuk to sit only at the lower part (Sharma 1956a, p. 259).

Seating arrangements are more than polite distributions in space, they symbolize authority arrangements and power relations. The Brahmins sitting at the head of the cot and the Thakurs next to them are expected by all to take the lead in the talk and then to express for all whatever consensus may be reached. The Dhanuk pigkeeper, from his place on the edge of the ground-sitters, is not expected and does not usually expect to be heard prominently, whether the talk is banter or deliberation. In some villages the Brahmin jati-group is small and relatively insignificant; it is given precedence but does not possess power. The Brahmin who speaks from his place at the head of the cot in such villages may have an influential voice only in matters of minor ritual performance, not in questions of weighty secular decision.

Separation in seating is but one detail of the permitted interchange and forbidden contacts among jatis. In some matters, notably marriage, there should be no interchange outside the jati. For other activities, such as smoking together, there may be a larger circle of permissibility. Those in the highest ranks are usually quite rigorous about avoiding close contacts with those of the lowest; they insist that the lowest groups use separate water sources, separate residential areas, and various other means of ensuring physical as well as social distance between the lowest and the highest jatis.

Rank-free Contexts of Behavior

Powerful and pervasive as is the order of jati rank, there are limits to its application. It does not enter equally into all activities; it is not constantly in the forefront of attention; it is not an itemized, ironclad code for interaction.

In certain activities, as has been mentioned previously, the relative rank of the participants is of less consequence than it is in others. Work in the fields, for example, is far less involved with ritual avoidances than is work in the kitchen. During the bustle of the harvest, people of widely different jati rank may work side by side and may come in physical contact in ways that are tabooed in the houses and streets of the village. People of every jati rank may work on the land, and they work together more closely there than elsewhere (Jagalpure and Kale 1938, pp. 393–394; Mathur 1958a, pp. 51–52; Silverberg 1959; Gould 1964, p. 32).

In play as in agricultural work, jati restrictions tend to be mitigated. Thus in wrestling matches between village teams in Mysore, young men of all jatis, except the very lowest, may lock arms in competition (Beals 1964, p. 107). The dramatic troupes that tour villages in western U.P. can include actors of different jatis (Gumperz 1964, p. 94). In some contexts of worship, especially in the devotional *bhakti* worship, differences of jati rank among the devotees are supposed to be irrelevant and to some extent actually are overlooked. Such latitude in work, sport, drama, and worship is old in India; the generally freer conduct outside the village, as at markets or fairs, is also of long standing. With the modern expansion of villagers' experiences with towns, commerce, government, and new forms of work, there has been an extension of the traditional leeway to these new activities.

Wide difference in rank does not preclude informal personal relations. A woman of a sweeper jati may come into a wealthy household of high status to do the menial cleaning, to remove ordure and the like. Her movements in the household are strictly bounded; she may not enter the kitchen or touch persons or come too close to the household shrine. But her daily visit may be most welcome to the women of the household who, being of high rank, are much restricted in their movements outside their house. Though their movements are restricted, their avid interest in the private lives of their neighbors is not. The sweeper woman goes about the village freely and visits different homes. She can be a prime carrier of gossip, a center of human interest, and she sometimes is a source of lively amusement.

In households that employ full-time servants, as Jyotirmoyee Sarma describes in a Bengal village in Hoogly district, the servants become members of the household even though they must keep to jati avoidances. Such servants of the low Bagdi jati cannot enter the inner rooms, must not touch or handle the water to be used for bathing or drinking, and must observe many other taboos. Yet the children of the household use terms of fictive kinship with them and such servants may be trusted with considerable responsibility (Sarma 1960, pp. 192–195).

Despite such limitations, jati rank does impinge directly on many aspects of village life. The tokens of rank often indicate real differences in power as well as in symbolic precedence, great differences in privilege as well as in forms of address. One villager's expectations about another's behavior are framed by the other's jati rank and customs. Their dealings with each other are constrained by the relative positions of their jatis in the local order.

On what grounds then, do villagers assume that there is a ranked order and how do they explain the rankings they make? The higher jatis, as is the way of the powerful everywhere, explain it on the basis of their inherently superior worth. Those of lower jatis are not always sure about that, but they are usually quite sure that their own jati is worthy of higher place than it presently enjoys. Villagers generally agree that the rankings involve ritual purity and pollution. The ritual criteria they note are indeed important; secular forces are also important factors in jati ranking, as will be discussed in Chapter 12.

Ritual Criteria: Personal Pollution and Purity

The traditional explanation is that people of higher jatis are less defiled and keep themselves more pure for purposes of religious ritual than are those of lower jatis. The lowest jatis are the most polluted and least able to have close relations with the higher gods and the higher jatis. Both pollution and purity are linked to a person's biological and physical acts; they are especially related to the bodily processes of men and animals. Perhaps explanations of social superiority and inferiority in all societies are ultimately linked to personal, corporal experiences. Certainly these experiences have been related to religious concepts in many. In Indian civilization these links are explicit and have been explicitly applied in the ordering of village society.

The main emphasis of the ritual criteria is on pollution rather than on purity. Becoming polluted bars a person from ready relations with man and god. He must keep his distance from people who are not so polluted as he is, lest his defect disable them also; he may not perform acts of worship because, in his defective state, he is repugnant to the deities. Any serious pollution entails avoidance and isolation.

There is, however, a vast difference between the two main kinds of pollution. One kind is temporary and personal pollution, to which every mortal is subject daily. The other kind is that permanent and corporate pollution ascribed to all in a jati, which is a main criterion in sorting out the social order (cf. Kane 1941, pp. 165–179).

The sources of pollution are many; the most potent of them are contacts with death and with bodily emissions such as blood and excreta. Every person is impaired by these defilements both regularly and sporadically. When a person defecates or urinates, he is thereby unclean. He must avoid ordinary relations with humans and must not approach the supernaturals until he has cleansed himself, if only by a token wash and perhaps a token prayer.

Every secretion and excretion that is separated from the body—as well as any separated growth of hair and nails—becomes a defiling object; by the act of severance a person puts himself in an impure state. "Faeces, urine, semen, menstrual blood, spittle, and parings of nail and hair are all ritually impure" (Srinivas 1952a, p. 104; see also Mathur 1964, pp. 103–105). These are not all charged with equal pollution potential. After touching one's own saliva, only a wash of the hands is necessary; at menstruation a woman must undergo much more prolonged purification.

Each person must put himself in the state of purity suitable to whatever activity he undertakes. A householder, in the Bengal village studied by Sarma, must wash and change clothes before touching cooked food, especially rice. Once having touched food, he is not in a fit state to turn to other activity until he has washed again. The act of ingestion puts a person in a state of mild disability; he must discharge himself from that state by a ritual wash before going on (Sarma 1955, p. 171).

Eating does not involve either bodily emissions or death, the principal sources of pollution, but like them it involves a transition from one ongoing state of being to another. Such transitions are sensitive states ritually, if not actually defiling.

Many villagers abbreviate or omit such daily rites of transition because they have neither time nor a change of clothes nor great concern with ritual niceties. Yet few ignore these daily transitions altogether; even poor villagers of the lowest jatis are sensitively aware of impure states. Harijans also guard, as best they can, against certain kinds of pollution. A Brahmin in this Bengal village does not omit certain ritual steps that others may omit. Thus he must change his clothes as well as wash after excretion. "Before changing clothes, a Brahmin may not enter his own room or touch any household objects, and if he touches even a low caste (untouchable) at such a moment, the latter will be defiled and will need a change of clothing" (*ibid.*).

The most dramatic emission of all is childbirth. After a birth, mother and child must remain in seclusion for a specified period, have the proper ritual acts performed for them and undergo purificatory rites to mark the end of the seclusion period. Thus purified, the mother may resume normal relations within her family and village; the child can emerge into society as he has into the world. Other members of the household are affected by the event of childbirth; they too must undergo some ritual restoration to their normal status.

Pollution is not the only reason given for seclusion after childbirth. The seclusion may be thought of as a means of protecting mother and infant during a period when both are particularly vulnerable to untoward influences, much as infants in a hospital nursery are secluded from unhygienic visitors. In other rites of transition also, the ritual acts are done for several reasons, but purification is always one of them.

Death in a family is the most traumatic transition and brings disabling effects upon the surviving kin. These effects must be expunged by ritual before the close relatives can reenter normal life. Proximity to death imperils a person from the supernatural sphere and disables him in the social sphere. Funeral rites are directed toward restoring all those who have been so imperiled and disabled to a condition of relative purity, of social safety and normality. Among the Kotas of the Nilgiris, for example, widows and widowers must undergo purificatory ritual and the whole lineage must be cleansed and restored. The very corpse and spirit of the deceased are not finally pure, able to take their proper place in the cosmos, until the proper rituals have been enacted (Mandelbaum 1954b, pp. 89–90). So is it generally in village India; all and everything that has been close to the event of death must be ceremonially restored to normalcy.

Every person thus must go through a cycle of impairment and restoration both regularly and sporadically. Bodily excretion imposes a daily cycle; other biological facts—of sex, of menstruation, of cutaneous growth, of birth, of death—entail recurrent disability and require periodic restitution. When a person is brushed by the death or birth of a close kinsman, the experience charges him with ritual disability, which must be discharged by the appropriate ritual acts. There are, to be sure, great differences in the purification practices of different jatis. But virtually all villagers, rich and poor, high and low, lackadaisical as well as orthodox, observe some such biologically-induced and ritually required purification.

A state of purity must be voluntarily induced, a state of pollution is usually involuntary or the consequence of biological processes. There are various degrees of both pollution and purity. One's normal state is neither especially pure nor defiled; "a mild form of impurity" is one description of it (Srinivas 1952a, p. 107; see also Stevenson 1954, p. 50; Harper 1964, pp. 152–155). From this mild state a person's ritual condition can be changed in either direction. The two stages of ritual purity that are recognized in the Telengana region of Andhra Pradesh are described by Dube (1955c). The most pure state is attained through protracted ablution procedures, including the cleansing of teeth and bathing. Clothes that have been washed and dried under conditions of complete ritual asepsis must be worn.

So sanctified, a man may perform a major rite of passage, such as the initiation ritual by which boys in the "twice-born" varnas assume full adult status. In this pure state, he may also celebrate the offering of the morning meal to deity. The state of high purity continues while the food is being cooked and served. As soon as the celebrant eats, his ritual condition is transformed. It then is at the lesser degree of purity, attainable through bathing and the wearing of silk and sufficient for such lesser rites as marriage ceremonies and the preparation of evening meals, which do not entail a sacred offering (Dube 1955c, p. 188). Those high degrees of purification are immediately dissolved by acts of urination, defecation, and sexual intercourse, by touching an impure animal or a person not ritually clean, by touching unclean objects, such as leather or even clothes that have not been specially washed.

Whenever any villager prepares for formal worship, he must make himself properly pure for approach to the supernatural. He abstains from polluting personal acts, he avoids contact with defiling persons and objects, he bathes and performs other preliminary acts. Even those of the lowest jatis, whose touch can temporarily disqualify others from entering the precincts of the high gods, are also careful to be in a fit state before entering their own sacred places. They usually have shrines of their own in a village, even though modern legislation has removed the legal bars to their entry into the great temples.

Roles That Require Special Purity

Certain kinds of people have to be particularly meticulous about ritual purity. These include priests of all jatis and widows of the higher varnas. Priests are ritual leaders and must observe more stringent purification than do laymen since they approach close and frequently to deity (cf. Harper 1964, p. 176). Among the jatis of the Brahmin category, those whose traditional calling is that of priest usually rank below those whose men traditionally devoted themselves only to learning. Service in a temple, Baines wrote, is not undertaken by the "better class" of Brahmin; it is held to be degrading and is left to those Brahmin jatis that are lower in station (1912, p. 27). Bhattacharya pointed out that while the scriptures recommend "the performance of priestly functions for the superior castes" as a proper vocation for a Brahmin, the work of a priest is not esteemed. It involves "almost menial service" in worship, it does not require knowledge, and those whose jati function it is to "study the original works that regulate these rituals, can find fault with the priest at every step, and reserve for themselves the higher functions of the critic and superintendent" (1896, p. 25).

Priests at large temples, through which flow a mixed concourse of worshippers, are especially exposed to contamination from visitors of unknown habit. For this reason, among others, some of these priests are not highly respected and are suspected of laxity in diet and demeanor. A village priest is more under the public eye and usually keeps himself more guarded ritually than do the laymen whose rites he leads.

Not all, nor even most, members of a Brahmin jati of priestly vocation need actually act as priests; they follow diverse occupations. There are also jatis of the Brahmin category in which the men do not provide priestly services for others, but are landowners and cultivators. Not all Brahmin jatis are vegetarian; K. N. Sharma has pointed out that vegetarianism is more a value of the

Vaishnava practice of Hinduism than of "Brahmins as such" (1961a). But the practices of jatis of the Brahmin category are expected to be purer than those of other jatis of their local systems. None in a Brahmin jati can practice such abominations as removing night soil or handling carcasses, which would tarnish their whole jati.

Widows of the higher varnas are also expected to be more stringent about ritual purity than other people need be. Such a widow is permanently debarred, by reason of her indissoluble link with a dead man, from many of the social and ritual functions she could perform as a wife. She must be more fastidious in ritual observance than she was while she was a wife because her widowhood has altered her social and ritual position for the worse (Stevenson 1954, p. 59). Yet, paradoxically, widows may undertake defiling tasks that wives will not, perhaps because widows have less to lose by temporary defilement. One widow of high jati whom I knew assisted at the delivery of an untouchable woman having a difficult and dangerous time in childbirth. Among the Havik Brahmins of Mysore, widows help at childbirths because, it is said, it is less inconvenient for them to remove severe pollution (Harper 1964, p. 175). Widows of lower jatis are also under some ritual cloud, but they may remarry and resume the role of wife again.

These pollutions, both from biological functions and mortal demise, are temporary and personal. They bring about only temporary avoidances and isolations which can be lifted (Stevenson 1954, pp. 51–53). Their contagious qualities may be spread by physical contact, but they are personal to the defiled person or to those of a close kin-group; the contagion does not radiate more widely and more automatically than that. Such pollution does not directly affect the ranking of jatis.

Corporate Pollution and Jati Rank

The kind of pollution that does influence rank pertains to an entire jati. Lasting and pervasive disabilities fall equally on all members of a jati who, because of their traditionally ascribed practices, must deal with death or with bodily emissions. The defilement of death falls heavily upon those who have to do with animal carcasses and with the products of the carcasses. The residues of dead animals, like those of humans, contaminate.

The most sacred animal of all, the cow, carries special potency both for purification and for pollution. The products of a dead cow, its meat and hide, are more defiling than are the products of other animals (cf. Brown 1957). Those who are vegetarians by jati practice consider themselves ritually purer than those who eat such carcass products as mutton and venison. Most defiled of all are those Hindus who eat beef (or whose jati fellows are reputed to do so), or who will handle any product derived from dead cattle. Among animals, swine are highly defiling because they will eat excrement; those who keep swine are tarred by that defilement.

Those whose jati occupation is to wash clothes, who handle clothes that are not only soiled but soiled with the exudation of sweat, are therefore consigned to low jati rank. More defiling still than sweat-soiled clothes are clothes that have been stained with menstrual blood; washermen who launder the former may not want to touch the latter.

There are differing degrees of jati pollution. Those villagers who wash clothes usually are ranked above those who remove dead cows, eat their flesh, work with their hides. The degree of a jati's permanent pollution is a prime factor in ascertaining "who may cook for or eat with whom; who may work for whom, or work with whom, or worship with whom…" (Stevenson, 1954, p. 50; also see Ghurye 1961, pp. 1–27).

Permanent pollution is contagious and corporate within a jati. A barber incurs pollution when he attends to the bodily growths of others. Women of the barber jati, in many places, attend at confinements. A man who gets a shave bathes ritually afterward to cleanse the barber's touch. A new mother undergoes a longer purification but she too is restored to her previous ritual and social status. But those who provide the services for pay incur permanent social disability, and that stigma marks every person in their jati.

One born into that jati ranks with barbers and midwives even though he himself may never have given a shave nor his wife ever assisted at a childbirth. If a barber family takes to shaving men of a jati inferior to its own—perhaps leatherworkers who have prospered and are ready to pay well for services they have not hitherto been able to get—the other families of the barber jati may strongly object. They fear that their own jati rank may be further demeaned if one of their families puts itself in an inferior position to so low a group. But, as we shall see, some of these prospering groups eventually do secure the services of others, and not only of barbers but of Brahmin priests as well.

A jati's ritual pollution is not lessened by the ritual cleanliness of individuals within the group. Even if some members of a low-ranking jati lead lives of exemplary purity, people of higher rank must still keep them and all their jati fellows at the proper social distance. The lowest jatis either carry on defiling practices presently, or are alleged to have done so in the past, or are supposed to be descended from ancestors who incurred permanent pollution. In the middle ranges of a local order there may be jatis whose members have no such discrediting marks, real or alleged. The ritual criteria alone do not explain why they should be ranked lower than others who may in fact not maintain as high a degree of ritual purity as they do. Other factors enter into the ranking as we shall note later. However, ritual pollution is commonly used by villagers as a blanket explanation; they are likely to think of some pollution-related rationale when they feel pressed to tell why they should rate one jati as higher than another.

Ritual stringency also varies by jati. Scriptural edicts direct the "twice-born" to perform more sacraments, and those more austere, than the sacraments performed by people of the Shudra category. In actual practice, villagers of the highest jatis do commonly devote more time, wealth, and energy to ritual observances than do those of low rank. One reason is that the lower are often too impoverished to be able to spend much time or money on ritual performances (Dube 1955c, pp. 187–189; Mathur 1964, pp. 99, 106).

But this is only a general tendency. There are low-ranking jatis whose rituals are both elaborate and stringent. Some of the lowest in a local order may be more rigorous in ritual observances than are some of those ranked above them. In Totagadde village in Mysore, for example, untouchables are on the whole more strict about menstruation taboos than are a good many of the Shudra category. Harper suggests that this may be because of the greater familiarity with Brahminical customs which these Harijans acquired as indentured servants and also because they are now the most militant about improving their jati status (1964, p. 191).

Though there are many villages with similar instances of a low-ranked jati's being more meticulous than are some of the higher, it is generally true that people of the higher jatis are more guarded about personal and corporate purity than are those of the lower echelons. The concepts of purity and of pollution are basic features in the local systems of society and we examine them in some detail.

CHAPTER 11

The Social Relevance of Ritual Pollution and Purity

Pollution is a well-defined and clinging state of being. Purity is more evanescent and fleeting. It is the achievement of a transient elevation rather than any lasting presence of grace. Pollution overcomes purity. A person who has purified himself is, as it were, in a precariously balanced state of being which is soon undone. Being in a pure state is a temporary holding off of inevitable encroachment—encroachment from one's own biological functions if from no other source. In both high purity and deep pollution a person must be insulated from social contacts and isolated from society.

Pollution and purity are central to worship in that participants in religious ritual must make themselves pure for such acts. The purpose of much of ritual behavior is to make persons, objects, and animals less defiled and more pure than they had been before. Villagers apply their concepts of purity and pollution ritualistically, in symbolic and compulsive ways.

An experience in one sphere of conduct is symbolically taken to influence and to represent the whole range of social relations. If a man must be avoided in the religious context, he must be avoided across a whole range of possible secular contacts. These concepts are compulsively applied in that a defect in a part compels men to treat the whole as defective. If only a few families of a jati handle ordure, all families in the jati are so categorized. This is so because all members of a jati are related in a kinship frame, they may eat together and generally have closer contacts with each other than with those outside their jati. Hence villagers hold that a regular and serious defilement of some in the jati inevitably spreads, by contact, to the whole—unless normal jati relations with the defiled ones are cut off.

The Contagion of Pollution

Pollution is lasting and contagious. Personal pollution is believed to last until it is removed with ritual ablutions and invocation. All pollution is transferable by physical contact between a person or object that is more defiled and a person who is less defiled until the moment of contact. The mere presence of a powerful source of pollution may transfer defilement to others. The most quoted historical example of this is that of the low jatis of Kerala, whose members were not supposed to approach closer than ninety-six paces to a person of high jati status lest their nearness pollute him. This was reported by early European travelers in the region but even in the 1930s Aiyappan noted that the Nayadis, beggars of southern Kerala, had to keep a distance of from seventy-four to one hundred feet from a local Brahmin. "But in practice the Nayadis keep themselves at a greater distance than the prescribed minima" (Aiyappan 1937, p. 18; Raghuvanshi 1966, pp. 157–158).

The Nayadis presented an extreme example of avoidance even in earlier centuries, but the contagion of ritual pollution is still a lively concern for many. This is illustrated in an incident from the autobiography of a man of a merchant jati in Rajasthan. He is in government service and was once invited to tea by an official superior. When he arrived, he discovered that eggs were being served. As a strict vegetarian, he would not eat them. He tells of his dilemma, not about refusing eggs but about drinking his tea. "I did not like to see others touching my teapot with hands of eggs but could not help" (Carstairs 1957, p. 281).

Two kinds of events, birth and death, radiate pollution, not only through contact or presence, but also through kinship bonds. In all jatis, the "happy" pollution of birth falls on a smaller grouping of kinsmen and for a shorter period than does death seclusion. The members of a dead person's family become ritually and socially incapacitated from the moment of his death. They must remain in seclusion and undergo purificatory ritual over a time and in a manner prescribed by the custom of their jati. Commonly the members of the deceased's lineage are also touched with death pollution and must also refrain from normal activities, though not for so long a period as the members of the bereaved household (Mathur 1964, pp. 106–108; Orenstein 1965a; pp. 3–10).

Among the Havik Brahmins of Mysore, these family members are treated as untouchables during the mourning period. Lesser degrees of seclusion are prescribed for other kinsmen, both agnatic and affinal. As we have noted previously, these Brahmins carry the ramifications of death pollution to an extraordinary length, at least in their theory. They stipulate that if a man is related to the deceased through a common patrilineal ancestor as much as twenty-one generations removed, he is supposed to bathe on receiving news of the death (Harper 1964, pp. 161–167).

Each jati in a village is likely to have its own phrasing of the pollution-purity rules and the observance of these rules marks out jati membership and helps to integrate the jati as a social unit. Mathur notes this about the jatis of Potlod village (Indore district) in Madhya Pradesh. "One of the main purposes of the rules of pollution then, is to contain a person within his caste or *jati* and to keep him well integrated with this natal status group" (1964, p. 114).

Purity is precarious while pollution is sure. It is nontransferable while pollution is highly contagious. A Brahmin in a state of high purity cannot transmit his purity to anyone, but he can be defiled by almost everyone. Only in very few contexts can ritual merit be transmitted. One such context is when a man performs certain rites before the high gods. His wife cannot directly participate in them but she stands by her husband, touching him, and so derives merit through him.

Pure things, however, can be used to set up a field of purity that may ward off evil influences. Amulets are so used, as are also the products of the living cow. Cow's milk cannot be defiled and does not transmit pollution. However, if one drop of water should be mixed in with the milk, that drop may defile a drinker of high jati. That drop may have been from water defiled by contact with a vessel touched by an untouchable (Harper 1964, pp. 173, 188).

Purity is a more relative condition than pollution. An untouchable can make himself pure for his own worship; he can never become pure enough so that an orthodox Havik Brahmin, say, will worship side by side with him. Yet such a Brahmin, polluted by a kinsman's death, temporarily bears the same degree of ritual defilement as does the untouchable (Harper 1964, p. 194).

Extrapolations of the Ritual Criteria

It is not only people who are graded on a scale of pollution and purity. The sides of the body, for example, have different degrees of pollution and purity. The right side is the more pure. The right hand is used in eating rather than the left which is used for more menial tasks, as in washing the body after defecation.

Similar rankings are made of the species of animals and plants. Even physical materials differ in the inherent qualities of pollution and purity attributed to them. The nonhuman ratings may be used in grading the varieties of men. For example, in some localities there are two different jatis whose members make pots. A potter jati that uses bullocks for transport is superior to one that uses the donkey, "that useful, but in India foulfeeding animal" (Baines 1912, pp. 58, 65; see also Ketkar 1909, p. 20; Stevenson 1954, pp. 50–51; Mathur 1964, p. 99).

It is not difficult to see why animals that feed on leavings and excreta, as do swine and donkeys, should be defiling, and why those who keep such animals should be socially demeaned. But it is more difficult to explain why a particular plant or material should be rated above another in purity. The general explanation may be that Indian villagers project hierarchical classifications on all their world, and tend to attribute graded ranks to most of what they perceive.

Many scriptural treatises are devoted to the explication of hierarchical arrangements of all sorts, in which the taxonomy of grading is extended, embroidered, and ramified with great care. The ordinary villager does not command such detail, but he does know that pollution affects much more than mankind and that hierarchy is a characteristic of every part of creation, including the Creators. The supernatural powers, too, are ranked in an order of relative purity. Gods can become defiled; this indeed is one of the frequent motifs of scriptural tales. The continuum in purity from higher to lesser gods extends through to the grades of men (Harper 1964, p. 195).

Ingestion as a Ritual and Social Act

Some of a person's daily acts are particularly vulnerable to pollution, especially the acts of ingestion—eating, drinking, and even smoking. Food and water are susceptible to ritual pollution and so each villager must take care about the purity of what he eats and drinks. What he eats must be an accepted part of his jati's diet and cuisine. From whom he will take food and with whom he will eat express his jati's status relative to that of cooks or fellow diners.

In most village households today, the rituals of mealtime follow the essentials of the pattern laid down in ancient and medieval scriptures (cf. Kane 1941, pp. 757–806). That ritual was remarked early in the sixteenth century by the Portuguese observer, Duarte Barbosa, the first of his nation to learn an Indian language.[1] He understood and spoke Malayalam. Barbosa described the "custom as to eating" of the Zamorin, the ruler of Calicut, in these words:

> … no one must be present while he is eating, nor must see him eat, saving only four or five servants who wait on him. Before eating he bathes in a very clean and large tank inside the palace, where he performs his observances quite naked, worshipping thrice towards the east wind, walking round and dipping thrice under water, then he attires himself in fresh garments, clean and washed, and he proceeds to seat himself in a house which is cleared for his meals, which is plastered [i.e., with a purifying cow dung paste]…. He takes no food with his left hand. Then they place before him a silver ewer filled with water, and when he wishes to drink he takes this in his left hand, and raising it into the air lets the water flow from above into his mouth without its touching the ewer…. And when he cleans his hands he makes no use of a napkin or any other cloth, and when he finishes his meal he washes himself (Dames 1921, pp. 22–23).

The modern editor of this account added the note that

> Barbosa's description of the Zamorin's ordinary rice meal is, excepting the appurtenances of state, an accurate description of any decent Malayali's mode of eating and drinking (Dames 1921, p. 22)

.A householder of some leisure and of an orthodox bent still takes his main meal in much this pattern, having a preliminary bath, wearing ritually clean clothes, sitting in a ritually clean place, eating food untouched in its preparation by anyone of lower jati rank, and concluding with a final rinse.

Even a poor man of lowly jati follows certain of the main ritual precautions that Barbosa noted long ago for the ruler of Calicut. All eat with the right hand. Even among the Nimar Balahis, a very low-ranking jati of Madhya Pradesh, "Food is taken only with the right hand, while the left hand can be used to hold the cup when drinking. The left hand should not touch food because it is used for cleaning after a call of nature" (Fuchs 1950, p. 370). The left hand can be used to handle one's food, but it should not touch the lips. Water is poured into the mouth; its passage through air is considered, by those who expound the reasons for ritual acts, to be a purifying process (cf. Stevenson 1954, p. 54; Mathur 1964, pp. 135–136).

In every household, the place where food is prepared is a sensitive area, which must be specially safeguarded. The observance of ritual purity is particularly focused on the kitchen. Thus in a village close by Bangalore city and rapidly changing, "no caste permits any individuals other than close relatives of the same caste to enter the kitchen" (Beals 1955, p. 134).

All that concerns one's food and drinking water is important to personal purity because whatever is incorporated into the body has great potency for pollution. Such internal pollution is a more

[1] Many travelers before Barbosa had noted the great concern of Indians about the act of eating. In the fifteenth century the Russian, Nikitin, observed that some Indians cover themselves with a kerchief when they eat so that no one may see them (Nikitin 1960, p. 114).

serious danger than that incurred externally by touch. Water that can be used for external ritual cleansing may not be pure enough for internal use (Stevenson 1954, p. 57).

Jawaharlal Nehru, in assessing the consequences of these standards of purity, saw them as both good and bad—good in their promotion of bodily cleanliness, bad in their "fantastic lengths" of "touch-me-notism" (1946, p. 251). But for those orthodox Hindus who are mainly concerned with the fate of their soul—in their view the only worthy concern—these standards and rituals enable a man to reach, as closely as he may, toward the true good and to avoid the false, the fleeting, and the worthless. Purity is not merely ceremonial purity, an Indian scholar has written, it is the principle of "the varying degrees of dominance of the soul over the senses, the dominance of the real man or God in man over the animal in man" (S. C. Roy 1934, p. 86).

For most villagers it is the social meanings of eating practices, rather than the theological concepts, that are of main consequence. The company in which one eats is of great social importance. Eating together is a sign of equality among individuals and groups, second only to intermarriage. Those who take their meals side by side, eating food from the same cook and kitchen, thereby show that each has equal ritual status with his fellow diners. And those who eat together are apt to act together and support each other, whether as family group, faction, lineage, or jati.

Sheer physical proximity while eating is very important. At village feasts where diners are ranged in seated rows, those of a higher jati will not tolerate those of much lower rank to sit in an unbroken line with them. And guests of one jati are content to be in the same row as those whom they acknowledge to be higher, even if they must sit, as it were, below the salt (cf. Harper 1964, pp. 157–158).

Who handles the food while it is being prepared for eating is a matter of high concern, because it is then in a pollution-vulnerable state. How food stuff is handled while it is raw, dry, unpeeled, or unmixed does not much matter. Directly it is taken in hand to be made edible, it becomes imbued with the same degree of pollution as inheres in the cook who touches it. Hence a person may not eat from the hand of anyone who bears greater pollution, personal or jati, than himself. That is why the cook for the King of Calicut was a "Bramene" and why Brahmins are desirable as cooks for households of most jatis. A cook's jati purity does not flow through the food to the eater, but whatever pollution he bears can contaminate food. A Brahmin cook suffers no ritual hurt if the lowest eat of his cooking.

Food can be ritually affected by other influences besides the cook's touch. Polluted utensils can conduct defilement. A clay pot is more easily polluted than a brass pot and is less readily reusable after being dirtied. This, according to one explanation, is because the more porous substance cannot be as thoroughly cleaned. In some households, servants of low jati are allowed to handle the brass utensils but not the pottery.

Drinking water may not be drawn by servants of the lowest jatis. Even though water is purified by being poured through the air from cup to mouth, water which has been carried by defiled hands is beyond such purificatory redemption. A chart of who will take water from whom, as given by Sharma for a village in Kanpur district, is a useful index for a local hierarchy. The acceptance of water there "is basic and most important" (1956a, p. 236). And Baines' comment holds true widely in India, that water is the element, above all, through which personal contamination can be conveyed (Baines 1912, p. 67).

Some foods have special purity, either inherent as in milk, or instilled as through frying. Food that has been fried, either in oil or, preferably, in ghee, is thereby made much less vulnerable to pollution (Mathur 1964, pp. 128–129). Such fried stuff, called *pakka* food, is usually taken by those of high jati in North India from the hands of people of quite low (though not the very lowest) rank. Thus a traveler will commonly eat fried food that he has bought from a roadside vendor, from whose hands he would never take *kachcha* food, that cooked in water, mixed with water, or baked. In South India this distinction between ghee-fried and unfried food is not as clearly made. Even in North India, frying only mitigates the cook's touch, it does not convert tabooed food. So even if meat were fried in ghee, it would be meat all the same to one of vegetarian jati.

Food that is left on a plate after a meal, as occurs at feasts, is tabooed to all but the lowest jatis, because it has been defiled by having been touched to the lips of another person. But leavings from the plate of one's father or husband, or leavings from offerings to the gods are in quite a different class (cf. Carstairs 1957, p. 80). It is good to eat them; in so doing one does not violate proper relations of subordination and authority but in some degree thereby partakes of the good qualities of his human guardians and divine mentors.

Harper discusses these practices as "respect-pollution." He mentions an extreme case of this among the Havik Brahmins whom he has studied. It is that of a widow who had become accepted as a *sadhu*, a holy person. When she visited the village of Totagadde, some of the Brahmins drank of the liquid in which her feet had been washed (Harper 1964, pp. 181–183). Such acts of respect-pollution seem to desecrate the deepest tenets of food and drink pollution but they symbolically affirm the larger order for which these rules are used. They affirm the proper hierarchical relations, both among people and between man and holy beings.

Villagers of all jatis accept these broad ritual criteria. Those who are disadvantaged by them do not usually deny that there should be such criteria although they do commonly deny that their own practices are really as demeaning as their neighbors contend. Those of a meat-eating jati do not argue that eating meat is ritually irrelevant; they usually have only vegetarian food on their most sacred occasions. They eat meat, partly because they are accustomed to do so, partly because their jati's station in society does not require the sacrifice of this taste. They may be from a jati of warrior tradition for whom the eating of boar flesh, say, is quite seemly, or they may be so poor that they cannot afford to forego any nourishment—even from a carcass no one else will touch. Non-vegetarian villagers can usually get meat only very occasionally, and the proportion of meat in their total diet is minute, but it is for them a welcome addition to the common grain-and-vegetable staple. Welcome as it is for a special meal, it is not a ritual asset.

The Balahis are meat-eaters; many are so poor as to be quite used to starvation-rations. They eat meat from slaughtered or diseased cattle when they can get it; it usually is cheaper than goat's meat or fowl. Their diet is a main reason why they are treated as untouchables, their practice of eating the leavings of others at a feast is something for which higher jatis have "equal revulsion as to the eating of beef" (Fuchs 1950, pp. 357–359).

Yet there are many kinds of food Balahis will not eat, including domestic pork and horsemeat. Moreover, even these lowly, bone-poor Balahis "consider taking a meal an important act," make suitable ritual preparation for a meal, and preserve certain ritual safeguards during it. Nor is the eating of beef taken as an indifferent act. "After eating beef, the Balahis feel polluted and must take a bath of purification. Such a bath is necessary if afterwards they want to worship their gods or perform any other act for which ceremonial purity is required" (Fuchs 1950, pp. 369–370). For men and women at all social levels, what is eaten affects their personal purity and therefore their roles in social interaction. With whom and from whom they take food has social consequences for their jati's place in the local order.

Alcohol is a special vector of pollution. The drinking of strong liquor is abhorrent in the Brahmin tradition, perhaps because a drunk man is apt to forget ritual precautions, to touch what should not be touched, to take in what should be kept out, and to trespass where he should not go. In other jatis, especially of the Kshatriya category, there is a more easy-going tolerance of liquor. People of lower jatis are more likely to drink liquor and may even make alcoholic libations to their deities. Those whose jati occupation is the making of liquor are thereby of low rank. Alcohol is thus doubly loaded against a man of higher jati, being defiling in itself and having been handled by polluting people (Mandelbaum 1965, pp. 283–284).

The Ritual and Social Bearing of Sexual Acts

Sexual relations also induce ritual impurity. After conjugal relations a purificatory bath should be taken though even the generally orthodox Havik Brahmins postpone this until the customary morning bath. In Totagadde village gleeful stories were told about one especially orthodox wife who rushed out to take a cold bath immediately after intercourse with her husband, thus announcing to village gossip the exact schedule of her sexual relations.

Abstinence from sex is prescribed before important ceremonies or before any approach to deities (cf. Srinivas 1952a, p. 103). Marital intercourse does not bring on a high degree of ritual pollution, but leaves a person in a bodily state that must nevertheless be purified. Intercourse between a man and a woman of different jatis, however, can have great social consequences. A man does not usually suffer great loss nor must he make ritual recompense if it becomes known that he has had an affair with a woman of a jati not very different in status from his own. His wife and relations may make him smart, but his jati fellows usually do not consider that they all have been defiled by his dereliction (cf. Dube 1955b, p. 144). Such jati taint is felt, however, if it becomes publicly known that a man of highest jati has consorted with a woman of the lowest. If a woman of high jati rank is discovered in sexual connection with a man of low jati, she may be cast out forever from her family, her jati, and her village.

Dire punishments, ranging from heavy fines to death are prescribed in Sanskrit scripture for sexual partners of unequal rank. "In general," Ketkar summarizes the texts on the subject, "the higher the varna of the woman contaminated the greater should be the punishment to the guilty man; the lower the varna of the man, the more severely he is to be treated" (1909, p. 153; Orenstein 1965a, p. 9). Sexual relations between a man of higher jati and a woman of somewhat lower jati are often deplored by village opinion but are not usually taken to undermine social structure as would cases of open interdining or intermarriage.

The usual distinction made between commensal and consexual relations is shown in the previously noted instance of the Nambudiri Brahmins of Malabar. Only the eldest Nambudiri son could marry, and younger sons established regular and recognized sexual relations with women of the Nayars, a group of warrior tradition whose kinship organization was strongly matrilineal. A Nambudiri man would visit the home and bed of his Nayar beloved regularly, but he would never eat of her food, nor would she eat with him (Rao 1957, p. 106; Miller 1954, p. 413; Mencher and Goldberg 1967).[2] Eating the same food would imply a marriage relationship, it

[2] Barbosa's account, written about 1516, notes an interesting qualification to a Nambudiri man's choice in establishing a relationship. "The brothers who remain bachelors sleep with the Nayre women, they hold it to be a great honour, and as they are Bramenes no woman refuses herself to them, yet they may not sleep with any woman older than themselves." The obligations of respect which a younger person owes those older affected even a man's relation with a woman of different rank. Nayar men, in their turn, could customarily carry on sexual relations with women of

would mean that the couple were of equal ritual status. The Nambudiri man would then suffer a permanent status loss rather than the temporary, removable incapacities that he incurred by contact with a non-Brahmin.

Means of Purification and Ideas about Pollution

Against pollution that is removable, certain agents of purification are available. Flowing water is a basic solvent for ritual impurity. Habits of ablution in India were noted in the seventh century by a Chinese Buddhist pilgrim. "They are pure of themselves and not by compulsion. Before every meal they must have a wash… before they have finished ablutions they do not come into contact with each other; they always wash after urinating" (Watters 1904, p. 152).

Twelve centuries later, similar ablution habits are still practiced by villagers, especially those of the higher jatis and wealthier families. Very few Indian villages are models of hygiene and villagers are no more hygienically clean than are rural folk in impoverished circumstances anywhere. But the ritual wash is part of villagers' daily routine. In Potlod village, for example, Mathur observed that "every morning most of the Hindus of Potlod took a bath and changed into clean clothes." Being unwashed and physically dirty, Mathur comments, is generally considered to be an impure state, though being physically clean does not necessarily mean that one is ritually pure (1964, pp. 98, 103).

Villagers often try to get defiling tasks done during the early morning. They bathe during mid-morning and then are fit to take their meal. The morning ablution rite is commonly an abbreviated affair, though those who have the time and inclination can protract the rite for hours. Handbooks on ritual procedure are available in bookstalls for those who want to perform full purificatory devotions (cf. Diehl 1956, pp. 66–95; Harper 1964, p. 153).

Water and washing are necessary but not sufficient for purification. The washing must be done in a proper formal manner and must be accompanied by ritual acts of speech and gesture. Other agents of purification are also used; fire, sun, and Ganges water are among the most potent (Mathur 1964, pp. 100–103). Most commonly used for purification are the products of the living cow. Cow dung, usually mixed with water, is applied as a general means of ritual cleansing and prophylaxis. The housewife cleans her kitchen regularly, using that mixture. With it the priest purifies the places where he performs his rites. Such use of cow dung entails the respect-pollution which we have noted above. As Harper puts it, "The cow's most impure part is sufficiently pure relative to even a Brahmin priest to remove the latter's impurities" (1964, p. 183). The most potent personal purification of all is the ingestion of a mixture containing five products of the cow, namely milk, curds, ghee, dung, and urine.

These vectors of purity and of pollution are known among all villagers though each group has its own ritual idiom, its particular combination of the main elements and their interpretation. All believe that contacts with death and bodily emissions are polluting, beliefs which can be interpreted as their expressions of a general apprehension about transition states. Death and birth are, of course,

---

still another group. Of the jati who laundered clothes Barbosa observed, "Those born of this class do not mix with others, nor others with them, save only that the *Nayres* may take their women as concubines if they bathe and change their clothes" (Dames 1921, pp. 35, 58).

major transitions. Menstruation and even the cutting of body hair can be seen as transitions from one state of physical being or of physical wholeness to another.

The impairment of previous wholeness can make objects as well as people vulnerable to pollution. Fruits and nuts, as long as they are whole, are not considered subject to ritual defilement. Thus even an orthodox Brahmin can take a whole plaintain or coconut from a person of lower jati. But once the coconut is broken or the plaintain cut, he cannot do so (Harper 1964, p. 156).

The transitions of the heavenly bodies create a parlous state for mankind. The days of the new moon and of the full moon are times when the immanent supernatural powers are more imminently present, and so are more powerful and more dangerous. The time of an eclipse, a visible transition, is a time of great vulnerability during which special precautions must be taken (Harper 1964, pp. 170, 188).

The ranking of jatis is explained, not only on the basis of their relative pollution and purity, but also by reference to the scriptural concepts of *karma* and of *dharma*. These concepts will be discussed again in later chapters, we need only note here that karma has to do with the transmigration of souls and with the supernal merit or demerit earned by a soul in its previous incarnations. One's station and jati in present life derive from one's conduct in previous existences. Further, to improve his soul's karma for future incarnations, a man is bound to fulfill properly the obligations of his current status, especially of his jati roles. Even the most polluting work, if selflessly done as a matter of jati calling, can enhance one's karma. "Because *karma* carried out in this manner, and this alone, does not pollute the individual soul, even though the *karma* (particular to one's caste) happens to be unclean or polluting" (Mathur 1964, p. 87).

That is the explanation commonly given by those of higher jati, and so a vast array of Hindu scripture and scriptural exegesis propounds. But villagers of the lower jatis may have a different understanding of pollution, karma, and dharma. In the southern village of Kumbapettai, in Tanjore district, "... the non-Brahmins, although they are aware of them, view the Brahmanical theories with nonchalance." The Pallans, landless laborers, "when questioned denied them with merriment" (Gough 1960, p. 54).

In the village of Senapur near Banaras the sweepers know and accept these concepts. They also argue that their jati really deserves high status on the basis of these standards but that their ancestors had been tricked and cheated out of their proper rank (Kolenda 1964).

Many villagers of all jatis, whether or not they subscribe to the explanations of Hindu scriptures, agree that there is an order of rank in their locality and that the respective ranks have to do with a jati's pollution and purity practices.[3] The ideas about pollution and purity, as we have discussed them in this chapter, are characteristic of those who observe the indigenous religions. However, the followers of the introduced religions—Muslims, Christians, Jews, and Parsis—also share some of these ideas and practices, though in what degree will be known only after more studies of these groups are available.

The ritual criteria provide broad standards for esteemed conduct and general guides for rank assignment in villages through most of the land. But although the ritual criteria are indeed important factors, they are not the only influences that determine jati rank. The order of jatis in a locality is also shaped by the influence of power and wealth as exerted within the local community.

---

[3] One questionnaire study found that the great majority of 100 subjects who were questioned believed that untouchability "was mainly due to the unlawful acts of the upper caste people, tradition, and other social factors" (Rath and Sircar 1960a, pp. 305–306). Such views may be increasing and may now be held by certain groups, such as university students, but the results of this study have not been confirmed by carefully conducted village studies.

CHAPTER 12

Secular Criteria and the Attribution of Jati Rank

The wealth that the members of a jati can marshal and the number of men they can muster for their jati purposes are not supposed to have great bearing on social ranking. In the ideal of scripture, it is ritual purity that counts. When jatis joust for precedence, each side invokes ritual reasons to justify their respective claims. This norm is expressed by Ghurye in his comment that the status of a person in Hindu caste society depended not on his wealth but on the traditional importance of the caste in which he had the luck of being born (1961, p. 2). Similarly, Prabhu writes that in Hindu India a dissociation was attempted, and even achieved, between wealth and status (1954, p. 117).

The ritual standards are used as a reference frame for the social order, but interaction among villagers of different jatis is strongly influenced by secular considerations. The Abbé Dubois recognized this in his classic account of South Indian peoples in the early nineteenth century. "Thus the caste to which the ruler of a country belongs, however low it may be considered elsewhere, ranks amongst the highest in the ruler's own dominions, and every member of it derives some reflection of dignity from its chief" (1928, p. 23).

Villagers still apply the ritual criteria to mark broad limits within which a jati may be ranked; they follow secular considerations to determine the status a group receives within these limits. There is, moreover, a difference to be noted between formal precedence and actual influence. The members of a ritually high jati may elicit overt gestures of respect, but its men may have little power in village affairs. Those however who combine secular dominance and ritual eminence possess authority that is doubly fortified.

The Application of Secular Influence

Secular influences are brought to bear on social ranking in several ways. Among several jatis of relatively similar ritual practice, the one whose people have the main power and wealth usually ranks highest. Secondly, the ritual shortcomings of a secularly dominant jati tend to be leniently interpreted by others in their locality. Finally, a low-ranking group that acquires wealth and power characteristically uses its strength to change its demeaning practices and to raise its jati rank.

The preeminence of the powerful among their ritual compeers is illustrated in Rampura village in Mysore. In Rampura the jati called Peasants by Srinivas are the dominant landowners, and their "local dominance gives the Peasants a high status among the castes in the middle division" (1955b, p. 25). Another group studied by Srinivas, the Coorgs of South India, illustrate how the ritual deficiencies of a powerful jati tend to be less harshly interpreted than are similar faults of a poor and weak group. The Coorgs ate pork, drank strong liquor, countenanced the remarriage of widows, did not practice menstrual seclusion—usages that might well degrade a group hopelessly in other parts. But the Coorgs were the dominant people in their territory, a strong and numerous set of landowners and warriors (1952a, pp. 32–37). Hence, they were accorded very respectable status among the peoples of their hill area.

In their warrior orientation, they resemble Rajputs and other North Indian groups that glory in their military traditions. The men of these jatis follow the martial, extrovert model for conduct rather than a ritual, ascetic model. They acknowledge the religious superiority of the Sanskritic ritual standards but do not themselves feel compelled to adhere to all Brahmanical injunctions. "The martial Rajput," writes Hitchcock, "regards it as a kind of warrior's dispensation that he is permitted to hunt, eat meat (except of course for beef), drink liquor and eat opium" (1958, p. 220).

In some places the families of martial style so far overshadow everyone else that the local Brahmin jati may count for very little in village life. This occurs in a village near Delhi where the dominant landowner-cultivators are Jats, belonging to one of the larger jati-clusters of North India. By ritual criteria, these landowners rank well below Brahmins, but here the Brahmins are few in number, tenants with shaky rights and generally subservient to the overlord group. The ownership of land, with the power of eviction, enables the landed jati to prevail over other villagers, including the Brahmins (Lewis 1958, p. 60).

An extreme example of the glossing over of the ritual deficiencies of the powerful is reported by Dube from a village of Adilabad district in Andhra Pradesh. The dominant landowners there are Raj Gonds, a jati of tribal origin. When Dube studied the village in the early 1950s, the Raj Gonds were still performing cow sacrifice and eating beef, traits that would have consigned them to the lowest depths of defilement among other Hindus. But in this village Hindus of all but two jatis took water from them and the lower jatis also took food from them. We will note, in a later chapter on tribal people, the special reasons for the unusually strong position of the Raj Gonds of this place, including their advantage in having been favored by the Muslim rulers of their territory, which had been part of the princely state of Hyderabad (Dube 1955a, pp. 189–190). The example of the Raj Gonds indicates that under especially strong conditions of power, even the most heinous of polluting acts can be overlooked by otherwise orthodox Hindus.

The third mode of secular influence, the use of wealth and power to bring about a rise in rank, is discussed in later chapters on social mobility. However high the people of a jati may aim, whatever righteous ritual they may observe, their aspiration for higher rank can scarcely be realized unless their claims are backed up with solid wealth and power.

The Sources of Power

Local power flows mainly from the land. Land is the prime good in this agrarian setting; land is the main source of wealth; land is a main need for a jati on the rise. "Of all village values, the most important and permanent is not money but land." So commented S. S. Nehru in his survey of 54 U.P. villages (1932, p. 47), and this is a common fact in village India to the present time. Land is the primary, scarce, productive resource; control of land means control of livelihood.[1] Under British rule, land became even more precious because population increased, because some artisans were forced into agriculture, and because cultivable lands—available even in the mid-Ganges valley in the first part of the nineteenth century—were quickly taken up (cf. Mandelbaum 1949). In a stable political regime, land is power because the landowner has a secure base for his livelihood and because he can control the livelihood of his tenants. Alternate sources of occupation and of power have greatly increased in recent decades but still are relatively few; hence having money is good, owning land is better (cf. Bailey 1957, pp. 239–246).

Any landowner's power is safeguarded if he belongs to a numerous and unified jati-group and jati. Then the force of many men can reinforce their economic and legal rights. Yet numbers alone do not guarantee jati power. A low-ranking jati in a village may include many people, but their loyalties may be so fragmented among their patrons and their poverty may be so deep and debilitating as to block joint action for self-improvement. Whenever a group—whether jati, jati-group, or lineage—is relatively numerous and is economically secure enough to call up concerted action, its members can forcefully argue the justice of their ritual claims. Such arguments become all the more persuasive to others when the strong, united voices are those of the landowners.

Power may also accrue to a jati when its members have effective connections with the power of the state. The Abbé Dubois noted that a jati's standing was enhanced if the ruler was one of their own. This was so even if the ruler's dynasty was founded by a gross marauder of low degree. A ruler had lands and favors to distribute and usually did not stint his jati kinsmen. He had his royal dignity to uphold and it was better upheld if his jati-fellows were also elevated.

When British officials became the paramount rulers, those who had regular access to them benefited. Such access could be obtained by fulfilling local offices, as of headman or policeman. But this was a relatively minor way of tapping the power reservoir. More ample access could be obtained through acquiring Western education. Education is still a good avenue to local influence. A villager who can write a petition in English or in the literary version of the vernacular and who can speak

[1] It has not always been so. In earlier centuries, good new lands were available to be brought under the plough. Especially after great famines or epidemics, the scarcity was that of cultivators or of cattle rather than of land. Even into the twentieth century, some groups in sparsely populated places, as the Wynad taluq of Kerala, are more concerned with another kind of scarce productive resource, ploughing oxen, than they are with land (Rooksby 1956).

with the administrator in the language of officials is much better off than one who has to make his way through a thicket of interpreters, scribes, and open-palmed underlings.

A person who qualifies for an administrative post or is elected to important office comes closest to governmental sources of power. Hence a jati that has Western-educated men in number is believed to have great advantage. It does not matter much that the actual favors granted by an official to his jati-fellows may be few and trifling. Most villagers are impressed; such achievements by the educated men of a jati usually shed luster, by a halo effect, on the local ranking of all in the jati.

These are some of the ways in which the secular forces of land, numbers, office, and education influence social ratings. The ratings are supposed to be based, according to both scriptural and vernacular theory, solely on ritual criteria. In theory also, the ratings are made by the ritual leaders, especially by the local Brahmin jatis. In practice, the men of a powerful jati have often been able to persuade their ritual superiors to bestow on them the prerogatives of high rank.

The Reciprocal Use of Ritual and Secular Resources

Yet such men cannot change ritual limits immediately or entirely. For one thing, there is a considerable inertia in ritual ratings. No matter how high a jati may rise, there is a long—sometimes a centuries-long—memory of jati origins. Secular power may elicit gestures of esteem; it is more difficult to command that unquestioned, implicit respect which is given to those who combine long-established ritual eminence with present power.

Moreover, even the more ambitious villagers do not want to upset the ritual standards completely. A man appraises himself and his jati by these standards. He usually tends to make the most favorable appraisal possible, but there are appraisals that are not possible for him to make. There have been rulers whose ancestors were of quite humble jati origin; such a Maharaja could wield firm power over a large dominion, but he might well have difficulty in finding a bride of suitably high rank for his son.

It is true that an able individual of quite low jati status can sometimes attain influence in village affairs. Thus in Rampura in Mysore a man of the toddy-tapper group has gained considerable wealth and power (Srinivas, 1955b, p. 17). But the jati affiliation of such men excludes them from the full measure of respect and of ritual participation that is attainable by able and successful men of the higher jatis.

A villager of Kishan Garhi in U.P., Marriott observes, can much more readily increase his *izzat*, his personal prestige, by his personal accomplishments than he can affect the status of his jati: "In Kishan Garhi, a man's caste rank counts for little more than seven annas in the sum of his prestige; wealth and political affiliation together count for nine annas. Thus although nearly everyone in the village would agree that the caste of Brahmins is to be ranked at the top and the caste of Chamars ranked far down toward the bottom, still most persons would rate certain well-to-do and respectable Chamars as higher in individual prestige than certain pious and impecunious Brahmins" (1959b, pp. 102–103).

Instances of men of very low jati attaining very high prestige are not common, but are more frequent now than before. However, it is still a limited prestige in village life because in such crucially important relations as interdining and intermarriage such a man's personal status must be subordinated to his jati's level. Seven annas is less than half of the old rupee of sixteen annas, a marked reduction of the traditional influence of jati rank on personal prestige. But it is still a large portion of a man's social worth in his present society.

The religious respect that was given to people cf Brahmin jatis helped to bolster their secular wealth. Sanskrit scripture teaches that it is meritorious to give to Brahmins; many an unlettered potentate dutifully followed this scriptural injunction. William Ward reckoned that the greatest means of support of the Brahmins he saw in Bengal were the properties given directly to Brahmins or donated to the gods and managed by and for Brahmin families. Ward wrote, "The donors were former kings, and men of property, who expected heaven as the reward of their piety" (1822, p. 88). Ward was not the most sympathetic or reliable observer of Bengali life, nevertheless he was quite right that Brahmin families were often supported by the income from such gifts. And supplementing their direct and prebendary income, some Brahmins also receive fees or jajmani returns for services rendered as household priests and teachers.

In addition to lands so received and inherited, a Brahmin family may be given advantage in the ordinary acquisition of land. Thus a more recent observer, S. S. Nehru, noted that the Brahmin is generally a *persona grata* in the villages he surveyed (mainly in Rae Barelli district of U.P.). He reports that Brahmins there were able to buy land at lower prices and could lease land at lower rates than could other villagers (1932, p. 51). Sharma offers another instance, from Gamras village, Kanpur district, where twenty of the twenty-six Brahmin families made their living from cultivation at the time of his study, and have long been landowners. "Many of them received land as gifts from their *jajmans*, while some of them purchased land to maintain their social status in the village" (Sharma 1956a, pp. 103–104). In the discussion of social mobility below, it will be noted that Brahmins who became poor often had an alternate occupation open to them as priests for lower jatis. In taking such service they remained part of the Brahmin varna.

Sometimes, when Brahmin jatis exerted strong double hegemony, both spiritual and temporal, they roused bitter resentment and even retaliation from other villagers. In earlier history these protests often took a religious form; latterly there has been political counter-action. In Madras state especially, non-Brahmins have been politically successful in reversing what they consider to be undue Brahmin advantages (Irschik 1969).

In general, ritual and secular influences have been reciprocally used. High ritual status has often brought secular rewards which, in turn, helped maintain ritual eminence. More significantly, when the members of a jati could increase in secular resources, they could generally augment their ritual status.

The Attribution of Rank According to Jati Blocs

The ranking of jatis is thus a main feature of interdependence within local systems. How and by whom is ranking determined? The short answer is that a jati's rank is often set in a rough and ready way, as part of a lump classification. It is set by the members of a united, dominant jati-group, where there is one, whose men calibrate the local order in the course of the exercise of their dominance. But where there is no such authoritative group, no exact order of precedence is set. In such villages, and there are many, conflict about who outranks whom is common. Yet the people of these villages have been able to carry on their community functions without a consensus about the detailed order of rank. Moreover, social mobility has long been a recurrent feature of village society, so at any one time there is very likely to be considerable disagreement about the proper rank of a jati whose members are in the process of changing their rank.

The assessment of rank within a village has to be rough-hewn, just as the varna and jati-cluster assessments used across villages have to be gross classifications. Villagers would have to perform prodigious feats of calculation if every status-relevant trait of a jati's members had to be computed. The roster of a jati's practices often includes some of relatively pure and some of relatively defiling character; within any jati, members differ in their ritual stringency and secular affluence.

In Gaon village (Poona district) for example, one of the high jatis practices the low custom of widow remarriage. One of the Harijan jatis there has some prosperous families who have raised their status enough to acquire the services of Brahmin priests. Within all the larger jati-groups there is considerable variation in family wealth (Orenstein 1965a, pp. 120–149).

A villager of Gaon does not make an analysis of such multiple variables in order to decide what his proper relations with a person of a particular jati should be. Nor is there any clear consensus in the village about the precise order of rank. Indeed, the same villager may make different rankings on different occasions. But there is considerable consensus and consistency about the main blocs (as they are termed here) into which the village jatis can be classified. There are four such blocs in Gaon, the jatis in each bloc are taken as of about equal status for most purposes. Some do not care for the way their neighbors classify them, but they too use the same bloc ordering (Orenstein 1965a, pp. 136–138).

A bloc is mainly a local classification, unlike such groupings as jati-cluster and varna. In Gaon, eight jati-groups are placed in the bloc called "the high castes," which comes just after the topmost bloc of Brahmin jatis in ritual precedence. One of the eight is the Maratha, the local representation of the jati-cluster widespread in Maharashtra. Marathas have a military tradition. Yet classed in the same bloc with them in Gaon are the barber and blacksmith jatis; neither of these is in the same varna tradition nor classed so high in most other regions.

Although there is no fixed table of social precedence jati by jati which holds good in all villages, the top and bottom of the local order in most villages are usually quite clear. A Brahmin jati is often given highest ritual rank by village consensus and the jatis of Harijans are at the other extreme. Some psychological reasons for this clarity of the extremes are suggested in a cross-cultural comparison of caste behavior by George DeVos (DeVos and Wagatsuma 1966, pp. 332–384). Harijans are examples of the pollution that each person must cope with in his own life. They are a living demonstration of the degrading effects of ritual defilement. Perhaps people of other jatis have insisted on keeping them so low because in so doing they have been proving that ritual pollution really is debasing and to be avoided and expunged. Brahmin jatis, by the same token, exemplify the rewards of ritual purity.

In between the blocs at each extreme, several blocs of jatis are ranked. The blocs are taxonomic devices; they tell nothing about cooperation among the jatis that are classed together. In fact, the most bitter rivalries may be between jatis of the same grouping. Nor are these groupings clear-cut, well-defined categories. They are rather divisions which villagers make in a rough way, often because the people in each bloc have similar standards of accepting food and water from others. And while two jatis may follow similar patterns of food acceptance, their jati customs may be quite distinct.

In sorting out the local jatis, villagers are influenced by the varna classification, especially in the ritual eminence of Brahmin jatis. Frequently, however, as in Gaon village, the classical categories do not fit well with the actual groupings that are used. Thus the people of Kishan Garhi village (Aligarh district, U.P.) generally agree that the twenty-four local jatis are placed in five or six ranked blocs labeled the highest, the high, the low, Muslim, the very low, the lowest of all. Marriott comments that this grouping of jatis in blocs is reflected in much interjati behavior, as in forms of greeting, arrangements for eating, smoking, and sitting. "Within each major bloc, the ranking of separate castes must be estimated by villagers according to minor ritual criteria; estimates of precise rank within the blocs are not consistent or well agreed" (1959b, p. 102).

Similar groupings within a local system have been reported from all regions.[2] Sharma's account of a village in Kanpur district, U.P., illustrates the kind of rough classifications that villagers tend to make. In that village, the Brahmin jati-group is the most numerous (104 out of the village population of 697 at the time of the study) and is without question ritually superior to the other jatis. Yet five of the Brahmin men will eat meat although most of their jati fellows do not. This is no sudden departure; some elderly Brahmins confided that this had been done in their father's generation also. These meat-eating Brahmins had had military service, and perhaps this had something to do with their deviance, or perhaps the military service was only another expression of a personal deviation from what is expected of a Brahmin. Sharma notes other divagations from high Brahmanical conduct (1956a, pp. 181, 241).

Yet some Brahmins continue to officiate as priests, and the whole jati does not appear to be degraded by the derelictions of some of its members. In theory, it should be; in practice, their priestly tradition plus their numbers override such deficiencies. As a jati-group they stand fifth from the top in average per capita income, and their numerical strength has been weakened by warring factions. The next highest jati, the Thakurs, do not accept *kachcha* food from those Brahmins whom they consider to be of dubious personal purity. For all that, this Brahmin jati continues to command ritual eminence.

The four families of the Kayasth jati—scribes by traditional occupation—have been rich and influential in the village for a century, particularly because of their tenure in village administrative posts, such as in the keeping of the land records. But the local Brahmins and Thakurs still recall that the Kayasths were anciently reckoned among the Shudras. With only four families, the Kayasths are not a numerous band in the village. The jati's situation in this village is similar to that which Kayasths have had to struggle against in many other villages of North India. Despite their outstanding wealth, political influence, and respectable ritual practices, "the Thakurs do not concede them an equal or nearly equal social status" (Sharma 1956a, pp. 242–243). The Brahmin and Thakur jati-groups have long managed village affairs in this place, but their control has not prevented the Kayasths, or even some of the very low jatis, from claiming higher privileges than the managing groups are willing to concede.

Through much of the round of village activities, a precise, definitive order of precedence for all jatis is unnecessary. When disputes about jati rank do arise, they should be settled, in the ideal view of the higher jatis, according to scriptural precepts. Since the most learned in scripture are usually

[2] In a village of West Bengal, J. Sarma noted eight such grades (1955, p. 168). Among the villages with five such blocs are Gamras, Kanpur district (Sharma 1956a, p. 240), Potlod in Madhya Pradesh (Mathur 1964, pp. 68–71), Shamirpet in Madhya Pradesh, with Muslims a sixth grouping (Mayer 1956, pp. 121–124). Six are reported from a Telengana village (Dube 1955c, p. 182), four from Gaon in Poona district, with two jatis outside any bloc, (Orenstein 1965a, pp. 136–139), three from Kumbapettai in Tanjore district (Gough 1955, pp. 82–83), six in Malabar villages (Miller 1954, p. 411).

the men of the local Brahmin jatis, they ought to settle disputes about the relative rank of two lower jatis. Sometimes they do. But more often, as will be discussed in the chapters on councils, the facts of a case remain unclear or the learned men disagree or their opinion carries little weight or they are not consulted at all.

Consensus and Dissension about Rank Order

Where there is a strongly dominant jati whose members live up to respectable ritual standards, whose families are landed, numerous, and powerful, and whose men speak with one voice of authority, then the leaders of that jati judge a group's worth and define its ritual precedence. If such a dominant jati is not Brahmin, its men may listen to Brahmin advice on certain ritual matters.

Often, however, no single jati of a local system is strong and united enough to exert such rule. There need not be, and often is not, any compelling ritual authority in a local system. Brahmins have presumed first rights to such authority among Hindu villagers but the local Brahmins may not be allowed to exercise these rights.

A local system does not disintegrate in the absence of an authoritative, rank-allotting group. Villagers still distinguish among blocs of jatis and regulate their own relations with those of other jatis according to these blocs. Villagers of all levels hold to the belief in a social hierarchy based on ritual standards. The men of two higher jatis may be in bitter opposition, yet they will commonly unite to keep a ritually inferior jati in what they consider to be its proper place.

Disputes about precedence between two jatis of the same bloc are not uncommon. Thus in the account of Ramkheri in Madhya Pradesh we find that "one caste may say another caste eats from its hands, the second caste denying this" (Mayer 1956, p. 121). And Srinivas, in discussing the jati he calls Peasants in Rampura, Mysore, writes that it is alleged by some that the Peasants in neighboring villages eat the domestic pig, but any public statement to this effect before a Peasant would lead to unpleasantness. "It is also well known that the poorer Peasants in Rampura and around eat the field rat and water snake, but this again would be denied. Only a few of those who drink alcoholic beverages would admit to it" (Srinivas 1955b, p. 21).

Nor is there monolithic agreement about such matters within a jati. One man of the Peasant jati in a village may rank the blacksmith group, say, as higher in the scale than will his jati-fellows, perhaps because he has had unusually cordial relations with a blacksmith family. All jati-fellows are likely to share a complimentary opinion of their own jati, but, even in this, one man may have higher aspirations for his group than does another.

In the jockeying for better rating, the insignia of rank prerogative—trivial though they may seem to an outsider—can be given supreme importance. Many contemporary instances of this will be noted later; one example may be cited here from a seventeenthcentury account by the Dutch missionary, Abraham Roger. He wrote (the English translation is by L. H. Gray) that among Shudras there are many and diverse groups "whereof each pretendeth to surpass the others; and therefore it doth ofttimes hap that great strife ariseth in the land, insomuch as one caste or another, be it in marriage or in burial of the dead, goeth beyond what is the custom."

In January 1640, he recalls, the city of Pulicat was in tumult "for that the Palijs, which is the caste of poulterers, spread a cloth upon the earth while burying one of their dead, to the end that the corpse might be covered thereover." This the "Cauwreaes" would not allow them to do because it was a privilege of their group. They obstructed the funeral, and the corpse remained unburied until the local governor had the body put away. His ruling incensed the "Palij" who began to attack the other side. Groups of artisans, such as carpenters, smiths, and goldsmiths "who must hold with them in time of parlousness" rallied to the aid of the Palijs. There were months of unrest in the locality," nor was the matter ended without effusion of blood, for in the month of March fifteen Palijs and Cauwreaes were slain in fight, so that ye may see how nicely each caste of Soudraes standeth on its own" (Jackson 1907, pp. 242–243).

The advantages of respectable rank, then and now, are considerable, hence the frequent struggles about the tokens of rank. A man of high jati is not so apt to be pushed around or brushed aside by others, whatever the situation, as is one of weak and low jati. For those at the lowest levels, improvement in status can mean the freedom to live in more desirable locations than those to which they are often confined or the freedom to use water points denied to the lowliest. "For others it is mainly a matter of self-respect—the Bhilala wishes to smoke freely with the great mass of upper castes, the Teli to eat on equal terms with Rajputs and so to have many eat from his hands who will not now do so" (Mayer 1956, p. 140).

The pulling and hauling about rank has made for a relatively labile social order of the jatis of a locality within a relatively fixed set of cultural standards. The disputes about rank probably helped to reinforce villagers' ideas that high rank was indeed very important. But along with the competition and dissension about local rank, there has also been a degree of consensus about jati endogamy and about the ritual criteria.

That necessary, minimum consensus allows for some quite wide variation, both by individuals and groups. In this general survey, individual life histories cannot be studied in detail. It may be well, however, to mention here the case of one woman who did not abide by the conventions, who manipulated the system for her own highly unconventional purposes, who has not followed the cultural script for her role as a woman, a Brahmin, and a widow.

She is a widow of a Brahmin jati in the village of Kanpur district U.P. studied by K. N. Sharma. She refused to accept the austere role prescribed for Brahmin widows and carried on an affair with a Thakur man. Becoming pregnant, she ran off with him, managed an abortion, and then returned to the village, where the two lived as man and wife though without benefit of clergy or approval of the respectable people. Well-to-do families in this region customarily send gifts of food, *sidha*, to Brahmins on certain occasions. About ten years after this widow's first escapade, a leading Kayasth, Lala Shiva Prasad, acting on the advice of Brahmin elders, stopped sending her this token of jati esteem. She objected violently to this lapse, arguing that her Brahmin birthright overrode her personal failings. "Then she began to abuse him and other Brahmins of the village. Lala Shiva Prasad gave a *sidha* to avoid unnecessary trouble" (Sharma 1956a, p. 433).

A less determined Brahmin widow would have slunk far off with her shame; a more determined Kayasth, especially if prodded by strong Brahmins, would have faced the woman with wrathful and righteous rejection. As it was, she violated tenets that must be inviolable for others if the system is to continue, transgressed in ways that bring drastic punishment to similar transgressors, yet she brazened it out, withstood disapproval, even insisted successfully on some of a proper Brahmin's due.

Such cases are exceptional. Villagers shrug them off as exceptional and carry on with the village order despite such individual contradictions. But it is important to take notice of them, not only because such abnormal instances help define the norm but also because the irregular, untypical, and contrasystemic cases may portend important social change.

A whole jati or a group of jatis may be treated as a special case by others in a locality. They are not fully incorporated into the local system but yet do not threaten its operation. For example, a jati's ranking may be held in abeyance for a time. In discussing the commensal order in Ramkheri village, Mayer observes that "the Ahirs are recent immigrants from the North, and at present eat from nobody; neither does any caste take food from them" (1956, p. 122). We shall see later how certain artisan groups of South India have for centuries acted as though they belonged in the Brahmin category, while most of the others in their villages did not accept their self-styled rank.

In some places, however, dissent about ranking has had to be periodically resolved. There were ceremonial occasions when the rank order was set forth plain for all to see. On such occasions there was a clear—if temporary—settlement of the rank order. Fewer villages now have such occasions, mainly because a settlement is more difficult to reach.

At a ceremony in which all the village jatis participate, the distribution of festal food symbolizes the order of local society. What groups eat next to what other groups and who is served before whom at the feast show agreement about the order of rank, or at least show how current disputes about rank have been settled for the time being. In the ordinary round of village life, villagers commonly use the acceptance of food and water as the best guide to the order of rank. A jati's place is thus defined at a feast in which all local jatis join—by where its members are seated, by what other jatis will take cooked food from its members and from whom they will accept food. But even when such clear ranking is publicly made at a village ceremony, some particulars of that order may be contravened in another context or at a different time, and ranking is likely to be somewhat different in other villages of the vicinity.

The order of rank, nevertheless, is a matter of great and continuing consequence to many villagers. Some studies have attempted to formulate a general scale of rank in a village by asking village informants to arrange in rank order a set of cards, each bearing the name of a jati of the village (Freed 1963b). The answers are mathematically combined to give a general result. But this mathematically derived listing, Berreman has commented (1965), may not be very relevant to actual behavior because it does not take into account the various criteria for ranking and the different contexts in which rank influences interaction. Another approach uses questions about actual situations to formulate ritual distances among jatis by a multiple scaling technique (Kolenda 1959). This does take contexts and criteria into consideration but is limited to a relatively few of the many that are actually used.

How a jati's practices are evaluated by other villagers, and the bloc in which a jati is classed, depend on such considerations as the power of its families and the popular stereotype of their conduct, as well as on the ritual quality of the practices. Though the appraisals of rank are full of fine nuances, they are made on the basis of a few generative principles. Purity and pollution, wealth and power are major considerations.

CHAPTER 13

Cultural Variations and the Jati Order

The hierarchical order of jatis in a locality is further bolstered by cultural differences among the jatis. The higher groups characteristically follow domestic and religious practices that they hold to be far superior to those of the lower jatis. The people of the lower jatis do not necessarily agree that their own customs are abysmally inferior, but once they are able to do so they emulate the more prestigious ways of the higher jatis. The process of emulation is discussed in the later chapters on social mobility; we note here some common cultural differences within a local order.

Villagers expect that each jati will have some unique traits and that these will characterize all in the jati. In practice there can be considerable variation in customs within a jati. In some jatis, the traditional occupation is followed by very few of the jati members. Further, there may be only slight cultural differences between one jati and another in a locality. Nevertheless, the villagers' concept is in some degree borne out in practice; there are typically certain customary ways unique to each jati.

There are, moreover, cultural differences among the main grouping of jatis. The scriptural, ritual differences appear most clearly in the contrast between the topmost and the bottommost blocs in a locality. Brahmins and other high jatis are purer in their diet than are the lowest—who may not be able to forego the occasional dietary windfall of a carcass. The highest jatis tend, on the whole, to be more fastidious ritually than are the lowest—who may not be able to afford, or may not know about, all the ritual niceties. Diacritical details of costume, such as the sacred thread, usually distinguish the higher from the lower. Men of the Brahmin jatis are—or are supposed to be—familiar with some of the main scriptural concepts, or are linked in other ways with the great, sacred, literate tradition of Hinduism. This is in contrast to people of the lowest jatis who do not, and formerly could not, presume to sacred scriptural learning.

This learning is more appropriate for men of Brahmin jatis than for those of the two other "twice-born" categories, but jatis of all three higher varnas, as we shall note in discussing models for mobility, are expected to differ from those of lower rank in style of life, in daily ritual, in jati ceremonial, and particularly in conjugal relations. Among groups at the top of the social scale, a woman at marriage enters a permanent inviolable relationship that must endure through all the here and the hereafter. Widows must never remarry; divorce is prohibited. No such taboos lie upon women of the lower jatis, who may divorce and be divorced and who may remarry whether they are divorcees or widows.

Brahmins tend to put more emphasis on the rites performed by males for their ancestors, an emphasis that makes sons especially prized in a family. Writing about non-Brahmins in Mysore, Srinivas notes that though a son is preferred, a daughter is not unwelcome. Girls are in demand among them and there is no religious duty to get a girl married before puberty. The code under which a woman has to live is not so harsh among them as among the Brahmins (1956a, p. 485).

Not all the proprieties practiced by Brahmins have clear sanction in scripture. Sanskrit scripture is not a single, coordinated corpus of holy writ. Earlier texts differ from later ones; widely different interpretations have been made of the same text or of a particular directive. But scriptural exegesis is of small concern to a villager. The important and prevalent belief is that holy scripture is the font of purity-pollution concepts and related conduct. To most villagers who know anything at all about the literate tradition these concepts are now and forever established; they have been revered in all preceding generations; they are revered even in this untoward age.

Differences in Religious Practices

There are significant differences between the scriptural, transcendental aspects of religion, which are mainly in the keeping of the high jatis, and the pragmatic aspects, which are used by all but are kept up principally by people of the lower jatis. These differences are discussed below in the chapters on village and civilization and on the accretion of tribal peoples; to indicate the nature of the cultural separations in religion among social strata, some of the distinguishing features of the two aspects should be mentioned here.

Animal sacrifice is one of the contrastive traits; it is more commonly performed by the lower jatis than by those who follow the "twice-born" models. There are scriptural precedents for certain kinds of animal sacrifice, but these are considered irrelevant to present-day Sanskritic worship by the learned, quite as clergy in the Judeo-Christian tradition wave aside Old Testament prescriptions for blood sacrifice.

Possession is another differential trait. In many regions there are persons who regularly become possessed. When a man (or more rarely a woman) becomes possessed with a deity or a spirit, the voice of the supernatural speaks through him, answers questions about illness and personal problems, and gives commands or advice for remedying what has gone wrong. These shamans are mainly from the blocs below the highest; rarely does a Brahmin become possessed in this way (cf. Harper 1957b; Carstairs 1957, pp. 92–94).

A comparison of worship in various social levels of Kishan Garhi village shows clearly that scriptural deities figure more prominently in the devotions of the higher groups than in the worship of the lower. The rites of the lower jatis are more concerned with the local godlings. "Forty-five percent of the deities worshipped by Brahmins are Sanskritic; 35 percent of the deities worshipped by members of ten high castes below the Brahmins are Sanskritic; but only 15 and 19 percent, respectively, of the deities worshipped by members of the low and lowest castes are Sanskritic deities" (Marriott 1955b, p. 209).

These figures illustrate significant differences in religious emphasis and also show considerable overlapping, especially in that Brahmins worship a number of local spirits and godlings, as do women of all jatis. Although these figures are only about relative numbers and not about the relative importance attached to the different deities, it is significant that these Brahmins hold in reverence many deities unhallowed in scripture.

All in a village can appeal to local deities for certain specific purposes. Thus in Kumbapettai village, in the Tanjore district of Madras, the village deity is the spirit of a Konar (cowherd) woman who died of smallpox. Her priest is a non-Brahmin. Besides being a deity of the Konar, propitiated by them at their annual festival, this goddess is worshipped by both Brahmins and Adi Dravidas ("Original Dravidians," a more acceptable term than "untouchables") at specific times of the year. The shrine of the goddess stands on a boundary of the village and "is believed to protect the whole community from crop failure, infectious diseases, female barrenness and deaths in child-birth." People of any jati may propitiate the goddess when illness, barrenness, or insanity afflicts their households. The chief village festival is celebrated for this local deity (Gough 1955, p. 89).

Cultural Contrasts and Their Social Effects

In Kumbapettai village the cultural differences between the top and the bottom of the local order are especially marked. In the 1950s the local Brahmins were, as they had been for centuries, the ritual superiors and also the strongly dominant landowners. The two jatis of Adi Dravidas are mainly poor landless laborers (Gough 1956, pp. 826–827).

These Brahmins place great importance on the continuity of the lineage and on a man's tight nexus with his immediate ascendants and descendants. Lineal descent is highly important to them because it determines the control and inheritance of land. To the economic significance of lineal relations is added the great religious necessity for sons. A dead man's soul does not find secure place in any afterlife unless it is fed regularly with ritual offerings made by a son. After his death a father is supremely dependent in this way on the son; while he is alive the son should be greatly dependent on him. The asymmetrical relation, in which the father or father surrogate is in complete authority and in which the junior male is the obedient disciple, is one that is highly prized and idealized.

The Adi Dravidas, at the opposite end of the local social scale, have no land; inheritance is not of paramount interest to them. Grown sons must fend for themselves and they break away from the father's authority soon after puberty. They are not much concerned with religious duties for departed souls. They do not stress a long and close relationship between father and son, nor do they idealize a state of dependency. Their emphasis is on the solidarity of peers, on the equivalence of brothers and of sisters (cf. Mandelbaum 1941; 1955). It is on the ties that a man has among a wide compass of his contemporaries rather than, as with the Brahmins, within the narrow range of his immediate forebears and descendants. They find it feasible to act together as peers of a jati group and to be represented by their headman. Conversely, the Brahmins of this village find it much less feasible to take joint action and to agree on a single chosen representative for all (Gough 1956, pp. 840, 846).

These different emphases are reflected in kinship terminology. The Brahmin terminology makes plain a person's relation to those of his lineage; there are relatively few terms for affinal relatives. Adi Dravida kinship terms are laterally extended over a wide range of affinal and cognate relatives (Gough 1956, p. 848).

A Brahmin woman in Kumbapettai works only in the home, does not own land, and at marriage her social personality becomes closely assimilated into that of her husband so that, for example, she adopts her husband's terms in addressing his kin. A bride's family must transfer wealth to the groom's family to ensure a stable marriage and the couple must live in the husband's natal household. The scriptural ban on divorce and on widow remarriage transfers the bride into her husband's social position for all her life.

Adi Dravida women are much more independent—economically, socially, ritually. They work with the men in the fields and are paid separately and individually. At marriage it is the groom's family that transfers wealth to the bride's rather than the other way around as with the Brahmins. Residence after marriage need not be strictly patrilocal. A woman remains much more of an independent social personality after marriage; she does not take over the same kin terminology used by her husband; she retains greater affiliation with her natal family and its social ties. Marriage is not an irreversible commitment. Adi Dravida women may divorce and remarry. They have greater spatial and social mobility than do Brahmin women. This is not to say that a wife rules the roost in these jatis; she must, overtly at least, be relatively submissive. But she, much more readily than a Brahmin woman, can pick up her children and go home to mother, leaving behind—perhaps permanently—an impossible husband.

The Adi Dravidas of Kumbapettai do not value sexual asceticism as do the Brahmins. Further, their men can more readily give vent to their aggressions, can trade blows and later forget the quarrel. Brahmin men may not explode into physical aggression in the same way; a physical fight among the men of a Brahmin family would be a most shameful, unforgettable event (Gough 1956, p. 847).

This comparison between the Brahmins and the Adi Dravidas of Kumbapettai village provides a particularly vivid contrast. In most villages there is not so great a disparity between highest and lowest, but some such differences are common. There are relative differences in culture and also certain sharper differences.

In the highest jatis there is relatively more worship of the scriptural deities, and among the lowest jatis relatively more assistance is sought from shamans. In families of top rank, as was noted in the chapters on family roles, there is relatively more deference to elders and less independent status for women than in families of lowest rank. A jati that is ritually highest in its local order may not be vegetarian, but its members are usually more meticulous about their diet, more selective than are their social inferiors. The local Brahmins may not be very learned, but they are more learned than their neighbors. Those who cherish a Kshatriya tradition take pride in being fiercer warriors than all others. Those of highest ritual status are relatively more scrupulous in ritual observance than are those of lowest rank.

The sharper differences are in such traits as *being* a shaman and *performing* an animal sacrifice. Those of superior status may willingly share the benefits of a seance or of the sacrifice of a goat, but it is rare for one of them to become possessed or actually to wield the sacrificial blade. And as between highest and lowest, a woman's lot in marriage has been different—no divorce, no widow remarriage, prepuberty weddings (though postpuberty nuptials and consummation) in the top rank; easier divorce, unquestioned remarriage of widows, postpuberty marriage at the lowest echelon.

Cultural differences have been the trigger and symbol of great social disturbances, as in the conflicts between right-hand and left-hand Hindu factions early in the nineteenth century or the riots between Muslim Sunnis and Shias early in the twentieth. But such upheavals have been limited in time and space; they have not been characteristic of the ordinary round of village life in which cultural differences are routinely accepted.

Certain understandings about society are shared by villagers no matter what their religion or jati status may be. There is usually implicit consensus in a village that there is and should be a hierarchy of ranked endogamous groups, that this hierarchy is very important, that it is based on criteria of ritual pollution and purity. These common beliefs form a broad, monistic frame for social organization. Within the limits set by this frame, cultural pluralism is allowed and expected.

Differences are not, in themselves, suspect. A Brahmin may abjure widow remarriage for Brahmins but he will not care whether the widow of his sweeper remarries. The Harijan shaman, when possessed by the spirit of a village godling, does not usually decry the gods worshipped in the great temple, nor do devotees of the scriptural deities ordinarily try to wipe out worship of the local spirits. The gods of the Sanskritic pantheon are held by Hindus to be universal deities, but they are not accorded monopoly over all the village, nor do the *dei loci* demand exclusive rights within their own locale.

In later chapters other cultural differences will be examined, such as those of sect, religion, and region. Within a village, differences between one sect and another may seem extraordinarily minute to an outside observer but may, on occasion, loom large in the view of villagers. Conversely, the differences in dogma that separate Islam from Hinduism may, in the ordinary round of village life, result in relatively little difference in the daily life of Muslims and Hindus of the same social level in the same locality. The premises of jati organization require some degree of differentiation in custom among jatis; villagers can tolerate quite wide cultural divergences within a local system so long as the basic tenets are not perturbed.

Résumé

"The institution of caste provides a common cultural idiom to Indians: wherever one may be in India one is in a universe of caste." Studies done in all parts of the land confirm this statement by Srinivas (1958, p. 573), yet as we noted in Chapter 1, students of caste have been mindful also of the problems involved in formulating the grammar (not to say the lexicon) of this idiom and of mapping the dimensions of this universe.

A scholar of an earlier generation, Emile Senart, asked in his book on caste, which appeared in 1896, whether we should abandon the difficult attempt to give a picture of the caste institution as a whole. Senart's answer, together with the fifteen chapters that follow it, asserts that the attempt should be made. Any such attempt, Senart said, will be incomplete, but will not necessarily therefore be false and misleading. "It will be enough to remember that no assertion should be regarded as absolute, that the relationship of facts leaves room for a multitude of fine shades of difference, and that only the most general characteristics are common to the whole domain" (1930, pp. 19–20). With due regard for the warning about absolute assertions, we review the characteristics of jatis and of relations among jatis that have so far been discussed.

Most of the peoples of the subcontinent have lived in jati-based social order, yet no single hierarchy has ever regulated all of Indian caste society. Caste organization has flourished as a vast series of local systems, each partially independent of others, each intricately related to others.

Each local system is centered in a village or a close set of villages. It includes those who come in from other villages regularly to perform jajmani or other functions. A person normally participates as village member in the local system that centers on the village of his residence. He participates as jati member in other localities where his kin and jati fellows live. In both capacities he perceives much finer social distinctions among those who are close to him than among those with whom he has less intimate relationships. Outside the marital and household sphere a person needs to recognize only broader social divisions. A landowner may be in frequent relation with his barber, washerman, and field hand for a lifetime without knowing much about their respective clans or the position of the jati of each within a jati-cluster of barbers, washermen, or laborers.

The broader social divisions are of several kinds. We have used the term jati-cluster for a grouping of several jatis under a common name with close enough ties of culture and communication to foster some feeling of mutual identity. Villagers also sort the jati-groups of their village into a series of blocs, groupings of different jatis lumped together and similarly treated. Sometimes the blocs are essentially the varna categories plus others, such as Muslims, who are not mentioned in the varna scheme. But a bloc may include jatis whose members follow quite different varna tradition, yet are similarly treated by other villagers. Nevertheless, villagers try to reconcile the main blocs with the varna classification, which not only transcends locality, but also is hallowed by the eternal and universal ambience of scripture.

Taken as an empirical formulation of Indian caste society, the varna outline is easily shown to be deceptively oversimplified, even misleading. Seen as the villagers' model of their social structure, it appears as a useful, even a necessary, social device. Using it, a person can maintain and establish relations with people belonging to a great diversity of groupings within his local system, and with the vaster diversity of jatis beyond this his home locality.[1] Peoples of a complex civilization need a simple social theory; in India such theory is taken from Hindu scripture.

Groups that are divergent by reason of religion or sect are fitted, as will be seen below, into the local order of caste. The field of hierarchical force generated by a local system draws in and adapts groups of all sorts, even those that have been formed on the grounds of antagonism to caste. A villager does not necessarily feel threatened by cultural differences among his neighbors nor impelled to change their ways to his. He does object if others try to take on what he considers to be his jati's prerogative. The fact that there are regional differences in caste order and criteria does not disturb villagers, even if they are aware of such differences.

All the variations—among regions, within local systems, within a person's repertoire of caste roles, in his perception of social divisions—are played out in a kind of counterpoint to the constant themes of jati organization. These themes have to do with ritual pollution and purity and with their consequences for social relations, particularly for endogamy. They entail the ritual and secular

[1] The extent of that diversity can be judged from the various and incomplete census attempts to count the number of caste groupings. In the 1901 Census of India, the counted number of "main castes" (mostly jati-clusters in our terms) came to 2,378. Ten years before that there had been some counting of the subdivision within certain main castes; for Ahirs there were more than 1,700 entries, for Jats a similarly large number, for Kurmis there were nearly 1,500 names.

In the 1931 Census, more than 15 million Brahmins were returned. In the hill state of Tehri-Garhwal, with a total population of only 350,000, there were counted 387 "subcastes" of Brahmins and 1,025 of Rajputs (Davis 1951, p. 166).

attributes of jatis, their interdependence and order. Certain personal practices, especially those having to do with eating and other bodily functions, affect a person's ritual pollution and purity, and this regulates the relations that he may have with other people. Such regulation is made within the family when one member is temporarily more polluted or is more purified than are the others. These temporary, ritual inequalities within a household arise and are mitigated daily.

Permanently, all in a household are ritual equals because of, and by means of, their intimate interaction. Similar ritual equality prevails more widely for all families among whom intermarriage may occur. Endogamy bounds the jati, which is kept as a firm unit by the strong taboo on marrying out of the jati. If we coin the term excest for this taboo, we can say that the horror of excest in village India is almost as powerful as the horror of incest. Genetically, a jati is a breeding unit as well as a unit of social reproduction. The genetic aspects of jati organization remain a relatively unexplored part of the study of caste society.

Each person is born into a jati, into one and only one jati. He and all the others in his jati are considered by their neighbors to have certain attributes, commonly including a traditional occupation. These attributes affect the permanent pollution or purity of the jati members and therefore affect the kinds of relations they may have with people of other jatis, who carry greater or less permanent pollution-purity than their own. Villagers rank those jatis they consider to be the purer as higher and accord them greater jati prerogatives; those seen as more polluted are ranked lower, with greater ritual disabilities. The ritual criteria for rank are, in practice, combined with the secular factors of a jati's wealth and power in the overall assignment of jati rank. Commonly all in a village agree that there is a social hierarchy and that it has certain outlines, but there is often considerable disagreement concerning at least some details of the rank order.

The jatis are both independent and interdependent. The members of each are held apart from all others in certain matters, by jati differences and avoidances. All are bound together by their dependence on each other; typically no jati is sufficient to itself either economically or ritually. Although there have long been important fields of village life in which jati rank was largely irrelevant, and these activities are rapidly increasing in scope and in importance, most villagers still identify strongly with their jati and conduct many of their relations with their neighbors with consideration to jati rank.

These thematic patterns provide the basic rule of the social game in villages through most of the land. For many centuries they have been bolstered by the ideology of Sanskrit scripture and its vernacular versions, which encompassed diverse local orders in a common frame. Villagers of the lower ranks have had little formal acquaintance with doctrinal concepts, but they have shared in scriptural stories and concepts. In sum, people at all levels and in hundreds of thousands of villages, have shared a similar image of society as a whole. They also have shared similar ideas about relations within their jati.

PART IV

RELATIONS WITHIN THE JATI

CHAPTER 14

Alliances and Sections within the Jati

Jati members cooperate in many ways, as kinsmen, as ritual equals in certain contexts, as political allies in others. Some aspects of this collaboration have already been noted, others will be discussed in the next few chapters. But there are also formal restrictions and implicit limits upon cooperation among the people of a jati.

The range of a person's relations within his jati depends on such matters as its size, his own social and economic status, and the formal subdivisions of the jati.

In a very small jati, such as the Gayawal (who number about one hundred twenty families in the town of Gaya), a man can know and relate to most others of his jati (Vidyarthi 1961, pp. 53–57). But many jatis are spread across scores or hundreds of villages, and a man can maintain jati relations with only a small part of the total. This part has been called his "effective jati," comprising those with whom he actually maintains such relations (cf. Mayer 1960, p. 151; Klass 1966, p. 954).

A villager's compass of jati relations usually varies according to his wealth and education. Srinivas notes that an elderly, uneducated Okkaliga of the Mysore and Mandya districts in Mysore State might not consider Okkaligas of other districts as belonging to his jati at all. His effective social span would include the Okkaligas within a radius of about twenty-five miles of his village. "But an Okkaliga lawyer or doctor would regard all the divisions as Okkaligas, and he might give his daughter in marriage to the son of an urbanized and educated Okkaliga from distant Shimoga in the west" (Srinivas 1966, p. 115). What the uneducated villager sees as separate jatis of the Okkaliga jati-cluster, the educated professional man now takes to be one jati.

In addition, the people of a jati commonly group themselves into subdivisions that limit the possibilities for full jati cooperation. Some jatis are formally subdivided on the basis of the marriage rules of hypergamy. Another kind of subdivision, one which is usually not formalized but which occurs frequently, is between opposing alliances. Jati members can be competitors and rivals for status as well as comrades and allies. Membership in a ranked section of a jati is inherited; joining an alliance is more voluntary.

Hypergamy and Hypergamous Sections

Women are generally expected to be more strict than men are about domestic ritual observances and niceties of domestic status. They are likely to feel more vulnerable than do men to breaches of such observances. Parents may be willing to arrange the marriage of a son to a girl from a family a bit lower than theirs in prestige and status but are usually unwilling to marry a daughter into a family of lower status within the jati. That course not only consigns their daughter to an inferior family but also lowers their own prestige in the eyes of their jati fellows.

This common preference to marry a daughter for better and not for worse is formalized in some jatis as a rigid rule of hypergamy. Under that rule, a woman must marry into her own section or into one that is higher but must not be married into a lower section of the jati. A man may take a wife from a lower section.[1] These ranked sections are hereditary, but section affiliation is reckoned in different ways. The sections of some jatis are made up of lineages; in others the ranked units are made up of clans or villages or territorial divisions.

Among Rajputs, the far-flung and numerous jati-cluster of northern and western India, clans are so classified and ranked in a complex fashion. There are four major sets of clans, named after the Sun, Moon, Fire, and Serpents; for purposes of hypergamy, the sets are generally ranked in that order, though with some questions about the relative ranking of Fire and Serpents sets (Karve 1965, pp. 165–171).

A Rajput clan often is associated with a geographic region and there is a concomitant rating by region. Although a Rajput man, and especially a ruler, could marry into a clan far lower than his (or even take a non-Rajput wife), in practice hypergamous marriages are made mainly between Rajput families of clans that are not far apart in the clan ratings, as these are understood by the families contracting the alliance. (There may be much the same difference of opinion about the relative ranking of Rajput clans in a locality as there is about the relative rating of some of the jatis in the caste system of that locality.)

Hypergamous ranking by clans also occurs among the Marathas of western India. The highest, most exclusive set includes the smallest number of clans; a clansman of this set may take a wife from any of the other sets down to the one that is lowest in position and that includes the greatest number of clans. Dr. Irawati Karve describes five such sets of Maratha clans (1965, pp. 176–179).[2]

---

[1] The rule is propounded in scriptural sources. Marriage between a man of higher position and a woman of lower is called *anuloma* ("with the hair"), and is, within certain limits, approved. The reverse, a woman marrying beneath her position, is called *pratiloma*, against the grain ("against the hair") and is strongly disapproved (Ghurye 1961, p. 54; Bouglé 1908, pp. 122–126).

[2] Arrangement into five sections is not found among all the jatis called Maratha. Thus in the villages of Poona district that Henry Orenstein has studied, clan hypergamy among Marathas is much more loosely arranged (1963, pp. 5–6; 1965a, pp. 126–128).

Among the Patidars of Charottar in Central Gujarat, sets of villages are ranked. "These circles are arranged in a hierarchy such that Six Villages at the top of the Charōttār Pātidārs will take brides from any other village if the father is able to pay a substantial dowry but they refuse to give their daughters outside the Six Villages" (Pocock 1957b, p. 21; also see Fukutake *et al.* 1964, p. 59). Patidar husband and wife must come from different villages.

Many North Indian jatis observe village exogamy, as was mentioned above in connection with rules of marriage, and in some places people of all jatis in a village follow the same pattern of hypergamy in arranging marriages with a family of another village. This occurs in Kishan Garhi (Aligarh district, U.P.). If a Kishan Garhi man—of any jati—has taken a wife from village A, then that village is deemed an inferior one for marriage alliances by all in Kishan Garhi. No father in Kishan Garhi will give his daughter in marriage to a man of village A. In this area, the northern villages are generally regarded as the superior, and brides at marriage usually go north to the groom's village.[3] "Marital relationships are formally one-sided and unbalanced: the boy's side is the high and demanding side, while the girl's side is the low and giving side" (Marriott 1955b, p. 176). The village from which the bride comes is inferior, for purposes of marriage arrangements, to the village into which she is married.

Often mentioned in discussions of hypergamy are the Rarhi Brahmins of Bengal. They are divided into four ranked sections, of which the Kulin is the highest. (The term "Kulin" is used widely for the highest unit in any ranking having to do with hypergamy.) A woman of the Kulin section may marry only a Kulin man, while a Kulin man may marry into one of the lower sections (Bhattacharya 1896, p. 38; Risley 1915, pp. 163–171; Hutton 1961, p. 53; Majumdar 1958a, p. 337).

The Kanyakubja Brahmins of Uttar Pradesh carry their internal jati stratification to a highly involuted extreme. A table listing forty-six sections of the jati is presented by Sharma as an illustrative but not a complete list. Each of these forty-six sections is characterized by a unique combination of attributes, such as *Upadhi* (surname), *gotra* (clan), grade (one of four categories), *Asami* (a famous person in the genealogical line), residence (traditional locality), and an evaluative order number called *biswas* (Sharma 1956b; Khare 1960).

The matrilineal Nayars of Kerala also followed the rule of hypergamy. The Nayars were classed into four ranked groupings, the royal and chiefly lineages, five groups of temple servants, five of commoner Nayars, and three of temple menials. A commoner woman could choose a temple servant man as her spouse and a temple menial woman could choose a commoner man. But royal and chiefly men had relations only with commoner women, not with women of either temple grouping.

A Nambudiri Brahmin man, as was noted in discussing family relations, could have an alliance with a Nayar woman of any status. At the other end of the local social scale, below the lowest Nayar jatis, were the "polluting" jatis of the locality; there was a sharp cleavage between them and all Nayars. No Nayar or Nambudiri man could have any kind of intimacy with women below this line. These hypergamous relations, Kathleen Gough comments, probably strengthened the unity among the ruling groups of an area against the lower jatis and also against external attack (Gough 1961c, pp. 319–321; 1965; Thurston 1909, vol. 5, pp. 300–303).

---

[3] In the Ganges-Jumna valleys, upstream is the superior direction in marriage alliances. This is north in the region of Kishan Garhi; it is west after the Ganges changes the main direction of flow.

In general, hypergamy makes possible the internal stratification of a jati without completely ending endogamy.[4] It is a kind of qualified endogamy. Formal hypergamy has been used, as will be noted later, as a step in social mobility. Families of an upwardly mobile group begin to set themselves apart from the other, less fortunate families of the jati by establishing hypergamous relations between themselves and the others. They still will take brides from the other families but will not give their girls to them in marriage. The others may protest vigorously, but sometimes the wealthier, more powerful families have succeeded in establishing formal subdivisions of their jati. In time, the memory that there was such a struggle for higher status is forgotten and those of the high sections are likely to say that their eminence within the jati was ordained from on high.

Contests for advantage and status among jati fellows still go on. How a family's status is, in some degree, tested on the occasion of a marriage of a child of the family has been noted. There are many other occasions when the prestige of a family or of a lineage within the jati is felt to be in the balance.

Such contests frequently occur among the men of a jati-group who are dominant in their village. The dominant jati-group splits into two or more opposing sets of families. These subdivisions within the jati are not formalized or freely acknowledged as are the hypergamous sections, but they are often more potent factors in the lives of the people so divided.

Alliances within a Jati-Group

The members of a jati-group are both kith and kin to each other. Day-to-day cooperation among jati fellows takes place mainly among those who live in the same village or cluster of villages. A villager's political activities are centered in his village; it is the scene of his livelihood and the daily stage for the enactment of his principal roles. Hence his relations with the people who are both neighbors in the village and kinsmen of the jati have a particular and a political importance to him (cf. Gould 1964, p. 26).

The political importance is likely to be especially marked in a jati-group whose people are numerous and economically strong enough to dominate their village. The common patterns of such domination are noted in the later discussion on the internal regulation of the village. But in their own jati affairs, the members of a large, dominant jati-group are likely to be split. In a small jati-group, solidarity can be enhanced by close interaction, as when all participate in each family's ceremonies. In less powerful jati-groups all can feel themselves confronted, and so consolidated, by their status rivals in the village. But the members of a large jati-group cannot interact as intimately as can a group of only a few families, and they confront only themselves in the village, since as a jati-group they are already in a paramount position. So with them the pervasive struggle for power

[4] The principal distribution of formal hypergamy, according to W. H. R. Rivers' survey, is among Rajputs and other groups living close to Rajputs who have adopted the Rajput model. He attributes Maratha hypergamy to the example of the Rajputs. It is also characteristic of the Kulin (i.e., Rahri Brahmin of Bengal) and of those Bengal groups that have followed the Kulin pattern. Hypergamy occurs among some Punjabi Brahmins (Rivers 1921, pp. 12–16). It is found only sporadically in the former Central Provinces (Russell and Hira Lal 1916, vol. 1, p. 28). Apart from the Nayar and other Kerala cases, hypergamy is not common in South India.

and precedence is commonly carried on within the jati-group, among the several alliances of its families. They usually do unite solidly against a clear threat to their status as a jati, but ordinarily much of their competitive energy goes into competition among themselves. In the Bengal village of Govindapur (Midnapore district), for example, Mahisyas are dominant, having 63 percent of the population and 66 percent of the land. Ralph Nicholas notes that village politics are mainly carried on between opposing groups of Mahisyas; "political affairs in the village, on the whole, are *not* caste affairs" (1965, p. 31).

In a survey of the data on village disputes Cohn writes that splits in the "dominant-caste" group are reported for most villages so dominated (1965, p. 92; references there cited include Lewis 1958, pp. 114–154; Majumdar 1958a, pp. 114–123; Harper and Harper 1959, pp. 461–462; Bailey 1957, pp. 194–195; Opler 1959a; Mayer 1960, pp. 126–127).

These divisions within a jati-group have often been called factions; the term emphasizes their competitive, contentious functions. In this vein Nicholas has analyzed the characteristics of factions. He defines factions as conflict groups. The conflict is political competition for public power; factions are not corporate, enduring groups; members are recruited by a leader and are drawn in for diverse reasons and principles (1965, pp. 44–46; 1966, pp. 52–57). This is a useful analysis, but very often a group that may well be called a faction is also a cooperative group whose members help each other in ways that are not just the upshot of mutual opposition to rivals. The term "resource group" has been proposed in order to emphasize this collaborative function (Sharma 1963). Typically also, such a group has a hierarchical structure of authority and an acknowledged scope of influence; the word "domain" stresses this aspect (Hitchcock 1959). The terms "alliance" or "allied families" include both competitive and cooperative activities and they are used in that inclusive sense here. Several alliances may join forces for a particular purpose and for a limited period to form a coalition.

Within a dominant jati-group then, there generally are several alliances, each one a set of families who interact more often and more intimately with each other than with others of the jati-group and who act collectively in the internal competition for status and power. The family is the fundamental component of any alliance. Brothers occasionally join different alliances, but they do not thereafter long remain together in one family. Lineage is almost always relevant in an alliance. Commonly all in a lineage are in the same alliance and an alliance is often composed of one or more lineages. If a man joins an alliance different from that of his lineage, it is evidence of his estrangement from his close agnates.

An example of how seriously this can be taken is given in Scarlett Epstein's study of Wangala village in Mysore. Only one man of the dominant jati there had associated himself with a faction (the term Dr. Epstein uses) other than that of his lineage. He was the eldest of five brothers, Tupa by name, who wanted to be an independent farmer. But when the ancestral land was partitioned at his instigation, his share came to so little that he could not start cultivating independently.

He had hoped to get some of the land that his father had purchased separately from the ancestral lands, but the father refused to part with any of it, as was his legal right. Tupa then sought support from the faction to which his lineage is strongly opposed. He did get some financial aid and struck up a strong friendship with one of the leaders of this opposing faction. His own lineage excommunicated him. It would have been his ritual duty, at his cousin's wedding, to fetch sanctified water from the pond to the bridegroom's household. Tupa was not even asked to attend the wedding. His place in the ritual was taken by his younger brother (Epstein 1962, p. 130).

This instance parallels the kind of redressive action that is used at other levels of caste organization. To be sure, Tupa was not put out of his jati, but he was cut off from his lineage. No one approved his switch, not even those with whom he allied himself, and "his dereliction prevents him from achieving the prestige that he sought." Lineage ties are thus usually important but not imperative in the formation and maintenance of an alliance. A split in lineage alignment is not approved, but it can occur when divisive pressures in a lineage builds up.

An alliance is generally made up of a few core families and several dependent, client families. The core families are rich and powerful enough to generate a field of influence and to withstand challenges from other families. Their leaders can marshal unwavering support within the alliance and, importantly, the stronger family heads have reached an understanding so that they do not undermine each other. If these strong families falter, that particular alliance is likely to disintegrate. They can loan bullocks or money to the dependent families, offer them fields to cultivate on a share-crop basis, or give them honorable employment. Their leaders can dicker with an intrusive policeman, negotiate a government favor, or fight a court case.

Together, the core and the client families form a unit of power and manpower. Leaders of such groups in Khalapur say of their allies, "They are the real friends of the family; they would come to our support whether we were in the right or in the wrong." Hitchcock comments that the implication here is that the real friends of the family would come to its support either with quarterstaffs in the event of a fight or as witnesses in a court case (1959, p. 29). And in a serious contest, the allied families can usually mobilize assistance from some of their retainers of lower jatis. They may also find support from others in the jati and village whose interests at the moment and in the context of the particular struggle happen to coincide with their own.

The makeup of an alliance is visible when the men come in from the fields. In villages of the north, they cluster in small groups to share a hookah. The smokers who congregate in the same men's house or sitting platform are apt to be of one alliance. In South India, the allies gather on the verandah of a big house or under a special tree, talking, resting, looking, playing cards, passing their leisure time together. They are partners in recreation as in council, in the banter of the evening as well as in the heat of a quarrel. Their women too are close to each other but women's interchange is more limited and less visible publicly than that of the men.

In a village near Jodhpur in Rajasthan, the powerful Jats are split into two rival camps. The principal unit of alliance affiliation is the lineage; few men break with their lineage mates to join rival groups. The reasons given for associating one's lineage with a particular alliance are mainly those of kinship, especially because of affinal ties (Bose and Malhotra 1964, pp. 312–316).

A survey of the alignment of 255 families in two West Bengal villages (where Mahisyas are dominant) showed that for 28 percent of the families the alignment was based on kinship ties with alliance leaders and for 27 percent on economic dependence on them. Residential proximity to alliance leaders accounted for 21 percent, caste reasons 14 percent, and protection from a powerful enemy 10 percent (Nicholas and Mukhopadhyay 1962, p. 32; Nicholas 1966 p. 56).

In sum, an alliance within a dominant jati-group is commonly a federation of lineages but may also contain a few adherents who have split with their own lineage. The alliance is cemented by the patronage and protection of the stronger families and by the tacit concord among the stronger family leaders. Amity within an alliance is reinforced daily by intimate, informal relations, and its strength is mobilized from time to time for status defense or aggrandizement.

An alliance is more flexible but less perduring than a kinship sodality. An alliance may endure for decades but it may also be ephemeral or may alter suddenly, precisely because no formal and durable principle of allegiance binds its members together. It is not usually denoted by any special term, or if it is, the term is apt to be pejorative, fastening on the contentious functions. Nor is it a unit of society clearly recognized by the villagers as are lineage and jati. Yet it is a group of considerable importance in many villages, not only within a dominant jati-group but also, as will be noted later, among families of different jatis.

The Bases of Alliance Strength

The strength of the whole alliance rests on its resources in wealth and in manpower, and on its access to wider sources of power, especially those of government. Wealth, as we have seen, is still primarily wealth in land. With enough land a family can be assured of its own livelihood and can provide for dependent families, no matter what the factional opposition may be. With the money from the yield of the land, it can buttress its power and prestige. But although land is a chief component of wealth, other sources of wealth—whether from trade, religion, raids, or government—have on occasion been mainstays of alliance power. Modern enterprises are increasingly important, their yield often being used for alliance purposes in quite the traditional ways.

One set of Patidar families in Gujarat has formed a flourishing corporation that provides petrol and oil used in irrigation pumps. Through the company they also operate tube wells and pumps and sell water to farmers. The rise of this alliance illustrates how dynamic families may now increase their wealth and in so doing expand and strengthen the cohort of their allies.

The company of these Patidar families buys land on the outskirts of a village area that is not irrigated or only little irrigated because the cultivators cannot afford a tube well and pump. These lands usually belong to the poorest Patidars who are therefore willing to sell, especially since they know that the rest of their poor land, if irrigation is available, may become much more fertile. After the pump is in operation, all the village farmers want water from it, but they may not be able to pay immediately or may fall behind in their payments and go into debt to the company. Although water rates are supposedly fixed there are times in the year when a villager must either pay heavily for water or see his crop ruined. So once the company is established in a village, which is to say once the alliance is thus established, it extends its business and also its power. "Customers are also clients. Upon this socio-economic base a web of power is spun and if the need arises, shall we say in some future business project, the company has widened the army of its allies" (Pocock 1957a, p. 303).

Wealth, aggressively wielded, begets more wealth and power. In Khalapur village (Saharanpur district, U.P.) for example, there are many more families of the dominant Rajputs than of the service and retainer jatis. So a family of potters, say, serves a number of Rajput families, some affluent, others poor. The wealthier Rajput families can provide more favors for their retainers, fodder for their buffaloes, wood for their fires, and generous amounts of food on ritual occasions "and by the same token, of course, are in a position to threaten them with deprivation." Hence a wealthier family, provided that its men are militant, gets better service than does a poorer family and the benefits spread to its allies. It reaps economic benefits especially at harvest time when there is a shortage of labor. The powerful families usually can get the field workers they need when other cultivators cannot and moreover they can get them at the time when they most need them (Hitchcock 1959, p. 28).

Manpower is another fundamental resource of alliance power. It permits the rallying of hands for peak labor demands and putting on a brave display at festive occasions. Even more, it provides the capacity to mobilize fighters if blows are to be exchanged. The use of force is a constant possibility, even if a latent one, in the opposition among alliances. Men who seek to maintain and improve their position in the village must stand ready to defend or attack with force. Members of an alliance usually see their own use of force as defensive, even when some of their people set fire to a hay-rick under cover of night, stealthily spoil an opponent's crop, or divert his cattle. In many villages, blows, beatings, and ambushes figure in the history of opposed alliances and in many, also, an occasional factional murder can be recalled. Even when the men of a dominant jati-group do not engage in violent acts themselves, they may not discourage their retainers or clients of other jatis from carrying out violence on their behalf.

Nonviolence has been an influential religious doctrine in certain places and contexts, especially as applied in Gandhian passive resistance. But in the context of most village struggles, violence is a stark fact of life that is partly controlled, partly exploited, partly manipulated, but always a potential factor with which a responsible man must reckon.

The third element of alliance strength is the ability to bring sources of influence from outside the village to bear in its behalf. Thus if the alliance leaders are eminent devotees of a religious sect, as is true of the Patidar magnates just mentioned, their fellow devotees will usually give them at least moral support in any dispute with others (Pocock 1957a, p. 302).

By far the most important source of power beyond the village is government. The holder of a village office, such as headman or revenue collector, gives advantage to his alliance. The villagers' presumption is that the higher officials with whom he deals will favor his cause and that of his alliance, or at least will give him the right of first hearing and the benefit of any doubt—provided that he has fortitude and skill to wield the tool of office. The ability to sway the police in one's favor is a prime asset in a dispute and is an immediate necessity in any serious outbreak of violence (cf. Epstein 1962, p. 289). In a protracted contest, the capacity to use the courts as a weapon and as a battleground of one's own choosing is an almost indispensable asset. Adversaries can be balked, their thrusts parried, their material resources exhausted through adept use of litigation. Many an alliance has prospered in its village because its leaders were skilled in the use of police and courts, and by the same token, many have fallen victim to these skills of their opponents.

An educated villager has considerable advantage in dealing with officials. He can fill out the myriad forms for himself; he can find out whom to see about what; he can speak to officials in terms they like to use; he can make his own way through bureaucratic procedure; and he feels less like an awkward bumpkin when facing officialdom. With government grants and aids becoming increasingly significant, those who aspire to respectable status usually find that they must have at least one educated member in their family or alliance in order to hold their own.

Education drains men from the village and the alliance. An educated son, if he has a secondary-school education—and all the more if he has a college degree—tends to make his career outside the village. But he is not entirely lost to his family and its alliance; whatever success he has redounds to their prestige, and he himself may remit cash and influence. A village family of wealth and power generally likes to have at least one son educated enough to deal with the officials and their papers. It is better if he lives in the household, but if he is employed in a place not too distant, he can still provide liaison services when they are urgently required.

An alliance is more apparent to an observer when its members strike out as a faction than when they interact as a cooperative group. When two powerful sides in a village are locked in struggle, each trying to defeat, forestall, and derogate the other, each trying to recruit as much help as possible in order to get its way, then villagers can scarcely avoid the subject of the contest, much as they may want to present a smooth face to a visitor. Even when the rivalries are less blatant, talk of them tends to come repeatedly to the attention of the observer after he has been in the village long enough to hear more than the *politesse* offered to a casual visitor from the city or from a foreign country. Cooperation among alliance associates goes on less obtrusively in such activities as the exchange of labor, the giving and taking of loans, and the choice of marriage partners.

Alliance Cohesion

The extent of collaboration within an alliance is illustrated in H. S. Dhillon's study of Haripura village, near Mandya in Mysore. This is a village of Vokkaligas (Okkaligas), the landowning cultivators who are dominant in many villages of this part of Mysore. Of one hundred thirty-five families in Haripura at the time of the study, one hundred twenty-six were Vokkaligas, sorted out into six alliances, which the author calls factions.

A main topic of Dhillon's inquiry was factional dispute, but he stresses the fact that hostility to other groups is seldom the only or even the major force that holds together the families. "The factors which bind members of a faction and enable it to function as a cohesive unit are the intensive kinship ties and the economic, social and ceremonial relations between faction members" (1955, p. 30). As elsewhere, members of a lineage generally belong to the same alliance and if some of them should line up with different alliances they seldom join sides that are bitterly antagonistic to each other. There are two strongly opposed sides in Haripura, each a coalition of two alliances. One of the six alliances is quite neutral, another is not fully engaged in the opposition between the main antagonists.

Dhillon looked closely at the amount of economic, social, and ceremonial interchange within an alliance as compared with that between alliances. He traced the major economic transactions (defined as sale or mortgage of land and major loans) within the village over a period of ten years. Of a total of 664 such transactions, 302 occurred within an alliance, only 30 were between members of two hostile alliances and in 22 of the latter the participants were linked by marriage ties. Most of the rest were between members of different but friendly alliances. In this total there were 22 mortgage transactions of which 12 were within an alliance; none were between members of opposed alliances. Of 55 land sales, 38 took place within an alliance and only one between members of two hostile alliances; in that one seemingly exceptional case, the men involved were married to full sisters. There were 205 intravillage loans in the list, of which 86 were negotiated within an alliance, only 10 between members of hostile alliances. The importance of affinal relations is reflected in the fact that of 222 loans between Haripura men and men of other villages, 80 percent were made with people of villages having numerous marital ties with Haripura. In sum, nearly half the major economic transactions were between members of the same alliance, and a great many in the other half were between members of friendly alliances (Dhillon 1955, pp. 59–65).

Ceremonial observances are also carried on mainly among alliance families although certain traditional obligations override factional cleavage. At a certain stage of a marriage celebration, for example, a Haripura family gives a feast for all in its division of the village. Those of a hostile faction who live in the same part of the village are invited and they do attend as tradition requires. However, they are not asked to help the hosts in the preparations, as with cooking. Such active participation is restricted to the host's alliance or those friendly to it.

Tradition further requires that on certain ritual occasions, in festivals for the village deity, all must participate together regardless of factional quarrels. This led to a stalemate in Haripura for several years. Animosities were so intense that the antagonists refused to let these rites be performed rather than join with their enemies in common worship. For several years the ceremonies were not held at all; then the hostilities were sufficiently mollified (though by no means erased) to allow the normal ceremonial cycle to be resumed (Dhillon 1955, pp. 67–75).

The most eloquent testimony of alliance cohesion lies in the arranging of marriages. Bride and groom may be of the same village, as is the South Indian custom, and 23 percent of the Haripura marriages studied (68 of 297 marriages) were intravillage matches. Among these 68 marriages, only 3 had been made between families that at the time had belonged to antagonistic factions and each of these three had resulted in a shift of alliance so that the families now linked through marriage were no longer separated by factional hostilities (Dhillon 1955, p. 74).

In other villages as well as in Haripura, cooperation among allied families has been noted in accounts that focus on factional dispute. Thus Lewis writes of the groups he calls factions among the dominant Jats of Rampur, near Delhi, "The small groups which we have delineated are held together primarily by cooperative economic, social, and ceremonial relations" (1958, p. 114). And in the hamlets of low-ranking cultivators in the Panchmahals highlands of Gujrat, Shah remarks that the faction (i.e., alliance) rather than the hamlet is the unit of all important social activities (1955b, p. 115).

A common feature of alliance affiliation is pressure for total commitment. Alliance leaders are usually not content only that a man have closer relations with the allied families than with others; they would prefer that he not have close relations with anyone outside the alliance. His social range in the village should be mainly within the alliance; his allegiance to and identification with others of the alliance should override any loyalties to those outside it. Above all, they insist that he must support the allies completely and unswervingly in a quarrel.

When hostilities between two strong alliances of a dominant jati-group are very intense, the opposing sides tend to dichotomize the village on the principle that a friend of my enemy is my enemy. Still, hostilities have a way of flaring and diminishing in intensity over the years, so that not everyone need be aligned on every village issue and there are often some neutral alliances and families in a given factional quarrel. Even within a closely knit alliance, a person generally can have some friendly relations with others who are not of his family's allies so long as they do not belong to an enemy alliance.

A villager need not take sides in every issue. In Haripura, for example, two men who are married to sisters but belong to contending sides, need not take active part in a quarrel between their respective alliances. But they must not give support to the other side and even this passivity is not tolerated if the fight is a very serious one. Similarly, a man may support either side of a quarrel where his own allies are not involved unless the leaders of his alliance take a firm partisan stand and then he must back them with full support (Dhillon 1955, pp. 51, 80).

A whole alliance may keep relatively neutral. One of the less wealthy alliances in Haripura does not carry on any active opposition at all, perhaps because its men do not feel strong enough to leap into the status fray. They do have some influence, however, and they are preferred on occasion by other alliances just because they are not active contestants. In Wangala village certain of the wealthier and prestigious lineages are relatively aloof from rivalries within the jati-group, perhaps because they feel secure and as yet unchallenged in their position. They too are influential in local affairs because they are not committed in advance and so can back either one side or another (Dhillon 1955, pp. 53, 59; Epstein 1962, p. 132).

Even strongly antagonistic alliances within a jati-group stop short of being full enemies. Their members are usually outwardly civil to each other when they must come together at public ceremonies, they all stand as one against danger to the jati-group from forces outside it. But beyond that, members of hostile alliances generally try to avoid each other. Sometimes their meetings are used for factional advantage. Hitchcock describes some leaders in Khalapur who wage factional struggle as a kind of game. They continually engage each other in trials of strength, which involve various forms of chicanery but not violence. Even though one of them may just have come from the police station where he tried to have his opponent recorded as a dangerous and criminal character, the two men continue to meet one another, smoke the hookah, and talk. "Needless to say the verbal exchange is often full of indirect and humorous aggression" (Hitchcock n.d., MS. p. 40).

More often there is precious little humor in the situation and the opponents do not go beyond minimal public civility. They stay away from each other as much as possible. In the Delhi State village of Rampur they will not attend each other's ceremonies, will not visit each other's homes, and do not smoke the hookah together except when visiting the home of a neutral villager. They can be "counted upon to marshal vicious gossip about rivals" in council meetings. While direct attack is rare, indirect attack is highly developed (Lewis 1958, p. 116). In a Rajasthan village members of the rival alliances among the dominant Jats do not attend each other's weddings nor do they participate together in other domestic, clan, or village ceremonies (Bose and Malhotra 1964, pp. 319–320).

In Haripura, members of opposed alliances among Vokkaligas do not usually visit each other's houses and they normally avoid speaking to each other. As we have seen they do not intermarry even though they could do so as jati fellows. The factions in Haripura are described as not very tightly knit and interfactional relations are not so strong or so sharply defined as in Rampur, but they are sharp enough to keep opponents apart in all sorts of social relations they might otherwise have, from casual conversations to formal betrothals (Dhillon 1955, pp. 31–32).

In Wangala also, Epstein describes factions as not rigidly opposed and as coming into play only in certain situations. Wangala, like Haripura, is in Mandya district of Mysore State, and in both places Vokkaligas are dominant. At the time of Epstein's study, members of opposing groups mixed freely in everyday relations and, except for a few leading members who never spoke to each other, the others would sit together at night and chat. Yet the situations where members of hostile alliances avoided each other were not insignificant. They did not celebrate festivals and life-cycle rites together. At one wedding, children of a rival alliance swarmed around when a particular delicacy was being served "but their elders insisted that they stay away and impressed on them the deep enmity that existed between the factions." Moreover, there had been no intermarriage between members of the opposed sides for ten years (Epstein 1962, pp. 129–136).

Thus there is a tendency for hostile alliances within a jati-group to treat each other in certain respects almost as different jatis. Those on one side observe a measure of social avoidance toward the other, they restrict mutual participation in ceremonies, they do not arrange marriages with adherents of the other alliance. All this takes place within the same jati, in which the ritual criteria for group separation are not relevant. Because the contests between jatis have often been waged for symbolic prerogatives, such as the right to wear the sacred thread, the ritual symbols overshadowed and masked what was essentially a struggle for general power in the village. This mask does not apply to the oppositions within a jati-group; there the political power struggle, without ritual trappings, is plain to see.

CHAPTER 15

Opposition and Cohesion within the Jati-group

What then is the opposition about? Why are there quarrels between alliances within the same jati-group? The manifest reasons are easily ascertained. There is a stock alliterative answer in Hindi which applies to conflict among men of different jatis as well as to our present concern with conflict among jati fellows. The causes of quarrels are said to be *Zamin, Zar, Zanani*—land, wealth, and women. Many fights do indeed spring from these sources of friction.

Land is the one main productive resource, scarce and costly. The possession of land gives independence and openings to power. Possession of land is schemed for, contrived, wangled, and disputed. Other kinds of wealth, like cattle or houses, are also sensitive matters, so that even a slight, perhaps an unintentional, infringement on a man's herd or house is likely to raise his hackles. Women are considered to be both submissive to and more highly sexed than men; the men, especially among the dominant jatis of the North, are supposed to be both personally venturesome and puritanically zealous of their women's honor. So Zanani really is a fertile source of trouble among men and alliances.

The old saying is borne out statistically in a tabulation of the causes of major quarrels over a period of forty-five years among the Vokkaligas of Haripura village. This count shows that land, women, and the inheritance of wealth were the leading causes. "Major" quarrels are defined by Dhillon as those fought between alliances and, we may infer, long and bitterly contested. Six of these major controversies were about land, five about illicit sex relations, five about inheritance. There were also four about procedure in festivals and three about adoptions. In "minor quarrels" land and inheritance were each involved in nine controversies; three were about illicit sex relations; three were over adoptions; and one was about festival observance (1955, p. 80).

The incidents that precipitate great contests in a village can be quite trivial in themselves—an argument about a scrap of land, a disagreement about minor details of a ceremony, a question of how a cow could have strayed into a standing crop. Such small and restricted disputes can blow up into great, bitter fights because, for one reason, the allies of the two immediate antagonists identify thoroughly with their respective partisan. So the one who wins brings victory to his whole alliance and the one who loses drags his whole coterie into defeat. Moreover, defeat even in a trivial matter can be taken to mean total submission, and the victory thus may be interpreted by the victors as a sweeping ascendency of their alliance. Such drastic, total interpretation conforms to the basic concept that most social action is hierarchically arranged. Ranked status is imputed to many contexts, and superior rank implies general, as well as specific, dominance over those of lower status.

Challenges and Realignments

Not every small village dispute escalates into a factional conflict. But when the people of two alliances are already poised as challengers and challenged, incidents that might otherwise sputter and fade become reasons for great quarrels. Such confrontations within a dominant jati-group recur because villagers usually accept subordination to men close in status only provisionally—even token subordination to others of the same jati. So families of lower status in a jati-group characteristically try for a higher as soon as their strength permits; those of higher rank oppose such attempts so long as their strength avails. Within a jati-group as among jatis, a family's gain in secular resources is often deployed for status rise. As Pocock comments in contrasting Paridars in Gujarat with those who settled in East Africa, "In Gujarat certainly wealth and power are important but there it is wealth and power for the purpose of standing in a particular system where, in a sense, it is status that makes life worth living" (1957a, p. 303).

As a family or a set of families gather resources, they first make symbolic assertions about themselves that do not directly threaten any specific group and so can scarcely become the subjects of argument. Such a crescive family among the Rajputs of Khalapur builds better houses, acquires showy bullocks (not necessarily efficient ones for farming), and gets fine clothes and jewelry. Such families now keep their sons in school. Because they are lavish in hospitality, more and more men come to spend time with them in their men's house. And they arrange good marriages and stage rich weddings for their children. Having prepared their base of power and prestige they can then challenge another alliance in local arguments, in court trials, or in elections. "In such quarrels the end sought is not so much material benefit—a few square feet of property, for instance—as the immaterial gains deriving from a demonstration of power which is relatively greater than one's rival" (Minturn and Hitchcock 1963, p. 256).

The more direct challenges are often about ritual prerogatives and village offices. These are usually in the possession of the lineage or alliance that was formerly supreme in the village. When others of the jati-group gain strength, they resent the disproportion between their economic and their ritual status. There are, for example, two prospering lineages of the dominant jati in Wangala whose men are relatively recent arrivals in the village and so do not hold any office in the traditional rites. "We find here an imbalance between economic, political and ritual status in the village and since ritual status is regarded as the ultimate criterion of social status, the 'progressive' faction is led continuously to bring its ritual status into line with its economic dominance." Whenever council meetings are held to discuss plans for a forthcoming ceremony, the leaders of the "progressives" try to get some formal place for their own lineages. The entrenched lineages resist this, all the more sharply because their own secular power has declined (Epstein 1962, p. 132).

In like manner, an imbalance of power and status among families within an alliance tends to disrupt previous relations. We have noted that an alliance characteristically includes core families and dependent families. But in time families may change in power. A talented, ambitious, driving man may come up in a dependent family and lineage. If he is additionally favored by the lottery of biology so that he inherits considerable land as sole son or survivor and yet has enough kinsmen to afford a firm base of support, he may gain quite rapidly in power.

Leaders of the core families do not joyously welcome a previous dependent as an alliance leader. Thus in Haripura village "the leading families within a faction do not tolerate any rise in the economic status of families which lie at its lower rungs and which depend on them for many of their needs" (Dhillon 1955, p. 32). These leaders treat a rising dependent in much the same way as lineage fellows or separated brothers treat each other. They are bound to help him when he is in clear and present danger and when his defeat would impair their interests, but when his difficulties do not threaten them they can be quite aloof.

The leaders who are expected to maintain unity in the alliance are not, however, "supposed to sacrifice their vested interests for other members of the faction." Thus when a man is involved in serious litigation, his alliance characteristically gives him moral encouragement, physical security, help in raising loans, and aid in marshaling court evidence. But if he loses the case and is financially ruined, they usually make no special effort to help him regain his previous economic position, as by giving him loans without charging interest (Dhillon 1955, pp. 32–33). The top families are generally interested in keeping up the power and ritual level of the whole alliance but otherwise they are more concerned with keeping their position in the alliance as it exists, knowing that a dependent family may well try to challenge their leadership if it can.

The cleavage of an alliance, as of a joint family, tends to be hastened if there is considerable increase in its numbers. Among the Mala and Madiga, the main Harijan jatis of Andhra, it has been noted that a hamlet of about fifty houses will split into two sets of allied families because, for one reason, a man celebrating a marriage cannot feed all in so large a hamlet (Reddy 1952, p. 258). Though our previous examples have mainly been of dominant, landowning jati-groups, Harijans also sort themselves into separate alliances of families within their segregated hamlets. There may be a certain critical range of size for an alliance.[1] Less than a certain number of families will be too few for the requisite self-sufficiency and more than a certain number will make it difficult to keep the alliance intact.

To answer the question at the beginning of this chapter, recurrent conflicts within a jati-group, especially a large and dominant one, stem from the common quest for wealth and power. Like so many village people in the world, villagers in India are apt to see the supply of good things as limited and not susceptible of growth or expansion (cf. Foster 1965, 1966). Hence if one man gets more, another must get less. To be more, to get more, to possess more, one must contend always with others, even with one's jati fellows and neighbors. Underlying these contests is the pervasive drive for status that sharpens and accelerates competition not only in the economic arena but also

[1] In a survey of six U.P. villages, 175 "factions" were counted among 3,125 households. The average number of households in a faction was thus 17.8; the largest faction had 43 or 44 households (Singh 1961, p. 9).

in many other contexts. Status competition may be waged within a jati-group at the bottom of the social hierarchy as well as at the top, as witness the example of the Malas and Madigas of Andhra, but the alliance relations within dominant jati-groups are often politically central in their villages.

Alliances are formed because a man and his family need close interchange with others beyond the lineage. A family must have allies if it is to succeed at all in status competition; a strong family needs dependents, a weaker one needs a protector. Lineage bonds alone are usually insufficient for these purposes. The number of a man's agnatic allies is generally too small for his needs, even though there is some flexibility in amassing such allies. Moreover, lineage relationships cannot be assumed or abandoned as readily as political manipulation may require. Yet an alliance can be quite a stable group, lasting over years, sometimes decades; usually some of its members are bound together by lineage ties and others by mutual interest, mutual support, and continued interchange. But the very force of status competition and of protector-dependent relation that helps cement an alliance also works in time to disrupt it. As talents and resources are reshuffled, alliances split. New contestants and allies take the place of the former ones; new alignments and new arguments arise.

Alliance Development and Variations in Alliance Formation

The process of alliance combination and recombination, which on the village ground seems to be the result of merely local forces and personal motives, is actually shaped by large demographic, economic, and political movements. Thus the steady increase in population since the 1920s may well have unsettled previous alignments in many villages, making some of the former alliances too large to be viable. The introduction of irrigation, cash crops and other new sources of income has permitted ambitious and able men to become much more prosperous than their fathers were, and this also makes for rearrangement of allies. Land reform legislation and the electoral franchise have contributed to the reallocation of resources and so of alliance loyalties.

Some broad regularities in the history of alliances can be seen in three widely separated villages for which we have historical information. One is Radhanagar, a village in northern Bihar where a Brahmin jati is dominant; Brahmin families own 90 percent of the land though they are only 28 percent of the population. Another is Rampur in Delhi State where Jats are 60 percent of the population and own practically all the land. The third is Haripura, south of Bangalore, where the Vokkaligas are some 95 percent of the inhabitants and own all the land. The Jats of Rampur have much the same rank as do the Vokkaligas of Haripura, both are Sudras in the varna scheme and both brook no infringement on their sovereign status within their villages.

The historical record in all three villages begins with a dual division within the dominant jati-group in the late nineteenth century. Factional conflict existed, changes in alignment of families all occurred within a two-party frame. Then came a period of intensified conflict; there was a good deal of shifting about, and in recent years new alliances have emerged in addition to the original two.

In Radhanagar the old moiety arrangement, with two Brahmin alliances in contention, lasted until 1937. Then the Brahmin opponents were forced to unite against a challenge, inspired by the Kisan political movement, from the other jatis and from a few dissident Brahmins. The traditional overlords finally won this contest through a court case in 1942 but the dual alignment was disrupted. There followed a period of unstable alignments. By 1959 there seemed to be some stabilizing of factional alignments with a return to two or three alliances (Roy 1963).

In Rampur and Haripura the dual division was altered at about the same time; 1915 is the date given for the change in Rampur, 1919 in Haripura. In both places there followed several years of intense conflict and jockeying, after which each jati-group settled down to a number of new alliances. The realignment took place about 1939 in Rampur, about 1942 in Haripura (Lewis 1958, pp. 142–147; Dhillon 1955, pp. 82–94). The development suggested by these three case histories—from dual division through a period of intensified conflict and shifting alliances to fairly stabilized multiple alliances—may have wider application and should be tested when more evidence is available (cf. Cohn 1965, pp. 97–98).

The present evidence does indicate certain main variations in the nature of alliances within the jati-group. One variation is between North and South India, another between villagers who have been more affected by newer, urban influences and those less affected by them. The differences in alliance functions between Rampur in North India and Haripura in South India are noted by H. S. Dhillon, who was in a particularly good position to make the comparison because he had participated in the study of Rampur and then went south to conduct the study of factions in Haripura.

Dhillon observed that the factions in Rampur are more cohesive units than in Haripura and the hostilities between them are stronger and more sharply defined. The reasons are rooted in the differences between Northern and Southern social structure and particularly in affinal relations. In the South a woman maintains closer relations with her natal family after her marriage than she is able to do in the North and, since the men of her natal family are not total inferiors to her husband's family as they are in the North, they are more likely to take some part in her husband's affairs. A man's feminal kindred in Haripura do intercede in his relations with his brothers and with his lineage mates whereas in Rampur "such cognate relations are expected to have absolutely nothing to do with the affairs of a family" (Dhillon 1955, p. 77).

In Haripura hostilities are considerably reduced in duration and in vehemence, because adversaries usually have feminal relatives in common and these—true to the welfare functions of feminal kinsmen—often succeed in pacifying the angry ones. Moreover, Haripura women can take the initiative in restoring friendship within an alliance, while in Rampur women cannot take so active a part. Another difference is that in the southern village more disputes occur over festivals, perhaps indicating a greater weighting of religious and ritual matters.

The diminished bite of hostilities in Haripura decreases the number of coalitions and enmities across villages, as compared with the situation in Rampur (Dhillon 1955, pp. 32, 77–82). But even though alliance opposition in Haripura is less protracted and pervasive, alliance loyalties are still quite durable. Dhillon writes that although most quarrels within a faction are settled in the course of time, "as many as 12 cases of shifts from one faction to another as a result of these quarrels were noticed during the period of the last 60 years" (1955, p. 78). Twelve in sixty years is not very many.

Sometimes villagers are caught between loyalty to their agnates and concern for their feminal kin. Dhillon learned of five such dilemmas in Haripura, in four of which the families involved remained relatively neutral; in council meetings they showed preference for their lineage allies but in private they helped their feminal kin with loans and tried discreetly to recruit support for them in other villages. This was a reasonable compromise in view of the cultural norms: agnates form more of a corporate, public body; feminal kin are more concerned with private, personal matters. In the fifth case, the man openly helped his sister's husband as against his own agnates and he was forced out of his alliance. He did not go over to its chief opponents but joined another alliance whose members were nevertheless favorable to the side of his sister's husband (Dhillon 1955, p. 79). Although alliance cohesion is less strong and alliance hostilities are less bitter in the southern village than in the northern one, among the Vokkaligas of Haripura a man's alliance still holds his strong allegiance and gives him strong support.

A second variation in alliance formation occurs in South India. Brahmins there are less inclined to form stable, cohesive alliances than are villagers of other South Indian jatis. In North India, Brahmins do maintain staunch alliances, as we have seen from the example of Radhanagar in Bihar. But in the South, Brahmins tend to be more atomistic, and opposition among them is more often between strong individuals than between alliances.

This is exemplified among the Havik Brahmins, overlords in Totagadde village of northwestern Mysore. Harper observes that a Havik is likely to have very close relations with one or two other men of his jati-group and hostile relations with perhaps one or two. Such enmities are common and they are commonly long continued, but they are more like feuds between two individuals than factional struggles between two sides. In feud as in faction, the tactics can be rough. Though physical violence is not used by the opponents themselves, each may formally accuse the other of breaking the law and may try sorcery against him. These feuds arise between men of comparable status, in the usual focus of rivalry between two men (or two alliances or two jatis) who are close in rank within the local hierarchy. One of these feuds between two prominent men verges on factional alignment.

Each leader has some men who support him, but most Haviks are not aligned with either group and not all the close friends of each leader give him factional support. For the most part, quarrels among Haviks are between individuals; a man's kinsmen and friends do not feel bound to support him against his opponent (Harper and Harper 1959, pp. 460–463).

This social atomism arises from each man's strong sense of his independence and equality. Men have authority over other men of this jati only as their seniors in a joint family that owns property. In all other situations, Haviks fiercely cherish their equality with all other Havik men. "A junior male in one property-owning group is the equal of the senior male in any other." Alliances cannot solidify when no man is willing to be a follower or dependent (Harper 1963, p. 165).

The same individualism characterizes the dominant Brahmins of Kumbapettai village in Tanjore district. There also, quarrels are more often between individuals and families than between alliances. The men of a lineage may unite against another lineage, perhaps to secure some prerogative, "but in a short time, affinal and matrilateral ties between their members serve to mitigate the group-conflict" (Gough 1960, p. 37). As Gough analyzes the values of these Brahmins and the child-rearing practices that inculcate the values, it appears that their most prized personal relationship is a dyadic one, held with someone much senior in age and much superior in status. They do not attach great importance to solidarity among peers, as we have noted before, even though fraternal concord is extolled as a formal ideal. They do not maintain powerful leaders because so few Brahmins are willing to be in any way subordinate to another Brahmin. Therefore they do not display the kind of alliance cohesion that non-Brahmins do.

A third variation in the nature of alliances comes about because some villagers have adopted new status symbols and procedures that are not part of the traditional game of status rivalry. This is exemplified in Epstein's contrast between Wangala, where the traditional oppositions are carried on in traditional ways, and Dalena where they are not. Both these Mysore villages are chiefly populated and dominated by Vokkaligas.

Wangala, as has been noted before, has prospered through the advent of irrigation and sugarcane cultivation. Its prosperity was fostered by the managers of the local sugarcane factory, who laid down the rules and provided the main requirements for cane production; all that the Wangala farmers had to do was follow instructions, work hard, and reap a rich harvest. They did not have to venture abroad, choose among economic alternatives, or make contacts in town and government. Hence their way of life has developed into a prosperity-intensified version of what it was before.

The two principal alliances compete vigorously for symbols of ritual status, the "progressives" trying to redress the balance between their new power and lack of ritual office, the "conservatives" trying to prevent them from doing so by keeping the ritual offices in their own possession. In their heated opposition, both sides implicitly agree on what things are worth fighting for. The challenging alliance does not want to change the traditional ritual pattern but only to secure a better status position in it for its own people (Epstein 1962, pp. 129–137).

The irrigation canals stopped short of Dalena but a number of its men have prospered because of their own vigorous efforts. They have secured land and jobs outside the village and have established contacts in the nearest town. Here, also, the chief opposition is between "progressives" and "conservatives," and the conflict affects all village issues and every dispute. The leaders of the "progressives" are three enterprising men who have close knowledge of town manners and government officials. These innovators are more concerned with status symbols in the political and social spheres beyond the village, where their economic interests are now vested, than in the traditional signs of prestige within the village. They are not much interested in carrying on village rituals and so many of the traditional ceremonies are no longer performed at all in Dalena.

In Wangala, the clashing sides agree so thoroughly on the importance of village ceremonies that a duplicate set is performed because of factional disagreement. In Dalena even the "conservatives" do not fully carry on the traditional ceremonial cycle. In Wangala, all the villagers close ranks to face a common danger, as from drought or disease, but in Dalena there are now fewer threats that the villagers see as a common danger to be met by common defense. It is not at all that any leader in Dalena has lost interest in the status quest; it is only that some have shifted their sights from the traditional symbols of status to the new array in the wider social field of district and state (Epstein 1962, pp. 284–290). Although Dalena social life has been affected by this shift, it has not been disrupted by it. In some places, however, this shift has been quite disruptive because while the new standards of status have not yet been fully assimilated, their impact has undermined the worth of the traditional patterns.

Such an inchoate state of village affairs prevailed in Namhalli, a village near Bangalore, when Alan Beals observed it in 1952–1953 (Siegel and Beals 1960a, 1960b). Namhalli is not dominated by one jati-group, but there was discord within each of the main jati-groups of the village. Pervasive factionalism, as Beals calls it, prevailed. Few cooperative activities of any kind for the benefit of the village as a whole were carried on. All agreed that certain things badly needed doing; the village roads should be improved, irrigation facilities maintained, ceremonials and dramas conducted, government subsidies obtained. But all efforts to accomplish such projects failed.

The villagers would not and could not cooperate because they so mistrusted each other, and they nourished past enmities so zealously that even an attempt to settle a dispute was usually used as a way to resume waging an earlier dispute. The traditional ties of allegiance did not bind people together as they formerly had—it was not unusual to find brother ranged against brother in a public argument—and the traditional ways of healing social differences foundered. Villagers changed sides frequently. The victory of one faction over another generally accomplished nothing more than the temporary humiliation of those who were defeated. "Victory was usually followed by betrayal and renewal of hostilities along new alignments" (Siegel and Beals 1900a, p. 397; Beals 1959, p. 433). A main reason for this disorganization, according to the authors, was an excessive degree of internal strain, uncertainty and conflict, about appropriate forms of behavior in situations that required cooperation or mediation.

When Beals returned in 1960 to have another look at Namhalli, he found a different state of village affairs (1962, pp. 92–97). In these few years, the strain had been mitigated, and the pervasive factionalism was quite abated. Villagers cooperated effectively for the common good. This happier condition came about mainly because a number of the villagers had secured jobs in the city, many of them in one of the largest of the new factories. They not only learned new skills, they also learned about new ways of organizing the village. The new financial technique of the "chit-fund" proved an effective way of launching both personal and community enterprises. It provides a farmer with capital for improved seed and fertilizer, and it is also used as a way of raising money for such enterprises as a bus trip for school children or the rebuilding of a village temple.

The people of Namhalli have come to have much easier relations with government officials than they did before. Membership in a labor union has given some of the villagers a sense of access to political power. Formerly they were wary of police and eager to keep them away from the village and out of village conflicts. It was not until 1959 that a complaint was lodged with the police by a Namhalli villager about the acts of neighbors. When a policeman visits now, the leaders chat with him as with an old friend. "If he threatened anyone or tried to collect bribes, he would be reported, and officials of the factory and the labor union would complain to the higher ranking police officials" (Beals 1962, p. 95).

The traditional way of life in Namhalli has by no means been abandoned but has been "reworked, reformulated, and enriched." Jati and jati-group are still important in matters of family, home, and religion, but are of less account now in livelihood. All social relations in the village are much more stable than they were in the period of pervasive factionalism. The Namhalli example illustrates a development from general disruption toward integration and also shows that urban influences can make for either condition, depending on how and to what purpose the urban forces are channeled.

Forces for Jati-group Cohesion

Despite the common cleavages within jati-groups and the major variations among them, the members of a jati-group do maintain a unity and present themselves as a unit for certain important purposes. Their common ritual status provides a main cohesive force. All in the jati-group share a common dependence on other jatis for certain services. In that sense they must deal together with the people of the other jatis in the village and its vicinity. Their village neighbors, in turn, deal with all in a jati (and often of several jatis) as though they are all equal members of a ritually defined unit.

The rites performed by the members of a jati-group also foster their solidarity. Certain rites are explicitly intended to transcend secular antagonisms. Funeral rites are commonly so interpreted; antagonists will often participate together in the mourning rites of a lineage-mate or a jati-fellow. Certain jati festivals are quite manifestly rites of consolidation and affirmation in which enmities are formally laid aside.

Both funerals and festivals express a kind of defensive unity—of society against man's biological fallibility in funerals, of society vis-à-vis the supernatural powers in festivals. Such observances reaffirm the solidarity of the jati as a coherent and supportive entity. At a funeral, for example, the lineage fellows and the closer feminal kin of the dead person attend to carry out the general functions of mortuary rites (of. Mandelbaum 1954b, 1959b). Commonly also at least one representative of every lineage or family of the jati-group must attend the funeral of a member to symbolize the sharing of the whole jati in the family's grief and the support of all in re-establishing normal social relations. Such consolidating mechanisms do not always work, of course, but many villagers still have the feeling that they should (of. Dhillon 1955, pp. 69, 71, 87).

Conflict within the jati-group is not something paraded before an outsider. Others of the jati are not keen to marry their daughters into a jati-group that is a hot battlefield, just as they do not like to send daughters into a squabbling family. Further, a smoothly co-operative jati-group is a matter of pride and prestige while a plainly discordant one is not. So although it may not take long for a visitor to discover that there are real rifts in the ideal of jati solidarity, it is not something he can usually find out through the first question. Ralph Nicholas has written that it can be taken as a general principle for the parts of Bengal where he has worked that the statement "there are no factions (*dal*) in our village" means exactly the obverse. Furthermore, it is likely that those who make this statement are themselves intimately involved in the factions (Nicholas 1962, pp. 172–173).

Yet the unity of the jati-group is not merely a cosmetic cliché; it can be a vital reality under certain circumstances. Characteristically, when the people of a higher jati feel their status threatened by a lower or when those of a lower feel that their just rights are being axed by a higher, then internal conflict is summarily dropped and all stand as one against the menace. This immediate, united defense takes place in other social echelons, notably in the whole village when all in it feel threatened together, and also in a whole jati; but the tightening of defense is more common in a jati-group, since most challenges to status are laid down on the local ground. Thus when the lower jatis of Radhanagar in Bihar challenged the political dominance of the local Brahmins, the two Brahmin sides at once gave up their long and bitter enmity, joined together to fight a protracted court case and won (Roy 1963). In Senapur in eastern U.P., the ruling Thakurs several times dropped their factional opposition in order to suppress the leatherworkers' attempt to improve their social position (Cohn 1955, pp. 68–72).

In a Kota village of the Nilgiri Hills of South India, I found active hatred between the Kota reformers and conservatives. But when a leading light of the reform party was beaten up by men of a stronger jati because of his reformist ways, all his fellow villagers, the die-hard conservatives among them, rose up together to claim, and get, reparations from the jati of the assailants (Mandelbaum 1960).

An episode in Wangala illustrates the unified response of a dominant jati-group against an assertive gesture by a lower group. In dramas staged by the Harijans of the village, the actor in the role of king traditionally does not sit on a prop throne but squats, in order that his head may not be higher than those of the people of higher jati in the audience. When their drama company let it be known that in a forthcoming production a stage throne would be used, there was a strong reaction. All the Vokkaligas stopped employing Harijan laborers. Eventually the Harijan headman sued for peace and his people had to pay a fine. The assertion and its purpose were defeated, at least for the time (Epstein 1962, pp. 183–189).

Not every altercation between jatis galvanizes jati-group unity. In Rampur, for example, the several Jat factions united when the Chamars first refused to pay the traditional house tax. But some years later when Chamars disputed the ownership of a plot of land with one of the Jat leaders, two of the Jat alliances openly supported the Chamars in the court case (Lewis 1958, pp. 74, 141). What rallies a jati-group at one period and under certain circumstances may not do so at others. But at any juncture there will usually be some kind of act that can impel members of a jati-group to drop internal quarrels, if only temporarily, and react together in joint defense.

Conflict within a jati-group is thus limited, but it is not formally channeled. Conflict is as inherent as is cooperation in a large, dominant jati-group, but while the cooperative functions of lineage and alliance groups are clearly and formally expressed in ritual, the competitive functions are not formally recognized or plainly avowed. This is one reason factional infighting so frequently seems to an outsider to be an anarchic hurly-burly. There are few, if any, occasions when latent conflicts between groups can legitimately be crystallized and expressed, as in competition in ritual games or in regular political engagements. The government law courts do serve on occasion as a means of resolving conflict but in general they have been used by villagers more to wage conflicts than to settle them.

An Indian anthropologist once remarked to F. G. Bailey that villagers are not in a face-to-face community; the more typical posture is back-to-back (Bailey 1965, p. 6). Each side in a major village dispute may attract some supporters who join in not because of kinship or alliance loyalty, but to get even for a loss in a previous and often quite unrelated tussle (of. Atal 1963). Coalitions of alliances are quickly made and may be just as quickly unmade. A few men may hover around the edge of any major quarrel seeking whatever may be to their own gain. Free-lance advisers, usually claiming connections to higher powers, are ready to give help for the justice of the cause and for some kind of fee.

The contestants operate according to a game theory directed toward the same goal as that involved in making marriage alliances; that is, higher status in the local hierarchy. But while in the making of marriages all are supposed to gain, in the exercise of internal jati-group conflict someone must lose if anyone is to win. In this winning and losing many are passionately involved. Even those men who stand apart from the contests usually follow them with enormous interest. For the principals, it is a most earnest game, sometimes acted out in dead earnest.

Though these struggles are seen by villagers as disruptive of the harmony that should prevail among jati brethren, they are not entirely disruptive for the jati-group. In the contests, a man of ability can gain covered laurels; through them he can reaffirm the values of the jati. By means of such contests, the "moving oligarchy" of a dominant jati-group is maintained, with the jati remaining paramount in the village but with successive actors and alliances coming into control (of. Hitchcock n.d., MS., pp. 51–55; Cohn 1965, p. 97).

In sum, the jati-group is a fundamental unit of village society, a category of attribution, a field for cooperation, and sometimes a unit of group action. Within a small jati-group, numbering only a few families, relations among the families are not much different from those within a lineage. But when a jati-group is larger, with perhaps a score or more families, alliance formation often begins to appear. And when a jati-group is both large and dominant in the village, then the relations among its alliances take on some of the features of relations among jatis, except that ritual criteria are not entailed. Thus there can be great status rivalry among alliances, avoidance of one by the other, totality of commitment to one's own group, and even the casting out of a transgressor. And this is done under the cover of an ideology that disparages competition within a jati much as the popular varna theory of caste discounts competition among jatis. Though the alliances of a dominant jati-group may be embattled against each other, together they control the village in the sense that they respond together to a challenge from villagers of other jatis.

Alliance rivalries, wide disparities of wealth and prestige, can occur within jati-groups at every level of village society. At every level also the families of a jati-group feel bound together by their common rites and traditions, their common ritual standards, their mutual economic interests and treatment by others. They acknowledge their cohesion and have agents and agencies for maintaining it.

CHAPTER 16

Maintaining the Jati: Leaders and Panchayats

A jati does not just hang together like the parts of a cat, it must be actively maintained. To do so, men assume certain roles and support certain agencies. Central to jati maintenance are the leadership roles and panchayat patterns that are used at every level from family and lineage to regional council. These roles and patterns are highly formalized in some jatis, as in those whose headmen are ceremoniously invested with the office and are given distinctive insignia and regular duties (of. Blunt 1931, pp. 107–109). In other jatis there may be no formal headmen at all and such jati organization that exists may be quite informal. Organization need not be ineffective because it is informal; both formal and informal organizations have their respective advantages for social maintenance, as will be noted again below, and one task for future research on the subject is to sort out the conditions favorable for each in the Indian context.

The modern trend is for the traditional jati organization to become less formal and for the newer caste associations to become more formalized, with set parliamentary procedures and prescribed office bearers. Yet in many villages the traditional jati leaders and councils are still powerful means of jati maintenance. One anthropologist, S. C. Dube, was impressed with the power and skill of a jati-group headman in the Andhra village of Shamirpet whose handling of a recalcitrant young man Dube witnessed.

"You bastard," this headman stormed at one point, "You seem to have developed great notions about yourself." He went on to rake the offender in terms and for reasons noted later, ending with "If you have the cheek to answer me back I shall make life impossible for you in the village. You have a long tongue, but if you wag it against us we shall pull it" (Dube 1955b, p. 204).

Leaders: Tasks and Motives

Both rough and smooth methods are needed for effective leadership at all jati levels. In a family, the senior man is expected to see to it that family quarrels do not get out of hand, that family members behave properly, that the family gives the appearance of a reasonably harmonious household. Among the senior men in a lineage, there is commonly at least one who tries to keep the whole lineage on an even keel, who attempts to calm stormy encounters and is alert to signs of impending trouble. Such lineage leaders warn a wayward youth or admonish a negligent father or cajole an embittered woman or ridicule an idle kinsman. They encourage lineage fellows to help gather in a sick kinsman's crop; they collect for lineage festivals; they take the complaint of an aggrieved kinsman before a council. The more influential of the lineage chiefs do the same for their alliance or for the jati-group as a whole.

At each level the leaders or elders assume the maintenance functions of trying to avert difficulties within their group and of containing and settling disputes when they break out. They also see to it that the normal activities of the group are properly performed. If a lineage has to help stage a wedding or a funeral, the lineage leader commonly is in charge of the arrangements or finds someone who will take charge. If the jati-group is responsible for a special part in a village festival, its leader oversees the performance of that part. He is asked to help supervise certain critical acts in a ceremony; when a large sum of money is handed over in a marriage, for example, it is given first to respected elders who count it aloud, "thus making the transaction public and stamping it with the seal of their authority" (Minturn and Hitchcock 1963, p. 252).

Another function is that of protecting and defending the group's interests against outside encroachments. A lineage elder is expected to be mindful of his lineage's prerogatives and to ward off any usurpation from other lineages. An alliance leader guards his supporters from the sniping of opponents. The headman of a jati-group similarly protects the rights of all the group and comes to the defense of anyone in it who may be threatened or abused.

Yet another function expected of a leader or elder is to act as a link between his group and larger social echelons. Thus the more influential men speak for their lineage in a jati-group council. The eminent men of the jati-group represent it in the councils of village and jati. They also represent their groups before the highest echelon of all, the supernatural. The head of a family performs homage to the ancestors on behalf of all the family; an elder of the lineage leads in the rites for the lineage deities and clan rites in those jatis that have them. When a feast is given in expiation for ritual trespass, the leaders partake first, initiating the restoration of the offender.

These functions are intended to maintain and preserve the several groups, not to alter them. Leaders are not expected to be innovators, except when a change in practice will help raise jati status—and then the innovation is generally represented as a return to the jati's ancient custom. A leader is not usually able to commit his group to a new activity or decision. His capacity as representative is more to protect the group's interests and to communicate group sentiments than to launch a course of group action. The headman of a jati-group must first canvass the lineage and family heads for their approval before he can effectively consign them to an action. A leader tends to have more leeway when he acts in clear defense of his group or when he judges a weak dependent for a gross transgression. There are occasional leaders whose personal power is great enough that they can take decisive action for their group and make the decisions stick. But generally a leader's independent powers are not broad.

Why then do men take on these roles that carry heavy responsibilities and bear limited authority? Some inherit an office of leadership, many aspire to positions of prestige, others find themselves laden with responsibilities for the group in the course of striving for quite personal advantage. It sometimes happens, for example, that a younger brother is so markedly more energetic, able, and enterprising than his elder brother that he gradually takes over the management of the family's affairs despite the formal authority of the elder.

Three such families are mentioned in one account of a village of Delhi State. In each the elder brother was quite content to let his clever younger brother take charge as family head and as lineage leader, and the younger made the relationship easier by giving symbolic deference to the elder while he controlled the family affairs (Gangarade 1963, pp. 5–6). Initially such a man takes charge so that the family's fields will be better kept, the yield more abundant, and selling more profitable. Then he may look to enlarging the landholdings and securing good marriages. If he is notably successful, he becomes known as the effective head of the family. When lineage or alliance affairs are to be discussed he is asked by the other family heads to attend along with his elder brother, and when he gives his opinion on a matter involving the welfare of the lineage the others listen respectfully to what he has to say. As the family prospers under his direction, his lineage mates increasingly seek his help in lineage affairs. So the younger brother, who began by attending more carefully to the bullocks and the weeding and the hired labor than did his other brothers, finds himself involved, say, with collecting money for the temple of the lineage deity or asked to help soothe a set-to within another family of the lineage.

Any family head who prospers and acquires dependents in the course of building up his own fortunes is likely to be pressed into taking concern for a larger group whether he likes to do so or not. He generally likes to do so; he likes the esteem and power given to a responsible and effective person. Prestige and power grow with public acknowledgment of them. As he climbs in personal status and wealth, he is consulted on affairs of wider and wider social consequence. Elders and peers bring him in because they need the weight of his influence to firm up any decision that may be taken, because without his active participation and that of other powerful men, no decision is worth much. But a man's rise to leadership in the village community is normally limited to his own social level.

A woman can take virtually no overt leadership, though some women exert considerable influence through their men. A Harijan leader may be preeminent in his jati, but he can have only indirect influence, if any at all, in the affairs of the village. At any level, an able man presents a larger and more tempting target to detractors as he rises. He must assuage or cope with those who feel threatened by his rise in order to fulfill the functions of leadership.

Attributes of Leaders and Methods of Leadership

In their personal qualities, the leaders in a jati generally follow a characteristic pattern (of. Dhillon 1955, pp. 118–126; Lewis 1958, pp. 125–130, 149–150). They need to have enough wealth and family support to back up their word. It is well if the man's family has an ancient and honored reputation, but it is even more necessary that his family be united behind him. One eminent leader in Khalapur lost his influence in part because he could not get his own nephew to obey him (Hitchcock MS. 1959, p. 41; Retzlaff 1962, p. 43). Further, a leader commonly has to have the time and the interest to keep himself closely posted on what goes on among his jati fellows. A man who keeps abreast of the gossip, rumors, and facts—and can skillfully distinguish among them—can anticipate and control trouble.

Unless a man has wealth enough to afford the leisure for this kind of participation, his interest in doing so will not avail. Moreover very few young men can spend their time in garnering local intelligence nor will the kinsmen and neighbors of a younger man give him the respectful attention that they give to an elder man. So the term "elder" is generally a valid synonym for leader. Age alone is not sufficient to qualify a man for leadership but youth is a disqualification and reasonable maturity as father and manager is necessary.

Similarly, wealth is necessary but is not in itself sufficient. To be an effective leader, a man must use his wealth properly in extending hospitality, in entertaining many visitors, and, as we have noted above, in staging generous family and jati rites. A wide net of connections with powerful people is an advantage, so too is some education, which presumably gives entree to holders of power. Because an effective leader must communicate effectively, fluency and cogency in public speech are great assets. In addition, the rising leader of a jati should demonstrate that he intends to use these assets for the general good before he is regularly, widely, and spontaneously invited to help maintain the whole jati.

As in many another society, a man who seeks to be a leader best presents himself as an unostentatious person, more interested in the welfare of his jati kin and neighbors than in personal aggrandizement. If he does not do so, his public judgments and acts will be suspected of being in his own selfish interest. That suspicion is usually not far distant in any case and a leader in the jati or village frequently has to make his way against a rolling drumfire of gossip and innuendo.

A main attribute of an effective leader is the ability to switch personal styles of conduct, to adapt readily to differing situational requirements. This is a hallmark of effective leadership everywhere; in the context of jati relations, it means that a man must be aggressive and selfishly partisan while he consolidates his wealth. But when, as a prominent man, he gives judgments in council on jati affairs, he is expected to be unaggressive, judicious, unselfish, seeking the jati's good rather than his own, upholding the values of the brotherhood (of. Dhillon 1955, p. 107, Hitchcock MS. 1959, p. 44). Though he is not required to sacrifice the interests of his family, he should also not act as a fervent partisan of his kinsmen in jati council. In order to link different levels of society a leader should be able to change gear in this way, acting in terms of one pattern vis-à-vis the smaller group, using another in relation to the larger.

In addition to the active leaders, there may be more passive leaders in a village, men of moral prestige whose advice is sought at critical junctures. These men have influence and functions separate from those of the other leaders, as Orenstein has noted in Gaon village, Poona district.

Two of the leaders there are Brahmins who make no effort to interfere in the actions of others. Because they are esteemed for their high moral conduct they are sought out as mediators and have influence in that capacity. The eight active leaders of Gaon are deeply occupied with status competition and do not feel impelled to live up to the ideal moral standards. There are also three "unsanctioned" leaders in this village, men of a higher jati who support and lead the Harijans against the higher groups and do so by strong-arm methods (1959, pp. 422–425).

Any jati-group of more than a few families usually has acknowledged leaders and, as was mentioned at the beginning of this chapter, the role is quite informal in some jati-groups while in others it carries a title, specific obligations, and special rewards. The advantage to the group of having a formal headman is that a particular person is thereby clearly and continually responsible for group maintenance. These headmen usually have ritual as well as secular duties so their secular leadership tends to be bolstered by their religious functions.

Such leaders are not the same as the so-called headmen who are arbitrarily selected to transmit messages from the rulers to the ruled (of. Dumont 1957b, p. 293). A government official or a landlord may appoint someone from a Harijan hamlet to carry orders to his jati fellows. That man may or may not be the real leader of his jati-group. A main disadvantage of formalizing the maintenance roles, for jatis as for empires, is the problem of succession. Formal succession is usually hereditary; the inheritor may be quite incompetent and become an easy target for others to the detriment of group solidarity, so the actual influence of a formal headman of a jati or jati-group depends greatly on his personal ability.

An able man is in a favored position to wield influence, but one who is uninterested or inept will make little of the office he has inherited or will allow a kinsman to wield the power latent in the office. The latter course occurred in Wangala in Mysore where a younger brother took over authority from his elder brother, in this case the authority of hereditary headman of the dominant jati and so of the village. The elder was weak and incapable, the younger had, in abundance, the qualities expected of a headman. So the younger acted as the real leader; the villagers called him "chairman," using the English term. He headed the council discussions and was recognized as the chief arbitrator in village affairs. But the more formal duties of headman, as in collecting taxes (and retaining the fee) continued to be done by the elder brother. The son of the elder brother would succeed to the headmanship, and if there was no longer any need then to delegate the headman's authority, the new office and title of chairman might well disappear (Epstein 1962, pp. 126–127).

In Dalena, the contrastive village of the same district of Mysore, the hereditary headman has also allowed much of his traditional duty and authority to be taken over by another man, also called chairman. The reasons here arise not from the headman's failures but from his economic success. He is an extremely capable man who has a flourishing business outside the village. Hence he is not much interested in village affairs; the villagers, for their part, do not trust him, particularly because he does not veil his business success, as a leader should, by expressions of humility and of frequent concern for the general welfare. So the villagers give their confidence to another able man who better fulfills their requirements for a leader (Epstein 1962, pp. 280–283).

In these two villages the partial displacement of the hereditary headman has been accomplished with reasonable smoothness. But it does not always happen that an incompetent inheritor has a talented younger brother to whom he is willing to hand over effective authority. Even more rarely does an able man become so engrossed in affairs outside the village that he is content to let another perform his inherited duties within it. So although there is flexibility about hereditary succession, there have also been bitter struggles in many a village about the inheritance of the formal role of leader.

The jati-group headman of Shamirpet, whose deliberate tirade to a disobedient young man was quoted above, combines the prestige of hereditary office and the power of personal ability. The way such a leader operates is sketched in Dube's study of this village near Hyderabad (Dube 1955b, pp. 47–49). Each of the seventeen main jati-groups in the village has a hereditary headman who is held responsible for the good conduct of his jati-fellows. His authority is not clearly defined and he must depend on the force of his personality rather than on any consensus about his legitimate powers.

At the time when Dube studied the village, most of these hereditary headmen were not very effective. Some of them were only nominal members of the village council; others merely represented their jati-groups. But the man who was quoted, headman of a middle-ranking cultivator jati, was both the formal and the real leader of his jati-group. Though he was then only in his late thirties, other villagers listened respectfully to him. He had great influence in the village council as well as in his own jati. There was another able and influential man in his jati-group, and it is a measure of this headman's skill that their relations were quite cordial.

Dube tells that this headman intervenes when a son in his jati-group does not show due regard to his parents or a husband and wife quarrel too often and too publicly. Similarly, if one of his fellows fail to fulfill the terms of his obligations or in any other way brings dishonor to the group, or if boys get unmanageable, or girls earn an evil reputation for easy virtue, "he effectively enters the scene, gives suggestions and advice, admonishes people if they do not seem amenable to persuasion, and in the case of adolescents and young boys may even inflict light corporal punishment" (Dube 1955b, pp. 48–49).

One day while Dube was in the village this headman came to the aid of a younger brother who had quarreled with his elder brother. The two brothers were living alone together, their parents being dead, and the elder was one of a band of young men who had taken to gambling, drinking, and generally "planning mischief." He earned little from their land, spent most of it on himself, and was saving nothing for his brother's marriage. The younger brother had already complained about him to the jati elders and on this occasion ran to the headman for help.

When the headman went to their house and summoned the elder brother, he was greeted with this volley, in Dube's translation of the Telugu (the original was probably racier), "Have you nothing else to do? What brings you here? Is it because of jealousy that you cannot see our welfare and prosperity and you are instigating my brother to separate from me?" At this, the usually calm and sedate headman switched into another mode of address, which included, in addition to the charges quoted above, the rebuke that "After spending a few months in the city—and with the support of that band of rascals—you think that you can defy the authority of the village elders. I will show you what it means to be impertinent to me." A crowd collected, other leading men of the jati-group came up and supported the headman. The other elders then induced the young man to apologize, which he did rather reluctantly, and they set the sum that he would have to provide for his younger brother's wedding (Dube 1955b, pp. 203–204).

An able headman continually prompts cooperation within his group, soothes hurt feelings, calms cranky kinsmen, sniffs trouble and tries to divert it. His success, as with all leaders, depends on the willingness and cooperation of the followers, as well as on his own motivation and ability. This day-to-day influence is highly important for the group—whether lineage, alliance, jati-group, or village—but it is not particularly visible. It is exerted in private conversations (though the case above blossomed into a public affair), in incidental actions, in quiet but firm suggestions.

When, however, a transgression has been committed, when a dispute cannot be sidetracked, or when a group enterprise must be arranged, the leaders can no longer act privately and individually. Then they meet in council and act through the role formation called the panchayat.

Panchayat as Pattern of Action

The term "panchayat" literally means a group or council of five. In village usage it refers not only to the group that convenes but also to a set of processes for resolving conflict, for redressing transgression, and for launching group enterprises (of. Cohn 1965, pp. 90–91). The pattern of panchayat action is triggered by a problem that people feel must be tackled and that cannot be handled by individuals acting singly. The issue may be one that touches only the families of a lineage or it may be one that concerns all in an alliance, a jati-group, or a jati. The responsible men of the group gather to discuss the issue. Their number, the timing of the meetings, the sanctions that may be imposed, all depend on the nature of the problem rather than on any fixed specifications or schedule.

It should be noted at once that this traditional panchayat pattern is quite a different thing from the recent, legislative use of the term panchayat. The recent usage refers to a statutory local body, recruited through elections, given legal powers, and charged with certain governmental functions. The relation between the traditional panchayats and the new institutions requires a separate analysis; the focus in this chapter is on the traditional panchayat as a means for maintaining the jati.

The panchayat pattern may be brought into play for so small an instance as the quarrel just described between the two brothers of Shamirpet. One brother appealed to the headman of the jati-group who hurried over to set things right. As voices were raised in anger, other elders gathered; such elders are usually of the same lineage and live within earshot of a family fracas. Together these elders assessed the case and made recommendations on the spot; their judgment was backed by the possibility of more formal and severe action if their recommendations should not be followed.

Such on-the-spot arbitration has been called an *ad hoc* panchayat and so it is; most other panchayat meetings are also *ad hoc* in the sense that they are called to deal with a particular problem. Some problems can be resolved by quick arbitration, as when a lane is blocked by a cart or a woman is slightly hurt in a quarrel; others, such as family arguments about partition, typically drag on for a long time, through many sessions, with changes of position by the disputants and changes of recommendations by the arbitrators (of. Epstein 1962, pp. 120–122; Srinivas 1952a).

The scope of a panchayat meeting and the participants in it depend on the nature of the issue that brought on the session (of. Cohn 1965, p. 100). A family quarrel is normally considered first in a meeting of the leaders of its lineage. Where strong alliances confront each other, as in Haripura, each side gathers its own panchayat to settle disputes among alliance members and to collect funds for village festivals and public works (Dhillon 1955, pp. 109–110).

For some problems a panchayat of the whole jati-group must be convened, including leading men of all lineages and alliances. Thus if a man is seen in town eating in low company or a woman of the jati is discovered with a man not her own, no time must be lost in gathering a jati-group panchayat to preserve all from the ritual peril raised by the delinquency of one. Or if village servants refuse to perform a traditional service for the overlords, a panchayat meeting of the patron jati-group is called to bring their power to bear on the recalcitrants. Conversely, if the privileges of a lower, serving jati are curtailed, their men gather in panchayat to determine how to bring their united strength to bear on the landowners.

Quarrels between jati fellows of different lineages or alliance are taken up in a panchayat of the jati-group. If a quarrel among brothers cannot be settled at the lineage level, any one of them can take the case before the jati-group panchayat, though he may risk decisive loss if opinion there goes against his claim. The planning of joint enterprises, as well as arbitration, may be the business of a panchayat meeting. The jati-group's participation in a village festival, its contribution to a jati temple, its share in village improvements are determined in a council of its elders and leaders.

In a village where one jati-group is strongly dominant, its council is, in effect, the village panchayat. But in a village where several jatis are strong, the leaders of each meet to take up problems affecting the village as a whole. Shamirpet is such a village; in it there is some overlap of jurisdiction between the panchayats of the village and of the jati-group. Serious offenses are laid before both panchayats; cases of incest or of beef eating so threaten both the jati-group and the entire village that they are taken up at once by both councils. Both give judgments to restore the whole community to its normal social status (Dube 1955b, p. 55).

Certain problems require elders and leaders from more than one village. If a betrothal is broken and one side feels injured by the break, its men look to a panchayat for satisfaction. That panchayat must include elders from the two villages. So also with divorce cases, not uncommon in the middle and lower jatis, when a council must adjudicate questions of return of marriage payments. When a particularly heinous transgression becomes known, as when a Hindu villager kills a cow (even if inadvertently), then more than his jati-group stand endangered by the deed. A council of his jati from a number of villages is convened. In some jatis the killer must be made outcaste, at least for a time, whatever the circumstances of the killing.

Any offense for which a person is likely to be cast out of his jati requires an intervillage council of the jati, so that the punishment can be widely known and totally supported. Councils of larger scope are also held for a variety of larger problems, disputes between jati-groups, promotion of jati festivals, reform of jati practices and, latterly, education for the jati's youth.

The number of villages represented in a jati panchayat varies by the organization of the jati and the gravity of the issue (of. Cohn 1965, pp. 93–94, 99–100). Some jatis have quite well-defined panchayat circles and notices are sent to each village when a problem for the larger council arises. The Rajputs of Ramkheri, for example, are part of a tight set of five villages within a radius of four miles of the center village; their council meetings must be attended by elders from all five villages. The weavers of Ramkheri belong to a circle of fifteen villages; attendance from all fifteen is not compulsory in their meeting but the three hereditary leaders in this weavers' circle must be present.

The larger councils of most jatis in Ramkheri are held at any large gathering of jati-fellows, mainly at marriages or funerals. At such times, when many jati brethren have come together from a number of villages (from five to twenty-five or more), the elders assemble to judge a case that has been put before them (Mayer 1960, pp. 253–255). Occasionally a wealthy family will summon a special jati council to hear its complaint and will invite jati fellows from all the villages where their kinsmen live. But the summoners must be able to feed a large concourse and to bear other expenses of an extraordinary council.

The tale of such a grand council is told among the Balahis, who are Harijans in Nimar district of Madhya Pradesh. One of the sons of an important family had been most grievously insulted by his mother-in-law—she hit him with a shoe—and the family brought together Balahis from eighty villages to hear their complaint. The council excommunicated the whole jati-group of the offensive mother-in-law. Those who were outcast resisted the verdict for a while, but after a few months declared their submission and had to stage an expiatory feast for an equally large gathering, also from some eighty villages. Nearly a ton and a half of wheat cakes were required for this feast, Balahis say; other expenses were proportionally large (Fuchs 1950, pp. 41–42).

This unusual convocation was remembered vividly twenty years after the event, and it would be unusually large even for people of higher, wealthier jati. The geographic range represented in a traditional jati panchayat is usually limited by the means and speed of transportation as well as by the kinship radius of the conveners. The potters of a village in Lucknow district belonged to a formal jati circle that included more than fifty villages. This size was found too unwieldy and extensive so they regrouped into smaller circles (Majumdar 1958a, p. 98).

Some jatis support yet a higher council, of broader geographic scope, which usually is more concerned with the jati's external relations than with internal disputes. Thus several of the jatis in Ramkheri maintain temples in Ujjain, the sacred center of the Malwa region. The rites at such a temple are not specific to the jati that supports it nor are they offered particularly for its members, but there are pilgrim lodges attached to a temple to which jati fellows come from a wide territory during the main religious festivals at Ujjain. At such times and in the facilities provided by the pilgrim lodge, the temple committee may convene a large meeting to propose jati policies. At one such meeting of a barber jati, the assembly resolved to fine and, if necessary, outcast a jati fellow who poached another's clients, if the client had not paid all that he owed to his previous barber. The meeting also set a maximum fee for matchmakers who arrange a remarriage (Mayer 1960, pp. 255–256).

Such traditional centers and assemblies are not maintained by all jatis, but a jati that has developed from a sect is particularly likely to have such organization. This is partly because devotees feel special need for regular convocations of the true believers, surrounded as they normally are by a vast ocean of unbelief, and partly because sectarian jatis tend to maintain their own sacred centers to which believers come annually from far places. The regional center is also the seat of the spiritual head of the sect who may be endowed with temporal as well as spiritual powers. Before him are laid serious disputes and major transgressions. His decree is accepted as final, above any judgment of a council, though he may be assisted by a council. Some of the Jain and Lingayat jatis maintain such leaders, and certain jatis that are not of sect origin, such as the Havik Brahmins of Mysore, also revere a guru whose judgments are final in jati affairs (Sangave 1959, pp. 101, 111, 330–335; McCormack 1963, p. 63; Harper and Harper 1959, p. 465; Hutton 1961, pp. 97–98; Dubois 928, pp. 284–285).

With the upsurge of political participation in the twentieth century, regional assemblies have been developed by a good many jatis, more rationalized and formalized than the originals, and made possible by great improvements in communication and travel facilities. The organization of these regional assemblies is usually modeled after the structures of Indian political parties and governmental agencies. Thus the Telis, oilmen, of Puri district in Orissa have an elaborate table of organization for the fourteen thousand Teli families in the district. They are organized into six "dominions," each dominion is further subdivided into a number of regions, each region into villages and each village into one or more wards.

The "dominion" assembly takes up the same kind of cases that a less formalized jati panchayat would consider, but it also discusses matters of wider policy as a council of traditional form and scope would not be likely to do. This modern, more elaborate organization of Telis thus performs traditional panchayat functions and also goes beyond them.

A still higher level of organization has now been added, the congress of oilmen from the various districts of Orissa. In 1959 an All-Orissa Teli Congress was held, including representatives from the three major Teli jatis of Orissa. Among the proposals suggested was that the Orissa Congress of Telis should enter into close relations with a still broader organization, the All-India Oilmen's Association (Patnaik and Ray 1960, pp. 76–77). At these conventions, as we shall discuss below, the main concern is for educational advance, economic improvement, jati reforms, and status elevation. This is far removed from the traditional functions of a jati panchayat, but these are still carried on, among Telis as among many other groups, by the more localized councils.

The Jats of Meerut Division did not have to create a new organization for these modern functions, they had only to revive their ancient regional council. Before 1850 that council had been maintained for centuries to provide for the common Jat defense, to collect revenue, and to administer some governmental affairs over the hundreds of villages within this Jat-dominated area. After a lapse of a century, this council was convened again in 1950 and has continued to meet, not for the old military, revenue, and administrative functions, but for the modern purposes of jati reform, lobbying, and regional welfare.

These Jats, as depicted by M. C. Pradhan (1965) have long had an unusually complex yet clearly conceived organization with a graded series of panchayats that have functioned continuously. There are other jatis in this Meerut region but the Jats are the dominant landowners, and their organization sets the style for and, in certain respects, includes the other jatis.

There are nine levels of Jat organization; a social unit at each level is made up of smaller units of the level just below it. Panchayats are assembled for groups of every kind. If a serious case cannot be settled by a panchayat of a smaller unit, it may be taken up by a panchayat of the next higher level. Issues between groups at one level are adjudicated by a panchayat of a unit at the next higher level.

A fundamental unit in this series is the lineage. As we have noted above, Jat lineages are strictly localized, in that a certain tract of land in every village is the property of a particular lineage. Only members of the lineage may own that land, no others may share in it. Because of this cohesion factor, these lineages are larger than those in most other parts. The minimal lineage is the same as the lineage we have previously discussed, a set of families whose men are closely related because of their common descent from a known ancestor, perhaps three to four generations removed from them. The maximal lineage among the Jats comprises all those families who have rights in a particular part of the village land. Their men are also descended from a common ancestor, but at a much greater generational distance (Pradhan 1965, pp. 1822–23).

A panchayat of the minimal lineage is convened to settle disputes of the kind that close relatives and neighbors are apt to get into. The partition of joint family property is a common issue before such a council. Other issues are quarrels about irrigation, borrowed farm implements, thefts, and repayment of loans. Several minimal lineages may together have common interests and so may assemble a panchayat of their elders to protect their interests. For example, the people of one set of minimal lineages became much annoyed with their genealogist and agreed in a panchayat session to fire him.

The panchayat of the maximal lineage takes up the more stubborn cases that the councils of its component minimal lineages have not been able to resolve. This panchayat is able to outcast an offender as the smaller units cannot do alone. And since the families of the maximal unit cultivate contiguous lands, that council also deals with land management problems, like the sale of their sugarcane or the voluntary building of roads. A maximal lineage is also a political unit, in that its men feel strong obligation to stand together against other lineages.

A village panchayat is convened to hear disputes between maximal lineages or between different jatis in the village. Since the village is an administrative unit, this panchayat deals also with representations to government or with activities related to the larger organization of the jati.

That larger organization includes units ranging from five to eight contiguous villages and, at the next higher level, units of as many as twenty villages. The principal higher unit is that of the clan-area; Pradhan mentions one clan tract that covers 84 villages. Elders and leaders from this clan-area assemble to consider serious problems—flagrant incest or adultery, difficult quarrels between maximal lineages or villages or between two jatis within the tract. An aggrieved man may appeal the judgment of a lower panchayat before this council (Pradhan 1965, pp. 1856–1857).

A range of enforcement sanctions are available to this council, provided always that there is strong and nearly complete agreement among the leaders sitting in council. Offenders may be fined and made to undergo explanatory rites. Sometimes they must express their repentance by touring the villages of the tract and asking the forgiveness of the elders in each village. To bring a recalcitrant offender to heel, a panchayat of influential men may assemble at his very door. They will discuss his case and refuse to accept any hospitality from him until he complies with their judgment. Few can resist such pressure.

Those who still hold out may be made outcaste. Even their whole lineage may be ostracized with them, if they support the defaulter. But in recent decades the outcasting has been almost always temporary. The transgressor asks for pardon and after suitable explanation is readmitted (Pradhan 1965, pp. 1859–1863).

Beyond outcasting, there is a greater, final penalty. It is the curse uttered by a panchayat. This may be inflicted by a council at any level, but when done by a high-level panchayat it is a particularly fearsome blow. Thus one man in his fifties entered into a marriage that had been forbidden by a high panchayat. That council then cursed him with the dread bane that he should have no sons. Twenty years later, in his seventies, he still had no son to his name. Pradhan comments that belief in the power of the curse is still fairly common even among educated and urbanized Jats; to a Jat villager it is a considerable inducement to bow to a given panchayat decision (Pradhan 1965, p. 1863).

In addition to the traditional functions, a panchayat of a clan-area now takes up such enterprises as the improvement of education for the children, the elevation of jati rites, the maintenance of communal harmony. And at the highest level of organization there is the revived regional assembly of eighteen clan-areas, which meets at intervals of several years. The modern effect of these Jat assemblies will be noted in later discussion of social mobility; like the grand congresses of Orissa oilmen, these assemblies pass resolutions for jati reform and political improvement. Enforcement of these resolutions devolves mainly on the lineages, but the regional assembly is increasingly a force for mobilizing jati strength in the halls of government, as its ancient prototype once mobilized jati armies for the field of battle (Pradhan 1965, pp. 1855–1864).

At every social level, panchayat action begins when leading men of a group, whether it is a lineage or a jati, meet to deal with a problem that affects that group. The meeting is convened by those who feel endangered or discomforted by the problem and it is attended by those who feel involved in it. Different kinds of issues induce councils of different kinds, from impromptu gatherings of lineage elders to planned convocations of people from many villages.

A vexing problem that cannot be resolved by a panchayat of first jurisdiction may be laid before a council of wider representation, often one gathered specifically for that purpose. There is usually no formal or regular mechanism of appeal from a judgment made at one level to a council of broader scope. A principal who is dissatisfied with a judgment, however, can bring his case to a larger council if he has influence enough to persuade elders to consider the case again and if he can afford to pay the costs of gathering and feeding them when they assemble.

Panchayat Participants and Procedure

The participants in a panchayat include those directly involved, either those accused of a transgression or both sides in a dispute. In an extempore meeting within a lineage, at least two or three elders should hear out the matter. For a summoned council meeting, all the effective leaders of the group involved should be present to concur in a judgment. If any are absent, by chance or by choice, a judgment may not be enforceable until they agree to enforce it.

There can be little electioneering for the position of indispensable elder because the position is a consequence of a man's power and influence. If he is influential, then everyone who is concerned with resolving the problem will be eager to invite him to sit on the council. His actively seeking the role implies that he may not be worthy of it, since a truly important man will know that the council cannot be effective without him.

A council meeting usually attracts a number of other men, some related to the principals, some who are particularly interested in the issue or who simply enjoy speaking in council discussions and listening to them. These come without special invitation. As jati fellows they have a right to hear and—if they are adult men—to be heard. Respected outsiders may be invited to attend in order to lend an aura of objectivity and authority to the proceedings. If it is an issue within a lineage, perhaps a wise elder of a friendly lineage will be asked to sit in; if it is a jati-group council, a respected man of another jati may be invited, often of a higher jati or of the dominant jati in the village (cf. Dhillon 1955, p. 106; Mayer 1960, p. 252; Minturn and Hitchcock 1963, p. 253).

The judges may be recruited on the spot, as when a sobbing woman rushes to an elder displaying the bruises from a beating by a neighbor. But in serious affairs, a council is summoned more formally and a date is set, perhaps for a time when many of the jati will gather to attend a festival or a wedding. Then messengers of a low jati are dispatched with written invitations and with a symbolic gift, perhaps of tobacco or areca nut. Within the village a crier—also of low jati—goes from place to place loudly announcing the meeting and its business. The venue is commonly in the vicinity of a temple, partly because it is an accustomed meeting place, partly to bring home the often quoted saying that where there is a panchayat, there also is God.

Elders demand respect for a council, whether it is an impromptu gathering or a jati conclave. Thus Srinivas tells that in the village near Mysore city that he studied, any house verandah will do as a place for settling ordinary disputes: "I have heard an elder, sitting in his verandah, sharply reminding a loose-tongued woman, party to a dispute, that she was in a *nyaya-sthana* (place of justice, court)." But when a serious dispute, one involving important people and several villages, is to be settled, the meeting is usually held before a temple, and every speaker begins and frequently ends his statement with a reference to his "soul as witness" or to "God as witness" (Srinivas 1954, p. 159).

No set agenda or order of presentation is required. The meeting usually goes on until every man has had his say and all are too tired or too replete with talk to add anything else. The session begins when the senior elders see that enough people are present, which is to say when all influential men who may be expected to come have arrived. There usually is no great concern about who shall preside. A particular man may take the lead on opening the council, either because he has a traditional right to do so or because he is the most senior or the most forward of the prominent men who are assembled. But any elder may take the lead in the discussions or interrogate as his interest prompts and as his fluency and pertinacity avail (cf. Dumont 1957b, pp. 293–294).

At the beginning there is apt to be an eloquent display by plaintiff and defendant and a heated exchange between them. An accused states his case and typically proclaims his innocence. Then the adherents and supporters of each side take part, offering whatever evidence and witnesses they can muster. The legal phrases and flourishes of government courts are so familiar that villagers commonly use them in panchayat discussions.

Now the men who take special interest in jural affairs also come in. They are self-appointed experts, but some of them are nonetheless trenchant, effective speakers (cf. Cohn 1965, p. 106). A panchayat is often the scene of impressive oratorical and legal performances. One ethnographer, describing a council meeting full of fine rhetoric in a case of suspected adultery in a Harijan group of Madhya Pradesh, waxes rhetorical himself, "… the men spoke with an eloquence and volubility, with a variety of superb gestures and suggestive change of voice, now pleading and imploring, then stern and firm, all of a sudden sarcastic and ironical, so that I could not but admire their oratorical talents" (Fuchs 1950, p. 35).

The place of council discussions in the life of many villagers cannot be grasped unless one understands that they are more than means for maintaining the peace and order of the group. As Dumont notes for the Kallar, a speaker often takes pleasure in unraveling a delicate and complicated case and in finding an elegant solution for it: "L'esthétique indigène est pour une bonne part verbale et juridique" (1957b, p. 293).

When the facts of a case are in dispute, each of the disputants is usually required to take a solemn oath attesting to his version of the story and invoking supernatural retribution if he speaks falsely. A crucial question of fact may be put before a deity in the temple. Lots may be drawn before the image, or some other method of finding the true facts may be used. An accused who protests innocence of a serious offense may be required to undergo an ordeal (cf. Dubois 1928, pp. 661–662; Hutton 1961, pp. 105–106). These oaths, omens, and ordeals do not always yield definitive answers, because both plaintiff and defendant may swear the same mighty oath to contradictory testimony, or the omen-taking may be inconclusive, or the ordeal subject to different interpretations.

The panchayatdars, the elders-in-council, usually do respond quickly and impartially when the ritual status of the whole jati is clearly in danger. Then they are likely to pin down the exact offense and the offender with objectivity and candor. But when there is a case involving two powerful alliances or two strong jati-groups within the jati, then their own interests may be drawn into the whirlpool of the dispute.

The role of the panchayatdar does not obliterate obligations of kinship; the panchayat member remains a kinsman though as councilor he should not join in partisan argument. Some sage councilors are above partisan involvement, others conform to Dube's comment on councils in Shamirpet. He says that outwardly all show an attitude of objectivity and impartiality, although in reality the rival factions within the council try to influence the procedure "so that the evidence may later be construed in such a way that it may prove advantageous to the client to whom they have already promised their support" (1955b, p. 202).

The most influential men ordinarily say little at the beginning of a council meeting. After others have had their say, the leaders start to put their points and questions, trying to steer the council into some compromise or course of action. Here, as Mayer notes, lies the value of a leader's flair for oratory and his firmness of temper and character. These qualities count more at this juncture than his hereditary position or wealth. The leaders size up the feeling of the council and estimate whether they can get a consensus. "If it is unlikely, they say less and less until the meeting peters out and it is understood that the matter will be taken up again later—there is not, in my experience, any formal postponement made" (Mayer 1960, p. 257).

A judgment is not usually reached unless there is unanimity or near unanimity among the presiding leaders. If they do not agree, the council meeting is dissolved with no decision taken; there is little point in pronouncing a decision unless it can be enforced, and it can be enforced only if the wielders of power determine to do so. Although some national leaders have written eloquently on the moral value of the striving for council consensus, F. G. Bailey has pointed out that councils in any society whose members have to implement their own decisions are impelled to search for such consensus. If the society provides a separate executive, then it is much more difficult for a disgruntled minority to block the majority decision in a council (Bailey 1965 pp. 8–9). But panchayats are not equipped with any separate executive officers. Hence in the village view it is generally more important to achieve broad agreement, even if it takes many meetings, much discussion, and considerable compromise, than it is to reach a decision quickly and to take action forthwith. There are, however, some kinds of cases in which decision and action follow in rapid succession.

The difference between protracted and speedy cases is illustrated in Scarlett Epstein's account of the formal panchayats that were held in Wangala during her year of residence there (1962, pp. 122–215). In that Mysore village the council of the dominant jati-group (Vokkaliga) is also the village panchayat. Among the protracted sessions were three that were held to discuss arrangements for village festivals. All three ended in a deadlock over how much food and firewood each household was to contribute and who was to prepare the food. One meeting was held to discuss the electrification of the village and the repair of the temple for the village deity; this too adjourned inconclusively because there was no agreement as to how much each household should contribute to the cost of these ventures.

Quickly decided, on the other hand, were two issues on which delay would have altered the circumstances. One was a straightforward medical emergency. An epidemic among the village buffaloes had in one day taken off twelve animals, more than ten percent of the total number. The panchayat met and decided on the steps to be taken immediately to prevent further deaths. Action was swift and effective. The other issue concerned a social emergency. It was the case, mentioned in discussing jati-group unity, in which the drama troupe of untouchables decided that the actor in the part of the king should sit on a prop throne rather than on the floor of the stage, as was customary for any untouchable actor (Epstein 1962, pp. 183–189). The Vokkaliga elders met this by declaring a boycott of the performance and a lockout of untouchable laborers. When the time came for the performance, the show was marred by a sudden rain as well as by the lack of a proper audience. The lockout was successful enough so that the village Harijans asked for relief and paid the fine decreed by the Vokkaliga council.

In all, this jati-group council effectively disposed of four of nine cases during the year. In the other five, factional differences came into play and each alliance blamed the other for unjustified obstinacy. Nevertheless these deadlocked meetings had an important societal function, Epstein points out, because panchayat meetings are one means of working out the relative strength of the respective alliances. The succession of seemingly inconclusive meetings served to demonstrate which men were now allied and which were in opposition. Although a particular plaintiff may not get his just due, the conduct of a case contributes toward clarifying the balance of alliance powers.

The egalitarian aspects of the traditional panchayat seem to pose a paradox. The need for unanimous consent and the right of every man to be heard appear dissonant to the leitmotif of hierarchy. If villagers are predisposed to view most social relations as being between superior and subordinate, why do they not implant a clear superior in the panchayat pattern? They might maintain a jati guru, as indeed some do, one chief who would pronounce a final ruling. The answer seems to be that most define a jati council as a council of peers. In it one family head usually feels himself quite the equal of any other, and so equally entitled to a voice in the discussions. It is true that a son will not contradict his father in open meeting, a young man will rarely ridicule or revile a respected elder, nor will a humble dependent readily stand up against his wealthy patron. Yet in the context of the panchayat meeting a family head tends to feel more as one among equals than as a subordinate. Therefore even a poor man will speak up if he feels moved to do so.

Any powerful man can ignore the wishes of the majority if he has not participated in a decision or has not agreed to it. He sees no more reason to subordinate himself to a particular number of his peers than to any one of them. Thus every issue must be extensively discussed until critical disagreements are eroded by the flow of talk and compromise becomes possible.

"The act of talking seems to relieve some of the aggression built up in a dispute," Cohn writes of the Chamars of Senapur, near Banaras, and this remark about Chamar councils applies to many others. A meeting may last for three or four hours; anyone can raise almost any problem without being cut off; issues that seem to have no bearing on the case are aired. When a meeting adjourns inconclusively, the leaders do more talking to the principals before the next meeting, trying to mediate. "Eventually a 'compromise' will be suggested, and even though it may be more favorable to one party, as long as it can be defined as a compromise in a rhetorical sense, both parties seem to be satisfied" (Cohn 1959a, p. 86).

Often a council meeting called to discuss one dispute will turn to adjudicate another that lies behind the antagonism and comes to the surface in the course of the discussion. The Chamars, Cohn observes, do not segment their lives into neat compartments and they see no point in trying to decide a dispute only on the basis of an immediate situation (1959a, pp. 85–86).

Quite a different pattern for group action, but also a traditional one, is used for certain other purposes. This pattern is more like committee procedure, with restricted membership, delegation of authority, and an expectation of firm decisions. It was commonly followed in the management of large temples, for looking after temple lands and endowments, for distributing temple perquisites, and in planning temple festivals. Mayer calls this the committee form (*Samiti* in the terminology of Ramkheri villagers) in contrast to the more common panchayat form (1960, p. 122). The committee model is the one now required for activities related to government, but the council procedure is still fruitful and congenial in many villages.

Dhillon's description of leaders (Yajmans) as councilors in Haripura applies widely. "Thus in this traditional panchayat, there is no delegation of powers for a specific period to an elected group. The *Yajmans* must make decisions in consultation with all concerned, and the confidence in them must be constantly reaffirmed by the people" (1955, p. 107). So panchayat procedure is a way of forming public opinion; through council discussions critical issues become known and sentiments crystallized. It is also a way of making public opinion effective for group maintenance.

Leaders have to be in close touch with their colleagues and followers if their leadership is to be effective. Leaders, whether lineage elders or jati headmen, help to hold their groups together; they help to overcome the social friction that is inevitable in any living group and to keep them functioning as groups. A leader's ordinary, daily efforts in these respects are not highly visible. When such quiet efforts become insufficient and leaders gather in council, their maintenance efforts then become necessarily and deliberately visible to their fellows.

CHAPTER 17

The Uses of Panchayats

The common village saying, "Where there is a panchayat, there is God," might also add that where there is a panchayat, there also is the group. Because it is mainly in panchayat sessions that the nature of a group—whether lineage, jati-group, or jati—is made clear. There the group's boundaries are defined, its cohesion maintained, its standards set, its common action planned, its purposes shown. Panchayat meetings are a major means of assuring the internal order of a group, of correcting ritual transgressions and secular offenses, of smoothing the disturbance of disputes. Counterchange action within the system of village society is thus largely carried out through panchayats. They are also used in defense against external challenge.

The members of a lineage meet in panchayat when they must defend their group status within the jati; a jati-group protects its place in the village through its panchayat meetings; a jati guards or advances its standing in the local order through the jati panchayats. Further, the members of a group set up cooperative links with other groups and liaison with other social echelons in their panchayat discussions. A lineage council discusses its participation in jati affairs; a jati-group council plans its part in a village ceremony; a jati council takes up relations with agencies of the state. Finally, as described in the following chapter, panchayats are used to advance group enterprises and to adapt to changing conditions. We shall note the special features of village panchayats in later chapters on the village.

There is much variation among jatis in the degree to which the panchayat pattern is used. The people of some jatis—notably the very poor and the strongly dominated—traditionally made little or no use of panchayats; others used them frequently. The present trend is toward lesser reliance on panchayats for some purposes, especially for those in which government agencies have become increasingly influential. At the same time there is a tendency toward much greater reliance on the modern version of the jati panchayat, the jati association, for entrepreneurial and adaptive purposes.

Redress of Ritual Lapses

A panchayat function that is still of high importance for many villagers is the redress of ritual lapses, which is also the maintenance of ritual standards. The ritual integrity of the jati is most precious since a grave transgression by one individual can affect all in his jati. In this matter there is absolute equality, not hierarchy. Every member must equally adhere to the jati's minimal standards of ritual purity. These standards differ from one jati to another, and are generally more exacting among the higher ranks, but people of all jatis—even the lowest—try to maintain and enforce such standards.

Anything that defiles an individual so that he contaminates those who have normal relations with him as jati fellows, comes within the purview of a panchayat. This includes such acts as eating improper food or eating proper food in improper company. Incest discovered or endogamy openly violated are pressing matters for a panchayat. A man who takes up an occupation inexcusably beneath his jati's dignity must be checked or rejected by a council. One who is beaten with a shoe is so defiled, in the traditional view, that he cannot continue as a member of the jati until the pollution is dissipated. A Hindu who kills a cow is so debased that only long ritual restitution can redeem him to his jati.

In such serious cases of defilement the offender's intent or his innocence of motive do not dispel his deep pollution. Even though his involvement in the defiling act may have been involuntary, he is nevertheless contaminated and his corruption is contagious to all who treat him as a jati fellow. This is true even of one who inadvertently has social relations with an outcaste jati fellow. A Chamar of Mohana village near Lucknow was once visited by a Chamar from another village. The host hospitably shared his midday meal with the guest. The visitor had not told anyone in Mohana that he had been made outcaste and when this became known there, the panchayat of Mohana Chamars felt that they had to expel (even though temporarily) the man who had merely acted with customary hospitality (Majumdar 1958a, pp. 94–95).

The contamination radiated by an outcaste can reach very far. Thus one washerman in a Mysore village found himself charged before a panchayat of his jati for arranging what he thought was a perfectly suitable marriage for his niece. But the bridegroom's mother's sister, it appeared, had been made outcaste some twelve years before for living with an untouchable. The crucial question before the panchayat was whether the bridegroom's mother had resumed social relations with the outcaste woman, her sister. If so, she was as defiling as the original culprit. Her son was as tarred as his mother since he lived with her, and the man who gave a bride to that son was also derelict, if the charge were true. The panchayat was little interested in the accused's intent or knowledge of the situation, the point at issue was whether there actually had been a circuit of contamination (Srinivas 1954).

This case took a fresh turn when the bridegroom's mother threatened to beat the accuser with her sandals, "a great insult indeed, involving both the aggressor and the victim in temporary loss of caste" (Srinivas 1954, p. 155). In this jati, which is not one of the higher, any one who is so beaten—a single slap on the face or head with the sole of a shoe is sufficient—becomes ritually degraded, even if he is the mistaken victim of a misguided attack. He must undergo purification and readmission to the jati. The attacker may also be thrown out of the group, but a desperate or vindictively determined person may use the threat of shoe beating as a weapon.

The mere threat of being beaten with shoes can endanger a man who is so threatened. This happened when a potter of Rampura village in Mysore sat in a teashop one day angrily cursing Putta, a Lingayat priest, for not repaying a loan. Finally he reached a crescendo of anger and said, "May I sleep with the priest's wife." May I sleep with his mother." Although this kind of abuse is not uncommon, the potter then added something that is much more rarely said and much more seriously taken. He said, "I am going to beat him with my sandals, and I am going to beat him till five pairs of sandals wear out."

The last bit was only added bravado but the utterance made the matter a much graver affair and more difficult to settle than it would have been otherwise. It could not be informally or quickly adjudicated because a council of the priest's jati would have to consider him as ritually contaminated. "Putta is a priest and in an important temple at that, and the potter's threat to beat him with sandals was likely to be interpreted by the caste elders as equivalent to the act itself" (Srinivas 1959b, pp. 193, 205).

So whether a ritual breach has been committed deliberately or unwittingly, the culprit (or victim) is a continuing menace to all in his group. The group, acting through its panchayat, must protect itself. If the transgression is a minor affair, the councilors will assess a fine of a few rupees to be paid into the common fund and will require that the offender purify himself by a simple ritual ablution. He should also give assurance publicly that he will err no more.

If the offense is major, however, the group itself must first be purified by expelling the one who is polluted. This initial step for redressive action is also the ultimate sanction in the power of the traditional panchayat. If the offender then recants, pays the proper penalties, and undergoes the proper purification, he can usually be taken back into society. Some ritual crimes, however, can never be wiped away. For example, a Brahmin woman who goes to live with a Harijan is usually beyond redemption to her jati and is totally cut off from her former kinfolk. In many cases of outcasting, however, there is the possibility of subsequent incasting.

A person may be cast out of all sorts of groups; exclusion from one group does not necessarily mean total rejection by society. A family may sever relations with one of its members yet neither its jati-group nor jati need follow suit. In Ramkheri village, for example, a Rajput woman once openly lived with her Brahmin lover. Her family would have nothing to do with her but they did not demand that all similarly reject her. Though many in the village strongly disapproved, no formal judgment was made. The others were content to leave things as they were since the family had not demanded further action. If she had taken up with a man of lower jati, however, her jati-group could not have passed over the matter in the same way (Mayer 1960, p. 260).

Similarly, an offender may be cut off from normal relations with his jati-group and village but still be able to maintain relations with jati fellows in other villages. Thus in Totagadde of western Mysore one Havik Brahmin was so ostracized because he refused to make his married daughter return to her husband. Another Havik incurred this penalty when he refused to pay his share of road repair costs and of the costs of the guru's visit. In these cases the village council is said to "build a fence" around the offender. He then cannot hire local laborers; a priest will not perform domestic ceremonies for him; no one in the village will visit him; often he endures petty thefts and damage to his crops and fields. Yet such a person remains a member of the jati. He may resist for a while, but he is usually forced to give in and ask to be readmitted on the council's terms (Harper and Harper 1959, pp. 463–464).

Outcasting, expulsion from the jati, is the extreme form of group withdrawal, imposed for extreme ritual offenses. The Abbé Dubois, who lived among Tamil-speaking people, has a poignant passage on the fate of an outcaste: "It renders him, as it were, dead to the world, and leaves him nothing in common with the rest of society. In losing his caste he loses not only his relations and friends, but often his wife and children, who would rather leave him to his fate, than share his disgrace with him. Nobody dare eat with him or even give him a drop of water" (1928 edition, p. 38). Since this passage was written, in the early years of the nineteenth century, outcasting has become more rarely used; it is entirely obsolete in some jatis and even when it is imposed the one who is made outcaste can find some refuge, perhaps in a city or in a very low-ranking group. Yet in more than a few jatis the threat of the penalty still has the dread air of final social extinction about it that the Abbé expresses in his description.

Modern examples of outcasting are not lacking. When in 1955 a Havik Brahmin widow of Totegadde village was discovered to be pregnant, she was formally expelled from her jati (Harper and Harper 1959, p. 465). Social boycott is described for two Bengal villages in the 1960s. "Villagers will not speak with the offender; serving castes will be prevented from going to his house; daily laborers will not work for him, and he will receive no help at the time of marriage, death, or even starvation at his house" (Nicholas and Mukhopadhyay 1964, p. 22).

Outcastes who have no hope of readmission to their own jati may possibly join a Harijan jati, such as the Balahis of Madhya Pradesh, who take in people fallen from higher status. Such newcomers are in time enrolled on the register of a Balahi genealogist and may even found a new Balahi clan. But joining a Harijan group does not relieve or exempt an outcaste from jati requirements; it only changes some of the stringency and certain of the rules. The Balahis bear out Gandhi's saying that the untouchables have their untouchables; the Balahis have the Mehtars, who are sweepers. A Balahi may be expelled by his jati panchayat if he should sit with a Mehtar on the same bed or bullock-cart (Fuchs 1950, pp. 18, 61).

A panchayat can rejoin as well as reject. The sentiment of a panchayat does not usually incline to the social extinction of transgressors but to their redemption; the councilors generally want not to lose a jati fellow but to keep the jati intact. Hence there is provision for incasting as well as for outcasting. Among the Chamars of Senapur, Cohn notes, the longest period of outcasting was for twelve years, the penalty for incest.

During the time a Chamar is kept out of his jati all social relations with him are interdicted. No one will eat or smoke with him, allow him to use the well, lend him food or implements, or participate in domestic rites with him. Later, he and his family are allowed to pay a fine to the common fund and to give one or two feasts. They may then be under partial ostracism for a time—allowed to draw water from the hamlet well and to get fire from a neighbor's hearth but not to smoke a hookah in Chamar company or attend celebrations—until the full rituals of readmission have been completed (Cohn 1959a, p. 84; 1965, pp. 100–101).

A formula used in many jatis for setting the amount of the fine emphasizes the supremacy of jati over miscreant, of custom over aberration, of society over sinner. The council spokesman announces a fine much larger than the culprit is really expected to pay. The guilty one, who now accepts the verdict, prostrates himself—either literally or figuratively—before the panchayat and humbly begs that the amount be reduced. It is, but to a sum that is still much larger than the expected fine. This is repeated thrice or more until an acceptable and payable amount is reached. Each time there is public reaffirmation of the redressive action that has occurred. A surly or recalcitrant petitioner will not be let out of his troubles until he goes through this rite of submission (cf. Nicholas and Mukhopadhyay 1964, p. 22; Dumont 1957b, p. 298).

Such a rite on a grand scale was performed in 1961 by the Sikh leader, Master Tara Singh and by nine of his colleagues. He had vowed to fast until death unless his party's demand for a separate Punjabi-speaking state was granted (it was established in 1966). But government representatives persuaded him to stop his fast whereupon other Sikh leaders urged his expulsion from party and community because he had broken his vow. The matter was placed before five eminent Sikh religious leaders who decreed a five-part punishment for Master Tara Singh and lesser penalties for his colleagues. He had to arrange for scriptural readings and offerings at a temple. He himself had to recite certain prayers for a month and for five days he had to clean temple utensils and the shoes of the congregation. Further, the whole community had to be ritually purified through the gathering of a large congregation of Sikhs who recited prayers together. All this was duly done (*The Tribune*, Ambala, October 1–December 5, 1961; *Hindustan Times*, New Delhi, October 1–December 5, 1961).

Ritual readmission in any jati entails public expiation and purification. One means of purification described in Sanskrit scripture, is the ingestion of *panchgavya*, a mixture of the five products of the cow, milk, curds, ghee, cow dung, and cow urine (Ghurye 1961, pp. 92, 101; Hutton 1961, pp. 88, 108). The penitent may be required to travel to a holy center of pilgrimage there to purify himself in the most sacred precincts. There must also be a final rite of social restitution performed in the sight of the jati brethren (cf. Fuchs 1950, pp. 45–49). The pilgrimage may be omitted and the purification ablutions much curtailed, but the public drama of re-entry is not usually neglected. The final phase of readmission is a feast, given at the offender's expense, in which the former outcaste eats with his jati fellows, especially with those who hold hereditary offices. In this way they demonstrate that his sin has been properly expunged and that the jati's integrity has been successfully maintained.

Problems of Enforcement and Jurisdiction

Not all want to recant. Some resist the judgment of a panchayat, and a determined, strong man occasionally even defies formal expulsion from jati. I saw such a struggle going on for many years among the Kotas of the Nilgiris Hills in South India. As I have described elsewhere (1941, 1960), Sulli, the first Kota schoolteacher, was so set on reforming Kota custom that he had his long hair cut off. It was a portentous gesture since a Kota man's chignon was then the hallmark of being a man and a Kota. In response, the elders of the seven Kota villages met and made him outcaste. He remained in the village and kept fighting for his reforms even though he was for a time completely isolated from all his jati fellows. His brothers avoided him; his wife was whisked back to her father's house; his lineage mates deserted him. Because he had a job as a teacher he could continue to make a living. He was a vigorous entrepreneur and had saved money that he used in his defense, unshakable in his conviction that he was right.

After a time his wife returned, his close kin resumed relations, and a few supporters came to his side. He had powerful weapons with which he struck back. He released voileys of petitions to the local government authorities; he harried his chief opponents with endless litigation; he pried adherents loose one by one through various stratagems—a favor for one, a service for another, a loan for a third. After a few years he had collected an alliance and when I saw him last, nearly thirty years after the council's decision, only a few stubborn old men still considered him to be outside of Kota society. There are not many who are as determined and resourceful as Sulli. More commonly, when a large panchayat rules that a transgressor must be thrown out, the guilty one feels compelled to sue for mercy and restoration.

A firm and determined ruling by a jati panchayat will usually be respected by others of the locality. Villagers of other jatis, whether patrons or clients of the offended ones, will help enforce the judgment lest the wrath of the united jati be turned against them also. A landowner will not usually want to employ a sweeper who has been outcast lest he find himself without the services of other sweepers and embroiled in a series of annoying difficulties emanating from the sweepers' hamlet. The ruling of a council may be eroded, however, if it turns out that there is only indifferent support for its decision. The enforcement of panchayat judgments depends on united public opinion and action; enforcement is not assigned to specific officers who have legitimate recourse to force. The use of force is always a lurking possibility but it is rarely a deliberate, overt prescription for the carrying out of panchayat judgments.

Personal considerations figure largely in the making of a judgment and in its enforcement. In assessing the facts of a case, the character of a principal or of a witness is an important consideration. A villager has clear ideas about the worth of his jati fellows and, as Cohn writes of the Chamars of Senapur, he sees no reason why he should not include this knowledge in his evaluation: "Some come from honorable Chamar families, some are educated, some have travelled, some are loose morally, some are stupid, some lazy—all these personal characteristics are known, enter into the adjudicative process, and need not be made explicit" (1959a, p. 86).

The probable consequences of a ruling are also considered in making a judgment. A powerful man may be judged more leniently than a man who is poor and inconsequential, because the important man may resist or even nullify the decision. In two Bengal villages studied by Nicholas and Mukhopadhyay, there are three powerful men who are not even brought before a council for their offenses. One keeps a concubine, another lives with his elder brother's widow, a third has a mistress who is the wife of his sharecropper. All these sexual irregularities are well known and might well incur penalties if they were the acts of less influential men. These three, however, are exempted from panchayat scrutiny (Nicholas and Mukhopadhyay 1964, p. 22).

The same situation is noted in a decision of 1796 by a court of the East India Company in Bengal. Two powerful men openly kept mistresses, which theoretically should have caused them to be made outcaste by their jati fellows. "They dare not, however, take notice of their faults, nor even contradict them and much less expel them from their caste" (cited in Cohn 1965, p. 101).

Still there are limits to the leniency for mighty ones. The most wealthy and exalted personage of a jati could hardly get off scot-free if it became surely known that he had committed incest, or taken a woman of low jati to wife, or killed a cow. He might be readmitted to caste relations more readily than a poor man, but his jati fellows could not overlook his trespasses (cf. Fuchs 1950, p. 37).

A heavy weight of evidence can tell against a considerable weight of influence. Thus in a case in which one washerman accused another of having relations with an outcaste woman, the verdict went against the accuser, even though he was a powerful man. He was even fined for making a false accusation when it became clear in the council session that he had trumped up the charges (Srinivas 1954, p. 161). Similarly, in Khalapur a Rajput who was ordinarily quite immune from panchayat action was made outcaste and driven out of the village when it was proved that he had impregnated a village "sister," then tried to kidnap and sell her off to a distant place (Minturn and Hitchcock 1963, pp. 255–257).

All are held to be answerable for serious ritual and secular offenses, but all do not get equal treatment for equal offenses nor is this really expected. The councilors' first charge is to maintain the group. They cannot be oblivious of the facts of power because that is part of the makeup of the group.

Another relevant fact is the relation of the judged to the judges. When an elder is considering an affair in his own lineage that involves a culprit whom he knows well as a kinsman, his inclination is to smooth things over somehow and get the errant one back to normal relations with as little ado as possible. But when he sits on a jati council and judges a person whom he does not know personally and with whom he has no close ties, then he may be more of a stickler for the jati proprieties and press for a full measure of punishment and formal restitution.

The kinds of offenses for which a jati panchayat is summoned are usually the more blatant ones. In Ramkheri, for example, an inter-village council of a jati deals with the offenses "which are most easily apprehended and over which there is unanimity as to the appropriate punishment." The cases dealt with by the jati-group or village council "tend to be those which are harder to prove, over whose seriousness there can be varying opinions, and over which there is not much unanimous feeling about the correct punishment" (Mayer 1960, pp. 261, 262). In Shamirpet in Andhra Pradesh, the different panchayats tend to give different penalties; the jati-group council rarely outcasts a person, while a jati council often does. And in Rampura in Mysore the council of village elders is characterized as being more friendly and lenient than is a council of jati elders (Dube 1955b, p. 210; Srinivas 1959b, p. 207).

Different judgments are occasionally given by the two councils, that of the jati-group and of the jati. This happened in Ramkheri when a man of the farmer jati began living with a widow and cultivating her lands. Her deceased husband's kinsmen objected, ostensibly because of a jati rule that a dead man's brothers should not meet his widow's second husband—that is to say, he should not live in the same village as they do—but more importantly because they wanted her land. They called a jati-group council, which ordered the pair to separate or to move, and when they refused, the council declared them to be outcaste. A jati council should have been convened to reaffirm that decision, but the jati fellows of other villages kept aloof from this matter. They said that the jati rule had not been violated since the man was only the permanent lover and not the wedded husband of the widow. Whatever his relationship, he had friends and supporters in the other villages and was able to resist the boycott decreed by the jati-group council (Mayer 1960, pp. 263–264).

Another example of a divided opinion on a ruling comes from Gandhi's biography. After he returned from his studies in England he had to undergo ritual purification, as was then customary in many jatis. This was done not only because of the scriptural prohibition against travel over oceans but perhaps even more as a general prophylactic measure. One who had sojourned in places far from home might have been exposed to polluting influences and to unsuitable ideas. Expelling him from the jati and then, on his humble petition, readmitting him ceremonially, ensured that he was ritually fit and morally attuned for normal jati relations. On Gandhi's return from abroad his brother took him directly to the sacred center of Nasik where he performed the purification rites. His jati fellows in his home town received him back, but the jati leaders in Bombay and in Porbander (his birthplace) refused to accept him as one who had been reinstated into the jati (Gray and Parekh 1931, p. 8; Pyarelal 1965, pp. 223, 281–284).

Generally such disagreements between one part of a jati and the others are resolved or eroded in time but they can also lead, perhaps more as symptoms than as root causes, to sharp cleavages in a jati or even to the formation of a new jati by those who have split off. Thus in Ramkheri, a council of barbers was convened about the disappearance of jati funds that had been entrusted to a man who had recently died. His son disclaimed any knowledge of the money and any responsibility for it. Finally the men from the son's village and from half a dozen settlements near it got up and walked out of the council meeting without waiting to eat of the feast that had been prepared. This was doubly insulting; not only was the walkout an affront to the council but it was also an insult to the host and a waste of his food. Thenceforth, at least for the several years that had intervened from the date of the council to the time of the study, each side formed separate jati councils and did not join in the same ceremonies (Mayer 1960, pp. 258–259).

When such quarrels involve serious differences about ritual matters, the split is likely to be more complete, so that the two sides no longer form a single endogamous entity. This has happened among Rajputs in the region of Ramkheri. The Rajputs of some twelve villages had together been adjudged guilty of a ritual infraction and all were cut off from the rest of the jati. They stood steadfast together and so have formed what is, from the point of view of the other local Rajputs, an outcast jati (Mayer 1960, p. 260). Such jati fission has been a common process in the recurrent change that we discuss later.

Withdrawal by an individual or a group is used as a weapon as well as a punishment at every level of village society. An important person can threaten to impair a ceremony by not participating in it. An important group can use this social leverage. Conversely, a group can exert pressure on an individual through various kinds of withdrawal, from not inviting him to a ceremony to cutting him off from society. In some of its uses, withdrawal is a political measure that entails the redefinition of groups and group action. Yet it is a political means that does not rest on the use of force. A person or a group declared outcaste is subject to social, not physical pressures and suffers through the withholding of interchange rather than from the inflicting of force.

Thus a panchayat of the Jats of Meerut Division may order beating as a punishment for certain offenses and offenders. For capital offenses there was never formal capital punishment even though these men reveled in their warrior traditions and fighting tempers. Their most severe punishment was not the taking of life but the taking away of social support and—through the curse of the panchayat—of supernatural support as well (Pradhan 1965, pp. 1862–1863).

Dispute Resolution and Government Courts

The secular matters that are laid before a lineage or jati panchayat are mainly about family and sex, land and livelihood, theft and assaults. Certain passages in a family's career are liable to be stormy. Cases of joint family partition are apt to be pending for council arbitration at almost any time in any village.

Betrothals sometimes run aground, perhaps because one family has discovered a hitherto unknown flaw in the other, or has uncovered the possibility of a better match, or is simply being difficult to make sure it is held in proper esteem. Disagreements between the contracting families at the wedding must be reconciled on the spot lest large damage ensue. Divorce and second marriages, inheritance and adoption, often require the ministrations of a council to calm domestic discord.

Certain sexual lapses are only secular, others require ritual redress. An irate husband complaining to a lineage panchayat that his wife has strayed with a lineage fellow presents a matter of only secular consequence. But if she were found with a man of her own natal lineage, then the affair smacks of incest and no simple patching up of marital relations will suffice.

Quarrels about land are often brought, at least at the outset, before a jati-group panchayat. The quarrel may be about the shifting of a boundary, or the encroachment of a path, or the trampling of a crop. Councilors try to keep such disputes from spreading to others in the village and to jurisdictions beyond the village. Water can be as bitter a subject of contention as is land; the use of a well, the diversion of irrigation flow are frequent causes of contention. Assaults and thefts committed by one jati member upon another are also taken before jati elders to the extent that outside authorities can be kept out of the affair. Among those jatis in which robbery was a regular source of income, a sharp distinction was made between the robbery of outsiders and of jati fellows. The latter crime was taken before a jati panchayat to be vigorously and righteously judged (cf. Dumont 1957b, p. 303).

Many of these secular problems also come under the cognizance of official governmental law. The government's laws and courts have influenced village life, but were generally viewed by villagers as adventitious forces which had to be coped with and manipulated. The intervention of state power in jati affairs, within certain limits, has long been accepted. In the ancient legal scriptures, the king is enjoined to maintain the social order, to prevent "the confusion of castes" (cf. Kane 1946, vol. 3, pp. 3, 57; Ingalls 1954, p. 42; Smith 1963, pp. 297–300). Even during the British regime, a Maharajah might settle disputes between jatis about precedence and might hear appeals from individuals who felt that they had been wronged by their jati councils (Hutton 1961, pp. 94–95; Cohn 1965, pp. 101–102).

There was a main difference, however, between the personal intervention of an Indian prince and the majesty of British law. The prince generally viewed his intervention as one element in a complex process of social maintenance. The British law for India did not take full account of that process or of the social order that was actually maintained. Soon after the British took control of large parts of India, they felt the need of using indigenous law in administering their new domains. At first they employed Brahmins to tell them what the Hindu law was. Later, when they discovered that Hindu law was very different in character from British law and that clear usage often was taken to outweigh written law, they tried to compile manuals of customary law. But this effort too, distorted the indigenous practices because British judges interpreted customary law much more rigidly than Maharajahs or village councilors ever did (Maine 1881, pp. 71–73; Cohn 1965, pp. 105–113; Galanter 1964). The distinctions that British Indian law did allow, such as those between Hindu and Muslim personal law, among several regional varieties of Hindu law, and the special customs of jatis, did not reconcile the fundamental differences in procedure between law as the British rulers thought of it and the actual jural practice of village society.

When a district officer on tour applied official law in the village, he might well understand and take tacit account of the real processes of social maintenance. But when the same officer was appointed as a judge and presided over court sessions in a headquarters town, he was then restrained from fully using his understanding of the unwritten village law by the rules of evidence, the formulae of legal procedure, and all the written and codified dicta that supported justice in England.

As the courts did not recognize most indigenous law-ways so, in their turn, villagers could scarcely accept the British legal apparatus as really relevant to justice and to the upholding of their society. British law assumed a social organization that villagers did not have and took little note of the organization they did have. It postulated values alien to village society and was conscientiously blind to some of the villagers' fundamental assumptions. It could not be ignored; the state and its police were, after all, very powerful and could be ubiquitous, but their actual jurisdiction could be held down to a certain minimal scope (cf. Cohn 1965, p. 105).

Cases of murder, of crippling assault, and of grand theft might be brought to the attention of the police in British times, especially if the attackers were of another jati or village than the victims. Alleged delinquencies of debt and breaches of contract were also brought to court, particularly when plaintiff and defendant were of opposed alliances or different jatis.

In most disputes internal to a jati, the villagers' inclination was to keep the matter out of the courts. Only large expenses and irrelevant judgments would be forthcoming there; most problems were better settled in council. While some villagers took to litigation early and avidly as a means of gaining personal advantage, many felt that courts could only hinder the settlement of important jati matters. Thus disputes about adoption in Haripura village were not taken to courts until about 1945. In Totagadde the first time a family of the middle jatis had recourse to a court was about 1949. In the 1950s no Harijan of that village had taken a case to court, having neither the knowledge, the money, nor the temerity to do so, although the Brahmins of the village had used the courts for longer than anyone in the village could remember. There was a "moving legal frontier." British law took hold more readily in some matters than in others and was used more quickly by some groups than by others (Dhillon 1955, p. 108; Harper and Harper 1959, p. 464; Galanter 1964).

Many jural issues could not be taken to a government court because the court could not assume jurisdiction over them.[1] Thus the redress of ritual offenses was—and still is—largely outside the official law. The social order of jati and village could not be maintained without provision for such redress. Government law offered no such provision nor feasible alternatives. Villagers felt they had to keep their own jural processes as free as possible from contamination by the government's legal system. They could not keep the two entirely separate, partly because courts soon came to be used as prime weapons in the status quest.

Four of the chief discrepancies between British law and village law-ways are sketched by Bernard Cohn for North India (1959a, pp. 90–92). They hold broadly true throughout India. The first discrepancy is between the villagers' hierarchical view and the basic precept of British-based law of the equality of the individual before the law. When people appear in court they are to be judged in terms of their stripped-down roles of plaintiff or defendant. Who they are outside the court, what other roles they fulfill, how society appraises their status—all this is not supposed to count, or at least not very much. To villagers generally this is not quite nonsense—legislators and judges naturally have their own jati customs—but it is unsuitable for jati or village purposes. They know that in their society men have widely different inherent worth. A man cannot and should not divest himself of all but one narrow role. A Chamar laborer knows that he is not equal to the Thakur landowner. "He may want to be equal, but he knows that he is not. The Thakur cannot be convinced

[1] When persons who were made outcaste sued the outcasters in the courts, the courts tended to apply the English law relating to expulsion from a club. A Calcutta court, however, ruled that on grounds of "natural justice" legal protection was more necessary for expulsion from caste than for expulsion from a club, and therefore cases of outcasting were cognizable by the civil court. But when the matter was taken to the Privy Council, the analogy of the English law pertaining to clubs was upheld (McCormack 1959, pp. 34–38).

in any way that the Chamar is his equal, but the court acts as if the parties to the dispute were equal" (Cohn 1959a, p. 91). It renders its verdict on these grounds and frequently the verdict is promptly negated by the actualities of village power.

A second discrepancy is between status and contract, as Sir Henry Maine showed. In official law the relation between landlord and tenant is a contractual one, limited to use of land and payment of rent; actually it is a multiple relationship, involving many obligations. A judicial decision that deals only with the contractual aspects must ignore such critical elements in the relationship as the tenant's obligation to assist in the wedding of the landlord's daughter or the landlord's obligation to pasture the tenant's cow. "People must continue to live and work together in the multiple society. So decisions of the courts based on ideas of contract do not fit the value system and social structure of the Indian village" (Cohn 1959a, p. 91).

A third disparity concerns the necessity for a decision. The procedure of official law requires a firm and reasonably quick decision; in any given case there should be a winner and a loser. The whole sense of the panchayat pattern is contrary to this. A common panchayat purpose is to delay, to talk, and to wear away the differences until a compromise satisfactory to all sides in a quarrel can be evolved. A man who feels that he has a strong case or who is overwhelmingly more powerful than his opponent may press for a quick decision in order to demonstrate his power, but a councilor should try to establish at least a fiction of compromise. The dignity of each disputant should appear to be preserved, so that the council promotes social maintenance rather than status victory.

Lastly, official procedure requires that in any legal case only that case is to be settled, related disputes are not directly relevant. In panchayat procedure nothing is irrelevant if it can bear in any way on the cause of the difficulty. The case that is ostensibly the crux of a dispute brought before a panchayat may turn out to be only a minor expression of a long-standing antagonistic relationship between two families. Elders in a panchayat believe that they must get to the root of the trouble if they are to judge effectively. An official court, on the other hand, can deal only with the case that is the symptom and is not allowed by its rules to probe from symptom to cause.

The official law could maintain the state, it could not and did not maintain the jati or the village. Governmental officials suppressed banditry, established better communications, ensured the collection of revenue, regularized land records, eliminated armed uprisings, and protected markets and trade. These consequences of the British regime had important effects on the whole system of caste and on its local manifestations.

Even though British officials did not want to get involved in caste matters and refused to allow caste questions to come formally to the government courts, they did in effect rule judicially on many caste issues. Among the cases in which they had to take jurisdiction were those involving varna classification, jati offices, and interjati relations (Cohn 1965, pp. 113–114). But for the most part government law could only set certain limits to social action. Within these very broad limits it either did not attempt to trespass or was kept out.

The Domains of Court and of Panchayat

The courts were well suited, however, to serve one aspect of village society, the waging of status competition. Individuals could gain superiority over their opponents, one alliance could establish supremacy over another, a jati could force advantage over others, if the rivalries could be framed as issues over which an official court could take jurisdiction. To succeed, the framers then had to win the court cases. Such use of the courts by individuals is illustrated from Totagadde village in Mysore, where courts are frequently used as tools in personal feuds. A man brings a case to court when he believes he can score better over his antagonist there than by laying the case before a panchayat, where the true facts are more likely to be ascertained and the record and personality of the disputants weighed in the balance (Harper and Harper 1959, p. 464).

Litigation figures also in the struggles between alliances in Kishan Garhi village (Aligarh district, U.P.) where, on the average, a new court case is entered each month. There were usually about three such cases pending at any one time when Marriott studied the village (1955b, p. 175). Struggles between jatis as well as alliances are waged through the courts by villagers of Senapur (Jaunpur district, U.P.). A landowner of the dominant Thakur jati who takes a case to court usually anticipates not just one quick case but a series of legal battles, adjournments, appeals and counterappeals, by which a poorer competitor can be ruined. "Since British procedure and justice appeared capricious to the Indians, someone with a bad case was as prone to go to court as someone with a good case." The prestige of a family was much enhanced by success in litigation and its power was heightened if it could ruin competitors through the agency of the courts (Cohn 1959a, p. 93).

Only the stronger competitors can afford a trial of strength at official law. Moreover, it is a more ruthless way to gain advantage, as Dumont points out in discussing courts and panchayats among the Kallar of southern Madras. A Kallar uses an official court when he seeks to ruin an adversary by any means, because the panchayat is too reasonable, too well informed, too careful of reconciliation "pour servir ce romantisme de la querrelle…" (1957b, p. 306). Only the stronger families or alliances can purchase the legal services needed to draw up charges and to steer a case through the courts. Only they can mobilize the manpower needed to stage a legally convincing scene and to supply suitably briefed and staunchly unwavering witnesses. Occasionally a poor Kallar will resort to the courts, but only if he is particularly stubborn and foolhardy, and unusually convinced of the merits of his case.

Villagers sometimes fabricate a legal complaint as a means of enforcing a panchayat ruling or of exerting pressure. In Sirkanda, a hill village near Mussoorie, three of the disputes analyzed by Berreman were so concocted. "In each case grievances which could not be successfully brought to a court of law were resolved by manufacturing a case which could be decided by the courts." In one case a man involved in an illicit sexual affair was brought to court on a charge of assault and rape and was punished by the court; it was the only case of rape, either actual or alleged, ever known in this locality. In another case villagers resented one man's prosperity; they hid liquor in his house and then told the police that he was dealing in illegal liquor. The third case was of a villager of lower jati who was considered to be intolerably insolent by men of higher rank; he found himself in court charged with theft (1963, pp. 270–272).

Civil proceedings are also staged for competitive advantage. Land can sometimes be pried loose by litigation. In one West Bengal village it is a main way of obtaining land. "Thus, a well-to-do man who finds some claim, however ephemeral, to the land of a poorer man, may consider it a wise investment to pursue the matter through the courts." The poorer man, knowing he cannot sustain a long legal struggle, may sell his land at a reduced price to another man who does have the resources for a court fight. This sets two prominent villagers at odds with one another or strengthens an already existing rivalry (Nicholas and Mukhopadhyay 1964, p. 28).

The British judges who had to apply the official law were generally aware of its shortcomings. The author of one of the earlier works on Hindu law examined the legal opinions delivered in every court of the Presidency of Bengal from 1811 to 1828 and found that "at least nine-tenths of the opinions were ascertained on examination to be erroneous, doubtful, unsupported by proof or otherwise unfit for publication" (quoted in Cohn, 1961c, pp. 624–625). The author of a modern compendium of Hindu law comments that "a surprising amount of 19th century case-law is only partly competent, or even, frankly bad. The student should not look at any pre-1930 case in Hindu law which is not mentioned in this book; and even where one is cited he should approach it with reserve" (Derrett 1963, p. 6).

A former member of the Indian Civil Service, Penderel Moon, wrote about the puzzlement felt by a young officer when he recognized how the law actually worked: "Litigation has become a national pastime and the criminal law a recognized and well-tried means of harassing, imprisoning, and even hanging one's enemies." He found that every official who had anything to do with the criminal administration was aware that the courts were "a sham and a mockery," each one deplored it, and yet nothing could be done about it (1945, pp. 53–54).

The judges were honest and villagers could count on that. The judges could not be manipulated, but the law could be. Once the legal framework of a case was properly contrived, the judge had little or no alternative but to issue the verdict desired by the contrivers. It was too much to ask of government officials, whether British or Indian, that they give up the postulates and procedures of the official law and it was impossible for most villagers to accept postulates and procedures that were so incongruent with the realities of their society. Since independence, there have been notable changes in official law, but thoughtful and responsible officials still deplore the gap between the purposes of the law and the results of its use in the village milieu.

If the law has indeed been so ill-adapted to the maintenance of village society, how could it serve to maintain a state whose people are, in great majority, villagers? The answer is partly that the official law and the customary law have been used as parallel codes, each influencing the other, but each sovereign in a different domain and neither absolutely inimical to the other.

Just as individuals or alliances will wage the competitive struggle with their rivals through the courts, suitably transposing the issues into terms a court will comprehend, so a jati or an allied set of jatis may carry the struggle for higher status into the courts. During British rule, court rulings were handed down on the varna status of such jati groupings as those of the Kayasths and Marathas, and of such sect-based jatis as the Lingayats and Jains (McCormack 1959, pp. 23–30).

Fighting the jati's good fight in the legal battlegrounds is seen by villagers as an entirely proper thing to do, but hauling a jati fellow to court over an issue internal to the jati is not generally approved. It is done frequently enough, but usually in the face of social pressure against taking an internal affair into the external lists (cf. Cohn 1965, p. 107). This pressure is sometimes explicitly stated, as it was in an assembly of Mahanayaka Sudras, cultivators in Puri district, Orissa. At a meeting of this assembly in 1935, one of the recorded decisions was that no member should file legal proceedings in connection with caste observances. "In case one does so he will be outcasted till the Assembly of Nine-Regions decides one way or the other. No assembly of any single region or sub-region or an area will have the right to lift the boycott" (Patnaik 1960a, p. 88).

The difference between court and panchayat powers is illustrated in the account of a dispute between two Vokkaligas of Wangala village. The quarrel had been going on for five years when Scarlett Epstein observed it in 1954–1955. It was about the ownership of a quarter-acre of land.

One claimant, Kempa, had strong support in the panchayat. The other, Timma, had won a number of legal appeals and was entitled to get police protection if anyone interfered with his cultivating the plot. But when Timma's wife began to plant seedlings, Kempa and his brothers stopped her. Timma brought a policeman from town who warned Kempa that he must not interfere. Yet after the police had gone Timma still did not dare to use the land. Police protection is a sometime thing; the danger from village antagonists is constant.

Shortly thereafter a compromise was suggested in a panchayat meeting: that the plot be equally divided between the two. Both men had already spent at least double the market price in legal fees, but neither was yet ready to compromise. Kempa belonged to a leading lineage and a strong alliance. Timma was of an inferior lineage and had to make recourse to the law because he had little power in the village. Kempa's strength had effectively blocked the legal writ. When Mrs. Epstein left the village, the case was still unsettled and the disputed land remained uncultivated (1962, pp. 123–124).

As a member of the jati, a man generally prefers to have disputes settled through the jati panchayat. But as a partisan in a contest, he feels he should avail himself of whatever means will advance his cause. If he believes that he can gain personal advantage through using the courts, he is likely to do so despite his contrary views when he is an interested onlooker rather than an engaged contestant.

Now that more villagers can use the law and government laws impinge ever more deeply into village affairs, the competition for status and power is increasingly staged in the arena of the courts. Nevertheless, much of the settlement of internal disputes and of the redress of ritual breaches continues to be handled by jati fellows through their own jural resources rather than by external legal agencies.

CHAPTER 18

Jati Enterprises and Functions

The people of a jati do more collectively than regulate their internal affairs. They commonly carry on joint enterprises; they usually work together to advance and defend the jati's status in its local order. In addition, they take the jati as a prime focus of personal identification and as a primary cultural social unit.

Jati Enterprises

The annual rites for lineage or jati deities, among those who have them, require joint planning and preparation. If there is a jati temple, subscriptions may have to be collected for its upkeep. If the jati-group has a part to play in a village festival, its panchayat assigns the various roles and sees to the provision of needed materials and facilities. A feast is commonly a salient feature of such festivities. A panchayat arranges for the food and for the special cooking utensils that are needed. These utensils are group property; their care is entrusted to a respected and reliable member of the group. In such ceremonial activities people see their group physically defined; each one's place in it is made manifest in action. In a lineage rite only brethren of the lineage are active participants; all others are spectators. The boundaries of the lineage are then clearly defined and the hierarchy within the lineage clearly demarcated as elders, juniors, and women have their respective parts to play (cf. Mandelbaum 1954b). During village ceremonies in which several jatis cooperate each jati has its traditional assignment. Jati members can take pride in the honor of the assignment and in the merit of its performance. If there is argument between two jatis for a ritual privilege, each side gives battle in a spirit of jati solidarity.

Secular enterprises are occasionally undertaken by a jati-group or jati although they tend to be more in the province of the village council. The Harijans in a village generally use separate wells. Where there is more than one sizable jati-group of Harijans, each likes to have its own well. The sinking of such a well is the concern of the jati-group. Among the Balahis the decision to do so is made at a panchayat meeting. The headman is authorized to collect a share of the expenses from each family and he assigns the work to be contributed by each adult. "Whoever fails to pay his due or does not appear for work, is excluded from the use of the well after its completion" (Fuchs 1950, p. 40).

Among the Kotas, work parties would be organized to complete a specific task, as the laying of a roof, which needed more labor than a single family could muster at one time. Each family was expected to send a worker, usually one of the younger people. The work was done with singing and ribald repartee and was capped by a feast. This kind of mutual help has largely lapsed, labor is now mustered by wages rather than jati obligation, but many an old villager in the mid-twentieth century fondly remembered the good times he had, in retrospect at least, as a participant in the work parties of his youth.

Efforts to preserve or improve jati status are not matters of nostalgic reminiscence; they are lively, ongoing, common occurrences in village life. When a panchayat of a low-ranking jati meets to defend its rights, the principal weapon at its command is the boycott. The council may decree that all members of the jati should withdraw from jajmani relations, trusting that the need for their services will bring the other group to terms. Such strike action by a jati-group requires backing by a jati panchayat; otherwise the recalcitrant patrons may get the goods and services from other villages. It also presumes that the patrons cannot get along without these services. But as alternate sources of supply have become increasingly available, this power of the artisan and serving jatis has diminished. Thus in a village of Delhi State, the dominant Jats decided to reduce the fees paid to a family's barber for his part in the marriage arrangements. The local barbers refused to accept the reduction, whereupon the patrons entirely dispensed with the function of barbers at Jat weddings. At this the barbers stopped all their services to the Jats, including shaving and hair cutting. Some Jats began to shave themselves, others found willing barbers elsewhere, and the barbers' strike was broken (Lewis 1958, pp. 66–67, 82).

Another example of the breaking of a strike is from Khalapur in western U.P. There an untouchable group refused to perform their traditional task of removing dead cattle. The dominant Rajputs were inconvenienced, but, more important, "They saw the move as a threat to the social order."[1] There are deep factional cleavages among the Rajputs of this village, yet they stood together against the recusants. The Harijan house sites belonged to the Rajputs, and even though government rulings have set aside claims to this ownership, the villagers still feel that the Rajputs can evict others from their houses. Also the Rajput landowners can, if they like, prevent people of the lower jatis from using the fields for latrine purposes or for gathering fodder. The unified Rajput reaction quickly restored the traditional carcass-removal service by the Harijans (Minturn and Hitchcock 1966, p. 48).

The spur to much of a jati's joint enterprise is the pressure for advancing or defending jati status. Such efforts are examined in the later chapters on social mobility. Villagers of lower jatis commonly

[1] When the dominant Havik Brahmins of Totagadde in Mysore were confronted with the same kind of refusal, they did not interpret it as did the Rajputs of Khalapur. Although they seem to be as strongly dominant in their village as the Rajputs are in Khalapur, and more ritually meticulous, they found a scriptural passage that, as they interpreted it, permitted Brahmins to remove dead cattle. Therefore they did not take drastic steps against the recalcitrant Harijans (Harper 1968).

feel that their jati is inherently entitled to a higher place in the order than is generally assigned to it. As soon as they think they have the resources to do so, they try to make good their claims. From their viewpoint, they are not asserting any new status, but only restoring the rank that had been theirs in earlier times. So when Harijan villagers try to throw off debasing customs and to take on more elevated practices, they are not attempting to replace the highest jatis in their local systems and still less to do away with the hierarchical order, but rather to be accorded honorable place in one of the levels above the lowest.

The thrust for status rise is reflected in some of the early Buddhist writings concerning guilds of artisans. A guild had many of the functions of the later jatis. It fixed rules of work and wages, standards and prices; it had juridical authority over its members and that authority was upheld by king and government. Each guild was jealous of its prerogatives; each pressed its claims against competitors of other guilds, sometimes to the point of street battles and riots (Basham 1954, pp. 217–218). In more recent times, the records of the court of the Peshwas in the eighteenth century show that many jatis protested to government about being restricted to unduly low jati practices (Ghurye 1961, pp. 186–187).

The traditional methods of jati improvement have been expanded in modern times. Improved communications have contributed to the widening of social horizons, as have new economic opportunities and the new possibilities of political power. Education for the jati's youth has become an essential feature of a program for jati improvement. Jatis of a close cluster tend to merge and so give added strength to jati endeavor. In order to take advantage of the newer means of jati elevation, a different kind of organization is required, with elected representatives and empowered officials, regular meetings and jati publications, all usually fashioned after the models of government agencies or political parties. These modern jati enterprises are also discussed below in relation to social change.

Variations in Jati Organization

Jatis vary greatly in the extent and effectiveness of jati organization. We have mentioned this in connection with internal alliances; it applies as well to their external relations. Hutton reports, "It has frequently been observed that the lower the caste in the social scale, the stronger its combination and the more efficient its organization" (1961, p. 99). This generalization was based mainly on the observations of British administrators; it is borne out by some of the anthropological studies.

Thus in a village of Kanpur district (U.P.) the highest ranking jatis do not have intervillage panchayats while most others do (Sharma 1956a, pp. 298–301). Similarly, in Totagadde village in Mysore, the formal jati organization—both intravillage and intervillage—of the Harijans, "who are repressed by all other castes," is more tightly knit than that of the jatis of the Sudra category. Most loosely organized is that of the Havik Brahmins (Harper and Harper 1959, p. 461). The reason for the greater unity, the authors suggest, is that the lower jatis need to muster their strength against the dominant landowners, while the men of the dominant jati, firm in their power, do not have such a need. Yet in another Mysore village, Wangala, the Harijans have no panchayat organization beyond the village (Epstein 1962, p. 118), perhaps because they are even worse off than are the Harijans of Totagadde.

When a jati-group is very poor and totally dependent, its people cannot afford to organize at all beyond the village. This holds true of whole villages where all the inhabitants are poor and quite completely at the mercy of outside landowners. In the parts of West Bengal, for example, where village lands were owned by a few dominant landowners or a single one, the landowners made most decisions and panchayats of any kind were rare and feeble. In those Bengal villages where land ownership was more widely shared, there was a corresponding increase in panchayat activity and effectiveness (Nicholas and Mukhopadhyay 1964, pp. 36–38).

Rivalry, rather than poverty or dependence, is a main cause for the looser cohesion of many higher jatis. For example, the Brahmin landowners of Kumbapettai village (Tanjore district) maintained little in the way of jati or jati-group organization at the time of Gough's study of them. Quarrels between families of the strongly dominant Brahmin jati "drag on in a desultory manner for months, sometimes years, until both parties are weary or kinship or ceremonial obligations draw them together again" (Gough 1955, p. 44). These Brahmins would gather in council to preserve a ritual norm or to punish rebels of low jati, but this was not often necessary. As for other matters, a Brāhmin landowner does not particularly need to cooperate with his peers, either economically or socially. He is trained from childhood to value the dependent relation of son upon father rather than the cooperative relationship among brothers. In the low jatis, as we have noted, a father's authority is relatively short-lived; it is broken shortly after a boy's puberty, when the boy becomes an independent wage earner. In such jatis the main emphasis is on the equivalence and solidarity of peers and on the solidarity of the jati-group and jati (Gough 1956, pp. 845–846).

Some social variations and cultural differences within a jati are to be expected. Jati fellows do not always march as a close social company, hewing to a set direction, fulfilling given functions, and mechanically correcting deviations. Commonly there are differences in wealth and power, in goals and ideals, in worship and occupation. But in certain matters, particularly those that involve permanent pollution, the people of a jati impose sharp limits on possible deviation by any of their fellows.

Jati as Means of Identity and as Social Unit

Despite such variation within his jati, a villager typically holds strong feelings of jati identification and cohesion. He feels so strongly identified with his jati in part because there are few or no alternatives to claim his loyalty, but mostly because he has been identified as a jati member by others through all his life and he identifies himself as such. He does so because a very large part of all his social relations are within his jati. It is, first of all, the harbor of his kin; all his kinsmen are of the jati, none are outside it.

The valence of kinship helps to hold a jati together, despite the rivalries that beat at its unity. Men of one village may be at odds with their jati fellows in another village. Yet each side may well have affinal relatives in the other locality, and a man does not like to be long estranged from these kinsmen. So it goes through the intricate web of kinship. Thus disunity in the jati is diminished, if not always and for everyone, still often and for many of the jati.

There is, further, the bond of common interest in work and livelihood. A potter does not have the same economic concerns as does an astrologer, nor does a farmer find as close understanding with a merchant as he does with another farmer of his own jati. Even if only a few in a jati-group actually practice the traditional occupation, most are apt to be in a similar economic range of occupation. A man's friends in the village are most often of his jati; all the more so for a woman, whose movements and social contacts are more restricted.

The great ritual events of the life cycle, marriages and funerals, bring together gatherings of kin, that is, of jati fellows. When a person goes to another village he usually visits with his jati fellows there. Communication between villages is largely between people of the same jati. Within a village, different jatis or blocs of jatis may use different dialects as their home language (Gumperz 1958, 1961; Bright 1960; McCormack 1960).

A child learns quite early to discriminate between his jati fellows and those of other jatis. He absorbs the self-image of his jati in countless ways. A Rajput boy learns about the martial style and regal tradition of his group by the bearing of his elders, by their contemptuous references to lesser breeds, by the tales, proverbs, and ballads he hears frequently. He may later reject that ethos, but he is not often indifferent to it (cf. Hitchcock 1958). Similarly, one who was reared as an orthodox Brahmin may later deliberately leave behind his early training, but it does not usually leave him. He tends to prize learning, to disparage physical aggression, and to be personally fastidious, quite in the manner of his jati.

It is not only the higher jatis who entertain flattering views of themselves and have heroic tales to prove it. One of the great folk epics of northern India, the Lay of Lorik, is sung by Ahirs about one of their forebears. Ahirs are traditionally herdsmen and are not ranked among the higher jatis (Deva 1958, pp. 87–89). Even the very lowest jatis have explanatory tales telling how they fell from a higher state through no great fault of their own (cf. Reddy 1952, pp. 334–341; Fuchs 1950, pp. 235–237). The essential message of the origin legend of the tribal Konds, as summarized by Bailey, is duplicated in the origin myth of many lower jatis: "Konds belong to the same community as the rulers; Konds are a dominant caste; they have fallen because they are a little stupid and unlucky, and have had to come and live in the jungle, but in origin they are warriors and the associates of kings" (1960b, p. 161).

So a villager identifies closely with his jati because much of his social world is encompassed within it and because his concept of himself is part of his jati's idea of what kind of people they are. Coupled with this self-identification is his constant identification by others as one of his jati. Jati is a principal referent in village life and although one villager deals with another in terms of grosser categories jati is nonetheless at the basis of reference. Moreover, a villager's drive for higher status is tied to the status of his jati. He cannot rise much higher than its level and if his jati should fall in status he is bound to decline with it. From the inside view of the villager, his allegiance to jati is inevitable, necessary, and morally proper.

When jatis are surveyed from the observer's analytic view, the jati is seen as a main cultural and social unit in the larger system. On close examination many jatis turn out to be much less firmly bounded and distinctive than their members take them to be. Culturally, some jatis are indeed quite distinctive within their localities, but many more differ only slightly in ways of life from other jatis of the same level and vicinity. Whatever the actual degree of cultural difference may be, the salient factor for the system is that villagers think of jatis as culturally distinct from one another. This accords with their view that each jati is socially separate from all others in kinship matters. We have noted that jati boundaries are sometimes blurred in reality and that the exact range of jati membership is often unknown to its members. This does not impair the social system, however, principally because villagers assume that jatis are firm units. The fuzziness of jati boundaries has helped give flexibility to the system; because of it jatis could form and reform adaptively.

People use themes of behavior within the jati similar to those that they use in relations among jatis. Moreover, when a man acts to maintain a component of his jati, say his lineage or jati-group, he is thereby also helping to maintain the whole jati. Similarly, when he acts to uphold his jati, he is also contributing to the maintenance of the local system of relations among jatis. The main social context for these relations among people of different jatis is the village; it is another of the chief components of the social system.

VOLUME TWO

CHANGE AND CONTINUITY

PART V

VILLAGE, REGION, CIVILIZATION

CHAPTER 19

The Village: Separate Hearths and Common Home

A jati cannot stand alone. Its people necessarily cooperate with some people of other jatis; commonly they compete with still others. The main locale of this cooperation and competition is the village. The groups involved are primarily the families and jati-groups of the same village and its vicinity, rather than whole jatis of a region. To a villager then, his village is far more than just a collection of houses, lanes, and fields; it is a prime social reality. To the student and observer it is a principal unit for the understanding of the society. Yet some observers have doubted the significance of the village either as a corporate group or as a useful unit for analysis (e.g., Dumont and Pocock 1957, pp. 25–32; 1960, pp. 88–89).

These doubts arise, in part, in reaction to the exaggerated notions of village autonomy that once were current. They may also stem from the complexities of the relationship between the multi-jati village and the multi-village jati. Moreover, village discord is apt to strike the observer's eyes and ears more stridently than does village concord.

The standard quotation, often reprinted, on the Indian village as a monolithic, atomistic, unchanging entity is from a report by Sir Charles Metcalfe, one of the founding administrators of British rule in India. The passage begins, "The village communities are little republics, having nearly everything that they want within themselves and almost independent of any foreign relations." It goes on to tell that wars pass over it, regimes come and go, but the village as a society always emerges unchanged, unshaken, and self-sufficient. Later writers of considerable influence, among them Sir Henry Maine, Karl Marx, and Mahatma Gandhi, reiterated this idea and suggested that the village was so perduring because it was so self-sufficient (Metcalfe 1833, p. 470 or 1832, p. 331; Srinivas and Shah 1960).

When modern field studies came to be made, however, they showed quite a different situation. An Indian village typically is hardly a republic; it has certainly changed from time to time; and it clearly was not and not self-sufficient. The whole nature of traditional society militated against the independent isolation of a village. In earlier days there was a good deal of coming and going among villages, even though roads were poor and travel dangerous. Marriage affiliations were commonly made between families of different villages, and each marriage would set in train a lifetime of visiting between the two families by the married couple and at least another generation of such visiting by their children.

Such visiting still continues, as do other long-standing reasons for frequent movement among villages. Economic needs send people in and out of the village. Few villages have a complete roster of resident specialists. Senapur, near Banares, has twenty-four jatis, but a family requires services provided by from thirty-five to forty jatis. So there is constant movement for work and trade. Each local area is a kind of labor pool; some villages in it utilize the surplus labor of others; villagers with special skills circulate through the locality (Opler 1956, p. 7). Certain services are available only in the nearest towns. Bricklayers and lime-workers, goldsmiths and coppersmiths, florists and genealogists tend now to be found in towns or larger villages.

Markets are a major reason for travel within a locality. It is a rare place where no one is outward bound for market weekly, unless the village is itself the seat of a market concourse. A good many villages have been involved in an interregional market economy for centuries, producing crops that were transported across regions and states (Srinivas and Shah 1960, pp. 1376–1377).

There are also the religious attractions of other places. A village ceremony may bring visitors from hundreds of other villages. In every region there are holy places to which people go on fixed days or at any time when impelled by a pressing need. And there is the magnetic pull of the great centers of pilgrimage which draw millions yearly.

All these movements have been intensified and sped up in recent decades. New reasons for travel—education, administrative business, litigation—have augmented the traffic. To be sure, not every villager travels; many a village woman seldom leaves her neighborhood and some men stir forth only occasionally. But for most of its people the village is not by any means an isolated unit. Villagers are closely bound into a larger social sphere and have long been so joined. For example, Opler writes that the articulations of Senapur people with other communities and far-flung places is "not a recent development or a consequence of modern systems of communication or transportation. They rest on ancient practices and patterns" (Opler 1956, p. 8).

Just as a villager is bound to many other people with multiple strands—deal with one person and processions of others follow—so his village is linked by many ties to other villages, towns, cities. A village is not a neatly separable social and conceptual package but it is nonetheless a fundamental social unit. When an observer first comes to live in a village, the internal cleavages claim attention at once—in the very settlement pattern, in the daily avoidances, in the division of labor and of power—so that the signs of village solidarity tend to be overshadowed.

Village Solidarity

Yet such solidarity typically exists and comes alive for certain purposes and under certain circumstances. Villagers live close to each other; they see each other and interact more frequently than they do with people of other villages. They share the same familiar life-space and share also common experiences of famine or harvest bounty, of flood or epidemic, of village fast or festivals. A village is usually an administrative and revenue unit. This in itself provides some common experience in the school, in the post office, in revenue collection. A man commonly has his closest economic associates within his village—as patrons or clients or workers or customers—with whose help he makes his livelihood.

When a man goes outside his village, he is apt to be identified first of all by his village rather than by jati or other reference category. As two strangers meet at a weekly market or in town and begin to talk, one of the first questions they may ask of each other is, "To what village do you belong?" Long after a family has emigrated to a town, its members still know and can identify themselves by their ancestor's native village. In Maharashtra, Mrs. Karve reports, the village is called "White mother earth," the habitation area being so distinguished from the black fields, and a man uses this term in taking a solemn oath. If he is excommunicated he must beg forgiveness of all in the village before he can be taken back (Karve 1958a, pp. 83, 87).

If a village gets a reputation in its locality for a particular characteristic, all those in it are then dubbed with a common label, whether as simple, or hard-working, or tight-fisted. These stereotypes do not ordinarily have great importance, though a quarrelling mother-in-law and daughter-in-law, perhaps even husband and wife, may belabor each other with the less complimentary epithets of their native villages. Sometimes the village reputation becomes a more serious matter. Carstairs tells of an incident in a Rajasthan village in which a youth, urged by companions as a dare, ate a bit of human feces. This became known immediately, with sad results for the boy. Even more, all in the village came to be known as being from the place "where they eat feces" (Carstairs 1961, pp. 105–106).

The immediate judges and enforcers of jati ranking are the people of one's village. They follow the standards of the region and the civilization and will not depart too widely from these norms. Nonetheless, it is they who perform the acts and give the opinions that place a person's jati in a particular local niche. As we have seen, this varies from locality to locality. Thus in Bisipara village the washermen are ranked among the clean jatis, but in the neighboring Boad territory, in the same district of Orissa, they are considered untouchables (Bailey 1963b, p. 129).

There may also be certain differences in rank assignment from village to village in the same close locality. When a man of Ramkheri village, for example, attends a ceremony in a nearby village, he observes the rank order of the place where he is a guest, although it may differ from that in Ramkheri. But he does so within certain limits. One such limitation is that a guest will not take food from anyone from whom he would not take water in his own village. That is, a guest may adjust his conduct to the extent that he may take food from a person from whom he would ordinarily accept only water. To illustrate this variation from home practice, one Ramkheri villager cited the example of two men, one of Rajput and one of farmer jati, who went together in a wedding party to another village. The two could not eat in one line at home, but in the other village this was done. "We shall also eat in one line; and it will not be a matter for our Ramkheri caste councils, because it is the custom of that village." The author comments that a man going across the boundary to another village automatically sheds his status as a resident of his own village and can conform to the commensal rules of the host village. In this respect "the village is very much a reality" (Mayer 1960, pp. 49, 159). In other parts of India as well, the village, in minor but still appreciable degree, is the arbiter of its own ranking practices.

Out of these common standards, identifications, and practices comes an allegiance to one's village that is expressed in many ways. One way is through the feeling, held widely though not universally, that all in the village share something of a kinship bond. This is directly shown in the fictive kin relations and the village exogamy that we have noted for North India. In the south also, a marriage can be of concern to the entire village. This is particularly true in a small village like Gopalpur where, Beals writes, a marriage is seen as a victory in the competition among villages. Every marriage of a child of Gopalpur activates more kinship ties and facilitates future alliances for the people of Gopalpur. "For this reason, the village as a whole must sanction any marriage that takes place between Gopalpur and any other village, and the village as a whole undertakes the responsibility of ensuring that people from other villages get value received when they arrange a marriage in Gopalpur" (1962, p. 28).

Not all villages of South India, by any means, display this kind of interest. In some, especially where there is a vast social distance between highest and lowest, those at the top could hardly care less how the Harijans mate. But even in such places the topmost are still concerned that no one in their village should bring an evil reputation to it.

Village ceremonies are commonly an expression of village solidarity. In the region of Gopalpur this is explicitly demonstrated in the festivals called *jatras*, given by all in a village to honor their village deity. The host families invite relatives from other places and regale them with food and entertainment. Wrestling matches between teams from different villages are a principal feature. As each contestant grapples with his opponent, he is cheered on by his teammates and fellow villagers. Young men of all jatis (save the very lowest and perhaps the Brahmins) participate as teammates for their home village, their usual differences and cleavages forgotten for the occasion. Two men who had sworn to murder each other took part on one such team, their sworn intentions dropped for the sake of village victory. "In the hand wrestling as in other aspects of the jātra, intra-village differences of status are minimized in order to create a representation of village unity" (Beals 1964, p. 107).

A jatra festival is supposed to show the host village as a good, friendly, and cooperative place in which to live. Those who succeed in establishing a favorable reputation for their village gain advantage in marriage negotiations as well as in trade and employment. Hence most people in a village try hard at festivals to please the guests as well as to honor the deity. Women visitors "exist inside happiness" at these occasions, in good measure because fathers and elder brothers provide a plentiful supply of drink to their daughters and sisters who come back for the festival. Far into the night groups of women gather, sing, and pass the bottle.

The men guests, for their part, do not really want to be convinced that their hosts' festival is better than their own, so there is a great deal of criticism and faultfinding. "Visitors leaving a jātra talk about 'our village,' and about how well 'our village' behaved, and about the superiority of 'our village jātra.'" This competition between villages occasionally becomes so intense as to lead to riots.

Beals notes that a village that actually is free of serious conflict does not need to demonstrate the fact at great cost. Hence a village advertising its state of harmony by holding a jatra may be one that is not particularly harmonious. Yet in staging a successful festival, the people of a village build up and demonstrate—to themselves as well as to others—their village loyalties (Beak 1964, pp. 109–113).

Village solidarity rites are common to many parts of the land. In Ramkheri, for example, there is a ceremony at which all forty-four shrines in the village are honored in succession as the concern of the entirer village (Mayer 1960, pp. 101–102). Where a local deity is worshipped as the tutelary spirit of the whole village, there are special rites in which all villagers may take part. In Senapur the village deity is supposed to protect all its people and animals from external dangers. But he (or she) does so only "if they are willing to cooperate by obeying the accepted religious, moral, and spiritual discipline of the community"; at least once a year each family must worship the village deity (R. D. Singh 1956, p. 11).

Particularly dramatic expressions of village unity vis-a-vis supernatural forces occur in the cattle-curing rites, called *Akhta*, which are held in parts of North India. As described for a village of Delhi State (Freed and Freed 1966), during this rite the whole village is sealed off from the outside world for forty-two hours. No one may come in or go out, not even a bus may pass through. Every soul in the village must observe stringent taboos on the use of iron, wheat, and salt, and all must abstain from other customary activities as well. The daily routine of every inhabitant is abrogated; each one must be aware of and concentrate on the rite.

The ceremony is held when there is an epidemic among the village cattle. Its purpose is to cure the sick animals and to ward off disease from all the useful domestic animals of the village. The rite begins after dark on the first day when a group of men visit each house and cattle shed spreading smoke from a pot of burning incense and cow dung. The incense is believed to have cleansing and purifying powers. On the next morning every animal in the village—cattle, camels, pigs, donkeys, even chickens (though not, apparently, dogs and cats)—is collected at a given place and then driven in three circuits around the village with much shouting and splashing of water.

Following the herd comes a man holding the pot of burning incense. After the last round he runs through the motley herd and on across the fields to bury the pot in the land of another village, symbolically transferring the dikase from his own village to another. In the ceremony that the Freeds witnessed, the pot was buried on what was probably government-owned land; if the people of another village had come to know of an intention to plant the pot in their grounds, they would have been "ready with sticks" (Freed and Freed 1966, pp. 682–689).

The whole rite symbolizes the village as a defensive unit against malevolent supernatural forces. Villagers stand together then, apart from all the rest of the world. Together and alone they marshal their collective strength through collective discomfort. Together, without distinction of jati rank, they perform the prophylactic rites for their animals and ritually transfer the evil influence from their corporate body into that of another village.

There had been opposition to performing this rite in the village where the Freeds were living because such practices are contrary to the teachings of the reformist religious movement, the Arya Samaj. Most families of the dominant landowners are followers of this movement though only a very few observe all its precepts meticulously. One man said that his father was against it because if the village held Akhta, the observers would consider them foolish people (Freed and Freed 1966, pp. 682–683). The Freeds replied that they had never seen Akhta and would like to see it.

Later, after more cattle had died, the village council decided to hold the ceremony, though in somewhat modified form, to conciliate some of the objectors. This rite is generally being held less often than formerly, not only because of reformist opposition, but as much because other means of coping with the threat of epidemics are becoming known and used.

Village festivals of all kinds are fading out in a good many places (cf. Nath 1962) partly because internal dissensions make it difficult to arrange for them and partly because alternative events and channels have become popular. But even when the ritual manifestation of village unity diminishes, that unity may be shown in other ways.

One common way to show village unity is to repel incursions by outsiders. If the forces of government threaten all in a village, or if strangers attempt to harm a fellow villager, or if the people of another village assault one's own, fellow villagers may well rise to the joint defense. An example of this occurred in Rampura, near Mysore City, when the state agricultural department ordered that fishing rights in the village tanks should be auctioned off. The villagers had been fishing in these tanks whenever they wanted to, and they felt that this order was an encroachment on their rights. So when a government official came to the village and opened the auction there were no bids. The villagers had seen to it that no one from their village or from any other place could approach to buy their rights (Srinivas 1955b, p. 32).

A similar episode occurred in Wangala in Mysore when the Revenue Inspector announced the auction of an acre of good land because of delinquent taxes. The land belonged to a poor man who had suffered a series of misfortunes. Land is precious and scarce in Wangala and ordinarily, eager bidders would not be lacking. Yet the leader of a rival alliance declared that no one should attend the auction because "to bid at such an auction would be supporting the Government against a man of one's own village." This was decided at a panchayat meeting; the auction was later canceled and arrangements were made for the owner to borrow enough to satisfy the tax arrears. Village (and jati) unity overrode factional differences (Epstein 1962, pp. 143–145).

Two such incidents are told for Shamirpet, near Hyderabad. One day some soldiers from a nearby cantonment rode into the village in two army trucks and began loading firewood belonging to a villager. It was obvious that they did not intend to pay and when the owner remonstrated, they beat him up. Word of this spread quickly through the village; men armed with staves came rushing up to stop the looting. At this the soldiers retreated and threatened to come back with reinforcements to destroy the whole village; they did not.

On another occasion, water for Shamirpet fields was diverted under cover of night to the fields of Aliyabad, a nearby village. "Next morning an organized team from Shamirpet attacked Aliyabad." The Aliyabad people said that the water had been diverted by mistake; probably they had bribed the guards and had overreached themselves by not allowing any water at all to flow into Shamirpet. "But in the dispute itself the two villages had forgotten their internal differences and dissensions and each of them had acted as one body" (Dube 1955b, pp. 210–211).

These three villages, Shamirpet, Wangala, and Rampura, appear to have relatively little internal friction. So their people may be more likely to rally defensively than would those of a deeply divided village. But even a fractious village has a certain unity simply because it is a node for the activities of its inhabitants. Typically, as was shown above, the village is where a man grew up, where his close kin live, where his work partners and helpers are, where his friends are found, where he worships, where he is known and placed. He shares with his village neighbors the lore of the village, that detailed inside knowledge that no others have.

It has been said that the village is a unity because of its extensions, not in spite of them (Singer 1956b, p. 4). That is, the villager's relations with other people take place so largely in the context of his home village that he is socially and psychologically involved with the village as a whole. This is not to say that the village is always or even usually a unified community; it is to say that it is important to its people.

Some observers have stated that a villager participates in two kinds of unity, one "vertical," the other "horizontal"; the village is the vertical unit and is made up of horizontal layers, each of which is a jati. This may be too static a view of a villager's affiliations and actions. His support of one or another social group varies by context and by circumstances.

Thus in Rampura there are occasions when many men of the village stand together, as they may in a fight against another village during a festival involving a number of villages. Yet a Brahmin of Rampura would not be likely to be attacked there by the enemies of his village because he has a special ritual position as a Brahmin. An untouchable or a Muslim of Rampura would be involved in the fight more because of his attachment to a particular patron who was also in the fray than because of village patriotism. The same three groups, Brahmins, Muslims, and untouchables, are not given important formal roles in the annual village ceremony of Rampura but still their cooperation is sought in staging the ceremony (Srinivas 1955b, p. 33).

Just as the occasions for "vertical" unity do not necessarily engage every last man and group, so the occasions for "horizontal" unity do not necessarily bring in every man and family of the jati-group. Loyalty to jati sometimes conflicts with loyalty to village. An elder participating in a village council, as we have noted, must sometimes tread a narrow line between what is good for the village and what is to the advantage of his jati kinsmen. The common suspicion is that kin ties are placed over all, but one test of an able leader is whether he can somehow reconcile the two, preserving the public good while not neglecting the cause of his kin.

The relations among jatis in a village are ways of "being together separately," as Beals puts it. That phrase applies to the human condition anywhere; each person is an individual in his family, a member of one group in a collocation of groups, a part of a local society in a larger social order. But for Indian villagers the togetherness and the separateness are largely carried on in the same locale, with much the same set of people and with the ritual separations pervasively significant. Separation often is a ruling concern, yet separation must always be mitigated by the fact that a jati cannot exist by itself. In Gopalpur, "The belief that jatis are related to each other, like brothers, and that all jatis provide essential services for each other creates a unity within the diversity of jatis" (Beals 1962, p. 41).

A village is clearly an important and viable social entity to its people, who also take part in the larger society and share in the pattern of the civilization. Hence the question raised by some students of Indian society as to whether the village is an isolable unit for study requires no absolute answer. In some ways it is, in others it is not. The people and culture of the village should be studied both in their local milieu and in wider perspective (cf. Marriott 1955b, pp. 171–182).

Settlement Patterns and Solidary Relations

Two important influences on village solidarity are local geography, especially the settlement pattern, and local economy, particularly the means of land management. These affect the ways in which the people of a village pull together or do not, yet it should be emphasized that the feeling for one's village is usually strong whatever the geographic or economic variations may be.

There are three main types of settlement pattern. Most common is the nucleated village, a tight cluster of houses surrounded by the fields of the villagers, perhaps with an outlying hamlet or several satellite hamlets. A second type is the linear settlement, in which houses are strung out, each surrounded by its own garden or compound, with little or no physical demarcation to show where one village ends and where another begins. This type occurs in Kerala, in Konkan, and in the delta lands of Bengal (Miller 1954; Karve 1958a, pp. 74–75; Nicholas 1963; Mencher 1966). The third type is simply a scattering of homesteads or clusters of two or three houses, again with no necessary physical indications of the limits of any one village. This type is found in hill areas, as in the

Himalayan foothills, in the highlands of Gujarat, and in the Satpura range of Maharashtra (Shah 1955b; Karve 1958a, pp. 76–82; Nandi and Tyagi 1961). In each type, both houses and fields are included in the people's definition of village.

Despite the blurring of geographical markers in the two latter types, the people of such villages know who belongs to their village and what it takes in. This may or may not coincide with the government's definition of where the bounds of a particular village lie, but the villagers themselves know who belongs to what village grouping. Thus in Sirkanda, in the Himalayas, about half of the villagers live outside the central settlement, mainly in field houses (called chans) which are some distance from the village nucleus. These outlying people readily identify themselves as belonging to Sirkanda and are so identified by others. "This in spite of the fact that they no longer reside in the village, that other villages may intervene between them and Sirkanda, and that they may be surrounded by the chans of other villages" (Berreman 1963, pp. 34–35, 260).

So also in northern Kerala where the line of houses of one village merges into another and the outsider can see no obvious boundaries. "The boundaries are nevertheless known to residents, and social relations are generally more intensive within than without" (Miller 1954, p. 411). In parts of the Bengal delta, houses line the higher ground at the edge of the waters; a village there is one segment of a long chain of houses, yet is a distinct social entity. In two such adjoining villages in Midnapur district, some houses of one village can only be reached by passing through a part of the other village. People of one are served by jatis of the other; men of one village own land in the other; at the boundary, adjacent families on both sides consider themselves to be part of the same neighborhood, "Yet the villages are quite distinct from one another." Each has its separate headman, its own meeting pavilion, its own temple. Each is maintained as a separate jural segment; its people convene their own council in settling disputes (Nicholas and Mukhopadhyay 1964, pp. 15–22).

In all three settlement types the village is an important social unit. But having said that, we must also emphasize that settlement patterns—and the factors that go into the making of them—affect social organization. For example, the dispersed villages of Kerala are more loosely organized than are the compact villages of Madras (Mencher 1966, pp. 143–146).

The effect of settlement pattern on village organization is further shown in a comparison of a linear village of the Bengal delta with a nucleated village of West Bengal. The nucleated village, called Chandipur (Murshidabad district), has one hundred sixty houses and one thousand people crowded in about five acres of habitation site. The other village, Radhanagar, has about one hundred houses along some twenty miles of winding settlement chain. Both villages share a generally similar culture although the nucleated village is much older and most of its land is held by the locally dominant Brahmins. The other village has recently been reclaimed from the waters; its settlers are mainly people from middle and lower jatis who dared settle on this frontier because of their hunger for land. Landownership is much more evenly distributed, there are fewer jatis of artisans and servants, there is less social interaction because of the dispersal of the houses, and less elaborate distinctions are made in caste ranking.

The contrast in political organization between the two is particularly marked. When a dispute is to be settled or a public decision made in the village of the delta frontier, the headman calls together a council and "eight or ten prominent men are sure to attend every meeting because no decision can be taken without them." In older Chandipur the headman is much more the supreme authority; he is by far the largest landowner in the village, the head of the most powerful faction of the ruling jati. He decides who is guilty, he decrees beatings and collects fines. "Others may come to watch and influential men may even express opinions, but it is the headman who makes decisions" (Nicholas 1963, p. 1195). Such concentration of power is not likely to develop under the greater dispersal of land ownership and of habitations in Radhanagar. The village is a viable unit in both instances, but a strung-out or scattered village is less amenable to close control than is a tightly packed huddle of houses.

The layout of a village generally reflects something of its social structure. Harijans commonly live in a separate quarter, removed from the main site by some open space and equipped with a separate water point, thus forming a distinct hamlet. Where there are two sizeable Harijan jati-groups, each tends to have its own locality. Nowhere in the Andhra villages observed by Mrs. Karve do the two main Harijan jatis there, the Malas and the Madigas, live in one section of mixed housing; she finds this true, also, of the Harijan jatis of Maharashtra (1958b, p. 137). Not only Harijans but any other jati-group may inhabit a separate hamlet for particular reasons of village history.[1]

The central village is typically divided into several sections, which may be formally demarcated as wards or more vaguely recognized as separate neighborhoods. In either case, particular jati-groups or lineages tend to reside in each section, giving some social distinctiveness to the several parts of a village. The distinctions are very marked in Sripurum village of Tanjore, where the three main social levels are mirrored in the residential pattern. The Brahmin jatis all live along one long street; the Adi Dravidas (the untouchables) live across a main road and jatis of the middle blocs labeled "non-Brahmins" are located between the two. The Brahmins' street is their exclusive domain, others do not enter it unless they have some particular business there. Nor do Brahmins ordinarily set foot in the Adi Dravidas' street; if they do they must bathe before resuming normal activities in their houses.

People of the three divisions are quite segregated from each other except in economic interchange. Most of the village land is owned by Brahmins; most Adi Dravidas are landless laborers; the non-Brahmins are mainly tenants and artisans. So the residential divisions parallel division of jati rank and economic class (Béteille 1962, p. 142). Social and physical separations have been particularly strong in Tanjore district villages because the Brahmins as dominant landowners could enforce rigorous ritual separation (cf. Gough 1955, pp. 47–52).

A family in most parts of the land prefers to live near its close relatives, partly because of the convenience of freer interchange in food and in all manner of things, but also because there is mutual protection in living together, especially for the smaller, weaker groups in a village. "A man feels safer in the *keri* (ward) of his caste," Srinivas says of Rampura in Mysore and this is widely so (1959a, p. 5). If there are many families of a jati, those of the same lineage cluster together. If there are only a few, the cluster includes the whole jati-group. Villagers have said (and I, for one, have reason to believe it is true) that even the dogs know their ward and try to chase out animals or strangers who amble in from elsewhere (cf. Smith 1952, p. 54).

The social ties of neighborhood are illustrated in the account of the wards of Ramkheri village (Mayer 1960, pp. 132–139). There as elsewhere a ward contains its own social nuclei. The participants in each nucleus may be found sitting on special platforms where the men smoke of an evening, or on favorite verandahs, or in workshops, or simply at good vantage points from which to see what is going on. To find a man, one goes to his accustomed leisure ground in his ward. Since

---

[1] The number of these satellite hamlets is said to be larger in eastern India, from eastern U.P. to Bengal, than elsewhere (Nath 1961, p. 142; see also Spate 1954, pp. 171–181).

women stay closer to home than do men, their daily interchange is all the more restricted to their own quarter of the village. They usually make good use of the trip to the well where women of various wards may gather, but there is a limit to the time that can be spent in this refreshing way. At harvest time, those whose fields are contiguous or close share one threshing floor and this provides an informal bond among villagers of different jatis in Ramkheri.

A good deal of informal cooperation normally goes on between neighboring households. People borrow utensils or staple foods from their neighbors in the ward and men exchange daily labor. Neighbors attend the minor household rituals of a family, those rites that do not bring in a large visitation of kin from other places. They also help in those rites where nonkin are necessary, as in a bridal procession, when women are needed to sing songs for background music and to provide foreground badinage.

Although neighbors do not necessarily belong to the same alliance, there is some tendency for an alliance to be centered in a particular quarter, partly because lineages and jati-groups tend to be similarly centered. Propinquity can breed enmity in village India as elsewhere, but, in general, village neighbors are likely to share at least some neighborhood interests and loyalties within the bounds of the whole village (cf. Dhillon 1955, pp. 43–45; Nicholas and Mukhopadhyay 1964, pp. 27–29).

Economic and Other Influences on Village Organization

A key factor in the relations among the families and jatis of a village is the nature of landownership. The following chapter deals with the kind of village in which one jati-group owns most of the land and thereby controls much of the village. Economic aspects of such control are illustrated in a comparison of two villages in Uttar Pradesh that are similar in area, in the number of jatis, and in general culture. In one, Madhupur, families of the dominant jati own 82 percent of the land and have long ruled the village. The other, Ramapur, has two leading jatis, the boatmen and the Brahmins, each of which derives considerable income from pilgrims to nearby Allahabad. These two jati-groups are at about the same economic level, and neither owns much land; most of its village lands were held by an absentee landowner at the time of the study. Though there is theoretically great ritual distance between the Brahmins and boatmen, social distinctions are not actually as sharply made in Ramapur as they are in Madhupur, where one jati-group dominates. There the dominant landowners kept other jati-groups in strict subordination and quelled attempts by lower jatis to raise their status (Opler and Singh 1952, pp. 188–190). Though jati relations in different villages are set in the same frame of ritual hierarchy, differences among villages in distribution of economic power make for considerable differences in these relations.

The effect on ritual relations of economic power is also shown in a brief comparison by Alan Beals of six villages in northern Mysore (1962, pp. 84–97). Though the six are only a few miles apart, there are notable differences among them. One is markedly conservative, another clearly progressive; jati lines are sharply drawn in one and in another they are more relaxed. In one, called Chintanhalli, there is a particularly great gap in wealth between the landowners and the rest of the villagers; that village has the most authoritarian social structure of the six. Chintanhalli lands are irrigated, are very productive, and are much too expensive to be purchased by farmers with little capital. Its garden crops require continuous, intensive labor. The landless laborers cannot oppose the landlords in organized, open conflict, because the landowners can defend their position too well with beatings and arrests. The laborers do express themselves through theft, murder (three in five years), and migration. This kind of conflict is not common in the region, and Beals concludes that it rises from the unusually great economic disparity in this village. In those villages of the sample with less disparity in wealth, there is also less rigid and pervasive stratification. Thus gross differences in wealth within a village, as in Chintanhalli, seem to make for more rigid stratification and authoritarian dominance. These conclusions are drawn from the preliminary study of only six villages. They are worth testing much more extensively.

Two other villages of Mysore are included in Beals's comparative observations. One village illustrates the effect of a peculiar ecology and of a strong sectarian religion; the other illustrates the influence of a nearby city. The first village, called Elephant, is situated in an isolated hill enclave. Most of the inhabitants are Lingayats, members of a sect-based jati. The Lingayat religion, more than the jati, seems to dominate in the village. "The people consider themselves among the last upholders of jati purity in an impure world." The village is a theocracy ruled absolutely by its priest and a few influential men. These rulers sometimes argue among themselves, but they permit little conflict, sin, disobedience, or theft in their village.

Elephant also "bears a peculiar cross" in that its men have to be especially considerate of their wives. There is no drinking water available in the village during the dry season, and water has to be carried up five hundred feet, over a mile of steep stone staircase, from a valley below. Families do not want to marry their daughters into so difficult a place. So the men of Elephant make the special concession of helping with the carrying of water and of wood. "Wives are treated with the greatest circumspection, for should one leave, it would not be easy to find another" (Beals 1962, p. 91).

The other village, called Namhalli, is dominated not by a sect dating from the twelfth century but by a telecommunications factory dating from the mid-twentieth century. Namhalli, as has been noted before, is near the city of Bangalore, and as the city has grown the village has become a quasi-suburb. Buses come every day to pick up and deliver the villagers who work in the factory. Yet, although Namhalli has been considerably affected and has recently benefited by the extension of the city, it is still essentially a village and the people follow the basic patterns and values of village life.

Beals writes that the villagers in Gopalpur, Elephant, and Namhalli share the same culture. "They all recognize the significance of jati, they all believe that it is sinful to disobey one's older brother, and they all hope to marry their sister's daughter" (1962, pp. 92–96). These clues indicate that proximity to the city for centuries did not greatly alter the usual village standards; proximity to and employment in factories has affected the villagers, as will be noted in the following chapter, but has not as yet altered these characteristics.

Urban influence does not seem to have affected village social structure greatly, although a strong impact of modern urbanization may yet come. In a review of the impact of urban areas on village life, Lambert concludes that the principal changes in village life do not stem from urban sources particularly but follow on general changes in the society. The social structure, he finds, is most sensitive to changes in land rights and the effect of the urban areas is "less than might be expected" (1962, pp. 129, 138–140).

This is further illustrated in Majumdar's study of Mohana, a village just eight miles from Lucknow. Two miles of rough cart road separate Mohana from a paved highway to the capital city and during the rains these two miles of mud discourage travel. Nonetheless, there is considerable contact with the city for trade, marketing, worship, and education. Yet the social order of Mohana does not differ appreciably from that of other villages of the region that are much farther from the city and have fewer contacts with it. The people of Mohana see themselves as villagers, supporters of a better, simpler, more pious way of life than they think prevails in the city. They may seek help from those who have special knowledge of the town and they may admire them for their experience, but most "regard the village as distinct and socially distant from the town" (Majumdar 1958a, p. 329). There may not be that much difference between town and village society, but many in Mohana believe there is, and are staunch for the village ways.

A factor that does carry great potency for change in village society is the advent of irrigation. This is well documented in the comparison, noted several times before, of two villages in Mysore—Wangala whose fields received irrigation, and Dalena whose lands did not. In Wangala the managers of the sugar factory took charge of most economic matters relevant to growing the new cash crop. As Wangala farmers prospered by producing sugarcane, they had no reason to venture beyond the village, and they intensified their local society and culture. In Dalena, no such farming potentials were created, no outside experts were provided, and the men had to seek opportunities outside the village if they were to keep pace with the increased prosperity of the more favored villages of the locality. They did seek such outside support and quite successfully. In doing so, they have given up some of the traditional goals, or at least modified them, and have taken to ways and standards that they have met in the town. This has indeed affected village social relations, but less because of the inherent attraction of the town than because of the economic forces that sent Dalena people to town (Epstein 1962, pp. 311–335).

Only a beginning has been made in classifying types of village social structure. The earlier studies, like those of Maine (1881) and Baden-Powell (1896), served their authors' purposes but are no longer adequate. Bose (1958c) has noted certain indices for classification including the degree of concentration of artisans or tradesmen and patterns of social change. Alan Beals has classified villages in relation to internal conflict; his guidelines have been adopted in Bernard Cohn's survey of dispute resolution to distinguish four village types. The first is the small village of only one jati. The three other types are multicaste villages with, respectively, a single head, a dominant jati, and no single dominant jati (Cohn 1965, pp. 83–98). The nature of village leadership is a salient element in this typology. The appointed officers of a village may or may not assume leadership roles but the functions of each office are important ones in maintaining the village community.

VILLAGE OFFICES: THE HEADMAN

The social establishment of a village normally includes an official headman (or headmen) and a keeper of land records the accountant. Both are agents of external authority, appointed by government and answerable to it. The headman is a member of the village who has specified duties and receives some pay for fulfilling them. He is usually a landowner, or at least one of the more substantial personages in the village. As a permanent resident he is subject to whatever social pressures his fellow villagers can exert on a co-resident. The accountant, however, need not be a member or old resident of the village, and in some states, the Punjab for example, it was official policy that he not be posted in his own village. In such places, and wherever the accountant is a sojourning stranger, the power he can wield for his own purposes tends to be great.

The headman's office goes by various names; its official functions are much the same throughout India. He is first of all the collector of land taxes. For doing this he receives a commission on the total amount collected or gets some rent-free land for his use. Secondly, he is the local link with the police. He is charged with keeping order in the village, and if some disorder occurs, it is he who must report it forthwith to the nearest police station. If the village employs watchmen, he supervises them; if the police require a weekly report, he has to send it in, naming any strangers in the village. Should a fight be in the making, he is supposed to try to break it up, and if he foresees an outbreak of violence he should call in the police before it occurs. In some places he reports the vital statistics; everywhere he must look after visiting government officials and should give them the impression that their orders and desires will evoke quick response. He is expected to act as the representative of the villagers when they want something from the authorities.

The position of headman is usually hereditary, though government officials can remove a headman for cause and shift the office to another family. The appointing officials may decide that there should be more than one headman—in Ramkheri village there are three, each responsible for a different part of the village. In Maharashtra, there are usually two, the revenue headman and the police headman. In the Kondmals region of Orissa, the village headmen have the police function, but the taxes are collected by a headman who has charge of a number of villages (Bailey 1957, p. 148).

With the headman's official duties go nonofficial functions. A headman may not be one of the actual leaders of his village or even of his jati-group, but the fact of his connection with police and officials can give him an advantage. In village eyes it endows him with potent influence, as it often does in fact. Police and other officials regard a cooperative headman as their man in the village and they are inclined to listen to him and to back him.

Because of this aura of influence, a headman may be called on to arbitrate disputes. He sits on the traditional village council, and is likely to be its chairman, insofar as there is a chairman. Often he leads in village ritual, functioning for all the inhabitants. This is especially true in the larger ceremonies in which all the villagers collectively stand before the gods (cf. Mayer 1960, pp. 112–114). When a group goes from the village to the district headquarters with a request for some village project, or attends on a political notable, or seeks a favor of a high official for the village, the headman is expected to be with them.

The actual influence of a headman depends partly on his personal abilities and social qualifications, which are quite like those we have noted for an alliance leader, and partly on the social structure of his village. Thus in Kumbapettai of Tanjore district, the headman is a nonentity. He is one of the dominant Brahmins there and they do not take kindly to any special preeminence of one of their number. They traditionally ruled the village without need for an effective headman (Gough 1955, pp. 43–44). In contrast, there is the headman of Chandipur in West Bengal. As the richest man of the ruling jati, he runs the village like a rustic dictator (Nicholas 1963, p. 1195). Supreme, also, but more in village esteem than in actual power, is the headman of Gopalpur in northern Mysore. Beals notes that the average villager of Gopalpur sees the headman as one who is wise and admirable and in every way superior. They take their disputes to him to be settled and are glad to obey him, even though many realize that he has a good many faults. For them he is "our Gauda," our headman. "Gopalpur creates its Gauda because the village has a need for a superior being, one beyond the ordinary"; that his life is really one of "loneliness, misery and fear" is of little concern to them (Beals 1962, pp. 53–63).

Most headmen are not ciphers or autocrats or presumed paragons. They are more often like the headmen of Shamirpet in Andhra or of Ramkheri in Madhya Pradesh, well-to-do men of respectable lineage and eminent jati. Their jati need not be ritually high but is almost always one that is powerful and respected in the locality (Dube 1955b, pp. 45–46; Mayer 1960, pp. 96–97). Such headmen maintain their influence by consulting with jati or alliance leaders on any issue of consequence; their power is tempered by the need for support from the leaders of their own and of other jatis. The appointment of a headman from among its members generally strengthens the power of a jati-group that is already strong. The office supports its power and can be used to increase it.

As new agencies for social and economic development come into a village, the headman does not have quite so strong a hold on communication with governmental authority. Other villagers come to have regular contacts with officials. The headman's grip weakens further when more villagers become educated enough to deal effectively with officials. Nevertheless, the village headman is usually someone to be reckoned with in village life. A visitor who ignores him may be resented not only by his close partisans but also by those villagers for whom he represents the village as a whole community.

Village Offices: The Accountant and Others

The accountant's office is quite a different one, more narrowly restricted to the one function of keeping the land records. It is one of the very lowest ranks of the government bureaucracy and is about as poorly paid as is the post of schoolteacher. The accountant is officially subordinate to the headman, and yet in his own sphere he may be one of the most powerful men in a village. This is because he is the sole guardian, sometimes the only interpreter, and the single recorder of the official documents that give rights to land.

The ordinary villager, as Lewis observed in Rampur, has no way of checking on the accuracy of the accountant. In order to challenge any record that he makes it is necessary to go through extremely costly and time-consuming litigation, perhaps up to the High Court (Lewis 1958, pp. 330–337). Moreover, any changes in the records which the accountant slips in without the owner's knowledge, may become legal if they remain unchallenged for a period of years—four years in the Punjab, five or seven in other states. Since even a literate, well-educated man cannot easily follow the accountant's quite technical details, a villager can hardly afford to antagonize the accountant.

The power of the accountant is vividly sketched in the Wisers' study of Karimpur village, east of Agra. There the accountant's records include the crop grown on a plot of land, its value, and the various rights held on it. He notes all changes in ownership, inheritance shares, mortgages, rents, and sales. Because many in the village cannot read and check his accounts, he possesses "powers which he, as a low-grade agent, could hardly be expected to disregard." In one case he could threaten, by indirect but unmistakable hints, to drop the name of one of the five owners of a grove. The unfortunate one had to pay something to him, else in a few years the omission of his name from the record would cost him his rights in the grove. "The possibility of its detection amid the masses of records are slim. Once when such a discrepancy was noted by an examining officer, the accountant blamed the carelessness of his assistant."

In another case a widow rented out her land for a term of five years. While she was on a lengthy visit to her relatives, the accountant transferred title to the land to the renter for a payment of fifty rupees. In this instance the widow took the case to court and, showing unusual diligence, won back the land. But the accountant was only reprimanded (Wiser 1963, pp. 107–111).

An accountant's common tactic is delay. If a man needs a copy of his title to some land, or if a sale or a mortgage must be recorded, the accountant can easily claim that he is swamped with work and hold off until the additional fee he demands, beyond the usual unofficial fee he always gets, is paid. In Rampur the purchase price of a plot is commonly recorded at a much higher price than was actually paid. This is a kind of title insurance because others may later challenge the sale and claim prior ownership on some legal technicality. But even if they win the case, they must give back to the purchaser the price which was recorded. The entry of this inflated price calls for another emolument for the accountant (Lewis 1958, pp. 332–333).

So villagers try to keep on the right side of the accountant. He gets gifts of grain, vegetables, milk, and fuel; often he has a good house rent free. For special transactions he gets a cow or a buffalo or even land. Some of his bills may be forgiven by a village merchant who is also a landowner. It is not only the small tiller of the soil who treats him with respect. Large landowners, even high officials, are sensitive to his power.

An officer of the Indian Civil Service, Mr. B. S. Grewal, in discussing this subject with me, told of calling on the Speaker of the Punjab Legislative Assembly in the days before independence. This eminent personage, knighted by the King-Emperor, was sitting on a cot beside a village man and was addressing him respectfully by a highly honorific title. After the villager had gone, the host explained that his visitor was the accountant in his ancestral village, where he owned land. Without the accountant's good graces, even he would be at a loss in his village. Mr. Grewal added that from his experience as Financial Commissioner of the Punjab in the 1960s, he found that the accountant was then still a very powerful figure in Punjab villages.

An accountant, for his part, can remind the villagers that he has to bear extraordinary expenses. In Karimpur, the accountant had to pay his immediate superior the equivalent of a month's salary. He had to appear before officials at district headquarters and this required more expensive dress as well as travel expenses. More to the point, however, is that his official association with educated people gives him motivation to improve his status, to give his sons an education, and to marry his daughters expensively into educated families.

Though at a disadvantage in any dispute with the accountant, villagers are not entirely helpless. They may take the records to court, as the Karimpur widow did, and get them corrected or, as happened in a village of Poona district, the villagers can get the accountant transferred. The accountant in Poona had overreached himself by using the office for the improvement of his jati as well as of his purse. He was a Harijan and he provided a public celebration on the birthday of the Harijan leader, the late Dr. Ambedkar. He procured contributions from non-Harijans for the purpose, but he soon was removed (Orenstein 1959, p. 421). And in Rampur, accountants "who overstep themselves are in danger of being killed by disgruntled groups" (Lewis 1958, p. 332).

The accountant in Rampur is in a special position of strength because he happens to have some of the functions performed by village headmen elsewhere. He is the sole representative of the revenue department in that village and is the main contact between villagers and other government officials. In other places, where the office is hereditary and the incumbent is a resident of the village, as is true in South India generally, his unofficial powers seem to be much diminished (cf. Srinivas 1955b, pp. 6, 12). Presumably he can aid one alliance rather than another, but apparently he does not levy tribute quite so heavily as does an accountant who is posted to a village for a few years and feels he must mine the territory while he can.

The new programs of land reform and of consolidation of holdings have given fresh opportunities to the accountant. Where there is a maximum limit to the amount of acreage a family can cultivate, it is he who can report the distribution of holdings that is to the family's best advantage. And when tenants receive rights to a plot after cultivating it for a certain number of years, the accountant can see to it that the actual period does not become a matter of record. When Mrs. Wiser returned for another look at Karimpur after thirty-two years, land was even more difficult to obtain than before, and one of the ways of getting it was "by bribing the village land recorder to alter a record" (Wiser 1963, p. 155).

Yet the accountant's monopoly is being weakened as more men can read the records and more dare complain to higher officials about a faked record. And when the accountant is drawn into responsibility for village welfare, his powers change. Thus in Wangala the accountant is a hereditary official of a Brahmin jati, as is common in that part of Mysore. His superior officer, called the Revenue Inspector, can join with the village accountant in giving or withholding favors. He can turn a blind eye to the cultivation of waste lands belonging to the village; he can be permissive about overdue taxes or illegal land transactions.

In recent years, however, the Inspector and his staff have been given the task of encouraging villagers to be progressive. For this an Inspector needs the cooperation of the villagers and on such cooperation depends his promotion. So for weeks before a scheduled visit of the Deputy Commissioner of the district, the Revenue Inspector, in his city clothes, was seen persuading the villagers—who in this prosperous place are not much concerned about official visits—to sweep the street and put up a decorated arch of welcome. At this time the Revenue Inspector is most amenable to requests from the villagers. On one occasion he had to meet a quota of land to be given as part of a Bhoodan campaign for voluntary redistribution of land. A deal was arranged whereby two acres of useless land were donated, and one acre of the village's common land, potentially very productive, was quietly transferred to a magnate (Epstein 1962, pp. 142–143).

Such stirrings among revenue officers, however, are still small, and in very many villages the accountant retains a good deal of negative power to hamper land and crop transactions and positive power to augment his income. One effect of these powers has been to lift the status of the local jati from which accountants are recruited. Moreover, the accountant's role has commonly been understood by villagers as that of a government servant who is alien to the village even though he resides in it and has power over its inhabitants. This may have set a pattern for such newer roles as that of the tubewell operator, also a government servant, also an alien, and also one whose power must be parried with cash.

The schoolteacher is another government employee who has long been a fixture in many villages. He too, is often a stranger who temporarily resides in the village but, except when he is a person of outstanding personal ability, he generally has little power or influence in the place where he teaches. A schoolteacher may be dedicated to his profession, but his pay permits little concentration on it. He must scrounge about for extra jobs—writing petitions, tutoring, keeping a store. If a teacher has land in his own village he is usually off just as soon as his school duties are over to look after it. The schoolteacher could be of much more consequence both for the village and for the whole society if he were a more effective link between the village and the larger culture, as other functionaries act as links between village and government. But the educational administrative system is such that the schoolteacher is more often a part-time caretaker of children than a full-time agent of the civilization.

There are other village servants, such as watchmen, scavengers, a number of functionaries to serve visiting officials; they are commonly given the use of land in return for their services (cf. Dube 1955b, pp. 51–53). Their duties have more to do with the inside organization of the village than with its relation to the wider society.

Villagers Together and Apart

Day-to-day relations between people of different jatis are usually economic and ritual transactions rather than friendship or other voluntary exchanges. A man's economic dealings are centered in his village and the villages of the close vicinity. As has been noted, any one village does not usually include all the needed specialists. The locational aspect of jajmani relation is illustrated in an account of Sherupur village (Faizabad district, U.P.); most of the thirty-five persons who render jajmani services for Sherupur do not live in the village itself, but in settlements within a two-mile radius (Gould 1964, pp. 26–28).

A landowner maintains relations with some specialists who live at a distance. One may be the genealogist who, in some parts, appears periodically to bring his register up to date, extol the merits of the line, and collect his fee. There may be a goldsmith in town to whom the householder regularly goes when he needs jewelry. Often there is a roving beggar or holy man who makes the rounds of his own begging circuit. But all these are occasional relations; the main locale for economic interchange and ritual services is within the village and its close neighborhood.

Considerations of local supply and demand affect this interchange as we noted in discussing jajmani relations. When the one barber in Totagadde in Mysore died leaving no successor the landowners searched about for a replacement, found one, and installed him in the village. He then demanded and received several increases in pay. The village leaders reluctantly agreed to his demands rather than go to the trouble of finding yet another replacement (Harper 1959b, p. 770).

In Shanti Nagar, near Delhi, the supply of barbers is limited because barbers find more lucrative employment in the city. The only person available to shave the village men, when I visited the village, was an eleven-year-old boy. He fulfilled the duties of his jati with on-the-job training and while he was doing so, Stanley Freed observed, a good many of the village notables would appear with bloody, hacked faces after their morning shave.

Sometimes the supply is greater than the demand. In Sirkanda, for example, the artisans have lost a good part of their clientele because of the competition of bazaar goods and have had to turn to such ancillary occupations as brewing illicit liquor. The competition among them for clients has made for bitter hostilities among artisans (Berreman 1962b, p. 390). The classic case of oversupply is that of weavers. They became superfluous all over India as cheap factory-made textiles became available. Many had to become landless laborers and in some areas their jati status declined as a result of their impoverishment (cf. Baines 1912, pp. 62–64).

Supply and demand also operate at the other end of the social scale. There is typically an increased demand for the services of Brahmin priests where families of lower jatis prosper. One characteristic act of their mobility efforts is to secure priestly services that they previously could not get because they were too poor in purse and too polluting in jati practice. Conversely, the services of Brahmin priests may be dropped, as the Jats of the Delhi area did under the influence of the reformist Arya Samaj movement. The priests there had to turn to other occupations (Lewis 1958, pp. 77–78). Such continual adjustments in jajmani services, whether of Brahmins or of washermen, have been worked out in the context of the village locality.

Most of a villager's informal social relations are characteristically with others of his jati or of a jati of the same bloc as his. There are usually few voluntary associations that might foster friendship across jati lines. The possibility of such friendships depends partly on the size of the village and of the jati-group as well as on the rigor of social separation. In contrasting two villages of different size, the smaller village of Gopalpur with its larger neighbor Gannapur, Beals notes that "In Gopalpur, friendships are frequently developed between people belonging to different jatis; in Gannapur, friends tend to come from the same jatis" (1962, p. 87).

Friendships across the main jati blocs are virtually unknown in Sripuram in Tanjore district, where people of each of the three main divisions keep rigorously apart. Friendships are made between men within each division and not between men of different divisions. Several young schoolteachers of different Brahmin jatis in the village are friends, but "I have not come across a single instance of such personal friendship within the village between a Brahmin on one hand, and a non-Brahmin or an Adi-Dravida on the other" (Béteille 1962, p. 145).

Much the same situation is shown in the responses to a questionnaire survey on relations within a village carried out by Karve and Damle in three Maharashtra villages (1963). Though the three are very different from each other, the survey results in all are quite similar.[2] In residence patterns, the "nearest neighbors tended to be agnates or affinal kin. The larger circle of neighbors consisted of caste fellows. Then came other touchables."

Each Harijan jati occupies a separate section, segregated from the other untouchable jatis as from the houses of "touchable" jatis. A villager has most interaction with those who are kin as well as neighbors, next greatest is with those of the same jati or jati bloc. Tenants are mainly of the same jati as their landlord (except in one village), but the borrowing of money and other economic transactions are not so much confined within the jati. Jajmani relations—called *balutdari* in Maharashtra—were then being carried on in all three villages, though the traditional pattern was changing. A majority of those interviewed found them useful and necessary. When a family needs help, whether in the field or in the home, it gets help first from kin in the village, then from jati fellows, and only for a few particular needs, such as medicines, from any others.

Almost every family entertains guests or gives hospitality to fellow villagers, but the guests are almost entirely from one's own kin and jati. Friendships are with people of one's own jati "except

[2] One of the three villages, Vorkate in northern Satara district, is a "typical Maratha village with many castes," nucleated in form and located in relatively flat terrain. The second, Ahupe in Poona district, is a more scattered village in hill country; its people are largely of a jati that is "semi-tribal." The third, Karal on the coastal strip of Ratnagiri district, is a dispersed village of separate garden-compounds with no single jati in the majority, unlike the other two villages. Included in the survey also were families from a modern farm colony near Poona. In all, members of 343 families were interviewed.

extremely few genuine friendships across the caste."[3] And in these few friendships, the man of lower jati may be entertained with tea and food in the house of his higher ranking friend, but he washes his own dishes and they are kept separately from those of the household (Karve and Damle 1963, p. 73).

In all, a very large part of a man's, and even more of a woman's, social relations in these Maharashtra villages are with his kin and within his jati-group. "Thus we find that most of the intercourse of an individual was confined to kin-groups and the inter-group intercourse was regulated by the caste code" (Karve and Damle 1963, pp. 71–75). Some friendships are maintained between people of different echelons of rank, but the difficulties in the way of doing so are considerable in these as in most other villages, so that most friendships are between villagers of about the same social level.

This is also noted in Gumperz's discussion of communication in Khalapur (Saharanpur district, western U.P.). Khalapur villagers of all jatis came into regular contact with those of other ranks, but "interaction among different groups is limited to certain neutral spheres." Free discussion and interchange of opinion go on mainly in the social nuclei of men who regularly come together in a certain man's house or other place. There are no comparable places or occasions for frequent daily communication. Even the communications for development workers and other agents of government are mainly transmitted through these groups.

Such a social nucleus is usually, but not always, made up of men of the same jati. Gumperz comments that "intercaste friendships are fairly frequent among touchable classes with roughly similar positions in the hierarchy" (Gumperz 1964, pp. 91–92). In another account of Khalapur, close friendships are said occasionally to cut across "caste group lines, though they never existed, so far as we know, when ritual distance between two men was very great" (Minturn and Hitchcock 1966, pp. 32–33).

These close friendships in Khalapur frequently begin in school and are maintained by former classmates in adult life. This is becoming increasingly common through the land, and as educational opportunity widens so does the likelihood that a man's fast friends will be drawn from a wider circle than that of his jati. So is it also with broadening economic participation. As economic participation becomes less closely bound to jati occupation, so do mutual economic interests bring together men of different jatis. But these trends are not yet very far advanced and the intimate interchange and free cooperation of most village men are still mainly with jati fellows and status compeers.

Even so, an Indian village is not the "sink of localism," of invidious discrimination and ruthless exploitation, that Dr. Ambedkar, revered leader of the Harijan movement, said that it was, nor is it the harmonious, resilient "little republic" that Sir Charles Metcalfe supposed it to be (Ambedkar 1948, p. 39). It is home for those who live in it. Despite the many allegiances that each one in it has with kin and jati mates in other villages, with specialists, mentors, or patrons in towns and other centers, and in spite of the deep and sometimes bitter cleavages among its inhabitants, it typically remains a real community. As McKim Marriott has written after depicting these fractionating forces, "But I am still compelled to go on to say that the village of Kishan Garhi is like a living

[3] From the tables given by the authors, it appears that 230 villagers of touchable jatis answered a question asking each respondent to name six friends. Of these, 155 named friends only in their jati, 63 included names from other touchable jatis, 3 named only kinsmen, while 9 (just under 4 percent) gave some names of untouchables (Karve and Damle 1963, pp. 236–239, 475–476).

thing, has a definable structure, is conceptually a vivid entity, is a system—even if it is one of many subsystems within the larger socio-politico-religio-economic system in which it exists." Marriott goes on to tell how Kishan Garhi, like most other Indian villages, is a vital nucleus of economic activity, a main nexus of social activity, a principal stage for political striving (1955b, pp. 176–178).

Our preference for the term "villagers" for most of the people included in this study is founded on just these functions of the village in Indian society.

CHAPTER 20

The Village: Internal Regulation

In those villages where one jati-group is clearly the most powerful, its leaders and panchayat are likely to manage the whole village. They may not be able to manage themselves very well; as we have seen, a dominant jati-group may well split into bitterly opposed alliances. Nevertheless they characteristically unite against a threat to their controlling power and so maintain their joint control over the other villagers.

In villages where no single jati-group is in firm control, several jati-groups or alliances vie for local power and, on occasion, unite for the village welfare. The arena for such contests and the vehicle for village solidarity is commonly the village panchayat. The panchayat, for a village as for a jati, is better understood as a pattern of dialectic, decision, and action, rather than as a formal political body with clearly defined duties. A panchayat helps in crystallizing and formulating village opinion; it is an agency for maintaining village order and is often also a means of reflecting and eventually legitimating changes in the local order. A dominant jati-group exerts control through its panchayat.

Dominant Jatis

In his listing of the "dominant castes" of India, Baines classified them as a special kind of land-holder (Baines 1912, pp. 42–46). Although land is usually the basis of their position, their power rises not from one but from a combination of forces. For a jati to be truly dominant, its members must not only be numerically strong in the village or locality, but they must also be prepared to exert their economic and political power. They are able, if necessary, to field a band of determined men who will discourage dissidents by force (Srinivas 1959a, pp. 1–2). Usually they are of respectable ritual rank. Nowadays some of them are likely to be educated enough to deal with officials and so to facilitate the holding of power. Importantly, they think of themselves as entitled to rule the village. Some jati-groups that are numerically large in their villages are nevertheless not dominant, not so much because their members are deficient in economic strength and social status but mainly because they lack a self-image as rulers.

The families of a dominant jati-group usually control a good proportion of the village land.[1] The ruling landowners tend to feel that they really are the village and all others in it are there only as their dependents or hangers-on. "In a sense, then," Lewis says of Rampur near Delhi, "the other castes, even the Brahmins, are in the village at the sufferance of the *Jats*" (1955, p. 155). It is possible to speak of "the" Jats in the village—even though there are deep factions among them—because they can stand as one if they see a real challenge to Jat authority and will unite against any who dare challenge Jat supremacy.

Because they control the principal means of production, the dominant families can dispossess other villagers of their livelihood. Thus the dominant Rajputs of Khalapur can threaten to take away house sites, fodder supply, even latrine areas from other villagers (Minturn and Hitchcock 1966, p. 48). The dominant Thakurs of Senapur determined not only the kinds of service that their clients should give them, but also what these clients were required to give to each other (Rowe 1963, p. 42).

In Rampura near Mysore City, each patron of the dominant Okkaligas is a combination of master to his clients, landowner to his tenants, creditor for village debtors, and main employer of a retinue of dependents. He thus holds a multiple economic grip on villagers of all jatis (Srinivas 1955b, pp. 26–31). This jati-group is firmly in control. Its leaders settle disputes, both small and large; they plan and oversee joint activities; they represent the village to outside authorities. A disputant who deliberately tries to take his quarrel outside the village for settlement is declared guilty of slighting the local patrons. "His action is, in effect, a declaration of 'no confidence' in them, and he will soon be made to realize that he has incurred their wrath. Nemesis is swift in an Indian village when people are bound to each other by a multitude of ties" (Srinivas 1959a, p. 9). Also, magnates in other villages are likely to support the local patrons, whose help they may need in arranging a match, securing a loan, or keeping their own political premises tidy.

These Okkaliga leaders—whose jati is classed as Shudra—rule over the local Brahmins, yet they take care to show formal respect to them. When a Brahmin of the village is in difficulties, he is apt to go to one of the Okkaliga patrons for help and advice. Should a Brahmin challenge the power of the village leaders he may be called to task. The headman of one village of the region once disciplined an arrogant Brahmin priest by imposing a boycott on him. "The high ritual position which this Brahmin occupies does not free him from the secular control of the dominant caste" (Srinivas 1959a, p. 8).

So strong and esteemed are the Okkaliga patrons of Rampura (Srinivas uses the term "Peasant" for their jati name; we take his terms for this and the other jatis) that they are asked to settle affairs internal to other jatis. When a Lingayat priest brought two loose women to live with him, the indiscretion was really his own affair and that of the local Lingayat jati. But when these women tried

[1] The Brahmins of Gamras near Kanpur are both ritually highest and numerically largest in their village, but, as was noted earlier, they are not the dominant group. They are relatively poor, fifth among the village jatis in per capita income, and they are internally at odds. K. N. Sharma writes in a personal communication that only two of the Brahmin men are listened to respectfully by other villagers on secular matters.

In another village of U.P., Karimpur in Etawa district, the Brahmins do control much land and they also control the village (Wiser 1963, pp. 14–19).

to join with the proper wives of other Lingayat priests at a ceremony it was too much. One of the Lingayat priests appealed to the Okkaliga headman to see to it that the loose women did not join in the sacred cooking, and the headman did indeed stop them.[2]

Similarly, the Peasant elders of a nearby village arranged the terms by which a Muslim divine would serve his congregation. When later these Muslims could not agree among themselves, they informed the Peasant elders that they would thenceforth bring their disputes to them. "This highlights a feature of rural social organization in this area, the council of the dominant caste tries to create a structure of authority within each group it has to deal with, though its efforts frequently fail" (Srinivas 1959a, p. 12). They feel responsible for village government because of their paramount position and so they try to devise ways of maintaining the several parts of the village order.

Still, they do not attempt to reach into every dispute. When a council of washermen from several villages met in Rampura, no Peasant leader attended, holding that the matter under dispute was for the washermen to thrash out among themselves. The untouchables of the village try to settle their own disputes without recourse to their patrons. The patrons in turn are very reluctant to have untouchable children in the school and to allow them to improve their position. They want to keep the cheap labor and the menial services that the untouchables provide (Srinivas 1959a, pp. 4, 8–9).

On occasion the dominant landowners may interfere drastically in another jati's domestic affairs; a patron is especially likely to intervene if one of his favorite clients is in danger. Srinivas mentions one Okkaliga panchayat that imposed two fines on a fisherman accused of making false charges against a kinswoman. The larger fine was to go to the Okkaliga common fund and the smaller to the fisherman's jati council. They also threatened the fisherman with expulsion from his own jati if he repeated the allegation. Such a threat is quite extraordinary; the leaders of one jati are rarely in any position to impose outcasting in another. The powers and presumption of this dominant jati are unusually great (Srinivas 1959a, p. 11).

Another example of a strongly dominant jati-group is that of the Brahmins of Kumbapettai village in Tanjore district. Their rule has been loosened in recent years, but they were still the actual managers of the village when Kathleen Gough studied the village in the 1950s. Their council would intervene in disputes within other jati-groups. In family quarrels in the other jatis, if one of the parties to the quarrel was not satisfied with the judgment of his own elders he would carry the matter to his Brahmin landlord. That patron then would consult with other landlords whose clients had an interest in the matter and together they would arrange a settlement.

The dominant jati-group can also impose collective punishment. The lower jatis of the village have strong organizations for the speedy settlement of disputes, and this partly because the overlords may punish the whole jati-group if a quarrel among them results in serious trouble. These Brahmins do not have a strong jati organization of their own, but "the fact that they are the administrators is itself a source of unity among the Brahmins." No matter how acrimonious their own disputes may be, they generally unite against offenders from the lower groups. Thus when some Harijans broke the traditional order of precedence at the harvest festival in 1952 and drove their cattle through the

---

[2] Rampura has had an unusually stable and firm village government, Srinivas observes, because the two principal Peasant leaders have been friends rather than opponents. Their fathers were also powerful men, but they were enemies and headed two of the main factions. Friendship between the two present leaders was founded "in the teeth of their fathers' opposition" and has resulted in advantage for the village as well as for the jati-group (1959a, p. 7).

streets before the non-Brahmin jatis did so, the Brahmin elders fined all the Harijans of the village collectively. As in Rampura, these dominant landowners try to keep agents of their authority within each jati-group. They reserve the right to depose a headman of a lower jati if he displeases them in any way (Gough 1955, pp. 44–47; 1960, pp. 37, 47–51).

Yet dominance is always tempered by dependence. A ruling jati-group needs the help and services of the other villagers; patrons cannot afford to alienate their clients completely. Even in so tightly controlled a village as Kumbapettai, the power of Brahmins is limited in several ways. A Brahmin offender who has trespassed in the Harijan quarters or who has been caught in sexual relations with a Harijan woman may be punished by the Brahmins themselves. These Brahmins may even look the other way if a youth of higher jati is beaten by those whom he has offended. Another constraint on their power can be felt when a tenant of low jati is pushed beyond the limits of endurance by a repressive landowner. He stands before the temple and invokes the curse of the goddess on the oppressor. Brahmins who know that they have pressed too hard greatly fear the curse. As do other dominant landowners, these claim to have a kind of paternal affection for their tenants and servants so long as the lower jatis stay in their traditional place (Gough 1960, pp. 49–50).

In Khalapur at the other end of India, the dominant jati of Rajputs is also strongly entrenched. They too recognize their dependence on the jatis who serve them. In one instance they gave way a bit to a complaint from a sweeper who had been beaten by a Rajput whose potatoes had been damaged by the sweeper's cow. The sweepers of the village stand together; they perform services that the Rajputs are very reluctant to lose. Hence the sweepers were able to extract the semblance of an apology from the Rajput who had done the beating (Minturn and Hitchcock 1966, pp. 48–49).

There are always some limits to the power of a dominant jati in its village, but how greatly that power is constrained by dependence on other jatis rests in good part on the strength, unity, and will of the subordinates.

Dynamics of Dominance

The three examples of Rampura, Kumbapettai, and Khalapur are all villages that are managed by a strongly dominant jati-group. There are many villages in which no single jati-group is dominant over the others.[3] Thus in Bisipara in Orissa, two jati-groups confront each other as rivals for leadership. In other places one alliance of jati-groups competes for power with another alliance (cf. Bailey 1960b, p. 260; Nath 1962, p. 1877; Atal n.d., pp. 5–6).

Such competition occurs in Ramkheri (Dewas district, Madhya Pradesh), where the Rajputs are the traditional leaders but their authority is not overridingly powerful. They own more land, animals, and equipment than do members of any other jati-group and are also the largest employers. But there are rich families in other jatis also, and a few other jati-groups are nearly as well off as the Rajputs. The Rajputs, with 12.9 percent of the population, are second numerically to the Khatis, farmers who made up 19.8 percent at the time of the study. (The Okkaligas of Rampura constitute nearly half their village, the Brahmins more than a third of Kumbapettai.)

[3] In a survey of five regions of India, Marriott characterizes the upper Ganges region as one in whose villages "political and economic powers are generally diffused among many independently acting families" (1960, p. 39).

The village headman in Ramkheri is a Rajput; Rajput elders are called on to help in judging disputes between jati-groups, but elders of other jatis are also asked to help. The Rajput leaders do not interfere with affairs internal to another jati, as the dominant leaders of Rampura do, nor is there any particular stigma, as there is in Rampura, about taking a dispute elsewhere than to the Rajput elders—even to the courts. These Rajputs are allied with nine other jatis in Ramkheri whose people follow their lead and emulate their manner. As against these allies, there is another set of jatis in the village, of which the Khati farmers are the most prominent, who are vegetarian and who in general follow an ascetic-ritual style of life rather than the Rajput model (Mayer 1958a).

The traditional Rajput leadership is being challenged, mainly by rising men of the oil presser (Teli) and farmer (Khati) jatis. The Rajputs are becoming concerned with consolidating their old adherents and with attracting new allies (Mayer 1960, pp. 125–131). Although the Khatis are well based for leadership, only a few of their men seek to supplant the Rajputs. As a group the Khatis prize jati exclusiveness and purity; they emphasize thrift and work. The Rajputs pride themselves on their largesse and are always ready to drop their own work when some village activity is going on. The Rajputs think of themselves as civic leaders and rulers; the Khatis, as yet, do not. Mayer suggests that when some of the Khati villagers become headmen and civic leaders, the interests of other Khatis may well be different. "The behavior of a village caste group may, in fact, be found to vary with the responsibilities (and dominance) it has in the village" (1958a, p. 414).

The dynamics of dominance in a village parallel the dynamics of eminence within a jati. Given the pervasive perspective of hierarchy and the belief that one's own group is worthy of higher rank than it presently enjoys, a locally strong jati-group tends to reach for dominance over the other villagers. Once the members of such a group acquire a good measure of dominance, they feel impelled to consolidate and strengthen their control against potential challenge. To gain and to hold paramount power in a village, they need economic strength; in the traditional village economy strength resides in land.

All are not equally ambitious to rise and become dominant. Most of the Khatis of Ramkheri are not particularly interested in becoming big fish in the village pond. Yet at any given time some men in a village are seeking greater power. That power, once acquired by some families, tends to be extended to their jati-fellows in the village because powerful men are inclined and expected to favor their kinsmen. They also encourage the idea that one can be a leading influence in the village. Thus some Rajputs of Ramkheri are poor and insignificant men, yet they stand on their group's political prestige. These poorer Rajputs take care to act publicly in the manner of their leading lights. If one of the chief Rajput leaders is present at a meeting his jati-fellows defer to him, but when no influential Rajput is present, the lesser Rajputs take over and assume direction of discussion. Since Rajputs attend to village affairs more assiduously than do men of other jatis, they are apt to take charge of whatever concerns the whole village. "For the Rajputs, village leadership was a caste thing, for the other castes it seems to have been the role of one or two 'big' men of their caste" (Mayer 1960, p. 113; 1958, p. 425).

Once a jati-group can unitedly exert economic power its men tend to seek control of village political and ritual matters. "The more forms of dominance which a caste enjoys, the easier it is for it to acquire the rest" (Srinivas 1959a, p. 3). Its leaders may intervene in the internal affairs of other jati-groups and its council may assume jurisdiction over everything that concerns the village. Because of this tendency, some observers have said that the solidarity of the village is only the solidarity of its dominant group (Dumont and Pocock 1957b, p. 29). This is not really so, for the people of a village like Gopalpur can show considerable cohesion on occasion, although there is no strongly dominant jati-group in it (Beals 1962, pp. 33–41; 1964, pp. 103–104). Even stronger statements on the importance of the dominant caste have been made by F. G. Bailey. "The traditional system contains one dominant caste which alone has a corporate political existence: the other castes are its dependents and are not politically corporate" (1960b, p. 191, also pp. 169, 258–259; 1961, p. 12). This is not always so, as several case examples cited in this chapter illustrate. Thus in Khalapur in U.P. and in Rampura in Mysore, both villages with a strongly dominant jati, there is still scope for councils of other jati-groups and jatis. These councils regulate their own affairs and can have some effect on village affairs.

In Khalapur there are more than thirty jati-groups, each with its own panchayat. Each council tries to protect its members' interests and to uphold "its pattern of social behavior and religious values." The village council of Khalapur takes a wider jurisdiction, over disputes between people of different jatis and over cases of theft and other breaches of village peace and order (Retzlaff 1962, pp. 18–21). Neither in Khalapur nor in most other villages traditionally dominated by one jati does the dominant jati wipe out all independent corporate action by the subordinate groups. Such action has indeed been confined largely to their internal jati affairs. But the evidence does not support Bailey's view that the traditionally dominant jati was the sole corporate political entity in a village and that this was completely different from the modern situation in which any large jati can be a corporate political body (Bailey 1960b, p. 191). A dominant jati may now find it more difficult to encroach on the internal affairs of subordinate jatis or to cut them off from a voice in village affairs quite so completely as was formerly possible. It is still true, however, that a dominant jati's coercive powers can yield a kind of forced solidarity that otherwise may be lacking.

A dominant jati-group that is not Brahmin does not usually try to demote the Brahmins from their high ritual status. Their leaders may take charge in ritual matters, as in determining the order of precedence at a ceremony, but they generally do so with some display of deference to the officiating Brahmin. They do not seek to usurp his ritual role and sacred status. For the most part, they do not want that role for themselves, although they esteem it. The local Brahmin is the symbol and often the exemplar of the principles of purity. In honoring him they honor the ritual principle by which much of their domestic and social behavior is regulated. "The dominant caste," Dumont and Pocock write, "is consciously subject to Brahmanic axioms but once the latter have been accepted and the Brahmins have been 'fed,' the less conscious royal model comes into play" (1957b, p. 33).

A paramount jati is likely, as has been noted, to separate into competing alliances. Where no single jati-group is preponderant, an alliance includes families of several jati-groups. In the long run there is a continuous process of challenge and response among village groups, not only in a Toynbeean sense, but also in a direct face-to-face way. The challenge comes from those who have been subordinate and who have gathered enough strength to think that they can strike for higher place. The reaction may wreck the challenge; the superiors and their descendants may continue to rule in the village and the region for centuries, but a driving force in the system is that new challenges continually arise as new sources of strength are found by potential challengers.

This dynamic favors the emergence of a dominant jati in a local system. In older settlements of the delta region of Bengal, for example, one jati has commonly risen to be the dominant one; in the newer villages on recently reclaimed lands clear dominance, even when one jati is numerically strong, is not so evident (Nicholas 1963, p. 1189). Yet even in these relatively egalitarian frontier villages, the people's cognitive expectations are for hierarchy and that inclines their village organization toward stratification and dominance.

Thus in Radhanagar village (Midnapore district) 86 percent of the population of some 600 are of about the same ritual rank, indeed 77 percent of the village belong to the same Mahisya jati. There is not much differentiation in wealth among the village families, yet they regard their community as stratified (Nicholas MS. 1967, p. 7).

In their annual village festival several of the villagers are made into "temporary Brahmins," as Nicholas puts it, so that there may be a proper sacred hierarchy. Evidently the few and poor Brahmins resident in the village do not suffice for the hierarchical needs of this grand occasion (Nicholas MS. pp. 18–20). Nicholas points out also that in adopting token dowry payments and in the conduct of panchayats, the people of this village demonstrate their inclination toward hierarchy. "When the principal men of the village, acting as judges, mark themselves off as 'superior' to the general public, they take an important step toward legitimating the decisions which they hope to reach" (Nicholas MS. p. 32). Both in ceremonial and in panchayat activities, Nicholas finds, the people of this village believe that social hierarchy is necessary for legitimate social activity and that without it such events are imperfect and ineffective.

Village Panchayat

The elders and leaders of a village assemble in panchayat to cope with problems internal to the village and to deal with external threats or opportunities. If the internal order of the village is challenged, the council sessions serve as an arena for ascertaining public opinion and mobilizing power alignments. If a change in the power structure has clearly been accomplished, the village panchayat provides a means of publicizing and of validating the change. A panchayat is also gathered to face external incursions. Increasingly, a village panchayat takes on some of the entrepreneurial functions urged by government agencies.

Modern political leaders have placed very high importance on village panchayats as means for grass-roots political participation. This is reflected in H. D. Malaviya's scholarly and comprehensive volume on village panchayats in India, written under the auspices of The Economic and Political Research Department of the All India Congress Committee. In it the author mentions that the very last document Gandhi signed was a draft constitution based on panchayats (1956, pp. 254–255).

The form and procedure of a traditional village council is like that described above for a jati council. It consists of all those men whose participation is needed for the assembly to reach a judgment that will hold. The number of participants depends on the nature of the issue for which a meeting has been convened. A falling out between two retainers of different landlords may require only an *ad hoc* meeting of the patrons to straighten out the quarrel. But a problem that seriously affects the whole village, one that perhaps endangers the reputation of all in it, requires a convocation of many of the household heads.

When there is a strongly dominant jati-group, its panchayat tends to be also the panchayat for the whole village. Their leaders decide both jati and village affairs. Elders of other jatis may attend a session but more as givers of evidence or receivers of information than as full participants. Where no one jati-group is paramount, a broader representation of leaders is needed for effective judgment. This broader base still does not include all groups and classes. Harijans usually attend only to serve as messengers. Women very rarely participate. And certain jati-groups may not want to participate. In Bisipara, the shopkeepers keep aloof from the village council in which the other touchable jatis participate. Their interests lie mainly beyond the village and they neither associate nor dissociate themselves with village affairs (Bailey 1957, pp. 192, 203).

The influence exerted by village leaders rests on the same attributes that were mentioned for jati leaders; most village leaders are the men of greatest influence in their jati as well. Typically they have the qualifications of wealth and family support, suitable age, and a history of proper use of their wealth; they also have time and interest for village affairs. A leader gains in influence if he is an effective speaker and if he presents himself as a firm, reliable yet humble person, or at least one who is not voraciously ambitious. To be effective a village leader must balance off competing claims and should be able to switch personal styles, now being the loyal kinsman to a relative, now the amiable helper of authority, and altogether the friend and guardian of the whole village (cf. Hitchcock 1960, pp. 267–268; Minturn and Hitchcock 1966, pp. 15–16).

Assembled in panchayat meeting, the village leaders seek to redress ritual offenses, to calm secular disputes, to organize group enterprises. A jati-group council has similar functions, but the two have differing though overlapping jurisdictions. The jati-group council takes cognizance of cases having to do only with their own jati practices or only with their own members. People of other jatis, especially the higher ones, are not particularly concerned with such matters.

The difference between the two jurisdictions is illustrated in Rampura by the kinds of questions that each kind of council typically entertains. The jati-group council, Srinivas writes, considers such questions as: "Should R be thrown out of caste for having sex relations with an untouchable woman?; and, should J be granted a divorce from M?" The village council takes charge of such questions as these, "Who stole grass from X's field?; who set fire to Y's straw rick?; and, is Z speaking the truth when he says that P owes him a hundred rupees and not fifty?" (1959a, p. 7).

Some village councils assume executive and legislative as well as juridical functions. Thus over one year the council of Bisipara village in Orissa arranged for the regular cleaning of public places, saw to the upkeep of a temple, organized the repair of a dam, and decided on invitations to a village festival. It abolished certain perquisites of washermen and barbers, and it transferred rights to provide music from one Harijan jati to another. The council also listened to complaints by a herdsman against a washerman.

Though this is a vigorous council, there are some affairs over which it will not take jurisdiction. When a young Brahmin quarreled with his mother's brother, the council tactfully refused to intervene and simply put off discussion of the matter. Should a village man have "an indiscreet liaison" with a woman of lower rank, then it is his jati-group and not the village that takes notice and prescribes action. His indiscretion endangers the jati not the village; only his jati fellows will share in his defilement. The woman's jati may ignore her or, if the group's sense of self-respect has been touched, may punish her. But the affair is not normally turned into a dispute between two jati-groups; each is concerned only to discipline its own members. If, however, the woman has been taken by violence and against her will, that is quite another matter; it is comparable to any other kind of assault and can be taken to the village elders for redress (Bailey 1957, pp. 191–195).

An especially heinous misdeed may be taken up by both village and jati councils. Some offenses are so enormous that the reputation of the whole village as well as of the transgressor's jati is imperiled by them. As we mentioned on page 184, in Shamirpet incest in a family is one such crime, the killing of a cow (almost always accidental) by a Hindu is another. No single jati-group is dominant in Shamirpet yet the village council, at the time of Dube's study, was a strong one. It took over matters that might otherwise have been for a jati council. Because the village panchayat is sufficiently aggressive, "it has arrogated to itself a considerably wide range of powers" (Dube 1955b, p. 55).

In northern Kerala, two tiers of village panchayats were maintained because of the special rigor of jati separation in that region. The lowest jatis of a village were under the jurisdiction of the local Tiyyas, then small tenants and laborers (toddy-tappers by traditional occupation), who were themselves subordinate to the landowning Nayars and Nambudiris. The Tiyyas took some responsibility for maintaining order among the low jatis. Cases that could not be settled by the Tiyya elders were taken upward again to the landowners. One of the reasons for this delegation of dominance was that the distance pollution then observed in Kerala made it difficult for an arbitrator of higher rank to come close enough to a dependant of lowest rank to find out what the case was all about (Miller 1954, p. 413).

In addition to internal, judicial functions, a village panchayat commonly takes external, executive responsibilities, especially when the defensive unity of the village must be rallied. A panchayat is a means of gathering, consolidating, and giving effect to public opinion. If all in a village feel themselves threatened, public opinion is readily consolidated, especially, as we have seen, against the forces of government or of another village.

In Bisipara, for example, a post office had been experimentally established for five years. At the end of the period the Postal Department found that the office was running at a loss and decided to close it. The villagers not only would be inconvenienced by this; they also would lose the prestige of having a post office in their own village. They petitioned against the decision, and the postal authorities replied that the service would be continued if the village would make good the loss for the five years past and guarantee that there would be no loss in the future. The village council met; no hint of faction divided them over this issue. "They replied by asking this question: If the post office had made a profit over the past four years, would it have given the money to the village?" (Bailey 1957, p. 193.) The author does not tell us whether the council succeeded in this effort, but he makes plain that all sides in the village were as one against the postal officials.[4]

Procedure in a village council follows that outlined in Chapter 16 for a jati or jati-group panchayat. Discussion of a problem is usually continued until a consensus satisfactory to all (or almost all) of the most powerful men is reached. If it appears that no agreement is possible at a session, the council meeting disbands and another is called later when some change of view may have come to pass (cf. Retzlaff 1962, pp. 23–25). One such change may result from the very act of arguing, as we have noted for the jati council of Chamars in Senapur; it occurs also in village councils. Even if a side loses its case, the act of venting its grievance and stating its justification apparently makes it easier for the members of the losing side to give their consent, albeit reluctantly, to a judgment that goes against them. Their tacit consent is usually necessary because voting on a proposition "with a

[4] Other Bisipara cases that are discussed without reference to jati or factional interest are those in which the issues and the evidence are so clear-cut "that there can be little debate about who is in the right and who is wrong." Thus in the case of a young man who wrongfully abused a widow, there was no dissent in the council about fining him because he was obviously at fault. He belonged to a faction opposed to that to which the widow belonged, and perhaps that was why the matter was not brought before the elders of their common jati. In the village council hearing no factional consideration entered (Bailey 1957, pp. 193–194).

majority carrying the issue and thereby binding the minority to that agreed decision, was and still is completely alien to the system" (Retzlaff, p. 24). A decision, if it is to stick, must have the consent, even though it may be reluctant or unspoken, of the main groups involved in the dispute.

After such general consent is obtained, the leaders try to enforce the decision. The powers they command are of the same kind that we have noted in the jati panchayat. They can impose penalties and fines and occasionally physical punishment. They can decree that the offender must provide a feast for the villagers before he is fully reinstated. Should the culprit refuse to submit to the judgment of the council, they can coerce him in many ways, as we have seen that a jati council may do. His axe may disappear, his cow get lost for days, his crop may be trampled. The services of washerman or carpenter may be stopped—or rendered so badly that it might be better to have none at all. His hay rick may catch fire, and he himself, however wary, may be waylaid on a dark night and beaten painfully. Nonviolence has been an important doctrine in the intellectual centers of the civilization and has a certain place in village ideology; violence has been a potent sanction in village as in jati politics.

The most dire penalty in the power of a village council, however, is not retributional violence, but the expulsion of the offender from village society. One who is so cut off is not necessarily also cast out of his jati; he may find shelter with jati fellows in another village. For gross transgressions, the offender may be cast out by both his village and his jati councils. A village council is inclined to go along with a jati council's strong verdict. But jati members are less apt to follow the village council's lead against a jati fellow.

Village leaders must show a high degree of outraged unanimity if their ostracism is to be successfully imposed and honored in other villages. Bailey found that in Bisipara such strong unanimity is evoked only in exceptional cases, as in the punishment of persons found guilty of keeping malignant spirits. In one such hearing, the defendants had to take a prior oath that they would abide by the council's decision and not call in government authorities to evade punishment if they were found guilty. "The plaintiff in such a case cannot get justice (as the village conceives justice) out of a Government court: the case must be conducted within the traditional juridical system." Four men were found guilty and fined. The one who had the largest fine, a washerman, demurred and was boycotted until, after two months, the council reduced the amount of the fine and he then paid it (Bailey 1957, pp. 157, 262–263).

When the village boycott of a man is effective, it is a most potent means of counterchange; yet occasionally an offender refuses to recant. He may feel strong enough to hold out, as some have done for jati boycotts (see pp. 196–199 above). A case of this kind occurred in Ramkheri when a prospering oil presser came in conflict with the Rajput leaders of the village mainly about some grazing land that he had begun to cultivate against their wishes. The economic issue did not come to a head directly but was fought out over quite another matter, about the kind of dramatic performance that should be staged at the Holi festival. The Rajput leaders decided to put on a much bawdier kind of play than some others could approve. After a confrontation on this matter, those who objected to the racy performance were threatened with ostracism. They all gave in with the exception of the oil presser, who had had a number of previous quarrels with the Rajput elders. He refused to yield and was boycotted, ostensibly because he would not agree to the choice of the play, actually because he was challenging the established powers.

At first no one would smoke with him or invite him to ceremonies; no craftsman or laborer would work for him. But he managed to keep going, and when Adrian Mayer was in the village, some four years after the boycott had been declared, he had survived and had partly broken the sanction. His lineage mates came to his domestic rites, which was excused because the ritual duties of agnatic kin are acknowledged to be paramount. But others had also resumed relations with him, "people who have ambitions of leadership in the village, who resent the present dominant group because of this, and so show their independence by accepting the invitations of the boycotted household" (Mayer 1960, p. 124).

Village Alliances and Changes in Power

Such resistance to panchayat decree usually indicates a change in power relations within the village. A successful challenge by one family encourages other challengers, who may well consolidate their forces against the previously ruling group to form a new or newly strengthened alliance. Participants in multi-jati alliances within the village, like those within a dominant jati, support each other for a variety of reasons.

One common reason for mutual support is economic; the dependents of a patron are also likely to be his adherents in village disputes. Another is kinship; the closer kin of a leader or challenger are apt to be his supporters. Jati is another factor in alignments; when alliance leaders who are of different jatis confront each other, each is likely to be backed by his jati fellows in the village unless they are his declared rivals. Common residence in the same neighborhood or ward occasionally impels a man to join one alliance rather than another. Having a common foe in the village is a great alliance binder.

Enmity within a jati-group and consequent adherence to rival alliances is illustrated among the potters of a delta village in West Bengal. The families of a potter lineage quarreled about marriage and land; four households came to be boycotted by the others of the lineage. These four then joined the alliance of the village headman, separating themselves from the alliance to which most potters belong, which opposes the headman and his jati. The jati of the headman, the Mahisya, is strong in this village. The Mahisya are cultivators, who elsewhere in the region rank fairly low and are ritually inferior to the local potters, but in the Mahisya-dominated villages, the potters are placed lower than Mahisyas. "The Potters feel that the Mahisyas have usurped all the positions of power and authority in the society, and they are subject to the will and whim of the dominant caste" (Nicholas and Mukhopadhyay, 1964, p. 29). Yet some potter families support Mahisyas because of the quarrel in a potter lineage.

Allegiance to a multi-jati alliance can be shifted just as adherence to an alliance within a jati-group can be. A man does have some option in his alliance affiliation. Usually only a strong personality or a highly incensed man will dare oppose the group to which his close kinsmen and jati fellows belong, but this does occur. Examples of alliance shifts can usually be found wherever opposed village alliances exist, as they do in a great many villages. Malcolm Darling, who knew Punjab villages well cites a knowledgeable estimate given to him in 1930 that only about 25 per cent of the villages of Rawalpindi district were free of deep factional splits and most of those only because they were too small to support rival sides (1934, pp. 41–42).

Alan Beals has analyzed some of the variables in factional conflict (1965, 1966). One variable is village size. From a survey of conflict in thirty villages of Gulbarga district, Mysore, Beals suggests that opposed factions cannot exist unless the village community is large enough to be divided into two viable segments. Villages of less than fifty households, he finds, do not support opposed alliances. "Life in such an infinitesimal community may provoke insanity or flight, but it is not likely to provide a suitable setting for party conflict" (1965, p. 18). Further, Beals finds that prolonged factional opposition will occur if the landowning jatis contain more than fifty households and represent over 50 percent of the village population (1965, p. 19). These tentative conclusions from a limited survey have to be tested against wider evidence, but they are in keeping with similar findings that were noted in Chapter 15 (Reddy 1952, p. 258; Singh 1961, p. 9). They indicate one possible variable in the incidence of village conflict.

An impressive case study, which highlights a different set of forces, is given in the previously mentioned account by Beals of conflict in Namhalli village, only a few miles from the city limits of Bangalore. Namhalli in 1952 had 603 persons living in 106 households; by 1960 it had 542 persons in 113 households. Economic conditions had improved in that short span so that more people worked and lived outside the village (hence the population decline) and more could set up separate households. With economic improvement came a marked betterment in village cooperation and a decrease in village conflict. When Beals lived in Namhalli in 1952, the village was in a condition of pervasive factionalism in which almost no villagewide cooperation could be managed. Hostility among the villagers was rife. An attempt to stage a village festival in 1952 ended in a series of grand quarrels between two alliances, which lined up some jati-groups against others and which split some of the larger jati-groups.

The year 1952 was a difficult one for the people of Namhalli. The period of prosperity that had begun in World War II had come to an end. There was a severe drought; some realized that opportunities for outside employment were shrinking and the traditional agricultural economy of the village could not possibly support the enlarged and continually swelling population. No fresh solutions were proposed. "On the contrary, old patterns of conflict merely became intensified, to the point where almost every meaningful interpersonal relationship became affected" (Beals and Siegel 1966, p. 128). The old patterns for resolving conflicts, within the family as within the village, could not be used effectively; mutual distrusts and enmities remained rampantly unresolved.

However, even when village cooperation was at a low ebb as it was in 1953 and 1954, most of the men rose to the common defense when there was threat of robbery by outsiders. They collaborated also when such major crimes as rape or poisoning were suspected. But the ordinary work of village maintenance was not done.

This condition continued until 1958 when several fortunate trends greatly eased the tensions. Jobs became available in nearby factories and bus service was provided to them. Agricultural income rose, partly because of the expanded market in the city. A new way of raising capital for village needs as well as for personal requirements, the chit fund, was successfully adopted (Beals and Siegel 1966, pp. 136–138).

By 1960, when Beals again studied the villagers, the roads were well maintained and the wells promptly cleaned. Although the village festival had not been resumed, there was less conflict within the village and more cooperative activities. The kind of close solidarity that used to be expressed in the village festival may no longer be required. "In the same way, village unity, being no longer a condition of survival, had ceased to be expected" (Beals and Siegel 1966, p. 138).

This Namhalli example illustrates how antagonism between alliances in a village can change over time and that alliance members can change toward a more solidary condition, just as individuals can change their alignments and drop old enmities. Alliances are not required features of village social structure as families and jatis are, but they are very common elements in it. Moreover, there is something of the same feeling about factional opposition in a village that there is about fraternal opposition in a family. Both are generated by forces in the social system and many villagers take part in them. Yet these same men, when their own particular quarrel is not in question, decry the prevalence of rivalries. Thus in Gopalpur where opposed groups are called parties, "Lineages, jatis, clique groups, and neighborhoods are regarded as desirable by people in Gopalpur; parties are considered to be a symptom of social disorder—the village divided against itself" (Beals 1962, p. 44).

The struggle for village power is not unique to village India. Wherever there is power there is contest for it. The contest in Indian villages is sharpened by the prevailing perspective of hierarchy, which sees any strengthening of one's status rivals as a demeaning of one's self and one's side. Therefore any proposal or act of a rival that may redound to his advantage, even if it may also be of advantage to the whole village, is likely to be obstructed by his opponents. The situation in Senapur in the 1950s was like that of Namhalli in the early 1950s, when no faction and no leader or group of leaders was strong enough to organize the village for any sort of constructive action. Yet each faction was strong enough to block any decisive action on the part of the opposing groups (Cohn 1955, pp. 68–76).

Such impasses are very familiar to those who have worked in Indian villages. Yet there are also many villages, more like the Namhalli of 1960, in which villagewide enterprises for the common good are regularly carried on. We have noted that in Rampura in Mysore two of the most powerful men are allies and friends rather than rivals and enemies, to the benefit of the village; in Bisipara in Orissa two jati-groups are in confrontation, yet a number of joint enterprises are accomplished; in Shamirpet in Andhra the village council is an effective body, even though there are factional rivalries in the village.

An effective village council fulfills both short-range and long-range functions. At any one time it maintains village order and helps keep the particular social order of the village. But as that social order changes the panchayat sessions reflect the new social facts; the council eventually validates the changes, adapts them to the local society and the society to them.

In the recurrent process of maintaining village order a council has power to act in such matters as theft and assault, working in conjunction with or in evasion of the official police. Ceremonies of the annual cycle are arranged by the council. These are mainly agricultural and protective rites for the whole village. (Rites of the life-cycle are staged by kinsmen rather than by the village.) The council also looks to the relations among the jati-groups, especially to those status claims which seem to threaten the village order, as when Harijans try to reject their traditional, polluting services and to take on higher practices.

If the village council (in which Harijans rarely figure) does not itself take positive action, its members may tacitly condone any violent action taken. Thus the Balahi of Khargan and Khandwa districts of Madhya Pradesh, in the 1940s, were able to ride buses and trams, to send some of their children to school, even to draw water from a few village wells put in by government. Nevertheless, they were usually confined to separate residential sections of a village and often were not allowed to walk freely in the streets of higher jatis. In some villages a Balahi did not dare to wear a clean shirt or a waist cloth draped in the style used by the higher groups. Further, "several cases are known of Balahis who have received a severe beating because they refused to eat carrion or the leavings of a high caste dinner" (Fuchs 1950, pp. 58–59).[5]

---

[5] The author adds that the Balahis treat people of jatis "a shade lower than their own" with equal severity. "The Balahis are the first to complain if in school their children have to sit with children of a lower caste and they keep

The economic as well as the ritual rise of a Harijan is often resisted. Thus the stoneworkers of Gopalpur, who are categorized as "unclean meat eaters" because they will eat pork (though not beef), are ranked close to the bottom of the local hierarchy and have to live separately on the outskirts of the village. Yet by the 1960s some had acquired land and had achieved a middle economic position. There is far more friction, however, when a stoneworker tries to improve his economic position than when a man of higher rank tries to do so. When a group of stoneworkers bought some good land (their other lands are inferior) and one of their men began ploughing it, a number of higher ranking villagers attacked him with clubs and beat him severely. The attackers apparently had little to fear from council action because "repercussions are likely to be slight when a Stoneworker is beaten" (Beals 1962, pp. 37–39).

Such violent reactions probably are triggered by deep symbolic meanings as well as by direct economic or ritual rivalry. We have suggested that Brahmins generally receive at least lip homage from others in their village because they exemplify the purity principle by which all villagers—in some degree—regulate their lives. It may also be that Harijans exemplify the pollution principle, the inseparable counterpart of ritual purity, which equally is used to govern conduct. In the person of Harijans, other villagers have constant proof of the detriment of pollution. So long as they must guard themselves against pollution and yet be defiled by it daily, they are likely to resist allowing the exemplars of permanent pollution to divest themselves of that status because that brings into question a fundamental postulate of their social and personal life. The special inertia against Harijan rise will be considered again in the discussion of social mobility.

Although a village council helps to maintain order in the village and the social order of the village, the same order of power and rank is not preserved indefinitely. In the long run there are shifts and adjustments; some groups rise, others fall. Some of the lower and subordinate manage to garner secular resources and use them to raise their ritual rank. The village council is one locale in which this process becomes openly acknowledged and, if successful, where it is clearly validated.

This process is illustrated in Wangala in Mysore where the village council must include the heads of the major lineages in the dominant jati of "Peasants" (Vokkaligas). Eight lineages are regarded as major, and the participation of their elders is considered essential for a valid council judgment. Other Peasant lineages and households in the village are of lesser importance in council. One of these minor lineages came to be a major lineage through the efforts of its leader, one of the richest and most influential men in the village. His father had acquired wealth and this leader increased his patrimony. Through his economic strength he could exert pressure in village politics.

Being intelligent and purposeful, he was able to establish a firm political following on the basis of his economic strength. He spoke up in council meetings, and as a number of the council members were in debt to him they listened when he spoke. He became an integral part of these meetings and, without any particular discussion of the matter, his lineage has become recognized as one of the major lineages because he is clearly a major member of the council. This case shows, as the author notes, that economic mobility is based more on the individual's achievement while

---

their distance from a Mehtar more carefully than any member of a higher caste" (Fuchs 1950, p. 59).

political mobility is more closely involved with a man's group (Epstein 1962, pp. 119, 127–128). It also indicates how the economic success of one man can benefit his kinsmen in the village.

This can occur for a whole jati-group as well as for a lineage. When one member becomes exceptionally prosperous, he is likely to see to the welfare of his jati fellows in the village, at least to the degree that they are his staunch allies rather than his challengers. Together they can use their wealth to take positions of greater influence in village politics. Over time their economic strength and new political influence are reflected in, channeled through, and therefore validated by sessions of the village council.

Such sessions can be very stormy because in them the throes of adaptation to changing circumstances are worked out. The forces for change may arise within the village or may impinge, as they often do, from outside the village. We look next at the external relation of the village, that is the regular relations of villagers with networks and centers beyond their village bounds.

CHAPTER 21

The Wider Ties of Village: Centers and Regions

Outside the circles of his kin, his jati, and his village, a man carries on more intermittent social relations that are nevertheless of high importance for him and for the whole social system. Most men make regular trips to a nearby market, occasionally visit more distant sacred places, sometimes have direct contacts with government officials. Specialists from outside come into the village; there are merchants and hawkers, touring religionists and peripatetic beggars, inspecting officials and policemen on circuit. Some men in each village take link roles, connecting the village community to the wider spheres of economics, religion, and government.

Each of these wider spheres can be described separately by the analyst for purposes of descriptive clarity. But each is also part of a larger whole and the nexus should not be neglected. In previous chapters jati and village have been examined separately, but we should note again here that the two are component subsystems within a local social order. A villager usually moves without difficulty from one subsystem to another, taking the roles appropriate to each as the situation warrants. For some purposes, especially those of hearth and home, he acts as a member of his family and jati-group. For certain economic, jural, and defensive purposes, he acts in the capacity of a fellow villager. Occasionally he may be uncertain about the proper role to take, as when he wants to join an alliance opposed to that of his lineage mates. But in general the obligations of each set of relationships are not greatly in doubt.

Neither is viable without the other; each provides necessary inputs for the other. For the village community, the jatis provide and maintain the main components, the jati-groups. For the jati, the village provides the social matrix of specialization each jati requires. Thus village and jati are indeed separate when used for certain purposes by the participants and when analyzed with reference to those purposes by the observer. In other contexts of action and of analysis, the two are reciprocal subsystems within larger systems. The next larger systems, in turn, can be described as separate entities, but they should also be understood as subsystems within a total field of society and culture.

Main elements in these larger contexts are the relations among villages and especially between village and center. Kinship bonds, as has been noted, require much travel among villages. Within a closer radius, jajmani exchanges necessitate many short trips. People circulate to attend panchayats and other jati affairs.[1] There is usually constant coming and going among the people of several contiguous or nearby villages (cf. Smith 1952). Within such village clusters, whenever news and influences from a center reach one village they are quickly known in the others. Influences from various centers are regular and important factors in village life and in the lives of most villagers.

Centers and Hinterlands: Villagers and Townsmen

Almost all in any village have been to the nearest market center, which is usually within a few hours' round-trip journey; a good many will go there regularly. Within a similar radius, if not in the same location, there is usually a holy place that attracts the villagers on ceremonial occasions or for personal exigencies. The nearest administrative center and the modern educational and medical facilities may not be so close but they also attract villagers from many villages roundabout.

Each local center has a hinterland of clientele and each is in turn part of the hinterland of a larger center. The trade center of smallest scope in a locality is usually the market held once a week in some convenient open space. Surajit Sinha studied such a market in Singhbhum district of Bihar at intervals over ten years (Sinha *et al*. 1961, pp. 131–163). It is held weekly at a village called Bamni. Customers come from about a five-mile radius, most of them from within three miles of Bamni. Some of them visit other weekly markets as well; there is one on Sundays three miles away and another on Saturdays four miles away. There are twelve weekly markets in the 634 square miles of the subdistrict; Bamni is among the largest of them.

Products of the immediate locality—vegetables, lentils, fish, pots, sweets—are sold, as well as goods brought in from other places—cooking oil, salt, kerosene, tobacco, onions, matches, and sugar. Some buyers also bring their own produce to sell or barter. Most sellers come from a greater distance than do the buyers.[2] Goods and services of some sixteen artisan jatis are available as well as products handled by specialized traders of still other jatis. In this part of Bihar, an average number of jatis in a village is only about six.

---

[1] For two adjoining villages in Faizabad district, U.P., thirty-three specialists come from six different hamlets within a two-mile radius. The eight settlements form a jajmani unit although they fall within five different village administrative units (Gould 1964, pp. 20–27).

The circulation occasioned by jati affairs in Rampur, near Delhi, includes council meetings in a unit of four villages and in the larger unit of twenty villages. These in turn belong to a league of 360 villages (Lewis 1958, pp. 29–31).

[2] Some merchants cover a circuit of 7 markets within 10 miles of Bamni; those who deal in manufactured goods come from places more distant, from as far as 20 miles away. A sample of the people at the market showed that buyers came from 24 different villages, sellers from 52. Those who visited principally to buy represented 19 jatis among the 125 people interviewed, sellers represented 32 jatis among 314 interviewed (Sinha *et al*. 1961, pp. 142–144).

The Bamni market, like others of its kind, also serves political, recreational, and general societal purposes. During the time when Sinha observed it, the most powerful local leader customarily sat on a cot in the market surrounded by his close associates, the influential village headmen in the locality. An ordinary farmer did not dare go near that cot, much less sit on it. Gentry of the higher jatis could speak with the leader on nearly equal terms. "All people attending the market would immediately recognize him as the lord of the land and as representing the peak in the regional power hierarchy." In this market, villagers could plainly see who the main leader was and who were his closest associates (Sinha *et al.* 1961, p. 154).

A good many of the visitors, especially in the slack season for farm work, came only for the fun of meeting friends at the market. New contacts could be made there. Given a few encouraging clues, a young man knew how to proceed. A girl's coy smile could easily bring her a fond pinch in return, and should that produce nothing more discouraging than a gay frown, a gift of betel chew and perhaps more intimate exchanges followed. Older people sought out their friends and relatives to exchange news and gossip; they did not seek to establish new social relations at the market.

Jati considerations were not central in market transactions but they were not entirely irrelevant either. While visitors to the Bamni market patronized tea stalls, sweetshops, and betel-chew sellers without much concern for the stricter avoidances of their home villages, yet none of these vendors were Harijans. Tradesmen were of many jatis. The main cash product, *lac*, was handled by traders of twenty-one different jatis. Manufactures, however, were sold or serviced mainly by artisans of the jatis traditionally involved with them. "From all these it becomes clear that even today, a greater part of material transactions in the market closely follow the traditional division of labour in terms of caste" (Sinha *et al.* 1961, p. 140).

Traders now come from a wider range of jatis than before, but in general the functions of markets like Bamni continue. Local products are sold or bartered; commodities from afar are on sale; specialists find the customers they need and villagers find there the full assortment of specialist jatis. As travel improves, the smallest markets lose attendance to the larger, but a market like that at Bamni flourishes. It is much more than a center for economic transactions. It is a chief place for recreation and a main node of local communication.

Beyond such local markets are those of wider scope. There is a larger market center nine miles from Bamni; it is a Tuesday market located on a railway line and a paved road. This draws more tradesmen from greater distances than does Bamni and also more buyers, possibly because it is the only cattle market in the subdistrict. While Bamni market draws from some fifty villages, the cattle market at Balarampur brings buyers and sellers from about 600 villages (Sinha *et al.* 1961, pp. 157–162; see also Patnaik 1953; Mukerji 1957).

Larger markets are often specialized. A marketing study of a Punjab locality showed that the farmers were inclined to take their wheat to one market, *gur* to another, and cotton to a third (Neale *et al.* 1965, p. 166).

There are, in addition, periodic centers that attract great numbers. They are mainly religious fairs and festivals during which a village or town honors its special deity. Thousands, even hundreds of thousands, then throng to the celebrated place. With them come merchants, hawkers, dealers, amusement purveyors in numbers. The report on fairs and festivals in Gujarat in the 1961 Census of India lists 1521 annual fairs in that state, with an estimated attendance of more than seven million (Trivedi 1965). Other accounts of fairs and festivals in the 1961 Census volumes (Part VII-B of each volume) testify to similar numbers.

Major influences flow from the permanent centers, the main towns. The district headquarters is usually a center for trade as well as of administration. It is often also a center for educational and medical services and of religious observances.[3]

A villager's visit to town follows patterns familiar to him. His dealings in the town bazaar are much like his dealings with a village shopkeeper. He worships in the great temple using the same ritual idiom that is appropriate in the village shrine. This familiarity does not mean that a villager is an easy participant in town life or that he feels completely at home in town, but rather that there are typically established relations with villagers and a regular place for them in the town setting.

Towns and cities are ancient in India and the relations between townsmen and villagers are also of ancient standing. Townsmen in the traditional centers have not been so very different from villagers in their social organization and general way of life. The Jatavs, leatherworkers of Agra City, for example, organized themselves in groups of related households that resemble the localized lineages of the villages, save that the emphasis was more on common locality than on lineage affiliation. Such a group maintained its own headman and panchayat; it was a unit of close cooperation and of frequent interaction. Several of these groups constituted a *mohalla*, a section of the city that was the functional equivalent of a village in that it was a unit for personal identification, for actual and fictive kinship, for panchayat functions, and a unit of exogamy (Lynch 1967, pp. 143–150).

Such common ground between villager and townsman of similar social level does not usually induce visiting villagers to want to settle there unless economic need impels them to take work in a town. But a villager's visits to a town are eased by the ample precedents for such trips, by the experienced companions or suitable guides he can generally find for his first ventures into that wider world, and by the traditional similarities between town and village culture.

True, what is part of everyday routine for a townsman may be a special occasion for the visiting villager. Many a villager looks forward eagerly, from one visit to the next, to the delights of the town—whether the heady distraction of shopping, the exaltation of grand ceremony, or the more mundane pleasures of cinema and restaurant. In the context of the town and under cover of anonymity a man from the village may relax his jati's standards for dining and drinking, and for personal contacts.

These visits are made more by men than by women. A woman does not often travel beyond the villages of her kin. She may go to the local market and on great occasions to a festival or a pilgrimage center. But the contacts between centers and village are mainly in the keeping of the men.

LINK ROLES

Regular contacts between village and large center are maintained by those villagers who take on link roles; some do so because of ascribed office or jati occupation, others for personal gain. One official link role is that of the village headman who is required to transmit information, requests, and orders between the village and governmental authority. He is expected to be spokesman for the villagers to official authority and also the agent of that authority in the village.

---

[3] Of a total of 310 districts in India, 216 were larger than 4,000 square miles and had more than a million population in the 1951 census. Each district is administratively divided into subunits, called *taluka* in some states, and a *taluka* is further subdivided into groupings of villages, called by various terms, *hobli* in Mysore, *firka* in Andhra (Rao and Bhat 1960, pp. 3–9).

Other bridging functions are performed in the regular course of a jati's calling. A tradesman brings goods into the village, acts as a broker for the crop or as agent for a broker in town. A Brahmin priest is supposed to share in the learning developed at the great centers and some are indeed learned enough to bring scriptural ideas and stories to their village clients.

Link roles can be lucrative and so ambitious men seek them. An energetic man of almost any jati may try to be a broker for village products. Those who are exceptionally successful may have considerable influence as wealthy men in their jati and as entrepreneurial innovators for the village. One Oraon tribesman who had been hired by a merchant and so was able to learn about the ways of the market, enriched his own locality when he introduced potato cultivation and also a more efficient way of trapping (D. P. Sinha 1963; 1967).

On another level of linkage are the religious-esthetic brokers who come into the villages. Some are themselves villagers who organize a dramatic company and stage plays in the villages of their vicinity (cf. Hein 1958). Cultural specialists from the centers are imported for grand occasions. A wealthy magnate may bring in a famous performer for a wedding or festival; a renowned sage may be brought as an act of merit.

One of the most famous of Madrassi performers of song and recitation, Saraswati Bai, had been an artist for forty-eight years when Milton Singer interviewed her in 1955. She frequently performed in villages before audiences of thousands. "I have not spared a single village and not a single village has spared me." Her presentations combined devotional lessons with dramatic performances of great esthetic appeal (Singer 1958, pp. 361–364). Traveling performers and sages have linked villagers to the artistic and religious centers for centuries, disseminating the ideas and precepts of the larger civilization (cf. Singer 1964; Geertz 1960). In the nineteenth century these ties were strengthened by improved travel, railways, postal services, and printed matter. More recently the ties have been enhanced by cinema and radio.

Another type of middleman is the self-appointed agent of liaison with government who offers his services for a fee. Such experts—there is commonly at least one in a village—claim special knowledge of bureaucratic ways or special advantage with an official, if only with the peon who guards the magistrate's door. One such middleman is mentioned by Srinivas in an account of a family dispute in Rampura village of Mysore. This man, called Kulle Gowda, urged that the family register a deed of partition, rather than settle the dispute without formal legal action, pointing out all the advantages to the members of the family in doing so. He was interested in having these legal steps taken because it would mean one or two trips to town for him as the family's representative. "The brothers would have to bear the expenses of these trips, and besides, Kulle Gowda would be able to charge them other expenses, real or imaginary—the clerk to be paid a certain sum for doing the work quickly, and so on" (Srinivas 1952b, p. 18).

Some years later, when I was with Professor Srinivas on a day's visit to Rampura, Kulle Gowda told us of a trip he had taken not long before to the city of Madras. He had lifted his sights considerably by then for he described how he had interested a movie magnate in a script on village life that he was writing and trying to sell.

Village and center are thus linked by many agents and channels of communication. What is transmitted through them is another matter. One of the few studies which bear on this question is by Y. V. Lakshmana Rao (1966). He has examined the different kinds of communication in two villages of Andhra Pradesh and has found a marked differential between the relatively abundant and diverse communications of the prospering village and the sparse communications of the economically stagnant one. Further studies of this kind will illuminate the detailed processes of modern relations between village and center. For the society and civilization as a whole, however, it is clear that the traditional networks of communication have brought about certain broad effects.

Regions: Of the Observer and of the Participant

The broadest effect of these long established networks is that certain root concepts and practices, such as the varna concept and the purity-pollution practices, have come to be shared across the subcontinent. Other concepts and practices have become characteristic of particular parts of the subcontinent, mainly because closer communications are possible within geographic barriers than across them. To be sure, mere frequency of social interaction does not automatically create cultural resemblances; much depends, in India as elsewhere, on the nature of the relations and the views of one another held by those who are in communication. Nevertheless, cultural similarities within a region indicate that there has been relatively closer social interaction within its borders than across them.

The term region here refers not only to a geographic tract but also to common characteristics of culture and society held for some length of time by the people of a territory, especially as such traits are contrasted with features characteristic in other parts of the larger geographic entity. Two kinds of social-cultural regions should be distinguished. One kind includes those delineated by trained observers; the other includes those which the people in the society perceive and which may command their loyalties, identifications and actions. The two are not mutually exclusive categories, although the regions denoted by analytic observers are not necessarily recognized by those who live within them.

The inhabitants of an observer's region may be quite unaware that they all belong to a territory in which important cultural and social elements are shared. Thus the four main zones of kinship practices formulated by Mrs. Karve for all of India (1953, 1965) are very useful taxonomic concepts for social scientists, but few, if any, residents of the respective zones have any notion that they can be so classified.

On the other hand, if a number of people strongly feel that they share a regional identity, that in itself is a common feature, which observers must take into account. Government authorities may denote a new political entity, which then may become one of the importantly perceived regions for the people within it (cf. Schwartzberg 1967, pp. 90–91).

Taxonomic regions can summarize a great deal of information and so can be useful for economic and social planning as well as for a general understanding of cultural distributions and social processes. The nature of such regions depends on which traits are selected as significant and what purpose the formulation is intended to serve. Any village and each family can be subsumed within differently postulated regions, each valid for its purpose.

To take just the matter of religion, Srinivas has noted that the people of Coorg—a relatively small but geographically and culturally distinctive hill district between Mysore and Kerala—can be classified as practicing a special variety of Hinduism as contrasted with that practiced in adjoining areas. In a larger view, their Hinduism belongs in one region with that carried on in the larger tract comprising "Malabar, South Canara, and Coorg Proper." That, in turn, belongs to a region he calls "Peninsular Hinduism," which itself is part of the vast region of "All-India Hinduism" (1952a, pp. 213–215).

The geographic spread of what is denoted as a region thus varies according to the criteria and purposes selected by the analyst. For certain criteria and purposes the whole subcontinent can be treated as one region, as Emeneau has done in respect to certain linguistic traits and as Kroeber has done in regard to civilization (Emeneau 1956; Kroeber 1947). For other purposes a tract like Coorg, which at the time of Srinivas' study had less than 200,000 people (fewer than 50,000 of them speakers of the Coorg language), living in a hill territory of some 1500 square miles, can validly be considered a separate region, both to the observers and to the participants. Even much smaller tracts and populations can usefully be denoted as regions for still other purposes. The present discussion deals mainly with regions of larger compass, those that take in very large blocs of the Indian population and terrain.

In previous chapters major differences have been noted in social organization between northern and southern India—more accurately between Hindi-speaking people of the upper and central Ganges Basin and the Dravidian speakers of the southern part of the Indian peninsula (cf. Karve 1965, pp. 242–252; Srinivas 1956b, pp. 218–219; De 1967, pp. 66–68).[4]

These differences are basic, yet in the distribution of other traits the north-south division is not so clear or so important. For example, Bose and Sinha have traced variations across the country in 14 material items having to do with village form, house types, diet, dress, utensils, and carts. Cohn's analysis of these data shows that three of the traits have quite a mixed distribution; six fall into an east-west classification, and only five into a north-south division (Bose and Sinha 1961; Cohn 1967, pp. 19–21).

Three macro-regions of India have been formulated by Selig Harrison in his book on political unity and diversity. "The political history of India can be viewed as the history of three large geographical arenas—North, Deccan and South—set off from one another by profound physiographic differences" (1960, p. 15). The principal criteria Harrison uses to distinguish those macroregions are historical and geographic. They are historical in the sense that they are based on continuities in broad political development and on the present awareness of those continuities. They are geographic in the sense that the morphology of the landscape inevitably affects communications, and the nature of the communications, as has just been noted, affects (though it does not determine) the nature of cultural resemblances and social loyalties.

The most detailed mappings yet made of the regions of India have been done on the basis of geographic and economic criteria. The 1965 report on regional development by the Registrar General, Ashok Mitra, generally follows Spate's comprehensive treatment of Indian regions and adds data from the 1961 Census of India (Mitra 1965; Spate 1954; A. T. A. and A. M. Learmonth 1958). The projects for a National Atlas and for the new India Gazetteer use a similar outline. Additional criteria have been taken into account in J. E. Schwartzberg's map of the cultural regions of the subcontinent which utilizes linguistic and other cultural variables as well as physiographic and economic features (1967, pp. 102–111). This work is being advanced by the author and his associates in the project for a historical atlas of India.

Such maps do what maps are intended to do, they illustrate variations and gradients of the social terrain. They can, for example, illuminate regional differences among groups bearing the same

[4] An interesting sidelight on North-South differences comes from a World War II study in military psychiatry. Dr. A. H. Williams reported that his patients from North India tended to show different symptoms from those shown by patients from the South. The South Indians, both Hindu and Christian, had more schizophrenic symptoms. The soldier patients from North India more often had other psychiatric disorders (Williams 1950, pp. 139, 167).

name and status. They can summarize the influence of a dominant jati; they can trace isograms of social structure.

Some regions are stamped with the characteristics of a strongly dominant jati. Thus in the parts of the Punjab (now Haryana) where Jats are dominant, they typically make up most of the village community, with few other jatis represented and those few having a relatively small population. This characteristic may well stem from Jat landowning customs that assign almost all the village land only to Jat lineages (Pradhan 1965; Schwartzberg 1965, pp. 488–489).[5]

Another example of the regional influence of a dominant jati is from Dewas district of Madhya Pradesh. Rajputs are strong in many villages there, but are not dominant in all. Other jatis that have dominance are generally allied to Rajputs. Mayer comments that "where the caste which may most clearly be called dominant does not control all or even the majority of villages in a region, these other villages will tend to be under the authority of castes which are sympathetic to it, and which adopt its ways in order to identify themselves with it, and then become its commensal equals and allies" (1958a, p. 419).

A few studies have taken social structure as the main criterion in regional mapping. Marriott has analyzed the degree of caste elaboration in five selected regions, examining the number of jatis and the consensus about their ranking rather than jati customs and functions. This study indicates that among the five areas, there is most elaborate ranking and greatest consensus about rank in Kerala. In decreasing order of rank elaboration and consensus are the Coromandel, the Upper Ganges, the Middle Indus, and the Bengal Delta areas. Although questions remain about the causes and correlates of these variations, the structural differences of jati ranking among the five areas have been indicated (Marriott 1960; Cohn 1962; 1967, pp. 8–9; Mandelbaum 1962).

Another feature used for mapping Indian regions is their historic character. Some have been nuclear centers of influence over long periods; others have been route areas; and still others have been relatively isolated (Cohn 1967, p. 12). Whatever criteria are selected, the analyst does well to heed Schwartzberg's comment that what should be of prime concern is not the periphery of a region but its core, that part in which the variables defining it are well expressed (1967, p. 94).

Of all the observers' classifications, the most generally useful are the major linguistic groupings. Mrs. Karve has noted that the contiguous territory inhabited by speakers of a main language and its dialects also shows relative homogeneity in social organization, in material culture, and in religious practices, as contrasted with the practices of another linguistic region. She has used such regions extensively in her analysis of kinship organization, and other scholars have made similar use of linguistic regions (Karve 1951, p. 1; 1965, pp. 1–6; Srinivas 1962, p. 98; Stein 1967, p. 42; De 1967, pp. 52–54).

These linguistic regions have come to be much more than useful taxonomic devices for scholars and administrators; they have become potent participants' regions as well. Some popular leaders have taken their linguistic region as a main category for self-identification for political and cultural symbolism. Many now perceive it as an important unit, all the more because state boundaries have been redrawn to adhere more closely to linguistic boundaries.

---

[5] As was noted in earlier chapters, the ranking of a jati can vary from place to place. Thus in much of Midnapore district, West Bengal, the Mahisyas are in the large majority, outnumbering the local herdsmen and potters. The order of jati ranking follows this fact. "Like the Potters, the Herdsmen generally in Bengal rank higher than the Mahisyas but must accept their dominance in Midnapore" (Nicholas 1965, pp. 37–38).

Regional Identification and Situational Context

A villager recognizes and feels potentially identified with a whole series of regions and other groupings; which of them motivates his action at any given time depends on the situation, especially on the context of confrontation with those of other regions or groups (cf. De 1967, pp. 52–56). Thus a person may see himself as a member of a particular lineage, alliance, jati, village, village cluster, district, state, language region, and nation. But he does not perceive and cannot participate in all at once.

When a dispute between his village and another is in question, he is likely to act as a village member; when he believes that the rights of those of his language are jeopardized, he may rally with others of the same language. Srinivas comments that solidarity with one's group, whatever it may be at a particular juncture, seems to require a certain amount of rivalry with parallel groups. So a man is a member of his jati vis-à-vis other jatis and a Hindu when in confrontation with non-Hindus. Similarly, he is an Indian in relation to non-Indians, so that "irrespective of his village or caste or region he reacts like an Indian when the problem of Goa or Kashmir crops up…. Tensions and conflicts at a particular level maintain the identity and separation of groups of the same order but these groups can and do unite at a higher level" (Srinivas 1962, pp. 110–111).

This process has been noted several times in preceding chapters. What needs to be clarified by future research is the sequence of choices that a man commonly faces and the points at which he must select among alternate loyalties. The pattern of such choices changes over time and as a villager's social space and intellectual horizons expand through wider experience and education, he finds himself aware of more potential identifications than his forefathers could recognize.

A person becomes especially aware of his region when he is out of it. Surrounded by people of different speech and manner, he typically feels in need of friends of his own kind. Migrants to a city, as was noted, generally find shelter and help from city residents from their own locality. A hotel manager in a northern town once told me that he enjoyed especially friendly relations with a university professor of the town because both of them were from Kerala. Regional clubs are common in the major cities, places where a man far from home can come to speak his home language, to meet his regional compatriots, and to enjoy familiar food, gossip, and humor.

Regional self-identification is usually strongest in a geographic enclave that is relatively isolated from outsiders but whose people are quite conscious of outsiders. An extreme example is a village of Kulu district north of Simla in the Himalayas. It has some 500 inhabitants who are so cut off by mountains from the rest of the world that they speak their own language, maintain their own customs, and have very little identification or contact beyond their remote wild glen (Rosser 1960).

A pocket of some 10,000 people exists in the hills along the Madras-Mysore border near the Kruvery River. For centuries the people of this enclave had little contact with outsiders; their lives and loyalties were concentrated within the villages of their hill territory. They were nearly self-sufficient economically; marriages were rarely contracted out of the territory; their leaders managed their own political affairs. Yet, as in other isolated parts of India, they were culturally a part of the main. There were several jatis among them and the dominant Lingayats carried on a full sectarian way of worship and conduct. In their infrequent contacts with outsiders they presumably felt themselves to be very much the distinctive inhabitants of a distinctive territory; inside the territory, jati differences were maintained (MacLachlan and Beals 1966).

Jati differences have been maintained in other isolated hill tracts. While the intensity of social relations within an enclave provides a base for special territorial identification and customs, it does not do away with cultural and social distinctions among the jatis of the enclave. The four peoples of the Nilgiri Hills of South India were largely isolated from villages on the nearby plains until the mid-nineteenth century. Together they formed a separate social system; there were constant, even daily, relations among members of the four groups, yet they remained completely distinct both culturally and socially (Mandelbaum 1956).

How and with whom a person identifies regulates the ways in which he shapes his conduct. He takes certain groups and categories as reference models to emulate. Other groups he sees in negative reference and is unwilling or unable to be like them. In later chapters reference models are considered in relation to social mobility. The mention of reference models is relevant here in that regional groupings in India often carry either positive or negative reference in the eyes of other people.

This reference behavior is exemplified in Berreman's account of Sirkanda village in the Himalayan foothills, located within a day's journey of the town of Dehra Dun in one direction and of Mussoorie in another. Sirkanda villagers speak Pahari, the distinctive language of a thousand-mile-long belt of the Himalayan hills; they share the major cultural features of Pahari speakers; they think of themselves as Paharis as against the people of the towns and the plains villages. They feel at a disadvantage when they have to deal with non-Paharis because they believe that the others are more knowledgeable and sophisticated than they are. "As a result, Paharis do not identify themselves as people who can learn or benefit from the ways of people of the plains"; they have frequent contact with non-Paharis but have taken over relatively little from them (Berreman 1960b, pp. 775–780, 783).

Their regular visits to large centers have had little effect on them because the town is too strange, the town traits too alien for any great cultural impact. Sirkanda men usually go several times a year to Dehra Dun or Mussoorie for marketing or other purposes. But their visits are usually brief and often uncomfortable sorties. They have no one to stay with in town and must bunk down in a temple or shop unless the visitor can get to a Pahari village before dark. Trips are scheduled, when possible, so the traveler can stay the night in a friendly village rather than in the alien cold town. Moreover, hill villagers feel conspicuous in the large centers because of "their rusticity and distinctive dress, language, and behavior." They are sensitive lest they be objects of ridicule. All this is not conducive to ready adoption of town manners.

By contrast, the Sirkanda people have much more intense and frequent interchange within their own hill locality, an area of some sixty settlements within a four-mile radius of Sirkanda. Eighty percent of all marriages are contracted within this locality; two markets are within it and the most important annual fair for these villagers takes place in their own territory. So there is considerable cultural homogeneity among the people of these 60 settlements. Their jatis are relatively few, with most people belonging to the higher jatis. There are cultural differences among the jatis, but they are not very great, partly because families of the lower jatis have been thinly dispersed among the settlements of the higher jatis. This is quite unlike the Nilgiri situation, in which each group was concentrated in its own settlements and so could maintain and develop its own cultural bent.

A few hours' walk from Sirkanda across a watershed to the north, there is another enclave whose people have somewhat different customs and are suspected by the Sirkanda villagers of practicing witchcraft. Both factors impede social relations between Sirkanda and these people. The Sirkanda people have more cordial relations with villages to the east of them, where the better lines of communication lie, than with those to the north and west, where there are not only more difficult geographic and cultural barriers but also a sharp dialectic boundary (Berreman 1960b, pp. 778–781; 1963, pp. 294–318).

What is illustrated among these hill people holds true elsewhere, that the wider social relations of a villager are directed by both objective and subjective factors. Objectively, there are the facts of geography, economics, social divisions, or cultural similarities. Subjectively, there are the identifications that a person makes of himself and of others. With some groups he feels able to identify, at least on some level, able to cooperate with them socially in some situations, and able to learn from them in some contexts. Others are defined as outsiders or enemies or aliens, with little likelihood of social cooperation or cultural assimilation. Migrants to a new region have usually resisted such assimilation, clinging tenaciously to the speech and customs of their original region. Thus the Tamil-speaking Brahmins who moved into Kerala have long continued to use Tamil as their home language (cf. Iyer 1909; Béteille 1962).

Influences of the region of residence do in time erode the practices of the region of origin. Mrs. Karve, however, once witnessed this process in a Maharashtrian village as it was occurring. A jati council of Gujars had been convened to judge a case of cross-cousin marriage, which was prohibited by their own jati tradition but practiced by their present neighbors. The Gujars are a pastoral group whose main locale is to the north of Maharashtra. These Gujars had maintained the marriage patterns of their northern brethren; their panchayat still imposed a fine for cross-cousin marriages. But this was on the way to being changed; a Gujar elder commented to Mrs. Karve that "One cannot resist the customs of the land in which one lives. After all a fish cannot wage a feud against water" (1953, pp. 9, 162).

Regional Change and the Rise of Regionalism

The region changes over time. One contributing factor is that centers rise and fall, their clientele and hinterlands shift. The town of Deoli in Rajasthan, for example, formerly the capital of a Maharana's state, has become an empty shell since the ruler's power was assumed by the present government. Its residents are now part of the political hinterland of the district headquarters rather than actors at the right hand of state power. The old feudal loyalties are now disintegrated (Carstairs 1957, pp. 15–27). Other towns have risen influence. Thus the commercial importance of Bolpur in West Bengal has steadily increased as it has grown—from a small village to a railway station, to a rice market, to a milling town—until it has become a trade center for a large area (Bose 1958a, p. 151). As Bolpur grew, the nearby river port, Supur, declined (Fukutake *et al.* 1964, pp. 103–140).

The people of any one village normally participate in centers of several different kinds. Thus Ramkheri village is seven miles from the district headquarters town of Dewas in Madhya Pradesh, and so the villagers go to Dewas to trade and for governmental and political business.

Dewas and its village hinterland are, in turn, part of the larger tract known as Malwa which contains the religious centers of Ujjain and Manud, respectively some thirty and one hundred miles from Ramkheri. The fame of Ujjain is ancient; its location fixed the prime meridian of Sanskrit geographers. Its temples still draw throngs of worshippers, among them people from Ramkheri. That center and that religious identification have not changed for the Ramkheri villagers. Nor have the commercial attractions of the city of Indore, twenty-two miles from Ramkheri, lessened for them. What has changed for them is that the new administrative and political center at Bhopal has become important. Bhopal is now the capital of the state of Madhya Pradesh. As the people of Ramkheri become increasingly engaged in larger political affairs, some of their leaders have become increasingly involved with officials and politicians whose center is at Bhopal (Mayer 1960, pp. 11–14; 1962, pp. 271–276; Spate 1954, p. 578).

Beyond the rise and fall of particular centers, the general trend for villagers is toward wider experiences and broader social horizons than they previously had. This induces broadening of jati boundaries through the kind of caste associations that are discussed in later chapters. Those who take active part in such associations become aware of the greater political arenas of state and national affairs. In those arenas one's region is in competition with others and regional allegiance is likely to be a powerful rallying influence, reaching on occasion into the villages as well as to the political centers.

"Regionalism" has become a major political factor for several reasons. One is simply the creation of the independent nation within which sectional interests vigorously compete for shares of the nation's substance and for symbols of regional eminence. Another is the growth in importance of the regional languages, in the number of people educated in those languages and their increased self-identification with the language and the region. This began in the nineteenth century when local leaders deliberately propagated indigenous regional speech, literature, and practices as ways of opposing the language and influence of the elite, whether they were English and colonial, or Persian and Mogul (cf. Cohn 1967, pp. 21–25; Brass 1967; McDonald 1968; Srinivas 1962, pp. 98–103; Irschik 1969).

The regional language is only one of the speech forms commonly used by villagers and townspeople. For each of three levels of interaction—within a village cluster, within local centers, and at regional centers—there is, as John Gumperz has noted, a corresponding level of language. More marked linguistic differences occur between adjoining regional languages than between dialects of adjoining village clusters. This linguistic separation between regions is another element in sharpening loyalty to region.

In a village and its close vicinity, the people usually speak the same dialect although particular jatis may use a special variation of the village dialect in their homes.[6] The regional dialect, as distinct from the village dialects, is used over a larger area. It is "the native language of small town residents" and is spoken by villagers when they visit the local centers. They use it to communicate with townspeople and with other villagers whose dialects differ from theirs.

There are variations between one town and another in the region, Gumperz notes, but these are minor in comparison with the much greater differences among the village dialects. Some of these regional dialects have in the past been literary languages much as Braj Bhasa, spoken around Agra, Avadhi spoken around Lucknow, and the Konkani spoken around Goa. At the present time literary works are written mainly in a regional language rather than in these regional dialects (Gumperz 1957, pp. 72–73).

The regional language is that which is used, in literary and colloquial versions, at the principal center, usually the capital of the state. The literary form is the more elegant version taught in the higher schools, and used in writing and formal speeches. The colloquial form is spoken by the uneducated in the main center and by the educated in home usage and for special purposes, as in humor

[6] The Sweepers of Khalapur village have a distinctive dialect which they use with each other; two other untouchable jatis in the village have their respective dialects. There are six dialectic variations in all, each used by a different group of the village. But all in Khalapur also know and use the dialect that is standard in the locality (Gumperz 1957; 1958; Gumperz and Naim 1960).

or to underline verbally a certain kind of message. The regional language is the usual speech of the educated people throughout the region. Townspeople in the smaller centers know both the regional dialect and the regional language quite well, but at home they speak the regional dialect.

The transition between one regional language and the next is sharpened by the way each is taught—as a separate language and culture vehicle—in the schools. But the dialects intergrade in complex ways. Gumperz gives a hypothetical example of two villages, A and B, on either side of an administrative border, such as the one between Bengal and Bihar. The dialects of the two close-lying villages may differ very little, but in village A the regional language will be Hindi and in village B it will be Bengali. "A villager from A can easily talk to a friend from B in the local dialect, however the two will not be able to exchange letters unless one knows both languages" (1957, p. 76).

The range of a regional dialect is commonly also the span of jati endogamy. Apart from border areas, even people of considerable education and wealth tend to marry within the area of the regional language. All other kinds of social interchange also decrease sharply across the spatial edge of a regional language.

Linguistic differentiation is an old feature of Indian civilization. In ancient Sanskrit drama, the parts were written in different languages and dialects for characters of different social status. It seems likely that there were commonly regional language cliques in the courts of ancient kings. But linguistic regionalism has been given a new importance by modern developments. What were mainly observers' regions of classification have increasingly become participants' regions of identification.

The linguistic regions of India were comprehensively mapped by Sir George Grierson in the Linguistic Survey of India, a work that began in 1898 and was concluded with the publication of the final volume in 1927. Long before that, learned men in India had a general knowledge of the major linguistic divisions. At the religious supercenters pilgrims from any corner of the country could be directed to that quarter where others of their regional tongue could be found. But the social force of linguistic identification did not develop greatly until communications within the regions improved, until the regional language was propagated for educational, literary, religious, and political purposes, and until local political leaders felt a need for supralocal alliances in order to swing political weight.

Regional interests have lately been seen as so opposed to national unity that some commentators have considered this opposition as a major, perhaps the greatest, issue confronting the nation (Harrison 1960). Some tensions between local loyalties and larger interests exist in all complex societies; they have been constant issues in all great states. Both kinds of identification and loyalty are necessary and some conflict between them may well be inevitable. The question is not whether such tensions should exist at all but rather how well the social system provides for their management.

Regional Loyalties and Wider Identifications

The management of conflicts of loyalty has had to be worked out anew in recent decades, particularly because of the rise of new political units since Independence. It has not been easy. Material resources are scarce in relation to expectations of regional political leaders and there is severe competition among sectional interests. There is also the general inclination to rank social units of all sorts, regions included, so that the people of one see themselves in status competition with those of others.

Villagers usually participate in regional rivalries only indirectly, through those who fill the link roles with the centers. But villagers often engage in similar rivalries at a more local level. Their several kinds of affiliations are not necessarily mutually destructive forces. A person does feel that he is a member of a particular jati, village, region, state, and religion "but these loyalties can represent a hierarchy of values and are not necessarily inconsistent with being a citizen of the Indian Republic" (Srinivas 1962, p. 110).

There is a traditional basis for the larger national identification. It is the idea, mainly engendered by Hindu religion but shared by those of other religions as well, that there is an entity of India to which all its inhabitants belong. The Hindu epics and legends, in their manifold versions, teach that the stage for the gods was nothing less than the entire land and that the land remains one religious setting for those who dwell in it. That sense was and is continually confirmed through the common practice of pilgrimage.

In most villages there are likely to be some who have been on pilgrimages, perhaps to distant centers. A count in one village, Sherurpur in U.P., showed that 49 pilgrimages had been made among a total population of 228. The nearest religious center is 20 miles away and it had attracted 28 pilgrimages; the other pilgrimages were to centers from 100 to 540 miles distant. Men and women higher in rank traveled more; villagers of the four higher jatis had made nearly twice as many pilgrimages as were made by those of the other four jatis of Sherurpur (Gould 1959, pp. 10–13).

Sacred centers range from those that attract visitors from a few score miles, to those that bring devotees from an entire linguistic region, to the great supercenters that draw people from all parts of the land.[7] A graphic, enlightening account of a pilgrimage to Pandharpur, a main center for Marathi-speaking people, has been written by Mrs. Karve. She tells how vivid a learning experience it was for the pilgrims. All recited the poetry of five centuries every day of their long march together. That poetry embodies a basic religious philosophy; "People speaking many dialects sang the same verses and thus learned a standard language. Their learning was achieved in a massive dose but without pain or compulsion."

The days of the pilgrimage are a joyous time; at halting places along the route there are continual performances by members of the vast moving congregation in music, dancing, drama. Some of it is bawdy, for all levels of esthetic and intellectual taste are represented. The bereaved and the suffering feel able to unburden themselves to their fellow pilgrims and so find relief. "The whole atmosphere was full of joy." Yet, as Dr. Karve observes, despite the comradeship of the pilgrimage, pilgrims of widely different jatis kept separate, especially in eating (1962, pp. 19–23).

Pilgrimages to the supercenters reinforce religious precepts but also impress the pilgrim with the vastness, the diversity, and—seemingly paradoxically—the oneness of the society. When I met the Indian anthropologist, L. K. Anantakrishna Iyer, shortly before his death in 1937, he had just returned from a long circuit of the great sacred places of pilgrimage. Even so learned and experienced a scholar as he was impressed afresh with the deep unity of Indian society and culture, and he spoke eloquently of that unity.

[7] The seven supercenters usually include five in the state of Uttar Pradesh—Banaras, Prayag (Allahabad), Mathura, Hardwar, Ayodhya—and Dwaraka in Gujarat, and Conjeeveram in Madras. Some Hindus include Ujjain in Madhya Pradesh or Nasik in Maharashtra in the list. There are still other variations on the list of the seven most sacred places (Bharati 1963).

A villager is also likely to return from a distant pilgrimage with an enhanced sense of the India-wide tenets of his religion and society. He has seen a variety of custom and a diversity of peoples—yet all gathered for the same purpose, acting on the same assumptions and focussed on the same rites and symbols. Some of the rites specifically underline the social unity of the whole country, as when a pilgrim to Rameshwaram in the far south, bathes in the sea and then takes a pot of sea water to be emptied into the Ganges (Srinivas 1962, pp. 105–106; 1966, pp. 22–23, 130–132; Bharati 1963).

Perhaps pilgrims can readily assimilate the idea of the whole India because of the very fact that they consort with others of their region in the great center. They are received by local guides who cater to visitors of their kind, so they are not totally bereft of their regional moorings in the vast strange concourse. Even a scholar who sojourns in Banaras for years can live and study with others of his region and language. "A priest from the region of Maharashtra," Cohn and Marriott write, "who travels a thousand miles north to Banaras for learning the Vedas resides in a Maharashtrian school and studies Sanskrit under Marathi-speaking teachers…" (1958, p. 7). Regional custom and cuisine are quite compatible with transcendental rites and concepts.

Members of other religions, Muslims, Jains, Sikhs, Christians, go on pilgrimage to their own sacred places. They too experience an amity and identity there that surpasses locality. In a later chapter the social orientations of villagers of these religions will be discussed.

A sense of national identity is now consciously inculcated in all Indians through education, through national ceremonies and observances, through the mass media, through the speeches and examples of prominent national leaders. Many in India had been prepared for this secular message by the tradition of their religion. Either they themselves or someone they knew had been personal witnesses to dramatic displays of conduct that transcended local and regional affiliations.

There has not been in India the kind of dichotomy between rural peasantry and the town elite and literati that prevailed in some other civilizations. Jati specialization in the villages paralleled specialization in the centers. A village Brahmin could consider himself as pure ritually as a Brahmin serving in a renowned temple and as worthy of reaching the highest pitch of scriptural learning if he had the ability to do so. Village tradesmen maintained commercial links with higher centers; they could and some did become great merchant tycoons if capacity and fortune favored. So also with able men of the warrior-ruler tradition. More than a few founders of dynasties were village bred and battle elevated.

In this respect the society of closed jatis was, in some degree, open. Within their jati's calling, whether religious, mercantile, or military-governmental, talented villagers occasionally did move from their village to live in a center. Only a very small proportion in the higher jatis did so, but many who remained in the village maintained regular ties with a large center. The vast mass of cultivators, artisans, and laborers lived their lives within a narrow locale. However, people and influences from the centers came into that locale, and the villagers themselves might have experienced the vivid lessons of the pilgrimage. Those lessons bound village to center and center to village in the shared concepts of the civilization.

CHAPTER 22

The Villager and Some Perennial Problems of Civilization

Within the village and outside it, Indian villagers have to cope with problems that are inherent in any civilization. Some of them have been noted above, such as those arising from specialization and from the relations between village and center. There are other constant forces that pose perennial problems in any complex society and in the culture of such a society, that is to say, in a civilization.

To begin with, there are forces from the encompassing natural systems of biology and ecology. Every social system, whether relatively complex or simple, rests on these natural systems. The people of a civilization, however, direct and exploit these forces to a far greater degree than do primitives. These natural systems can be called "parasocial systems" in the sense that they constantly and directly impinge on social relations.

In India as in most of the world man's control over biological and ecological forces has greatly increased in recent times. This has been possible because of the establishment of global social-cultural systems, as of technology and science. These newer systems may be termed "megasocial systems" in that they surpass any one national society and affect all of them.

Within each complex society there are certain problems characteristic of such societies. One basic problem is that of providing for both broad personalized relations and narrower impersonalized relations. We discuss here a duality in role relations in Indian villages arising from this perennial problem, especially in economic, political, and religious activities.

Yet another problem indigenous to civilization is that of providing legitimate special roles for exceptional persons. Discussion of these roles leads to a general consideration of role definition and of fields of action among Indian villagers. Much of the discussion of this chapter applies not only to villagers but also to modern-educated, mainly urban people as well. A person's leeway of choice in his roles and field of action brings the discussion to the subject of the following chapters, the study of social and cultural change.

LARGER SYSTEMS OF BIOLOGY AND ECOLOGY

Both biology and ecology are usually treated as parameters in social analysis; that is, they are taken as constant factors in studies of social interaction and culture change. And it is not only the analyst who takes these forces as given. Villager and observer alike assume that there will be a flow of infants into a society, that they will grow up through the biological stages of the life-cycle, that the sown fields will yield and the seasons properly turn. But under certain circumstances these systems cannot be taken as parameters because forces from them obtrude strongly into the social routine.

Villagers deal with such obtrusions, say epidemics or crop failures, as best they can through empirical and supernatural means. The observer has to deal with such obtrusions by expanding his frame of analysis, by taking direct account of forces that he ordinarily relegates to other scientific fields. Thus illness can be taken as a parameter in the study of village society until we have to account for those social changes that result from the decrease in the incidence of fatal illness and the consequent rise in population.

Expanding the frame of social analysis to include such topics as demography, disease, genetics, and the biological life cycle also limits opportunities for neatly circumscribed well-integrated analyses. This matter of the scope of one's inquiry has been discussed in respect to social anthropology generally by Devons and Gluckman (1964) and by Bailey with specific reference to his work in India (1964), both with inclinations toward clearer circumscription rather than expansive exploration. In the present discussion, we can only acknowledge, and that all too briefly, the social potentials of these parasocial factors.

Among the most powerful of such factors are those of ecology, which in this agrarian culture mainly involves the technology of land cultivation. The subsistence basis of jati and village is postulated on plough agriculture. Those in India who use a different kind of cultivation, usually maintain a different kind of society. There are a good many tribal peoples living in remote, usually hilly, areas who practice swidden or "slash-and-burn" cultivation. The wild growth on a plot of land is cut down, burned over, and seeds sown in the ground fertilized by the ashes. Since the fertility of such soil declines sharply after a few seasons, the cultivator leaves it and begins the cycle again by clearing a new patch of overgrowth.

Swidden agriculture can be quite an effective way of adapting to a hill-jungle environment through a "canny imitation" of the natural landscape rather than by a bold reworking of it as in wet-rice cultivation. But the yield of swidden agriculture is always quite limited. Additional increments of labor or capital do not proportionately increase the crop, as they do with rice cultivation. The estimates of the number of people who can subsist on swidden fields range from 20 to 50 per square kilometer. Whatever the number in any particular locality, the carrying capacity of swidden land is far below that of ploughed land (Geertz 1963, pp. 15–37). Swidden agriculturalists in India typically maintain a tribal rather than a caste society, perhaps because caste organization implies a certain density of population that swidden methods cannot sustain. Some tribal groups do use ploughs or have a combination of plough and swidden methods, so the adoption of plough agriculture is not a sufficient cause for adopting caste organization although it does seem to have been a necessary condition for its historical establishment (cf. Bailey 1960b, pp. 63–68).

This subject is examined more extensively in the later discussion of tribal societies, and the symbolic importance of the role of swidden cultivator is noted there. The point here is that the one kind of relationship to the land provides a viable subsistence base for caste society while apparently the other does not. Swidden cultivation is rarely, if ever, the principal support of a caste village.

Another kind of ecological influence affects the intensity and flow of social relations. This influence has been noted in the previous discussion of village settlement patterns, particularly in Nicholas' comparsion of two villages of West Bengal whose people have quite the same culture but who live in two markedly different terrains (1963). One village is situated on the marshy, low-lying land of the active delta where houses must be strung out in long lines along the embankments, the only feasible house sites. The land has been newly reclaimed; each village is a kind of frontier settlement. As was noted in the discussion of village settlement patterns, social interaction within this village is relatively limited, jati composition and jati relations are relatively simple, and there is very little dominance by one jati over the others. The other village is in an area of ancient habitation, termed the "moribund delta." The settlement is in the usual compact cluster, permitting a good deal of jajmani and other social interchange within the cluster. The jati order is much more complex and rigid than in the frontier village; in this part of Bengal dominant jatis are common.

Not all of these differences are direct outcomes of the ecology. The marshy, frequently flooded terrain does dictate the strung-out settlement pattern and this does impede frequent interchange among fellow villagers; the relative simplicity of the jati order is a more indirect result. Those who are attracted to this new ground are mainly from the lower jatis of cultivators and are often from the poorer families among them who do not have enough to live on in their home villages. Better-off cultivators, artisans and other specialists are not usually drawn to a chancy frontier locale. The delta ecology limits certain kinds of relations and encourages others. It limits social interchange and fosters a relatively simple jati order.

A similar ecological contrast, on a broader scale, is given in Joan Mencher's comparison of Kerala and Madras as ecological and cultural regions. Kerala is a well-watered land, lush and green, whose villages consist mainly of spatially separated homesteads. Most of Madras has less adequate and dependable rainfall; irrigation works were built there in ancient times.[1] Villages are nucleated, partly because of the requirements of water management. In the compact Madrassi settlements, village organization can be tighter than in the dispersed houses of a Kerala village (Mencher 1966, pp. 137–152).

As for caste organization, Mencher says that "ecological factors have led to an elaboration and development of a relatively constant caste system in somewhat different directions" (1966, p. 163). In Kerala, the direction was toward authority focused on person-to-person relations, toward jati and rank proliferation, toward small, weak states and toward rigid spatial standards of pollution because of the close proximity of different jatis in a small homestead. In Madras the ecological influences made for group-to-group authority relations, less jati proliferation, larger bureaucratic and state organizations, and less need for stringent distance pollution (Mencher 1966, pp. 163–165).

As villagers take up modern agricultural technology and gain greater control over ecological forces, such traditional differences among regions are being modified. The new technology requires multiple, dependable social ties in order to assure supplies of water and fertilizer, of vaccines and

[1] The shift to intensive irrigation cultivation, as Dr. Mencher notes, fosters the kind of monumental social adaptations that have been discussed in many works, notably those of Karl A. Wittfogel and Julian H. Steward. A brief note on this subject by Henry Orenstein suggests some of the main activating forces in these changes (Orenstein 1965).

transport, of all the complex flow of goods and messages that modern agriculture demands. Since the government provides much of the frame for these new economic and social relations, villagers have to be increasingly involved with government officials in all regions. The spread of modern agricultural technology seems, in the short run, to be terribly spotty and agonizingly slow, but in the long run it is likely to be steady and massive. Great changes in agricultural methods bring notable changes, in India as elsewhere in the world, in social relations.

As for biological factors, the consequences of the new social controls over disease have been much discussed in the demographic literature and need only be mentioned here. These controls have been made possible by the megasocial system of medical science and have been mainly implemented by governmental agencies. Their success makes necessary new social adaptations of many kinds, a principal one being for greater controls over the biological forces of procreation.

Modern science and technology are affecting every phase of Indian village society. We return to this theme later, but now turn to three of the subsystems of village society.

Dual Functions in Economics, Politics, and Religion

Villagers have traditionally distinguished religious, political, and economic activities in the sense that there are separate specialists and social patterns for each of these subsystems. Each includes two sets of functions and roles, one for the more local personal, and immediate purposes, the other for more distant, societal, and long-range purposes.[2]

In economic relations, there is on the one side family production and internal village exchange, and on the other the flow of village-center trade. Cash crops, such as cotton, turmeric, and areca nut, have been traded through centers for centuries.[3] Different styles of behavior go with differing economic functions. The jajmani relationship, as we have seen, tends to be a multiplex bond in which two families share a long series of rights and obligations. They share in ceremonial as well as economic exchange, their association implies broad mutual support as well as specific transactions. In contrast, the trade relationship between villager and town merchant is more narrowly confined to the transaction itself.

---

[2] A similar distinction has been made by Srinivas and Béteille (1964) in contrasting a person's "close-knit" network of relations within the vilage to the "loose-knit" network outside his village.

[3] Because we are apt to think of wide-ranging trade as a recent development, it is well to recall that such trade is ancient and integral in Indian culture. The people of the Indus civilization, dating from the third millennium B.C. maintained trade links with Central Asia, Northeastern Afghanistan, Northeastern Persia, and South India. Indeed the whole existence of this civilization depended on a regular trade between hinterland villages and centers. The main centers such as Mohenjo-Daro and Harrappa, were key elements in the development of civilization. The large grain storehouses at these sites indicate that the concentration of specialists was made possible by the establishment of regular commerce with a wide hinterland (Wheeler 1953, pp. 28–33, 58–62). The classical manual of statecraft, the *Arthasastra*, of perhaps the third century B.C., details the duties of the official who supervises trade. In more recent times, nineteenth-century accounts show that there was a considerable amount of indigenous interregional as well as village-center trade. The temporary blocking of the flow of cotton into the English markets as a result of the American Civil War brought sudden, though temporary, prosperity to cotton growers in India (Kautilya 1951, pp. 104–106; Drekmeier 1962, pp. 276–277; Srinivas and Shah 1960; Leacock and Mandelbaum 1955).

These distinctions are not always clear cut. Thus certain tasks are arranged on a specific contract or cash basis even between jajmani associates. Conversely, many a villager has a personal relationship with a town merchant. In Totegadde village of Mysore, cash transactions have long been used in marketing the traditional crop of areca nuts, yet multiplex role relations are still important (Harper 1959b, 1961). In general, economic relations within the village are more often carried on through roles of multiple function, while in extravillage relations, the roles are likely to be more restricted to narrowly economic functions.

In political functions there is a duality between the politics of power within the village and the maintenance of administration by state authorities. We have previously discussed the characteristic political contests within a village and the manner in which agents of the state were kept out, insofar as was possible, of intravillage relations. Villagers rendered to agents of the state the revenue and deference that was their due; they did not want them meddling in the village nor did they usually think of themselves as active participants in state affairs. This is reflected in the differences between villagers' behavior in their own panchayats and in formal law courts. In the one milieu villagers emphasize the settlement of conflict, in the other the emphasis is rather on worsting an opponent. The two spheres are complementary in many ways: advantageous contacts with administration make for power in the village; dominance in the village helps to smooth relations with state administration.

In religion the duality is between the transcendental and the pragmatic functions, between those beliefs and practices that deal with the needs of society and those that are more directed to the immediate needs of the individual (Mandelbaum 1966, pp. 1174–1179). The transcendental complex is used to assure the long-term welfare of society, the maintenance of the social and of the sacred systems, and the proper transition of individuals from stage to stage within these systems. It is concerned with the ultimate goals of man. The pragmatic complex is used for personal benefits and local exigencies—to cure a sick child, for success in family ventures. The one is connected to religious centers far beyond the village as well as to places of worship within the village; the shrines of the other are mainly within the locality. Different forms and practitioners attach to each, as was previously noted in Chapter 13.

The transcendental deities are conceived as being universal in scope, their message for Hindus given in Sanskrit texts, their rites and ceremonies staged in a regular round. The practitioners of the transcendental complex are mainly, though not exclusively, Brahmins, and are hereditary priests of high jati rank. They are accorded prestige because of their jati and its calling and they are presumed to be exemplars of ritual purity.

The deities of the pragmatic complex are considered to be local in power and in residence. Their messages and stories are transmitted in the folklore of the vernacular. Some of their rites are cyclical but a good many are impromptu, staged when an urgent need arises. Some of their practitioners are priests, religious technicians, but they are generally shamans also, who become possessed by the deity and through whom the deity speaks, something that does not usually happen with the Brahmin priest and the high gods whom he serves. The shaman's calling is an achieved rather than a hereditary one. Any prestige that a shaman gains through his powers accrue to him alone, not to his jati. He is often of low jati and his clients are not bound in jajmani relations to him as a Brahmin priest's often are. They call on him as their need arises and their desire inclines. The pragmatic practitioner is not an exemplar but rather a demonstrator of the presence and powers of the local deities (Mandelbaum 1964, pp. 8–11).

The two complexes are used in complementary relation, each for its own purposes. Traditionally there was little rivalry between them. The Brahmin priest did not decry the services of the shaman, and the shaman, whether in possession or not, did not revile the services of the priest and his gods. Doctrine did not pit one against the other as might seem likely from a literal reading of scripture. The transcendental doctrines of karma, of the soul being held in moral account from one transmigration to the next, and of maya, of the immateriality of the flesh and all earthly things, did not prevent a Brahmin or any villager from trying to enlist the help of the local godlings to cure his sick child and for similar mundane but urgent purposes.

Each complex is clearly distinct from the other, but neither is kept as an absolutely exclusive category. High gods may be invoked for quite pragmatic purposes; local deities may be petitioned to look after transcendental affairs. A local deity or ceremony can gradually be assimilated into the scriptural pantheon and identified with Sanskritic rites. Conversely, a god from the scriptural roster may be transformed, by the people of a particular locality, into a pragmatic and local spirit. Marriott has discussed these processes under the terms universalization and parochialization (1955b, pp. 211–218). These transpositions change the particular details within each complex; they do not usually do away with the distinction between them.

In religion, as in economics and politics, people of different social levels participate in different ways. Those of poorer and lower jatis have less to do with transcendental rites and more to do with the pragmatic. This is in part because pragmatic needs press urgently upon them, in part because they have little responsibility for, or freedom to engage in, matters of larger and longer concern. Yet they do participate to some extent in the worship of transcendental gods, just as villagers of high jati, especially women, seek benefits from the pragmatic deities.

The worship of the high gods, as was noted in the previous chapter, takes many villagers to distant places. The regional centers are part of the general transcendental pattern, sometimes specifically designed after a supercenter. Thus the town of Wai in Maharashtra was built up to be a kind of "Southern Banaras," its temples, festivals, and bathing ghats consciously modeled after similar places not only in Banaras but in other important religious centers as well (Cohn and Marriott 1958, pp. 6–7).

Non-Hindus maintain a similar religious duality. There is, moreover, considerable mutual use of local deities by villagers of different formal faiths. So Hindus and Muslims alike pray for favors at the tomb of a particularly revered Muslim whose spirit is thought to watch over a locality; Muslims in turn may seek the aid of a Hindu shaman (cf. Beals 1962, pp. 47–48).

The same duality is seen in art, which is inseparable from religion in village life. Traditional art forms are integrally connected with religion and the major ceremonial occasions also provide for esthetic performance and enjoyment. Folk dancing, for example, goes with ceremonies of the local deities and the literary arts and architecture are in the province of the transcendental complex.

Education once was part of religion, specifically for the maintenance of transcendental religion. In pre-British times, education was loosely organized, confined to the higher jatis, directed to maintaining traditional ways and learning. It was so heavily weighted toward preservation of the sacred word, that a child's education characteristically began with many months, even years, of nothing but sheer rote memorization. Over many centuries that system of education effectively fulfilled the purposes for which it was intended. The scriptures were preserved intact, the learning was transmitted unimpaired. After the establishment of the British regime (and far more under the independent government), education has become widespread, more formal, more organized, and secular. It is now intended as a prime means of innovation rather than as the great instrument for conservation.

With the enormous expansion of modern, secular education, educational administrators have had to face difficult problems involving, among other things, the duality of role relations. Many educators believe that education ought to be carried on through personal rather than impersonal relations between student and teacher. Yet with masses of young people now being educated, impersonal mass roles rather than personal multiplex roles have to be taken.

Such tensions between differing role requirements are inherent in complex societies; individuals require at least some personal, non-contractual, supportive, multiplex relations, but the demands of maintaining a complex society impel toward impersonal, contractual, simplex roles.[4] Different civilizations have evolved different ways of coping with this tension. Kinship roles usually provide much of the personal dimension; the duality in kinship roles in India has been noted above, some of the agnatic roles rather paradoxically being more impersonal than certain affinal roles. The dual sets of roles in economic, political, and religious activities are the means evolved by Indian peoples for meeting a problem inherent in all civilizations.

SPECIAL ROLES

Another perennial problem of complex societies is the kind of role to be accorded to persons who do not fulfill the normally expected roles. Some social provision is usually made for the accommodation of exceptional personalities. These include men who insist on carrying out the ideal precepts of religion so literally as to impede ordinary social relations. In India, Hindu nonconformists may take special, and honored, roles in which their singular personality does not clog the normal processes of social life.

A man who wants to do so may cut himself entirely loose from his local society and completely vacate all his roles and statuses within it. He becomes a *sanyassin*, a religious devotee who consecrates himself to deity, takes no social responsibilities, lives by alms, and often wanders about without fixed home. Scripturally such a role is enjoined at a certain stage in life for men of the three highest varnas; in practice a man of almost any jati can throw off his ordinary costume and identity, and take on the ochre robe and the asocial character of the sanyassin.

A man who did not fit in with his society, who "was out of joint" with the social institutions, Nehru wrote, became a sanyassin (1946, p. 249). The lack of fit may rise from a powerful vocation for religion or for any number of other reasons, but whatever their motivation such men are considered to be outside the social norms expected of others and they act in that way. One of the early European observers, Barbosa, wrote in the sixteenth century that these devotees did not observe food or touch taboos (Dames 1918, p. 323).

This freedom from expected norms still obtains. On becoming a sanyassin a man discards the insignia of his previous identity, a Brahmin puts off his sacred thread, cuts off the tuft of hair that the

[4] The disparity is acutely felt in medical services. Thus in an analysis of medical practices in Sherurpur village, Gould writes, "The peasant sees hospitals and clinics as places where he will be compeled to wait endless hours in congested anterooms, castigated and mocked by officious attendants, and finally examined and treated by a doctor who will show no personal interest in him whatsoever." But the same villagers welcomed modern medical services when "medicine was being integrated into patterns of social interactions which they understood and which did not drain from them every ounce of their self-respect as the price of being benefited by what the modern world has to offer" (Gould 1965b, p. 208).

orthodox wear. Occasionally the family of such a man conducts funeral rites to mark his symbolic departure from earthly affairs. And when a sanyassin does actually die, he is buried, in the sitting position proper for religious meditation and dedication, rather than cremated (Ghurye 1953; Karve 1953, pp. 297–298). These persons are both pure and polluting. Carstairs tells that in Deoli town in Rajasthan a Brahmin will bow down and clasp a sanyassin's foot, but will not sit to eat with him, even if he had been of the highest caste before becoming a sanyassin. By leaving taboos behind and associating with persons of the lowest castes, "he carries a threat of pollution for one who is still committed to the dialectic of pious observance versus defilement which is inescapable in everyday life" (Carstairs 1957, p. 102).

Some sanyassins settle into one place rather than wander, and direct their efforts toward religious-social improvement as well as to their personal salvation. Such an ascetic came to a village of the tribal Reddi along the Godavari River and there established an *ashram*, a religious retreat, in a garden he laid out. His reputation as a holy one spread to towns far from his retreat in the jungle-clad hills, and visitors of wealth and high rank came to him from afar to share in the merit of his presence. He required his visitors to contribute toward the welfare of the Reddi and when the anthropologist Fürer-Haimendorf was in that village in 1943, the sanyassin had founded an organization for the "poverty relief" of the local tribal peoples (1945, pp. 269–275). Two decades later a young anthropologist drawn to visit the village because of its anthropological rather than sacred renown found the ashram and its founder still in vigorous condition.

Other devotees remain in their home villages, especially those who take on this role in their later years. Some who discard personal ties at a relatively young age remain in the region of their home, sometimes attached to a village temple, and despite their worldly nonattachment, still exert influence over the villagers, especially women, to the point of taking a strong though usually indirect hand in village politics (Gough 1956, pp. 838, 842). K. D. Gangrade has studied a village in the Delhi district in which the sanyassin resident in the village temple exerts a strong, though covert, influence on alliance politics.

A modern monastic order of sanyassins, the Ramakrishna Mission, is directed toward works of social welfare as well as to the spiritual elevation of its members. It is quite unlike the traditional orders—the term "monastic order" implies much more organization than they usually had—whose members would preach to the laity and answer their questions but would not engage in social enterprises. The scholar, Agehananda Bharati, tells how he came to India from Vienna, where he was born Leopold Fischer, to join the Ramakrishna Order. But after a novitiate of two years he left that group because of doctrinal and other differences and was initiated as a sanyassin by a venerable monk of one of the traditional orders. His account of his experiences as a wandering mendicant vividly illustrates the relationship between itinerant sanyassin and villagers (1961, pp. 157–173).

Although the disengagement from society is not necessarily total severance, almost all sanyassins live a life of overt asceticism. Of this religious dedication, N. K. Bose writes, "The price demanded from the individual was indeed heavy. He had to surrender all the benefits normally derived from collective life. Only when he was prepared to put up with the starkness of such a life, was he assured a degree of freedom and prestige not enjoyed even by the sacerdotal caste. The sanyassin was put beyond the operation of social laws" (1953a, p. 181).

Not all the mendicant devotees are universally respected; villagers may grumble, especially when a number of them come through their village, that the holy state is becoming a kind of racket for some. Nor does every man who takes to the role stay with it until death. Some, either replenished with spiritual achievement or depleted by sparse alms and rigorous wanderings, revert to their previous social niche. But a man who feels stifled by social duty can still become a sanyassin and thereby attain social release as well as spiritual gain. "We may imagine," Bose concludes, "that this safety valve was responsible, to a certain extent, for the stabilization of the Hindu order of society. Those who suffered from a feeling of oppression, could escape and leave the organization itself to work as before" (Bose 1953a, p. 182). Individuals who might have created considerable friction in a local system could in this way remove themselves from it.

While the sanyassin is not a member of any social group his role is recognized as moral and legitimate by the society he has renounced. Dumont and Pocock note that this holy state "counterbalances in a way the existence of castes and is rightly included in a definition of the system" (1957a, p. 17). One who deliberately cuts himself off from every social group must, nevertheless, keep to certain social prescriptions for the role, as in style of dress and of hair and in ascetic practices: A sanyassin casts himself in a zero social role but that role nonetheless has social position, social shape, social weight. The role of alienation itself is part of the system of society.

Roles and Fields of Action

Roles are not straitjackets; a villager has room for some individual variation even in the more rigidly prescribed roles. A woman's roles generally allow for less variation than do a man's, a young bride's far less than a mature matron's, but all role behavior is subject to the actor's personal touch. All role behavior is also subject to social change. When actors in large numbers begin to alter particular role behaviors in consistent directions, they thereby begin the course of social change. A role, as formulated by the observers, includes both expected behavior and the actual behavior with specified others as that behavior is regulated according to certain norms (cf. Gross *et al.* 1958, pp. 48–67; Parsons 1961, pp. 41–43; Banton 1965).

Moreover, a person switches his style of behavior as he takes different roles. The same man who feels constrained to be a rather aloof father to his adolescent son commonly shifts to being a more friendly, supportive person when another youth, his sister's son, comes into view.

The expectations held about any particular role are far from uniform. A certain minimum agreement is necessary in order to maintain interaction but beyond that minimum there often are considerable differences of view (cf. Levinson 1959). In the traditional jajmani roles, patron and artisan typically take differing views of what should be tendered by the other, the landowner stressing loyalty and devoted service, the artisan stressing the protection and regular rewards due him from the patron. The artisan tends to have a grander notion of the importance of his position than does his patron. What is important for the maintenance of jajmani relations is that there be just enough agreement so that the exchange of goods and services can continue.

A person's field of social action includes those role relations that he carries on commonly and centrally, as with his family, and those that are more occasional and peripheral, as with a town merchant or a priest of a distant temple. In addition to the actual field of interaction there is the potential field—those roles that a person may possibly actuate under certain circumstances. Actual and potential fields of conduct are illustrated in the distinction between kin of cooperation and kin of recognition, which was noted in respect to the uses of kinship. The former are kinsmen with whom a person maintains actual relations and the latter are more distant kin, either genealogically or geographically distant, with whom kinship interaction may be established if one of the potential kinsmen becomes wealthy and ambitious enough to expand his field of actual kin, or if both of them do.

A person's kinship field changes over time as births, marriages and deaths alter its composition; it may be changed also through voluntary extensions or contractions. The combined kinship fields of the members of a jati-group (the kinship region, as Mayer calls it), include all those "populations within which marriage can take place without enquiries as to credentials of membership" (Mayer 1962, p. 268). Rising families may expand that kinship region, making marriage alliances farther afield than before, or they may contract their endogamous circle by hiving off from the larger jati and deciding to marry only with those families who meet new and higher standards.

A villager may activate his potential roles in any aspect of his life. The extent to which he can do so is dependent on a series of conditions, attributive, cognitive, motivational, expedient. Attributive factors constrict the possible roles that can be taken. Men of the lowest jatis had, and to a considerable degree still have, a very constricted range of roles, actual or potential. They could not take overtly active roles in village politics; they were debarred from large parts of the transcendental complex of religion; they were usually too crushed by poverty to be able to take any but the most elemental economic roles.

Cognitive factors also delimit the range of possible roles. A villager's fields of conduct are obviously limited to the roles he knows about or can know about. Not all of those he knows are open to him or attractive for him, but he cannot take on new roles unless he knows something about them. People whose education, travel, and information are very limited have small role potential; those whose horizons of experience and knowledge are wider have greater fields for potential relationships.

Motivation to expand one's roles and relationships is not in short supply, at least, not among some men of almost any village. The process requires a firm base of material and social resources; an ambitious villager is commonly in middle age by the time he has established a base above that which he inherited. Hence much of his role expansion is done through his children, by enlarging their potential fields by means of formal education and by arranging socially advantageous marriages for them. Expediency in marshaling resources for a particular purpose is characteristic of such men. They are able to translate potential relationships into actual services, to command loyalties of diverse kinds and to bring them to bear on specific issues. A successful alliance leader in a village commonly does this, gaining his ends—whether to calm a dispute or add to his land—by calling forth support from people of different jatis, lineages, and interests.

The people who are called upon, and respond, in order to help a man achieve his purposes constitute his resource network (Sharma 1963). The term "network" has also been used for those people in a group's actual field of social relations who are deployed by the members of the group for certain purposes (cf. Jay 1964; Mayer 1962; Srinivas and Béteille 1964). Through the contacts of his resource network, a man may reach far beyond his usual field of relationships. Village leaders have long manipulated these resource networks to gain their ends, but in recent times the reach of such a network from the village can be remarkably extended.

Thus in Sripuram village of Tanjore district in Madras, a Brahmin landowner wanted to have his son admitted to an engineering college in the city of Madras. He proceeded first through his own father, who practiced law in the nearby town and who had as a client an eminent businessman, a non-Brahmin in Tanjore city. The landowner from the village could thus discuss his problem with the businessman who, in turn, had influential business associates at the state capital, Madras. Through these city magnates the village landowner was put in touch with a member of the committee of the college to which his son was later admitted (Srinivas and Béteille 1964, p. 166). Such manipulation of social resources for one's family is laudable by traditional standards, but in the context of a modern establishment it is open to criticism by other standards, criticism that is expressed in such epithets as favoritism, nepotism, or even corruption.

Village, Civilization, and Change

These four chapters on the village have examined salient features of internal and external relations, the ties among village, center, and region, and villagers' responses to certain problems of civilization. The overarching concept of Indian civilization consists in large part of the fundamental, prevailing ideas about man and society; some of these have already been discussed, others will be noted in succeeding chapters. Scholars have sketched the outlines of the civilization, but much of the analysis remains to be done (cf. Raghavan 1956; Brown 1961; Singer 1964). It is an analysis needed for comparative studies of civilizations as well as for an understanding of Indian civilization (cf. Kroeber 1944, pp. 480–686).

The idea of Indian civilization is known in villages, but it is not a concept that is in the fore of villagers' perception. However, when there is confrontation with people of other civilizations, this latent concept—now couched in modern nationalist terms—becomes in important force, as it did in the struggle for national independence.

The village, in sum, is a basic feature of the civilization and continues to be a viable community for its inhabitants. A person's village provides him with one source of his self-identification, with a nexus of his activities, a stage for his status, and an arena of conflict. Observers can view it as a system comprising component jati-groups and functional activities, and also as a subsystem of larger social systems. The people of a village have used the panchayat pattern to facilitate interchange and effect counterchange. Alliances are commonly important to a village system, though villagers are usually reluctant to avow that alliances are proper and legitimate factors in village life.

Those of any one village have ties with people in many other villages and centers. Their relations with centers are important cohesion factors in maintaining the precepts of the civilization. These precepts, together with the other elements of the society and civilization, have been altered over time and are now in a vast process of change.

In the preceding chapter it was observed that a villager can choose to identify himself with one or another of his groups and groupings according to the context of action in which he is involved at a particular juncture. In the same way he has some choice in selecting one role or even one subsystem of action rather than another in order to gain his purpose. The choice of system for action and selection of role within a subsystem is often quite clear and straightforward to the participant. For one of the dominant "Peasant" jati in Wangala, as Mrs. Epstein writes, it is the context of a social situation that determines to which unit he feels and expresses his allegiance. "In his everyday economic activities he regards himself as a farmer or farmhand; on ceremonial occasions he acts as a member of a faction; in his relation with other castes and untouchables in Wangala he acts as a member of the Peasant caste; and in his relations with the Administration he acts as a Peasant of Wangala" (1962, p. 145).

But there are other occasions when the choices are not so clear and when alternative possibilities can be manipulated. Thus Bailey tells of a villager of Bisipara who is an untouchable by jati, a minor official by appointment, and a quite affluent trader by his own efforts. His trade is carried on with men of the Kond tribe who are rated as a clean jati by the neighboring Oriyas. When this man, Nrusingh by name, visits Konds in his capacity as a minor official he overplays that role, hectoring them more than do other minor officials who are not untouchables. The Konds, on their side, "do not hesitate to rub in Nrusingh's untouchable state." But neither wants to allow their mutual animosities to stand in the way of their trade relationships; their other roles do not contaminate the roles of buyer and seller. The Konds may treat Nrusingh in any one of his three capacities but not all three at the same time because the roles are in some situations contradictory. "In every situation the actors have an element of latitude and may choose the way they will behave in order to further their own ends. The Konds can humiliate Nrusingh by treating him as an untouchable or they can flatter him by treating him as an official, whichever suits their purpose" (1960b, p. 209).

Whether Nrusingh is humiliated or flattered signifies very little even in his own small remote village, but the principle and fact of choice among roles and systems is of the highest importance in such villages and essential to an understanding of the whole social system. We have so far focused on the main roles, groups, and systems of village society, on the rules of the social game. Although changes and choices have necessarily been mentioned before, we now turn to a more detailed examination of the dynamics of the social order.

PART VI

RECURRENT CHANGE THROUGH SOCIAL MOBILITY

CHAPTER 23

Jati Mobility

Choices, decisions, alternatives, confront a villager when he comes to take responsibility, whether for his family or lineage, for his jati or village. A man is then impelled to be something of a manipulator of his culture and society as well as a creature and carrier of it. To be sure, the actual decisions may privately be influenced by the women or the younger people, but the men, the heads of family, the elders and leaders, must give the signal and initiate action.

Some kinds of decisions occur only a few times in the lifetime of the decider and may set in train a series of events that he does not foresee or desire. But from the wider perspective of the observer most of these decisions can be seen to lead into cycles which are regular processes of the social system. Such cycles follow on decisions to choose one girl rather than another as a bride for one's son, to keep a joint family together or to part, to join in an alliance affray or to remain aloof. The cycle of family growth and dispersal is one kind of recurrent change.

Our main interest in the chapters of the following two sections is with recurrent change in the social order through jati mobility, religious regrouping, and the movement from tribal to caste society. We begin with jati mobility, looking first at the underlying pressures toward status competition among jatis, the conditions required for a successful mobility campaign, the cultural adaptations that ambitious villagers typically make, and the social tactics they use to secure their purposes.

Competition among Jatis

Recurrent change among jatis arises from consistent efforts by members of lower jatis to raise their ranking. The higher jatis usually oppose them in order to preserve their own superior rank, but some of the lower do succeed in time in raising their status. Occasionally a higher jati may fall in rank. Such shifts are positional not structural changes. The social structure remains quite the same even though one group now is accepted as higher than its former superior and its members outrank those of a previously higher set (cf. Srinivas 1965, p. 8).

The political contests involved in this process in village India have been called routine politics by F. G. Bailey in contrast to the "politics of change"; this contrast is like that which Max Gluckman has drawn between rebellions and revolutions in African societies. Routine politics are repetitive, in the sense that whichever side wins, similar conflict at once emerges, and the system goes on as before. "The logistic, factual, and jural rules of this type of conflict are such that when one group wins it is immediately faced with a similar conflict, where the same rules apply, and so on down the infinite corridors of structural time, until something happens to change these rules" (Bailey 1965, pp. 23–24).

The "corridors of structural time" are also corridors of power, because repetitive politics are basically about power, about who gets what and who controls whom in the local system. Village political contests were traditionally expressed as disputes about jati rank and as struggles about the insignia and prerogatives of rank. Men who accrued wealth or new political resources typically tried to translate them into a gain in ritual rank in order to legitimate their rise and fix it against the passage of time. In that sense jati mobility included both economic and political mobility.

Status contests, as has been noted, can be carried on as vigorously within a jati as among jatis. But such internal contests are usually superseded by united defense if the rank of the jati as a whole is at stake. A prospering man normally tries to enhance the standing of his family and lineage within the jati. But unless that jati can command a suitable degree of local respect, his gains are incomplete. He is likely to try to band together with his jati confreres to raise the jati, and—as they see it—to restore it to its proper place.

Individual mobility, by itself, is limited and ephemeral. It is limited because even though a man may become wealthy and personally powerful in his locality, his neighbors of higher rank still deal with him according to the ritual attributes of his jati. It is ephemeral because members of a rising family must find brides and grooms for their children from comparably eminent families. Unless other families of their jati have risen in similar proportion, the status gains of one family may fade away after a generation. Hence mobility in rank must be collective if it is to be fruitful and durable (cf. Srinivas 1966, pp. 44–45).

The drive for collective mobility is of surpassing concern to many villagers because they believe that greater power and material rewards are won by those who succeed in gaining higher rank. The grounds for this belief are particularly clear to members of the lowest jatis. The people of an untouchable jati are usually landless and are highly dependent on the will of the landowning patrons. Other jatis commonly resist the acquisition of land by untouchables lest on becoming less dependent, they no longer will consent to do polluting tasks. Untouchables who can somehow lift themselves to a higher social level may be freed of many economic and personal shackles. Untouchables can aspire to higher ritual rank because they share the pervasive ideas that one's own group is entitled to higher place in the social hierarchy than others accord it and that the higher position is worth struggling for.

This valuation of self and of society is an important factor in the striving for jati mobility. The people of a jati typically hold to an origin myth that tells of their descent from noble or divine ancestors, or from some of each kind. These accounts not only reflect the common self-image, they also serve to justify efforts to regain one's noble and rightful heritage.

Villagers cherish two different origin myths, one for the society as a whole, the other for their own jati. The account for the whole society is that discussed previously of the four varna categories as given in *Manu* and in other scriptural sources. The people in each of the four categories are fixed by that account in their respective rank, the order is immutable and the ranks are not competitive one with another. The scriptural concept of *dharma*, of one's sacred duty, asserts that each person should fulfill, dispassionately, the obligation of his station in life. That station is given to him for the duration of one lifetime as a result of his soul's *karma*, the supernal merit or demerit that his soul has accrued in previous existences (cf. Karve 1961, pp. 91–101).

The other account, that of one's own jati origin, does not contradict the first in any single particular, but taken in conjunction with it encourages constant competition among jatis. Their jati myth assures the members of a lower jati that they really belong to a higher rank; hence, if they are truly to perform their sacred dharma, they must struggle to get that loftier rank formally and permanently acknowledged by others. The myth also implies that they must keep jatis below them in the proper lowly position to which local society and their respective karma assigns them.

The reigning, ideal principle is that of social immutability while the ruling, actual principle is that of social competition among those close to each other in rank. Some observers, basing their views on the ideal principles, conclude that caste in India is essentially a noncompetitive system (cf. Leach 1960, pp. 6–7; Bailey 1963a, pp. 121–122). Others see an apparent paradox or contradiction between the ideal rule and the actual condition (cf. Pocock 1964). To the villagers, little contradiction is involved; each principle is applied where it is relevant for oneself and one's group. Jati rivals do not worry much about the validity of their opponents' story of origin; it is the validity of one's own that must be fought out and justified in the village arena.

Competition among jatis may well be ancient, but only a few historical studies of the subject have yet been made. Rivalries among ancient guilds resembled contemporary jati rivalries. There is evidence of jati mobility from the Gupta period, as when silk weavers, perhaps still organized as a guild, moved across to another region and rose to new, more respectable occupations (Thapar 1966, p. 153). In medieval South India, there seems to have been considerable social mobility by families. This too was accomplished mainly by geographic mobility. New land was available for cultivation (as it was in many parts of India well into the nineteenth century); ambitious people could move to a new place, put untilled land under the plow, become landowners in a new settlement, and so establish a new social identity for themselves. This obviated some of the intense rivalry of more recent times, when new lands were not so readily available (Stein 1967).

A seventeenth-century report by the Dutch missionary, Abraham Roger, mentions jati rivalries quite like those of the twentieth century. Roger lived in Pulicat, north of Madras, from 1631 to 1641. In one passage he describes the jati called "Wellala" and then notes, "The other castes I shall not here set forth according to their order, for that there is no unanimity among them as to which precedeth, but each mightily claimeth and pretendeth that his own caste is best" (translation by L. H. Gray in Jackson 1907, p. 244).

From the more ample European sources of the eighteenth century come numerous references to competition for jati rank. In his review of these sources, V. P. S. Raghuvanshi cites examples from various parts of the subcontinent, commenting that some of the South Indian accounts "look as if there were a constant scramble for superiority among the various trading, artisan, and cultivating castes at certain places" (1966, p. 167).

The Abbé Dubois, who lived in South India for some thirty years at the end of the eighteenth and the beginning of the nineteenth centuries, tells of a quarrel between "Pariyas" and "Chucklers" that threatened the peace of a whole district. The dispute concerned the right of the Chucklers to wear red flowers in their turbans on ceremonial occasions (Dubois 1928, pp. 26–27). Such antagonisms between two untouchable jatis have been carried on in modern times as well, for example between the Malas and the Madigas of Andhra. Similar rivalries are found at every social level; the land-owning Kamas and Reddis in Andhra have been such rivals (cf. Frykenberg 1963, pp. 2–5; Harrison 1960, pp. 206–213).

Even the top jatis of a local order are likely to jostle for higher status among themselves. If there are several Brahmin jatis within a village, each may claim and strive to be the highest. Sripuram village of Tanjore district holds 12 separate jatis of Brahmins, in a Brahmin population of 341 (Béteille 1965, pp. 72–79). They are differentiated by the language used in the household (Kannada, Telugu, or Tamil), by priestly occupation (of the Siva and Vishnu temples), and by doctrinal affiliation (several jatis of Smarthas and several of Iyengars). Most of them oppose the non-Brahmins' drive for political power in the village, but they are divided among themselves and indeed believe that the present decline of Brahmin power is a result of their disunity.

The evidence, however, is that they are not any more at odds now than they were in the past. Béteille indicates that in the 1880s "they quarreled bitterly among themselves over ritual and other matters." As for the present order of rank among these Brahmins, "it is doubtful whether a definitive answer can be provided even after detailed consideration of political, economic, and other 'interactional' features" (Béteille 1962, pp. 143–144).

Brahmins in all regions naturally emphasized those stories that reminded others of their sacred obligation to acknowledge Brahmin superiority with proper respect and gifts. These were not always and everywhere readily forthcoming. In parts of the Punjab, for example, a good many Hindus gave little more than lip service to their local Brahmins (cf. Tandon 1961, pp. 76–77).

Yet Brahmin jatis were acknowledged as belonging to the highest varna among all Hindus and among many they were supported with material gifts as well as with gestures of respect. Nevertheless the Brahmin jatis were not, and are not, immune to status competition. Where several live in the same locality, claims and counterclaims of higher status among them are commonly pressed. Harijans may have more at stake in their push for mobility, but the competitive drive animates people at all levels of village society.

Conditions for Mobility

Aspirations for jati rise are common; achieved aspirations are much less common. To achieve a rise usually takes time measured in generations. Ambitious members of the jati must first be able to command ample wealth and power. The process typically begins when a good many families of a low-ranking group secure such resources, usually through long and hard efforts. They use them to improve their ritual purity and then to secure public acceptance of their claims. Mere reform of jati practices, in itself, does not usually bring about much gain in rank.[1]

Wealth and power are used for jati gains in ways similar to those noted above in the status competition among families, lineages, and alliances within a jati. Assets in the political system, such as friendly connections with officials, facilitate gains in the economic system. And those who amass wealth are inclined to develop political connections to make their wealth more secure. Both

[1] The Mala of the Telengana region of Andhra, for example, do not eat pork or carrion as do other untouchables in these villages, yet they are firmly classed as untouchables "and rank only just a little higher than the carrion-eating Madigas" (Dube 1955c, p. 190).

economic and political assets are typically invested in the higher form of village security, namely augmented jati status.

Occasionally an able, persevering man, even though of poor family and lowly jati, becomes rich. Such success stories are widely known, though the number of such instances is small. Even an untouchable can become relatively wealthy; one such man in Bisipara village in Orissa became a middleman in the sale of hides. He began with nothing and prospered until he came to own land worth more than that held by all the others of his jati-group (Bailey 1957, p. 159).

But a few wealthy men do not make a mobility campaign; that requires concerted use of wealth and power by many families. It is helped along if they can mobilize enough force and courage in their villages to withstand threats of violent reprisal (cf. Srinivas 1959a, p. 4).

A whole jati can gain in wealth when favorable economic opportunities open in the jati's occupation. One historic example is that of the Kayasths, a jati-cluster whose members are widespread over North India and whose traditional occupation was that of scribe. Writing was not an accomplishment highly prized by Brahmin scholars of earlier ages, who saw it as a useful device but one mainly necessary for clerks and merchants; a true scholar committed scripture to memory. When the Mogul emperors established administrative procedures based on written records kept in Persian, the ability to use these records became important and lucrative. Many Kayasths, following their traditional occupation of scribes, became proficient in Persian. A good many of them showed high ability and intelligence and were appointed to influential posts. Their capabilities became all the more useful during the British regime; a number of Kayasth families rose high in public service as well as in education and wealth. Thus strengthened, eminent men of several Kayasth jatis fought long legal battles to have their social rank recognized as being above the Shudra category to which earlier tradition had assigned them (Bhattacharya 1896, pp. 175–191; Baines 1912, pp. 38–40; Karve 1961, p. 45).

A more recent instance of jati rise through occupational opportunity is that of the Noniyas of Uttar Pradesh. Their traditional occupation was the extraction of salt and saltpeter from saline soils. Since the handling of salt for profit is ritually a dubious business, they were ranked quite low. In Senapur elderly villagers recalled in the 1950s that when they were children the Noniyas were "almost untouchable," and Bhattacharya noted in his all-India survey that "generally they are regarded as semi-clean Sudras" (1896. p. 265). During the last part of the nineteenth century some Noniyas prospered greatly. When better salt than theirs became available, they turned to other kinds of work with earth: some took to agriculture, others to building watercourses, wells, tanks, roads, and to making bricks and tile.

When the British greatly expanded irrigation facilities, roads and other public works, there was a great expansion of demand for the skills that the Noniyas possessed and for the bricks they produced. Some Noniyas became contractors to government and grew wealthy. A small but powerful Noniya elite arose; these families campaigned vigorously for higher status. "The changing opportunity structure in colonial society, with the emergence of a newly prosperous group within the caste and the resulting incongruence of their ritual and economic ranks led to the founding and financing of a self-conscious caste mobility organization" (Rowe 1968, p. 70). In Senapur they are now placed by the dominant Thakurs as ninth or tenth from the top among the twenty-four jatis of the village, well above their earlier rank.

In some villages of eastern Uttar Pradesh, the local Noniyas are almost entirely landless and are still heavily dependent on landlords of other jatis. These poor Noniyas see the organization for Noniya improvement "as a distant and not very real entity." By contrast, there is a small group of well-to-do men in Bombay, also of Noniya extraction, "who would appear to the superficial observer as well-established, middle-class professional men of a Kshatriya caste" (Rowe 1968, p. 68).

There is a saying among Indian Muslims which, in various versions, expresses the relation between growing wealth and mounting ambition. It is told about weavers or butchers or other low-ranking groups. "Last year we were weavers, this year we are Shaikhs, and next year if the harvest is good we shall be Sayyids" (cf. Misra 1964, p. 170; Ibbetson 1916, p. 10; Baines 1912, p. 63).[2] Wealth makes augmented purity possible; enhanced status may then follow. The reverse does not hold. Many a group has purified its practices and still remained poor and lowly. Greater purity is usually costly, requiring the giving up of previous sources of income or the assuming of expensive new customs. Such assumption, if seen as a threat by those in a higher niche, raises opposition and hostility, which has to be countered by still more expenditure.

Gains in political power have usually opened the way for economic advantage and eventual rise in jati rank. In medieval India, rulers of low social origins were commonly accorded Kshatriya status after they seized power (Stein 1968, p. 79; Panikkar 1956, p. 8; Srinivas 1966, pp. 30–42). To capture or found a state, a free-booter had to have staunch allies, usually his clan and jati mates. Once he was installed in power, his comrades-in-arms became wealthy landowners. They then could afford the appurtenances of higher ritual rank and could quell any opposition to their claims.

A ruler's grace and favor could also affect the status of jatis other than his own. In some princely states this influence continued into the late nineteenth century. A British official who had served in Punjab hill states wrote that "it is within the present writer's own experience that the Raja of Lambagraon… readmitted to the twice-born status certain Kolis who had been ousted from it more than a century earlier by the Raja of Kangra, as a punishment for disrespectful behavior." He noted also that the Rajas of Chamba similarly had conferred the right to wear the sacred thread, with a step up in social rank, in return for gifts or special services (Maynard 1917, pp. 93, 97). This occurred in the South also; in the same article, Sir Sankaran Nair is quoted as giving an instance from sixteenth-century Kerala. The Charmas, "a servile caste," had been raised to the station of the military Nayars by the Maharaja of Cochin as a reward for military services (Maynard 1917, p. 93; Srinivas 1966, pp. 40–42).

When the British took over direct rule, they refused to intervene in caste affairs in this way. Hence manipulation of political power for jati mobility became more circuitous; it was done through long litigation about jati prerogatives or through the education of sons who might become government officials. Their positions then enhanced the prestige of the jati, even though as officials they might not bestow more tangible rewards.

Special Resistences to Change in Jati Status

There is a certain inertia to jati ranking, as was noted in discussing village power relations. Untouchables find it particularly difficult to move to the other side of the untouchability barrier, as the Holerus of Totagadde village in Mysore have found. As in most areas, the landowners there

[2] A similar Tamil saying is "Kallan, Maravan, and Ahamudiyan by slow degrees become Vellala. Having become Vellala, they called themselves Mudaliyar" (Béteille 1965, p. 98).

were strongly opposed to allowing untouchables to own land. One Holeru recalled that the elders of his jati were even fearful of going to speak to a Brahmin (Harper 1968, p. 57). They had neither the skills, the education, nor the capital which might enable them to be anything other than unskilled laborers.

Nevertheless these Holerus have in recent decades thrown off some of the more degrading practices. They no longer eat beef, they will not remove dead cattle, they will no longer supply wood for funeral pyres. But these reforms are depreciated by the Havik Brahmins who are dominant in this village. On one occasion a Havik loudly asserted, in the hearing of his Holeru worker, that the Holerus were dirty and degraded because they ate beef. When the anthropologist to whom he was speaking questioned this, the Havik asked his servant if the statement were not true. The reply was that the Holeru council had prohibited the eating of beef for jati members some thirty years before. The Havik triumphantly said, "You see, I told you that Holerus are a dirty caste—they used to eat beef" (Harper 1968, p. 36).

Holerus are further bound into lowly status through their very quest for respectability. A Holeru family feels that it must give elaborate weddings for its children, each costing the equivalent of from one to two years of a man's income. The money usually is advanced by a Havik landowner; in return the Holerus pledge themselves as indentured laborers for years. Harper notes that of all things in the world, they value most that of which they have the least—prestige—and they strongly believe that a group's rank is in part based upon the elaborateness of its marriage rites (1968, p. 61).

They delude themselves. It is true that in staging a lavish wedding a Holeru family demonstrates how completely it shares in the values of the higher jatis. But despite such demonstrations and notwithstanding the reform of their customs, Holerus remain at the bottom of the local hierarchy. The landowners continue to advance marriage expenses to Holerus because they need field hands at peak demand periods and that is one good way of insuring a reliable labor supply. A good many Holerus are in constant debt and so are bound fast in the nethermost depths of social rank. But they are beginning to revise their mobility tactics and may yet succeed in narrowing the social gap between themselves and the other villagers.

As an untouchable jati must overcome special resistances in order to rise, the fall of a Brahmin jati is slowed by special inertia. If a Brahmin family loses its means of livelihood, its members may turn to performing some less honorable priestly tasks, such as funeral rites, or may act as priests for prospering families of lowly jatis who had not previously been able to afford the services of Brahmins. In Kumbapettai village of Tanjore district the dominant landowners are Smartha Brahmins; none of them would act as household priests for families of low rank.

In this region there are also Telugu-speaking Brahmins who traditionally were household priests to the local aristocracy. When the princely courts and courtiers were dispossessed, many of the Telugu Brahmins had to officiate for lower groups who "in their efforts to rise in the ritual hierarchy, were glad to employ impoverished Brahmins as household priests." One such Brahmin came to Kumbapettai in 1947, rented a house there and "ekes out a livelihood by conducting marriage, funeral and ancestral rites for those non-Brahmin families of the village who care to pay his fee" (Gough 1960, p. 31).

Brahmin jatis whose members officiate professionally at funeral rites or who take clients of low status are ranked lower than other Brahmins. Those euphemistically called Mahabrahmans, "great Brahmins," were considered to be so impure that in Punjab villages of the nineteenth century they were not allowed to come inside the village gate save for funerary purposes

(Ibbetson 1916 p. 221). However, the contemporary Mahabrahmans of Ramapur village near Allahabad, mentioned previously, are very favorably situated because the sacred center there draws many worshippers who require their services for the memorial rites which are best completed at that holy place. A Mahabrahman of that locality is apt to be relatively wealthy, but in spite of his Brahmin status, most Hindus treat him in some ways as an untouchable and will not accept water and food from his hand. "He may not live in many villages" (Opler and Singh 1952, p. 185).

There are jatis of so-called "degraded" Brahmins in most parts of India (cf. Bhattacharya 1896, pp. 118–131). Generally they are recognized to be Brahmins, entitled to wear the insignia of their varna, to officiate at rites, especially funerary rites, to receive gifts due to Brahmins, but yet they are Brahmins who must be kept at a social distance by most other villagers. To be taken as Brahmins worthy of higher esteem, they would have to give up officiating at funeral services and this they are presumably reluctant to do because it is so lucrative. One such Brahmin jati obtained a rescript in the nineteenth century from a revered religious leader which certified to their true Brahminhood. Despite this document, their village neighbors continued to treat them as before (Bhattacharya 1896, p. 93).

An entire Brahmin jati may decline in status. The Gayawal are the main temple priests at the great pilgrimage center of Gaya. In recent decades they have come on hard times. Others have encroached on their clientele and the total number of pilgrims has fallen off considerably. The Gayawal have lost income and, from the evidence of L. P. Vidyarthi's account, they have diminished in ritual rank as well. They are still indubitably Brahmins, but are no longer as respected and influential as they once were (Vidyarthi 1961, pp. 86–110).

Impoverished Brahmins may descend to giving less prestigious services but they rarely, if ever, drop below the Brahmin category. Even a man who is cast out of a Brahmin jati may still, somehow, maintain his status as a Brahmin. One such case, recounted by Bhattacharya, is that of the ancestor of the Tagores. When this Brahmin was made outcaste, he left his village and settled in the town of Jessore. His descendants moved to Calcutta, which was then a kind of new frontier. Caste credentials were not too closely examined. The new elite there considered that "A Brahman is a Brahman though outcasted by his clansmen" (1896, p. 122). The Tagores were able to establish themselves and rise to the top of the new secular elite though, as is noted in Chapter 25, it was a very long time before they were fully accepted as unblemished Brahmins. It was possible for them to remain Brahmins, but difficult to restore their former ritual standing among orthodox Brahmins of Bengal.

Personal Ambitions and Systemic Counterchange

In sum, social mobility is possible at all social levels, though it is more feasible for some jatis than for others, more propitious under certain circumstances, and more eagerly sought by some men than by others. Ambition to improve one's status is very common though some villagers display relatively little and others display little else. An ambitious man does not neatly differentiate among the various levels of his social aspiration; he tends to see the rise of his family, of his lineage, and of his jati as being all of a piece. Specific efforts for one or the other advance may have to be directed in different ways, but he hopes that a status rise at one level will advance efforts in the others. The basic conditions for a successful rise are similar at each level as is illustrated by the previously noted examples of lineage mobility in Wangala village and of the mobility of hypergamous sections among the Patidars of Gujarat.

In Wangala, Scarlett Epstein observes, the main contests result from an imbalance between the secular and the ritual status of lineages in the dominant jati. The size of a family's landholdings can shift drastically in a relatively short time. A man can build an estate in his own lifetime or conversely, a large estate can be dissipated in a few years, fragmented among numerous heirs. Formal lineage status is hereditary; descendants of eminent lines cling tightly to their hereditary lineage rights when their material fortunes decline. The rivalry between the "conservative" and the "progressive" factions in Wangala stems from such imbalance and since ritual status is regarded as the ultimate criterion of social status, "the 'progressive' faction is led continuously to bring its ritual status in line with its economic dominance" (Epstein 1962, p. 132).

Similar contests occur among the hypergamous sections, the "village circles" of the Patidars of Kaira district in Gujarat. Each jati-group belongs to one of these circles, and a daughter should be married into an equal or higher village circle. As a family prospers, it invests its wealth in symbols of prestige, especially buildings, and tries to contract the most prestigious marriages possible in its hypergamous range. Sometimes a family becomes wealthy enough to break into a new marriage bracket and others in its village try to do the same. They may succeed if the whole jati-group has prospered. "When any particular village makes more money as a result of a few good years of tobacco harvests, it may well endeavor to cut its ties with the other villages of its marriage circle and attempt to be included in the next highest circle" (Pocock 1957b, pp. 22, 29–30).

Efforts to raise one's lineage or jati-group do not preclude efforts in behalf of the whole jati. Each effort is made in the context suitable for it. Lineage leverage is tried when only jati brethren are involved, jati leverage is used when confronting other jatis. Promoting a whole jati is the more arduous task, if only because jati fellows who are scattered in many villages have to be mobilized and directed.

The goals of a jati campaign are to have the higher jati status ritually legitimated by local Brahmins, affirmed by all villagers in daily life and on ceremonial occasions, and confirmed, if necessary, by village panchayats.

The members of a rising jati have made good their claims when those who formerly would not eat with them or accept cooked food from them, now do so. Mayer notes that in Ramkheri the commensal seems to be the key relationship for a moving caste to establish, "for besides having ritual significance, it is reciprocal" (1956, p. 142). Eating together is a public and unmistakable gesture.

To attain these goals, the people of an aspiring jati usually have to reform jati practices and refurbish the jati origin myth. Villagers in India are no more versed in their actual history than are villagers anywhere, and they may ignore what they do know when it reminds them of what they would rather forget. But they are far from indifferent to statements about their past that can be enshrined in myth. Myth and customs may be suitably adjusted in a generation or two if economic conditions favor and unified efforts avail, but the opposition of higher jatis often lasts longer. And even when a jati has seemingly clinched a higher place, the memory of its former, lowly position is apt to linger on with the other villagers through more than one or two generations.

Those who try to raise their jati status are in one sense attempting to alter the local system. Those who resist their efforts are applying counterchange pressure to restore the previous order of that system. But in the larger view, a mobility drive is a way of bringing about closer parity between a jati's secular powers and ritual status. It is thus a means of restoring a local system to the state toward which local caste orders in India repeatedly gravitate, namely to eliminate great disparity between a jati's secular power and its ritual rank.

In that wider sense then, a prospering jati's struggle to rise is part of the counterchange of the system, although on the local ground it is the opponent's efforts that appear as counterchange pressure. The acts intended to disturb an existing, static order of rank, simultaneously serve to maintain the dynamic, adaptive system of jati relations.

CHAPTER 24

Cultural Adaptations and Models for Mobility

As the families of a jati, in sufficient number, accrue a strong power base, and as their leading men become united enough to move together for higher status, they typically step up their efforts to improve their jati customs. They try to abandon demeaning practices and to adopt purer and more prestigious ways. They usually want to drop their old name for a better one.

A modern instance of this traditional process, that of the Yadavas, has been illuminatingly described by M. S. A. Rao (1964). This example illustrates a mobility effort which combines traditional and modern modes of disengaging from degrading customs and associating with respectable practices. The term Yadava has been taken by many different jatis, mainly of North India, whose traditional occupation was cattle keeping. They now maintain a national organization which has published a well-edited and well-produced volume entitled *The Divine Heritage of the Yadavas* (1959). The book was originally written by V. K. Khedkar, a schoolteacher who rose to be private secretary to a Maharaja, and was later revised and enlarged by his son who was a surgeon. It argues that the jatis whose occupation was cattlekeeping and milk selling are descended from the deity Krishna through a number of royal dynasties.

These jatis, among whom Ahirs are a widespread and numerous contingent, have usually been held in considerably less glorious repute by their neighbors. While an occasional warrior of a pastoral jati did establish his own state and dynasty, cattlekeepers are ranked in many localities among the lower blocs of the Shudras. This was partly because they wandered about with their cattle and so their purity practices (so the explanation ran) could not be checked; partly because they performed castration operations on animals, and, perhaps mainly, because they were involved in the sale of milk (Baines 1912, pp. 56–58). The production of milk for one's family is entirely proper, but economic transactions in the sacrosanct product are thought to be unseemly. A cow's milk, like mother's milk, should be for one's children, not for customers and cash.

As some herdsman families became prosperous in the late nineteenth century, the campaign to take the Yadava name and Kshatriya style was begun, backed largely by a new business elite. Some men from these jatis, long accustomed to trading at cattle markets, became successful city tradesmen; others, who had traditionally contracted for the care of animals, became wealthy as contractors to government for the same purposes.

The book by Khedkar combines a traditional origin myth and a highly modernized improvement campaign. It postulates divine and noble ancestry for a good many jatis in several language regions covering hundreds of thousands of people who share little more than a traditional occupation and a conviction about their rightful prerogatives. The editor's introduction begins by giving the credentials of the authors, including the eight British diplomas, degrees, and certificates garnered by Dr. Khedkar. The editor also tells that the authors' manuscript was corrected, revised, and brought up to date by one Professor and two Assistant Professors of Indian History from the University of Allahabad. (It must be said that a very modern apparatus of historical scholarship is shown in the footnotes and references of the text.) A final chapter, added to the original manuscript by Dr. B. N. S. Yadav, states that the ancient Yadavas upheld "republican ideals" as against imperialist movements. The writer concludes that "In this way we find that in the hoary past the Yadavas were associated with a political ideology which is considered to be progressive" (1959, p. 200).

This contemporary mobility drive was preceded by many earlier struggles carried on separately in various localities. At one stage Ahirs in the Punjab and U.P. joined forces to improve Ahir status (Marten 1924, pp. 231–232). Parallel but independent efforts were being made at about the same time in other linguistic regions. Representatives of the separate organizations met at Allahabad in 1924 to found the All-India Yadav Maha Sabha (the "great league" or "great assembly" of Yadavas). This association has published a journal ever since, and its resolutions urge that all adherents conduct themselves in a life style befitting the name Yadava.

Certain components of this improved life style are quite like those traditionally prescribed by the jati panchayat of almost any ambitious group. Jati fellows are told to discard demeaning practices, particularly the eating of meat and drinking of liquor. They are urged to take on prestigious customs and symbols, one of which is the wearing of the sacred thread. When a good many Ahirs in Bihar actually began to wear the sacred thread there was intense, sometimes bloody, opposition from the dominant Bhumihars and Rajputs (Marten 1924, pp. 231–232; Lacey 1933, pp. 267–268; Rao 1964, p. 1440).

Other reforms urged by the Yadava Sabha are more rooted in modern social and political conditions than in the traditional ideals. Thus the delegates to Yadava Sabha conventions have frequently resolved that dowry payments among their members should be lowered, the age of marriage of their children raised, the duration and cost of weddings lessened, and marriage alliances between families of different Yadava jatis increased. The wealthier brethren are encouraged to contribute to Yadava welfare causes and, as M. S. A. Rao reports, "They gave liberal donations to build schools, colleges, hostels, hospitals, and temples, to scholarship funds and toward the expenses of running caste journals and of holding conferences and meetings" (Rao 1964, pp. 1441–1442). With popular elections, opportunities opened to put fellow Yadavas in office in constituencies where Yadavas are numerically strong. By 1964 there was a "sizable group" of Yadava legislators in both the Bihar and the Uttar Pradesh assemblies, and some twelve members of the central legislature were Yadavas. At the top, "there is an Ahir Minister in the Union" (Rao 1964, p. 1443).

A new proposal for Yadava improvement came as a result of the fighting of 1962 in the Himalayas. One company that fought gallantly was the 13th Kumaon composed entirely of Ahirs. One hundred fourteen of this company were killed; their brave stand received wide sympathy and admiration in the Indian press. It stimulated the Yadava Sabha to press for the formation of a Yadava or Ahir regiment in the Indian Army (Rao 1964, p. 1440).

The modern Yadava campaign includes many more people, uses more rationalized techniques, and seeks broader achievement than a more traditional effort waged by a single jati to improve its local lot. But in essence the modern campaigners follow similar patterns of action for similar purposes. On the one front they must disengage themselves from low jatis and their demeaning customs. Hence there is still the plea to give up meat and liquor. On the other front, they seek to associate themselves with the more prestigious customs and groups. Putting on the sacred thread is a gesture of self-association with the category of the twice-born, although this symbol no longer is as important to young men as it was to their fathers and grandfathers. Refining the jati's origin story is another traditional move. Other reform proposals associate the rising group with the educated and modern elite.

Change of Name and Customs

In both the older and the newer means of cultural adaptation for jati mobility, a characteristic step is to change the name of the group. Either a respectable term is added to the old name, or an entirely new name is proposed.

A case in point is that of a sheepherding jati of the Poona district in Maharashtra. A number of families in this jati have become landowners and have given up their rather lowly former occupation, claiming the occupation of landowner, soldier, and village headman, and assuming the sacred thread. Known formerly as Sagar Dhangar, the latter being the term for shepherd, they now call themselves Sagar Rajputs. Orenstein reports a speech given by an official of their caste organization, who cited the "historical" reasons that they are not Dhangars and should not be so called. He demonstrated, to the loudly voiced satisfaction of his fellows, that they are really Rajputs (which links them to the mythology of the martial nobles) and also Marathas (which links them to the dominant jatis of Maharashṭra). The historical contradiction involved in their claim to be both was as irrelevant to his appeal as the fact that historically they were neither. His peroration was, "Then tell everyone that you are Marathas!" (Orenstein 1963, pp. 6–7).[1]

Similarly, in parts of Bengal the dominant cultivators are called Mahisyas, a name that has come to be the standard term for them only in the past fifty years. "Previously in Midnapore and still in parts of Bengal where they are not dominant, they are known by the despised name Kaibartta or Hali Kaibartta (ploughing Kaibartta) in order to distinguish them from the lower-ranking Jali or fishing Kaibartta, with whom they now admit no connection" (Nicholas and Mukhopadhyay 1962, p. 19).

[1] In this locality both terms are used to mean all jatis whose men follow the Kshatriya model. The term Maratha may refer either to a specific jati of the Maratha cluster or to any "high caste whose rank was more secularly based as against those whose rank was based more on ritual purity." The specifically Maratha jatis are traditionally soldiers, landowners, cultivators, and the newly ascendant. Sagar Rajputs emulate this reference group in certain ways (Orenstein 1963; 1965a, pp. 143–146; also see Karve 1961, pp. 44–45).

Such name changes are an old story in India. In eighteenth-century Gujarat, members of the Kunbi group who became landlords and revenue collectors were called Patidar, the title for revenue officials. This title carried such great prestige that in time Patidar became the name of the jati-cluster (A. M. Shah 1964b, p. 90; Srinivas 1966, pp. 35–38; Pocock 1955, p. 71).

When a decennial census was established, it provided a new arena for mobility efforts, especially in the matter of name changes. At the time of the first nationwide census, taken during 1867–1871, some groups formally registered their claims to a grander name than that commonly given them. Two jatis of cultivators in Madras, for example, asked to have varna terms affixed to their jati name. Vaishya in the case of one, Kshatriya in the case of the other.

In the 1901 Census, information was collected and published on the relative ranking and varna affiliations of each jati. This had the effect of certifying that the Census was indeed an arena for mobility struggles and precipitated a new phase of the competition. Many aspirant jatis thereupon concentrated their mobility efforts on the census operations. By 1911, census officials were inundated with petitions for name changes and other status certifications; one officer reported receiving about 120 pounds of petitions from the districts he covered (O'Malley 1913, p. 440).

A count of the claims for higher rank in four census regions of the 1931 Census (United Provinces, Bengal and Sikkim, Bihar and Orissa, Central Provinces and Berar) shows 175 such claims, of which 80 are to Kshatriya status, 33 to Brahmin (including two untouchable jatis claiming Brahminhood), 15 to Vaishya. There were 37 requests for new names without specific varna reference; 9 Muslim groups asked for new labels. Twenty-three groups entered more than one claim; a few claimed two or three prestigious names, perhaps in the hope that one would stick (Srinivas 1966, p. 99). In the 1941 Census and thereafter, the listing of jati and varna names was largely eliminated, terminating the use of the census as a tool for jati mobility.

Only certain elements of group custom are deliberately altered for mobility purposes. A great part of the jati's life style is kept quite the same, partly because of economic necessity and habitual response, partly because the members of an aspiring group see no need to make completely sweeping changes. If they are farmers seeking to be known as Kshatriyas rather than as Shudras, they commonly take pride in their work on the land, perhaps seeking to add a bit of martial luster to their yeoman status or to be known as overseers as well as tillers. Their aspirations do not require that they abandon farming. Many of the artisan jatis too, are not necessarily eager to give up their respective crafts, but rather to have traditional carpenters (or masons or whatever) recognized as practitioners of a high-ranking calling. Rising families do not try to change those domestic practices that have no deleterious implications (cf. Marriott 1959a, pp. 67–68).

All agree that certain practices degrade the practitioners. Hindus who seek a social status above the lower echelons avoid the eating of beef or of any carrion meat, the disposal of corpses or carcasses, the handling of products of dead animals (particularly cows), and the disposal of excreta. Muslims have different but parallel standards. Although there is solid agreement about what should be avoided, there is less consensus as to what should be emulated. Alternate models of prestigious conduct are available; different strategies for social rise are possible, and a combination of models may be feasible.

In sorting out the processes of mobility, it is useful to distinguish reference categories, that is, general principles for proper conduct, from reference groups, actual exemplars of conduct. A main reference category is that of the "twice-born" varnas in the three classic variants. Another is that of modern, educated, elite conduct. Each category is invoked in certain contexts and has particular appeal at certain stages of mobility. Commonly the two are combined, as when a jati organization exhorts its members to become strict vegetarians and also to be zealous proponents of college education for the children. The reference principles are usually interpreted according to the living example of a prestigious reference group. These are people whose life style can be seen and copied by those who seek similar rank, privileges, and respect.

VARNA AS REFERENCE CATEGORY

"Twice-born" is a generalized category. Ambitious families of Shudra or Harijan category select one of the three varna models to emulate, but all three models share common elements. The general label for the three is from the scriptural sacrament of the second "birth," the *Upanayanam* rite, at which a boy is formally separated from his preinitiation status and takes a last meal as a child, with his mother. He undergoes a token transition status, acting for a few moments or hours as an ascetic student bound for the great religious center, Banaras. He is incorporated into his new status when he receives a sacred verse from his spiritual mentor and is invested with the sacred thread worn across the left shoulder (cf. Kane 1941, pp. 268–316; Stevenson 1920, pp. 27–45). All birth rites proclaim a child's legitimate membership in society; this rite of second birth endows a boy with an important aspect of his full status and identity.

In religion, the "twice-born" are expected to show greater concern for the transcendental complex than do other folk and to have less to do with the pragmatic complex. Rites conducted by any of the "twice-born" should not, and rarely do, include blood sacrifice. If they want to propitiate local deities by such sacrifices they should contribute indirectly or vicariously. They are expected to follow the main tenets of Sanskrit scripture more closely than do others; their customary diet is supposed to be more pure than that of the lower orders in their locality. Those of Kshatriya status need not be vegetarians and teetotalers, but they still do not eat the lower forms of flesh, especially beef, nor do they offer alcoholic liquor in religious ceremonies. They usually have closer jajmani relations with local Brahmin priests than the lower jatis can have.

Closer adherence to scriptural teachings entails more stringency in family relations, especially for women. A girl should become a wife as early as feasible and a mother as soon as possible. Her fate depends on her husband; as a wife no divorce is open to her, as a widow no remarriage is possible. "Among Hindus generally, there is a preference for virginity in brides, chastity in wives, and continence in widows, and this is especially marked among the highest castes" (Srinivas 1956a, p. 484). This last phrase is important. It is not that people of the upper varnas can claim exclusive rights to these family practices, as traditionally they did to the sacred thread, to the initiation sacrament, and to Sanskrit learning; it is rather that they should carry out these practices in purer fashion than do others.

The division between "twice-born" and all other Hindus was reflected and probably reinforced by the way in which British courts interpreted Hindu family law. For the purposes of British-Indian law there were only two kinds of Hindus, the "twice-born" and the Shudras. Any Hindu whose jati did not qualify as being of the three upper varnas had to belong in the fourth. The converts to Hinduism and untouchables were classed as Shudras. One kind of law was enforced for Shudras in matters of marriage, succession, and adoption and another kind for the "twice-born." The chief legal tests for the higher category were whether the sacred thread was customarily worn and whether marriage ceremonies followed Sanskritic patterns. If there was evidence that widow remarriage, inheritance by illegitimate sons, and divorce were allowed this was taken as an almost decisive index of Shudra status. In various legal decisions, other criteria were mentioned as indicating membership in the higher rank. These pronouncements tended to focus the reform efforts of mobile groups on these criteria (Derrett 1963, pp. 28–29; McCormack 1963, pp. 68–69; Galanter 1963, p. 545).

The process of cultural adaptation to these higher standards has been called "Sanskritization" by M. N. Srinivas. He defines the term as "a process by which a 'low' Hindu caste, or tribal or other group, changes its customs, ritual, ideology, and way of life in the direction of a high, and frequently, 'twice-born' caste" (1966, pp. 1–45; 1952a, pp. 30–31; 1956a). The concept has been a fruitful one, which has stimulated a number of further explorations (e.g., Chanana 1961b, Gould 1961b, Barnabas 1961, Singer 1964, van Buitenen 1966), but the earlier formulation of it has drawn criticism, notably that there has been great regional and historic variation in the content of "Sanskritic Hinduism" (Staal 1963).

That is quite so. Sanskrit scripture is vast; different sources lay down differing standards for conduct; the same source has been held by different interpreters to sanction different action. The Bhagavad Gita testifies to this (Edgerton 1952, vol. 2, p. 103). In Sir Edwin Arnold's translation of the relevant passage it is rendered as follows:

> "Look! Like as when a tank pours water forth
> To suit all needs, so do these Brahmins draw
> Texts for all wants from the tank of Holy Writ.
> But then, want not! Ask not! Find full reward
> Of doing right in right.

Doing right, as we have seen, is taken by many to mean trying to raise one's jati rank; their superiors in rank usually view such striving as being quite wrong.

Yet most villagers agree that certain canons of conduct should be followed by those who legitimately count themselves among the "twice-born." These standards have long been upheld by the higher jatis and they do underlie the many varieties of Sanskritization. These themes of conduct are repeatedly brought home to villagers, as has been noted, through religionists of many kinds, visiting entertainers, itinerant preachers, revered mentors. Some of the most effective agents of Sanskritization, paradoxically, have been devotees of anti-Brahmanical sects. In their missionary zeal, these sectarians reached into groups which were not already imbued with the scriptural standards for the "twice-born" and were sometimes as successful in implanting these ideas as in making converts to their opposing sect. This was true for Lingayats of Mysore in earlier centuries and for the Arya Samaj in North India in the twentieth century (Srinivas 1966, pp. 21, 101).

Mrs. Karve has commented that among the illiterate people of Maharashtra, there is far greater knowledge about the literary tradition of the last seven centuries of this land than among the people who have received their education in schools and colleges. Through village channels there has been effective communication of the "fundamental theoretical framework underlying the social structure" (1961, pp. 117–119). This is true in other parts of India as well; religion remains a propitious code for communication (Gumperz 1964).

People of the "twice-born" varnas are thus differentiated from the rest of society by standards that are based on scripture and accepted by most villagers. When a group becomes resentful enough about being classed as Shudras or Harijans, powerful enough to do something about it, and united enough to launch effective action, its members change their personal habits and jati manner to conform to a particular varna model. The model is also a marker. If such a group can succeed in being accepted by their neighbors as a jati of the higher varnas, they have arrived. Untouchables do not usually try to become Shudras; they aim for one of the higher categories, most frequently Kshatriya. Those classed as Shudras do not often use that term for themselves, though other villagers do (Karve 1961, p. 47); when they gather strength for a mobility leap, they generally aim for one of the "twice-born" categories, rather than for higher place among Shudras.

Which category is selected by those of an aspirant group depends on such factors as their origin myth, the attraction of a locally dominant group, and on calculation of the most feasible strategy for status gain. Whatever model is chosen, the general requirements for each are well known throughout village India. In simplest terms, jatis classed as Brahmins are expected to stress purity, piety, learning, and priesthood more than do others in their locality. Kshatriyas, for their part, emphasize honor, virtue, force, and masculinity. Vaishyas pride themselves on steadiness, thrift, intelligence, as well as on purity and piety.

These various features are known in the remotest corners of the land because, together with the basic "twice-born" standards, they are presented, assumed, and repeated through all the media of the civilization—in sacred stories and plays, in local tales and anecdotes, in the information picked up by pilgrims, in the talk of genealogists and other professional visitors to the village, in daily interchange. A villager knows from his everyday experience that there are considerable variations of occupation and custom in every varna category. Yet certain directives for behavior are postulated for each varna category and they do regulate the conduct of those classed in it or of those who aspire to be so classed.

Kshatriya Models

The warrior-ruler model of the Kshatriya has been the most popular for ambitious men of lower jatis. It best accommodated those who cut their way up with their swords in earlier centuries (Karve 1965, p. 116). Under the Pax Britannica, it remained a popular and feasible model. In the sample from the 1931 Census, there were 80 claims to Kshatriya status made by lower groups, as against 33 claims to Brahmin and 15 to Vaishya standing (Srinivas 1966, p. 99). Those who proclaim themselves as Kshatriyas are expected to be ready to use force to gain their honorable purposes and to be zealous in defense of their honor. It does not much matter, for purposes of the Kshatriya ideal, if they be slow in learning, lacking in wealth, deficient in ascetic piety. In those jatis whose men pride themselves on their warrior tradition, the beau ideal of the Kshatriya is absorbed from childhood; a youngster learns it from his elders' frequent reference to the glories of their own kind and to the craven conduct of others. It is lovingly and lengthily depicted in stories and dramas from the Epics. A man of true Kshatriya breed should be easy to anger, hard in combat, magnanimous in victory, freehanded with his possessions, closefisted with his honor.

Rajput jatis have particularly upheld and cherished their Kshatriya character. A sketch of the martial Rajput as seen in Khalapur village ninety miles north of Delhi, is given by John Hitchcock. He writes that a Rajput who faithfully follows the warrior tradition looks a bit old-fashioned now to the educated young men of his jati, but even they share some of his attributes. The older Rajput still dresses the warrior part, with a long mustache and a high turban; he goes always armed with a heavy, wire-bound staff, which he stands ready to wield with skull-cracking skill. He considers himself to be one of the rulers of society by birthright and natural endowment, and "regards it as his duty to see that the proper relationships between all castes are maintained, and that the hierarchical order of society is preserved." He takes great pride in his warrior ancestry and has fine scorn for all who do not share his heritage and tradition. If he acts rashly, he explains it as a sign of his valor; if he grasps for power, it is evidence of his destiny to be a ruler. As for ritual piety, he "regards it as a kind of warrior's dispensation that he is permitted to hunt, eat meat (except of course for beef), drink liquor and eat opium" (Hitchcock 1958, pp. 216–221).

Other Rajputs across northern India take a like Kshatriya posture. In a Gujarat village the Rajput overlords are described as being dedicated to the achievement and maintenance of power; they proudly say that a Rajput who bears an insult commits a thousand sins (Steed 1955, pp. 114–115). In a Madhya Pradesh village the local Rajputs run village affairs and are considered to be "the prime Kshatriya caste" (Mayer, 1960, p. 63). According to a description of the Rajputs in a Rajasthan town, "their traditional duties are to rule, and to fight" and although they did not have much good to say for their hereditary ruler "every Rajput insisted on his loyalty to him: if it came to fighting, even those families which were out of favour would claim the privilege of carrying arms in his support" (Carstairs 1957, pp. 106–107).

A Bengali version of the martial style is the Ugra-Kshatriya jati, Ugra meaning "hot-tempered." They are characterized in Lal Behari Day's novel of 1872 about his village in Burdwan district as "a bold and somewhat fierce race, and less patient of any injustice or oppression than the ordinary Bengal raiyat." An account of the same village as of 1962 quotes this passage and comments that the Ugra-Kshatriyas ("a strong, courageous community") still show the same characteristics. Their origin myth (from *Manu* X.9.)[2] told of their descent from a Kshatriya man and a Sudra girl, and so they were not given unequivocal Kshatriya standing, but "they are now claiming themselves to be Kshatriyas and are trying to acquire the status of the twice-born themselves" (Basu 1962, pp. 24, 36).

Bold, ambitious, pugnacious men have found little difficulty in taking on Kshatriya attributes. No great revisions of diet or of routine are required in doing so. People of the Kshatriya category are not expected to be as stringent about food, drink, and ritual niceties as are Brahmins, nor as skilled in trade or crafts as are Vaishyas. What is required is a display of force and fortitude, useful qualities in any event in a struggle for higher rank. Ambitious cultivators frequently own to these qualities, and the Kshatriya ideal is based on control of land.

Moreover, it is not difficult to construct a mythical or even historical association with warrior ancestors. During millennia of battles many warrior bands rose to power and many also were toppled and dispersed. A genealogist can usually manage to find one such forgotten ancestor for an ascendant group (Srivastava 1963, pp. 264–265). K. M. Panikkar indeed concluded that practically all Indian rulers had been successful fighters who were then elevated to Kshatriya rank. "Every known royal family from the time at least of Mahapadma Nanda in the fourth century B.C. belonged to non-Kshatriya castes" (1956, p. 8). So sweeping a statement may be doubted by other historians and challenged by proud scions of the former princely houses, but there is no doubt that once a group fought its way to power, it was likely to be reclassified from Shudra to Kshatriya status.

---

[2] The same myth episode was used to explain the origin of the Coorgs in South India (Srinivas 1952a, pp. 33–34, 219–220; Hopkins 1884, p. 306).

Such reclassification has occurred in many a village scene. In the village of Gaon of Poona district, for example, two jatis assert that they are Kshatriyas. One is Maratha, of the jati-cluster dominant in the region. The other is known as Sagar Rajputs, whose change of name was mentioned above. They are dominant in Gaon village and its vicinity. Other villagers of Gaon tell that not so long ago (as the older people well recollect) the present Sagar Rajputs were Dhangars, shepherds by traditional occupation and Shudras by traditional classification. They grew in strength and ambition to the point where they were able to change their name, declare their Kshatriya status and wear the sacred thread. One of them hired a genealogist who proceeded to trace their ancestry to a chief officer in the armies of the great Maratha leader, Shivaji. Those of the Maratha jati in Gaon, much longer and more securely established in their warrior repute, are apt to sneer at these claims. And the Sagar Rajputs have not fully adopted certain Kshatriya practices, particularly the ban on widow remarriage. They counter Maratha aspersions about this by accusing Marathas of covertly allowing a widow to be unofficial wife to her dead husband's brothers. Most of the other villagers take the Marathas' view about Sagar Rajputs' claims, but they do so more in private than openly because the Sagar Rajputs are quick to take offense and ready to beat up the offender (Orenstein 1965a, pp. 145, 159).

Yet Marathas themselves have not always been universally accepted as Kshatriyas. In the nineteenth century they were labelled as Shudras by some Brahmins (*ibid.*, p. 145). Mrs. Karve cites an account, dated 1697, of the elevation of Shivaji to the category of Kshatriyas. A Brahmin found a suitable genealogy for him and counseled that the sacrament of the sacred thread be performed as was the custom of the northern Kshatriyas. "So in a sacred place Shivaji had the thread ceremony performed on him and was made a pure Kshatriya and then crowned King in the year 1674" (Karve 1961, pp. 43–44; 1958a, p. 88).

In the Dravidian-speaking regions, there were not many jatis that had long-standing claims to Kshatriya or even Vaishya standing (cf. Dubois 1928, p. 15). The Nayars of Kerala, warriors by preference and profession, were classed as Shudras by the Brahmins of the region, and only the ruling lineages among them were known by the term Kshatriya (Mayer 1952, pp. 26–27). During the nineteenth century, several Tamil groups began to declare Kshatriya affinities. One of them, the Padayachis, petitioned for the title of Kshatriya at the time of the first census in 1871, and by the 1891 Census, they had produced a book on their rights to the name and rank. To judge by their ranking in Tanjore district, their efforts have not been wholly successful; there they still are placed below the jatis they were trying to surpass (Béteille 1965, pp. 87, 97).

The Coorgs are an example of a people who have effectively secured their reputation as Kshatriyas, as was noted earlier, despite certain lapses from the usual Kshatriya standards. They were a compact body of warriors and landholders and as they became more closely incorporated into the mainstream of the civilization they retained these characteristics, fitting well into the category of Kshatriya (Srinivas 1952a, p. 33).

Brahmin Models

Some ascendant groups take to the Brahmin rather than the Kshatriya style. They stress ritual purity and purifying ritual, they become more meticulous about avoiding pollution. They do not have to perform priestly services or acquire scriptural learning because many Brahmin jatis do not provide such services and a great many Brahmins have little learning. A Brahmin jati needs mainly to be more ritual-directed and purity-focused than are the other local jatis. Their degree of purity is always relative to the practices of the others. Many Brahmin jatis are strictly vegetarian, especially those of the South and those of Vaishnavite sects. There are also many Brahmin jatis of North India whose members do eat meat and fish (Sharma 1961a), but they do not eat the more defiling kinds of meat and although their diet is not vegetarian it is still at least as pure as the customary diet of jatis in their locality, and usually more so (cf. Carstairs 1957, pp. 115–116).

As for learning, the ideal of the scholar was wholly fulfilled by relatively few Brahmins. Yet the ideal was and is revered by Brahmins more than among other village jatis. Kshatriyas may consider a very learned Brahmin, one who has a whole Veda in his memory or who is accomplished in scriptural exegesis, as worthy of respect but scarcely of emulation. Brahmins and would-be Brahmins see the scholar's pursuits as an exalted version of their own; Kshatriyas do not. In the traditional Brahmin view the earth belonged to Brahmins, but Kshatriyas were allowed to rule it so that Brahmins could avoid the necessity of taking life and could devote themselves to ritual (Ingalls 1958, p. 212).

Those who aim their mobility efforts in a Brahmin direction need not stress power over others but rather control over their own group so that its members are uniformly disciplined to Brahmanical standards. This discipline is a standard theme in the pages of caste journals. N. K. Bose gives a characteristic example from a Bengali caste journal of 1908, the journal of the Namashudra, cultivators and boatmen, who despite their name have waged a long struggle to win recognition as Brahmins. In translation this passage reads, "prompted by envy or anger, people may dislike us; but if one observes our clean Brahminical way of life as practised generation after generation, they will have to admit unanimously that the Namashudra caste is descended from the ancient sages and *Rishis*, i.e., from pure Brahmins."

Another Brahmin-oriented group in Bengal are the Yogis, weavers by traditional occupation. Their caste journal began advocating Brahminhood from about 1911; by 1921 the priestly section among them claimed Brahmin status and in the Census of 1931, the leaders of the jati claimed that all Yogis were properly of Brahmin status. Discrepancies between Brahmin standards and Yogi practices were thrashed out in their publications. The question whether Yogis who had taken the sacred thread could still be farmers was answered with a clear "yes," but on the former Yogi custom of allowing widows to remarry there was some disagreement. Those who took the stricter Brahmanical line wanted to forbid it, but other members of the jati were not so sure, perhaps because they saw new respectability for the old practice under modern Western influence (Bose 1958b, pp. 86–88).

Some jatis emulate the Brahmin model without campaigning actively for Brahmin rating; others take the warrior-ruler model without trying to be known as Kshatriyas. In two of the jati blocs of Ramkheri village in Madhya Pradesh, for example, the several jatis of each bloc are accepted as being about equal in ritual rank; both blocs are ranked just below the local Brahmins. The people of one are vegetarians and teetotalers, those of the other eat certain kinds of meat and drink liquor.

The leading jati among the vegetarians is that of the farmers (to use the author's terms), the other vegetarian jatis are gardeners, carpenters, smiths, tailors, and Bairagi. All these are most confident of the superiority of their style of life. Mayer notes that "They are supported in their contentions by the emergence of popular Governments since 1948 which are dominated by vegetarian castes, and they look forward to national policies which will eventually ban all animal slaughter and so bear out their superiority" (1960, p. 45). Whether the government has actually been so dominated or whether such influence may long continue does not affect the confidence that these jati-groups have derived from the Gandhian movement and its political consequences. They are oriented to the Brahmin mode yet do not claim membership in the Brahmin category.

Rajputs are most numerous in the other bloc and set the tone for the seven jati-groups who are their firm allies in the village. These allies consider the vegetarians to be "weak and effeminate" and take pride that theirs is the style of the former Rajas and, as they believe, of the meat-eating rulers of Western countries. They scoff at the farmers' prudence and exclusiveness. Rajputs are more generous, civic minded, and outgoing; they present a model that men of lower jatis feel they can readily emulate. The origin story held by these jatis lets them circumvent the question of old Kshatriya status. It is the story of the god Parasurama who scoured the country, looking for Kshatriyas to kill. In their flight from this supernatural scourge, Kshatriyas took to different occupations as a disguise. Hence when Parasurama came upon a Kshatriya working as a gardener, he spared him and that man's descendants became the gardener jati. Rajputs alone carried on their martial occupation; the others can then claim to be ex-Kshatriyas if they wish, or avoid the question as many do (Mayer 1960, pp. 44–45, 60–62, 88).

A similar example from South India is from Sripuram village, Tanjore district. There, also, two blocs of jatis display different life styles, one prizing force and rule without raising the Kshatriya banner, the other following a more ritualized pattern without claiming to be Brahmins. Each set is known by the name of its leading jati, Kalla and Vellala respectively. Kallas are described as being physically larger and as having a distinctive "domineering" appearance. "They can be distinguished particularly from the Vellala group by their close-knit organisation (their 'tribal' character, as some call it), the comparative unimportance of Sanskritic elements in their culture, and their tradition of lawlessness and violent life which still makes them feared by the generality of people" (Béteille 1965, p. 84). Vellalas follow a more ritualistic, "Sanskritic" style of life and proclaim themselves as Vaishyas. While the Kallas are the more important politically, the Vellalas are the more influential ritually (Béteille 1965, pp. 82–85; Gough 1956, p. 827).

Artisans, in many villages of the South, show a special kind of mobility striving. The five allied jatis of artisans have made long and insistent claims to being Brahmins. They say that they are Brahmins of a special and most superior kind, descended from the god *Visvakarman*, builder and architect of the heavenly realm. Included under the collective title of *Panchala* are jatis of goldsmiths, copper and brass workers, carpenters, stonemasons, and blacksmiths. Through much of the Tamil-, Kannada-, and Telugu-speaking areas, these artisans are allies. They tend to spurn the proper Brahmins, those so recognized by the rest of the local society, and they do not seek priestly services from them, relying instead on priests of their own jatis. They disdain Brahmins as a reference group, but identify thoroughly with Brahminhood as a reference category.

Men of these jatis wear the sacred thread; they are so ritually meticulous that they will accept food and water from few if any other jatis; they use Sanskrit gotra names for their clans; they observe scriptural sacraments; some of them have even studied the Vedas. Yet despite all their scriptural ways, they are not taken as equal to proper Brahmins by their neighbors. In some places even untouchables will not take food and water from blacksmiths, though they are vegetarians. Perhaps the very audacity of their claims has led to special discrimination against them (Epstein 1962, pp. 162, 294; Srinivas 1955a, pp. 22–24).

Their claims are not new. Accounts of the seventeenth century hint at them (Jackson 1907, p. 243; Ghurye 1961, p. 6). Dubois noted at the beginning of the nineteenth century that the five classes of artisans "refuse, in some districts to acknowledge Brahmin predominance." They were also principal partisans of the Left-Hand faction, arrayed against the Right-Hand faction of the higher Shudra jatis and their allies (Dubois 1928, pp. 23–25). Reports from the beginning of the twentieth century note their continued assertions that they are Brahmins of the purest water and highest degree and the continued response of their neighbors that they are no such thing (Baines 1912, pp. 58–60; Thurston 1909, Vol. III, pp. 106–125).[3]

These artisan jatis of the South adapted culturally to the Brahmin category but failed socially. Perhaps they were able to keep themselves ritually isolated and relatively pure because they had a grip on the economy. Without the services of carpenter and blacksmith, other villagers would have difficulties in farming and without the services of goldsmith, coppersmith, and stonemason, other parts of village life would be impaired. Hence when blacksmiths took on the sacred thread, other villagers could not maul and harass them lest the next harvest suffer for lack of tools and repairs. Yet the artisans did not have enough power to compel others to respect their claims. For several centuries there was a standoff. The local systems worked quite well, these artisans and cultivators maintained jajmani relations with other jatis for economic purposes only. The unresolved controversy apparently was not a great impediment to the functioning of the local caste systems.

Vaishya and Shudra Models

The Vaishya model, like the Brahmin, is ritualized, stringent, and ascetic, but it includes, as the Brahmin does not, a mandate to engage in a mundane occupation, commerce. (cf. Srinivas 1966, pp. 31–32; Carstairs 1957, pp. 119–120). Those who seek Vaishya status can keep any clean occupation and still show their Vaishya affinity whenever they market their produce or open a shop.

The Telis of Orissa, traditionally oil-pressers and ranked as Shudras, have insisted that they are really Vaishyas whose trade was halted by external circumstance; they had to fall back temporarily on the less respectable occupation of extracting vegetable oils. In the resolutions passed by the Teli caste organization there is regular mention of this origin story.

The resolutions also include rules about the kind of trade proper for Telis. For example, they may sell betel leaves but may not sell betel prepared for chewing. The former is a respectable wholesale trade carried on by growers, the latter smacks of the petty peddler's traffic. "Those of our caste who earn their living by cultivation of betel leaves, may sell leaves at the plantation. On no account should they carry baskets of betel leaves to distant markets either on their heads or in bullock carts." A resolution taken at another meeting allows for selling betel leaves in a shop but not "by wandering from place to place." Several resolutions indicate that some Telis continue to carry on inferior kinds of trade, and they are urged to transact only the more honorable kinds of trade, those suitable for people of Vaishya status (Patnaik and Ray 1960, pp. 31–32, 34, 42).

Farming as well as trade is permitted for Vaishyas. The Vellalas, farmers who lay claim to being Vaishyas, stress the purity of their practices rather than the pursuit of commercial profits (Béteille 1965, p. 97; Gough 1956, p. 829; Thurston 1909, p. 366). But other jatis take to the Vaishya category just because of its mercantile feature. The numerous and influential Patidars of Gujarat are shifting from Kshatriya to Vaishya affiliation, as we noted above, mainly because of their increasing involvement in trade and because of the high prestige that businessmen have come to have in Gujarat.

[3] Baines notes similar tendencies among artisans of Bengal and Maharashtra, though these claims were more modest and less militant. More recent studies from these two regions indicate that some artisans continue these assertions (Nicholas 1962, p. 130; Orenstein 1965a, p. 212). Artisan jatis of the Gangetic plain have not generally advanced such claims.

The term Patidar, meaning landowners who had a particular kind of tenure, became the name of the jati-cluster. For several generations Patidars proclaimed themselves as Kshatriyas; they argued that they, like the local Rajputs, wielded political power. Like Rajputs, they supported genealogists to create and keep ancestral records and they became fond of the blood-and-thunder recitations of the bards. But in recent generations, a good many Patidars have been giving up the genealogists and their tall tales. They now prefer to have the same status as the local Baniyas, the trading jatis who are indubitably Vaishyas. When the kingly model was dominant in their region they adhered to it, but it seems a bit obsolete to them now that many Patidars have been successful in trade. Both Baniyas and Patidars took to English education at an early date; both have prospered and, in general, have adapted to modern conditions more successfully than have people of the traditional Kshatriya jatis of Gujarat. Hence a number of Patidars see little to gain by clinging to the old kingly model and have shifted their adherence to the model which is now more suitable, realistic, and profitable (Shah and Shroff 1958, pp. 268–270).

The fourth varna, the Shudra, is rarely taken as a goal for mobility, though presumably an untouchable jati could try to rise by claiming Shudra status. In the sample taken from the 1931 Census, twenty-six untouchable groups gave themselves Kshatriya status, five claimed Vaishya, and two even claimed Brahmin titles. Thirteen untouchable groups demanded to change their jati names without giving a particular varna. None in this sample of 148 claims argued for Shudra status (Srinivas 1966, p. 99).

Not all rising Shudra jatis lay claim to a higher varna. One such group, the Mahanayaka Shudra of Puri district in Orissa, convened caste assemblies in 1935 and again in 1959. In the published reports of these meetings there is no mention of superior varna. There are, however, many resolutions for improvement and reform, as for more meticulous birth ritual and stricter endogamy, against prepuberty marriage, for the education of poor boys of the jati, and against demands for exorbitant dowry gifts, like a gold ring or a bicycle (Patnaik 1960a, pp. 81–118).

Both traditional and modern elements are typically included in such resolutions; recommended ritual improvements are from the "twice-born" repertoire, educational uplift is from the modern sector. There are other reference categories used by particular groups. As we shall note in a later chapter, rising Muslim families attempt reforms in special Muslim terms while also calling for secular improvements and purer practices much as do ambitious Hindu families.

Reference Groups

When jati brethren change their ways to raise their status, they not only adopt a reference category but also follow the specific example of a reference group, a life model. They insist, however, on keeping their own group identity. They do not want to merge with those whose rank they esteem and whose ways they emulate. They feel no need, therefore, to copy all features of their reference groups, but only those they need for better rank. The standards of behavior for the reference *categories* are learned, indirectly as it were, from books, rituals, tales, schooling, dramas, and latterly from movies, newspapers, magazines, and radio. The standards of the reference *groups* are vividly seen as enacted in life.

The life style of a strongly dominant group generally influences others in its area. We have mentioned the example of Gujars in a Maharashtrian village who were changing their marriage patterns to conform with the ways of the locally dominant Marathas. Some of the Brahmins of Maharasthra also follow the Maratha practice of cross-cousin marriage, even though it is against scriptural prescriptions and is contrary to the common practice of Brahmins. Excommunication for this offense was decreed in the eighteenth century under the Peshwa government but such marriage arrangements among Brahmins are still known (Karve 1953, pp. 9, 17, 162; Raghuvanshi 1966, p. 149).

In Gujarat, Rajputs are taken as a prime reference group by the jatis known as Koli. The term Koli, as A. M. Shah and R. G. Shroff explain, once covered about a quarter of all Gujarati Hindus and refers to an assortment of people who owned little land and who were presumably of tribal origin. In recent years, prosperous Kolis have employed genealogists who provided ancestral records linking them with Rajput history and prehistory, and ultimately showing divine provenience. They have taken clan names and some of the marriage customs of Rajputs, and now have Brahmin priests to guide them in the sacramental rituals performed by Rajputs proper.

These Kolis, Shah and Shroff observe, are "fast Sanskritizing as well as Rajputizing themselves." One of their genealogists commented that they still pay less than do Rajputs and do not know the niceties of Rajput hospitality, "but they have great reverence for us." This reverence has declined or vanished among many of their former clients, notably Patidars. As is true elsewhere, the Kolis are adopting practices from a group whose members are discarding the same practices for others that they deem more estimable (Shah and Shroff 1958, pp. 264–268).

An example of these tendencies comes from two villages in central Gujarat, which are only a few miles apart. In both places Patidars are dominant and set the cultural style for other jatis, particularly for the Baria (formerly Kolis). The Patidars of one village have become wealthier than those in the other, they belong to a much higher hypergamous section of their jati, and they have departed more widely from the former Patidar devotion to Kshatriya symbols. The Barias of each village take their cues from their own Patidar neighbors, modeling themselves in the one after the more traditional Kshatriya pattern and in the other after the ways of the newer elite (Pocock 1957b, pp. 25–27).

The cultural influence of socially dominant groups was strikingly demonstrated among Hindus in what was the North-West Frontier Province. Hindus were a small minority among Muslims there; the tradition of Muslim rule and prestige remained strong even under the British. Brahmin priests were not much used among Hindus; they commanded little reverence and less learning. A Hindu of "twice-born" varna would eat meat and eggs "even in the bazar, generally put on the sacred thread only at the time of marriage, recited no *mantra* (save Rama-Nama), knew no Sanskrit and sent his children to the local madrassa run by a Maulvi." Hindu children taught by a Muslim teacher in an Islamic school grew up to be deeply influenced by Islam. But with a shift in political tides these Hindus turned to greater interest in Hindu scripture and acquired it chiefly through the non-Brahmanical Arya Samaj movement (Chanana 1961b, pp. 409–411).

Though the attraction to the life style of the dominant group is strong, it is far from total. The Hindus of the northwest frontier remained Hindus, observing some scriptural ritual even if in attenuated form and maintaining jati differentiation. Where the Rajputs were the overlords, not all the lower jatis emulated them. As we have seen in Ramkheri, some chose the ascetic rather than the warrior model.

The Kshatriya model in all regions includes the broad characteristics of devotion to honor, rule, and martial valor. The Rajput version of that model adds certain traits, such as hypergamous clan organization. That version itself is observed in different regional varieties; Rajputs of Gujarat differ in certain ways from those of Rajasthan or Uttar Pradesh (Baines 1912, pp. 29–33; cf. Steed

1955; Carstairs 1957; Minturn and Hitchcock 1966). So the men of a rising group who chose the ruler-warrior road of mobility adopted Kshatriya principles for conduct, oriented themselves to, say, Rajput standards, and actually guided their conduct according to the example of those Rajputs whose behavior they could see. The example of the visible reference group is usually much more influential than are abstract principles of scripture or indirect examples in legend and literature.

Modernization as Reference Category

Such cultural adaptations were part of recurrent changes. The overall system of society remained relatively constant even though (and partly because) there was continuous struggle for higher rank. The pervasiveness of these struggles within local systems and across the land, helped to reinforce a villager's conviction that higher rank was attainable and was eminently worth the struggle for it.

In the nineteenth century, European influences began to reach strongly into village society. Villagers were confronted with new conditions, of police and government, for example, with which they had to cope and which had somehow to be fitted into their social organization. There was some adjustment of the system. When the new temporal rulers would not intervene in caste ranking as indigenous rulers might, the ritual criteria came to be more rigidly applied and litigation became a main instrument of caste manipulation. Yet the structure of the villagers' social order was not drastically altered, the mobility efforts observed in the mid-twentieth century are similar in process and phases to those reported in the eighteenth century (cf. Raghuvanshi 1966, pp. 167–169).

Modern influences, however, especially those that came with political independence, are cumulatively bringing about long-range changes, which we will discuss later. Village society was not static under the colonial regime; there were some systemic adjustments, but generally villagers tended to assimilate the main innovations in government, technology, and communications into the established pattern of jati relations. British culture was too alien from the village world to provide a new reference category and British society in India was far too isolated and aloof from village life to yield a new reference group for mobility.

A few quite exceptional Indian groups did adapt their ways to an English model, as some Coorg landowners did to the example of the English planters, but this was far from common and even the Coorg adaptation was limited to selected outer traits, as the club, plantation management, and men's recreational pursuits; it did not pervade religion or family relations (Srinivas 1966, p. 57).

Villagers of middle or low jati who gained assets in modern ways typically used them to acquire the accouterments of high status in the traditional ways. As they did so, those of the higher jatis who had also benefited from modern accretions began to revise their status symbols and standards. Hence ambitious people of lower jatis, as has been noted above, tend to take on traditional symbols of high status that are being relinquished by the higher jatis. The latter are adopting new symbols that are not only indicative of their modern sophistication but also serve as new indicators of their superiority. This is illustrated in Sherurpur village of Faizabad district of U.P. where one man of low jati has become wealthy as a contractor. "He has symbolized his new-found opulence not by becoming a 'modern man' but by building a residence in the village which outdoes the high castes in its traditional architectural style." He has also built a grand rest house for pilgrims, a gift traditionally made by benefactors of high jati rank. The local Brahmins and Rajputs "have little choice left to them than to turn to westernization as a means of maintaining the social distance between themselves and the lower castes which is no longer possible within the old order in the face of the latter's current ability to Sanskritize themselves" (Gould 1961b, p. 947).

The Brahmins and Rajputs here and people of traditionally high rank in other villages do not relinquish their respective varna standards, but add modern standards of education and occupation to them. They are no less eager for substantive privileges of high status; they have taken a new view of the proper symbols and content of that status. Nor do prospering people of low jati ignore the new standards. Many have taken to whatever modern ways they could assume (cf. Srinivas 1966, pp. 66–67). Some of the lowest jatis have struck directly for better status through modern political processes. Most aspiring groups now combine the older and the newer means of raising themselves in the social order.

The Yadava example with which we began this chapter shows the eclectic approach. Those who call themselves Yadavas are urged toward such traditional ways as the wearing of the sacred thread and abstinence from liquor and meat. Yadavas are also advised to abolish child marriage and high dowry payments, practices formerly honored but countered by modern influences. Intermarriage among all jatis now known as Yadavas is endorsed, even though such vast expansion of endogamy is quite contrary to former rules for marriage. The older preference is overridden by the prospect of united political strength which broader marriage ties may bring (Rao 1964, p. 1440).

To take one other example, the Telis of Orissa were notified through the 1959 constitution of their association that all the separate jatis calling themselves Telis should allow complete freedom of intermarriage among them, that high dowries and child marriages should be stopped, and that the children should be given more education (Patnaik and Ray 1960, pp. 73–76).

Some of these resolutions are more readily put into practice than others. Determination to wear the sacred thread in the face of opposition from higher jatis is usually much more appealing (especially when there is a good chance of overcoming the opposition) than is the advice to arrange marriages more broadly. While resolutions against lavish dowries and expensive weddings get resounding votes as tokens of devotion to social progress, it is quite another thing when a member, even a leader of the organization, has to marry off his own daughter and must then demonstrate his own family's status in the jati. Such contradictions between ideal and real practice, between scriptural standards and modern notions, are generally glossed over without much difficulty. The goal is clear. The purpose is to get more respect and esteem from others in the society. A rising group uses all its resources from both the traditional and modern repertoire in order to accomplish that purpose, and combines them in whatever way seems best suited to reach the goal.

The term "Westernization" has been used to refer to the modern repertoire, to those adopted practices and ideas that originated outside Indian civilization (cf. Srinivas 1966, pp. 50–56). But though these traits were originally introduced from European sources, this is not often relevant to villagers. Most of the patterns of government, technology, and communication that were first brought in by Europeans are now firmly part of the village world. Some of them have been so for generations. As far as the villager is concerned they are indigenous and long established. He certainly recognizes the difference between scriptural edict and modern law, between traditional ritual and national ceremonies, but no opposition among them is necessarily assumed.

Secular education, railway and bus lines, newspapers and postal service, introduced food and cash crops, are no longer seen as alien by villagers. Moreover, most innovations are soon adapted to the Indian milieu and take on characteristics notably different from those of the prototypes. Perhaps the term "modernization" avoids the unwarranted implications of "Westernization" provided it is not taken as a slogan of invariably good and desirable progress.

Villagers, in sum, are altering modern patterns, such as those proffered by government agencies or presented through the mass media, to suit village conditions. They are also rephrasing the still powerful reference models of tradition to accord with modern conditions.

CHAPTER 25

Mobility Tactics: Overcoming External Opposition

Cultural models induce social actions. Ambitious men usually have a clear idea of what they want to attain for their jati; getting it demands long, steady social maneuver. They face two tactical necessities. One is to press steadily against the external opposition, against those who feel that their own jati position is threatened by the rise of a lower group and so fight it. The other is to maintain sufficient internal unity to be able to overcome. External opposition may be circumvented through passing and percolation, or it may be dealt with by undertaking a straightforward jati campaign.

The individual villager, as we have seen, commonly engages in different mobility drives for his several social groups, pushing one more than another at a particular juncture, usually giving priority to jati defense over lineage or family aggrandizement. To a villager, his several affiliations are not neatly packaged, discrete entities. He tends to take them together as part of his general position in society. In North India, a man's view of his general position is called his *izzat*, his personal honor. Izzat has to do with a man's obligations and rights through all his social roles; it is the sum of his social credit; it includes all the values and attainments that others give him credit for—as he perceives that credit. Getting a prestigious groom for his daughter or a fine bride for his son is part of maintaining his izzat, as is the daughter's proper conduct and the son's manly behavior. Upholding the tradition of his jati is also part of personal izzat, as is the defense of jati rights against usurpers of lower rank. Thus an individual's izzat is linked to his view of his jati's proper place, power, and prestige.

Contingency and Individual Influence

Mobility tactics follow characteristic patterns, but the contestants themselves are more concerned with the contingency, with the unpredictability of the struggle rather than with its patterned regularities. The observer must focus on the regularities, but he must also recognize that it is the indeterminancy of a contest rather than its general predictability that impels the contestants to keep striving. In particular cases the will and determination of a few men are critical factors no less than are the social and cultural factors.

This has been true in one mobility contest I have observed over a number of years, waged by the Kotas of the Nilgiri Hills of South India. This contest was pressed most vigorously by one man, Sulli, whose life story I have sketched elsewhere (1941, 1960). For decades he had to fight a running two-front battle, with the opponents of Kota ambitions and with his opponents among the Kotas. He eventually won on both fronts; his long, tenacious fight certainly affected the status of Kotas during his life and has probably had long-run effects as well.

The Kotas are a very small group, one of the four aboriginal peoples of the formerly isolated Nilgiri plateau. When the isolation ended, the Badagas, the most numerous group of the four, grew prosperous as potato farmers and their leaders became zealous to reform Badaga ways. Many of them rejected the traditional interdependence between Badaga cultivators and Kota artisans; they began to treat Kotas more like complete untouchables than they had before. Kotas resented this, but only Sulli propounded a program of Kota reform that would counter the Badaga aspersions. The program he concocted for his small group was in essentials quite like the reform programs of the great caste associations. It entailed dissociation from degrading customs and association with elevating practices, of both scriptural and modern origin. Some younger Kotas took his side but many Kotas opposed him bitterly as a wanton violator of precious tradition. Badagas of both the reform and the conservative parties fought his proposals for greater rights for Kotas; both saw him as a threat to proper social order.

The opposition was formidable but Sulli was formidably determined. He divided his enemies and marshaled his strength against each in turn. When Badagas beat up Kotas he stood as champion of the Kotas. Sulli was the only Kota of his generation who knew some English, and so he could write petitions to authorities, use suitable persuasion to bring in the police, and initiate litigation to punish the Badagas' strong-arm men. When he asked for official protection, he portrayed his small, beleaguered, disadvantaged people as standing in desperate defense against the numerous and wealthy Badagas. Government officials, whether of the British regime or the independent state, could scarcely spurn his plea. Nor could Sulli's bitter enemies among the Kota try to undermine him at the very moment when he was defending the honor of them all.

When, on other occasions, the opposing faction barred Sulli from the Kota temples or when a Kota council decided to sever social relations with him, he brought litigation against them, effectively imported police into the village at times convenient for his plans, and appealed to officials as a progressive citizen oppressed by his reactionary brethren.

Sulli was a school teacher for many years, and since his income did not depend on his fellow Kotas he was not so bound by their council edict as an ordinary Kota would have been. As a school teacher he carried the fight for Kota respectability into Badaga villages. When he was appointed as a teacher in a Badaga school all the parents withdrew their children and the school had to be closed. But he tried again, and eventually, because he had the sympathy of some school officials, he succeeded in acting as a teacher to Badaga pupils.

Before the end of his life Sulli was able to see a number of his reforms accepted, his Kota opposition almost gone, and his own place among Kotas secure. If Kotas have not risen much in their local social order, neither are they as lowly as some Badagas would have had them be nor as impoverished as they might have become. An observer can see in retrospect that Sulli's success was likely because he was riding a favoring tide of national history and world events. This wide trend made for propitious official attitudes toward the disadvantaged. But at any one time the internal Kota quarrels and their external contests were touch-and-go affairs with the outcome almost always uncertain. Sulli suffered setbacks as well as victories, and had his determination flagged, his ambitions and reforms might have been frustrated.

Sulli's ambitions were always couched as ambitions for his people. He conceived of no future for himself apart from the fate of the Kotas. Though he disliked many of them and despised more than a few, he felt part of the same social body as all, and agitated in behalf of the whole group.

Individual Passing and Percolation

Leaving one's group and passing as a member of some other jati is a possible mobility tactic but, insofar as can be known, it is not often done successfully. For one thing, it is difficult to bring off; an imposter may be unmasked at any time. This happened to one man in Sripuram village of Tanjore district. He came into the village as a mason by trade and claimed to be by birth a Padayachi, one of the middle jatis. He worked in the village for three or four years, had access to Brahmin houses in the course of his work, and was accepted by men of other middle jatis at his claimed identity. Then one day a visitor saw him sharing betel with such men and expressed surprise. The mason, it turned out, was a Palla, an untouchable, and a jati fellow of the newcomer. The pretender was forthwith beaten and fled from the village (Béteille 1965, p. 81).

Even if those who try to pass move far enough away so that there is slight chance of being recognized, there are still great difficulties in settling into a different village (cf. Mayer 1960, pp. 27–28). The new neighbors want to know who the newcomer's relatives are and what his jati is. Since he cannot produce them readily or substitute convincingly, who will give him a daughter as wife? If he comes with a wife, whom will his children be able to marry? These questions arise in the city as well. A study of educated city people who are of untouchable origin (Isaacs calls them "ex-untouchables") shows that, although they are generally able to gloss over their jati origin in their professional or business practice, their family life and intimate relations are with similarly educated people of like jati birth (Isaacs 1965, pp. 143–149, 157–160). They have a way of passing in public while not passing in private. Isaacs quotes one such informant, who told him that educated people cannot separate themselves from their jati community because without such a community all a man's relationships are awkward. The quotation concludes with the italicized sentence "*In India you have got to be connected*" (Isaacs 1965, p. 147).

There are undoubtedly some who do manage to pass but there is no way of telling how many do so. Occasionally an instance of successful passing is reliably reported, for example, the case of a man from the Jatavs of Agra. Jatavs were formerly leatherworkers, and, as noted again below, they have succeeded in raising their rank considerably. This Jatav claimed to be a Brahmin, apparently with some success, because in 1962 he married a Brahmin girl from Rajasthan (Srinivas 1966, p. 73).

One Harijan, who had passed but later returned to become a political leader among Harijans, explained to me that his father had been a village boy who obtained an education at a mission school. After reaching manhood, he married, had children, and moved to a city, where he took a new name, and gave out that the family belonged to a middle jati. He did well in his profession, severed all ties with his kin, and even succeeded, through astute and costly devices, in marrying his daughters into the jati whose name he had adopted. His son, however, could not forget the family's origins. After he was educated and became a lawyer, he decided to drop the camouflage (with what results for his married sisters I did not find out). He abandoned the assumed name and worked for the Harijan cause.

Another kind of individual and family mobility is through the marriage of girls into a higher group. In large jatis that have ranked hypergamous sections, the more favored girls of the lowest sections are taken by higher ranking men. The young men of these low sections compete for the few girls of their own level who remain available or take a bride from the next lower jati. Thus the lower Rajputs of central Gujarat take wives from the higher lineages among Kolis; as was noted above, men of the lowest sections of the Patidars of this region are sometimes compelled to marry girls of a lower jati because of a lack of eligible brides in their own section.

Percolation also occurs when a girl of a lower jati in a jati-cluster is married to a man of a higher jati in the jati-cluster. Such matches are not approved but can be tolerated. There are two jatis of genealogists in central Gujarat, one using written records, the other relying on oral tales and ballads. When a young man of the latter group learns to read and write he may be hired as a clerk in a family of literate genealogists. In time he may be fully incorporated into their jati (Shah and Shrof 1958, pp. 252, 265–267; Pocock 1957a, p. 19).[1]

Through such channels of percolation, a family may become affiliated with a close but higher jati and may gradually become assimilated into it. No strong claims to high rank are announced and no strong countermeasures are aroused. Infiltration into higher rank rather than capture of it has probably been brought off by many aspirants. Percolation is a quieter procedure that has not yet been well described, partly because it draws less fire and notice, partly because those who take this path have been diligent in covering over all traces of their route to the higher niche.

The Jati Campaign

The mobility tactics of greatest social importance are those undertaken for the jati. Claims to higher rank are common; those who make good their claims must move from substantial secular gains to insistent symbolic assertions. Wealth alone, we note again, is no automatic guarantee of higher rank. Jati members must use it properly so that the jati's rank may be elevated for their children.

---

[1] The Coorgs of South India formerly permitted a kind of percolation into their jati that is not common among dominant landowners. In the nineteenth century whole families of non-Coorgs, some of quite high jati, were received as jati members. These were families who had settled in the then isolated Coorg territory and wanted to become assimilated to the dominant group. Apparently the Coorgs also took in some who had been excommunicated by their jati. Very low groups like the Nimar Balahis may do this, but the Coorgs were exceptional among landowners in extending such hospitality (Srinivas 1952a, p. 37; Fuchs 1950, pp. 18–20).

The more common pattern of percolation seems to be illustrated in Gandhi's family. His biographer, Pyarelal, writes that Gandhiji once said that when his father was to be married for the fourth time, there was some difficulty in finding him a bride of his own group probably because Kaba Gandhi was then nearly forty and because his third wife was still living. "As a result, he was married into a family considered to be inferior in the hierarchy of caste" (Pyarelal 1965, p. 186).

Secular gains are primarily the results of family efforts. A profitable transaction is brought off, another field is purchased, a good harvest enables the family to expand its operations. A jati's power increases almost imperceptibly, through prospering family units. An enlargement of economic opportunity in its occupation may enable a number of its families to become richer. As these families prosper, they are apt to favor jati fellows and so they accelerate the general prosperity of the jati.

Gains in ritual rank, however, are typically made by a group for the group. There is little point to wearing the sacred thread unless it is done as a matter of jati right. This is not to say that jati leaders wait patiently until their jati fellows have accumulated a given quantity of wealth and power. Low jatis may make high claims even though the power they have falls far short of that needed to press the claims successfully. Some try any possible opening: witness the untouchables who tried to get themselves inscribed in the Census under Brahmin or Kshatriya titles.

Others have set up confrontations prematurely and have been beaten down (cf. Cohn 1955, pp. 65–74). However, those who are defeated do not necessarily lose very much as a group. Some of the challengers (especially if they are untouchables) may be beaten up, a few possibly murdered. Some of their leaders may expend much of their wealth in the effort. Neighbors of higher rank may squeeze them a little more economically and scorn them a bit more socially. But for the group as a whole not much will change because of the failure of their attempt. If they are Harijans they cannot well be further degraded; their economic services will still be needed. If they are Shudras, they will still be treated as a jati of that category. There are limits to punitive conflict among jatis as there are limits within a jati.

In contrast, such limits are not observed in the status competition among the Swat Pathans of northern Pakistan and among similar peoples on the northwestern borders of the sub-continent. Among them, the competition is just as continuous but it is much more on an individual basis. There is little supervening framework as in a jati order, nor is there much corporate sharing of victory and failure. Hence the results of failure are much more serious; if a Swat Pathan loses the main criterion of rank, the ownership of land, he may sink to the depths of the social scale. Conversely, the rewards of victory are not translated to any long-term group prestige, so that a victory is valid only so long as it can be successfully and individually defended. Rife as is status competition in Indian village society, it seems not so sharp nor so much a matter of life and death as it is in the more atomistic society and more individualized competition of the Swat Pathans (cf. Barth 1959).

How much increase in wealth is required before an advance in ritual rank becomes feasible depends on such variables as the relative size of the jati-group in the village population. A large jati-group is likely to secure status gains more readily than one with few people on the local ground. Srinivas gives the example of one Mysore village in which fishermen are rated so low that they are not allowed to take their processions into the streets of the higher jatis, while in villages where fishermen are in the majority, they suffer no such disabilities (1959, p. 4). Numerical strength in many villages of a close vicinity gives added strength to the jati's cause in each of them.

Another factor is the position from which a jati starts its rise. An already respectable jati may need relatively little secular gain to win a higher ranking while a low group may gain considerably in wealth and still be judged low. In Gaon village of Poona district the jati whose members were temple servants, musicians, and beggars was ranked quite low in an account of 1868, but by 1954 they had given up music and begging and were ranked by their neighbors as being just below the local Brahmins. Their temple service and vegetarian diet enabled them to win higher place with relatively little increase in wealth or power. On the other hand, the leatherworkers have become markedly better off than they were and have reformed their practices considerably, but they have not yet made great gains in rank. Most people in Gaon consider them to be transmitters of touch pollution like the other Harijans.

The leatherworkers have succeeded, however, in getting some local Brahmins to conduct their weddings, though the Brahmin officiants avoid touch contact with the members of the wedding (Orenstein 1965a, pp. 146–148). Securing the services of Brahmins is, as we have noted, an important step in legitimizing a jati's status claims. A beginning is usually made by engaging some of the poorest and not too meticulous Brahmins; more effective legitimation comes when the more respectable Brahmins of the locality provide full sacerdotal services to the jati's members (cf. Srinivas 1966, pp. 24–28).

The small ritual advance of the leatherworkers contrasts with the rise, mentioned in the preceding chapter, of the dominant jati-group in Gaon, which has risen within a century from quite low shepherds to high "Rajputs" firmly entrenched as Kshatriyas. Some of their neighbors in Gaon are annoyed by this, especially so the Marathas who are dominant in the region though not in this village, but who dare not openly challenge the quondam shepherds. Others support their achievement and "their claim was respected to the extent that everyone referred to them by the Rajput title, whether they were present or not" (Srinivas 1966, pp. 145–146). These "Rajputs" have achieved for their jati what many a villager aspires to for his—legitimation of the higher rank by Brahmins, affirmation of it in the daily acts of their neighbors, and confirmation in formal panchayat.

Steps toward Higher Rank

Such success is achieved gradually, beginning with a series of steps to which others cannot well object, perhaps reform of the jati's marriage practices (how can others protest if the jati's widows are prohibited from remarrying?) or enlarging sources of income which others do not care to have (what harm if earthworkers take a government contract to dig a canal?). Later the ambitious jati members make more open assertions, which are more objectionable to higher jatis. The lowly earthworkers may decide to wear the sacred thread. It is at such a point that escalating aspirations and growing hostility come to a head; there is a confrontation, often followed by other physical, legal, and societal encounters.

In Ramkheri village, for example, the weavers and Bhilalas have taken the preliminary unobjectionable steps, while the oil-pressers have made more overt assertions. As Mayer describes the situation, the weavers (Balai) are untouchables who are quietly preparing to move out of that category. They have stopped eating beef and have dropped former demeaning practices. By occupation they are now laborers rather than weavers. "No explicit demand has yet been made for adjustment of their status, but many Balais maintain privately that they are now no different from other castes, and it is therefore unjust for them to be discriminated against as Harijans." Those of higher jatis are aware of this notion and "there is an undercurrent of feeling against those Harijans who try to assert themselves" (Mayer 1956, p. 139).

The Bhilalas (the name implies descent from Bhil tribesmen) are ranked in the Shudra category but they want to be accepted as Kshatriyas along with the local Rajputs. They proclaim their Rajput origins and play down their tribal associations. As one preliminary gesture, they decided to build a caste temple on the banks of the sacred river Sipra as higher jatis have done; their claim to be known as "Bhilala Rajputs" verges on overt assertion.

The oil-pressers (Telis) have shifted from covert preparation to overt demands. Although they are ranked with Rajputs for some purposes, they are not fully accepted in the Kshatriya category. When they asked to sit in the same line at a feast with the Rajputs they were refused. In reprisal for this assertion the Rajputs refused to smoke in their company, a privilege the Telis had previously enjoyed. But, as Mayer indicates, the oil-pressers will not readily be discouraged; some of them own land, some are educated and have urban contacts. The weavers and Bhilalas, on the other hand, have little land or education and so, like other ambitious but insufficiently strong groups, they must concentrate on bettering their ritual observances rather than on making overt demands (Mayer 1956, pp. 139–141; 1960, pp. 48–49).

At some point a mobile group is likely to perform an overt act that others will take as a clear challenge. Where no untouchable was permitted to own land, the mere purchase of land by a Harijan might be taken as an intolerable disruption of the social order (cf. Harper 1968, p. 46). In the example from Gopalpur village mentioned previously, the low-ranking stoneworkers were allowed to own inferior land but when some of them bought good rice-growing land and one of their young men began to plow it, he was severely beaten by men of higher jatis (Beals 1962, p. 39). Opposition to the ownership of land by lower jatis is passing in most places, but there are many other grounds for confrontations. Village festivals often occasion quarrels among jatis, as weddings may among families within a jati. Some village festivals have been abandoned mainly because they precipitated insoluble quarrels about jati rank.

The symbols themselves become differently interpreted in time. The Noniyas, the earthworkers, of Senapur village and vicinity decided at a meeting in 1936 to put on the sacred thread to show that they were really Chauhans by caste and Kshatriyas in varna. When some of them did so, the dominant landowners beat them, tore off the sacred threads, and imposed a collective fine on the whole jati-group. Subsequently, after their position in the village was stronger, Noniyas individually began to wear the sacred thread without any fanfare. This aroused no violent counter-measures. In recent years, Noniya young men have lost interest in wearing the sacred thread; a number of them have worked in cities and learned that other insignia, a wristwatch for example, are more prestigious than the traditional insignia of the "twice-born." When William Rowe studied the Noniyas, their oldest men did not wear the sacred thread because they were of a generation that had not been strong enough to do so. A considerable number of the middle generation wore it, but the younger men showed decreasing interest in doing so (Rowe 1968, p. 76). Noniyas now are accorded higher status than they were given formerly, and in that sense they have defeated the adversaries who once tore off their badges of higher rank. However, the adversaries themselves have become less concerned with these badges and more interested in other ways of symbolizing and maintaining their dominance.

Whatever issue may precipitate open conflict about rank, the men of a dominant jati are commonly among the main adversaries. They tend to see any alteration in the social order as a potential threat to their dominance and take themselves to be the guardians of that order. "The elders of the dominant caste in a village were the watchdogs of a pluralistic culture and value system," Srinivas writes, and he adds that when a low caste "refused to perform the services, economic or ritual, which it traditionally performed, or when it appropriated an important high-caste symbol, then punishment followed swiftly" (1966, p. 15). Other high jatis may be equally uneasy lest the lifting of a lower group mean the lowering of their own status. Lower jatis may also resent the rise, feeling that they are further demeaned if another jati is added to the number of their superiors. Where no single jati is dominant, the thrust of a lowly group may bring about a coalition of high jatis for the purpose of putting down the challenge (cf. Roy 1963).

To overcome such opposition, the aspirants commonly gather allies of their own. Just as an alliance leader within a jati secures the support of one man by lending him money, of another through the lease of land, of still another by giving him a patron's protection, so the prospering men of a jati secure allies for their jati's advance in the course of their workaday affairs. They attract and bind supporters through the redistribution of their wealth on ceremonial occasions. Their families invite many guests of other jatis to their weddings and, in turn, are munificent about weddings in other jatis. They will give handsomely to the rites for the special deity of a low jati, contribute generously to the temple of a high god, and will liberally support village festivals and other enterprises for the common good. Thus they gather strength for a test of rank. There may be a dramatic confrontation, like the temporary debacle of the Senapur Noniyas in 1936. More likely there are a number of successive encounters, the aspirants gaining in some and losing in others, their hopes only gradually becoming fulfilled and being securely established only after the passage of a generation or more.

The gradualness of this process is brought out in F. G. Bailey's account of the rise of the Boad distillers (Sundi) of Bisipara village in Orissa (1957, pp. 186–198). In the late nineteenth century, this jati was placed among the "Low Hindus" of the village, just above the line of untouchable pollution. By mid-twentieth century it held a firm place near the top of the "High Hindus," ranking just below the dominant "Warriors" (Sudo). The springboard for this advance was a sudden enlargement of economic opportunities when this jati was given a near monopoly of liquor manufacture in the area. This monoply lasted from about 1870 to 1910 and in those forty years the jati members came to have more average wealth per capita than any other jati-group in Bisipara. They bought land, farmed it with the aid of laborers, and became economically equal to the dominant landowners.

As they accumulated wealth, they sloughed off demeaning traits. Their women cast off a knee-length garment in favor of the long sari worn by Brahmin women of the village. They dropped the traditional occupation of distilling; most of them have stopped drinking liquor. They no longer keep chickens, as low folk do, and they wear the sacred thread as do the high-born. Like other newly arrived they exaggerate their ritual purity. They refuse to take water and food from certain jatis from whose hands even the local Brahmins accept water and food. Their neighbors of other jatis sometimes sneer at their pretensions, but at the same time they agree that the distillers are in the top part of the local order.

This ascent, Bailey emphasizes, probably was accomplished through a long sequence of steps, each a partial rather than a total bid for better position. For example, if you are a distiller (or of any other ambitious jati) and distillers rank below washermen, the first step is to persuade a washerman to wash your family's clothes. This will be for cash payment at first; perhaps later it may develop into the kind of jajmani arrangement that washermen have with high families. The aspiring men also get some untouchables to work for them, again on a contractual arrangement at first and gradually developing into a more permanent patron-client tie. Similar arrangements are established with families of barbers, herdsmen, and Brahmins. Should any of these village specialists refuse to provide their services, others of their occupation from a different village may be hired or may even be permanently imported for the purpose. But a washerman heavily in debt to a distiller would not spurn the distiller's request for a cash arrangement nor long defer jajmani exchange.

The success of the distillers has not altered the structure of the local order even though the specific order of jatis has been shifted. While they are now higher in ritual rank, they uphold the traditional standards of that higher rank. They have come to be about as powerful in village affairs as the "Warriors," and they comport themselves in the manner of the traditional landowners.

Different Routes of Advance

The distillers have followed the traditional upward path; they have emulated a standard reference category and a strong reference group to achieve a higher place in their village. But this is not the only route of social ascent; two others are exemplified in the same village of Bisipara. There is another jati-group of distillers there who have followed a Vaishya rather than a Kshatriya model and, most importantly, have taken as the social stage for their rise a wider area than the village vicinity. They have drawn power from the wider area and have won higher place in it. A third instance is that of the untouchable Pans. The members of this jati seek to rise not only in the village but in the political arena of their state and they have drawn power for their struggle in the village from the political sphere.

The two separate jatis of distillers migrated to Bisipara village from different places. The Boad distillers whom we have been discussing came from the Boad kingdom to the north. The Ganjam distillers came from the Ganjam plains to the south. There were five households of Ganjam distillers in the village in the 1950s, forming only 2 percent of the population as compared with 6.7 percent for the Boad distillers. These five households not only shared in the forty years of lucrative liquor monopoly but also engaged in very profitable general trade. As merchants they kept up their kin and trade connections with the Ganjam plains, unlike the Boad distillers whose interests were concentrated within the village.

The Ganjam distillers have also reformed their jati practices but they have entered very little into Bisipara village affairs, holding themselves politely aloof from the other villagers' pastimes, disputes, and concerns. They were able to do so because they dealt with their fellow villagers as customers more than as neighbors; they were not economically dependent on them because they had little competition as merchants and drew customers from a number of settlements. At the same time they took care not to offend villagers' sensibilities. The villagers in turn were reluctant to offend them because they were rich men with governmental and economic connections outside the village. Their status aspirations have been directed toward a wider sphere and toward a different arena than the village locale in which the Boad distillers won success (Bailey 1957, pp. 199–210).

The other rising group, the Pans, comprise about one-fifth of the village population and some of them have prospered despite their position as untouchables (Bailey 1957, pp. 211–227). British officials gave them advantages in schooling, farming, and government employment as part of a program of uplift, and after independence such aid was increased. As a result, some have become schoolteachers; others are in government service; still others have made money by trading cattle. A number of them own land, and several are as rich as the richest traditional landowners.

With this base the prospering Pans began to reform their jati practices as the Boad distillers had done. They too gave up defiling occupations, changed their diet, dress, and name. But they were not as successful as were the distillers in using their new wealth to secure allies and dependents. Part of the difficulty was that not enough of them were rich. To secure the services of others, from washermen to Brahmins, untouchables need much more wealth, time, and manipulation than do other jatis.

When Pans tried to enter a village temple they were rudely turned away and the higher jatis united solidly to repel them. There were other confrontations in which the Pans were rebuffed. They then turned to outside sources of aid—police officials, government agents, even to a Minister of Orissa State, who happened to be in the vicinity when a confrontation was being staged. Educated Pans, especially those who have been in government service, are much more adept at appealing to officials than are villagers of higher jati rank but with limited social and political experience. The latter were thoroughly intimidated, Bailey comments, by the long and impressive list of people whom the Pans were able to interest in their troubles; they said that the outside world in general and the Congress Raj in particular were on the side of the Pans. Although they were not by any means ready to grant ritual respectability to the Pans, they were far less prepared to oppose them openly. Instead, the higher jatis seemed to be withdrawing from events and circumstances in which a test might be made. This new challenge and the response may well presage a shift away from the traditional processes of recurrent change.

Low-ranking jatis in many other places have drawn on wider political forces to hasten their rise. The Jatavs (ex-Chamars) of Agra City, for example, have done this in a much larger, better organized way than have the Pans of the remote hill village. They have forged modern political instruments of their own, including a political party that has exerted considerable influence on the Agra scene (Lynch 1968).

Dominant jatis as well have taken to maneuvering through political parties in order to maintain and enhance their status (of. Srinivas 1966, pp. 111–113) This shift to a wider arena of power is not a totally new procedure; able and highly ambitious men have long done so, though the method has become much more common in recent decades.

A historical example of the mobilization of wider resources for social rise is that of the Tagores of Bengal whose efforts to expunge a group blemish were mentioned in Chapter 23 above. Their example also illustrates the strength of opposition to a rise. Despite their great secular achievements, it was well into the twentieth century before they overcame the ritual stigma that orthodox Brahmins of Bengal had attached to their name since the seventeenth century. The Tagores are descended from Brahmins called Pirali who were a separate and beclouded jati of the Rahriya division of Bengal Brahmins (Risley 1892, vol. 2, p. 176). An eminent Tagore wrote out the tale told about their degradation, that their ancestor was tricked into a defiling act by a Muslim official, one Pirali Khan, whom he had offended. This story is convincingly impugned by J. N. Bhattacharya on the basis of internal evidence (1896, p. 123). He conjectures that the ancestor in question was probably a surveyor in the service of Pirali and, as sometimes happened, made himself unpopular by attempting to usurp titles to lands of other Brahmins. Presumably the landowners banded together to ostracize him, perhaps on the pretext given in the account.

Whatever the reason may have been, the Piralis were treated as outcastes by other Brahmins of Bengal in the seventeenth century. In the last decade of that century, one of them moved to the place where the East India Company had established a factory and which was to become the city of Calcutta. Few Brahmins lived in Calcutta during its early decades, most of the prospering residents were weavers by jari origin with a few from the trading jatis. In this frontier town, as we noted, they accepted the Tagores as Brahmins. The family prospered greatly, grew into a proliferating and influential lineage, and became so prominent that they even stimulated a leading Brahmin personage to "form a party for degrading them" (Bhattacharya 1896, p. 123). But the Tagores, as by then they were known (from the anglicization of the honorific term Thakur), were not to be denied and continued to grow in prosperity, fame, and numbers.

By the end of the nineteenth century, members of the Tagore lineages had greatly distinguished themselves in government service, in traditional religious piety, in reform sects, in scholarship, in the indigenous arts, as well as in commerce and industry (of. Kripalani 1962, pp. 14–32). Their most illustrious son, Rabindranath Tagore (born in 1861) was launched on his career of immense productivity. But their origins as Piralis were not forgotten in spite of the unsurpassed brilliance of Tagore accomplishments. When his family sought a bride for Rabindranath in 1883, their choice was mainly limited to the daughters of a few Pirali families in the small town of Jessore (Kripalani 1962, p. 112).

One commentator who extolled their contributions was moved to write, "If they are denounced as outcasts, such outcasts are the ornaments of the country" (S. C. Bose 1881, p. 175). And in 1896 Bhattacharya wrote, "From a long time the Tagores have been struggling hard to be restored to caste." He observed that they are very orthodox Hindus—with the exception of one family, headed by Rabindranath's father, that belonged to the reform sect of Brahmo Samaj. They could sometimes marry their girls expensively, to Brahmins of the Rahdiya division, but the groom "is himself reduced to the rank of a Pirali, and always demands a heavy premium as a *sine qua non.*" Bhattacharya summarized their rank as of 1896: "But the Tagores are now fast rising in the scale of caste. Poor Brahmins now more or less openly accept their gifts, and sometimes even their hospitality; and Sir J. M. Tagore is on the way towards acquiring an influence on the Pandits which may one day enable him to re-establish his family completely in caste" (1896, pp. 119, 124). Their caste disabilities were later overlooked, if not totally forgotten. Perhaps one reason it took some eight generations for the Tagores to achieve respectable rank among orthodox Brahmins was the very magnitude of their accomplishments, which drew envy and enmity as well as fame and fortune.

In all three of these cases, a status rise was accomplished by drawing on resources far beyond the village and its land. The Ganjam distillers followed a more traditional, Vaishya, route in doing so. The untouchable Pans in their backwoods home and the illustrious Tagores in the metropolis both have drawn upon modern political and educational resources.

JATI LEADERS AND LEADING GROUPS

Those who now lead a jati to higher rank have typically had some modern education and some experience with a greater world than than that of the village and its vicinity. To take the case of Sulli again, as a schoolteacher he had seen much more of towns, of different kinds of people, and of non-Kota standards than had his Kota contemporaries. He understood, for example, that the traditional Kota man's chignon was a token of social inferiority in the eyes of others and not, as most Kotas saw it, the ancient symbol of being a proper Kota man. He realized also that their traditional diet and occupations doomed them to invidious treatment by outsiders. At that time other Kotas were little involved with the Hindus who had come into the Nilgiri area.

Such leaders transmit to their jati fellows the values of the wider Indian civilization, both Sanskritic and modern. The traditional mobility tactics are carried out on a wider scale than before.

"The drama of Sanskritization is played on many a village stage, but the script may be written elsewhere, the star performers are often a travelling company, and the critics represent a greater and growing public" (Marriott 1959b, p. 105). A few men rise above the mobility strivings of their jati. A man who attains state or national office cannot keep his jati affiliations in the center of his attention. One who becomes an industrial magnate finds more engrossing pursuits than the uplift of his jati, though jati considerations usually remain paramount in his family life. Such men typically stand ready to help in jati causes, but they are often remote from them.

Their personal achievements are nevertheless of great interest to their jati fellows. The most successful within a jati are held up as demonstrators of the true worth and level of all the jati members. Thus Yadava publications proudly cite not only their mythical progenitors and their historical Rajas, but also contemporaries who have become learned scholars, rich industrialists, and high civil servants (Rao 1964; Khedkar 1959).

Similarly, the example of those sections of the jati that have won higher place in their localities gives heart to others in the jati who are still battling for such place. "Members of minority castes in Rampura occasionally told me with pride that in a particular village their castefolk were numerous and wealthy" (Srinivas 1959a, p. 4). They were trying to identify themselves with jati fellows whom they regarded as having a higher position than themselves. And on a wider scale, the clear success of a low group in raising their social position has a "demonstration effect" on all the lowest peoples in their region. "It was as though they suddenly woke up to the fact that they were no longer inhabiting a prison" (Srinivas 1966, p. 91).

At each step of a jati campaign, in any route of advance, strains are likely to develop within the jati. All jati members do not improve their resources and local standing at the same rate. Some families and lineages, some jati-groups are much more successful than others, but their victories also bring on new problems for them. Marked success attracts notice and tends to unify opposing forces. Thus with success the problems of maintaining internal unity are apt to be intensified. The most advanced groups may have reformed their practices so much that they can hardly bear to be considered as jati equals of those sections who still carry on the demeaning customs. Moreover, the success of one group tends to arouse challenges from within. We have noted that an alliance may be disrupted by the same forces that once helped cement it, namely the desire to challenge those next higher. So is it also within a jati when one group has advanced much more rapidly than others. Overcoming external opposition, as has been noted, is only one part of mobility tactics; maintaining internal unity is the other.

CHAPTER 26

Maintaining Internal Cohesion: Fission and Fusion

To raise their rank, the people of a jati have to act in unison. They must coordinate their acts of association and dissociation and mobilize against opposition. They must also display enough uniformity in ritual matters to establish a suitable rationale for their claims. So the leaders of a rising jati try to keep all their jati fellows up to the ritual mark; they exhort the laggard to reform, cajole the powerful to be patient, threaten to punish recusants. The ritual homogeneity they actually achieve does not need to be complete, but they cannot afford flagrant disunity. If some in a jati persist in eating meat and performing servile work while others proclaim their vegetarianism and occupational respectability, the mobility campaign will be undermined. Any claim by the reformed to higher rank is likely to be hooted down so long as their relatives and ritual compeers are so patently low.

This holds true for the maintenance as well as for the advancement of jati rank. The members of a jati, as we have seen, cannot tolerate a flagrant transgression of their ritual standards by anyone in the group. If such a violation becomes publicly known, the transgressor must be penalized; if he is not willing to take his punishment and recant, he must be made outcaste. Outcasting is a means of restoring the jati as a proper unit by redefining the membership of the group.

Redefinition of boundaries is also used to help raise jati rank. In the following chapters four kinds of regrouping are discussed. Two of them, fission and fusion, are usually direct efforts toward mobility. The other two, regrouping on religious grounds and the accretion of tribal peoples, often involve considerations of mobility.

Fission commonly comes about when the more prosperous and ritually meticulous families within a jati stop intermarrying with the less advanced families and declare themselves to be a separate jati. Fusion occurs when people of previously separate jatis begin to interdine, intermarry, and merge their mobility efforts, their main purpose being to increase their secular strength. Religious regrouping has occurred when converts to a religious movement have become a new jati. Personal salvation may be the original impetus for conversion but as the individual converts gather together, they tend to develop into a jati. The quest for spiritual improvement has often led to the usual quest for higher rank. The fourth kind of redefinition involves the flow of tribal peoples into caste society. There are still many millions in India who maintain tribal forms of society, but there has been a continual transformation of tribal groups into jatis. Once a new jati is formed, through any of these processes of redefinition and regrouping, it is maintained in the same way as are other jatis of the same loaclity and of similar social level.

Fission

There are several reasons for jati fission. A common one is that some families have taken to a different occupation, have prospered beyond the others, and have gained a better means of acquiring power and education. Migration of part of a jati has often led to eventual fission. The outcasting of a whole section of a jati has sometimes occurred, as has the establishment of a new jati as a result of clandestine unions. Occasionally a jati has split because some have taken on a different reference model from that held by others of their jati.

Jati division because of occupational separation was noted by British observers of the eighteenth century (of. Raghuvanshi 1966, pp. 169–171), and continued to be mentioned in later ethnographic reports. In the Punjab report of the 1883 census, Ibbetson wrote that it was common for some members of a low group to change their occupation (as from scavenging to weaving) to separate from their former fellows, and thereby to gain in rank; "each caste throws out off-shoots into the grade above that which is occupied by the greater number of its members" (1916, p. 267). From Rajasthan, Baines cited the example of a jati of watchmen-raiders, some of whom became farmers and split away from the main group. Those who remained watchmen held themselves to be the superior at first, "Now, however, the cultivator has advanced in prosperity and refuses to recognize the older section as its superior or even as its equal" (1912, p. 82).

From Uttar Pradesh (then called United Provinces), Blunt listed a number of "relatively new instances of fission, having been reported for the first time at the Census of 1911." One new case was of tailors who took the name scribe-tailors (Kayastha-Darzi) "and have published a monograph on their ethnology" of the kind usually produced by groups trying to rise in the social scale (1931, pp. 54–55, 216). In an instance from Madras, O'Malley cited a report that among some Harijans "there is growing up a special superior caste known as Quinsap, namely those who have served and are descended from those who have served in the Queen's Own Sappers and Miners" (O'Malley 1934, p. 9).

Risley noted in Bengal a stage of partial separation among the Pods, a group of fishermen and cultivators of the districts near Calcutta. He reported that those Pods who were educated would no longer give their daughters in marriage to the noneducated although they would still take brides from them, perhaps because there were not enough marriageable girls among the families of the educated. "But this will right itself in the course of time," Risley was sure, "and they will follow the classic precedent of the twice-born classes and will marry only within their own group" (1915, pp. 164–165, also pp. 118–119, 157–158).

Although such hypergamous distinctions are known in Bengal, the complete break predicted by Risley in the case of the Pods had not occurred a half century after he made the forecast. The educated among the Pods did mount a mobility campaign of the usual type, as Jaya Datta Gupta reports (1959). They succeeded in changing the name Pod to a more mellifluous term, an end they had special reason to desire. As their leaders noted in a 1956 appeal addressed to the President of India, the Bengali term "Pod" is synonymous with "rectum" in English. "Even in this age of marked progress," their appeal stated, "wherever members of this community move in bazars or in public places, in villages or on farms, in every sphere of activities, they are purposely called and insulted directly or indirectly by this word 'Pod'" (Datta Gupta 1959, p. 126). They have been justifiably successful in changing this name, at least officially; their other mobility goals seem not yet to have been fully achieved.

Migration has also been a main cause of jati fission. A number of families move to a new locale, drawn by opportunities for land or work—sometimes driven by wars and famines—and gradually their ties with their original group become attenuated. They find it difficult to arrange marriages and keep up affinal relations over a long distance. If they have moved into a different language area, they may cling tenaciously to their original speech and customs through many generations, but even so they will adapt in some degree to the practices of their new region. Their cultural drift adds to the schism and they eventually become a wholly separate jati.

Although only a very small percentage of the population has migrated in any one period (except at the time of national partition), there has nevertheless been some migration throughout recent centuries.[1] Many tracts of land were brought under plow cultivation after the advent of the British regime. Migration to them was motivated more by a search for food and material security than by a quest for rank and ritual respectability, but if the migrants prospered in the new territory, they sometimes established a new jati that ranked higher in its local order than did the parent jati in the old homeland. A modern instance, mentioned previously, is that of the settlers on the reclaimed lands of the Bengal delta.

Families may migrate because of population pressure. There may be too many barbers or carpenters or laborers for a given locality to support; many a cultivator has found his land too small and has struck out for emptier spaces. A migrant jati usually maintains its separate social identity in the new locale, even though jatis of similar occupation and rank are also there. We have noted two jatis of immigrant distillers in Bisipara village. In Ramkheri the indigenous Malwa carpenters are separate from the carpenters who came into the village from Mewar, although the Mewari's genealogical records indicate that the immigration took place many centuries ago. The Mewari carpenters are themselves split into two endogamous bodies, of older and newer migrants (Mayer 1960, pp. 157–158).

Another kind of jati fission, exemplified in the villages around Ramkheri, is the creation of an "outcaste" jati. Whole jati-groups or lineages may be excommunicated quite as an individual or a family may be. In this locality the Rajputs of twelve villages were ostracized for reasons that were not divulged to outsiders. They became a separate endogamous and commensal group (1960, pp. 154–155).

[1] In medieval South India, families could raise their rank within a short time by moving to a new location. "A section which moved out became a separate endogamous *jāti* after the lapse of several years, and true to caste tradition, each such *jāti* claimed to be superior to the others" (Srinivas 1966, p. 44).

The villages of this vicinity provide an example of jati separation, if not exactly of fission, that has resulted from clandestine unions between members of different jatis. There is a jati called Rajgeria Khati (farmers) whose members do not openly intermarry with the other Khati of the locality. The Rajgeria Khati are said to be descended from offspring of Rajput landowners and their farmer servant girls. Liaisons between masters and servant girls have long gone on; the men may acknowledge their children and provide for them although they cannot take them into their jati. The children of such unions were presumably raised by their Khati mothers and so became a kind of Khati even though they could not be admitted as a member of that jati either. There is some percolation of the Rajgeria Khati into the main Khati group by the girls who may quietly be taken in marriage by men of poor families among the Khati proper (Mayer 1960, p. 155).

A similar group came into being among the Jews of Cochin in Kerala, as we shall note again in discussing religion-based jatis. They formed a third jati of Cochin Jews, called Brown Jews, separate from the White and the Black Jews. The Brown Jews were descendants of unions between White Jews and servant girls who lived in the Jewish households and followed Jewish practices. Hence their children grew up in the Jewish streets, attended the synagogue and the Hebrew school, although they were relegated to an outer annex in each (Mandelbaum 1939). Unlike the Rajgeria Khati, their main affiliation was with the jati and customs of their fathers.[2]

Jati separation has also come about when one part of a jati has taken a reference model different from that held by the rest of the group. This occurred among the Coorgs of South India. In November 1834, some Coorgs severed their ties with the others in a threadtaking ritual on the banks of the Kaveri River and took the name Amma Coorgs. The main branch of the Coorgs were then landowning cultivators of warrior tradition. The Amma Coorgs chose to adopt Brahmin rather than Kshatriya ways; those who participated in the rite became lay disciples of a Brahmin monastery. The Amma Coorgs have an origin story telling of their common descent from a Coorg father and a Brahmin mother; whatever the genealogical facts may have been, the jati was founded to follow a more Brahminized mode of life than that led by the other Coorgs. The Amma Coorgs, Srinivas comments, "exemplify a tendency which has always been present in the caste system: a small group of people break off from a larger whole of which they are part, Sanskritize their customs and ritual, and achieve a higher status than their parent-body in the course of a few decades" (1952a, pp. 34–35, 165–166).

The act of jati secession may be dramatically announced, as it was with the Amma Coorgs, although more usually it is quietly and tacitly effected; in either case, however, the split typically comes at the end of a series of strained relations and after a critical threshold for tolerance has been passed. There are countervailing pressures to remain as one jati, just as among a set of quarreling brothers, there are reasons to remain together. Not every jati splits whose families have taken to different callings and have very different fortunes. In earlier centuries families of highly disparate fortune remained in one jati and all in a jati did not follow the jati's ascribed occupation. So is it also

[2] During their existence, the Brown Jews were a very small group and finding marriage partners for their children was always difficult. By the 1960s the group was virtually extinct as a jati. Most of them had been quite well educated, one or two had married into the White Jews, the others had married spouses of similar education or profession from other Kerala religions and jatis. Although mixed offspring were traditionally ranked lower than either parent in Kerala (Alyappan 1937, p. 14), the modern education acquired by most members of this group enabled them to transcend the traditional barriers.

in modern times. To take some examples from the account of Ramkheri village, there is no ritual separation there between the Nai who remain barbers and those who have become landowners, or between the Nath who seek alms and those who have become farmers. Some of the village Chamars are farmers only but they maintain their connections with those who continue to work with hides and leather (Mayer 1956, p. 132). Studies have not yet been made as to why some jatis have split while others, under similar strain, have not. But some indication of the reasons are found in Pocock's comments on the history of the Patidar jatis.

The several jatis of Patidars in central Gujarat have not fragmented further, although in the census reports of the nineteenth century only a few of those who are now known as Patidars had taken that name and there was a wide gulf in manners and wealth between them and their jati fellows who had not yet changed their name. Pocock writes that a contemporary observer might then have reasonably anticipated more fission, which did not occur. One reason may have been their separation into ranked hypergamous sections through which ritual and secular differences could be marked within a Patidar jati without changing the idea of jati endogamy. Pocock suggests also that the increase in agricultural income throughout the region, especially from tobacco growing, helped all groups of Patidars and narrowed economic differences among them. Even famine and plague conditions at the end of the nineteenth century did not widen economic disparities among Patidars because poorer families were impelled to try their fortunes in East Africa where most of them did well. The earnings they sent back to their kin in the home villages helped to lift the lot of these formerly poor families (1957b, pp. 30–31).[3]

Jati Separation and Political Affiliation: The Jatavs

When cohesive forces do not prevail, those who break away exclude themselves from the previous relations with their former jati fellows, and try to include themselves with some other, higher category. The Jatavs of Agra City, as described by Owen Lynch (1968), provide an example of fission in the classical manner combined with modern political coalition. The purposes of their jati fission as well as of their political affiliation were the same, namely the status rise and material benefit of the group.

Jatavs number about one-sixth of the city's population and began as Chamars who performed the traditional lowly tasks of this jati-cluster, working in hides and leather, occasionally scavenging, mainly doing hired labor. Toward the end of the nineteenth century some of them managed to get a foothold as contractors for municipal construction in addition to contracting for hides and scavenging. Two brothers even became mill owners. Some few Chamars in Agra City thus lifted themselves out of the dismal poverty that was the usual lot of village Chamars.

In the 1920s there rose in Agra a shoe and leather industry of a modern kind (though it was far from a rationalized, integrated industry) which produced for a national, even an international,

[3] Patidars of central Gujarat were united also in their opposition to the local Rajputs, who had been rulers of the state in earlier centuries and were dominant in many villages. Gradually, Srinivas and Shah comment, they asserted their ritual superiority to Rajputs. "At the present moment, Patidars do not accept water or cooked food from Rajputs" (1960, p. 1377). In Chapter 27 we note how Rajputs have responded to this through the formation of a modern caste federation.

market. Chamar entrepreneurs were among the leading figures in this industry; their labor force was Chamar, and factory work became virtually the only occupation of their jati fellows in the city. As workers and owners they not only prospered but they had really shifted to a new occupation, one that was without jajmani implications or village sanctions, even though it still involved working in leather. Moreover, the industrial Chamars became more residentially segregated in the city and so were sharply separated from other Chamars both in occupation and residence.

They were now able to send their children to school. The sons of the earlier Chamar entrepreneurs had either attended schools run by missionaries or by the Arya Samaj reform sect, or government schools. The Arya Samaj was an important influence because it offered access to Sanskritic scriptures and practices. The educated young men seized on the ritual symbols and practices thus offered though they were not as enthusiastic about Arya Samaj advocacy of a casteless society. These educated men did not want to abolish caste society but rather to gain a higher place in it. They successfully founded organizations for their jati's advancement in 1917, 1924, and 1930. By 1924 they had also produced a book to prove that they were really Jatavs by name, of ancient Kshatriya heritage. They dissociated themselves from all who were Chamars and even rejected the claim of another rising Chamar group, called Guliya, that they too were Jatavs. When a Swami came to Agra and preached to them about the abolition of caste and endogamy, he was driven out of the city by the leaders of the Jatav movement.

They pressed vigorously in the 1930s to be listed as Jatavs in government publications and to be completely separated from Chamars in official procedures, and they eventually succeeded in this. At the same time, they insisted on being listed with the "Scheduled Castes," the government roster of disadvantaged groups, largely untouchables, who are eligible for special governmental grants and preferments. Many another low jati has been involved in a similar contradiction that is more apparent than real. To men of such jatis it is not an embarrassing contradiction at all; one naturally takes advantage of all that can be had from government, certainly under the British regime, and securing such benefits has little to do with the real sphere of jati relationships. The more serious contradiction for the Jatavs lay in the fact that they were still leatherworkers and while they might carry off a new name and improved ritual practices, they still were weighted down, in the traditional perspective, by the burden of a demeaning occupation. This may have made other means of social improvement, through modern political moves, all the more attractive to them.

The Jatavs began political participation in the 1920s when they petitioned government officials to appoint Jatav representatives to legislative councils and administrative boards. Such appointments were in the gift of the officials, mainly British, who thought it proper that qualified members of lowly groups should have a representative voice in these advisory and administrative bodies. As the nationalist political movement grew, the Agra Jatav organization took political stands and affiliated with similar groups. By 1944–45 the Jatav organization had joined politically with the Agra Scheduled Castes Federation, which was part of the national federation led by the great Harijan leader, Dr. Ambedkar.

In the sphere of party politics the Jatavs were thus allying themselves with some of the same untouchable people from whom they were strenuously trying to dissociate in the sphere of traditional ritual relations. Again the anomaly was more apparent to outside observers than real to the participants. The real issue to them was the material and social improvement of the jati and its members. With the growing postindependence realization of the power of the vote and of elected officials, the educated Jatavs became increasingly concerned with gains in governmental politics rather than with ritual symbols. Some of them followed Dr. Ambedkar's lead in calling themselves Buddhists, as a means of opting out of any system of caste, but this move has been discouraged by the fact that governmental grants to the disadvantaged are specifically for low-ranking Hindus, and they do not want to define themselves out of that category.

Agra Jatavs were prominent in the formation of a new political party, the Republican Party, which was based mainly on lower jatis and on those estranged from the dominant party. It included a diversity of groups—Muslims, Harijans of various kinds, as well as Jatavs; one of the principal leaders was of Vaishya origin. The Jatav coalition with these groups resembles the alignment of a jati-group in a contest between village alliances; it is short term, limited to purposes of political gain, and involves no redefinition of Jatav identity.

Jatav endogamy is not breached nor is Jatav solidarity replaced by allegiance to the Republican or any other party. If some of the symbols of higher jati rank are no longer as prized as they were, the jati as a main identity and focus of loyalty is by no means jettisoned. A rising group like the Jatavs seizes on modern mobility resources, particularly through higher education and political stratagems, but its members continue to hold themselves apart from, indeed to obliterate the memory of, any former associations that might impede their rise.

Forces for Fusion

As the advantages of consolidation became clear, *sabhas* (caste associations; literally, assemblies or leagues) were organized at every social level in all parts of the country. The great impetus to sabha organization came with the Census of 1901 (as was noted in Chapter 25) when the idea spread that the Census could be used as an arena for mobility efforts (Srinivas 1966, pp. 94–100). Jatis in the same cluster joined forces to change the name of their cluster and to press together for governmental advantages. Such associations usually aim for a permanent merging of group identities, unlike the temporary political coalitions of the Jatav case.

While modern democratic conditions have favored fusion, an example of the amalgamation of jatis was noted in the nineteenth century. The goldsmiths of northern India were consolidating their highly fragmented groups, which were "subdivided to an astonishing extent" (Baines 1912, p. 60). They were thinly dispersed, since even a large village could support only a few goldsmith families. When roads were poor and communications uncertain, only a small number of these families could join within a single compass of endogamy. As communications improved, they began to enlarge the area of their marriage alliances and so to enlarge the jati beyond an uncomfortably small number of families.

Caste associations are now established to advance the material welfare and the social status of all members. Their leaders commonly urge intermarriage among all jatis in the association as the main way to guarantee continuing unity and the benefits of unity. But such intermarriages usually come after other beneficial functions are well established. In the next chapter, some characteristic forms and functions of caste associations are discussed; it is useful here to note some tendencies toward fusion apart from the context of a formal association.

To take examples again from Ramkheri village in Dewas district of Madhya Pradesh, two jati-groups of oil-pressers (Telis) there have almost completely merged. Those who immigrated from the Mewar area and those indigenous to Malwa began to interdine and intermarry about 1915;

during the 1950s they sat in the same jati panchayat and shared in other jati functions, but still kept different names. Both were then adopting the same new name, however, and were on the verge of becoming one jati. The reason these two jati-groups have united, while two jatis of carpenters and two of goatherds in the village remain separate, may possibly be the strong mobility drive, noted earlier, among the Telis of Ramkheri. This kind of expansion of jati boundaries is comparable to the expansion of a kinship circle by an ambitious and prospering man who turns kinsmen of recognition into kinsmen of cooperation. Similarly he and his jati-fellows may take some who are recognizably close in ritual status into full jati relations.

Fusion also occurs at the top of a local order, for reasons relevant to family rather than jati mobility. Among the twelve Brahmin jatis in Sripuram in Tanjore district, two pairs are beginning to intermarry. Each merging jati is already close to the other in sectarian orientation, language and ceremonial practice. Béteille points out that the "general trend towards the contraction of structural distance between proximate segments" stems from secular and Western influences. The style of life of the different Brahmin jati has become more similar as it has become more secular and the importance of differences of ritual detail has diminished (1965, pp. 74, 78, 220).

Moreover, an urbanized Brahmin wants to have his daughter marry into a family of comparable education and wealth. If no such match is found in his own jati he will arrange for a suitable groom of a close Brahmin jati, much preferring that his daughter marry an educated boy of a not-too-different jati rather than an uneducated person of his own. He hastens the merging of jatis in order to maintain his family's status and his daughter's welfare.

A man's views of jati fusion are likely to depend on his education and social experience. This was noted in Chapter 14 where Srinivas' comment was cited that an elderly, rural, and illiterate Okkaliga in Mysore may not regard Okkaligas of other districts and divisions as Okkaligas at all. But an Okkaliga lawyer or doctor would regard all the divisions as equally Okkaliga and might give his daughter in marriage to the son of an urbanized and educated Okkaliga who lived in quite a distant part of Mysore, provided the family were educationally and economically of the proper status (Srinivas 1966, p. 115).

The wealthier members of a jati have long had a wider geographic radius of marriage than the poor, and now the more educated, who are generally wealthier also, extend their marriage alliances across jati as well as district boundaries. They rarely marry their children into families of a different varna or jati-cluster from theirs, but rather into a family of comparable modern attainments that shares similar jati status and ritual practices, and speaks the same language.

Resolutions which urge intermarriage among the several jatis of a caste association are commonly adopted at association conventions. These help pave the way for the widening of endogamy, but it is mainly a family's concern for the welfare of its children and the improvement of its status that actually brings about such marriages.

The quest for status impels coordination among close jatis in many other ways besides the ultimate test of endogamy. Resources from far beyond a local social order can now be marshaled to lift a jati in the social hierarchy. To command such resources—of government, education, commerce, and the professions—jati members feel that they need the strength of a broader organization than that of the jati alone. The main trend of jati regrouping, therefore, is toward fusion among close jatis, partly on the level of family unions but particularly through caste associations.

CHAPTER 27

Modern Means for Jati Improvement: Associations and Federations

Caste associations can be much more than just new means for carrying on the recurrent struggles for jati mobility. Some indeed are little more than that, but others have been built up into effective agencies for modern education and for participation in political democracy. As jati members become increasingly educated and involved in state politics, they are likely to alter their views about personal and jati goals. The modern forms of jati organization may have a formidable effect on Indian society. Just how formidable that effect has been and is likely to be remains to be gauged by further studies. It is useful to show here some of the bases on which these associations have been founded and some developing trends in their functions.

These associations have been founded on traditional organizations of various kinds, as is illustrated by the examples discussed in this chapter. The Jats of the districts north of Delhi have revived an old league for military defence. The Iravas (Tiyyas) of Kerala have joined together as followers of a réligious teacher. The Telis of Orissa have used their traditional panchayat apparatus. The caste associations in Kanpur City have been organized on several different social bases.

The beginnings of association functions are seen in the case of the potters of western Uttar Pradesh. The Vanniyar and Nadar associations of Tamil Nadu (Madras) show more advanced development, in which association members have had considerable political and organizational experience. Finally, a caste federation is discussed, that of the Kshatriya Sabha of Gujarat; this federation does not seek endogamous merging, as do many associations, but mainly the pooling of political strength.

Whatever the base for a caste association, its leaders generally use parliamentary procedures in their meetings and emulate the organizational style of the main political parties. Each association is intended as an agency for the welfare and uplift of its constituency. Improvement in the education of the children is a constant theme. Reform in both the traditional and the modern modes is urged. Communication is typically fostered by a journal that carries news of association activities and such items as advertisements for potential grooms and brides.

A Jat Confederacy Revived

An old organization that has been revived is that of the Jats in the districts of the Meerut Division of Uttar Pradesh (Pradhan 1965; 1966). These Jats maintained defensive leagues into the nineteenth century, but the leagues lapsed after the uprisings of 1857. After 1947 Jat leaders began to realize that large collective organizations were needed once again, to give strength to political representations and to bolster modern mobility efforts. Jats were still the dominant landowners in their territory, but they sensed the new conditions for power.

In 1950 the first large panchayat since 1857 was assembled, attended by the hereditary leader of all eighteen clan areas of the Meerut Division. This meeting concentrated on the reform of Jat marriage practices and resolved that the amount of wealth expended on weddings should be reduced and that the overweening superiority of groom's family to bride's family should be lessened in a general raising of the status of women. These resolutions, M. C. Pradhan observes, "have had a profound effect upon the people of Meerut Division" (1965, p. 1861). At the next convocation, in 1956, one leader estimated that the Jats and other people of the area had saved 750 million rupees (then the equivalent of some 150 million dollars) in five years. Allowing for forensic rhetoric, it seems quite probable that a considerable amount of wealth was made available for capital investment and other productive uses through compliance with the resolutions. Their enforcement produced additional capital; the fines collected from defaulters were given to existing schools or used to build schools in the clan area. By the third assembly, in 1963, the goals for Jat improvement were enlarged. Better educational facilities were proposed, specifically a girls' college and two military colleges. National, defense, increased agricultural productivity, and the removal of "caste distinctions and barriers" were espoused, as was also the protection of cows from slaughter.

One reason for the success of this revived organization is that the component lineages and clans had been kept as viable economic and political units after the military functions of the larger league had been abandoned. The Jats of this area continue to use their traditional panchayats rather than those elected under governmental auspices. The strength of Jat society is further demonstrated by the strong allegiance of educated Jats to their natal communities. Pradhan writes that Jats who have served in the army, in the civil service, or in other modern jobs outside their home area like to return to live in their villages when they retire. "I did not come across even one case where a Jat had sold his property in his native village and had settled down in a city" (Pradhan 1965, p. 1863).

A Religious Foundation: The Iravas of Kerala

Another strong caste association, but one formed at a different social level and cemented by religious appeal, is that of the Iravas of Kerala, who are also known as Ezhavas or Tiyyas and make up more than 40 percent of Kerala Hindus. Their traditional occupation was the making and sale of alcoholic beverage, an occupation that consigned them to low rank in the rigid hierarchy of this region.

In 1854 there was born into one of their families in a village near Trivandrum a child who became the great sage and reformer for all the Iravas. He became known as Sri Narayana Guru and, as Aiyappan writes, his history is the modern history of the Iravas. "Religion has been the greatest of all integrative forces in social life, and Sri Narayana's reforms which welded the Iravas into one powerful community were all through religion" (1944, p. 151). He preached open access to Sanskritic observances by all people and advocated a casteless society. His influence did not extend much beyond his fellow Iravas, but among them it had great effect and led to the establishment of a strong association, which has been used for political advance as well as for internal ritual reform.

Intermarriage among the several jatis of the Irava cluster has gone on for decades, in keeping with the appeal of their great sage. The religious appeal also brought about considerable reform of Irava practices. The opposition of higher groups was so strong, however, that their social rise was relatively slow until recent years, when they have been able to benefit from their voting strength and from the new political environment (Aiyappan 1944, pp. 151–162, 188–194; 1965, pp. 147–169; Gough 1963, pp. 192–194; Hardgrave 1964, p. 1847).

A Modernized Panchayat Organization: Telis of Orissa

The association of Telis in Orissa continues with its traditional maintenance functions while pressing for innovative reform measures. In mid-twentieth century Teli leaders were still engrossed in internal tasks and had only begun to take interest in external, political activities.

The Telis are traditionally pressers and sellers of oil, an occupation that is not highly esteemed in the traditional view. They are quite numerous in Puri and adjoining districts of Orissa and have long had an extensive panchayat organization. Their modern association is thoroughly rooted in villages through the old panchayat ties and seems quite well adapted for both the traditional panchayat purposes and for reform (Patnaik and Ray 1960). The traditional pattern includes formal panchayats of higher and of lower jurisdiction. In the 1950s these councils still assessed fines, prescribed purifications, outcast errant offenders.

Patnaik and Ray have analyzed 203 cases, dated between 1942 and 1959, in the records of a panchayat jurisdiction called the "Dominion of Eight-Regions," one of the six in Puri district. Two-thirds of these cases dealt with marriage problems, property and financial disputes, and with the violation of jati standards. Others had to do with sexual crimes, requests for financial assistance, and organizational matters such as the appointment of headmen. In one case the elders of a component jurisdiction were themselves declared outcaste because they had not stopped a woman from giving false testimony in a court case, presumably to the detriment of the jati's larger interests (Patnaik and Ray 1960, pp. 17–20). The council of this Dominion, which covers seventy wards of oilmen, not only assumes judicial jurisdiction over difficult problems but also is prepared to take action to enforce its decisions.

A central concern of council meetings and especially of larger assemblies is the program for Teli improvement and uplift. The preamble to the regulations adopted by one Dominion states that many evils have crept into their society, and so the officeholders are authorized to frame and implement rules to free the society from its present blemishes. The explanatory myth is then given, that Telis were formerly respectable, prospering merchants engaged in overseas trade, who, when the main

Orissa ports were closed (through no fault of theirs), were forced to resort to the less respectable occupation of crushing oilseeds. They lost not only their good livelihood but also their ancient level of education. "Everyone should therefore try to promote education and culture in our caste" (Patnaik and Ray 1960, pp. 25, 31, 44).

Education is vigorously advocated in resolutions adopted at almost every assembly; repeatedly Telis are told "that all boys of the jati must learn to read and that needy school boys should be helped from the Assembly's funds." An all-Orissa convention of Telis in 1959 adopted a resolution on education that opened with the comment that most Telis are very poor. "They feel keenly the need of educating their children. Let us encourage the education of children, and build up funds for the grant of scholarships" (Patnaik and Ray 1960, pp. 40, 74). The repetition of this resolution over the years, without mention of schools that have been built or scholarships granted, may indicate that there has been some lag in setting up educational facilities.

Ritual improvement has also been a constant theme in these resolutions. Divorce and remarriage are deprecated, sale of cattle to butchers condemned, peddling of pan (prepared betel leaf and areca nut) prohibited as a debasing occupation (Patnaik and Ray 1960, pp. 22, 29–36, 42–43). The repeated adoption of such resolutions through the years may also bespeak some failure to enforce them. The traditional name, Teli, with its disparaging overtones is rejected and a new, more respectable name meaning "merchants" is taken.

The general policy of most jati associations, that of combining traditional steps and modern measures, is summarized in a resolution adopted by the Teli association. "It is necessary [for us] to observe the old laws which have been in vogue from ancient times; while, at the same time, new regulations should be adopted in consonance with the times" (Patnaik and Ray 1960, p. 26). The two are not necessarily compatible, however; questions of priority arise. For example, there was heated debate at the all-Orissa meeting in 1959 on a proposed *dharmashala*, a pilgrims' lodge, in the pilgrimage center of Puri. To build such a lodge would be a traditional act of piety that would provide a center where jati fellows from various parts of the state could meet and become imbued, under religious auspices, with a spirit of jati solidarity (cf. Mayer 1960, p. 255). The proposal was opposed by younger delegates who argued "that instead of erecting a mansion which does not particularly serve the interests of the caste, it would be a hundred times better to build a hostel for students belonging to the caste" (Patnaik and Ray 1960, p. 72).

At the same assembly, free intermarriage among the three main jatis of Telis in Orissa was once again espoused. The anthropologist who attended this meeting happened to be sitting next to an elderly delegate as one speaker, a prominent Congress Party worker and a leader in the Sabha, was advocating the merging of the three into one endogamous unit. The old man whispered that it could not happen now, and, pointing to the speaker said, "I am a Haladia Teli by caste. Will he agree to marry my daughter to his son? He will then be outcasted. I will also not dare to give my son in marriage to his daughter from whose hand no one in my family would accept water" (Patnaik and Ray 1960, p. 77). Sabha collaboration for him stopped short of endogamy. But the younger and educated members of that assembly felt no reluctance and were beginning to arrange such marriages. The president of that conference even advocated the "establishment of friendly and marital relationships with oilmen in other parts of India." This association and others in Orissa had, in the 1950s, taken relatively little part in local and state politics as similar associations in Madras and in other states had done for decades.

Caste Associations of Kanpur City

In any caste association, the prime movers toward fusion and modern reform are likely to be those who have a modern education. They are concentrated in the cities, and the headquarters of an association is likely to be in a city. A study of eight caste associations in Kanpur City illustrates both their variety and their similarities.

The organization of the Kanya Kubja Brahmins was the first in the city in 1915. Its purposes were only those of education, and having securely established an Education Trust that maintains secondary schools the association became defunct. Brahmin concern with education was not new, but the push for modern education, which included education for girls and even night classes for women, was a departure (Nandi 1965, pp. 87–88).

The organization of the sweepers was the last to be founded, in 1957. But it began in strength, with aid from the All-India Sweepers' Association in Delhi, and with a government grant. The initial enrollment was 3000 members. It too provides education, especially primary education for children. A main reform purpose is to reduce the drinking and gambling habits of the jati's men. Other reforms are less emphasized, perhaps because they must await educational and economic improvements (Nandi 1965, pp. 94–95).

The other associations in Kanpur spread a wider net for reform. The Omar Vaishya tradesmen, for example, advocate educational and economic cooperation and also reform of marriage practices. Some of their resolutions have apparently been followed, such as the abolition of dancing by prostitutes at weddings. Others, like the reduction of dowries, have been given mainly lip service. The latter is a characteristic reform effort to reduce disparities within the group between the families of bride and groom. It may also be a gesture toward reducing the social disparity between men and women through upgrading the status of a bride and her family in relation to the groom and his family (Nandi 1965, pp. 91–93; Fox 1967, pp. 580–582).

Whatever specific reforms are urged at association conventions, more and better education for their children is almost always part of the improvement program. All agree on this, old and young, wealthy and poor, the better educated as well as the illiterate.

An Incipient Association: Potters of Western U.P.

Potters in the western districts of U.P. and in Delhi State have special difficulties in organizing. Though hundreds of thousands of them live in this territory, they are dispersed and are not numerically strong in any one locality; consequently they cannot hope to marshal decisive voting strength on their own. Moreover, the dominant landowners in many of their villages are Jats who, as we have seen, are quite effective in keeping control of the land.

These potters have little opportunity to obtain an economic base for jati mobility and they are, to boot, increasingly threatened by technological displacement. Blocked from economic opportunities, knowing little about the "twice-born" models and not much interested in them, their aspirations are focused on modern education. Very few of them have yet had much education, but it is the one glittering avenue of promise to better jobs, more prestige, and a higher standard of life for the individual and the group. Even with few educated people in their number, the strains between educated and uneducated leaders, which were noted among Telis and other groups, are already apparent.

Their incipient organization has been studied by Veena Monga (1967), who stayed in the potters' camp during one of the great annual festivals at Gadh Mukhteshwar on the banks of the Ganges. A great market fair takes place at the same time as the religious festival; the potters are especially active in the market for donkeys, mules, and horses, the animals they use to transport their wares. Potters stay in their own encampment during the days of this religious event. With several thousands in camp, they can call panchayat meetings to settle disputes and association assemblies to debate resolutions.

Their association has had a tenuous career since 1924; it lapsed and then was revived. In 1967 there was a Sabha tent in the potter encampment. About twenty men, who were addressed as "Pradhan," heads of their local associations, congregated there. Two of these men had some modern education—one was a librarian and the other a practitioner of indigenous medicine. Several other educated men were present and took part in the association discussions.

The educated are clearly the elite; their dress, speech, and manners are accorded highest prestige and respect. One of the richest potters in the camp lived quite like the poorer ones; none of his family had a single change of clothes nor were their meals any more sumptuous than those of poorer potters. The main difference was that the rich man was educating all his grandsons. So prized is education that in the potters' discussions Harijans are held up as "an ideal example" of how to secure educational benefits from the government.

The more traditional leaders, however, are not very easy about the educated among them. They feel them to be condescending and quite impractical. The educated, for their part, try to show some formal respect for the illiterate leaders, but hold themselves to be much better. Even an educated man must depend on his jati fellows; only with their children can he arrange marriages for his sons and daughters (Monga 1967, p. 1054). Endogamy remains a force, as G. S. Ghurye has noted in many writings, that binds the members of a jati, the educated as well as the illiterate, in all parts of the country (1961, pp. 209–210).

A division of function has begun to appear in the affairs of the potters' association. The older, uneducated leaders continue to settle disputes and maintain the jati's unity, matters at which the educated are not competent because of their lack of relevant experience and interest. The educated men are given the lead in initiating educational measures and reforms, and in relations with officials. At the time of Monga's observations these potters, as a group, had scarcely begun to participate in state politics. But as an association becomes more effective in internal cohesion and improvement, its leaders tend to look to improving its external relations, especially in politics. The political activities of the Yadava and Jatav associations have been noted above. Two other associations illustrate the development of such political functions.

Political Engagement: The Vanniyar Association

The Vanniyar and Nadar associations of Madras State share a similar political history. Both groups were engaged in mobility efforts in the first half of the nineteenth century; both achieved considerable economic gains and internal reforms in the first half of the twentieth century; both overcame strong opposition to their rise; both used their associations to gain political benefits; and both eventually withdrew their associations from party affiliation. These case histories illustrate a significant new social factor, the effect of the caste association in bringing its members into the processes of political democracy.

The Vanniyar number nearly 10 percent of the Madras State population, and in the four northern districts where they are concentrated they comprise about one fourth the population. Some are still landless laborers but many have become landowners, modern artisans, and tradesmen. The former jati divisions among them have been modified in recent times.

A record of 1833 shows that Vanniyars petitioned even then for an official decree that they were not "of low caste." They were among the first to use the Census for mobility claims, petitioning in 1871 to be listed as Kshatriyas. Their association was founded in 1888. By 1891 one of their educated men had produced the usual book to assert and document their merit, and by 1931 their former name no longer appeared in official records (Thurston 1909, Vol. 6, pp. 1–28; Rudolph and Rudolph 1960, pp. 13–15; 1967, pp. 49–63).

After national independence opened new opportunities for improvement, the Vanniyar association became politically active. Lloyd and Susanne Rudolph have traced the history and shown the results of their activities. The association pressed the Congress Party for jobs and preferment for Vanniyars. When that party did not respond to their satisfaction, they contested elections as independents. They were most interested in elections to the district boards, not only because they could muster decisive voting strength in certain districts but also—and this is generally true of the political efforts of caste associations—"because the subjects falling under the competence of district boards, especially educational and medical facilities and road building, were of the greatest local and political interest" (1960, pp. 16–17).

Vanniyars generally did well as independent candidates; in 1951 a Vanniyar political party was formed which soon split into two parties. Their candidates nevertheless could mobilize Vanniyar voters, using the traditional panchayat network. In the 1952 elections they won 13 percent of the seats in the Madras legislature. Vanniyars naturally voted for candidates of their name and grouping, who presumably understood their needs and shared their aspirations. In this traditional mode of alignment in a partisan context, they were repeating the initial, and often continuing, trend wherever democratic elections are established.

The two Vanniyar parties were later dissolved, their leaders joining other parties. But the Vanniyar association has flourished and has steadily pressed for political benefits. It has worked for educational gains, schools for the children, scholarships and academic support for the youth. It has sought civil service jobs and political appointments for Vanniyars. It has urged general development projects, hydroelectric schemes, roads, and land reform, which benefit all in the localities where Vanniyars live.

The Vanniyar secured some governmental advantage by having themselves officially classified as a "Backward Class" and so entitled to certain preferments. As was noted before, this formal classification as a disadvantaged, and presumably low-ranking, group is not seen as hampering the group's claims to higher status in the real ranking of village life. Vanniyars have markedly improved their ranking as well as their general political and economic position. A notable part of this rise has been accomplished through their caste association (Rudolph and Rudolph 1960, pp. 18–22). And even though Vanniyars have not voted solidly for any one political party, they have benefited from their general political participation. Thus in the elections of 1962 in the South Arcot district, all three major parties chose Vanniyar leaders (L. I. Rudolph 1965, p. 984).

Political Engagement: The Nadar Association

The Nadars have also waged a long, hard, and successful mobility campaign. Their traditional occupation was the same as that of the Iravas of Kerala, the making and sale of alcoholic liquor, the fermented product of sap ("toddy") tapped from a palm tree. The Iravas became unified under a religious leader and his doctrine; the Nadar achievement has been through secular, reformist, and political means. Some Nadars, as will be noted again in the discussion of religion-based jatis, did become converts to Christianity, but they number only about 150,000; the Hindu Nadars now number between one and a half to two million in Madras State.

In the early nineteenth century Nadars were ranked, in some localities, with those jatis whose women were not allowed to clothe themselves above the waist as women of the higher jatis did. First the Christian converts among them breached this rule and then some of the Hindu women among them followed suit. The higher jatis were outraged that these women should put on airs and blouses; they threatened violence and riots erupted. The Governor of Madras intervened in 1858 to grant permission to women "of the lower castes" to wear a cloth over the breasts and shoulders. The Maharaja of Travancore also felt moved to issue a proclamation on the matter, but he temporized a bit. He allowed their wearing an upper cloth in the manner of fisherwomen or "their covering their bosoms in any manner whatever, but not like women of high castes" (Thurston 1909, Vol. 6, p. 365).

In the latter part of the nineteenth century a good many became prosperous merchants. In 1874 these Nadars led an attempt to secure the right to enter the great temple at Madurai. They lost that round, but continued the struggle for temple entry, bringing a suit to the High Court in Madras and then to the Privy Council in London. They lost that case also; the judge was sympathetic and commended them for their "education, industry, and frugality," but he felt forced to rule that they should have separate but equal religious facilities (Raj 1959, pp. 87, 222, 261; L. I. Rudolph 1965, pp. 978–981; Rudolph and Rudolph 1967, pp. 36–49).

The Nadars' bitter opponents were Maravars, the jati just above them in most of their localities. The Nadars persisted in their claims to Kshatriya status, and the wealthier, merchant families called themselves Nadars rather than Shanars, the term for toddy-tappers. At first these wealthier families tried to separate themselves from their jati fellows who continued as toddy-tappers, but by 1910 many of them had shifted from a fission to a fusion strategy. They founded a caste association and their leaders urged the uplift and reform of all Nadars and intermarriage among the five Nadar jatis.

Their caste association soon became one of the largest and most active in Tamil Nadu. Its agents toured the villages to establish panchayats, schools, and cooperative banks. By 1921 the Census Commissioner announced that by order of the Government of Madras their former name would no longer be used in official records, all of them would be recorded under their preferred name, Nadar.

In the 1920s and 1930s their district organization began to take active interest in state politics. In one district where the Nadar merchants were predominant they backed the Justice Party as against the Congress, and when a young Congress worker, who was to become the most famed Nadar of all, Kamaraj Nadar, appeared at a meeting in the early 1930s, he "was stoned by the community as a traitor to his caste" (Hardgrave 1966, p. 616). However, Nadars in other localities supported the Congress Party, and by 1947 the great majority of them did so. The Nadar caste association aligned itself with the Congress Party.

Later, the association was taken out of party politics because there were strongly divergent party affiliations among its members. The organization continues to work for the uplift of all Nadars (Raj 1959, pp. 180–199), not all of whom are at the same level. In some localities the traditional occupation is still followed by most; in other places Nadars are mainly merchants. In the large cities many are in the professions and in government service as well as in trade.

Nadar political activities differ in each of these places, as Robert Hardgrave has observed (1966, pp. 618–621). Where Nadars are numerically predominant and are still impoverished tappers, politics are mainly factional, among different alliances of Nadars. Voting behavior there is an extension of traditional village politics within a preponderant jati. In another constituency the Nadars are mainly merchants and are a minority as against the dominance of their old opponents, the Maravars (cf. Baranov 1965). Voting alignments there are like village contests among jatis, with a smaller jati shifting its support about to gain greatest advantage.

In Madurai City, Nadar merchants are concentrated in two wards, and these generally return Nadar candidates to the city council. But in this city there are also Nadar factory workers and students, whose political affiliations hinge on their occupational interests, which are quite different from those of the Nadar merchants. This is all the more so in Madras City. "In Madurai and Madras, caste has by no means ceased to be an important factor in determining political behavior, but it is only one of a multiplicity of variables which affect the individual voter's decision" (Hardgrave 1966, p. 620).

Nadars are predominant among the merchants of Madurai, as Myron Weiner observed when he studied political behavior in that city in 1962. The Nadar merchants contribute a portion of their income to their caste association, which runs schools and a bank and issues a weekly newspaper in the city. Their civic concerns are lodged in their caste associations as much as in political activity; in politics they tend to take a utilitarian rather than ideological approach to the Congress Party. "Thus, although the Nadar merchants have displaced the Brahmins and Saurashtras at many levels of leadership within the party and within the municipality, they lack the party *esprit* which these other communities had" (Weiner 1967, p. 421). However, they are apparently not lacking in devotion to their own association.

The association was used as a direct political instrument when Nadars, as a group, either held power or were acting together against other groups. This use of the association is less feasible among urban and educated Nadars, who do not readily line up in a solid political front. Among them the association is used for a less direct but nonetheless effective purpose, that of bringing economic and educational advantages to its members. With those advantages, they can then acquire political influence according to their own party preferences.

The success of Nadar social mobility is summarized in Lloyd Rudolph's study of their political activities: "The community has breached the pollution barrier, changed its rank within traditional society and now occupies an important place in the modern society of Madras and India" (1965, p. 981). Rudolph gives particular attention to the contribution of caste associations in general to political development in India. His conclusions are reflected in the title of this article, "The modernity of tradition: the democratic incarnation of caste in India."[1]

Rudolph notes that caste associations have become vehicles for internal cultural reform and external social change; they have united jatis and have taught illiterate peasants to participate in modern politics. They have enabled disadvantaged groups to find advantage in their numbers. The result has been to make representative democracy meaningful and effective in the new nation and in caste society (Rudolph 1965, pp. 981–982, 985). All this, Rudolph continues, belies the predictions of Marx and of others that caste society could not adapt to modern conditions and that a totally new social structure would have to be erected.

---

[1] L. I. Rudolph's book of 1967, written with Susanne Hoeber Rudolph, includes much of the material in this article as well as treatment of other subjects. It bears the title, *The Modernity of Tradition, Political Development in India.*

It may be too early to assess this adaptation; the impact of caste associations is still in the making and relatively little detailed information about them is now available (cf. Bailey 1963b, p. 128). Some have taken a politically adaptive step beyond that of caste association; they have formed federations.

Federation: The Kshatriya Sabha of Gujarat

The advantages of association have induced some to press beyond the ready base of a jati-cluster. The Yadavas, for example, have tried to bring together all in India who were traditionally of pastoral occupation and of broadly similar tradition and status. Within Madras State, the leaders of three sets of jatis have begun to combine their respective caste associations under one name (L. I. Rudolph 1965, p. 984; Gough 1963, p. 193).

This kind of outreach has led to the founding of federations in which there is no emphasis on the merging of the component jatis as there usually is in a caste association. The leaders of a federation stress the mutual benefits that can come out of the united efforts of many jatis.

One of the most active caste federations is the Kshatriya Sabha of Gujarat. It dates from 1946 and includes several jati-clusters of the region, notably Rajputs, Bariyas, and Bhils. The federation tries to upgrade the customary ways of all who affiliate with it and to augment their joint political strength. A study of this organization by Kothari and Maru concludes that "it represents a step beyond caste association in Indian development towards a political community" (1965, pp. 34–35).

This federation of "Kshatriya" jatis in Gujarat had certain organizational assets from the start. Rajputs tend to be more concerned with secular power than with ritual niceties and so they welcome as allies (when they stand in need of them) all jatis who follow the Rajput model and the Rajput lead. In much of Gujarat the Rajputs felt in need of allies since many Rajputs there were poor, some were landless, and most were losing ground to more efficient cultivators, especially the Patidars.

When independence opened new avenues of politics, two Rajput leaders took charge. One was a powerfully persuasive figure, the other a very efficient administrator. The two led the federation for many years. Reforms were urged in the form of an interesting combination of traditional uplift, Rajput militancy and Gandhian nonviolence. Great feasts were staged at which people of all the federated jatis interdined in symbolic reduction of social distances. These distances had traditionally been great, from Rajput nobles to tribal Bhils. The federation even took the initiative in bringing Muslim Rajputs back into the fold.

The President of this Sabha told Myron Weiner, "We have taken all the backward peoples who are martial by nature and called them Kshatriyas" As the Congress Party had taken up the Harijans, he continued, so had his association taken up all the low-ranking groups of Gujarat who display "intense nationalism," who show "spirit and action." The other founder put it more generally by stating that the Kshatriyas are a class not a caste (1967, p. 97–99). Not all blue-blooded Rajputs could agree to this but their opposition was not great. Many of them could swallow a common meal with Bariyas and Bhils, if they could thereby resume the cherished Rajput role of political leader. The Bariyas, for their part, still revering the traditionally esteemed models, felt honored by tokens of equality from Rajputs and foresaw achievement of something like Rajput status through the Kshatriya association. They supported it in great numbers. Another unifying force, particularly in central Gujarat, was Rajput antagonism against Patidars. Many Patidars, through diligence and intelligent management, had prospered as farmers and merchants and had gained considerable local power. In a good many localities they had, in effect, ousted Rajputs from their former dominance, or so it seemed to many Rajputs and their allies (Kothari and Maru 1965, pp. 36, 43; Weiner 1967, p. 93).

For a time, the federation also included Kshatriya jatis in the adjoining region of Saurashtra, but this soon lapsed because the Rajputs of that region were still the dominant landowners. They were not then interested in the political measures advocated by the poorer Rajputs of Gujarat (Kothari and Maru 1965, pp. 38–39).

Within Gujarat, the federation gained important political influence. Its leaders backed the Congress Party at first but became dissatisfied with the response of Congress leaders to their requests. They expected the political party to give them direct compensation in jobs and political nominations in return for their support. The Congress Party leaders were perfectly willing to make the usual political calculations of ethnic and caste representation but would not consign a definite number of preferments to the keeping of a caste federation (Weiner 1967, pp. 106–109). In 1955, when the Congress Party resolved that its active members could not hold simultaneous membership in any caste or communal organization, the Kshatriya federation dissolved its political allegiance to the Congress Party and later aligned itself with the Swatantra Party. Since then the federation has swung its influence in various party directions. At one time it united with those Patidars who opposed the Congress Party. Then the Congress Party gave more attention to its problems with Kshatriyas and organized its own Kshatriya Sabha. In 1967 the principal founder of the federation was reelected to Parliament for the Congress Party (Weiner 1967, pp. 113–114).

Despite its organizational assets, the leaders of the federation have had difficulty in holding it together because primary loyalties remain with the jatis. A federation's problems of unity are even greater than those of an association (Harrison 1960, pp. 105–109; Rudolph and Rudolph 1960, p. 11).

Yet the Kshatriya Sabha illustrates the adaptability of contemporary men and of their traditional institutions. Many of the Rajputs of Gujarat still take pride in their ancient feudal tradition. Nevertheless they have accepted the modern version of social hierarchy and the revised rules for attaining social eminence. The traditional Rajput goal of being secular rulers may still be cherished, but the Rajputs are willing to fall in with the modern means for reaching that goal.

Wider Ties and Deeper Change

In sum, many villagers now press for higher status through caste associations and federations. Proposals for cooperation among closely similar jatis are usually accepted readily; effective joint action in at least a few matters has often followed. Merging through intermarriage meets more resistance and in any event cannot be consummated overnight. The power base of an association can relatively quickly be built up through mobilizing voting strength. As villagers become aware of the potential rewards of electoral victory, they rally increasingly to groups that lend themselves to political action. Well suited for the purpose is the jati-cluster—formerly a category of attribution, now turned into a group for joint action. The head of the Congress Party organization in Gujarat put the trend succinctly to Myron Weiner: "As soon as people become a little more conscious politically they become more caste-conscious" (Weiner 1967, p. 106).

Occasionally political gains and status advantages are still accomplished through fission. The Jatavs of Agra have split away from their former jati ties, but they are quite unusual in that they had a large concentration within one city. They too are now reaching out for wider alliances.

The Nadar case is more characteristic of contemporary trends. Nadars were waging mobility battles long before they organized an association to aid in their campaign. Some Nadars tried jati fission first, but changed to fusion and association when they realized that under modern conditions their purposes would be better served by uniting than by separating. A smaller group had less chance than a larger group had of building schools, of getting governmental preferments, and, latterly, of electing powerful officials. Moreover the traditional ritual symbols of high rank, which could be won by a smaller, tightly disciplined group, were losing some of their appeal. Once the Nadar association was made into an effective instrument, its leaders engaged the organization in state politics and then, in a subsequent stage, decided that the members' interests were better served by withdrawing the association from politics.

In all stages of association activities, among Nadars and among others, the grand strategy remains the same. The goal is to lift one's group in the social hierarchy. In the course of achieving this the more immediate strategy is switched from fission to fusion. This switch does not require great departures from traditional mobility patterns, as was noted in the case of Yadava adaptation. It entails familiar ways of attracting allies, parallel conditions for successful mobility, and, importantly, the same moral rectitude of striving for one's kin and jati. It does, however, sacrifice homogeneity in ritual symbols and practices in favor of material benefits and modern prestige symbols.

A caste association typically helps advance the traditional conditions for successful mobility. Secular resources can be strengthened by lobbying and through united economic efforts. Customary ways can be reformed, especially through modern education, which also yields economic benefits for the educated. The association leaders press for official recognition of the group's merit. The change of name used to be a main target; more substantive indications of worth are now sought, especially in the form of high positions and prestigious jobs for the group's members.

Government resources can help greatly in achieving social rise in the eyes of one's neighbors—who remain the critical judges of one's real rank. So a rising jati has a heavy stake in political power. Hardgrave writes that "As caste solidarity has increased, caste has been politicized and drawn into the political system as a major actor" (1966, p. 614; also Harrison 1960, pp. 132–136).

Jatis have long been politicized in their localities; what has significantly changed is the widening of political engagement from village and locality to district, state, and nation. Traditional jati panchayats usually tried to keep government out of jati affairs. This is still so in some measure, but caste associations now court government aid. Status advantage remains a motivating force and so competition among caste associations appears, not infrequently in political rivalries.

Competition among political parties is built into the present political order, but parties do not often command the kind of moral allegiance that a jati and even its association can elicit. A man who works for his caste association can be understood by villagers as helping his family and kin, as trying to establish the proper dharma of his whole group. There are, to be sure, dedicated workers for political parties and there are villagers who are imbued with a party ideology of moral justice. But most villagers understand the ideology of jati and varna better than they grasp the ideologies of political parties.

The trend toward fusion follows much of the traditional pattern, for jati mobility, but the new elements in the process may eventually alter the process itself. The arena of competition is larger, and government is a principal force in it. Methods of organization are shifting from the relatively loose, implicit organization of the jati to the explicit, formalized, bureaucratic organization of the association. The alternate models for mobility are beginning to be merged into one generalized model of educated, politically influential, and wealthy people. The social hierarchy tends to become much less differentiated in both social distances and cultural differences.

Modern education has become a prime source of both prestigious symbols and substantive power, so most aspiring groups put heavy stress on the education of their children. They need not simultaneously relinquish traditional symbols of high status, but their educated children are more inclined to bypass or modify these symbols. A good many caste associations maintain their own schools, college hostels, and scholarships. The associations allow people of disparate interests and background within a jati-cluster to work together. The educated (who provide the new leadership) and the uneducated cooperate in them, as do urban and rural members, and those of traditionally higher and lower status within the cluster.

The individual villager still tends to see his personal rise and the status of his family as being linked in considerable measure—though not so completely as formerly—to the rise of his jati. Social rank is still a central concern for many in the village. But as the moves for social mobility are modernized, the nature of the hierarchy is being altered. A headline in the *Statesman*, quoted by Lloyd Rudolph, referred to this trend, "Caste hierarchy declines, as casteism rises" (1965, p. 989).

The impetus to form a caste association comes out of the same motives that impel people to strive for their jati's rise. The leaders of an association commonly urge cultural adaptations, hold up models for mobility, combat external opposition, work for internal cohesion in ways similar to those discussed in the previous chapters on jati mobility. But the newer ways also differ from the more traditional maneuvers in being adapted to modern political and social conditions. In altering the traditional mobility moves, jati leaders may also be modifying the fundamental components and processes of the traditional social system.

Srinivas concludes that the trends toward political mobilization by jatis "all suggest that changes of a fundamental kind are occurring" (1966, p. 117). In assessing these changes, in asking whether they are likely to be recurrent or systemic, it is useful to consider them in the perspective of other kinds of major change that have gone on in Indian society for centuries. These are changes through regrouping on religious grounds and changes undergone by tribesmen when they shifted into jati society.

PART VII

RECURRENT CHANGE THROUGH RELIGIOUS AND TRIBAL MOVEMENTS

CHAPTER 28

Social Regrouping through Indigenous Religions

Religion has been, and continues to be, a matter of absorbing interest for many in India. "Theological discussions," Srinivas observes, "are freely entered into by people who meet for the first time in trains, in buses, in hotel lobbies" (1966, p. 143). The participants in these discussions do not restrict themselves to any narrow definition of theology; religious talk readily edges over into politics or medicine or anything else.

In former centuries no aspect of life was set apart from religion. Not every person was necessarily pious or god-fearing, but religion was taken as all-pervasive. All social relations were inevitably and legitimately suffused with religious ideas and acts. Hence social movements were couched in religious terms, and personal restiveness and social disaffection could best be expressed as religious strivings. As new social ideas were developed, they were offered under the aegis of religion.

Movements to reorganize society in India were therefore expressed mainly through indigenous sects and through introduced religions. Equality rather than hierarchy among all believers was a common theme, and in almost all these movements the devotees finally came to sort themselves into jatis and to act like other jati members in their local order.

Recurrent change through religion has typically been sparked by personal quests for salvation rather than by sheer mobility aspirations, but the social outcome of these personal quests has consistently turned out to be quite like the outcome of the mobility drives discussed above. Once a new dispensation becomes established as a sectarian jati, its followers may come to dominate their localities. Then their ways, including their religion, may be emulated by subordinate groups just as any dominant jati may be taken as a reference group. This kind of emulation or conversion should be distinguished from the process considered in this chapter through which persons become devotees, devotees form a cult, the cult becomes a sect, and the sect turns into a jati.

Straightforward emulation, as when clients are attracted to the religion of their patrons, servants to that of their masters, or subjects to that of their rulers, does not occur automatically. Many clients, servants, and subjects have steadfastly kept to their own religion through long periods despite (or because of) strong efforts by their superiors to convert them. We cannot here attempt an analysis of the conditions under which a subordinate will or will not be attracted to the religion of the superior, we need only note that such attraction has been effective in some cases and has been resisted in others. To cite one example of effective attraction, the report of the 1931 Census in the Punjab noted that a good many Hindus of lower jatis were becoming Sikhs because they "obviously considered that they gained in status as soon as they ceased to be Hindus and became Sikhs." An account of a Sikh village testifies that such conversions were going on there in the 1950s and for the same reason (Khan 1931, pp. 293–294; I. P. Singh 1961, p. 191; Srinivas 1966, p. 101).

Many were converted to the religion of temporal rulers, as to Islam when Muslims held power and to Christianity during the British regime. Though religious leaders have deplored this motive for conversion, it has long been a potent one. The direct status gain that converts derived was usually not great. Untouchables who became converted to Christianity, to Islam, or to Sikhism were not immediately taken as social equals by their coreligionists, and certainly were not treated more respectfully by neighbors of different faiths (cf. Béteille 1965, pp. 92, 98; I. P. Singh 1958, p. 485).

The original inspiration for much religious change has commonly come from a charismatic teacher who drew disciples to his revelation of the true path to eternal salvation. He characteristically taught some reform of social practice as the earthly counterpart of his fresh vision of eternity. As his words and example fired his followers and their numbers grew, they built a religious movement separate from their former society. Sooner or later that movement was reabsorbed into the system of caste society.

If seems almost to be a property of this social system that such movements well up periodically, develop through the cycle, and then devolve back into the system. This trend has often been remarked by scholars, though detailed comparative studies remain to be done (cf. Karve 1961, p. 109; Srinivas 1966, pp. 75–76; Weber 1958, pp. 19–20). Jawaharlal Nehru wrote ruefully about this process, perhaps with some concern lest his own valiant efforts for social reform be caught up in the same massive drift. He said that it was curious and significant that throughout Indian history great men have given repeated warnings against priestcraft and the rigidity of the caste system. Powerful movements have risen against them, "yet slowly, imperceptibly almost, it seems, as if it were the inevitable course of destiny," caste organization has grown and spread. "Rebels against caste have drawn many followers, and yet in the course of time their group has itself become a caste" (1946, p. 112).

"Inevitable destiny" is not an answer that really satisfied Nehru or suffices for other students of Indian society. We have to clarify, as best we may with the available evidence, how it was that those who held other ideas of a good society were repeatedly absorbed into caste organization and into the caste processes of recurrent change.

Individual Choice and Religious Change

Religious cults still rise in every part of India. A villager today joins a religious movement for reasons probably much like those that influenced earlier generations of devotees. To begin with, a villager finds in religion his (or her) principal opportunity for personal choice. Much in his life career is quite tightly prescribed, but he does have some option about which deity to single out for special devotion, how to express that devotion, and which personal mentor to select. Narrow though this choice may seem to an outside observer, religion does afford the villager a wider range of choice than is easily available elsewhere. Religion is generally seen as a benign field of conduct. So long as a person shows the recognized signs of behaving religiously, others give at least conditional approval to what he does. One member of a family may take a deity or a ritual not shared by others of his family. Some families worship in a different manner from their jati fellows without demur from the others, provided that their worship does not violate jati standards (cf. Karve 1961, p. 121).

Religion also provides alternate roles for those ill-suited to the roles they have inherited. One such person, a Rajput overlord in Gujarat village, has been described by Gittel Steed (1955). As a young man he inherited a position of responsibility and leadership, yet he was not comfortable with the role of martial Rajput. Unusual circumstances had given him an unusual upbringing; he was reared in his mother's natal family, surrounded by strong women. In any event, he is mild-mannered and retiring. After bouts of hysterical symptoms and of opium use, he has turned to intensive religious devotion. This is quite understood by his kinsmen and neighbors, and although he does not conform to usual Rajput conduct, he is not considered particularly deviant. "His recent preoccupation with religious practices was also well within a pattern of alternative choices that was common to the larger Hindu society" (Steed 1955, p. 143). As was noted in Chapter 22, a deviant personality as well as a gifted one can become a sanyassin, a holy person dedicated to a deity.

Religious cults were, and are, among the principal voluntary associations available to individual villagers. Hence they have been used as ways of expressing discontent with the established order, or of seeking political and economic change.

Religion answers many personal needs. A youth can gather with his agemates to sing sacred hymns; women can publicly express their inner feelings through special religious rites. A main religious search is that of finding a particular holy person in whom one can discover the real truth. To this person a man or woman can give unalloyed allegiance and from him he can receive inner strength.

The sheltering canopy of religion is best held over a man by his own mentor, his guru. Voluntary personal dependency is not invidious; dependence on a true guru is a great good. In his guru a man seeks, and often finds, a figure whose spiritual superiority is unquestioned, who is nurturant and noncompetitive, who can lift his disciple out of the abrasive tussles of everyday social relations. Very many village men seek out such a mentor. Dumont estimates that "A majority of Indian heads of families, of all castes, even Muslims, have chosen a *guru* who has initiated them while whispering a mantra in their ears, and who, in principle, visits them once a year" (1960, p. 60; cf. Ferguson 1963). A man may shift from one guru to another and his relationship with any one may be brief and tangential, yet he characteristically does not give up the search. Many a man finds a guru with whom he can forge a close bond and whose words are taken as guides to life. The guru himself is commonly the disciple of yet another holy man, often one who has departed the present life and who was one link in a generational chain of disciples preaching the word of some great soul of the past. The guru inducts his pupil into the way shown by the founder.

A modern example is the cult of Saibaba, a Muslim saint whose tomb and main shrine are in Maharashtra. Saibaba's teachings have many Hindu adherents in South India, including Western-educated people, and Srinivas reports that there are Saibaba prayer groups in several South Indian cities (1966, pp. 132, 143).[1] If these groups establish some regular communication, agree on a new ceremonial agenda, codify the teachings, and support professional religionists, they will then have developed into something more than a zealous set of cult adherents. The fact that Hindus are prominent among the devotees of a Muslim saint reflects the belief that a holy man's earthly background and affiliations are of far less importance than his spiritual achievements.

A sanyassin is expected to cut off his secular attachments, to abandon all considerations of kinship, jati, and village. Hence when a sanyassin acts as guru he is likely to pass lightly over such matters or to brush them aside entirely as inconsequential and positively harmful to the spirit. The circle of his devotees characteristically tries to ignore social distinctions in the context of worship. Joining with dedicated worshippers answers the personal needs of a man (or a woman) in ways acceptable to his kin and neighbors. It gives welcome scope for personal choice. It offers new or expanded roles, perhaps especially attractive because they are different from those thrust on him by others. Submission to a new religious discipline can enhance his sense of power and relieve his feelings of helplessness. Moreover, many in India find great personal reward in being the disciple of a guru and in gathering with fellow disciples.

Such groups are legion, most have brief existence and little social consequence. But some endure, coalesce with others, and regularize their religious activities; their participants become known as members of a cult. Occasionally a cult gathers strong momentum, perhaps because of favoring social or economic conditions (cf. Bendix 1960, pp. 202–205).

The devotees, inspired by success and fired with zeal, make the cult a pervasive force in their lives. They use it as their primary social identification and try to widen the influence of their guru. This requires organized effort; as their organization becomes established and their new identity becomes known and accepted, the band of devotees develops into a sect. Members of the sect tend to form an endogamous unit, which functions socially as another jati. In this way devotees from diverse social backgrounds come to redefine their jati identity so that it is one with their religious allegiance.[2]

A Modern Religious Movement in Madras City

Three historic religious movements are discussed later in this chapter, but first a contemporary example of religious movement in the making is examined. It entails both traditional and modern elements and may not develop into anything much more than it was in the 1960s. It is not yet an established sect, still less has it produced new jatis. But it may become an important influence in revising former groupings among the educated, wealthier people of Madras. The account of it by Milton Singer (1963) shows how traditional forces of religion are being channeled in modern Madras City.

---

[1] In 1968 I visited an old friend in a Badaga village in the Nilgiris, I noticed a new picture in the display of religious pictures in his home. My friend told me that it was a picture of Saibaba, whom he had seen, so he said, when the holy man had visited the Nilgiris a few years before.

[2] English observers reported the rise of a number of new sect-based jatis in the eighteenth century (Raghuvanshi 1966, pp. 169–170); most of these jatis are now forgotten.

This movement arises from an old form of worship called *bhajan*. The word means "prayer" or "devotional song" and also carries the meaning of a gathering of devotees to sing and worship. The traditional emphasis is on spontaneous meetings in which worshippers can communicate with the beloved deity, and with each other, in a free outpouring of songs, words, and acts. In Madras City five types of bhajans are held, ranging from informal weekly meetings in a private home to annual ten-day festivals with crowded agenda culminating in a marriage ceremony of the gods Krishna and Radha. Although such festivals resemble traditional performances, they are now elaborated in ways different from the older, traditional ceremonies.

Three gurus are credited with giving the ritual and philosophy of this Radha-Krishna bhajan its canonical form. All lived near Kumbakonam in Tanjore district in the seventeenth century. Their teachings were introduced into Madras City about 1900 through disciples from the Kumbakonam locality—one a former schoolteacher, another a government accountant, a third an official. They initiated others as followers of the Kumbakonam Gurus in the traditional manner by imparting a secret verse and a set of religious instuctions. One of the present leaders of the bhajan cult is a retired film actor who was so initiated.

Though the relation between guru and disciple is an intensely personal one, Singer notes that among the devotees whom he studied it can have important social consequences. "This evidence suggests that, far from being an independent mode of transmission which transcends the social structure and the culture, the guru-disciple relationship operates as the very lifeline of the culture and social structure" (Singer 1963, p. 207). It is a voluntary relationship, but it does not exist in a social vacuum. A disciple puts himself under a guru's guidance because he already shares many of the values that the guru teaches. There is room for innovation as well, and a guru can bring about certain adaptations in religious practice.

Some gurus and devotees in Madras City have promoted bhajans so successfully that from small, informal hymn sessions there have developed complex organizations. One of them stages a variety of religious performances, "elects officers, solicits donations, prints announcements and invitations, and issues an annual report with an audited account of its revenues and expenditures" (Singer 1963, p. 195). In 1958 the officers of this group called a conference of all leading bhajan devotees of the city. A federation of some forty-five bhajan groups was set up; it now holds conferences annually, conducts special festivals, and plans to include affiliates from the whole of the state of Madras. Other Radha-Krishna devotees will have nothing to do with this elaborate organization, holding that gatherings of devotees should be informal and unscheduled in order to maintain the spontaneous feelings of love and equality that should prevail in such sessions. But the majority of the bhajan devotees in the city find advantage in organization.

They are mainly professional men—government officials, business executives, doctors, university professors, accountants, and musicians—and are predominantly Brahmins. In one list of financial contributors only some 20 percent were non-Brahmins and about 55 percent were Smarta Brahmins, from the jatis following the intellectual philosophy propounded in the eighth century by the sage Shankara. Singer comments that it may seem strange that so many adherents of the emotional, personal, bhajan worship should come from an intellectual and scholastic tradition. But, as he points out, Smarta Brahmins have long been the most civic-minded among Tamil Brahmins, more concerned with the general polity of religion than with narrower sectarian interests. Their founder, Shankara, led the Hindu restoration against Buddhists and sought "to build an all-India Hinduism that could rise above the doctrines and practices of any particular group or region" (Singer 1963, p. 210).

Shankara's modern followers in Madras City may also be building a bulwark against challengers, especially their contemporary political assailants who take an anti-Brahmin line.

The *bhajan* groups bring together Brahmins and non-Brahmins. They dramatize aspects of the Brahmin tradition; they provide social nuclei for the new elite. They follow the ancient devotional pattern in ways that are adapted to the realities of modern city life. Professional colleagues, work groups, neighborhood associations have a new importance in the city. The basic bhajan group is a neighborhood group. The participants come together weekly in a private home; they also invite colleagues from their work or relatives who may live in another neighborhood. The host derives some prestige from the meeting; guests take this way of making friends in the big city. The participants find benefit in regular religious sessions even though these sessions are quite different from the intricate, time-consuming daily rituals practiced by their forebears. A monthly bhajan brings people of various neighborhoods together; the annual festival attracts crowds from all parts of the city.

The ritual stresses the equality of the devotees. There are mutual embraces and prostrations of each to all; people of different jatis mingle in an informal, friendly way. Singer points out that the equality shown in this religious context is not meant to be extended literally to other contexts. The devotees interpret the prostrations as expressions of humility and tokens of an ideal, not as indicative of habitual daily conduct.

The contemporary bhajans, like the caste associations, are adaptations of traditional patterns to modern circumstances. As village Brahmins in Tamil Nadu did not have strong jati organization, so their educated descendants in the city do not develop strong caste associations. Yet even though the bhajan movement is intended for the benefit of the individual soul and many adherents bear witness to the spiritual grace they derive from it, participation in it also has social consequences. Educated people of diverse jatis and geographic origins are brought together and establish friendly relations.

Although there is talk of a "casteless, sectless, ecumenical form of Hinduism," Singer observes that "already tendencies have appeared toward new forms of ritualization, intellectualization, and sectarianism which render such an outcome unlikely" (1963, p. 226). It may be that this bhajan cult or something like it will lead to structural revisions of caste and sect among its adherents. Systemic changes are in train in India, as they are throughout the world, and the ecumenical vision held by Indian sages may yet come to pass. However, the historical record attests that in the past such visions, in India as elsewhere, have become translated socially into a more parochial *oikumene* than the visionaries sought. If it does nothing more socially, the cult is likely to revise the divisions among Tamil Brahmins in terms of modern realities rather than of ancient doctrines.

From Casteless Cult to Sectarian Jati

The growth of this bhajan cult illustrates only part of the historical cycle of religious regrouping. The cycle begins with people who are restive in their faith and restless in their social order. They take the open option of religion to change their personal circumstances. It is an option available even to untouchables, who have produced many sectarian movements and some renowned saints. It is true that those who were most severely pinioned by poverty did not have enough leeway to take even the religious option. But some untouchables did, and many more of higher jati have changed their social identity through accepting a new religious dispensation.

A person makes this choice by placing himself under the guidance of a guru and within the tradition of a line of gurus. In a devotional tradition each soul is taken, in the ideal if not in practice, as an equal manifestation of divine grace and each person as an equal sharer in its beneficence. The fervor of surrender to guru induces a fever to gather with companions in devotion and to convert the as-yet unenlightened. These inclinations lead to concerted acts for social purposes.

In due time the cohort of devotees requires hierarchical leadership; the role of personal guru is developed into the office of guru for the sect (cf. Bendix 1960, pp. 202–205). This institutionalized guru may attract personal disciples but he is more likely to be a kind of religious headman who periodically makes a stately tour about the circuit of his faithful. He regulates their conduct, adjudicates their disputes, refreshes their sectarian allegiance. The faithful in their localities marry within their group, hold panchayats for the group, keep social distance between themselves and lower jatis, observe certain standards of pollution and purity, and in general fit into the local caste order. They have then come full circle, from being a member of one jati to being a member of another jati, this one based on sect.

Sectarian jatis are typically open to certain kinds of converts. In Ramkheri village, for example, there are three sect-based jatis. One centers on Shiva and is ranked with the Rajput bloc; another focuses on Vishnu and is allied with the vegetarian jatis in the village. Both accept converts, but only those of equal or higher jati rank. The third sectarian jati is classed with the Harijans; its members revere the teachings of Kaber, a saint of the fifteenth century (Mayer 1960, p. 28; 1956, pp. 118–119).

The local ranking of a sectarian jati, like that of any jati, depends on both ritual and secular factors. Lingayats in western Mysore are rated quite high because of their general ritual purity and secular strength, despite their deliberate transgression of certain standards, as in their refusal to have their women observe menstrual seclusion. In Bengal, the jati of Vishnu devotees is also treated as one of the higher, even though its members accept recruits from most other jatis, even from those of very low rank.

Only a few sectarian jatis have been studied closely and those mainly in their theological rather than in their social aspects (e.g. Allison 1935; Deming 1928; Kennedy 1925; Orr 1947). We do not yet have detailed analyses of the forces that have brought about this kind of recurrent change, but we do know the social outcome of the major religious regroupings in Indian history. The process is illustrated in the histories of three existing indigenous religions of India—Jainism which dates from the 6th century B.C., Lingayatism which began in the twelfth century A.D., and Sikhism, dating from the fifteenth century.

Indigenous Religions

Each of these three indigenous religions began with a founder who preached a new way of faith which his devotees took as a new way of life. In fulfilling the new precepts they separated themselves from established groups. All three founders emphasized the way of devotion over scriptural knowledge and ritual diligence, two other traditional avenues to salvation. Renou comments that in Hinduism "there is no sect without some element of *bhakti*" (1953, p. 93). But a founding guru could scarcely stress anything but devotion. If he is to open a new way, there is as yet no new scriptural learning or uniquely relevant rites developed for it. These follow later, but in the founding period it is devotion that must necessarily spark the movement. Devotion, moreover, can be given by any person, whatever his social degree. Each of the three founders accepted all devotees as equal; each proclaimed an ingathering of all regardless of status; each wanted no invidious social distinctions to be recognized among any of his faithful.

All three movements rose out of Hinduism and bore a social message that modified the Hinduism of the time. Each founding sage preached that caste distinctions did not exist in the sight of God and should not exist among his followers. His devotees deviated from the ways of their neighbors, opposed them and were opposed by them; but they had to operate within the same general society and had to use similar standards in doing so. So much did each of the three movements become social establishments that in time anti-establishment groups splintered from them, led by zealous reformers seeking to revive the pure principles of the founding guru.

The founder's social doctrine has not been abandoned in any of these three sects; it is embedded in the sacred writings and repeated in ritual prayer. But it is held as an ideal that must be tempered by the realities of society. This is not to say that this social ideology makes no social difference. Sectarian jatis do differ in being open, usually, to some recruitment by conversion. Their members interdine and generally interact more freely with others of the same faith. They feel themselves part of the same band of believers when they confront nonbelievers; their solidarity is based on their scriptures and sometimes is riveted by a tight organization. Nevertheless, the members of these sects also uphold the characteristic principles of caste organization. They maintain separate endogamous groups within the sect. They observe standards of pollution and purity that are in the main (though not in all specifics) like the standards observed by others of their region. They keep untouchables at a social distance, even those untouchables who have become committed devotees of the same sect. The system has triumphed over the revelation in that the devotees do indeed act as jati fellows in a caste order, but each sect also upholds its distinctive ideals in particular ways that distinguish its adherents from all other religions.

Jains

Jainism was one of the first of the indigenous religious movements. The great sage of the Jain religion, Mahavira, lived from about 540 B.C. to 468 B.C. and so was a contemporary of the founder of Buddhism (*ca.* 563 B.C.–483 B.C.). The two teachers had broadly similar life histories and their respective teachings have had great consequence to the present day. Buddhism is a vast force in Asia, but it was almost extinct in India until taken up in recent years by the backward-classes movement. Jain devotees have practiced their faith for more than twenty-five centuries and have created a large scriptural literature. (Modern scholars have particular appreciation for Jain monks who held that it was a deed of religious merit to copy and preserve any manuscript.) However, Jainism did not spread beyond the Indian subcontinent and eventually came to be centered mainly in the regions of Gujarat and of Mysore.

Mahavira's teachings concerned the relation of one's soul to the timeless cosmos. Only indirectly did he discuss the social order, less rigidly demarcated in his time than it later came to be. He and other Jain sages stressed that personal acts, not ascribed status, determined all that was important for the soul. "The doors of Jainism," Sangave writes, "were thrown open to all and equal opportunity was given to everybody to practice religion according to his capacity." This modern Jain scholar further comments that the ancient teachers of Jainism envisaged "a society wherein classes were not watertight compartments and complete freedom was granted to people to change to the class of their own aptitude" (Sangave 1959, pp. 67–70).

That social vision has yet to be realized among modern Jains. More than any other sect they have divided themselves into numerous jatis, some so small that they are en route to extinction. A 1914 directory of one branch of Jains listed 87 castes of which 41 had a population of less than 500. Sangave mentions "nearly sixty" endogamous groups, each with a population of less than one hundred (1959, p. 73).

Many Jains are tradesmen. A common explanation of this is that an orthodox Jain cannot be a farmer because Jainism places strict prohibitions on violence and on the taking of life, and ploughing crushes the life of worms. Although trade is a common calling for Jains, there are Jain jatis of diverse rank and occupation. Some are cultivators. Jains in South India rank themselves in four divisions, headed by those who are temple priests. The priestly jati acts in the manner of a Brahmin jati among Hindus, with the main exception that even these highest among Jains will interdine with all other Jains of their region.

Jains reflect the characteristics of their region of residence. In Gujarat they maintain hypergamous sections, as do other Gujarat jatis of similar social level. In South India, they have high priests who are like the chief gurus among other South Indian sects. Each high priest presides over a territory and is elected by representatives from the villages. One such high priest "has supreme authority over all Jainas south of Madras, but not over those of Mysore or South Kanara with whom the former have no relations." He periodically tours his territory, "settles caste disputes and fines and excommunicates the erring" (Sangave 1959, p. 111).

Perhaps because so many Jains were competitive, independent merchants, they have been inclined to split into very small exclusive groups. Thus one dogmatic difference separating two groups was whether their ascetics should use peacock feathers or cow hair to brush off insects. Territorial bounds also can be quite narrow; Jains in Ahmedabad City did not marry their daughters outside the city (Sangave 1959, pp. 62, 157).

Many reform movements have arisen in the long history of Jainism. Renou describes the annual assembly of one such group that was founded in 1760. Their ninth pontiff presided, "like a Mahavira redivivus," exemplifying the founder's severely ascetic rule. "It is not unusual to see one of them (as I have) freely choose to die in the way characteristic of the Jainas, ending a life of austerities by abstaining from food altogether" (Renou 1953, p. 124). Such sects within a sect tend to repeat the social cycle of the larger movement. Another such splinter group within Jainism numbers about 10,000. Sangave says of it, "Even though at present there are six castes among the Taranapanthis, they were really against the caste distinctions" (1959, p. 55).

The modern trend toward fusion is beginning to reverse the Jain predilection for fission. Some Jains have long intermarried with counterpart Hindu jatis. The counterpart jati bears the same name, follows the same occupations, and has the same characteristics save for the worship of Hindu deities. A woman generally takes on the religion of her husband in such marriages. When regional and national associations of Jains were formed, their leaders urged that intermarriage be arranged among Jain jatis rather than with Hindus (Sangave 1959, pp. 77, 86, 156). Jains, too, are beginning to consolidate into larger units and so the modern adherents of this ancient reform sect may be entering a new cycle of reform.

From a distance of nearly two and a half millennia, we cannot say much about the social origins of early Jainism. However, from the somewhat more ample data of recent years, we see that Jains have operated as a set of jatis, separate in identity but similar in form and function to other jatis of their level and locality. Their special characteristics include their propensity for asceticism, their inclination toward trade, their proclivity to extreme fission. These traits are now being modified, especially in the trend toward fusion.

Lingayats

Lingayats began as forthright reformers. They call their religion *Virashaivism* (that is, strong, stalwart devotion to Shiva). The term Lingayat comes from their rule that members must always wear Shiva's emblem, the lingam. A principal statement of their belief is the *baswa purana*, the teachings of the sage Baswa (or Basava), who may have been the main founder of the sect and certainly has been a central figure in it. These teachings tell that when Baswa was to be invested with the sacred thread when he was eight years old, he refused and said, "I am a worshipper of Shiva and do not belong to the generation of Brahma. I am the axe laid to the tree of caste" (McCormack 1956, p. 2). Lingayat reform was aimed at Jainism as well as at Hinduism. Since Jains were powerful at the time of the great rise of Lingayatism, Jain temples and Jain merchants became special targets of attack for zealous Lingayat converts (Renou 1953, p. 121).

Lingayats carried their egalitarian beliefs so far that they treated women as religious equals. They abolished some fundamental pollution observances of Hinduism, especially those of birth, death, and menstruation. Hindus who want to keep free of such pollution must keep their distance from Lingayats because they cannot be sure how virulently polluted a Lingayat might be at any time. In other ways, however, Lingayats uphold purity practices more stringently than do many Hindus. They are strict vegetarians, do not use alcoholic liquor, and are meticulous about personal ritual cleansing.

In the Lingayat heartland of northern Mysore, their jatis are of about the same variety as among the Hindus of the region. Despite the explicit rejection of caste-ordering in Lingayat scripture, Lingayats group themselves into ranked jatis. The highest are the Jangamas, hereditary priests and teachers. Those among the Jangamas who dedicate themselves entirely to the religious life as celibates and ascetics are the principal religious mentors. This is a feature of a number of sects. Some of the devotees choose to become living exemplars of the true faith and in doing so become active preservers of the sect as a social entity. Lingayat ascetics are particularly influential because reverence to one's guru is a central article of the faith. As one modern Lingayat scholar puts it, reverence to the guru has no limit. He is superior to father and mother since he is the cause of spiritual birth, which is far more important than physical birth. "He is considered to be worthy of more reverence than is due to Siva, the Supreme, because it is he who leads the soul to unity with Siva" (Nandimath 1942, p. 54). These priests-preceptors minister to all Lingayat jatis; they interdine with all save with those untouchables who profess to be Lingayats but are kept apart, because of their jati pollution, by others of the sect (Farquhar 1920, pp. 262–263; Thurston 1909, 4:251–252).

Lingayat jatis receive converts, but these must adhere to the puritan rule of the sect, including abstinence from meat and liquor. Hence there were few converts from the lower jatis when the Abbé Dubois observed the sect in the early nineteenth century (1928, pp. 118–119). There are also initiation ceremonies by which a Lingayat can rise from a lower to higher status within the rank order of the sect (Thurston 1909, 4:251).

Their organization links each Lingayat to a guru in his village and to a greater figure in a religious supercenter. Each family is hereditarily associated with a particular lineage of priests, Jangamas, from whom it takes its gurus. Each Jangama lineage, in turn, is associated with one of the five main Lingayat *maths*, monastic establishments, which are located in the five great centers of Shiva pilgrimage in India. When a Jangama boy is initiated, a representative of that center must be present. Each center has a *jagadguru swami*, a "world-master" who tours about visiting the Lingayats associated with his math. A visit from the great guru strengthens Lingayat solidarity in several ways. The deep reverence he commands enables him to settle disputes promptly and effectively; his visit provides status validation within the Lingayat groups; and the great pomp and ceremony mustered for the visit demonstrate to all, not least to the Lingayats themselves, the power of their sect (McCormack 1963, pp. 62–64).

Although they have flouted certain precepts, Lingayats have been the carriers of the basic Sanskritic principles to others, as to the Coorgs. In their evangelical vigor, they spread out and sought to affect others. Their emphasis on vegetarianism, on reverence for guru and scripture, and their general puritanism demonstrated to tribal and lower groups some of the main elements of the twice-born" as reference category, even as the Lingayat missionaries decried the "twice-born" jatis as reference groups (Srinivas 1952, p. 225).

Despite their ritual separatism, Lingayats are as concerned with their rank in a local order as are those of other jatis. Lingayats have also tried to use the Census operations as a means of raising their social status. In 1891 and 1901 they presented petitions to census officials and to the Maharaja of Mysore asking to be recognized officially under a high-sounding title and as a high group. By 1904 a Lingayat association was formed and grew rapidly. After independence, Lingayats came to be one of the two main political forces in the state of Mysore and they now maintain vigorous political as well as religious organizations. After eight centuries of development in one cycle of recurrent change, the members of this sect, too, are embarking on the new fusion-political process.

Lingayat history illustrates the cycle of sectarian development. Lingayats began as fierce opponents of the establishment. The principal members of that establishment were the inheritors of an earlier reform movement. The Lingayats vehemently opposed some parts of the Sanskritic tradition yet were instrumental in disseminating other essential elements of the tradition. They were, at the time of their beginnings, extremely egalitarian in certain respects and they built a particularly sinewy sect organization that bound Lingayats together over wide areas. Nevertheless, they were as sensitive to local ranking as were any others in their villages and they tried to improve and defend their rank just as did the others.

Sikhs

Sikhism is a relatively modern movement which was founded by Guru Nanak (1469–1539), the first of a succession of ten great Sikh religious leaders. Its roots lie in the Bhakti tradition of Hinduism and in the *Sufi* inspiration of Islam. Nanak started with the watchword "There is no Hindu, there is no Mussalman" and rejected all social distinctions among his followers. He is remembered by Punjabi villagers of all religions by such sayings as this: *Guru Nanak Shah Fakir, Hindu ka Guru, Mussalman ka Pir*. Guru Nanak, the king of religions, to the Hindu a guru, to the Muslim a saint (K. Singh 1953, pp. 25, 41–42; 1963, pp. 17–98).

Guru Nanak censured those who would condemn fellow men to untouchability. He himself chose as a close companion in religion a Muslim musician, who would have been regarded as an untouchable by Nanak's kinsmen and jati fellows. Nanak was probably of a Khatri jati, traditionally tradesmen and government officials in the Punjab, though the name Khatri is from the word Kshtriya. The nine Sikh Gurus who came after him were certainly Khatris.

Guru Nanak adopted a practical means of proclaiming his social doctrine by setting up free community kitchens at which all his believers ate together, whatever their caste origins. The tenth Guru, Gobind Singh, established the principal Sikh institutions. He dramatically and publicly initiated five of his followers, of different jatis, into the new fraternity which he named the Khalsa, "the pure." They drank together out of the same bowl and were given new names with the suffix "Singh" attached. This common surname later exasperated bibliographers and payroll accountants, but, with the abolition of distinctive jati names, all Sikhs were further made equal (K. Singh 1953, p. 30).

The faith spread in the Punjab (though scarcely beyond it) making mass conversions especially among the clans of Jats. As the believers increased in number and influence, they roused fears in the temporal rulers and were persecuted. They resisted, organized, and developed from a fellowship of reconciliation into a militant sect. A great military leader, Ranjit Singh (1780–1839) led the Sikh warriors to the conquest of the Punjab and beyond. After his death the state he had consolidated fell apart, the British took control over the Punjab, and Sikhism again became more a religious than a secular force.

The Sikhs, like the other sects, did not fully realize the egalitarian doctrines preached by the founding Gurus. In surveying Sikh history, Khushwant Singh writes, "If intermarriage is considered the test of equality, at no time was there much inter-caste marriage between Sikhs converted from different castes. The untouchable converted to Sikhism remained an outcaste for purposes of matrimonial alliance" (1953, p. 45). He was kept apart for other purposes also; Sikhs were recruited into the Indian Army by the British and, as Sir Athelstane Baines noted, a recruit from the lowest of Sikh jatis "makes a capital soldier, but has to be brigaded in separate regiments, as the other Sikhs, with their eye on the traditional calling, refuse to associate with the convert, even in religious ceremonies" (Baines 1912, p. 83). Whatever may have been the case in the old British Indian Army, jati differences among Sikhs are suspended in the village practice of religion; even the lowest sit in the temple.

Studies of Sikh villages document both jati separation and religious integration. In Daleke, Amritsar district, there are ten Sikh jatis, one Christian jati, and several Hindu jatis. Jat Sikhs are dominant, other Sikh jatis are those of agriculturist-merchants, artisans, potters, water carriers, washermen, laborers, sweepers, even barbers. Since orthodox Sikhs must not cut their hair, a jati of Sikh barbers might seem superfluous. But they mainly perform the extrabarbering duties done by traditional barbers; they are cooks, workers, and managers at all ceremonial occasions and they also serve as messengers and matchmakers (I. P. Singh 1958, pp. 480–482).

The main cleavage among Sikhs in Daleke is between the lowest, the Mazhbis, and all others. The Mazhbis live in a separate hamlet and have a separate well. Yet no miasma of touch pollution is attributed to them; they sit among others in the temple (though the more finicky women of the other jatis take care to sit away from them); they contribute grain to the temple kitchen and partake of the consecrated food prepared there. In the village they are not addressed as are other Sikhs by the honorific title Sardar (captain or military leader), but out of the village their beards and turbans mark them as Sikhs and they are addressed as Sardar (I. P. Singh 1961, p. 219). All other Sikh jatis in Daleke interdine, attend each others' domestic ceremonies and share in communal rites. The cultivator jatis hold themselves to be of higher rank than the artisan and serving jatis. Though marriage is generally within the jati, women may be brought in from lower jatis; there were fifteen women in the village whose jati was "not known." They face little disadvantage on that account and their children suffer none.

Complete abolition of jati divisions among Sikhs is still urged by itinerant preachers. One such reformer spoke in the Daleke village temple while I. P. Singh was there. A Mazhbi rose to ask whether any in the audience would receive his daughters into their families in marriage. "Practically everybody in the audience, consisting of all castes, raised his hand." But when he asked who would give girls in marriage to his sons, no one volunteered. Even under the eye of the preacher, no one of higher jati would make that gesture (1958, p. 487). But in ritual performance, even Mazhbis are equals. One of the *granthis*, the religious functionaries, of the village is a Mazhbi. He is given the same respected position as is given to the other granthis in Daleke, one of whom is of the washerman jati, another a carpenter, and one a Jat (I. P. Singh 1958, pp. 483, 487).

In another Sikh village, Nalli in Ludhiana District, there are seven Sikh jatis. Here also there is quite free interdining and interchange except with Harijan Sikhs. Only one couple had married across jati lines; a Jat Sikh had a wife of the water-carrier Sikhs. One of his clansmen suggested that because he was mentally defective and poor he had been unable to get a Jat Sikh bride (Izmirlian 1964, pp. 23–28). In both these villages, alliance divisions and factional conflicts are not crystalized along jati lines.

Each Sikh jati accepts Hindu or Muslim converts who are from a social level similar to its own. Among some Punjabi Hindus one of the sons in a family may be reared as a Sikh. Until recent decades, Brahmin priests were regularly brought in by Sikh families for their domestic rites. This is done much less often now; Sikhs are now inclined to stress the autonomy of their religion and the independence of the sect. In Daleke village the complete break with Brahmin priests came when a Jat Sikh married a Muslim woman who had been converted to Sikhism. The Brahmins could not tolerate this confusion of faith and threatened to break off all ritual services to their Sikh clients. Nothing daunted, the Sikhs publicly celebrated the conversion and marriage (I. P. Singh 1958, p. 484).

In this village as in others, Sikhs observe a vigorous round of ceremonial activities which help bolster their faith and serve to solidify the sect. The temple is the scene of many activities—discourses, teaching, scriptural readings, informal storytelling—as well as being the setting for the round of rites in which all Sikhs participate (I. P. Singh 1958, pp. 496–497).

As Sikh institutions became established, separatist groups split off, each under a leader who rallied followers to what he believed to be the true, pure precepts of the founding Gurus as against the current practices of the Sikh establishment. One such sect within Sikhism is called Kukas. The sect rose in the mid-nineteenth century under a founding seer who was succeeded by a gifted executive leader. Kukas are an austere group, more rigorously puritanical than are other Sikhs. They give themselves over to a euphoric kind of worship in which they voice loud *kuks* (shrieks). Most Kukas were converted from the lower jatis; they feel that they are the elect, the true, saintly fraternity, as against the other, impaired Sikhs. They number more than half a million and, though they admit converts, they do not marry outside the fold of Kuka believers (K. Singh, 1966, pp. 127–135).

This fissive trend of the nineteenth century was reversed in the twentieth, among Sikhs as among others, by the attractions of fusion. A main stimulus toward unity arose from resentment about the mismanagement of Sikh temples. The hereditary priests of the great shrines, some of them Hindus, asserted proprietary rights in the temples and in temple endowments. In 1920 a number of Sikh leaders organized and, after several years of lobbying, succeeded in having the temples placed legally under the trust of an elected committee, known as S.G.P.C. This committee became a kind of Sikh government within the national and state governments. Income from the temple endowments sustained it; the more militant adherents formed a pressure group, even a striking force (K. Singh 1966, pp. 193–216). Through this organization Sikhs exerted political influence, and in 1966 they were able to bring about the division of the Punjab into two new states of India, Punjab Subha and Haryana. Sikhs now form a majority in Punjab Subha, they were a minority in the undivided state. They are well embarked on the fusion-political process, though internal rivalries keep boiling up among alliances in the state capital as in the villages.

Sikhism began as a way of cultural fusion. The founder's ecumenical vision was directed toward bringing together Hinduism and Islam, Hindus and Muslims. Along that way, however, Sikh converts separated from their former jati affiliations and split again after Sikhism became an established religion. The modern fusion organization among Sikhs has gained notable strength, though it also has suffered the usual fragmentation pangs that come in the aftermath of power.

Personal Conversion and Systemic Stability

Religious movements offered the principal means by which people in this social system could regroup themselves in far-reaching ways. People in all complex societies sooner or later rearrange their social groupings in order to adapt to external change and internal development. Jati mobility has been one adaptive process in this social system, the rise of sectarian groups has been another. Once a sectarian rise had been accomplished, the new group continued in the common pattern of jati mobility.

Incipient sects had the advantage of being voluntary associations of like-minded, like-motivated people. A family, even an individual, could independently join such an association because of the favorable attitude toward a person's dedication to almost any religion, provided that the religion did not carry sinister social overtones. A religion that threatened jati standards and jati integrity was to be shunned. Within that provision, devotional differences were and are readily tolerated.

No wonder, then, that cults have mushroomed in the past and continue to appear. Most of them eventually die out. Some persist, grow until they reach a critical mass for firm establishment, and develop into organized religions. They can reach the later stages because of a combination of inspired leadership, self-sacrificing followers, and other fortunate circumstances—"blessed" circumstances, the true believers firmly hold.

As a cult becomes an organized sect, its people have to operate as a unit in the larger society. In India, villagers knew of no other way to participate in the larger society than as members of a jati. And so the regrouped devotees became members of a jati. What typically began as a deeply stirring religious experience felt by many, sometimes did stir the social system as well, but in ways that helped to preserve the fundamental structure of the social system. This is not to say that these indigenous movements had no effect in the society. Some have considerably affected the culture of their region; some have shaped the trend of political events; a few have influenced the civilization. But none has altered the basic system of jati relations.

In the twentieth century a change in the redistribution process seems to becoming about. The bhajan movement in Madras apparently is not developing quite in the traditional cycle, nor have such wider reform movements as the Arya Samaj done so. Other means for social redistribution and adjustment are becoming available; political and educational agencies are being put to these uses.

The sects discussed so far are indigenous. World religions were brought into India, attracted converts, and became established there. These, too, provided avenues for social regrouping, and converts to them also continued to maintain jati organization and mobility drives.

CHAPTER 29

Social Aspects of Introduced Religions: Muslims

Four scriptural religions, Islam, Christianity, Zoroastrianism, and Judaism were brought into India and became established there. The origins of each in the land are historically obscure though mythologically elaborated. Merchants seem to have been instrumental in each introduction. They came into India from abroad, settled there in small colonies, prospered and attracted converts, perhaps as much by the inspiration of their thriving example as by their proselytizing zeal. Zoroastrianism and Judaism continued in that way, carried by relatively small, localized groups.

Islam and Christianity, however, became more widely accepted in India, apart from the original settlements, after rulers of these religions conquered large territories. Emulation of the temporal rulers and the persuasive power of their resources had something to do with this acceptance though some became converts for essentially spiritual reasons and others were converted because of a desire for social regrouping.

The foreign merchants and rulers were too few or too aloof to induct converts into a new way of life as well as into a new mode of worship. They offered a reference category rather than a reference group. Converts lacked any new social base to go with their new scripture and had little alternative but to continue in the pervasive caste system. They became jatified (linguistic structure too can assimilate foreign elements) and reentered the typical struggle for social mobility. The Parsis, however, did not divide into separate jatis. There were some attempts among these Zoroastrians toward jati separation, but the attempts were overridden. Their rejection of jati division may help explain why they later took so successfully to modern social models.

The adherents of the introduced religions have responded to modern influences with search for wider alliances and identities. Their ways of doing so vary greatly. Large groups of Muslims have become more purely Islamic in their religious practices. Some Jews have emigrated to Israel. Many Christians look to modern education as the best avenue to wider affiliation, to the careers and broader associations open to the educated.

Islam and Christianity have had important influence in India, but village Muslims and Christians carry on their social relations in ways that are generally similar to those followed by their neighbors of other religions. Muslims and Christians participate in their local social orders as jati groups; their mobility drives are in the characteristic patterns and fall into the systemic process of recurrent change. However, religious affiliation does make for certain social differences as well as broad similarities.

Religious Differences and Social Similarities

Muslims in India are about one-ninth the national population; only Indonesia and Pakistan among modern nations have more Muslim citizens. Historically, the Muslims of the subcontinent have contributed notably to Islamic thought as well as to Indian civilization (cf. Smith 1957, pp. 256–291).

Muslim villagers are generally aware of the special career of Islam in India and of the distinctiveness of their religion among others in India. They believe that their social organization is different from that of Hindus. "Orthodox Muslims," Zarina Ahmad points out, "resent the word caste being used for the Muslim religious groups" (1962, p. 329). Though their doctrine and their popular theory assert that all Muslims are equal, the actual social practices of Muslim villagers usually parallel those of their Hindu neighbors. The differences between them can be of vast consequence in certain contexts—the partition into two nations is witness to that—but the differences do not necessarily lie where popular theory holds them to be.

Muslims in all regions of India class themselves into endogamous, hereditary groups which are ranked in relation to each other (cf. Ansari 1960; S. C. Misra 1964; Imtiaz Ahmad 1965; Kudryavtsev 1965). Hereditary occupations are usually attributed to each group; members of each traditionally participate in jajmani relations with families of other jatis in their locality. Where Muslim untouchables exist, they are so treated by both Hindus and Muslims. Muslims usually differ from Hindus in certain family practices, as in permitting parallel-cousin marriage or in allotting greater inheritance rights and stricter seclusion to women; but in other family relations they are usually like the Hindus of their place and social level. A Muslim group in a village maintains its internal cohesion much as does a similar Hindu group. In some regions the same term is used for a Muslim as for a Hindu jati (cf. Eglar 1960, p. 29; Misra 1964, p. 139). In all, it is not misleading for our present purposes of social analysis, to speak of Muslim jatis.

Yet the social differences must be recognized. Muslims of all groups in a village interdine freely (except possibly the local Muslim untouchables), they worship in the same mosques, they participate in ceremonies together. Village Muslims are strongly on guard against individual pollution, as in menstruation and childbirth, but their views of corporate, permanent pollution are more diffuse and are officially disclaimed.

Endogamy is relatively looser. There is apt to be greater latitude for hypergamous marriages; social percolation is easier. Secular power is brought to bear more quickly and forcefully in gaining higher rank. The ritual criteria include exalted ancestry, zeal for Islamic practice, scriptural learning, and freedom from defiling occupations and demeaning customs. These are important but are not as weighty in the Muslim ranking as are the ritual criteria in ranking among Hindus. Hence mobility into a higher rank tends to be more common and is achieved more readily by separate families. Prospering families still must take on pure and genteel practices in the usual mobility pattern, but there is less resistance to their rise in the local Muslim hierarchy, provided they have wealth and use it with proper discretion. Muslim villagers agree that certain Muslim groups are high and others are low, but they show perhaps even less agreement than do Hindu villagers about the precise order of ranking in the middle ranges. This is partly because the order of rank has little place in religion and lacks supporting ideology.

Other doctrinal differences between Islam and Hinduism are well known, even by villagers (cf. Mandelbaum 1947). Islamic doctrine, for one matter, is monotheistic, Hindu doctrine is more eclectic. But for pragmatic purposes of religion, Muslims and Hindus of a locality often use the same shrines and practitioners. This is noted in an account of a village near Hyderabad in Andhra Pradesh, where Muslims are about one-tenth the village population. These Muslims take only a nominal part in Hindu festivals but they "are active and enthusiastic in planning measures to ward off evil spirits, ghosts, and epidemics in cooperation with their Hindu and tribal neighbors" (Dube 1955a, pp. 189–190). Such cooperation is not uncommon. Hindus and Muslims in a village are usually willing to participate in each other's pragmatic rites, even though neither would ever worship in the mosque or temple of the other religion. Both use shamans of either religion, depending on the priest's reputation for effective practice rather than on his formal faith (Mandelbaum 1966, p. 1178).

In their social strivings Muslims may vie with other Muslims of a locality in the same ways in which Hindu families and jatis carry on their rivalries. Riots between Muslim factions have long been reported (cf. Martin 1838, Vol. 1, p. 144). Muslim and Hindu neighbors cooperate in some contexts and not in others. The differing contexts have not yet been studied closely although it is clear that whenever religious differences become salient social markers, the followers of each religion tend to see themselves as upholders of the one true faith, a tendency not restricted to Indian villages.

Indian Muslims share some of the basic social characteristics of the civilization, in their jati arrangements for example. They also share in the characteristics of the region in which they live and the social-economic level to which they belong. They see themselves as being distinctive religiously and they give a special phrasing to the traits they share with non-Muslims. Yet in many respects their social relations are quite like those of their non-Muslim neighbors. A vivid example is that of those Muslims in Kerala who were matrilineal in the Nayar manner, utterly unlike the patrilineal emphasis of Islamic scripture and of other Indian Muslims (Gough 1961, pp. 415–442; Yalman 1967, pp. 372–374).

In all regions, Muslims carry on their social relations in ways characteristic of their locality. Thus one account of a village in West Bengal reports that the three levels of Muslim jatis there "are very much akin to those of the parallel Hindu castes of the village." Here the Shaikhs are the highest and are completely endogamous. Cultivators make up the middle bloc and fishermen the lowest. The Muslim fishermen may not take water from the tanks used by the higher Muslims nor are they allowed to enter the village mosque (Guha 1965, pp. 168–169).

A review of village studies in East Pakistan concludes, "In summary, the Muslim caste-like groups are much like their Hindu counterparts, especially among the specialists and menials.

Nevertheless, if the Muslim group are to be called castes, it must be recognized that they are part of a considerably more flexible system of social stratification" (Beech, *et al*., 1966, p. 11).[1]

Some of the best studies of Muslim groups have been done in Uttar Pradesh and in West Pakistan. These studies further indicate that Muslims share in the social characteristics of their region, participate in the patterns of mobility, and enter into the processes of recurrent change.

Muslims of Uttar Pradesh

Muslim social organization in the state of Uttar Pradesh, with nearly eleven million Muslims in the 1961 Census, has been sketched by Ghaus Ansari (1960). He reports that U. P. Muslims group their jatis in several blocs, not unlike the varna categories. A main distinction is between the *Ashraf*, the "honorable," and all other Muslims, the *Ajlaf*. The division has been compared to the Hindu dichotomy between the "twice-born" varnas and other Hindus, but Imtiaz Ahmad (1967) stresses that the term Ashraf refers more to the esteemed style of life than to any specific jatis or blocs.

Those who are called Ashraf are usually held to be descendants of distinguished foreign, non-Indian, ancestors. They are traditionally the landowners, the civic and religious leaders, the wealthier and more purely Islamic among the Muslims of their locality. According to Ansari, four "classes" (i.e., jati-clusters) of Ashraf are found in Uttar Pradesh, of whom the highest are the *Sayyad*, "princes." This line is believed to come from the daughter of the Prophet and her husband, the fourth Caliph of Islam. Sayyads are further divided into some twenty sections; endogamy is common within each section but is not mandatory. Next are the *Shaikh*, "chiefs," believed to be descended from Arab ancestors who were among the first followers of the Prophet. Marriages may be contracted between families of their sections and Sayyads, but rarely with families of the two other high groups, the *Mughals* and *Pathans*. These two are reputedly descended from Mongol and Afghani conquerors in India (Ansari 1960, pp. 35–38; Z. Ahmad 1962, pp. 326–328).

At the bottom of the Muslim ranking are those Muslims who do scavenging, sweeping, and other menial tasks. In Uttar Pradesh they are commonly descended from converts who retained their former jati name, occupation, poverty, and disabilities. Muslims of higher status do not ordinarily take food from them. Sometimes they are not allowed to worship inside the village mosque but must stand and pray outside (Ansari 1960, pp. 50, 58). They are treated in much the same way as their Hindu counterparts. However, a high Muslim may choose to take food from them or worship with them without incurring the kind of penalties that a high-ranking Hindu might suffer for such transgression.

The middle ranks among Muslims of U. P. include Muslim Rajputs and the "clean occupational castes." The social distance between them and the highest Muslims is illustrated by Zarina Ahmad's observation that in the villages she studied no member of an Ashraf group will marry a non-Ashraf or even take food with one (1962, p. 327). There is broader interdining among Muslims elsewhere in U. P. Muslims of the Shi'ah sect are reported to be more stringent about food than are Sunnis. Shi'ahs are supposed to refuse prepared food from any non-Muslims but Sunnis will take such food from "clean Hindu castes" (Ansari 1960, pp. 40–41, 54–55, 58).

---

[1] Bengali Muslims are said by Karim to take particular pride in foreign ancestry. Distinguished forebears from anywhere outside of Bengal seem to validate Ashraf rank; if they were from outside India, "it is the better" (1956 p. 134).

Village studies from U. P. show that Muslims operate in their local social order much as do Hindus of similar status. In one village of Saharanpur district about half the land is owned and cultivated by the Hindu jati of Tyagis and the rest by Muslim Tyagis. They are descendants of a common ancestor and together they dominate village affairs (Gupta 1956, p. 31).

A study of kinship among Ashraf Muslims in several parts of U. P. concludes that their kinship terminology and inheritance rules are essentially similar to those of the higher Hindu jatis of the same localities (Vreede–de Stuers 1963). Muslim artisans provide services under the same conditions as do their Hindu counterparts and manage their jati affairs quite like a comparable jati of Hindu artisans (Ansari 1960, p. 56; Misra 1964, pp. 139–149).

An incident from a village of Lucknow district illustrates Muslim sensitivity to rank. One of the guests at a wedding in an Ashraf family was a woman of the *manihar*, bangle-seller jati who had just returned to the village after a long absence. Her husband had prospered; she wore expensive clothes, and, not being recognized as she came in, she was seated at a table with Ashraf ladies. In the middle of the meal, one of the Ashraf women recognized her; the other women "at once stood up and refused to sit at the same table with the *manihar* woman. It caused a lot of embarrassment, but the *manihar* lady had to sit and eat on the floor" (Z. Ahmad 1962, p. 331). In their precipitous, upright act these Muslim ladies were doing what Hindu ladies of high jati would also do in like circumstance. This is not to say that Hindus and Muslims in Uttar Pradesh have identical social views or that the views of either Hindus or Muslims remain unchallenged. Differences as well as similarities exist and must be taken into account; social changes are impending among Muslims as among Hindus.

Villages of West Pakistan

The establishment of Pakistan has had important consequences in the lives of its citizens. Yet studies of Pakistan villages since independence show a considerable continuity in the traditional social groupings. Thus Zekiye Eglar has described a Punjabi Muslim village in which "A child learns the caste it belongs to from the time it begins to speak and tells it when he gives his personal name. Very early, the child also learns that it can marry only within its own caste" (1960, p. 29). These villagers consider caste practices as having been borrowed from the Hindus and as referring primarily to inherited occupation, but they hold strongly to these practices nevertheless.

In this village of Gujrat district, West Pakistan, jajmani relations are like those among Hindu Punjabis, but high rank is more closely and immediately bound to the ownership of land. Very few artisans or servants own any land at all; status within the landowning group depends on the amount of land each family possesses. Eglar emphasizes the importance of gift exchange, called *vartan bhanji*, at all social levels and in all important contexts. These exchanges pivot around the daughters of a family, who are therefore central to social relations among families, jatis, and villages. Since the daughter is the central figure "one may say that a daughter is as crucial to *vartan bhanji* as *vartan bhanji* is to the whole of the traditional culture" (Eglar 1960, p. 101). Similar analyses of gift exchange in other villages have yet to be made. It may be as dominant a concern of women elsewhere in the land as it is in this Muslim village in the Punjab. Certainly women talk a good deal about this in other places.

An account of another Punjabi village illustrates the way in which Muslim villagers continue the life style of their ancestral Hindu group. In this case they are Jats, who are dominant landowners in a village of Gujranwala district, West Pakistan. Jats, whether Hindu, Sikh, or Muslim, pride themselves on their unvarnished manner, their straightforward response, their taste for a fight. The Muslim Jats here are in the same mold, believing that a person who has no enemy, whom nobody fears and whom nobody obeys, is worthless. Inayat Ullah, who has studied this village, reports that "The first question to be asked from a visitor is about his caste, as this information decides whether he is to be given a cot to sit on or is to seat himself on the ground; and whether a special meal is to be cooked for him, or whether ordinary food would be sufficient."

There are some thirteen artisan and laborer jatis among the village Muslims. They are mainly endogamous, though landowners occasionally take specially favored brides from them. Pride in one's jati is strong at all levels; brave deeds by a jati fellow are a source of pride; misdeeds, especially sexual lapses by women, disgrace all in the jati. "Usually, every member of the caste feels it his duty to defend his caste against every sort of accusation and to live up to the tradition of his caste" (Inayat Ullah 1958, pp. 170–174). Conversion to Islam has not dampened pride in jati traditions.

Pride in one's group is also strong in a Muslim village of Dadu district in Sindh, West Pakistan. There are some twenty-seven ranked groups in this village, the groups are called *zat*.[2] The four highest have produced an unusual number of scholars, teachers, and government officials; they have given the village considerable renown. Their motivation toward modern achievement, Honigmann believes, stems from their pride of rank and their drive to maintain it. As among other Muslims, wealth is requisite for such rank but does not necessarily command it. Observance of certain standards, as the seclusion of women, endogamy for girls, limited hypergamy for boys, are still relevant for high rank. A main attribute is noble ancestry, which means that the men of the group have long been wealthy, respected, learned, and free from any need to do manual labor.

Yet noble ancestry alone is not sufficient; there are four Sayyid families in the village who are not counted among the village leaders. Though presumably descendants of the Prophet, they are given respect "from the religious, not the social point of view." They are lacking in the kind of education and government service that are now important criteria for high rank (Honigmann 1960a, pp. 8–12; 1960b, pp. 833–839).

In these villages of West Pakistan, social relations are hierarchically arranged in the general pattern followed by most people on the subcontinent. Mobility drives, both in the traditional and modernized modes, are also broadly similar among Muslims and others of each region.

Social Mobility among Muslims

Prospering Muslims pass upward in the familiar pattern. Low-ranking families who become rich disappear from their former social niche and reappear in a higher Muslim stratum. Single families can do this over a few years; the rise of whole groups takes longer but the sequence of steps is broadly the same. "As soon as a lower class Muslim makes money, he puts his women in *purdah* (a practice observed only by the Ashrafs), starts going to the communal prayers in the mosque

---

[2] The author notes that Muslims do not employ the term "caste" with the meaning it possesses for Hindus. But his explanation of the terms used in this Sindhi village, called Pat, points up the parallel usages. "The leading families of Pat refer to themselves as constituting four or five 'castes' (English-speaking villagers and public records used the words 'tribe', *zat*, and 'community' interchangeably with 'caste').... Such castes are ideally endogamous, marriage into a *known* family bearing the same surname being preferred" (Honigmann 1960b, p. 833).

and goes to Mecca for pilgrimage" (Zarina Ahmad 1962, p. 329). Such families cast off inferior occupations, whether as weavers or barbers or butchers, become landowners and assume the manners of landowners. They give more assiduous attention to religion in ways that are beyond the means of those who work with their hands. They secure the services of a reputable ritual leader, a *Maulvi*, to conduct their life-cycle and domestic rites. Once they acquire some aura of respectable rank, they negotiate for prestigious marriages for their children. As they succeed in this, they place themselves in a higher bracket of rank among the local Muslims (Ansari 1960, pp. 38–39; Misra 1964, p. 169). Having done so among Muslims, they presumably acquire like respectability in the eyes of the non-Muslim villagers, though there have been few descriptions of the mutual ranking of Muslims and Hindus in a locality.

The case history of a rising Muslim family in eastern Uttar Pradesh is told by Zarina Ahmad. A new Muslim family came in to a village of Barabanki district, built a big house, and set up a large brick-making works. Their sons were being educated in town; their women were in strict *purdah;* their elders were constantly at prayers in the mosque. The family called itself Shaikh, but it soon became known in the village that they had been Julahas, weavers, in their former home. Most of the landowning Ashraf families of the village kept aloof from the newcomers, refusing to attend their social occasions. After a time a few of the Ashraf did accept their invitations.

With this small encouragement, the family "took a very daring step," and sent a proposal for their son's marriage to an Ashraf girl. The boy was well educated, the parents rich, the match attractive—save for the groom's origins. After a year of negotiation, the alliance was settled and the marriage celebrated with lavish pomp. The other Ashraf families of the village were much annoyed, not only at the fact of the alliance but also at its pretentious display. The new couple felt this animus and moved out of the village permanently, though the family remains and maintains its claims. "But, within a generation or two, these facts will be forgotten and they will become genuine Shaikhs" (Z. Ahmad 1962, pp. 331–332).

To repeat, in another version, the popular saying about mobility that was quoted earlier, "We used to be butchers and now we are Shaikhs. Next year if the harvest prices are good for us, we shall be Sayyads" (cf. Ansari 1960, p. 37; Blunt 1931, p. 184; Misra 1964, p. 170). Some aspiring Muslims change their jati names as other ambitious villagers have done. The 1931 Census report for U. P. lists three Muslim jatis with fresh claims to being Shaikh; formerly one was a weaver, one a musician, and one a butcher group (Ansari 1960, p. 38). Not all such Muslim groups seek to change their names, however. The Sunni Vohras of Gujarat were mainly farmers at the beginning of the twentieth century. They have since become predominantly traders and have much improved their jati practices as well as their occupation, but they keep the same name (Misra 1964, pp. 169–170).

Gujarati Muslims seem to have been particularly prone to fission. There are at least six jatis of Memons, tradesmen, and four of Vohras, cultivators. These are further subdivided by allegiance to different holy men. The families of one part of a jati may become adherents of a particular saint while others in the jati give allegiance to a different holy man; the two sides will have little to do with each other (Misra 1964, pp. 138–142).

New jatis have arisen from indigenous Muslim sects much as they did from indigenous sects of Hinduism. The two major sects of Islam, Sunni and Shi'a, were brought in with Islam itself. In India each of these major denominations was further divided. One of the offshoots of the Shi'ah are the Isma'ili, some of whom acknowledge the Aga Khan as their head. There are several Isma'ili jatis, the Bohras and Khojas of Gujarat being the major groups among them. Some of the Muslim sects indigenous to India developed quite eclectic doctrines. Khoja doctrine, for example, held at one time that the Aga Khan was an incarnation of the "glorious Tenth Avatar," the future manifestation of Vishnu (Khadduri and Liebesny 1955, pp. 117–119). One Muslim cult was founded by a Syrian of Jewish origin and included Jewish and Christian as well as Hindu rites; other Muslim sects gave honor to Hindu deities (Aziz Ahmad 1964, pp. 155–163).

A modern sect, the Ahmadiyas, was founded in the late nineteenth century by a powerful sage in a small town of the Punjab. His followers have become more than a sectarian jati they form a close-knit community engaged in economic activities as well as in vigorous missionary work. Their center has been described as a combination of modern enterprise and fundamentalist theology; their very activism has drawn attacks from other Muslims. Like the more vigorous Hindu sects, the Isma'illis and the Ahmadiyas have developed a particularly effective internal organization. This helps bring them prosperity which in turn eventually yields respectable status in their localities (Smith 1957, pp. 230–231; Spate 1954, pp. 189–192; Misra 1964, pp. 15–68).

Aspiring Muslims emulate their local elite as Hindus emulate theirs. One observer has described the Muslim process under the term "Ashrafization" (Vreede–de Stuers 1962). Such emulation is much more than just a way of social climbing; it is seen as a means to moral, transcendental personal improvement. Those who shift to a more devout Islamic way of life, who attend to prayers and rituals more assiduously, who give hours to reading or listening to the Koran, who school their sons to the beauties of Islamic literature, do so not only because they can afford to and because it is the path to higher status, but also because they want to be better men, finer servants of God. A Muslim who intensifies his devotions, like a Hindu who deepens his piety, is not only following the main chance in the game of social elevation, he is also pursuing the revealed direction toward the good of his eternal soul.

The spiritual gain does not lessen one's need for proper social maneuver. A rising family must take on other Ashraf ways, such as having the women observe strict seclusion. This is a sure sign of prosperity, since women so secluded cannot work out of the house and must be able to afford servants. Outer symbols must also be changed. The poorest usually wear the same dress as do the poor among non-Muslims of their locality. But among the wealthier and higher villagers, a distinctive Muslim costume is worn nowadays and rising families tend to adopt the distinguishing dress (cf. Misra 1964, p. 167). At a still higher social level, modern educated Muslims generally adopt Western-style dress and revise their domestic practices quite as do their Hindu counterparts. They may wear traditional Muslim dress on symbolic occasions and give some deference to Ashraf ways, but they have added new elite standards that combine Islamic precepts, Ashraf manners, and modern mores.

These elite standards are beyond an ordinary Muslim villager's knowledge and certainly beyond his reach. If he has status ambitions, he is intent on dropping debasing customs and on assuming respectable ones. He is likely nowadays to drop specifically Hindu customs, such as in the form of marriage or the *rakhi-bandhan* ritual between brother and sister. In modern times Muslims of higher rank frown on the use of specifically Hindu practices.

It was not always so, at least not in the Punjab. In the 1883 Census report for the Punjab, Ibbetson wrote that in the eastern part of that region, "conversion has absolutely no effect upon the caste of the convert. His social customs are unaltered, his tribal restrictions are unrelaxed, his rules of marriage and inheritance unchanged; and about the only difference is that he shaves his scalplock and the upper edge of his moustache, repeats the Mahomedan creed in a mosque, and adds the

Musalman to the Hindu wedding ceremony" (1916, pp. 13–14). Ibbetson did say that since the 1850s there had been a Muslim revival in the Punjab and that the adherence of Muslims to Islamic law and custom was growing stronger. But it was not only Muslims in the eastern Punjab who neglected their scripture, the Hindus of the region did not set great store by the local Brahmins or by Sanskritic scripture. In the twentieth century, however, Punjabis of all religions came to be less blithely eclectic and more observant of their respective doctrines.

The primary goal of ambitious Muslim villagers in all regions is to gain better status among the Muslim groups of their locality. If they achieve that they also rise in the general status system of the village and its locality. The bracket of Muslim jatis is articulated into the local system of rank. As we have noted, untouchables are treated as such by all in a village, whether they are Hindu or Muslim. A wealthy Muslim landowner of distinguished bearing and esteemed ancestry is generally given respect by all in his locality.

Islamization and Modern Adaptation

Relations between Muslims and non-Muslims were severely jolted throughout the subcontinent and completely severed in many places during the political developments of the 1940s. Then, as commonly occurs in times of general tension, the usual village rivalries were consolidated into larger oppositions. Status rivalries among particular jatis or alliances were relinquished for more massive encounters. The years before independence saw a steady increase, spurred by national forces, in mass confrontations between Hindu and Muslim villagers. In earlier periods, such antagonisms might flare when one side publicly celebrated its festivals. The adherents of the other religion were then particularly sensitive to any gestures or status claims made in the celebration that might disparage their own position, but once the day of struggle was past, villagers usually reverted to the daily round of interchange among jatis and families of all religions. National events exacerbated this antagonism and made it a continuous affair, even in villages, until it resulted in the climactic separation of nations (Mandelbaum 1947).

After independence, massive demonstrations of rivalry within each nation were elicited by various issues; one such issue has been the claims of linguistic regions for proper rank and recognition. Tensions between Muslims and Hindus have erupted in violence in certain places and times, but these tensions were not the paramount reasons for internal strife in either nation, nor have they become a dominant issue of internal politics.

Muslims in India soon resumed their efforts for group improvement and social mobility, as did non-Muslims. Many of the Muslim jatis have followed the general trend toward federation, reform, and political participation. Reform, as for Hindu jatis, entails a combination of traditional high practices and prestigeful modern ways. Reform among Muslim villagers particularly, means greater observance of their religious traditions and so there has been a marked turning toward Islamic practices and symbols.

This intensified Islamization is shown by the Meos, the dominant jati in some two thousand villages on the borderlands of Rajasthan and Punjab. They tilled a poor land and in earlier centuries often resorted to raiding. They became Muslims about the fifteenth century, perhaps in the hope that the Muslim rulers might then deal more leniently with them. After their conversion they continued as bearers of Rajput values and kept their Rajput customs, adding such Muslim practices as circumcision and burial of the dead. They maintained jajmani relations with Hindu artisans and with the Brahmins who conducted some of their rites.

After 1947, however, the Meos found the old relationships to be unworkable.[3] Their former clients and servants began to break away and to demand more money and independence. Meos realized that they needed better cooperation within their own group and with others beyond their territory in order to be effective in modern ways, especially as participants in state politics. They had been singled out as Muslims by others in their region, subjected to hostile gestures and even to clumsy attempts at reconversion. Proud of their identity as Meos, they received a most cordial reception from other Muslims while the non-Muslims around them were decidedly cool. Some of the Meos, perhaps a fourth, migrated to Pakistan but the rest remained in India. They have now become far more dedicated to Islam than they had ever been before. They are determinedly giving up Hindu practices and are diligently trying to take on Islamic ways, though they are not always sure what these ways may be. They have built new mosques; they wear a new style of dress; they have begun to eat meat, even buffalo meat. "It is not at all an exaggeration to say that the Meos have adopted more of Muslim practices in the last 17 years than they had in the previous 450 years" (Aggarwal 1966, pp. 159–160).

Their original conversion required no profound turn to scriptural Islam; they kept their former ways quite intact and only added an overlay of Muslim features. But if they are now to be as effective politically as are other organized groups, they need stronger internal unity than before and wider alliances. They look for both in the context of Islam, and so they have become stauncher Muslims, partly for reasons of religion, but partly also in order to become better participants in the democratic processes of the Indian nation.

Muslim groups in other parts of India have been forming political alliance with fellow Muslims much as caste associations and federations have been formed (cf. Wright 1966; Srinivas 1966, pp. 73–74). In the present trend Muslim leaders in India tend to emphasize the distinctive symbols of their religious heritage while striving to integrate their people into the national spheres of politics, education, and economics, and to gain a good place for them in these spheres.

[3] An account of recent Meo history as seen by one of their political activists is by Chowdhry Abdul Haye (1966).

CHAPTER 30

Social Aspects of Introduced Religions: Jews, Parsis, Christians

Judaism, Zoroastrianism, and Christianity have been rooted in India for more than a millennium. The followers of each religion have participated in their local social systems as jati members. The historical evidence on Jews and Christians in India is particularly useful in showing how the social themes of these religions came to be adapted to the prevailing mode of Indian society. Hence our discussion of Jews and Christians gives particular attention to their historical development.

JEWS: TWO SETTLEMENTS, FIVE JATIS

The ancient Indian settlements of Jews are in Cochin (in the state of Kerala) and in Maharashtra. Although both settlements were always numerically small, they were divided into jatis. The Jews of Cochin have been more extensively described than have those of Maharashtra.

The three jatis of Cochin Jews numbered about twenty-two hundred persons in the seventeenth century and there were fewer still in later times. Yet they have firmly maintained their religious identity for at least a millennium (Mandelbaum 1939). Their earliest documentary record is found in a set of copper plates of about the eleventh century. Inscribed on these plates are grants conferred in perpetuity by the reigning Raja to a Jew named Joseph Rabban. He and his posterity were granted a principality and all its revenue. They were also given such prerogatives as the right to ride an elephant, to be carried in a litter, to parade with a state umbrella, to be preceded by drums and trumpets, to have criers call out before their approach so that the lowly might withdraw from the streets. The date inscribed is not certain but has been interpreted as 1020 A.D. It is clear that a Jewish community must have existed in the Raja's domain for some time before the date of the grant. Such boons would not have been bestowed on a recent arrival (cf. Fischel 1967).

There is a Jewish tombstone in Cochin bearing a date equivalent to 1269 A.D. and there are historical records of the Cochin Jews from every century thereafter. A traveler's report of 1570 gives the first mention of their social organization as including "a Sephardi community and other congregations of the black Jews." The Sephardic families were almost all descendants of immigrants from Europe, North Africa, and the Middle East who had come in after the Portuguese opened the sea route from Europe to India in the early sixteenth century. But two families of the Sephardis, or the White Jews as they came to be called, were descended from Jews who had been in the region long before the first Portuguese arrived.

After the Dutch ousted the Portuguese from India, a delegation was sent by the Amsterdam Jewish congregation to conduct an enquiry into the condition of their coreligionists in Cochin (cf. Fischel 1962). The account of their researches, published in 1687, shows that there were then two jatis of Cochin Jews and that their relations were like those of a higher and a lower jati elsewhere in this region. The White Jews were generally lighter in skin color than the Black Jews, though some of the White were as dark as any of the Blacks.

The White Jews would not intermarry or interdine with the Black Jews and would not even count a Black Jew as one of the *minyan*, the minimum member of ten required for congregational worship. The Black Jews repeatedly challenged the assumed jati superiority of the White Jews. In the sixteenth century they sent petitions to rabbinical authorities in Egypt, asking that their claims to equal status with the White Jews be confirmed. There is a record of another petition for equality in the year 1723, this one addressed to the Raja of Cochin, specifically asking that women of the White Jews be made to wear the same headdress as women of the Black Jews. The Raja in his wisdom decreed that the women could wear what they pleased.

For a time there was a splinter group within the Black Jews reminiscent of those among the indigenous sects. One of their seven synagogues lacked its own ritual butcher and its members arranged with the White Jews to certify a member of that congregation for the office. Previously, candidates for this post were ordained only by Black Jews; the other congregations of Black Jews gathered in council and outcast all in the errant synagogue. For generations they were not allowed to worship with the others. Marriage to one of their girls meant that the groom could no longer participate in his former synagogue. But a single congregation was scarcely enough to form a separate jati, so the quarrel gradually lapsed and in the mid-twentieth century was almost forgotten.

A third jati did rise from converts made by the White Jews from among their servants. They were called by the Hebrew term *meshuhararim*, "the manumitted," and called "Brown Jews" in English. Conversions were still being made when I made a brief study of the Cochin Jews in 1937. One of them explained the process in this way. "The servant feels more secure in his master's house if he becomes a coreligionist of the employer." He went on to tell that many of the servants had spent all their lives in Jewish homes and had participated in the ceremonial cycle and daily practices of Judaism. "They feel associated with Judaism in every way, and want to become Jews in name also. And the servants who are born in Jewish houses sometimes have Jewish blood in their veins." He concluded that in the Passover ceremony, the convert sits at his master's table as an equal, in accordance with scriptural rule, "and so achieves a prestige which the non-Jews among the servants cannot attain."

In the twentieth century, the Jews of Cochin have shown the characteristic reach for wider affiliations. A good many of them have found it in Zionism and have emigrated to Israel.

The other ancient settlement of Jews in India is larger, with some 14,000 people, but it is still a tiny enclave in the Marathi-speaking region. These Jews now are known by the Hebrew term, Bene Israel, sons of Israel, but prior to the eighteenth century they knew almost no Hebrew and apparently had no knowledge of or contacts with other Jewish groups. They lived in several Konkani villages as oil-pressers. This is not a prestigious occupation and they did not rank high in their villages. They were distinguished by certain religious traits that were unlike those of any of their neighbors. For one thing, they were known as Shanwar Telis, Saturday oilmen, because they would not work on Saturday. They knew nothing of Judaic scriptural law, but they did observe certain Jewish festivals. They maintained some of the Judaic dictary regulations and practiced circumcision. Their one Hebraic formula was the Shema, the brief confession of faith, which they recited as an incantation at every ritual occasion (Strizower 1959, pp. 45–47).

Like oil-pressers in other regions, they attempted to improve their local status by such reforms as purifying their diet and prohibiting the remarriage of widows. After Cochin Jews established contact with them in the eighteenth century and after they came to know of other, foreign, Jews in Bombay City in the nineteenth century, the reference model of Judaism was opened for them. They took to it but did not relinquish their jati divisions.

Like the Cochin Jews but independently of them, the Bene Israel were separated into two jatis, the higher being called the Gora, the fair ones, and the lower the Kala, the dark ones. They too did not interdine or intermarry, though they did worship in the same synagogues. Those of the higher jati claimed purer Jewish ancestry; the lower, they alleged, was of mixed origins.

The separation continued into recent times, even in the city of Bombay. One woman of the Gora jati recalled, "My mother used to get furious when Kala came near her cooking utensils and would push them away. She would not allow Kala to touch any utensils which she used for food" (Strizower 1959, p. 49). Most of the Bene Israel now live in Bombay City; a good many of them have migrated to Israel. The barriers between the two jatis are far less rigid in the city than they had been in the Konkan villages, but even in the 1950s a betrothal across the two jatis raised family objections as well as some disapproval among the local Jews (Strizowei 1959, pp. 48–49, 56).

These Jewish jatis provide further examples of the gravitational attraction of the Indian system of caste. Similar influence is exerted by the social order of any civilization on the smaller, culturally divergent groups who live within it.

Parsis

The Parsis have not split into separate jatis. Their religion, Zoroastrianism, was introduced to India from Persia in about the 8th century A.D. Parsis were a small, little known mercantile community in the western part of India until recent centuries, when a number of their families became successful industrial entrepreneurs and merchant tycoons. Parsis as a group then acquired cultural and financial influence far beyond their modest number of about 115,000 people. Much of their culture, apart from religious rites, was like that of other trading communities of Maharashtra and Gujrat. Their internal councils resembled the panchayats of trading jatis, though perhaps they were more effective than most of these. In their localities, they constituted another jati, mainly of traders.

Though Parsi families strive for status as do families of other jatis, there has been little formal separation among Parsis. One short-lived separatist move occurred in the eighteenth century when families of hereditary priests decided to set up hypergamous relationships with lay Parsis, to take daughters from the laity as brides but not to give their own daughters into lay families. The incensed laity passed a resolution in 1777 that reversed this order; the quarrel grew until a government commission of three "English gentlemen" arbitrated the matter in 1786 and smoothed over the rift (Karaka 1884, pp. 219–233). Since the mid-nineteenth century Parsis have been among the leaders in the Indian trend toward modernization; their example has been emulated by other modernizing groups in their region and elsewhere in the country.

Christians of the Earlier and of the Later Foundation

Christianity was brought to India in two main movements separated by more than a millennium. The first movement occurred in the early centuries after Christ when Christian travelers, following the trade routes from the Levant, settled along the coast of Kerala, made converts, and established permanent groups of Christians there. The second wave began in the sixteenth century when Europeans seized political control over trade centers and eventually over the entire subcontinent. This second introduction of Christianity into India was different from the other religious introductions in that it was carried forward by missionaries, who were professionally dedicated to making converts. Their efforts, moreover, were bolstered by the powers of the state and by the obvious material advantages of their European culture.

The first advent of Christianity produced social results like those caused by the first entries of Jews and of Muslims along the west coast of India. The ancient Christian population of Kerala was much larger than that of the Jews but not so large as that of the Muslims. Known as Syrian Christians because their liturgy is mainly in Syriac, they long maintained intermittent contacts with centers of Christianity outside India. Like the Cochin Jews, they too possess ancient copper plates that confer privileges on some of their families; they seem to have been under the protection of Rajas in medieval times, perhaps because they acted, as did the Cochin Jews, as reliable middlemen in trade and as functionaries in government (Anantakrishna Ayyar 1926, pp. 50–57).

As tradesmen and government servants the Syrian Christians were ranked above the artisan and laboring jatis but well below the priestly and warrior groups. Their way of life, except for religious practice, was not notably different from that of their neighbors of similar rank and occupation. They grouped themselves into a number of jatis; the principal differences among them were denominational and territorial (Anantakrishna Ayyar 1926, pp. 60–61). The jatis of Syrian Christians jockeyed for status as other sectarian jatis have done, and like them they became part of the local caste orders.

The second, European, introduction of Christianity posed fresh problems to Indians. The religion was seen as an adjunct of a most powerful culture and society. The culture could yield great material benefits but it was so thoroughly alien that few Indians could imagine themselves as full participants in it. Hence the religion, freely proffered as the one part of that culture they were urged to share, seemed more the property and hallmark of the foreign rulers than the spiritual legacy for all mankind that their missionaries said it was. Some attributes of the rulers were not unattractive, but other attributes would undermine the fundamental ritual basis of high rank.

Moreover, although the Christian missionaries insisted that all believers were equal before God, they and other Europeans kept meticulously aloof—as much so as the haughtiest of indigenous sects—from any token of social equality, whether in everyday dining or in intermarriage. The equality they insisted on seemed confined to the hours of church worship and even then the padre sahib was unquestionably the actual first among putative equals.

The European administrators by and large were content to have it so. From the earliest Portuguese establishment to the high noon of British control, they found it useful to be accepted as a species of especially powerful and socially distant Kshatriyas who would not try to impose their own religion on all their subjects, though they would welcome and even favor converts. But some of the missionaries felt caught in a strong dilemma. Their sacred commitment was to bring as many heathen as possible into the fold, to change their lives religiously. But they soon found that to change lives religiously they also had to change them socially, since ritual and social elements were inseparable in the Indian view. And shifting their converts' social organization was a mighty task. The alternative was to accommodate the missionaries' standards to Indian social values.

One of the first to face this dilemma with courage and ability was Roberto de Nobili, an Italian Jesuit, scion of Tuscan patricians, a prodigy of learning in his youth, related to two Popes and nephew of the distinguished and influential Cardinal Bellarmine (Cronin 1959). De Nobili set foot on Indian soil in Goa in 1605 and died in Mylapore near Madras City in 1656. During the half century of his missionary work he did what no other European missionary had been able to do before and what exceedingly few did after. He set out to conquer Hinduism from within, to convert by colloquy with Brahmins in their sacred language and to convince all Hindus through the example of his ascetic life.

He lived that life as a sadhu, clad in the saffron robes of an ascetic, keeping to high standards of Hindu ritual purity in his diet, in his daily activities, and in his social contacts. Almost all his missionary efforts were carried on where there were few or no Europeans, where no European force could protect him should the local Raja or the populace turn against him. He learned to speak Tamil and other vernacular languages fluently so that he could convince the temporal rulers; he mastered Sanskrit and Sanskritic scripture so that he could sway learned Brahmins on their own theological grounds through the cogency of his arguments for Christianity. He believed that once he was able to make convinced Christians of those at the top of the social order, all the rest would follow.

He did have successes. He and his associates made a good many converts, 150,000 by the end of the seventeenth century, but there were also great difficulties. Near to his locality in Madurai, a mission of Portuguese priests had established a church among fishermen. Wearing their contaminating shoes, eating their polluted diet, ignorant of the language and the civilization, such priests could still do something for fishermen and others of the lowest jatis; they could do nothing but arouse disgust when they tried to come close to Brahmins and others who valued their own high status.

De Nobili could not associate with such priests and still maintain his reputation as a sadhu worthy of respect. He could not break totally with them lest his religious superiors take offense, as they indeed did from time to time. He tried visiting his fellow Europeans under cover of darkness and eventually had to face hostile formal investigations from both his own Church and from the indigenous authorities.

De Nobili's strategy for the conversion of India was an extension of that propounded earlier by Saint Francis Xavier and it was carried on for several decades after de Nobili's death. A set of instructions for missionaries given in 1659, as quoted by a contemporary Jesuit, offered these recommendations. "Ne vous efforcez pas de détourner les peuples de leur rites et coutumes, pourvu qu'ils ne soient pas ouvertement contraires à la religion et aux bonnes moeurs. Quoi de plus absurde que de vouloir remplacer ces coutumes par celles de la France, de l'Espagne, ou de l'Italie ou de toute autre partie de l'Europe? Ce ne sont pas ces coutumes qu'il faut implanter, mais la Foi, qui ne repousse les usages d'ancien pays, s'ils ne sont pas mauvais, mais veut au contraire qu'on les conserve" (Castets 1931, pp. 564–565).

These sage instructions could not be carried out for long. To keep the customs of this country meant that Christians, both the missionaries and converts, had to keep social distance among the jatis of their converts. For a time those who followed de Nobili's lead actually did this and a Catholic priest who ministered to Brahmins avoided any contact with a fellow Jesuit who worked among untouchables. But this accommodation to jati practices clashed too violently with European notions and it was banned in a papal decree of 1704. The same decree declared that Christianity should be presented to Indians in a form that was not repugnant to them. Catholic missionaries did generally make some attempts to respect purity observances, as in abstaining from beef and even other kinds of meat, but they were far from ritually pure by Indian standards (O'Malley 1941, pp. 50–53; Neill 1934, pp. 60–62).

After Protestant missionaries arrived in considerable numbers in the nineteenth century, their denominational conferences regularly discussed caste divisions among converts and passed resolutions condemning jati practices among Christians (Raj 1959, pp. 64–77). Some of the missionaries, both Catholic and Protestant, recognized how impossibly difficult was the rootless position of any convert who faithfully tried to follow their social as well as spiritual advice.

The Indologist Max Müller recognized this clearly, even though he himself never visited India. Indian converts were not admitted to what they saw as English caste, he noted, so a potential convert dreaded the prospect of an isolated position. Müller recommended that measures should be adopted to give converts something in place of the caste position that they would lose. "In a certain sense no man ought to be without caste, without friends who take care of him, without companions who watch him, without associates whose good opinion he values, without companions with whom he can work for a common cause." He added that the healthy life of a political body, meaning a modern political body, can only be supported by means of associations, circles, leagues, guilds, clans, clubs, or parties; "... and in a country where caste takes the place of all this, the abolition of caste would be tantamount to a complete social disorganization" (Müller 1868, p. 358).

Converts might have adapted the religion to the social system more smoothly, as indeed the Syrian Christians did, had it not been for the overseeing presence of the resident missionaries. These men were generally against the Indian social order yet were unable to provide feasible alternatives. As a result, converts were mainly made from very low jatis, from those who had nothing to lose and perhaps could gain something in status and livelihood. In the Punjab, as Khushwant Singh comments, Christian came to be synonymous with sweeper despite some conversions from the Sikh elite (1966, p. 138).

The Abbé Dubois sadly wrote about the low state of Christianity in India at the beginning of the nineteenth century, attributing the decline of Christians in number and in the quality of their devotion to the "immoral and disorderly conduct of the Europeans," who overran the country and provided horrid examples of Christianity. "A Hindu who embraces Christianity nowadays must make up his mind to lose everything that makes life pleasant.... He is abandoned and shunned by everyone" (1928, p. 301).

The Abbé was condemning the conduct of European soldiers and officials, but he implied that the missionaries too, in their disregard of Indian ritual sensibilities, made it hard for villagers to accept the religion. In spite of this, many did become Christians, though they were a small fraction of the population in most areas. The total Christian population in India in 1961 stood at some eight million. Some who were not untouchables were converted for reasons of factional advantage, others for the connection they might make with secular power and especially for educational opportunities, and some for essentially religious reasons.

One who became a Christian as a result of his spiritual quest was Narayan Vamen Tilak (1862–1919), a learned Chitpavan Brahmin. He became renowned among Christians in Maharashtra and wrote notable poetry in Marathi as well as numerous tracts, articles, and sermons. He did much to transpose Christian concepts into a language of poetry and prose that could appeal to the literati of Maharashtra. But by his day, the tide of Indian intellectual opinion was already firmly set against the proffered religion of the rulers (cf. Winslow 1923; L. Tilak 1950).

A Christian Jati: Nadars of Tamil Nadu (Madras)

In spite of the difficulties inherent in conversion to Christianity, functioning jatis of converts did take form and were articulated into their local social hierarchies. An example is the jati of Christian Nadars in Madras, who were noted above in the discussion of caste associations. From their traditional occupation of brewing and selling alcoholic drink, a good many came to prosper in more lucrative and respectable occupations, mainly as traders and money lenders. They became known for their industry and zeal for education. Contemporary Nadars, both Christian and Hindu, share the view that Nadars are hardworking, enterprising, thrifty, and reliable (Raj 1959, pp. 87, 222, 261).

Perhaps it was because a good many Nadars were enterprising and were very restive about their low status that some of them took the avenue of conversion as a way to better rank despite the outcasting and all the other difficulties besetting that road. One of the earliest Protestant converts among Nadars had previously been a leader in *Shaktipuja*, the cult in which caste barriers were formally broken in a ceremony of eating and drinking together by people of different jatis. He was the leader among the fifteen families in his village who, in the words of a contemporary account, "are attached to this kind of worship, and they esteem it a great honour to have renounced caste… but having heard the word of God, he has become a Christian and abandoned Saktipuja" (quoted in Raj 1959, p. 123). It may be that he found in Christianity a better instrument than *Shaktipuja* to accomplish the same mobility goals.

In any event, the number of Nadar converts grew steadily well into the twentieth century. Though the missionaries urged them to become one united body in the fellowship of Christianity, it was not possible for Nadars and other converts, especially in South India, to do so. Hilda Raj points out that the converts "were sorely in need of belonging somewhere socially and culturally." They could not possibly belong with Europeans in either respect and other converts "who had higher social status than the Nadars would not join with them, those from a lower social status would not be socially acceptable to the Nadars" (1959, p. 215).

Hence they had no alternative but to form a new jati once they had been received into the new religion and were consequently thrown out of their natal jati. The new jati became almost as rigorous an endogamous unit as their original jati. The Christian Nadars have much the same marriage preferences and affinal relations as do the Hindu Nadars; they use similar kinship terms and roles; they observe similar practices of ritual seclusion and purification (H. Raj 1959, pp. 183, 199, 207–212).

Splinter groups separated from the Christian Nadars as they did from other religion-based jatis. One schismatic sect developed briefly under a leader who preached that the European elements in Christianity perverted the true belief, that the New Testament was the chief purveyor of this taint and so true believers should revere only the laws and commandments of the Old Testament. The founder of this revelation accordingly called himself Rabbi and sought correspondence with Rabbis elsewhere. When Hilda Raj searched for this sect in 1956 it had disappeared without trace in the villages where once it had attracted followers (1959, pp. 131–135).

In the end, Nadars who became Christians did not gain status advantage in the villages over those who remained Hindus. But they did have easier access to education. A relatively larger proportion of them have qualified for professional positions and prestigeful employment; a good many have migrated to the cities.

The need for wider alliances also touched the Christian Nadars, and one effort at fusion has been the federation of Protestant denominations in the Church of South India. Another is the Nadar caste association, which we have discussed in an earlier chapter. Any Nadar, whether Hindu or Christian, may belong to it and Christian Nadars do participate in its activities.

Among the Christian Nadars, as among other Christian converts, the missionaries' exhortations that they change their social system could scarcely succeed (cf. Risley 1951, pp. 80–82). The exhorters had little appreciation of the nature of such change of the drastic personal consequences of attempting it. The missionary approach of de Nobili and his followers, that of accommodating to the caste system and working for religious change within it, was also not feasible because it conflicted at too many points with the standard of the European social system, especially in its colonial version. The second movement of Christianity into India seems to have had the greatest impact on Indian society through its efforts in modern education.

Religious Conversion and Recurrent Change

In sum, the introduced religions produced social results like those of the indigenous sects and for similar reasons. Converts were redistributed into new groups or revised the forms of worship of existing groups, but the groups functioned as component parts of the general social system and their members acted socially as jati members. In certain respects Muslims and Christians made special contributions to Indian civilization. They maintained links with coreligionists of other civilizations and were instrumental in the reciprocal influence between civilizations. The Muslims' contribution in this manner was greater in earlier centuries, the Christians' contribution greater in more recent times.

Those who adopted a new faith, whether the faith was an indigenous sect or an introduced religion, eventually reconciled their new doctrine to the traditional system. In doing so they completed the pattern of recurrent change through religion and also reentered the cycles of recurrent change through jati mobility.

In addition to these types of recurrent change within local systems and within the general system of Indian society, there has been another kind of repetitive process. It has involved the inflow of tribal peoples into caste society, a movement that required them to shift from tribal principles of social action to those of caste society.

CHAPTER 31

The Accretion of Tribal Peoples

The shift of tribal peoples into jati society has been going on for many centuries and it is still an ongoing, indeed an accelerating, process. More than thirty million people were counted as tribals in the 1961 Census of India. Many of them are taking on jati practices and are becoming integrated into local hierarchies in ways followed by other tribesmen long before them. Those ways form another process of recurrent change in jati society, not by internal regrouping as in religious movements, but by the gradual transfer of individuals and groups from a tribal kind of social system into local caste systems. Once a tribal group becomes a jati, its members are likely to enter the usual mobility drives as do members of sectarian and other jatis.

Tribesmen who adopt jati customs are, often unwittingly, changing some of their primordial principles of conduct. They are moving themselves and their groups into a different systemic level of culture and society, in which fresh potentials for further development become possible. Difficult choices and personal dilemmas are involved in that move, complicated by the new avenues to potential power and the newer models of the educated elite.

The discussion of tribal changes, in this chapter and in the next, deals with the nature of tribal social systems and the recurrent transfers from them into jati systems. This analysis also provides a contrastive perspective in which to view the whole system of caste society in India. That view in turn suggests some general differences between tribal social systems and those of civilizations.

TRIBE: OFFICIAL DESIGNATION AND ACTUAL CHARACTERISTICS

The shift into jati society is usually gradual and undramatic. There is no absolute cultural or social distinction between all tribal and all caste peoples, but rather a range of variation between tribal and caste traits. At the middle of the range there may be very little difference between a group that considers itself a tribe and one that claims to be a jati.

The requirements of law and administration, however, demand a sharp definition of who is to be counted as a tribesman. Article 46 of the Indian Constitution directs that "The State shall promote with special care the educational and economic interests of the weaker sections of the people, and, in particular, of the Scheduled Castes and Scheduled Tribes and shall protect them from social injustice and all forms of exploitation." Other articles of the Constitution confirm this directive and much legislation has been enacted to implement it. Special grants, scholarships, government preferments, have been made available to members of a scheduled group.

That schedule was initially promulgated by Presidential order and can now be modified only by an Act of Parliament. So the administrative definition of who is a tribesman was set by presidential or parliamentary decision without much social analysis. The courts have had to clarify some of the criteria in order to judge, for example, whether a man of the Moka Dora tribe whose family had, since 1928, claimed to be Kshatriyas should be allowed to take a seat in Parliament that was reserved for a member of a Scheduled Tribe (Galanter 1966b, pp. 631–635). But the court decisions have not materially altered the method of defining who is a tribesman by Presidential order.

The official schedule of tribes was used in the 1961 Census of India as similar designations had been used in earlier Censuses. Census officials have complained at regular decennial intervals that it is sometimes scarcely possible to draw a clear line between a tribal and a caste group (Ghurye 1959, pp. 1–9). The official listing, however, does cover the bulk of those whose culture can be placed within the tribal side of the scale by anthropological criteria. The spectrum of Indian groups called tribal, by official notification or popular usage, ranges from hunters and gatherers who are clearly outside of caste society, to settled village groups that function as jatis.

Some such groups are quite small; the Kotas discussed below are little over 1000 in population. Other tribal names are applied to millions; for example, the term "Santal" includes over three million. The larger tribal groupings are not organized entities; their tribal name refers to an array of groups who speak the same language and share certain cultural characteristics. They usually have little acquaintance with others of their name beyond their own locality. Within their villages and localities, however, most tribals have a strong sense of their distinctiveness and hold themselves to be quite separate from jati villagers. Language is a distinguishing trait for many tribal groups. The five million speakers of languages of the Munda stock are mainly tribesmen. But other tribal people do not have a distinctive language, and speak a dialect of the regional language.

Omitted from the present discussion are the tribal groups in the extreme eastern and western salients of the subcontinent. They were too different and too distant from jati society to have been much affected by it. The eastern groups, in what is now the North East Frontier Area, Nagaland, and adjacent sections, have ancient affinities with Southeast Asia in language and culture, though their more recent ties are with Indian culture and government (cf. Burling 1960). The Muslim tribesmen of the northwest are culturally closer to tribal peoples of the Afghan and Iranian highlands than to villagers of the Indo-Gangetic plains, though they too are now closer to their national government and society than they formerly were.

Most tribal peoples of India live in hilly or forested terrain where population is sparse and communication difficult. They are found from high valleys near the spine of the Himalayas to the hills of southernmost India. The main tribal territories are in the broad central belt of hill country from West Bengal, Bihar, and Orissa on the east, through Central India, to the upland parts of Rajasthan, Gujrat, and Maharashtra on the west. Although there are great cultural and social differences among the tribal peoples dispersed across India, some preliminary generalizations can be made about them.

Among none of these peoples is there the complete dichotomy between tribal culture and civilization which appeared when Europeans first confronted native peoples in the Americas, Africa, and Oceania. Even the most remote and isolated of tribal groups in India has certain cultural traits in common with jati people, as for example in the nature of ritual purity and pollution, in the worship of local spirits, and in kinship practices[1] (cf. Jay 1959, pp. 81–83, MS. 1961a, pp. 32–34).

Yet there are some broad distinctions between tribe and jati. Five aspects of these distinctions—social, political, economic, religious, and psychological—are discussed here, though it must be recognized that in actual behavior there are many nuances and gradations. Some tribals are closer to the jati side of the scale than are other tribal groups and, conversely, some jatis are closer to tribal characteristics than are other jatis (cf. Majumdar 1958b, pp. 355–361; Atal 1963; Dube 1960; Roy Burman 1960; Risley 1915, pp. 72–76; Vidyarthi 1967; Weber 1958, pp. 30–33).

Tribal and Jati Characteristics Compared

One difference between tribal and jati society is in the quality of interpersonal relations. In tribal life the principal links for the whole society are based on kinship. Individual equality as kinsman is assumed; dependency and subordination among men are minimized. Agnatic bonds form the fundamental web, affinal ties are of lesser significance. Lineages or clans tend to be the chief corporate units; they are often the principal units for land ownership, for defense, for economic production and consumption. Each man considers himself entitled to equal rights with every other. Although there is some subordination by age and sex, age dependency is relatively short and women's dependency relatively shallow.

An extreme example of individual autonomy in the tribal mode are the Paliyans, food gatherers in the hills of western Madras. Social cooperation among them is limited to nuclear families and even the families are not very cohesive. They live in small settlements, but there is little cooperation among the families of a settlement. Marriage an arrangement among equal families; marriages commonly founder because of suspected infringements of personal independence (Gardner 1966, pp. 393–397). There are very few tribal groups as starkly individualistic and atomistic as are these Paliyan. Most tribesmen have larger corporate groups than the family and wider social cooperation. Some even tolerate dependent groups in their villages; the tribal Konds of Baderi village in Orissa have a resident group of untouchables serving them. The great difference is that tribal people consider such dependent groups to be useful but dispensable adjuncts to their own society and not integral, necessary parts of it.

Jati members, especially of the higher ranks, hold quite different assumptions about kinship and society. The Brahmins of Kumbapettai village, for example, are not very far in miles from the jungle Paliyan but are at the other end of the tribe-jati scale. Kinship for them cannot possibly pervade all their society; they could not be Brahmins without subordinate jatis of laborers, artisans, sweepers.

[1] I became vividly aware of this at the start of my first field work in India when I reached a group of Urali who lived so deep in the Travancore jungle that they used tree houses to keep out of the way of the elephants and other wild animals with whom they shared their habitat. Yet these Urali, I soon discovered, would regularly pack their cooking utensils and set off for a day-long trip to market. They took their pots with them because, they said, they would not accept food cooked by anyone but an Urali (Mandelbaum 1939).

Far from assuming equality, they assume inequality in society; rather than minimizing dependency, they stress and try to prolong dependency in their families.

But the contrast is less sharp in other social matters and at other jati levels. In Kumbapettai, individual equality is asserted more within a low jati than among Brahmins, and personal dependency is slighted. Women of the lower jatis are less dependent and children are subordinate for shorter periods than they are among the Brahmins (Gough 1956, pp. 844–849). And even among Brahmins, equality among the senior men is strongly defended. A Brahmin householder considers himself equal to any other Brahmin head of family. He does not readily subordinate himself socially to any of them, and he is most jealous of his equal rights among the men of the jati.

Jati and tribe are similar units in that each is considered by its members to be an endogamous entity composed of ritual equals. The crucial difference is that jati members, on the one hand, believe they must have nonkinship relations with others in their society and that these relations must be arranged in an order of dominance and deference. Tribesmen, on the other hand, tend to see their society as held together by kinship bonds and do not insist on hierarchical ordering. Further, jati people expect their village society to be culturally heterogeneous, each jati following a unique combination of customary practices; tribesmen expect their society to be homogeneous or, at least, not necessarily heterogeneous.

In political organization, tribal people do not usually maintain strong, complex formations. These require specialized roles and dominant-subordinate relations, neither of which is congenial in the tribal view. Kingdoms were established among some of the more populous tribes, but most of them had only precarious support and the rulers often made use of specialists imported from caste society. Although tribesmen have often been under the nominal control of rajas, few have acted the part of faithful, steadfast, and subservient subjects (cf. Weber 1958, pp. 30–32).

Tribal lands tend to be vested in clans; the kinsmen of a clan together share a productive territory. This land-clan nexus is singled out as the main differentiating feature between tribe and jati in Bailey's analysis of the tribal Konds and their caste neighbors. The Konds have localized clans, "Membership of the clan is, under this system, a condition of holding and exploiting land in the clan territory. A right to land is not achieved by subordination to anyone else, but by equality as a kinsman" (1961, pp. 11–12).

Direct access to land, according to Bailey, is the prime test of tribal organization. The larger the proportion of a given group in India that has direct access to land, the closer that group is to a tribal kind of organization. Conversely, the author concludes, the larger the proportion of those in a group whose right to land is achieved through a dependent relationship, the more does that group maintain a jati organization (Bailey 1961, pp. 11–14; also Bailey 1958, 1960).

This test has been criticized by Louis Dumont (1962) as being too narrow and by Surajit Sinha as not corresponding closely enough with other criteria of tribal organization. Sinha would rather take the land tenure criterion as one among other distinguishing features (1965, p. 60). In general, tribal people believe that a productive territory should be shared by relatives of a clan or lineage and that every such relative has some rights to that territory. Most jati members hold no such assumption, though some in North India, as the Jats of Meerut division, share this basic concept (Pradhan 1965, p. 1823; Kudryavtsev 1964).

Another difference between tribe and jati in political organization lies in the mode of incorporating new groups, whether migrants or allies. The tribal Konds incorporated new groups haltingly, occasionally by making them into fictive kinsmen; they could cooperate effectively with agnates and affines but could not readily deal with nonkinsmen. The Oriya villagers had no such difficulties; they could have economic, political, even religious collaboration with others without disturbing the kinship spheres of their jatis.

Tribal societies are more "segmentary." Tribesmen see the component groups of their society as more autonomous, viewing each group as similar in function and status to any other segment of the tribal society. Jati societies are more "organic" in that each jati is part of an organic whole; its members provide necessary, specialized functions for the whole. Each unit is not taken to be autonomous or necessarily equal to any other (Bailey 1960b, pp. 243–248; 1961, pp. 12, 15).

In subsistence economy very few tribal groups still are hunters and gatherers, but some continue to practice shifting agriculture. This, as was noted in Chapter 22, is variously called slash-and-burn, swidden, or axe cultivation. A patch of jungle or forest is cut down, burned over, planted for several seasons until soil fertility declines. It is then abandoned as the cultivators move on to repeat the process on another nearby tract. There is a certain congruence between shifting agriculture and tribal organization. A swidden economy cannot support so many in a given locality as can be maintained by plough agriculture. A relatively low population density per acre can be supported by swidden methods, but added input of labor does not yield enough to feed added people. Accordingly, there was little need for incorporative social mechanisms under swidden agriculture. The constraints of the technology precluded the possibility of much incorporation (cf. Geertz 1963, pp. 1–37; Elwin 1964, pp. 48–56).

The greater social potentials of plough agriculture were demonstrated to the Konds when some of them switched from swidden cultivation. Many then came down from the hills into the valleys and concentrated in larger groups. Rice fields, being productive capital investments, were worth fighting for as swidden lands were not, and therefore political alliances were developed and strengthened (Bailey 1960b, pp. 63–68). A swidden economy does not provide a sufficient base for strong political leadership or enough surplus to support the specialists in crafts and religion necessary for a jati society. A plough economy does provide these and also fosters political grouping and action. However, the congruence of social and economic organization is not absolute; some people who are clearly tribal in social organization nevertheless practice plough agriculture (Fernandez 1965). Conversely, there are jati villages where population is sparse and agricultural productivity low, but where jati standards are observed. Plough agriculture was probably essential for the original development of the civilization, producing a surplus that could be used to support technical specialists, state government, and full-time religionists. The main economic differences between tribal and jati societies in recent centuries, however, have been more related to economic values than to agricultural technology.

Tribesmen place little value on surplus accumulation, on the uses of capital, and on market trading (S. Sinha 1958b, pp. 509–510; 1963). To cite an extreme example again, the Jungle Chenchus are gatherers and hunters whom Fürer-Haimendorf studied in their remote jungle area of what is now Andhra Pradesh (1943, pp. 57–83; 1967a, pp. 17–24). Their main subsistence at the time of the study (1940–1949) was from the day-to-day collecting of food from the jungle. They did not store food against an emergency and lived from hand to mouth in a nearly literal sense of the cliché. There was little economic cooperation among their families, each being an autonomous economic unit, though they did aid each other in illness or accident. A few of them cultivated small plots and kept cattle, but in general there was quick consumption of all that was produced. Any surplus or windfall was rapidly distributed and consumed.

They knew about settled village life and indeed some Chenchus of this Mahbubnagar district migrated to jati villages. But the others remained in the jungle because they preferred the life there even though they knew about the boons of the more foresighted, controlled village life. There are very few tribal peoples who take so little interest in tomorrow as do these jungle Chenchus, but in general, tribesmen are much more given to quick consumption and generous distribution than are caste villagers. Those of the lowest jatis in a caste village are sometimes accused of similar inclinations by their wealthier and higher neighbors. The high label the low as feckless and improvident, as caste superiors are apt to do elsewhere in the world. This is a convenient rationale for the superiority of the high and they may try to see to it that the low have little opportunity to be provident and purposeful.

It is generally true that the values of a tribal group, in the aspects here noted, are more like those of the low jatis in a locality than of the high. But though Harijans and tribesmen may be similarly disinterested in long-term planning, there is a main difference between them in the pursuit of wealth. The aspiring Harijan who accumulates wealth is acting in a way that is respected in his society, though he himself may face the most bitter opposition, but a tribesman who works hard beyond the call of tribal custom and who is closefisted goes counter to the values and opinions of his society. Tribesmen are not averse to accumulating food stores, to deferring consumption, to maximizing productivity, but they characteristically feel that these worthy pursuits should not be pressed so hard as to interfere with the prompt prospect of pleasure.

Tribesmen do not usually take to trading or to making financial transactions. The trader's role is counter to their preference for openhanded relations. Thus, as Martin Orans tells, some of the Santal tribesmen try trading, but "It is difficult to square the basic reciprocity of relations in a kin society like that of the Santal with the impersonal and contractual relations of the market." Fledgling entrepreneurs usually fail in business because they are overgenerous in extending credit and underinsistent in collecting debts. Most know something about the ways of the market and the common swindling manipulations. "But the traditional Santal, once at the market, is too eager a buyer, too poor a haggler, and too readily drawn into pleasant social intercourse to hold his own" (Orans 1965, pp. 40–41).

Government officials have long deplored the fact that traders from the plains almost always exploit the tribesmen with whom they deal. The tribal seller often gets absurdly low prices for what he has to offer and pays immoderately high prices, often forfeiting his land when it is worth taking. This happens because a tribesman usually prefers to act as a generous kinsman rather than as a self-seeking trader intent only on personal profit. Coupled with this is the priority tribesmen give to immediate enjoyment over deferred gratification.

Most tribal people can and do work diligently when necessary, but typically they do not find much pleasure in the sweat of labor, in the righteousness of abnegation, or in visions of future power. Perhaps, a tribesman may agree, the deferred rewards might be greater in the end, but who can tell when the end will come and what unforeseen difficulties may intervene?

In religion also there are differences between the tribal and the jati sides of the cultural scale. Tribals tend to stress the short-term, pragmatic functions of religion as well as long-term transcendental functions, and they do not differentiate these two aspects as sharply as do caste villagers. As was noted before, the transcendental functions have to do with the long-term welfare of society, with the explanation and maintenance of institutions, with the continuity of society by the proper passage of individuals through the life cycle from impending birth to departure of the soul. The pragmatic functions are for personal benefits, for immediate needs, for individual welfare. Jati people tend to maintain different forms, practitioners, and behavior patterns for each of these two aspects of religion. The transcendental complex is mainly in the keeping of the higher jatis and the pragmatic in the charge of the lower, though both complexes can be used by villagers of all jatis. Tribal peoples do not maintain two distinct complexes; they tend to use similar forms, practitioners, and patterns for both functions of religion.

In jati villages the priest, who serves the universal gods of Sanskrit scripture, is a religious technician quite separate from the shaman, who has direct, personal contact with local deities. The priest, often a Brahmin, holds hereditary office and high jati rank while the shaman is usually from the lower jaris and gains prestige through his personal achievements. The priest is supposed to be an examplar of ritual purity while the shaman is mainly expected to demonstrate the immediacy of supernatural forces. Tribesmen do not usually make such distinctions between shaman and priest, who may serve the same gods or who may be combined in the same person. Both help chiefly to deliver supernatural boons rather than to demonstrate the sacrosanct life (Mandelbaum 1966; 1964, pp. 8–11).

A tribal religion typically combines features of the tribal culture of the region with some from Hindu worship. Tribal peoples do not have direct access to the rich resources of scripture, and so their religions tend to be less systematized, less specialized and elaborated than is the Hinduism of the higher jatis. The lower jatis in a village may have as little direct knowledge of scripture as tribal people but their beliefs and practices are more directly influenced by scriptural Hinduism.

Asceticism is usually respected by tribesmen as a powerful way of exerting pressure on certain gods, but it is not elevated as the supreme path to the good life or to any blessed afterlife. Nor do tribesmen commonly set great value on puritanical modes of conduct in this life for the sake of a happier hereafter (cf. S. Sinha 1958b, p. 512).

This is well documented in Fürer-Haimendorf's comparison of moral concepts among the South Asian peoples whom he has studied. The results of his remarkably extensive fieldwork have been published in three of the major works on peninsular Indian tribes as well as in several books on the tribes of northeast India and of Nepal. He has also studied a Hindu jati, the Chetris of Nepal. The Chetris believe that supernal merit can be gained from "morally positive conduct"; most tribesmen have little or no such idea. "For although some of the tribes also believe in a sequence of lives, and others set great store on the acquisition of *social* merit which raises a person's status in this life, in none of the tribal societies did we encounter the idea that moral choices affect a person's fate in a future existence" (Fürer-Haimendorf 1967a, p. 168). The moral outlook under a tribal system of society is much more concentrated on this world; such a society has very little interest in any other.

Finally, there is a psychological factor that underlies the other differences. Tribal people generally take direct, unalloyed satisfaction in pleasures of the senses, whether in food, alcoholic drink, sex, song, or dance. The "twice-born" tend to be ambivalent about such pleasures; they are inclined to defer them or to refine them or to surround them with elaborate ritual. Kshatriya men (though not their women) are allowed more latitude for pleasures of the senses, but still in a more restricted way than tribesmen enjoy.

This contrast is well described by G. M. Carstairs, who studied it from his dual vantage as psychiatrist and anthropologist. He tells how his understanding of the higher jatis was sharpened when a band of Bhil tribesmen appeared in the Rajasthan town where he was working. They performed a three-day religious dance, and in the process provided Carstairs with the contrastive perspective he needed. "Here was clearly a people whose values were strikingly different to those cherished by my Hindu informants, as the latter indeed insisted" (1957, p. 126). The Bhils were boisterously demonstrative; they shouted, sang, laughed aloud, and were unashamedly drunk in public. Shocking to the townsmen was the open display of affection between a Bhil man and his wife.

When Carstairs later stayed in a Bhil village, his medical patients included many with venereal diseases. Not one, however, mentioned the complaint he had so often heard from other men, that they had suffered loss of strength through sexual relations. The Bhils have no use for celibacy or asceticism. They enjoy life zestfully, accepting pleasure and dangers as they come (they are a violent people), and in their homeland "they regard themselves as inferior to none, carry themselves proudly and look strangers squarely in the eye" (Carstairs 1957, pp. 132–136).

The capacities of tribal peoples for direct, spontaneous emotion and personal independence captivated a good many Westerners who came to know them. British officials were apt to feel protective about tribals—after they had crushed all traces of armed rebellion (cf. Hutton 1941). Special legislation was enacted to safeguard tribal interests and such legislation increased after independence. One eloquent student and defender of tribal peoples in India, Verrier Elwin, tells in his autobiography how greatly he was influenced by their style of life. The youth dormitories of the Muria tribe conveyed to him a message which, he wrote, is typically Indian. It is that human love and its physical expression is "beautiful, clean and precious" (1964, pp. 168–169). This is scarcely typical of the Indian ascetic tradition, but it is known to tribal people in India.

Tribesmen are drawn together by their bent for enjoyment. Martin Orans tells that when a Santal meets a fellow tribesman from a distant place, one of the first questions he asks, in the traditional custom, is "How is pleasure in your region?" He thinks of "pleasure" as preeminently a social experience—the festive atmosphere at ceremonies, the dancing, drinking, and comradeship that are enjoyed then. "Pleasure, as the Santal understand the term, is a shared understanding which creates immediate bonds with cotribals wherever they may be from." (1965, pp. 8–9).

This happy solidarity is one reason why some have resisted jati relations. There were other reasons as well. Until the nineteenth century most tribal groups had very little contact with jati villagers and civilizational centers. Many were additionally insulated because they spoke languages different from those used by the nearest jati people. However, some who have had long and near acquaintance with jati people have still remained tribesmen. The Konds of Baderi village have lived within two miles of an Oriya caste village for perhaps as many as eight centuries and have remained tribal Konds. There is a jati of Kond potters in the Oriya village, so not all resisted the pull of jati life. Many did resist, however, until recent decades when the movement toward the jati end of the continuum accelerated. Like any continuum, this one involves both differentiating features and common properties. The most remote of tribal groups carries culture elements of the civilization; the most sophisticated of jatis is also a putative kin group like a tribe.

The Shift Toward Jati Values

As a tribal people begin to take on jati traits, perhaps restricting their diet, they become involved in other jati values as well, as in restricting their social contacts (cf. Sinha 1958b, pp. 515–517; 1965, pp. 61–64). When members of a low jati alter their conduct in order to rise socially, they already have such values as asceticism or hierarchy embedded in their culture. They know about them; they are not reluctant to acknowledge and to enact them when they can. But in tribal life, little esteem is given to ascetic ways, to pervasive hierarchy, to other values of the "twice-born" model. There is apt to be, therefore, more internal struggle within a tribe about adopting a caste trait because it may be taken to symbolize, and rightly so, a shift away from tribal values. Among the Kotas, a change in men's hair style became a grave issue of factional conflict (Mandelbaum 1941 and 1960).

When a tribal group does become drawn into a jati order, its members, too, try to cast off demeaning customs and to adopt prestigious ones. At first they need not discard much, perhaps only such gross matters as cow sacrifice, but as they become more actively engaged in the competition among jatis, they feel pressed to alter more of their culture. Their tribal values become changed at different rates but in the same general direction.

In social relations, they shift from relative equality among kinsmen toward the hierarchy in which dependence is incumbent on everyone. Even those at the very top of a jati order must depend on those inferior to them. Role specialization does increase productivity, and social stratification does provide incentive for aspiration, but both require greater dependency than does the tribal norm.

In political affairs, tribesmen usually feel small obligation as subjects of a ruler or as citizens of a state. But with involvement in jati society they become more open to political influence from outside their communities, and their own village affairs tend to become more politicized. Factions and feuds are not absent from tribal society, but alliance politics seem to be more prevalent in jati society. Few jatis feel so securely entrenched that they can be oblivious of challenge from others; in a tribal society there are fewer positions of power to be challenged.

In economic relations, tribesmen shift from sharing liberally with all in a small community to more selective and directed sharing with those of a larger society. From dealing quite openhandedly with kinsmen, they engage in more limited transactions with jajmani associates and in the guarded games of commerce with customers and merchants.

The transition in religious outlook shifts a tribesman from a close and knowable cosmos to a vast universe that is unknowable in all its reaches. Much of the knowledge in the more complex religion is vested in scriptures that are in the keeping of specialist jaris. The daily discipline of one's own body and mind becomes a main arena of religious observance. In the course of the shift some elements of the tribal religion are incorporated into the pragmatic complex and others are merged with Sanskritic deities and rites. The pragmatic functions of religion are relegated from primary position to an important but secondary place. The local tribal godling may be transformed from an autonomous power to a subservient specialist. As tribesmen become drawn into the race for respectability, more of their tribal ways must be given up. Dancing at ceremonies, libations of alcoholic liquor, and youth dormitories are among the customs disapproved by religious arbiters, who teach that some acts are good or bad morally, quite apart from their immediate consequences.

Another kind of change is in self-view. A tribesman is inclined to see himself as an independent agent who prizes the sense pleasures through all his life. As a jati member a man must defer some pleasures, he must deny others for the sake of his jati's status in the village and of his personal fate through eternity. These constraints are supposed to yield future rewards, though tribesmen have often been dubious about that.

The assimilation of tribal groups has gone on for a very long time. The tribes of the Gangetic plain, according to D. D. Kosambi, were conquered by and assimilated into the kingdoms of Kosala and Magadha beginning in the sixth century B.C. (1965, pp. 120–132). From the third century B.C.

there are references to tribes in the edicts of Ashoka, as in this passage about Ashoka's benevolence: "The Beloved of the Gods even reasons with the forest tribes in his empire, and seeks to reform them. But the Beloved of the Gods is not only compassionate, he is also powerful, and he tells them to repent, lest they be slain" (Basham 1954, pp. 53–54). Tribal peoples in later eras were similarly warned that if they were to be the beloved of the Beloved of (other) Gods, they had best stop raiding the king's subjects and change their savage ways.

During the British regime, the raiding was largely quelled, but officials were not so enthusiastic about changes in other tribal customs. They frequently deplored the assimilation of tribal groups into jati society. Sir Herbert H. Risley noted the process in his report as Commissioner of the 1901 Census, having observed it since 1873. He wrote "All over India at the present moment tribes are gradually and insensibly being transformed into castes." He hoped that future studies would "throw some light upon the singular course of evolution by which large masses of people surrender a condition of comparative freedom and take in exchange a condition which becomes more burdensome in proportion as its status is higher" (1915, p. 72). This movement is generally irreversible. Tribes have often become jatis, only rarely and under exceptional circumstances have jati members turned to tribal practices.[2]

Attractions and Repulsions of Jati Society

To illustrate some of the ways by which tribesmen become drawn into jati society, examples from three tribal peoples can be considered. The first is from the tribal Reddi (not to be confused with jatis of the same name) of the Bison Hills in Andhra Pradesh; the others are the Raj Gonds and the Hill Maria Gonds.

The Reddi example centers on the activities of a single family, that of a headman. Reddi chieftains were appointed as headmen (called *muttadar*) by the British and given responsibilities for the collection of revenue. They received an income for their duties and had more contact with outsiders than did their fellow tribesmen. By 1941–1943, when Fürer-Haimendorf studied the group, some of these headmen had added plough cultivation to shifting agriculture and had taken Lingayat religious mentors. They were wealthier and held themselves to be superior to ordinary Reddis.

One such headman had gone further and had declared, as had his father before him, that he was not a tribesman at all. He asserted that he did not belong to any Reddi clan, that he was a "Raj Reddi" of Kshatriya ancestry. It was known that his mother had been a tribal girl, though a Brahmin had been hired to perform a special ceremony at her wedding that purportedly enabled her to eat with her husband.

This headman had married a girl "of his own caste" from a distant place, again with the benefit of Brahmin clergy. Other headmen sneered at his pretensions but "locally his claims to higher caste are generally recognized and his aloofness from the social and ritual affairs of other Reddis places him outside and above tribal life and distinguishes his status vis-à-vis his subjects from that of other muttadar, who live within the fold of Reddi tribal custom." The other Reddi headmen had begun

[2] One possible case is that of the Badagas of the Nilgiri Hills, who came from the plains of Mysore into the isolated Nilgiri area some time after the twelfth century. They presumably were a jati people at the time of their migration and adopted some tribal characteristics (Hockings 1965, pp. 12–13).

to bridge the cultural distance between tribe and jati; this one had, apparently successfully, crossed over through the unusual expedient of establishing his own family jati (Fürer-Haimendorf 1945, pp. 167–173).

Contrasting examples of the movement from tribal to jati society are from two divisions of the Gond peoples. The Raj Gonds have moved directly into high jati rank; the Hill Maria Gonds have tried to reject jati entanglements yet have become involved in them. There are more than four million Gonds in all; their language is of the Dravidian stock and their main locale is in Andhra Pradesh and adjoining states. The Raj Gond case was briefly mentioned above.

There were Raj Gond kingdoms in earlier centuries, though their Rajas did not alter the tribal character of the Gonds (S. Sinha 1962, pp. 61–65; Fuchs 1960). Raj Gonds are now the dominant jati in certain villages of Andhra Pradesh, one of them being Dewara in Adilabad district. When S. C. Dube studied this village in 1950, all the villagers acknowledged that leadership in local affairs was largely in the hands of the Raj Gonds. This was so in spite of the highly unusual fact that these Raj Gonds were still sacrificing cows and eating beef. Yet men of the other jati-groups, except Brahmins and some weavers, accepted water from them. The lower Hindu jatis also accepted food from them.

One reason for this exceptional latitude was that the Raj Gonds wielded strong power in their locality and long had done so. Another reason was that the district had been part of the dominions of the Muslim prince, the Nizam of Hyderabad, whose government, not unlike the British, was inclined to take the side of the tribals in any conflict with jati people. At the time of Dube's study, the princely rule had been deposed but the new governmental influence had not yet taken full effect (1955a, pp. 189–190). These Raj Gonds had entered into jati relations practically on their own terms. Other jatis were immigrants into their territory who had accepted their suzerainty, and their dominance had been further buttressed by the state.

The Hill Maria Gonds, by contrast, have kept themselves isolated from jati relations and have resisted Hindu influences. They show the kind of distaste for jati ways which has slowed the assimilation of some tribal groups. The Hill Maria Gonds are among the most isolated of the Gond tribesmen. They number about ten thousand people in the forested hills of Bastar, the largest district of Andhra Pradesh and one with exceptionally poor communications (Jay MS. 1961a; Grigson 1949). Hill Marias know about commensal taboos and about other jati restraints even though there are only a few families of jati people in their territory. They know that they may take food from some but not from others, and that there are jatis whose members will not accept food from them. That knowledge is useful mainly when Hill Marias attend a regional fair or market.

Their deep disinclination to change toward jati ways is shown in one village where good land for growing rice by plough cultivation is available. The staple of Hill Maria diet is millet, grown by slash-and-burn tillage. Though rice cultivation is vastly more productive, it is not feasible on the dry, steep slopes of most of the Hill Maria territory. But even in this village where rice growing is feasible and profitable, only a fourth of the families have given up axe cultivation. Most cultivate by axe as well as plough; they are reluctant to abandon shifting cultivation because it symbolizes for them the tribal way of life.

They suspect that if they go over to rice cultivation entirely they will also be going over to a different way of life, one in which they may lose much that they now cherish. Shifting cultivation "at once provides them with their daily sustenance and sets them apart as a people, separate from all others" (Jay 1961b, p. 1371). They want to be separate; the alternative they fear is to become a dependent, inferior, disoriented jati. They dislike jati people and think of themselves as being outside jati relations. Nevertheless, they are taking up some Hindu religious practices to complement their tribal religion and they are accepting other jati features. While they reject the religion of Hindus they are adopting important parts of it. “Thus we might say,” Edward Jay concludes, “that Marias are becoming Hindus in spite of themselves” (1961a MS. p. 39).

The attractions of jati society for tribesmen are manifold. Tribal leaders sense the promise of more secure power and eminence within their group. Hindu religious practices appear to be useful ways of invoking supernatural help. Some tribesmen attach themselves to jati villages because they can get food and work there (cf. Bose 1953b; Sachchidananda 1964; 1965). The changeover may take generations, but after it has been accomplished, those whose forefathers lived under a tribal system of society have shifted to a different system, that of jati. It is a different system not only because it is operated on different principles but also because it has different capacities. The tribal assumption that kinship ought to pervade all one’s society (those who cannot possibly be kinsmen can scarcely be fully men) is replaced by the concept that kinship is compartmentalized within a hierarchy of specialized, organically related jatis, with regular ways of relating to nonkinsmen.

The carrying capacity of the tribal system is limited just as the production capacity of swidden agriculture is limited. A tribal system cannot accommodate as many people acting cooperatively as can a system of jatis. Jati society can include a far more diverse and productive array of specialties and specialists. It can therefore include a far greater content of knowledge, because specialists can amass specialized skills and information and make them available for social use. Moreover, tribal social systems have much more limited capacities for adaptation; as tribal peoples the world over take on new technologies and ideas they find it difficult to adapt tribal systems to them, and many have to make quite abrupt social changes. Jati societies have been more adaptable to modern circumstances, as our discussion of recurrent change has indicated.

Tribesmen in India use various tactics to alter their former social relations, as the Reddi and Gond examples illustrate and as the case examples given in the next chapter show. These examples also show that all the varied tactics press in the same general direction, toward civilizational characteristics. What is to be rejected is frequently more apparent, to tribesmen as to aspiring jati villagers, than just what should be adopted. Tribesmen have been given special incentive to take to political means for mobility because government law and agencies have provided legislative seats and other advantages for them.

These provisions came before there was mass pressure from tribal peoples themselves for special political treatment. The benefits were established by the founders and leaders of the new nation because of their political beliefs. They were, and are, intent on reducing the more gaping social disparities within the nation. Designating tribes and low-ranking jatis as disadvantaged and as in need of government aid is a means of redressing the balance of Indian society, or rather of hastening a new kind of social calibration. There has been considerable criticism of the manner in which the proffered advantages have been administered and of the way in which they give a scheduled group a vested interest in continuing to be declared “backward.” Nevertheless these redressive measures have had effect. This new kind of political counterchange has quickened the absorption of tribal people into the mainstream of national life.

CHAPTER 32

Direction of Tribal Change

The direction of tribal change in India is clear and expectable. Virtually all tribes are now shifting toward jati characteristics, a movement which has greatly accelerated as communications have improved and external forces have impinged more closely. Seen from afar and in the large, when tribals are viewed as a culture type, it is quite certain that this shift toward jati society will continue apace. However, when we examine the change at close range, in particular tribes, villages, and families, we find much conflict about which cultural direction to take, considerable uncertainty about which values to cherish, frequent personal oscillation between the requirements of differing social structures.

TACTICAL PROBLEMS AND LONG-RANGE TRENDS

The direction seems clear in the grand sweep of the observer's eye. But the outcome of a struggle is typically far from certain to those engaged in it on the ground. There are many possible ways of adapting. The advent of political democracy has opened new possibilities for tribal people as well as for other villagers; tribal leaders, too, have seen the advantages in acting as voters and lobbyists.

Government authority used to sit lightly with tribal people. Foreign Rajas might claim territories inhabited by tribal groups but usually they were not strong enough to impose firm controls over them, nor were most tribal lands worth great conquering effort. British administrators quelled the more extravagant tribal customs, such as human sacrifice or the elimination of tax collectors, but for the most part they did not tamper directly with a tribal way of life save to try sporadically to preserve it. After political independence, however, the hand of government became more ubiquitous than it was before, and the arm of government stronger in the tribal villages. The opportunities to share in the body politic became apparent, especially at election time.

These changes have altered the choices before tribesmen and have sometimes added to their perplexities as well as to their advantages (cf. Bose 1964; Fürer-Haimendorf 1967b). Jati members face similar conflicts and uncertainties, but tribal peoples must cope, in addition, with the special problems of adapting tribal characteristics to modern requirements. To illustrate the choices and conflicts that tribal people now face, examples from five widely separated groups are given.

The first, from a Kond village in the highlands of Orissa, shows how tribal leaders now have to switch from one mode of conduct to another if they are to be effective. Effective adaptation may be hindered, as the example from the Kotas of the Nilgiri Hills shows, by a self-image that is no longer appropriate to their contemporary social scene.

Tribesmen are also switching their reference models; the Bhumij of West Bengal had gone far toward accepting the Kshatriya model when some of their leaders urged a turn toward the newly advantageous posture of a culturally deprived people. As such, they can obtain political and material advantages to attain more rapid social rise. This shift to a new model may be spurred by external circumstances, as is shown in the example of the Bhotia who were sped toward a modern model by the borderlands inroads of Communist China. The fifth case example is that of the Santals, particularly those Santals who live in the steel city of Jamshedpur and its vicinity. Their ancient antipathy toward jati people and jati practices has been bolstered by their industrial contacts. The reference model that their leaders ardently advocate is one that seems to entail a reversion to traditional tribal customs. The reversion is only in appearance; in actuality it provides a means by which Santals can adapt to modern political participation and social advance.

The agents of change in these examples include indigenous Rajas, religious mentors, secular teachers, government officials, tribal association leaders, Christian missionaries, and Hindu social service workers. Each kind of agent has tried to direct change in his special mode. Often enough, one kind of agent is violently opposed to those of another kind. Nevertheless, despite their diversity and antagonisms, all have wanted tribesmen to adopt similar, civilizational principles of conduct.

Konds of Baderi Village, Orissa

The dilemma faced by Konds is exemplified by a quarrel in which the headman of Baderi was the central figure (Bailey 1960b, pp. 197–237). One day the headman was an infuriated, unfettered tribesman who shouted abuse and threatened violence against the despoilers of his people from the jati village; the next day he listened meekly to advice from a Hindu guru and pledged to give up drinking. One purpose of his having a guru was to learn how to behave like a "Hindu gentleman" so that he could better deal with officials.

Baderi village is in the Phulbani district of central Orissa in the hill area called the Kondmals. There are well over half a million tribals who speak Kui, the Dravidian language of the Konds; most jati people in Orissa speak Oriya, a language of the Indo-European stock.

On the day of the quarrel at Baderi, the headman had been drinking when a man from the nearby jati village of Oriya-speakers came to see him about buying some turmeric roots. This visitor was the same Nrusingh whose several roles were discussed in an earlier chapter. Though a Harijan, he is one of the better educated in the locality and has become relatively affluent through his trading activities. He also holds a minor official post as assistant to the Oriya revenue headman.

On catching sight of Nrusingh the headman exploded with rage and abuse. A few days before, it had been discovered that Nrusingh had cheated one of the Konds by pocketing part of the tax payment that the Kond had turned over to him. Incensed by this incident and inspirited with alcohol, the headman aggressively made for Nrusingh who promptly fled out of reach. The headman's anger was then vented in a tirade against three men from the Oriya village who happened to be about, two traders and the local school teacher. That evening, still enraged, the headman vented his anger on his son and daughter-in-law. The couple appealed to the headman's Oriya preceptor. The next morning this preceptor visited the now sober headman, gave him advice, and got from him a promise to stop drinking.

This last act illustrates in miniature what seems to be a major contradiction in Kond behavior. On the day of his anger at Nrusingh the headman railed against Oriya evil; on the day of his sobriety he solemnly promised an Oriya that he would keep Oriya high-caste values.

Several impulses were compounded in his wrath. As headman he had the contradictory responsibilities of representing outside authority in the village and of championing his people against outsiders. The former obligation he ignored in this episode, the latter was demonstrated in great amplitude and emotion. His immediate target was an Oriya Harijan, but he reviled Oriyas of all kinds and jatis "with a coarse invective as liars and thieves who live only to make money by cheating others." Further, he charged, they use their better education and political power to extort money from the poor Kond tribesmen. These are two facets of the same grievance; Oriyas cheat Konds in trade and cheat them also through abuse of their political power. "It is their [the Konds'] standard complaint and it is in this area of social relations, rather than in culture that they see themselves different from and opposed to the Oriyas" (Bailey 1960b, p. 232).

Konds dislike trading while a good many in the Oriya village thrive by it. Konds consider trade to be "at once beneath their dignity and beyond their capacity." The proud Kond relegates business dealings with his produce to the untouchables in his village. Moreover, most Konds believe that they are not clever or wily enough to engage in trade successfully.

Trading was involved in the episode at Baderi village in that Nrusingh had come to buy some turmeric, the main cash crop raised by the Konds. But neither then nor subsequently did this specific relationship enter into the headman's attack. Trading and commerce, Bailey notes, are taken to be outside the other kinds of social relations. This is probably why the Konds, with their inclination to wrap all social relations in a kinship bundle, despise trade. Yet when they do engage in it, as in selling turmeric to Oriyas, they follow the logic of the marketplace and do not mix trade considerations into other social interests (Bailey 1960b, pp. 132, 185, 205, 226–228). They decry the isolating of trade from other social relations, yet they do isolate their business relations when they buy or sell.

The newer influences on Kond life are reflected in the headman's oscillation from one day to the next. His spiritual adviser is an Oriya who has a large clientele; this mentor's task with Konds is to teach the Konds the Hindu way of life. The headman listens to and pays for the guru's counsel not only for religious reasons, but also for reasons that have to do with the struggle for control of modern forms of political power. "It is an advantage in this struggle to be a Hindu gentleman and not an uncouth aboriginal." The headman functions at the grass-roots level of this struggle, but he is aware that unless he can take on certain manners and refinements, he and his people cannot have ready access to the fountain of political benefits (Bailey 1960b, pp. 235–237).

For centuries ambitious tribal chieftains have taken Hindu mentors in order to gain more durable power by learning to be proper Kshatriyas. This older tutelage was mainly intended to enhance the rule of a tribal chieftain over his own people; now, however, even a village headman seeks guidance from a Hindu preceptor, not only to solidify his own power but also to exploit the power newly available through political democracy. The headman of Baderi, who is a loud defender of tribal tradition, maintains his prestige and authority by "being at the same time both a traditionalist and a progressive" (Bailey 1960b, p. 237).

The Konds of Baderi have been situated within two miles of an Oriya village for perhaps eight centuries and so they share some elements of Oriya culture. The concept of pollution is held in both places, certain ritual traits are common to both, inheritance rules and such personal values as the immense need to have a son are similar (Bailey 1960b, pp. 91, 93, 133, 175). The Kond village even harbors four specialized groups, Kond smiths, herdsmen, and menials, and some families of Oriya herdsmen. The dominant clan of Konds deals with them in the manner of a dominant jati in a caste village. The Kond landowners, however, seem less concerned about their dependents than Oriya landowners are about the work and the deference they expect from theirs (Bailey 1960b, pp. 121–156).

These similarities have not blurred the strong sense of social distinction that the Konds feel, nor have they eroded the tribal features in Kond culture. The Konds are well aware of the contrast between their customs and those of Oriyas or of "Hindus" in general. They differ in visible, immediately apparent ways, as in language, in traditional dress, and house form. They differ also in the symbolism of their rites and ceremonies. In agriculture, Konds and Oriyas use the same techniques for growing rice but Konds also cultivate swidden fields on the mountainsides and the Oriya villagers do not. Bailey comments that the Konds say that they are Hindus like everyone else, but they make a sharp distinction between themselves and the Oriyas (Bailey 1960b, pp. 3–4).

Though Oriya rulers had anciently settled military colonies among the Konds and had tried to control them, the Konds would not become acculturated and remained very largely their own masters. They refused to be dutiful subjects, dependable allies, or dependent auxiliaries. They maintained the kinship base for their society, kept its religious autonomy, preserved its economic values and its psychological stamp. They gave limited homage to Rajas and tolerated specialized jatis in their villages, but they considered none of them essential to their way of life.

In the twentieth century this accommodation did not work so well as it had before. The Kond territory became much less isolated and much more open to influences from outside the Kondmals. Konds began to want some of the things Oriyas possessed and they began to form an association, as jatis have done throughout India. They organized an uplift association, called the Kui Samaj, which tries to do for the Kond tribe what the headman's guru was supposed to do for the headman of Baderi village. It is a self-preceptorial effort to enable Konds to gain advantages in the larger society with which they are now engaged. It is also intended to preserve Kond identity, to solidify Kond unity, and to deliver votes (Bailey 1960b, pp. 186–193). Konds are numerous enough so that they have much more to gain by remaining a distinctive group than by assimilating with some jati bloc or merging into a political coalition.

The new trend was still much in the making at mid-century. The Kui Samaj was not yet a mass organization and representative democracy was only sketchily understood by most Konds. However, Bailey tells us that an ambitious Kond does not now aim to rise only among his clansmen and villagers nor does he aspire, as his predecessors would, to be headman for a set of villages. Rather, he tries to get into the inner circle of the Kui Samaj, to work in a political party, "and eventually to reach the top by becoming a member of the Legislative Assembly" (Bailey 1960b, p. 186). In making his way toward the new top, he must appear to be both a tribal traditionalist and a political progressive, an appearance not easily maintained.

Konds now operate in three social-political arenas: they carry on some of the features of the tribal way of life, they are acting increasingly as a jati, and they are beginning to bid for place in the democratic polity (Bailey 1960b, pp. 269–272). Different rules are appropirate to each arena and Konds now find themselves in situations in which they are not clear about which mode of behavior is appropriate. This, to be sure, is part of every man's dilemma in any society. The uncertainties are greater for some personalities and at particular stages of each person's life cycle. But the personal choices are not made any easier when a man's society is in transition and a headman may act like a direct, unbridled tribesman one day, and then take the part of a dutiful disciple the next, in order to command power in an evolving political order on still another day.

Kotas of the Nilgiri Hills, Tamil Nadu (Madras)

The choices that are actually made are guided by a people's perception of themselves. Often these perceptions are legacies from an earlier period and do not serve the group well in adapting to contemporary realities, a lag sometimes found in great nations as well as among tribesmen in India. Thus the Kotas of the Nilgiri Hills generally hold a view of themselves as proud aborigines, entitled to special considerations because of their seniority on the land and the artisan skills they can provide. They are, in fact, a minute part of the present population of the district, unknown to many in the area. There are only seven small villages of Kotas, about 1100 people in all, yet they maintain their own language, religion, social organization, and lively sense of distinctiveness. The general processes of change noted in larger tribal societies go on as well within this little enclave. Their case illustrates how the self-image of a people can impede their adaptation to a current situation.

In my study of the Kotas, I have seen men vacillate between tribal and jati modes of behavior. In funeral ceremonies, for example, many buffaloes used to be sacrificed to speed the departed soul and to demonstrate the solidarity of the bereaved kinsmen. As the influence of jati practices grew, funeral sacrifices came to be deprecated. In the village of Kolmel all agreed to limit themselves to one buffalo for all mourners at the annual memorial rites. However, when this ceremony was next held a conflict arose. The mourners did not want to be so restricted. Each of them had been in favor of the limitation in the council meeting, but in his role as mourner he wanted to follow the old tribal practice and to sacrifice as many buffalo as he could afford for the honor of his family (Mandelbaum 1954b, pp. 82–84).

The factional rift between Kota traditionalists and the reformers led by the schoolteacher, Sulli was discussed previously (cf. Mandelbaum 1960, pp. 221–255). Kotas of both factions bitterly blamed their neighbors, the Badagas, for Kota disabilities. They still saw the Badagas as an integral part of the old order of the four Nilgiri tribes and not as the Badagas are today—an enterprising people, many of whom are seizing the new economic and political opportunities, and most of whom are uninterested in the former tribal relationships.

That old order of the Nilgiri tribes was, in effect, a caste order that was carried on in isolation from the centers and carriers of Indian civilization (Mandelbaum 1956, pp. 33–45). There was no knowledge of scripture to bolster it, no Brahmins to legitimate it, no Kshatriyas to rule over it. Yet the social order functioned well for centuries. Before the British came into the Nilgiri Hills in 1819 and opened up some roads to the plateau, the people of the region had few contacts with the villagers of the plains below their homeland. Each of the four Nilgiri groups was a tribal society in the main, yet each was specialized in some degree and dependent on the others for certain economic and ritual services.

The Kotas still think of themselves as an important element in that order. They were the artisans and musicians for the Badaga cultivators, for the Toda pastoralists, and for the Kurumba sorcerers. Families of each tribe carried on jajmanilike relations with families of the other three tribes. Badagas and Todas considered Kotas to be defiling inferiors because they provided music for funerals, handled carcasses, worked in leather, and ate the flesh of cows and buffaloes. Kota musicians at a Badaga ceremony were fed separately, used separate utensils, and were not allowed into the inner parts of a Badaga house or close to the sacred things. When a Kota met a Badaga or a Toda he used to make formal gestures of respect as from a subordinate to a superior.

Yet this deference did not, in earlier times, seem onerous to Kotas. Although they gave the gestures of deference, they did not feel totally subordinate. They had their own lands, did some farming, and kept some cattle and thus were not completely dependent on the Badaga farmers for grain or on the Todas for dairy products. They lived in their own villages, governed themselves, and were not under any daily rule by overlords. Moreover, they knew that unless they provided tools for the other groups the others could not carry on their work, and unless they provided music some of the main ceremonies of the Badagas could not be completed. When there was a falling out between Kotas and Badagas, the Kotas would withhold their services. The Badagas would feel the pinch enough to compromise and arbitrate.

The Badagas were and are the most numerous of the four indigenous peoples. In the first Census of 1871 there were 19,476 Badagas, 1,112 Kotas, 693 Todas, and 613 Kurumbas. By the Census of 1961 there were 85,463 Badagas while the other three groups were about as large as they had been ninety years before. In spite of these population figures, Kotas do not consider Badagas to be overwhelmingly more important than are Todas and Kurumbas. Their origin story tells that Kotas, Todas, and Kurumbas are descended from brothers who were put on the Nilgiri land by a creator father who assigned them their special tasks and mutual obligations. Badagas were latecomers (historical evidence corroborates Kota folklore in this) who fled to the hills from the Mysore region some centuries ago and were allowed to settle there by the permission of the ancient inhabitants.

As for all others who live in the Nilgiri district now and make up the bulk of the population, they do not figure much in Kota legend or historical reference. Thousands of migrants from Madras and Kerala have settled in the Nilgiris, attracted by the salubrious climate, fertile lands and opportunities for employment. In the Kota view, they are in the Nilgiris but not really of that area. In mid-twentieth century the older Kotas still perceived the Nilgiris as the vouchsafed homeland of the four tribes and saw themselves as a pivotal people among the four.

The facts have become far different. The Nilgiri district now holds some 400,000 people. Of the four indigenous groups only the Badagas have kept pace in numbers and prosperity. As they increased in wealth and education, many of them found that their traditional associations with the Kotas hampered their jati ambitions. They realized, for example, that people of respectable rank did not dance at funerals to Kota music as had been Badaga custom. When tools and utensils became readily available in markets, most Badagas found the traditional association with Kota families to be unnecessary and irksome. They had no further need to rely on Kotas, who were supposed to be inferior dependents but who acted more like independent claimants.

A main factional split in Badaga society came about 1930 on the issue of Kota music (cf. Hockings 1965, pp. 111–113, 134–138). The reform faction was against using Kota music at funerals; the conservatives were just as determined to keep it. At funerals of the promusic faction, antimusic zealots interfered. In 1936 there was a riot at one such funeral; police fired on the crowd and two Badagas were killed. By the 1960s the reformist Badagas had largely prevailed, only a few conservative Badagas used Kota services, and even they did not keep up the full traditional relationship. For a time Badaga reform leaders held a special animus against Kotas. To those Badagas who were anxious to shed all traces of their former, quasi-tribal state, the Kotas posed a threatening presence; they reminded the Badagas of what they wanted to forget, that not so long ago Badagas had followed customs unsuitable for a jati of respectable and educated people.

Badagas, conversely, appear as the main adversaries in the Kotas' view. The conservative Kotas resent the Badaga withdrawal from the old relationship which, as they understand it, was formed in the beginning of time and should not be unbound in the present mid-course of time. Though they would like to have the payments they used to get, they do have land and are not in dire need of Badaga patronage. Their resentment is mainly because the old harmonious Nilgiri order, as they nostalgically recall it, has been abolished, because the Badagas have reneged their ancient obligations, and because the Kotas now see no satisfactory place for themselves in the new situation. Moreover, some Badagas actively denigrate the Kotas, and, even worse, many Badagas ignore them.

The progressives among the Kotas resent Badaga opposition to their efforts to improve their social standing. Sulli fought against Badagas for decades, first to secure the right of a Kota to be a schoolteacher, later for the right to be served in eating places in town and for similar acceptance as a citizen with equal rights. In the main, Sulli succeeded in his struggles, but the next generation of Kotas, especially those who have had some education, seek a still better status for Kotas.

Eleven hundred people might be enough for a viable tribe or jati, but it is far too few to count for anything in the modern political arena. The Kotas feel the need for wider affiliations but as yet do not know with whom to form them. A few are beginning to realize that both Kotas and Badagas are caught up in the same current of great affairs, and that somehow Kotas have to revise their ancient images and adapt to the requirements of their present world.

BHUMIJ OF BARABHUM, WEST BENGAL

Those tribals who choose to reform face difficult decisions about how best to change. The Bhumij, a people who number about half a million in Bihar and West Bengal, exemplify such problems of choice. In a series of writings, Surajit Sinha has described how most of them had gone far toward becoming jati folk and had convinced themselves that they were Kshatriyas, when some of their leaders realized that the traditional Kshatriya way was no longer the best means for social advance. These men decided that there was more to be gained if Bhumij declared themselves to be tribesmen.

Such a reversal is not easy because the Bhumij had committed themselves so strongly to the Kshatriya goal. The dilemma is illustrated in an account of a 1954 meeting of Bhumij leaders. The majority supported the drive for Kshatriya status, which had been led by the large landowners for some forty years. But at this meeting contrary opinions were heard. One Bhumij, who had been an M.L.A. (a member of the state legislative assembly) said, "The programme for labelling our caste as Bhumij-Kshatriya should be abandoned. I know from my experience as an M.L.A. that if we claim to be Kshatriyas, then we shall get no facilities from the Government as *Adibasis*" (S. Sinha 1959, p. 24). Another speaker also urged that Bhumij proclaim themselves as *Adibasis*, members of an aboriginal tribe, and be officially listed as such. He pointed out that if they insisted on being Kshatriyas, they would logically have to give up doing their own ploughing, they should stop widow remarriage and shun rice beer. Despite decades of reform exhortation, many Bhumij still followed tribal practice in these matters. He ended with the question, "What shall we gain following the examples of our Zemindar class?" (S. Sinha 1959, p. 25).

Some Bhumij zemindars, the large landowners, had become accepted as Kshatriyas and had separated themselves completely from Bhumij society to form a new jati (S. Sinha 1959, p. 11; 1962, pp. 52–58, 72–75). The masses of Bhumij, however, were not wealthy enough to take that step—they could not afford the cost of Brahmins, genealogists, and special Sanskritic rites—nor did they want to foreswear all the pleasures of tribal custom.

The Bhumij speak Bengali and live in multijati villages in which they are often the dominant group. Their territories were not particularly isolated, so jati people have lived in their villages for centuries. One such village is Madhupur in Barabhum pargana near the Bihar-West Bengal border.[1] Of the six jati-groups in the village the Bhumij are the wealthiest, with about four-fifths of the land, but there are also some Bhumij in the village who are landless laborers. Even the poorest among them share the Bhumij self-view that they are the ancient inhabitants and present lords of their homeland. The wealthier families uphold more elegant standards of diet, drink and ritual, and they tend to marry into other well-off families. The poorest form yet another marriage class whose families have lower sumptuary standards (S. Sinha 1959, pp. 12–13; 1962, pp. 48–52). None consider themselves to be separate from the other Bhumij, however.

The Bhumij of Madhupur carry on jajmani relations with a half dozen or more specialist jatis; they meet people of some thirty jatis at the weekly market. They are so far assimilated to jati standards as to require services of Brahmins, barbers, and washermen. They regard themselves as a Hindu jati and are so regarded by most others (S. Sinha 1959, p. 10). But there are vast disparities of opinion among their neighbors as to where the Bhumij are to be placed. The people of the three other tribal groups in the locality consider the Bhumij to be among the highest of jatis, equal to or higher than the Brahmins. But the more prestigious of the local Brahmins rank the Bhumij far below Rajputs and traders, about at a level with washermen, weavers, and distillers (S. Sinha 1965, p. 74; 1959, pp. 10–11). These Brahmins will not officiate for Bhumij; even the wealthier Bhumij can persuade only hard-up, "degraded" Brahmins to minister for them. This may explain why some Bhumij leaders are quite ready to cast their political lot with tribal peoples among whom they are held in high esteem.

Bhumij are rated low by these Brahmins because, for all their aspirations, few of them have completely renounced tribal traits concerning diet, women, and death. Many still drink liquor and eat chicken; their women are free to remarry and even to dance at ceremonies; their dead are buried rather than burned, and the bones later reinterred in a custom common to many Indian tribal cultures (S. Sinha 1959, p. 11; 1965, pp. 75–77). Though Bhumij are the dominant group in many of the villages in which they live, they are still not wealthy and powerful enough to persuade the authentic

---

[1] Barabhum pargana was in the Manbhum district of Bihar. In November 1956 the bulk of this district was reapportioned to the Puralia district of West Bengal.

"twice-born" to turn a blind eye to their tribal failings. The higher jatis see them as a tribal lot who follow debased customs. Their tribal neighbors, however, see them as dominant landowners who uphold both Kshatriya and indigenous standards, so they place Bhumij high among the superiors in the region.

The reform movement has had some effect. Sinha writes that their gay sensuality has been slightly toned down in order to make a good impression on the higher Hindus (1965, p. 79). But the toning down has not been so great as to curtail their overriding bias toward a good time. Bhumij are generally diligent farmers, but they believe that the reward for work should be pleasure rather than the accumulation of capital.

Migrants into their villages, especially cultivators of the Mahato jati, are more inclined than the Bhumij toward cool calculations of future profit and less to the hot pursuit of pleasure. A number of these Mahato are thrifty and capital-oriented, and despite legal safeguards against the loss of land by Bhumij, some of the Bhumij lands have been passing to immigrants imbued with the ethic of hard work and capital gain (S. Sinha 1963). Following this ethic yields greater income, which is commonly redistributed to attain lasting symbols of rank. As an aspiring jati, the Mahatos in this area have organized an association that urges reforms quite like those proposed for the Bhumij (Das Gupta 1962).

Unlike the Mahato, a good many Bhumij seem less attracted by the future benefits of higher rank than by the immediate pleasures of festive celebration in jovial company.

The attraction of these pleasures has proved quite durable; Bhumij have known of the other standards for a long time. Jati models were introduced when Bhumij chieftains, probably between the thirteenth and sixteenth centuries, granted lands and privileges to Hindus of high jatis and induced them to settle close to the ruler. The Brahmins taught the chiefs how to be proper Kshatriyas and invested them with the panoply of that status complete with initiation, sacred thread, and noble pedigree.

Thus equipped, the Bhumij chiefs convinced themselves that their powers and legitimacy had been destined from above. Some did extend their power beyond the limited scope ordinarily feasible in a tribal society. These rulers also established transcendental rites in Bhumij culture. Tribal deities were elevated to world (and state) guardians; tribal rites became state ceremonies. Not much of the tribal culture was disrupted and new elements only gradually seeped into Bhumij villages. The Hinduization of the ruler and of his backwoods court helped him maintain a center of power even if his subjects continued to see him as a temporary first among permanent equals. As a Raja's rule became firm, tribesmen could travel farther from their home village, could witness the ceremonies at the court, and could meet new people at the weekly markets that were established as part of the civilized regime.

Village headmen usually led the rest in acculturation since they had wider contacts and greater income. A headman might perform the Durga Puja (a main Bengali ceremony); he would avoid doing manual labor and would keep his women restricted to the bounds of the village. Even the ordinary Bhumij cultivators were half-seriously called *Raja Lok*, "royal people," by others in their villages. They felt themselves connected with the rulers but they were too remote from the Raja's court to do much about transforming their tribal ways (S. Sinha 1957a, p. 31; 1962, pp. 38–55; Navalakha 1959).

This, then, was the condition of Bhumij culture when British administrators came into their territories. In 1833 one official visited the locality that includes Madhupur village; he described the Bhumij there as professing to be Hindus but without any respectable Brahmin to officiate for them. Fifty years later, in 1883–1884, H. H. Risley reported that the Bhumij of this area worshipped Hindu as well as tribal gods and that the "more advanced" among them employed Brahmins as family priests, though these were probably not "respectable" Brahmins. They were beginning, Risley noted, to forget their totemic clan divisions and he speculated that they would soon abandon the tribal groupings in favor of more aristocratic designations. "The tribe will then have become a caste in the full sense of the word and will go on stripping itself of all customs likely to betray its true descent" (Risley 1915, p. 75; S. Sinha 1959, p. 9).

The Bhumij did try to do this but the pace was not fast. It began to quicken in later decades; the history of Madhupur village illustrates the trend (S. Sinha 1959, pp. 12–30). In 1897 a holy man of a Vaishnava sect was induced to live in the village. The villagers had previously known that such holy men would initiate Bhumij devotees into a state of religious grace and would act as their preceptors. It was not until the widowed mother of the village headman decided that she needed spiritual initiation that they procured a holy man of their own. He preached the ascetic ideal, led in frequent hymn sessions, and conducted recitations at which the lessons of the Sanskritic texts were told in the vernacular. The villagers thus gained a resident tutor in Sanskritic lore. Some of the villagers rejected the guru's precepts and only a few were devoted enough to adopt all of his doctrine, particularly his central message that "The discharge of semen is the root of all evil."

This holy man moved to a nearby village in 1910, and in 1914 another was brought in. The replacement was thought to be even more learned in scripture than the first, but he preached a hedonistic doctrine. With relief the families that had stopped drinking liquor and eating fowl now took up such practices again and joined with the new preceptor in merry song and dance. The new guru continued to tutor the villagers in stories from scripture even though he stressed a different aspect of scripture than did the ascetic guru.

Then, about 1921, the villagers heard rumors that a new divine being had appeared on earth and preached the ascetic vegetarian way. So influential were these rumors that some in Madhupur forthwith disposed of their chickens and goats. Then came the news that the name of the heaven-sent Raja was Gandhi. In 1923 townsmen who were followers of Gandhi appeared in the locality and set the record straight. Mahatma Gandhi, it transpired, wanted the people to give up liquor and to wear homespun, but he did not ask them to give up meat or fish, so they said.

In the following years there were a number of meetings in this vicinity at which Congress Party volunteers lectured on political independence, on the use of nonviolent methods, and on how to live a clean life based on moderation. These lectures, moreover, revealed that people could formally organize for reform. The principal Bhumij leader of the locality was stimulated to convene a meeting in 1935 at which the association of "Bhumij-Kshatriya" of the district was founded. At the meeting resolutions were passed about reform of diet and about the proper conduct of women. In the next year officers of the new association toured the villages and levied heavy fines on violators. There was a great slaughter of chickens and a diminution of tribal rites, but after the first flush of zeal, chickens reappeared and liquor was brewed again. Still, there were certain tribal practices, such as group dancing by women, that were really abolished. In this way, the movement for national independence gave added impetus to the shift toward jati standards.

A great turn came with independence in 1947. Rumors of clashes with Muslims spread and Bhumij leaders were called together to hear an orator of the pantribal party, the Jharkhand Party. He urged them to take up their bows, arrows, and spears against the rumored danger. But the Bhumij were not much attracted to close alliance with other tribal groups; they thought of themselves as true Kshatriyas, perhaps only a bit manqué. When elections came to be held, the Bhumij association was used as a means of mobilizing votes. As government officers and political candidates came to their villages bearing gifts actual and promised, the Bhumij began to take a greater interest in political participation than in the refining of their ritual purity or of their women's deportment in dance. Sinha tells of a meeting of Bhumij he attended in 1958 in which only lip service was given to Kshatriya status and in which the emerging leaders were literate, educated commoners rather than the landed chiefs. At this meeting it was resolved to insert the term Adibasi, aboriginal, in the name of the association so that it became, rather paradoxically, the Bhumij Adibasi Kshatriya association.

Since the 1950s, Bhumij interest in being known as Rajputs has progressively waned, yet many Bhumij are loath to declare themselves as tribesmen because they and their forefathers insisted so long that they were Kshatriyas. Sinha points out that the Bhumij find it more difficult to adapt to the new situation than do others, less Hinduized, tribal groups. "With the unfulfilled craze for Rajput recognition still lurking in their hearts and a residue of the broken landed aristocracy yet remaining in their midst the Bhumij and the Raj Gonds find it hard to adjust to the current secular demands made upon them" (S. Sinha 1962, pp. 78–79).

They have not become "a caste in the full sense of the word" as Risley predicted, though in the first half of the twentieth century they shifted appreciably in that direction. The Bhumij Rajas had some acculturative effect, but important change began in the late nineteenth century when sectarian holy men came to live in villages like Madhupur. The influence of these holy men accelerated the shift toward jati standards, though they ostensibly preached a casteless creed, and this trend gained momentum when a Bhumij leader adopted some of the organizational techniques of the nationalist workers who came to the locality. Before many years had passed, however, the success of the nationalist movement brought about new conditions that made the Kshatriya campaign seem, if not irrelevant, then certainly insufficient to gain more assured power and better status for Bhumij.

The new men in power were opposed to some parts of the "Bhumij-Kshatriya" reform (the greater seclusion of women, for example); they were indifferent to other parts of it, such as the taboo on eating chicken; and they placed much greater emphasis on such matters as education and political organization. The stride of the old reform leaders thus faltered as their chosen road became obscured and new, swifter ways to social advance seemed available. Hence the conflicts and waverings that have appeared in recent Bhumij meetings.

The new political ways nevertheless have a good deal in common with the program of ritual reform. Both assume a desire to rise higher in a wider society than just that of Bhumij. Both require moderation, discipline, postponement of immediate gratification. The nationalist dispensation demands quite as much discipline as do the "twice-born" standards, but this discipline is directed more to acquiring education than to regulating diet and to developing political roles rather than to separating sexual roles. Both movements require that salient tribal values be dropped in favor of more constrained behavior and wider social relations.

The Bhumij who now want the group to be classified as a tribe do not aim to revert to a previous state of tribal isolation and cultural separation, but rather to push zealously ahead toward secular gain and wider social advancement. These goals were introduced through the Bhumij Rajas and were later reinforced by sectarian gurus. The holy men, who thought they were lifting the immortal souls of their followers, also sharpened their material ambitions by opening a wider world for them.

These ambitions were further heightened among those who received some modern education, who are urging the tactical shift to tribal classification within the same strategy of social mobility.

Bhotias of Johar Valley, Uttar Pradesh

The Johari Bhotias had little hesitancy about declaring themselves, in the 1950s, to be tribals entitled to special governmental protection, although they too had previously claimed Kshatriya rank and had done so quite successfully. There are special circumstances in their case, as Ram Srivastava has cogently shown (1962). First, these Bhotias live in the Johar Valley high in the Himalayas; their villages lie between 11,000 and 13,000 feet above sea level in the Almora district of U.P. Secondly, they are traders who traditionally have carried goods, mainly salt, between Tibet and India. Finally, any conflict they may have had about their status was vastly overshadowed by the greater conflicts that ensued after the armies of the People's Republic of China took over Tibet (Srivastava 1962).

There are both jati and tribal villages in the lofty valleys on the Himalayan edge of the subcontinent. The jati folk carry on an attenuated jati order, as was previously noted. The tribals in these regions differ from the jati people in the ways noted in the previous chapter, though the cultural distance between jati and tribe is usually not great. The perceived social distance, however, can be very great. In the four valleys in which Bhotia predominate, there are Brahmins and Rajputs of ancient residence and also "immigrant" Brahmins and Rajputs (the forebears of these immigrants have lived in the region for "anything between twenty to fifty generations"). Both kinds of Hindus look down on the Bhotia as tribesmen who will eat beef.

The term Bhotia in the Himalayan borderlands is used for any kind of trader who plies between Tibet and India, but the Bhotia proper are those (some 22,000 in 1961) who live mainly in the four valleys northeast of Almora town and speak a distinctive language of the Tibeto-Burmese stock. The Bhotias of Johar Valley are nearest to the towns and have had closer contacts with Hindus and Hinduism than have the Bhotia of the three eastern valleys. They have also prospered in trade, have become much more like a Hindu jati, and have claimed Rajput status.

Unlike the Johar Bhotia, the eastern Bhotia show only traces of Hindu rites. They continue to have "a nightly gathering of unmarried men and women who dance, drink, and sleep together" (Srivastava 1962, p. 66). This custom and their other tribal ways violate the sensitivities of pious Hindus who know them. When a zealous Hindu missionary came to one of the valleys (which is on a pilgrimage route), built a temple and schools, and organized a society for service to them, they did at first promise him that they would give up drinking, smoking, and the insouciant commingling of sexes. But after a few months the holier but drabber life suddenly palled and they burst into drink, dance, and pleasure again (Srivastava 1962, pp. 7–72).

Johari Bhotias, as befits a more acculturated group, carefully dissociated themselves from the eastern Bhotia. Their trading successes have made them the wealthiest among the 10,000 residents of the Johar Valley. They have secured the services of Brahmin priests and pride themselves on being stricter in their Rajput deportment than are the old Rajputs of the valley. But these Rajputs hold that their Bhotia neighbors must be low; if they are not actually beef-eaters themselves, they deal and possibly eat with Tibetans who are certainly beef-eaters (Srivastava 1962, p. 54). The Johari Bhotias responded to such slurs as other disparaged aspirants have done. They organized an association for reform; one of their leaders started a journal and compiled a genealogy which showed them to be true-blooded Rajputs (Srivastava 1962, pp. 68–69).

Their competence in trade is not as anomalous as it would be for other tribals. Tribesmen, as we have noted, prefer to couch all friendly social relations in the idiom of kinship. Since a trader can scarcely treat customers and suppliers as kinsmen, tribesmen do not usually make good traders. Moreover there is the inclination to share one's stock in trade freely when one sees an occasion for joyous celebration, which in the tribal view is often. The Johari Bhotia, however, carry on a trade that involves arduous travel across some of the highest passes in the world; it is not at all like a casual jaunt to the weekly bazaar. Their main stock in trade, salt, is not a commodity to be consumed in one festive burst. Moreover, the trade is not with fellow tribesmen, but with outlanders of different religion and manner. Hence this trade is more like a foray into alien territory than like a business deal in the grain or cloth bazaar.

An enterprising, traveled people, the Johari Bhotias sent their children to modern schools so that by the time of independence there were educated men and women among them who followed national developments and soon recognized the advantages of voting strength. They formed a "Kumaon Bhotia People's Federation," made overtures to the previously deprecated eastern Bhotias, and presented petitions to Government asking that regulations be enacted to protect all the Bhotias.

Then came the events that prompted them to look more anxiously to government protection. When the Chinese took over Tibet, they insisted that Tibetans deal with China rather than with India. This quickly stifled the Bhotias' trade. With this loss, the Johari Bhotias became all the more eager to share in any benefits their government might give. They began a campaign to be counted as a scheduled tribe even though the Uttar Pradesh government had decided that none in the state should be so listed. Johari Bhotias are not concerned about any opprobrium in this official designation. Their need for aid is all the greater because their own social campaign has been undermined by battles between great nations.

Santals of the Jamshedpur Vicinity, Bihar

Santal mobility efforts are aimed directly toward the new political power and status, passing over the traditional varna models. Santal leaders do advocate new standards for conduct but they present them as Santal virtues, sanctioned by Santal tradition and deities, rather than as a return to ancient Kshatriya or Brahmin models. This movement insists on preserving the ancient Santal identity and gods and deliberately rejects some of the most sacred elements—the sacredness of the cow for one—in scriptural Hinduism. The special quality of Santal mobility is illustrated in Martin Orans' comment that "Once I saw a young party activist who had grown up in the Jharkhand movement persuading an older Santal with a few years of education that he must take up beef eating again if he wished to preserve the Santal caste" (1965, p. 108).

The Santals are one of the largest of tribal groupings in India. There are well over three million who speak Santali, a language of the Munda stock, and who live in parts of Orissa, Bihar, and West Bengal. There was very little political cohesion among them but there was and is considerable cultural similarity and very strong feelings among all Santals that they are utterly different from Hindus (Culshaw 1949, pp. 15–24). This powerful sentiment was reinforced by the great event of their history, the Santal rebellion of 1855–1857, an uprising that is still commemorated in their songs and tales and holds a central place in their memory.

The rebellion was a convulsive attempt to wipe out the steady loss of land and livelihood to nontribal immigrants into their territories. Like other tribal peoples, Santals could not cope with the financial and legal procedures that the newcomers manipulated nor could they resist the blandishments that led them into debt and to legal loss of their lands. After years of fruitless complaints they united to rise in arms. With arrows, spears, and axes they slaughtered many of the immigrants, routed the police forces sent against them, and even held off an army unit (O'Malley 1941, pp. 421–430). But they were finally defeated in a series of bloody debacles and their leaders were imprisoned or executed. The rebellion has become a glorious memory of courage and unity against insufferable wrongs and has deepened Santal feelings of separatism.

Santal detachment is social rather than cultural. The Santal have kinship usages similar to those of Hindus of the region, they depend on artisan jatis for most manufactured goods, they bring in Harijan midwives to assist at births. Some even establish bonds of fictive relationship with jati people, though close ties with particular friends do not erase their opinion of jati people in general. Orans writes, "that portion of Santal culture shared by all Santal is so marked with Hindu traits that it would be a monumental task to indicate all of them" (1965, pp. 42–43; see also Datta-Majumder 1956, pp. 98–129; Kochar 1963, pp. 176–178).

Some of the wealthier, landed families took on "twice-born" practices; beef eating and cow sacrifice were abandoned, dress and marriage customs were changed. The significant fact is that almost none tried to become Hindu or to be known as a jati. Christian missionaries made some Santal converts, particularly the mission supported by Scandinavian and American efforts, which included over 25,000 Santal Christians in 1941. Among the Santals as elsewhere in India, a major contribution of the missionaries was to open educational opportunities for many who would not otherwise have had any schooling at all (Orans 1965, pp. 87–90; Culshaw 1949, pp. 161–174).

In 1908 the steel mill and the company city at Jamshedpur in southern Santal country were built. These establishments had important bearing on Santal adaptation. Both educated and illiterate Santals found suitable work there; in the industrial setting they saw no reason to try for higher ritual rank or to emulate the traditional models of high status. The outlook of the Jamshedpur workers became known to other Santals. "The aspiring Santal who was well acquainted with Jamshedpur might adopt Western clothes, an automobile or motorcycle, and a *pukha* house (one with modern facilities) rather than vegetarianism, teetotalism, and a sacred thread …" (Orans 1965, p. 101). Not many rural Santals are educated and wealthy enough to aspire to such heights, but they follow the lead set by educated Santals. One of the educated became a founder of a popular new religious cult and others are the chief supporters of the mass political party.

The cult was established partly in anticipation of the 1951 Census, to show Santal strength. Many Santals had previously been enumerated as Hindus by the census takers. The cult is called *Sarna Dharam Semlet*, Sacred Grove Religious Organization, after the main locale of the tribal deities and the site of religious ceremonies. A Santal high-school graduate was one of the chief creators of this religion and has been given the title of Esteemed Guru. He has written a long epic-heroic play that is a parable about the proper duty of the Santals, the iniquity of jati people, and the noble virtues of the Santal heroes. It indicates to Santals that they too are worthy of having a scriptural epic. Another educated Santal has adduced archeological evidence in support of the story; less sophisticated Santals say that the epic play was written as the result of a revelation. The Guru has invented a script for writing Santali and there are plans for an authoritative text of

Santal tradition written in the new script (Orans 1965, pp. 113–119). The new rites emphasize the main features of tribal worship, not only worship in the sacred grove, but also offerings of beer, dancing at ceremonies, and even the sacrifice of cows. In these matters, they make no concession to Hindu sensitivities, indeed they stress such distinguishing features as ways of differentiating themselves from Hindus.

In a larger respect, however, this revitalization movement has made a fundamental concession. Its proponents implicitly tell the Santal that the traditional tribal religion, which lacked scripture, preceptors, epics, and large-scale coordinated ceremonies, needs to be remodeled. It is being recast in a transcendental mold fashioned after the examples of Christianity and Islam as well as of Hinduism. This implicit acknowledgment is part of what Orans calls the "rank concession syndrome," the acceptance by tribal peoples of their social and cultural inferiority to jati society and their consequent attempts to raise their social level in their own terms and by their own means (Orans 1965, pp. 123–146).

One of the means to advancement is the Jharkhand Party founded by Jai Pal Singh, an Oxford-educated Christian of the Munda tribe. A proclaimed aim of the party was to carve out a new state of the Indian union in the Chotanagpur area in which tribal peoples would be numerically dominant. Although it was organized as a pantribal movement, it also helped unify the Santals within their localities. It gave them a contrajati cause and a program on which all Santals, educated and noneducated, landed elite and ordinary villagers, could agree. It reinforced their ancient separatism from jati people while it mitigated cleavages within their own Santal society. The area headquarters of the party were located just outside Jamshedpur and served as a rallying place for Santals as well as for other tribals in the city and surrounding villages.

For the Santals in Jamshedpur the party offers an important new basis for social interaction and solidarity. Their industrial jobs do not provide for their social needs; the traditional solidarity rites cannot well be carried on in the city. Marriages tend to be contracted between individual families and weddings are no longer great dramatic declarations of alliances formed between two large groups of kin. Although the old Santal ceremonies cannot be staged as they were in the villages, political rallies serve some of the same social functions. Plays are performed, traditional dances are arranged, songs and conviviality prevail. The rallies are pleasure occasions similar to the festive occasions so important in traditional Santal life (Orans 1965, pp. 93–104). And yet the pleasure is not really the same; the occasions are more scheduled and limited, and the leaders guide the celebrations through a tempered, sober program.

Although educated Santals set no great store by the high insignia of Hinduism, they have been disciplined by their schooling to accept certain of its scriptural values, such as the emphasis on deferment of gratification. They have been indoctrinated with the idea of the advantages of thrift, moderation, and hard work, or at least of a regular stint of work. This acculturation is increasing now that Santal children in the vicinity of Jamshedpur attend school. The changes Orans noted, particularly among Santal industrial workers, are likely to continue and to accelerate. One of the fundamental changes is an increased emphasis on work, study, and rank attainment and a concomitant discouragement of "pleasure" (Orans 1965, p. 109). Thus many Santals are finally taking on the attitudes and values of contemporary Indian civilization even as they are vigorously rejecting the traditional symbols of Hinduism.

Social Transitions and Systemic Stages

These case examples illustrate the general trend of change among most tribal peoples in India. Like the Kond headman of Baderi village, they are making a dual transition, shifting to traditional jati standards and, in midcourse, adding changes toward modern, especially political, conduct. Among the five groups we have discussed, the Kotas are handicapped in this effort by their small number and by their lack of a wider jati-cluster, of ready-made allies. This may be why some Kotas cling to the nostalgic and obsolete view of what their wider society was like. Tribal associations have been formed among each of the other four tribes discussed. To be sure, the mere existence of an association does not guarantee that it will have social impact; some remain empty forms, others quietly become defunct. Nevertheless, an association does indicate that some leaders have become aware of the need for a new kind of social organization to grapple with the new conditions of social hierarchy.

The Bhumij have had some difficulty in making the new adaptation because many of them find it hard to forget what they claimed to be. They had nearly nailed down their claim to be Kshatriyas when they were directed toward a different model and organization by the movement for national independence.

The Bhotias had few difficulties in turning about, but they had the added push of the modern expansion of China, which sent them rapidly toward the shelter of their government. Santal leaders, too, have not been reluctant to try modern political organization, although they have done so on their own terms. They developed their own sect and supported a tribal political party. Under the banner of tribal cultural revival, they are trying to alter their basic tribal characteristics to accord with those of Indian civilization.

Konds have been more typical of the present trend among tribal peoples. Their tribal association attempts to do for all the Konds what the headman's guru was trying to do for his disciple. In teaching the headman to be a devout Hindu and a "Hindu gentleman" the guru enables him to participate more effectively in the new mode of local politics. The tribal association, quite like a caste association, is trying to reform Kond customs, to improve Kond education, and to pave the way for political weight in state politics.

In certain ways modern standards resemble the old tribal characteristics. Educated people are usually in favor of a greater degree of personal equality, of individual independence, of marital choice, of dietary latitude than is traditionally proper for those of high jati rank. These modern values are closer to tribal than to "twice-born" standards. In many other ways, however, the modern values impose requirements that any civilization, including the traditional Indian civilization, imposes on elite classes. The requirement for self-discipline, for greater specialization of function, for differentiation of roles, and for the maintenance of widespread relations beyond those of kinship.

The several civilizational styles that have been pressed on tribesmen are alike in fundamental respects even though they differ vastly in content. Tribesmen have been exhorted by modern-day Hindu preachers to turn to the purer practices of the high varnas; Christian missionaries have advocated Christian values; welfare workers have explained the advantages of modern conduct and education. The protagonists of each give them similar advice; they urge them to defer immediate gratification for the sake of some greater, long-range good, to mask expressions of sensuality, to prize sobriety and hard work, to revere the written word and the learned code. Now their own association leaders urge them to show these values in their personal conduct for the greater good of their ancient tribe.

In the long view of human change, we see that the development from tribe to jati began in India several millennia ago when technological innovations, especially that of plough agriculture, made possible the social-cultural invention of civilization. The Indian version of civilization developed caste organization. Improved technology opened the possibility for civilization development, but civilization and civilized peoples did not overwhelm all tribal societies.

In recent centuries the intellectual revolution of science and the great technological revolutions have similarly opened many new possibilities for human development. Worldwide changes have been set in motion and the movement is influencing the lives of Indian villagers, whether they are organized in jatis or in tribes. Both jatis and tribes are far less isolated than they were, both are much more affected by world forces, both are much more closely bound into their wider, national society.

The closer social involvement brings cultural changes. Some tribesmen, like the Hill Maria Gonds, make the changes unwillingly because they feel disadvantaged by them. Like many other tribesmen of earlier times they feel that any gain in material benefits and social resources is offset by losses of firm identity, close solidarity, religious satisfaction, and emotional security. They do not want to slip from a proud tribe to an inferior jati. Such ideas have long influenced tribesmen to hold off encroachments of jati people and customs.

Now, however, the encroaching pressures are greater and the advantages of change seem larger. Tribesmen and jati villagers are being influenced in the same tidal direction of change. That tide does not wash away or wipe out difference among groups nor the considerable difference in the pace of their change. It does steadily press them toward a new kind of social organization and a revised set of cultural standards.

In the long view of caste society, the absorption of tribal peoples into jati structure is part of recurrent change. New recruits are incorporated; the overall social system and the component systems remain unaltered. But from the view of tribal society, the same events entail systemic change. Former tribesmen enter into a different kind of social system when they act fully as jati members. They then take on more differentiated roles and more specialized functions than they typically have under tribal organization. In comparison with tribal organization, jati organization makes it possible for a society to have a much greater carrying capacity in numbers of people and in productive content.

Jati organization, as we have seen, is being changed. Status advance can now be played out on larger social scenes than before, those of region, state, and nation. In the wider scenes, there is more differentiation, specialization, and carrying capacity than there usually is within a parochial jati hierarchy. This suggests that caste society may be undergoing systemic change to a new level of social organization. The systemic change in jati organization may perhaps be understood as recurrent change toward modern, global organization, just as systemic change in a tribal society can be seen as recurrent change into caste society.

PART VIII

CONTINUITIES AND TRENDS

CHAPTER 33

Psychological Forces, Social Processes, and Systemic Shift

The people who together engage in a social system must share certain critical psychological characteristics if the system is to work. The following summary of our social analysis therefore begins with a discussion of two psychological factors that are particularly important in this system. One is a cognitive assumption, the other is a personal motivation. The two are used as generative principles in the grammar of social action. Both are applied in much of a person's social interaction. These themes of personal behavior underlie the social competition that is carried on at all levels. The very acts of waging competitive conflict help to confirm the contestants' conviction that status is worth the struggle.

Contests for status are part of the adaptive capacity of the whole social system. Groups that came to be materially successful (whether through their abilities, or fortunate opportunities, or both) could rise in their local social orders and did not feel impelled to disrupt the general system. Also, a local order could be adapted to accommodate new groups and institutions. The people of a locality could set up relations with alien groups without feeling that their own social integrity and status were necessarily endangered by such relations. The groups that were absorbed socially generally became assimilated culturally to the precepts of caste society.

These processes resulted in recurrent change in local social orders and in the long-term stability of the fundamental system. The parameters of that system are now being altered and with them some of the systemic principles appear to be changing. The shifts may possibly affect the psychological modes of perception and motivation that have supported the traditional social concepts and structure. The psychological features of cognitive assumption and personal motivation have been mentioned in earlier chapters; it is useful to examine them together here.

Themes of Personal Behavior

The cognitive assumption is that most interaction occurs between a superior and a subordinate, or between representatives of a dominant and of a dependent group. One's society is therefore seen as a hierarchical order; that order defines the relative positions of the actors in a social situation in advance of their interaction. Dominance and subordination are fundamental dimensions in all societies, not only in India, and advance definition of social position is a requisite condition in all social systems.

In Indian village society the hierarchical assumption is applied particularly widely, stringently, and intensively. It is constantly reinforced by being linked to a person's bodily experience as well as to his religious beliefs. Each person's biological functions, especially his acts of ingestion, are in some measure the concern of all in his jati. If he falls below the jati's standards of ritual purity and pollution, then all may be in peril of sinking to a lower social position. His body thus becomes an arena in which weighty issues of group status are at stake. Each child learns that he himself becomes more defiled or more pure according to his daily acts and experiences. The criteria of ritual purity and pollution that mark off these different states of an individual's being are also used to demarcate the social strata of his society.

Some important exemptions from the hierarchical perspective have been noted above. Within the family, relations between brother and sister and between mother and child are construed with a different emphasis. A self-dedicated holy man, a sadhu, has presumably removed himself from the social frame. There are situations in which hierarchy is not a primary assumption, as among those who are struggling together against a common opponent, whether they are persecuted sectarians or college classmates. These and other exceptions are not few, but they are nonetheless exceptions to the prevailing assumption of hierarchy.

In relations among people of different jatis, the hierarchical assumption has been linked with postulated differences in ritual pollution and purity. One outcome of holding these linked assumptions is that the ritual superiority of Brahmins has been acknowledged by most of those who held secular power. Brahmins could legitimate power and sometimes made skillful use of this prerogative. Another reason Brahmins possessed such durable influence was that the dominant jatis (and the Rajas in earlier times), in acknowledging the ritual superiority of Brahmins, were also affirming the validity of the hierarchical principles central to their own conduct. For this reason also there has been considerable inertia about untouchables rising and Brahmins falling in a local order. In maintaining clear extremes of their social order, the people of a locality were also maintaining clear exemplars of the assumptions by which they regulated their lives.

Those assumptions are translated into a social map by the varna categories, to which have lately been added the overlapping categories involving modern conduct. Muslims, Christians, and Jews set up analogous divisions of their own. Ambitious villagers model their conduct according to the reference category of a high varna and, more particularly, after the living examples of the reference groups whose behavior they can see. In their emulations and mobility struggles, villagers demonstrate to themselves and to all their society, in the characteristic circular way, that their hierarchical assumption is indeed true.

Coupled with this image of hierarchical society is a characteristic image of one's self as worthy of being a superior within a close bracket of rank. A man does not typically feel impelled to challenge the superiority of those high above him in any hierarchy; dependency on such superiors is not deprecated, whether the superior is a revered guru or a powerful official. Subordination to someone in a proximal rank, however, is often felt to be uncomfortable and something to be changed as soon as possible. This personal motivation is the other source of the perennial press toward recurrent change.

How this motivation and confident self-image have been inculcated are matters about which we can only speculate, since detailed studies are not yet available. Certainly these ideas are absorbed early in childhood from family experience. Perhaps one factor is the great importance to a mother, at almost all social levels, of the birth of her child. The child, particularly the first son, becomes a kind of social savior for her; each of her other children, in turn, can be the subject of her open emotional expression in a milieu that provides few other approved emotional outlets for a young woman. It may be that this focusing of maternal attention and affection gives a child an especially strong sense of his own worth. Whatever the causal factors in Indian family life may turn out to be, it is clear that these motifs of personality have been widely shared by men and women of the various regions and social strata on the subcontinent. This same personal motivation bestirs untouchables at the bottom of a local order (provided that they are not utterly crushed by poverty) as well as the elite of the upper ranks.

The response to acts rising from this motivation is defensive. The same man who gathers his strength to challenge a superior knows that some of those subordinate to him are probably preparing to challenge him. This makes him very sensitive about the prerogatives and symbols of any superior status he may hold. It leads to a style of personal relations that I have elsewhere termed "aggressive defense" (Mandelbaum 1955, pp. 235–239).

As against the instability of proximal relations there is the relative stability of distal relations. Villagers not only agree that there is a hierarchical frame to society but also that certain parts and figures are outside the arena of open competition.

Within a family a man's father has the more distal role, his brother the more proximal role. Solidarity among brothers is apt to weaken once the authority of the father is gone. One brother challenges another, eventually the family separates, with added bitterness because each tends to blame the other for rupturing the ideal. Both also blame the women, partly to gloss over fraternal hostility, partly because the women of the family are also competitors among themselves. The young bride must be subservient to her mother-in-law, but as she becomes a mother and a matron she can begin to challenge her mother-in-law and to contend with any other of the sons' wives in the family. Although certain aspects of family relations do indeed differ by social level and by region, these family processes are shared across regions and jatis. When a low-ranking family begins to rise, its members tend to take on the family patterns of the higher jatis.

Beyond the family, one lineage of a jati may challenge another; the people of one village, under some circumstances, try to outstrip another village. The principal group for challenge and confrontation, however, has been the jati. It is, as we have seen, a main unit of a man's identification, a principal agency for individual and group power, the chief vessel of status. A villager's aggressive defense of his honor—the term izzat, as previously noted, expresses the concept for many in North India—combines defense of personal and family status with defense of the integrity, standards, and prestige of his jati.

Competition and Conflict as Systemic Processes

Competition among jatis is common and is better understood as an outcome of the basic motivation than as the root cause of village conflict. The importance of this motivation is shown when a jati or a jati-group is so firmly entrenched that its members fear no challenge from others. Challenge and conflict are then likely to come up *within* that group. Some of its members will feel subordinate to other members and will sooner or later dispute their superiority. The personal motivation toward challenge of immediate superiors is constant, and so is social competition.

It is a competition without end, not only because every superior feels that some of his subordinates will eventually defy him, but also because a man who is a superior in certain contexts generally feels himself to be a subordinate in others. He may be impelled to try to improve his position in those contexts while being warily defensive in others. The competition can yield enlivening rewards as well as nagging anxieties. A man may get considerable personal satisfaction from the results of his status strivings, as he does when he brings off an advantageous marriage in his family, or gains a precious ritual symbol for his jati, or helps put a kinsman into a position of power and prestige.

Competition is pervasive in many life situations, but there is also much in a villager's life that it does not pervade. As we have noted, there are exempt relations and situations. Relations between fully acknowledged superiors and reciprocally valued subordinates tend to be secure and assured (cf. Carstairs 1957, p. 106). The subordinate then prizes rather than resents his dependency. For some people religion is a secure resource against the abrasions of competition. In the scriptural ideal a man who has fulfilled his family duties opts out of the social competition and into religious devotion. There are also some individuals and groups who prefer to be neutral and who try to remain on the sidelines of any competitive arena. Often they succeed in doing so for a time, but they are apt to be nudged periodically into competition by forces of the social system.

Failure in mobility efforts is allayed by the very assumption of social hierarchy. A defeated group is not obliterated or condemned to complete helplessness. Some of its members may be beaten, a few even killed, a number of its wealthier families may lose much of their wealth, but the group is generally not much worse off than it was before. The victors are usually satisfied to have the defeated resume their subordinate positions. The superiors need their goods and services, and they also need inferiors below them to shore up their position as superiors.

The ideology of noncompetitive varnas is firmly believed while competitive social action among jatis is zealously waged. At any given time and place, some groups may be rising and others may be losing ground in their local order. This fluctuation is one reason for differing opinions about just where a particular group is to be placed.

Conflict within families is also disapproved in the villagers' ideology yet is inherent in their actual relations. In a family the stress point at which conflict is likely to erupt occurs when grown brothers, bereft of parental regulation, must reach some important decision about their domestic economy.

Among jatis, village ceremonies have often been occasions for outbreaks of conflict when each jati at the feast must be seated in order of relative rank. Such conflicts may consolidate each contesting group and reinforce the idea that higher rank is highly important. So quarrels about rank result from and also buttress the psychological themes.

Adaptive Capacities

The traditional social system was putatively closed and immutable but actually provided openings, if difficult and limited ones, for the rise of ambitious groups. The *Manu* version of fixed varnas was rarely denied, but the real possibility of status rise promised success to those who could best adapt. Adaptive success for a group within the society could be initiated by skillful development of economic resources, by military conquests, by settling new lands, by adroit trading or political acumen, or through any other fortunate exploitation of the environment. Military prowess has not been a means for jati rise for some time, but the other avenues to status gain are still in use. Few can achieve much ritual advance in their own lifetime, but they may raise their material base enough to glimpse the self-promised niche that may be occupied by their descendants.

A main adaptive feature of jati society as a whole is the capacity to absorb alien groups who then become contestants for rank and thus supporters of the whole system. Such groups could readily be absorbed because jati villagers did not feel threatened by cultural differences among their neighbors. They could carry on restricted relations with those of different customs without loss to their own standards or status. Tribesmen have been continually absorbed socially and then assimilated culturally; jati folk could accept them as low-ranking dependents or, if circumstances so dictated, as dominant landowners, without impairing their own caste society. Immigrants from another region of India or from outside the subcontinent were similarly accommodated. The early Christian, Jewish, and Muslim traders were absorbed into jati society and retained their religious identity. Foreign raiders who settled down to found dynastic kingdoms made their peace with the jati system. The British tried to keep aloof from the system of caste relations, but as wielders of paramount political power they did affect the system. Yet for all their influence on it they did not change the fundamentals or the pervasiveness of caste relations.

Jati people could cope with introduced institutions as well as with introduced groups. The British brought in new kinds of bureaucracy, law, learning, and technology; all were promptly utilized for jati as well as personal purposes. When the colonial bureaucracy was established, for example, there was not much question as to whether taking part in it was good for one's family and jati. Those who understood that they could get a respectable place in that hierarchy were usually far more concerned about how to get the highest possible place than whether it was good to participate at all. They took to the new institutions as providing auxiliary criteria of high status, new opportunities for attaining higher rank and additional channels for mobility.

Long before the impact of European influences, villagers dealt with strong outside influences—economic, governmental, and religious—without changing the bases of their social structure. The economic effects of irrigation, for example, were anciently felt in villages of the Tanjore area and the jati structure was fully maintained. It was maintained in Totegadde in Mysore where a cash crop has been grown for centuries. Such economic forces have had important consequences. They have affected the order of the jatis in a locality but they have not disrupted the jati order.

In governmental matters, villagers had ways of giving a Raja his minimal due while actually managing their local affairs through their own devices. British institutions of government were potentially inimical to the traditional system, but as we have seen, villagers quite successfully subsumed British law and police order within their own political code and jati order.

The introduced religions of temporal rulers, Islam and Christianity, attracted millions of converts and influenced the whole civilization. Their influence did not undermine the traditional social system. Moreover, the internal tendency toward religious revolt against the system created social groups that were regularly incorporated back into that system.

Social Mobility and System Maintenance

The system was used so adaptively because people applied the thematic principles both steadfastly and flexibly. They applied the hierarchical perspective steadfastly to new as well as to habitual situations; they applied it flexibly, not insisting on any single or completely calibrated hierarchy for all occasions. There is a certain flexibility even at the extremes of a local jati order. Most in a locality agree that certain jatis are lowest, but members of each of these low jatis typically insist that at least one of the others should be ranked below their own group. In this sense there is usually no absolute bottom to a local ladder of rank and in a parallel sense there is no absolute top.

Those who occupy the topmost rung are apt to compete among themselves for the best place along that rung, or they may look to a grander struggle in a wider arena. During the British regime, for example, a Maharaja might be the unchallenged suzerain within his state, with only a very few and broad constraints imposed on his conduct by the paramount British authority. Yet many such princes constantly tried to improve on the honors officially allotted to them at ceremonial occasions from, say, a ceremonial salute of nine guns to the eleven-gun class.

The drives toward social advance are quite constant, but the tactics for advance are varied. Different routes are possible; the traditional alternatives are in the three "twice-born" varnas. Though these reference categories are very different in certain respects, all three stipulate certain broadly similar kinds of behavior, as in the relations between men and women and in the discipline of conduct. Those who attempt to move up into any one of these higher echelons must conform to the broad standards required of all leading groups in Indian civilization. A convert to Islam or Christianity from a low jati is urged to discipline himself in ways that are similar in general, though different in details, from those he would follow in seeking high varna status as a Hindu.

Whatever route may be chosen, effective rise begins with the prospering of individual families. Hopes for higher rank are futile unless steeled with secular strength. Individual families can achieve real advance only as part of a larger group and so prospering families deploy their secular resources to achieve ritual gains for their group. To succeed, their leaders must simultaneously cope with external opposition and maintain internal strength.

Success against opposing jatis is usually achieved gradually, in a series of steps beginning with changes to which others cannot well object. As the aspiring villagers build a base of wealth and purity, they begin to make more open assertions that are more objectionable to those who rank above them. In Senapur village, the Earth-workers decided to wear the sacred thread. It is at such points that escalating aspirations and growing hostility to them come to a head and there is a confrontation, commonly a whole series of physical, legal, and societal encounters. The confrontation may be delayed if the higher groups have taken to modern standards and therefore set less store by the traditional symbols that the aspirants are trying to attain. The confrontation may be postponed but it is not annulled.

To overcome in such confrontations, an aspiring group must mobilize united effort. Unity is usually a difficult problem. All sections of a jati do not improve their resources and local standing at the same rate. The most advanced sections may have reformed their practices so greatly that they can scarcely admit to being jati partners with those who have not reformed. Moreover the success of some tends to arouse challenges from others within the jati.

If the more successful members find that they cannot muster enough cultural and social unity for their purpose, they may redefine the boundaries of the group. In the traditional process the more advanced or dissatisfied families split off and declared themselves to be a separate jati. Occasionally such sections joined with similarly mobile sections of other jatis in an action that entailed fusion as well as fission. With fresh unity, they then proceeded to battle for higher rank.

Individuals identify with different kinds of groups as different situations require and may compete for higher rank in each context. A vigorous villager strives mightily to advance and defend his family's rank among the families of his jati, but when he participates in a village panchayat on an issue affecting his jati, he is apt to be a firm proponent of the jati more than of his family. Should the repute of his village be at stake on some occasion, he is likely to identify with the village and to challenge those of other villages.

In some contexts he may fight to advance the status of his religion, or his region, or his language group. To be sure, he may not always know where to put the greater effort. He does not always switch identification smoothly; a village leader may sometimes be torn between advancing the interests of his village or that of his jati.

Moreover, an ambitious leader must be task-oriented as well as rank-oriented. He must focus on what is to be done for the village as well as on who gains rank advantage by what is done. The two interests are usually not completely separate; the one impinges on the other, but neither should be scanted if the leader is to be successful in an enterprise. Balancing off each consideration is a constant problem for leaders at all levels. This is indeed true in all complex societies; it is a particularly potent problem for village leaders in India.

Those who strive for social mobility do not challenge the hierarchical frame but believe rather that they are only trying to restore their proper place within it. Those who oppose them believe that the climbers are trying to alter the ordained order of society.

From the wider view of our analysis, the challengers are right, though not for the reasons they give. They are right because their efforts are part of the grand counterchange within the general social system through which secular power and ritual rank are kept in a broad parity. That parity, however, is not without exceptions. There are poor and ineffectual Brahmins, even whole jatis of them. Conversely, an occasional village Harijan may be rich and influential. Yet by and large, the higher jatis of a locality are the wealthier and more powerful, the poorest are also lowest in ritual rank. So, as we have noted, acts that are intended to disturb an existing, static local order of rank, simultaneously serve to maintain the dynamic, adaptive general system of jati relations.

Recurrent and Systemic Change

The system of society in India was changed in the ancient past; the earliest Vedic scriptures reflect a social order of relatively open classes rather than of bounded jatis. After the classic system of caste became established, perhaps a millennium ago, temporal rulers sometimes intervened in the ranking but did not alter the systemic principles. A freebooter who seized state power could enhance the rank of his own jati and could manipulate the village ranking of other jatis through grants of land and of privilege.

During the period of British rule, ranking seems to have become more rigid. Greater emphasis was apparently given to the ritual criteria for rank, and greater power apparently accrued to jatis whose men were already high and dominant. These were not really systemic changes. The major social units remained the same; the assumptions about high and low status were unchanged; relations among jatis were carried on in the same way; and mobility campaigns continued, though with some shift in mobility tactics.

Political independence has set in train a series of social and economic changes that are still very much in the making. In some ways the trend seems to be a return to the precolonial condition when state power could directly impinge on jati ranking. Modern political power is based, not on military conquest, patents of nobility, and grants of land, but on voting influence, official positions, and such boons as tube wells, roads, and import licenses. Changes in the avenues to wealth and power have brought about changes in mobility procedures. Some low-ranking groups, obstructed in their villages, have appealed to higher political authorities, have organized for voting purposes, and have acquired offices, grants, and local influence. They have detoured the traditional step-by-step procedure and have struck directly for respectable status through political action.

With the increasing success of such actions, there has come a consequent decline in the attractions of the traditional symbols of high rank. Thus those Noniyas who succeeded after long and bitter struggle in wearing the sacred thread now find that their sons are quite uninterested in doing so. Men of the higher jatis are no longer so concerned as they were about who wears this ritual badge because many of them, like the younger Noniya, are more concerned with badges of higher modern education than with badges of higher varna status.

Ambitious men now find the fusion of jatis for political strength more effective than the fission of jatis for ritual purity. Hence many jati leaders urge the enlargement of their endogamous group by encouraging marriages among previously separate, though similar, jatis. The trend is toward fewer, wider, better organized jatis. Villagers continue to assume that endogamy is a central factor for social solidarity, that social groups are ranked, and that one's own group must constantly try to advance or to defend its social position. The systemic changes that are in view do not point directly toward an unstratified society but toward fewer and more homogeneous social groups. These changes will not necessarily be rapid; much hinges on the rate of economic improvement.

The major changes in Indian society are in the same direction as that taken by broad changes in other contemporary societies. The general trend is toward the narrowing in cultural disparities and in social distances between groups in a society, though scarcely toward any total elimination of stratification. There is a general shift away from traditional status symbols to modern political and technological symbols. Disadvantaged groups at every level of society are entering the political arena as they had not been able to do before.

The common trends come out of the broadly similar influences of modern technology, industry, education, and communication. These forces set the parameters for the evolving social systems, though they do not determine the precise nature of any of them. But the parameters do frame a new type of social system, to which most of the former systems are being changed. This brings us back to the suggestion raised at the end of the previous chapter. It seems that the systemic changes within one major society, as in India, do appear as incipient recurrent change when viewed in the perspective of modern world civilization.

CHAPTER 34

Trends

Indian society is being changed in some major ways. These shifts are still in the process of being worked out and their full importance cannot yet be assessed. However, certain directions of social development are clearly apparent. We discuss these trends in this chapter, focusing on changes in family relations as illustrative of the general direction of social change and of a particular paradigm of change.

Drives and Hindrances to Social Change

Many in India now take government to be a principal engine of social change. Even those who are politically conservative agree that a good part of social change must be stimulated and directed by governmental agencies. Main responsibility for these innovative, reformist functions of government rests with the new elite, as M. N. Srinivas terms the growing class of educated people in India from whose ranks come those who manage the affairs of state (1996, pp. 69–82). Though members of this class vary greatly in their political views and social identifications, they share certain basic concepts about the desirability of social change and about desirable kinds of change.

The successes of new elite since independence are sometimes overlooked or underrated. A glance at the condition of other peoples who achieved new nationhood at about the same time shows that those of India might have fared a good deal worse if their national leaders had been less astute, dedicated, and able. Yet there are few, whether villagers or urban elite, who are satisfied with the achievements thus far or with the current rate of change toward the material and social goals that many in India want to reach.

The nation's potential for achieving these goals is handicapped by several sets of circumstances. One is the sheer magnitude of the problem of changing the ways of so large a population with so many living in deep poverty. There are, in addition, the inherent contradictions and inevitable conflicts that confront any people whose leaders seek rapid development—contradictions made less tractable in India by the size of the population and the extent of the poverty. Some observers have said that national plans have been hampered by misconceptions concerning the nature of Indian society—a hindrance that is of particular interest for our present study.

The magnitude of the effort required to direct fundamental social changes in a nation that includes about one seventh of the human race has been amply noted by many writers. Only a few of the main facts and conclusions need be cited here. Although economic output has been rising steadily, the gross national product is still relatively low. Within the nation, a large part of the population is abysmally poor.[1] Families that are so perilously poor—and there are many millions of them—can scarcely do much about raising their productivity or changing their social standards.

The problem of population growth illustrates one of the many contradictory situations that planners and legislators must face. Allocating substantial resources to improve health and lengthen life may well increase the pressure of population on the nation's economy and so diminish the sparse resources available for development purposes. Other contrary pressures arise between the drive for social equality and that for productive efficiency. Wider distribution of land ownership may, in the initial stages, lower production because of the disruption in agricultural management. A most important difficulty is that major development projects are long-term enterprises which take many years before they can pay off, yet political leaders come under public pressures to produce tangible benefits quickly.

Added to the popular pressures for swift material results are the ideological pressures for quick social results. The major political parties have held forth the promise of greater social justice as well as greater prosperity for the nation. National leaders have frequently depicted the caste system as the great obstacle in the way of achieving both justice and prosperity (e.g. Nehru 1946, pp. 112–113; Narayan 1958, p. 87). Such leaders feel that they must use strong rhetoric if they are to jolt the strongly entrenched social system, but the rhetoric tends to becloud the social perceptions of planners and legislators. If policy makers view much of the existing village society as absolutely inimical to national welfare and as a system that must be eliminated before long, they are not intellectually prepared to deal with that society in suitably constructive ways. They cannot quickly eradicate the social patterns they condemn and they are not likely to search for those forces in the existing society that can be channeled toward the constructive goals they desire.

Misconceptions about Social Change

Misconceptions about the nature of Indian society have been cultivated by some scholars. A volume of essays by an economist, K. William Kapp, entitled *Hindu Culture, Economic Development, and Economic Planning in India* (1963), is a case in point. One of Kapp's principal conclusions is that "… Hindu culture and Hindu social organization are determining factors in India's low rate of development" (p. 64). Kapp's views parallel those of Max Weber whose work of 1915 on the

[1] For example, a 1962 sample survey of 8,655 rural households showed that the poorer 50 percent of these households held about 7 percent of the total reproducible wealth, and accounted for about 22 percent of the total income. The households in the poorer half of the sample owned very little of the total land; 62 percent of them had incomes of less than $250 per year (Lokanathan 1965a, pp. vii, 112–121; 1965b, p. 3).

religion of India has influenced a good many of the later sociological and economic writings (cf. Weber 1958; Bendix 1960, pp. 158–211; Singer MS. 1969).

In a rebuttal to Kapp's arguments and to the Weber thesis, Milton Singer has pointed out that adequate empirical evidence for such conclusions is not given in the works proclaiming this thesis and that there is considerable evidence to indicate that Hindu culture and caste society have not had any great dampening effect on economic development. Moreover, Kapp's conclusions are largely speculative extrapolations from misunderstood scriptural concepts. These speculations, Singer says, are presented as if they were "a collection of proven generalizations from which far-reaching policy decisions should be drawn" (1966, p. 505). Singer notes that some policy-makers in India share these unproven and misleading ideas about the relation of Indian society to economic development. "In that case, these ideological commitments of a relatively small group of political and intellectual leaders may become as important a limitation on economic growth as any feature of the traditional value and belief system or of the social structure" (Singer, 1966, p. 502).

The common clichés about caste society and economic development appear in Gunnar Myrdal's comprehensive, and in some respects, most illuminating *Asian Drama*. Myrdal begins by stressing his commitment to "a broad institutional approach" (p. ix) but despite the cogency of his institutional analysis in economic terms, he underestimates the force of the institutions of Indian society. Thus Myrdal writes (p. 1081) that in the main there are no institutional spurs driving Indian people to work and work hard. Quite to the contrary, as the village studies show, the prevalent quest for status is a constant spur to hard work, though the fruits of diligent labor may be spent in expensive confrontations, in litigation, in conspicuous consumption, and in other ways that an economist might describe as uneconomic. These may well be disadvantageous in the economist's perception, not necessarily so in the villagers'.

When Myrdal states (p. 1692) that the masses in South Asia do not calculate rationally in terms of costs, returns, and maximum profit, he is neglecting their own social calculations which are as rational in their village milieu as the economist's calculations are in his milieu. In the same passage, Myrdal writes that the masses in countries like those of South Asia are not interested in raising their living standards and he adds that this is "confirmed by anthropological studies all over the world." Anthropological studies confirm no such conclusion.

Some of Myrdal's comments are cogent, some even startling. For example he notes that on the basis of all his information he believes that the masses on the Indian subcontinent live in worse poverty than did those in the Western European countries during the several centuries before the industrial revolution (1968, p. 688). He also concludes that the growth of population is the single most important social change that has taken place in South Asia since World War II. "It has been far more important than any reform or development efforts and it has done a great deal to thwart these efforts" (1968, p. 1530).

Yet some of his statements about Indian society and character are very wide of the mark (cf. Madan 1968). He says, for example, that to a Western observer the main source of India's weakness (presumably economic weakness) lies in the human factor. It is not, Myrdal continues, a lack of innate abilities or technical skills, but rather a lack of initiative, of interest in improving their economic status, of respect for labor—"the imprint of the caste system on their character" (p. 1148).

While some "Western observers" hold such opinions, as does Myrdal, other observers both Western and non-Western, have vigorously (and in my view, correctly) challenged these views (cf. A. K. Singh 1967; Morris 1967; Singer 1966; 1969). Moreover, studies of actual village life in India show little lack of initiative or absence of desire for improvement but rather reveal impediments to entrepreneurial efforts from the economic situation, the political environment, and the social apparatus. Pinning the blame on the "human factor" falls in with the common exhortations to villagers and townspeople that they work hard, reform their customs, eschew temptations, and rise above human fallibilities. There is an abundance of such moralizing; there is, however, a lack of clear understanding of the social forces involved, of the real nature of caste systems, and of the actual potentials for institutional change. Those concerned with economic and social development in India gain little by being told that India's greatest problem is the imprint of the (misunderstood) caste system on the people's (undefined) character.

Such notions, like the varna concept, provide an oversimple explanation of a complex situation. But unlike the varna theory, these ideas are more likely to undermine than to bolster the social purposes of those who hold them. To advance these purposes, the main problem is not how to kill caste relations most quickly but how best to channel the dynamic forces in village society so as to construct a new system of relations with greater advantages for all in the society. Radical extirpation is urged by some ideologists and commends itself to some activists as the only road to their goals. That road has well-known disadvantages as well as obvious attractions. When a political-social upheaval does occur in a society, the people have to develop any new relations and institutions largely on the basis of those they already know. A clear understanding of that social basis can surely benefit those—of whatever political persuasion—who are trying to direct change. The difficulties of Indian development can only be compounded if misleading notions about the nature of Indian society hold sway.

Particularly misguided is the notion that there must be inherent contradictions between established customs and modern innovations. As we have noted in previous chapters, there has been considerable cultural continuity along with modern social change. Villagers have generally extended their previous ways more than they have taken up totally new roles and institutions. They could do so because the people of India have maintained a complex society for many centuries; they had long possessed the capacities for maintaining a civilization when they met the ideas, artifacts, and representatives of modern Western civilization.

This is illustrated in an 1819 account of the village of Lony (now Lonikand) twelve miles from Poona. It was written by Thomas Coats, a surgeon who lived in Poona for seventeen years and had traveled extensively about the countryside. Coats's account was the basis for a restudy done in 1954–58 by G. S. Ghurye and his associates (Coats 1823; Ghurye 1960).

When Coats wrote his account of Lony, the village had been under British control for less than two years and had been little altered by that control. The villagers were thoroughly engaged in a monetary economy and in market exchange. There was a school for children of the higher jatis. Coats observed that even though the ordinary cultivators were not literate, they were minutely informed about everything that related to their calling and many of them had a "tolerable knowledge" of the leading events of their country's history. "On the whole, they are better informed than the lower classes of our own countrymen, and certainly far surpass them in propriety and orderliness of demeanour" (Coats 1823, p. 192).

In 1819, the year when these observations were written (the year also of Queen Victoria's birth), the villagers of Lony had recently been incorporated into the largest political domain that had ever existed. Yet some twenty centuries earlier, this locality had been part of another empire, that of

Ashoka, which was then one of the largest political domains that had ever existed. Although the Lony villagers did change their ways during the one hundred and thirty years when they were under British cultural influence and political rule, and although the pace of change has quickened since independence, yet much of the ground plan of their culture, as described by Coats in 1819, is still evident in Ghurye's book of 1960.

Recognition of such continuities diminishes the supposed antithesis between "traditional" and "modern" ways. So-called traditional patterns have not been held static and modern kinds of behavior are commonly fitted into long-standing patterns of action. To be sure, the continuities do not avert conflicts, contradictions, and dilemmas. Any major shift in emphasis inevitably discomforts some who have social and personal investment in the previous state of affairs.

To illustrate the trends of modern social change we next examine changes in family roles and relations. A social system tends to be stronger than any of its component groups and as weak as any of its fundamental principles. Particular groups—jatis, dynasties, sects, colonial powers—have come and gone in India without drastic impairment of the general social system. Certain units of society, the clan for one, have waxed and waned in importance at particular times and places, and the general system has remained quite the same. If, however, many in a society change their fundamental ideas about what their social order is and should be, then major change is likely to impend. Our discussion of family change is therefore particularly concerned with possible change in the integrating ideas about the family.

Family Changes and Continuities

The "breakdown" of the joint family in India has often been forecast on the grounds that joint families were suited to the old agricultural societies but are dysfunctional under present conditions. Hence a sharp break between the "traditional" joint family and the "modern" nuclear family is supposed to occur. This view has been challenged by studies showing that the form of the family is not so closely linked to the type of economic organization (cf. Kapadia 1966, pp. 273–308, 329–331; Singer 1968, pp. 423–424). Most students of the family do recognize that there is a general tendency in modern societies toward placing greater importance on the conjugal bond between husband and wife and toward decreasing the demands of the consanguine ties, especially those among siblings, but this is a long-term trend rather than a cause for abrupt revision of family relations. Because so many studies of family trends in India have been focused on the supposed passing of the joint family, there has been more counting of heads clustered in households than examination of continuities in family functions and values. A. M. Shah is one of the scholars who has sharply questioned the approach to family studies that assumes "an inevitable trend from large and complex (or joint) to small and simple households." He points out that the normal, cyclical development of an Indian family must be distinguished from basic changes in family organization (1968, pp. 133–134).

In that cyclical development, as we noted in the chapters of Part II, a nuclear family typically becomes a joint family when the sons marry and continue to live in the parental home with their wives and later with their children. That joint family eventually splits into smaller families, usually after the death of the father. The period of joint family living tends to be longer among owner-cultivators and among the wealthier and higher ranking families in general. It is shorter among the poor and also among those who receive a cash income, whether from the practice of modern irrigation agriculture or from the practice of modern professions. There are other variations, as among families in different regions of the country, but underlying all the variations are certain widely shared ideas. These ideas hold that the security and safety of the family group depend on cooperative relations among the men, between a father and his sons, and among brothers. The mutual loyalties among the men of a family should not be weakened by the loyalty of a son to his wife. The men of the family are expected to provide the durable continuity, the women are recruited into it from other families and are expected to pose a potentially disruptive force. Yet through the women of his family, especially from his mother's brothers, a man often gets great support and affection, given to him as a person rather than as the bearer of an agnatic role.

The family ideals have not always been carried out in full, but they typically have been strong influences on each person's family experience. In assessing the present power of these ideas, two studies provide useful information. One is by M. S. Gore (1968.) on Aggarwal families, traders and merchants by traditional occupation, living in and around Delhi. The other is by Milton Singer (1968) on the families of the leading industrial magnates in Madras City.

Gore's study is based on the responses to an extensive questionnaire which was answered by members of 399 families, including urban and rural residents and some from "fringe" villages near the city. Responses were also obtained from 100 additional families of professional men and office workers who did not follow the jati's traditional occupations. Their educational level was much higher than the average of the main sample in which the family heads had received relatively little formal education (Gore 1968, pp. 77–91).

The study, completed in 1961, presents two main conclusions. "One is that the sample as a whole still largely conforms to the pattern of joint family living in behavior, role perception and attitudes." The other is that urban residence and education "do seem to introduce a certain measure of variation." But the variation is more in the attitudes given in questionnaire responses than in actual conduct. Education through high school or college was a main influence in a respondent's readiness for family change; urban residence, by itself, was not. In fact, among families of traditional occupation and limited education, "the rural-urban differences were not apparent" (Gore 1968, pp. 151, 232). The answers on living arrangements and on the position of the women of the family showed that the great majority of families in the sample kept the traditional patterns in these respects. More than half of the families were nuclear at the time of the response (263 of 499), but 86 percent of the heads of nuclear families had previously lived in joint families. The members of nuclear families did not reject the ideal of joint family living, although they interpreted the ideal to mean filial rather than fraternal solidarity (Gore 1968, pp. 109, 235).

Similar findings have been reported from other jatis and from other parts of the country. The ideals of family life are still powerful ideas. The solidary relations are, in considerable degree, honored and maintained. Certain shifts are being made. Fraternal solidarity is not stressed as much as it was formerly. Women's position in family life is being changed. Thus among the Aggarwals there is less rigid separation of the physical space for men and for women. Yet acceptance of changes in family life is much more a matter of word than of deed. The most marked shifts, both in verbal answers and in social behavior, are among those who have had a secondary or higher education.

In his foreword to Dr. Gore's book, W. J. Goode sets the results of this study in the frame of world trends in family relations. Goode points out that the ideology of change may have significant effects before there is any strong impact from modern urbanization and that this ideology can facilitate subsequent urbanization and industrialization. Goode affirms the thesis that family systems throughout the world are generally moving in the direction of the conjugal pattern, but notes that the transformation may not take place swiftly (Goode in Gore 1968, pp. vii–viii).

In the study by Singer, nineteen of the leading industrialists in Madras City and members of their families were interviewed to learn how these men are adapting the old family ideals in the urban setting. These are families of educated, wealthy, and highly successful people. Their present family relations are decidedly different from those which each of these tycoons knew when he was growing up in a village or small town. Family size, the position of women, the daily family routine are different. Yet cultural continuity is also clearly evident, "families living in nuclear households continue to maintain numerous joint family obligations and, for the most part, continue to subscribe to the norms of that system" (Singer 1968, p. 438).

One of the ways of maintaining both persistence and change is through compartmentalization, the traditional mode of separating the standards of the work sphere from those of the domestic sphere. In their household behavior, members of these families tend to observe scriptural standards much more closely than they do in their activities outside the house. These industrialists separate the two spheres of action more sharply than was done in their boyhood homes and the scope of the work sphere is far greater, but the modern practice stems from ancient precedents (Singer 1968, pp. 438–444). This device, it must be noted, is not restricted to the industrial elite. Even the men who pull rickshaws in the streets of Lucknow similarly separate their standards for conduct in the work domain from those followed in their homes (Gould 1965a, p. 31). Another adaptive process is called "vicarious ritualization" by Singer. An industrial executive of this sample cannot faithfully fulfill his domestic ritual duties so he employs professional priests to perform the rituals for him and also encourages his wife and children to ritual devotions. He does not reject the familial aspects of his religion but delegates them to others.

In the management of their firms these industrialists have adapted some of the traditional patterns of family management. Control and ownership are separated in both business and family; the family head controls the business, the shareholders or coparceners defer to his authority. Singer comments that the practices used in the joint family "offer some distinct advantages for organizing an industrial enterprise (1968, p. 445).[2]

Whether the family practices of these first-generation magnates will be maintained in the following generations is an open question but it seems clear that joint family ideals and practices do not necessarily undermine economic development as some writers used to assert (cf. Goode 1963, p. 205). Villagers and townspeople are neither summarily rejecting the ideals of joint family living, nor turning headlong to the conjugal family. The proportion of nuclear households has increased among many groups, more because of economic factors than because of any spurning of joint family obligations (cf. Kapadia 1958, p. 260; Desai 1964, pp. 145–147; Driver 1963, pp. 41–56). Allegiance to these obligations may be weakened in time but as yet this sense of obligation continues to be strongly upheld by many in India.

---

[2] The paternal authority which one of these industrial leaders wielded is reflected in the fact that, as a believer in birth control, he himself had a vasectomy and then persuaded other male members of his family and about 3,000 of his male employees to do the same (Singer 1968, p. 435).

SHIFTS IN FAMILY ROLES AND OBLIGATIONS

More marked change is becoming apparent in the family roles of women. The women of a household are not so formally dependent on the men and so segregated from them as they used to be. A wife's fate is not quite so totally dependent on her husband's in that widows are now being allowed to remarry in some of the higher jatis in which widow remarriage used to be absolutely prohibited (cf. Goode 1163, p. 365; Gore 1968, p. 216; Kapadia 1966; pp. 174–179; Madan 1965, pp. 26, 122; Pocock, 1954, p. 201). Even divorce, now legally possible, is resorted to by a few from higher jatis (Deshpande 1963; Kapadia 1966, pp. 186–197; Ross 1961, p. 273).

Villagers are well aware of changes in women's roles as is illustrated in a report from Senapur village near Banaras. A team of anthropologists interviewed 29 men and women (all of them over 55) of Senapur in order to record their impressions of the major changes they had witnessed. "Without exception, all the subjects commented, sometimes at great length, about the relaxation of *parda*, or the seclusion of women" (Opler 1960, p. 94). In most jatis in Senapur a young woman had been obliged to demonstrate her subordinate position by strict avoidance of her father-in-law and elder brother-in-law, by demure deference to her mother-in-law, by staying close to the household and by not showing in public any special attachment to her husband. By the 1950s, as all the respondents agreed, the young wives of Senapur were much less careful about avoidance practices, they were going out of their homes more freely, and they were more willing to accompany and assist their husbands publicly. Both husbands and wives were less inclined to make a great secret of their intimate meetings.

The respondents were quite clear about the reasons for the change. It was initiated, they asserted, by the young men and especially by those men who had had experience outside the village and those who had a high school or college education. Men who had worked or studied in cities saw women there going about much more freely than did Senapur women. Some city women worked in offices and shops, some participated in the professions and in politics. The men from Senapur took these women's activities as part of higher and highly desirable social status. So on their return to the village they encouraged their wives to be less constrained and more outgoing. The wives of the educated men usually have some education also and they gain in personal confidence because of their education. Such women do not accept the complete subordination of the young wife as readily as did their uneducated mothers and grandmothers.

This is not to say that joint family ideals are obsolete in Senapur. In the 1950s there were twice as many joint families as there were nuclear families in the village and four-fifths of the people lived in joint families. Nevertheless, as the older people of Senapur are aware, the changes in women's conduct may well have important effects on the nature of family relations (Opler 1960, pp. 96–97).

Similar changes are indicated in a variety of studies. The age of girls at marriage in most parts of India is steadily and significantly rising (Kapadia 1968, pp. 158–199; Ross 1961, pp. 245–250, 282; Goode 1963, pp. 232–236; Kannan 1963, pp. 187–192; Driver 1963, p. 61). The bride who comes to live with her husband in his family's household is not often a youngster just a few weeks or months from her menarche, but is typically more of a young woman with some sense of her own abilities and personal rights (Kapadia 1966, pp. 327–328). Family members who aspire to prestigious status generally try to give their daughters some education. The pick of the potential grooms are educated boys who demand that their brides also have an education, though not usually to a level as high as their own.

The education of girls is increasing with great rapidity in villages whose leaders want to gain a reputation for being progressive. Mrs. Kamla Nath studied the women in one such village, Jitpur in

Ludhiana district of the Punjab. In a sample of eighteen households, the 14 women above the age of thirty-five were illiterate. There were 22 women below thirty-five; 12 of them, more than half, had had some education. Of the 18 girls of school age (6–14 years), all were going to school. There were 10 daughters-in-law of these households living outside the village because their husbands were in military service or held white collar jobs. All 10 of these women had been educated, presumably to about the high school level. Mrs. Nath reports that all families in the village are sending their girls to school and the more progressive are sending them to institutions for training to equip them for teaching or other careers. "Girls are being educated because educated men, who are in [government or military] service and who are the prized grooms, want educated wives" (Kamla Nath 1965, p. 815). An incidental result of this development is that young men of the village who are illiterate or barely literate have great difficulty in securing brides.

This switch in two generations within the sample households from totally illiterate women to totally literate girls is one indication of the general change in women's roles in this village. Thus many of the girls now ride to school on bicycles, in a way that "would have been unthinkable a generation earlier, when a girl was not allowed to go out of the village unescorted" (Kamla Nath 1963, p. 815). Jitpur is a particularly prosperous village in a progressive district, and the degree of change there is not typical of Indian villages. But the direction of change in women's activities in Jitpur is entirely typical of the trend that is seen throughout the nation.

One consequence of the increasing number of women who have had a high school or a college education is that an increasing number of them find employment in clerical, administrative, or professional work (Gadgil 1965; Chhibbar 1968, pp. 120–123). Their number is not large in comparison with the number of women who work on the land or in unskilled jobs, but educated working women are now numerous enough in the cities so that the idea of a woman of high status holding a paid job is no longer a startling or repugnant idea.

The family roles of men as well as of women are being changed. Men who earn incomes in their own right, whether as cultivators of cash crops, businessmen, employed workers, or professional men, can become independent of paternal authority at an earlier age than formerly. Even where such independent incomes are not significant factors, as among the Rajput families in Khalapur village, the family relations of men are being altered. A Rajput father there is expected to be a fairly stern and remote figure to his children but this is much less true now than it used to be. He is also supposed to be the disciplinarian of his children and, among the men of the household, his own father and brothers are supposed to be the child's defenders. A man was expected to have cordial relations with his brother's sons rather than with his own. This is still considered to be proper but actually seldom occurs. Now the brothers tend to separate and each man interacts with his own children (Minturn and Hitchcock 1966, pp. 118–119).

In many families across India, family elders seem to be less apprehensive than elders of the previous generation were about a son's relations with his wife; they seem to be less fearful that the conjugal relation may threaten parental authority and fraternal solidarity. More open relations between husband and wife are being tolerated and less drastic separation between the male and female spheres is widely accepted. Not only is there less stringent avoidance between a young husband and wife but there is less also between father and son.

For a man, earlier personal and economic independence should make the strains of family separation less difficult than they formerly were. For a woman, the transition from daughter to daughter-in-law may not be as traumatic as it used to be, though new kinds of personal problems may well arise in the new family situation. For the society, these changes in family roles are portents of systemic changes that may come. Among the bulk of the population they are still only portents. The long-established constellation of family roles is being modified in many families but most villagers follow the family cycle in much the same way as in previous generations, though they do change the duration of particular phases of the cycle.

K. M. Kapadia summarizes his extensive studies of family trends in India by emphasizing that the joint family ideal still has powerful influence on individual behavior. He writes that even a man who has himself broken away from his parental family to start an independent household will typically expect to maintain a joint family when his own sons marry. Married sons usually feel obliged to provide for their elders in case of need and to hold themselves responsible for the education and marriage of their younger siblings. "A person who fails in these duties is talked of as faithless and henpecked, not only by his relatives but also by his neighbours" (Kapadia 1966, pp. 332–333). Few can resist such pressures; characteristically the values of the family ideal are personally internalized as well as socially imposed. Another element of the traditional family pattern, the pressure to have children, especially a goodly number of sons, remain strongly felt by men and women alike.

Urban residence, as was noted in Chapter 3, does not necessarily accelerate changes in family relations; the wider ties of kinship are in some ways strengthened in the city. Villagers who come to work in a city often live close together in kin-based groups, which serve them as a refuge against the anonymity of city life and as a source of protection against urban dangers. In a study of rickshaw-pullers in Lucknow, Gould concludes that "compound kin groups are retained with great frequency in the urban environment regardless of occupation" (1965, p. 46). A similar conclusion is drawn by William Rowe from his study of 46 men from Senapur village who were working in the city of Bombay. All but one were living in tightly controlled kin groups; the groups were formed either on the basis of actual (though not necessarily close) kinship or through bonds of fictive kinship. The ideal that all men of a village are village brothers, Rowe comments, has greater meaning in the city than almost anywhere else (Rowe 1964, p. 21).

A considerable proportion of city families maintain joint family obligations with parents and siblings in a village. Many an urban household, Srinivas observes, is only the satellite of a kin group in a village or town several hundreds of miles away (1966, p. 138). Among city families, Srinivas adds, those of the new elite are most clearly changing their patterns of family life, in part because they may be separated from their closest kin by large distances and in part because they live in a social and cultural environment that is so greatly different from that of their village or small-town relatives. Such households often lack elders who would care deeply about traditional family customs; the parents' concern is rather with their children's success in the educational and career competition (Srinivas 1966, pp. 138–139). Yet among many families of the new elite, marriage continues to be a test of family status, weddings are still occasions for great expenditures, matches are commonly arranged by parents and kin, and endogamy is still a serious consideration.

Changes in Marriage Patterns

There has been much public concern about large dowry payments and inordinate wedding expenses. Newspapers editorialize on these subjects; political leaders discuss them; legislatures have passed laws aimed to regulate them. The practice of making dowry payments is not new, especially among the higher jatis of North India, and such payments have helped to ensure the stability of a marriage and the good reception of a bride by her husband's family (cf. Goode 1963, pp. 211–212). In recent decades dowry costs are said to have risen sharply in the heightened status competition for educated bridegrooms. The burden of dowry obligations falls heavily on families endowed by the biological lottery with a preponderance of daughters. Their outcry has long been heard (Ross 1961, pp. 260–264; Cormack 1961, pp. 113–114). Writers and reformers of the nineteenth century denounced the practice; more recent comments are no less critical. Thus Kapadia flatly says, "Education, instead of mitigating the evil, has worsened it to scandalous proportions" (1966, p. 137). In 1961 the Indian Parliament passed the Dowry Prohibition Act. "So far," Srinivas writes, "the Act has not had much success in combating the institution" (1966, p. 126). Nor is it likely to have great success unless many more people in India change their ideas about the central importance of family status and about the proper ways to maintain and raise that status.

The costs of wedding celebrations as well as the costs of dowries draw anguished cries from families caught in this kind of nuptial squeeze. Although these costs have regularly been denounced by intellectual and political leaders, heavy wedding expenses continue to burden many families. The wedding remains, as was noted in Chapter 6, a main event in the family cycle and a principal occasion for demonstrating and validating social ties. It may even be relevant to the family's future credit rating as is noted in an account of the merchant jatis of a town in Ambala district, Punjab. "The ceremonies of marriage and the public display of dowry serve as public statements of one's financial position and are meaningful to other members of the local community" (Hazlehurst 1966, p. 116).

Large wedding expenses, at all social levels, are intended to assure the social welfare of the family's children and to enhance the family's reputation. Family elders, especially the women, commonly believe that their economic resources can be expended in no better way than for these purposes. They argue that economic capital is not worth much unless it can be translated into social capital. Economists and planners have deplored these expenditures, vast in their totality, that do not help to increase economic productivity. Members of a family, however, typically feel that no investment deserves higher priority than investment in the social security of their children.

The choice of a spouse remains very largely a matter for negotiation and decision by the family elders. Young people, especially those with a high school or college education, are preponderantly in favor of securing greater freedom for themselves in the choice of a spouse (cf. Goode 1963, pp. 216–217; Ross 1961, pp. 251–260). Many of them have gained the right to see, perhaps to talk with, a prospective marriage partner. A few may veto a proposed match if they actively dislike their parents' choice. The extent to which the young principals participate in marriage arrangements has been variously reported. On the basis of her studies in Bangalore, Aileen Ross concludes that educated young people have few opportunities for such participation (1961, p. 279). B. V. Shah's survey in Gujarat, however, indicates that college students have come to take considerable part in the choice of their marriage partners (1964, pp. 80–104). C. T. Kannan's review of several relevant studies notes that such young people are now "fully consulted" before a decision on a marriage arrangement for them is made (1963, p. 198). In general, however, the initiatives and negotiations for the marriages of educated young people are largely where they traditionally have been, in the hands of the parents and elder kinsmen.

The wording of some of the matrimonial advertisements in newspapers seems to signify bold departures in marriage norms but analyses of such advertisements show that the great majority of them stipulate the traditional criteria (plus education) and the usual procedures for arranging marriages in urban middle-class society (Aiyappan 1955, pp. 121–122; Anand 1965; Gist 1953; Niehoff 1958; Reyes-Hockings 1966).

Although endogamy remains a major consideration in arranging a marriage, the boundaries of the endogamous group, as previously noted, are typically being enlarged, and marriage partners may now come from formerly separate jatis of the same jati-cluster (cf. Kapadia 1962, pp. 85–86). A few marriages do occur between spouses who openly acknowledge that they come from quite disparate jatis and Kannan's study of intercaste marriages indicates that the number of such marriages is increasing, but such unions are still very exceptional even among urban and educated people (Ghurye 1961, pp. 204–205; Gore 1968, pp. 204–207; Goode 1963, pp. 215–217; Kannan 1963, pp. 198–217; Kapadia 1966, pp. 118–119; Newell 1963; Patterson 1958; Ross 1961, pp. 270–273).

Marked changes have been made in the laws that pertain to family relations. K. M. Panikkar summarized the new thrust of legislation when he wrote that the Constitution of India "not only has assumed but has proclaimed in clearest terms its right and duty to legislate for social needs" (1961, p. 81). Among the most pressing of these needs is that for "equality of opportunity for men and women." Legislators have followed the constitutional mandate by enacting the Hindu Code and other acts that attempt to redesign Indian family life as no earlier governmental authorities have tried to do. The former rules for inheritance have been altered, as have such matters as the legal recognition of the varna categories and legal preference for joint families (cf. Galanter 1965, p. 79).

These far-reaching changes in family law have not, as we have seen, quickly brought far-reaching changes in family life. The new laws have removed legal obstacles to family changes but they have not imposed restrictions on maintaining joint-family relations (though some of the tax and land laws are alleged to do so). Derrett's assessment is that "So long as the father and his sons regard themselves as jointly and successively responsible for the maintenance of members of the family, the joint-family will remain, and the MHL [Modern Hindu Law] has not taken away its juridical framework" (Derrett 1962, p. 46).

Fathers and sons (and mothers!) generally hold to this concept of family responsibility whether they are urban professionals or village cultivators. As citizens or as legislators, educated people have generally been more ardent for changing family relations within the nation than for challenging old family values closer to their own homes. Their political ideology on this matter has commonly outpaced their family behavior. Nonetheless, they are generally shifting their family behavior as well as their ideas toward the kind of relations between the sexes, between spouses, and between parents and children that the new conditions of world civilization appear to favor.

A Paradigm of Change

At all social levels then, changes in family roles and relations are well under way. The direction of change is toward greater emphasis on the conjugal bond and toward lessening of the formal separation of men and women. The new ways of earning a living, the wider spread of schooling, the modern facilities for transport and communication, the post-independence climate of legislative action have all affected people's ideas about their families.

The degree of change varies not only according to education and jati but also according to the kind of ideas that are being altered. The new family law reflects the great change in the ideas held by educated people about how family relations ought to be carried on. The concepts that govern specific roles are also being changed. As we have noted in the critical matter of women's roles, ideas about the proper conduct of the girls and women of a family are being revised in the villages and these revisions may well affect the whole range of family conduct.

In the matter of the unspoken, pervasive, and deep-lying themes of behavior, however, the degree and direction of change are not so clear. While the more rigid hierarchical gradations within the family are being mitigated, status competition among families seems hardly less than it was in the past century. New symbols of family prestige and new content for family status are sought, but the perspective of ranking and the competition for prestigious standing, as noted in the matter of dowry and wedding expenses, seem undiminished. The new family ideals and the new laws have opened the possibility of systemic changes in family relations, in which the fundamental roles and processes will be redefined. Yet the motifs of behavior that underlie many social relations, including family relations, seem to be little affected. Perhaps these bedrock ideas will continue to underlie future systemic forms and processes.

Ideas about jati and village, about social mobility and political participation, are being revised in ways similar to those we have noted in family relations. People throughout India commonly keep to traditional social patterns while adapting them to modern circumstances. Abstract ideals are most readily revised; fundamental motifs of cognition and motivation seem little altered and are evident in the newer arenas of competition.

The jati continues to be the principal unit of endogamy, a significant attribute of identity, a common locus for interaction, and an important vehicle for social mobility. All these functions, as we have noted, are being reinterpreted. Not only is endogamy more broadly construed than it was before, but also personal identity is not so sweepingly a matter of jati membership as it formerly was. The members of almost every jati are becoming increasingly diversified in occupation, education, income, and residence. Such diversities have long·existed within iatis but they are now more consequential than before. Moreover, many more people now work outside their home localities and in activities for which jati considerations are not directly relevant (cf. Gist 1954; Kapadia 1963; Mathur 1959; Sharma 1961).

Villagers continue to see their local social order as being made up of ranked, interdependent jatis, but they are revising the criteria for the ranking and the meaning of the interdependence. The former jajmani relations, as noted above, have lately been much curtailed. Families of different jatis remain dependent on each other economically and frequently also ritually and politically, but the dependence is neither so great nor so mandatory as it was in the past century.

The cultural and social distances among jatis are being reduced. Vast disparities remain everywhere in India but there are now opportunities and new stimuli to better one's position in the local hierarchies. Those of the lowest jatis now have at least potential access to the Sanskritic traditions and to traditions of the modern, educated elite. Very few in a Harijan jati may actually know much about either high tradition but many of them will know of some members of their jati-cluster (or of one like it) who have triumphantly participated in both. The example of those who succeeded in making a great personal rise (Dr. Ambedkar is a prime example) encourages others in striving for jati and political rise.

The decrease in social distances among people of different jatis has been very slight in some places and quite significant in others, but the unmistakable trend is toward greater social rights for people of disadvantaged jatis. As their objective social disabilities are in some degree overcome, their subjective feelings of resentment tend to grow and to be more forcibly and openly expressed. As their social hopes rise, their acceptance of demeaning status falls. Some, following Dr. Ambedkar's lead, have tried to eject themselves from the system of ranked jatis by becoming converts to Buddhism.

Many in the lowest jatis remain abysmally poor and their poverty shackles their efforts to rise. The benefits of the general increase in national productivity tend to accrue to families of middle and high income, so the economic gap between the poor and the wealthy may have increased in many localities. Yet opportunities for economic betterment are now more open to people of the lowest echelons than they were before independence; as Harijan families manage to pull themselves up economically, they commonly expend some of their added income on their children's education as well as on the older tokens and ceremonials of higher status.

Land continues to be the major economic resource for most villagers and where the families of one jati own much of the village land they still tend to dominate village affairs. That dominance, however, is now subject to a new means of challenge through the power of the vote. Voters in India can be as misled and manipulated as those in other countries, yet the votes of a numerous jati cannot be ignored by those who want to manage public affairs, whether in a village or in a larger constituency.

In this way, a person's role as citizen and voter has become attached to his role as jati member. The realities of jati membership have been affected by modern ideals of social justice propounded mainly by educated people. Affirming these ideals, leaders of the new elite have brought about legal and political changes that have modified the previous potentials of jati roles. Jati membership has become an important factor in wide political arenas; in these arenas the contestants often display the kinds of perception and motivation that have characterized village contests.

The village typically continues to be the chief scene of the villager's activities and the main nexus of his social relations. While many villagers have had more experience outside the village than did their forefathers and know a good deal more about the world beyond their locality, their chief concerns are still centered within their village and locality. Many are aware that their village is changing. Because national leaders have recognized that the welfare of the country rests on democratic development in the villages, governmental activities in villages have been greatly increased. Elected village panchayats have been established as the local agencies for economic development and social betterment. The acts that set up these statutory panchayats were the expression of an ideal of village democracy held by the educated. As with other legislation based on such ideals, there have been considerable difficulties and delays in realizing the purposes of the legislation. Nevertheless, the statutory panchayats are beginning to work well in some places, though not many of them have achieved the high purposes for which they were established. These elected bodies have augmented the functions of government in the village; they have not usually augmented village solidarity. In some ways the added functions of government—as in providing water, schools, special grants—have introduced new reasons for conflict as well as for cooperation. The new village panchayats are developing modern means of cooperation but they also reflect the older struggles for status.

Contests about social mobility have long been at the heart of village politics. Mobility efforts have now become increasingly related to political participation in district, state and even national politics. The resemblance of political behavior at these higher levels to the style of village politics is not because state and national leaders are only village elders transposed, but because both villagers and the new elite stem from the same civilizational roots and share in the perceptions, motivations, and values that characterize the civilization (cf. Morris-Jones 1967).

A new phase of social development may well follow the rise of industry and the great improvements in agricultural technology. Both are still in beginning stages and only a few studies of their social impact have yet been made. The available studies of factory workers indicate that they may be changing their social patterns more rapidly than is generally true for villagers, but that jati considerations remain of importance to them, not only in domestic activities but also in the recruitment and management of industrial workers (cf. Lambert 1963).

As the people of India attain new levels of technological and economic advance they also meet fresh problems of social and cultural adaptation. A potential resource in coping with such problems is the intelligence that can be provided by students of society. That intelligence is more than knowledge of statistics, patterns, institutions; it also entails the process of acquiring knowledge about people, of testing ideas and expanding understanding through asking productive questions. Such questions are apt to be concerned more with social adaptation than with the supposed demise of tradition. The questions are likely to be more useful if they are based on the concept of people acting in social systems rather than focused on presumed failures in moral rectitude. Political and religious leaders have to speak out on moral issues but planners and policy makers must know that systemic relations as well as moral principles govern the behavior of men and women.

Each social system is more amenable to certain kinds of change than it is to others. The paradigm suggested in this chapter indicates one aspect of this differential: generalized ideals have been more readily shifted than have the concepts about specific roles and relations. These, in turn, have been altered more than have the implicit, but powerful, psychological motifs. It is the social scientists' task to test this suggestion and all other theoretical formulations in a wide variety of social contexts so as to expand and refine man's knowledge of human behavior. It is the task of those concerned with the welfare of people to use the current state of that knowledge toward the best advantage of the people.

Appendix: The Concepts of System and of Stratification

Uses of the Concepts

The use of the concept of system has the merit of eliminating some misleading dichotomies and of including crucial social factors in one model. Structure and process, concord and conflict are viewed in the same general perspective. Stability and change, norm and deviance can be examined together. There need be no treatment of social control apart from social conformity. The system is the social control; the feedback of counterchange is as integral as is the expected interchange. A people's main values are expressed in the kind of systemic order they seek and maintain.

Social structure is here taken as one aspect of social system. The concept of structure focuses on the component groups and their interrelations at a particular time. The concept of system adds the processes of counterchange among the groups and the systemic changes that they produce over time.

A social system is kept constantly in motion and can be adaptively changed. As an adaptive means, people use their systems, not merely to cope with their world, but also to elaborate their lives and to create new ways of life. The concept of system guides us to see a society as more than the sum of its parts, to try to understand it—in Redfield's rather paradoxical phrase—as an "analyzed whole." My own use of the concept has been informed by the writings of Homans (1950), Nadel (1951), Redfield (1955), Vogt (1960), Parsons (1961), and by the more recent syntheses by Buckley (1967).

Yet any concept that purports to embrace so much can explain correspondingly little specifically. It is a potent means of departure, not of arrival. Moreover, its use entails some lingering questions. Whose concept is it? Is it only in the eye and mind of the professional beholder or is it a verity of human life, part of the people's truth? As we use the concept here, it is both. The people whose society we study have quite lively ideas (not necessarily accurate ones) about the systemic nature of their society, which influence, if they do not determine, their social relations. Their ideas are important elements in our analysis.

Another question is about the boundaries of a system. A family, as we have noted in Chapter 1, is a component of a larger system of kinship. But kinship is also one of the subsystems of the larger society. If we focus on family relations, each family should be viewed as part of a general system of family relations. Similarly, religious, economic, and political activities can be considered as separate systems for certain purposes and as subsystems in other contexts of analysis. On this question, too, we are guided by how the people whom we study perceive various contexts of action and how they differentiate among them, though we must separate their notions of ideal conduct from that which they expect and that which is actually realized.

Finally, there is always some question about the application of any guiding concept, no matter how cogent or sound it may be. We tend to focus on the evidence that fits more neatly into the system concept and look past that which does not fit so well. Because we postulate counterchange, we produce the real evidence of counterchange. Because we postulate that there are systemic social relations, we do not test the utility of the concept at every step of the exposition. Because we postulate a general human preference for orderly relations and for a return to order, we may slight disorder and disarray in social relations, or interpret them as a means of attaining some new and more satisfactory order—which they may or may not be. However, the general test of the usefulness of a concept is whether it helps to clarify, explain, and assess probabilities, not whether its use surmounts all questions about it and gaps in it.

The subject of social stratification is more in the background than in the foreground of this enquiry. We are dealing with *the* classic instance of stratification as frame and focus for a civilization, yet we must also recognize that ideas about stratification are being changed in India in ways similar to those in which other peoples throughout the world are shifting ideas about social divisions. These grand changes are close to the nerve and bone of most modern nations. Hence intellectuals and political activists everywhere are apt to be absorbed with one or another aspect of the subject of social strata and the proper rights and rewards pertaining to each grouping. Stratification is considered to be the main distributive arrangement of a society accounting for who gets what, how, and why (Gould 1960a; Tumin 1967, p. 12; Lenski 1966, pp. 1–23). So it is no wonder, as Melvin Tumin comments in his survey of the subject, that the study of stratification has come to assume a central place in modern sociology. He notes that it has become a "dominant pursuit" of sociologists and is likely to continue to be, so long as inequalities are critical for the life-chances and life-patterns of people in different strata of a society (1967, pp. 10–11). Anthropologists have not been so heavily engrossed with this subject as have sociologists, but they well recognize its importance.

Some of the writings on stratification stress the objective criteria and the material forces that impel social divisions. Others emphasize the subjective views that the participants hold. Karl Marx set off great consequences with his testament of the technological causes and the objective criteria for social classes and his analysis of the inevitable conflict between classes. More recent sociological writers, Lloyd Warner and Talcott Parsons among them, have noted that a major factor is how people understand the nature of their society and how they consequently class themselves. Parsons points out that social relations inevitably involve value choices and moral judgments, and the way in which stratification is carried out depends on the moral evaluations made by the people (1953; 1961, pp. 42–44).

A much debated issue is between those who emphasize that stratification supports stability and those who view stratification as an inherent source of conflict. The former tend to dwell on order, rewards, interdependence, subjective satisfactions, the latter on power, exploitation, strain, objective causes for dissatisfaction (of. Lenski 1966, pp. 22–23, 441–443; Dahrendorf 1966, pp. 714–718). The manner in which this issue has been debated seems less apposite for an understanding of Indian society than for other societies. Social divisions in India most clearly follow both objective and subjective criteria; they involve both stability and strain, both cooperation and conflict. The problem is not whether the one kind or the other kind of influence prevails but how much of each exists and under what circumstances.

Another debated issue is whether highly stratified societies outside of South Asia can usefully be labeled caste societies, with the implication that they share important characteristics with the Indian systems. This idea has been explored by Barth (1960), by Bailey (1963a), and especially by

Gerald Berreman, who has strongly maintained that they do, drawing his evidence mainly from a comparison of India and the American South in the mid-twentieth century.

WHAT KIND OF SYSTEM IS A "CASTE SYSTEM"?

A caste system, as Berreman discusses the concept, is one that is composed of ranked groups. Membership in a group is only through birth. The groups are exhaustive, exclusive, and discrete; that is, every person is a member of such a group and of only one; he is clearly recognized by others as a member of his separate group. Membership in his group influences most of his roles and activities; there is a high degree of "role summation." No one should try to change his inherited membership and any attempts by individuals to shift themselves to a higher group are strongly disapproved (Berreman 1966, pp. 275, 285; 1967a, p. 48; 1967b, p. 355).

Relative rank affects almost all social relations. Most interaction among people of different groups involves considerations of superiority and inferiority, and superiority means greater privileges, precedence, and a larger share of the good things in life. Each group is a firm entity, named, bounded, self-aware, culturally homogeneous. Because interaction between people of different groups is limited and that within a group is more intense, the members of a group tend to share distinctive cultural characteristics. A caste system is therefore one of cultural pluralism (Berreman 1967a, pp. 46, 55; 1967b, p. 354).

The groups are interdependent; each needs the services or goods provided by others. But they are held together less by agreement about mutual needs and purposes than by the coercive power wielded by the superior groups. (Other students of caste systems recognize the importance of coercive power but do not consider it to be the sole cement of such a system.) The inferior groups conform in their actions, not necessarily in their ideas about the reasons for subservient behavior (Berreman 1966, p. 289; 1967b, pp. 352–357).

A general concomitant of such a system, Berreman notes, is that the higher groups explain their superiority in terms of a moral evaluation that shows why they are intrinsically more worthy. They take a paternalistic attitude toward the lower people, considering them to be childlike, irresponsible, incapable of finer feelings or higher achievements. The lower do not share these views but adjust to the superior power by avoiding conflict, by apathy and psychic withdrawal, or by overcompliance. Other concomitants are the restrictions on relations between people of different groups. Eating and sitting together, marriage and sex relations are rigidly controlled or are forbidden (Berreman 1966, p. 308; 1967a, pp. 59, 64).

The higher, privileged groups hold that the social order is static; the lower strive to improve their status. Any system of marked stratification is itself a source of mobility motivation as Veblen, Bendix and Lipset, and others have noted. Such mobility striving is a constant dynamic force in a caste system. Berreman discerns a difference between India and the U.S. South in that a lower group in India is usually more interested in achieving superiority for the group rather than equality in the society, whereas Southern Negroes, because the society of the deep South has two main divisions rather than multiple groups, have objected to the system as well as to their position in it. In this way there is more consensus about the proper nature of the social system in India than in the South, though Berreman stresses that in neither place do the lower groups accept the concept of their inferiority (1966, pp. 298, 308, 318; 1967a, p. 66).

The principal functions of a caste system, as Berreman sees them, are to perpetuate social and cultural diversities, and to enforce and articulate them. Privilege is protected through power. These functions, his discussion notes, are highly disfunctional in the modern world, irrelevant to human welfare and sources of unnecessary conflict and suffering (1967b, pp. 352, 356–366).

The critics of such definitions of "caste system" question whether the category is a useful one. Certain groups, such as the low-ranking groups in Japan, do not fit readily into the general definition (of. DeVos 1967). These critics point out, moreover, that specialization is essential in all modern societies and leads to some degree of stratification and ranking. Social and cultural diversities have to be articulated in all societies; each separate group tends to seek some privileges and power for its members. These processes are inherent in a complex society and, as processes, can scarcely be called disfunctional. The trend in most contemporary societies is certainly away from the inclusive, invidious distinctions of caste divisions but also it is away from cultural pluralism and toward a cultural conformity, which some deplore. Those critics add that the discussions of caste systems in general have done little to advance an understanding of caste organization in Indian civilization (Leach 1960, 1967; Dumont 1967; S. Sinha 1967; Cohn 1968, p. 196).

But at least these discussions of what is meant by a "caste system" help us to understand the systems of Indian society as part of the human continuum, as special phrasings and configurations of social processes common among much of mankind. It is especially important to understand the dynamic nature of the Indian systems, because they have so often been depicted as static in Hindu scripture and in villagers' concepts, as well as in much of the writing on the subject.

Bibliography

AGARWALA, B. R. 1955. In a mobile commercial community. *In* Symposium: caste and joint family. Sociological Bulletin 4:138–146.

AGGARWAL, PARTAP C. 1966. A Muslim sub-caste of North India: problems of cultural integration. Economic and Political Weekly 1:159–167.

AHMAD, AZIZ. 1964. Studies in Islamic culture in the Indian environment. Oxford: Clarendon Press.

AHMAD, IMTIAZ. 1965. Social stratification among Muslims. The Economic Weekly 10:1093–1096.

AHMAD, ZARINA. 1962. Muslim caste in Uttar Pradesh. The Economic Weekly 14:325–336.

AIYAPPAN, A. 1937. Social and physical anthropology of the Nayadis of Malabar. Bulletin of the Madras Government Museum, n.s., Volume 2, No. 4.

———. 1944. Iravas and culture change. Bulletin of the Madras Government Museum, n.s., Volume 5, No. 1.

———. 1955. In Tamilnad, Sociological Bulletin 4:117–122.

———. 1965. Social revolution in a Kerala village: a study in cultural change. Bombay: Asia Publishing House.

ALLISON, W. L. 1935. The Sadhs. London and Calcutta: Oxford University Press.

AMBEDKAR, B. R. 1948. Remarks on draft constitution. Constituent Assembly Debates, Official Reports, Volume 7, No. 1, pp. 38–39.

ANAND, K. 1965. An analysis of matrimonial advertisements. Sociological Bulletin 14:59–71.

ANANTAKRISHNA AYYAR, L. K. 1926. Anthropology of the Syrian Christians. Eranakulam: Cochin Government Press.

ANSARI, GHAUS. 1955. Muslim marriage in India. Wiener Völkerkundliche Mitteilungen 3:191–206.

———. 1960. Muslim caste in Uttar Pradesh: a study of culture contact. The Eastern Anthropologist (special number) 13:5–80.

ATAL, YOGESH. 1963. Short-lived alliances as an aspect of factionalism in an Indian village. The Journal of Social Sciences (Agra) 3:65–75.

———. n.d. Trends of change in village politics: a case study. Mussoorie: Cultural Institute of Study and Research in Community Development. Mimeographed, 7 pp.

BACHENHEIMER, R. 1956. Theology, economy and demography: a study of caste in an Indian village. MS., 11 pp.

BACON, ELIZABETH E. (editor). 1956. India sociological background: an area handbook. New Haven: The Human Relations Area Files.

BADEN-POWELL, B. H. 1896. The Indian village community. London: Longmans, Green and Co. (Reprinted by HRAF Press: New Haven, 1957.)

BAILEY, FREDERICK G. 1957. Caste and the economic frontier: a village in highland Orissa. Manchester: Manchester University Press.

———. 1958. Political change in the Kondmals. The Eastern Anthropologist 11:88–106.

———. 1960a. The joint-family in India: a framework for discussion. The Economic Weekly 12:345–352.

———. 1960b. Tribe, caste and nation: a study of political activity and political change in highland Orissa. Manchester: Manchester University Press.

———. 1961. "Tribe" and "caste" in India. Contributions to Indian Sociology 5:7–19.

———. 1963a. Closed social stratification in India. European Journal of Sociology 4:107–124.

———. 1963b. Politics and social change: Orissa in 1959. Berkeley: University of California Press.

———. 1964. Two villages in Orissa (India). *In* Closed systems and open minds: the limits of naïvety in social anthropology, Max Gluckman, editor, pp. 52–82. Chicago: Aldine Publishing Co.

———. 1965. Decisions by concensus in councils and committees. *In* Political systems and the distribution of power, F. Eggan and M. Gluckman, editors, pp. 1–20. London: Tavistock Publications; New York: Frederick A. Praeger.

BAINES, ATHELSTANE. 1912. Ethnography (castes and tribes). Strassburg: Trübner Verlag.

BANNERJEE, HEMENDRA NATH. 1960. Community structure in an artisan village of Parganna h Barabhum. Journal of Social Research (Ranchi) 3:68–79.

BANTON, MICHAEL. 1965. Roles: an introduction to the study of social relations. London: Tavistock Publications.

BARANOV, I. L. 1965. "Kastovyi bunt" v Ramnade ("The caste revolt" in Ramnad) *In* Kasty v Indii (Caste in India), G. G. Kotovshii, editor, pp. 262–273. Moscow: Akademiia Nauk SSSR. Institut Narodov Azii.

BARNABAS, A. P. 1961. Sanskritization. The Economic Weekly 13:613–618.

BARTH, FREDRIK. 1959. Political leadership among Swat Pathans. London School of Economics. Monographs in Social Anthropology, No. 19. London.

———. 1960. The system of social stratification in Swat, North Pakistan. *In* Aspects of caste in South India, Ceylon and Northwest Pakistan, E. R. Leach, editor, pp. 113–146. Cambridge Papers in Social Anthropology, No. 2. Cambridge: Cambridge University Press.

BASHAM, A. L. 1954. The wonder that was India. London: Sidgwick and Jackson.

BASU, N. B. 1957. Gango (an instance of Hindu method of tribal absorption). Bulletin of the Tribal Research Institute (Chhindwara) 1:40–47.

BASU, TARA KRISHNA. 1962. The Bengal peasant from time to time. London and Bombay: Asia Publishing House.

BEALS, ALAN R. 1955. Change in the leadership of a Mysore village. *In* India's villages, pp. 132–143. Calcutta: West Bengal Government Press.

———. 1959. Leadership in a Mysore village. *In* Leadership and political institutions in India, R. L. Park and Irene Tinker, editors, pp. 427–437. Princeton: Princeton University Press.

———. 1962. Gopalpur. New York: Holt, Rinehart, and Winston.

———. 1964. Conflict and interlocal festivals in a South Indian region. The Journal of Asian Studies 23:95–113.

———. 1965. Crime and conflict in some South Indian villages. Mimeographed 23 pp.

———. n.d. Dravidian Kinship and Marriage. Unpublished paper.

BEALS, ALAN R. AND BERNARD J. SIEGEL. 1966. Divisiveness and social conflict: an anthropological approach. Stanford: Stanford University Press.

BEBARTA, PRAFULLA C. 1966. Family type and fertility. Economic and Political Weekly 1:633–634.

BEECH, MARY JANE, O. J. BERTOCCI AND L. A. CORWIN. 1966. Introducing the East Bengal village. *In* Inside the East Pakistan village. (Asian studies papers. Reprint series, 2.) East Lansing: Michigan State University.

BEIDELMAN, THOMAS O. 1959. A comparative analysis of the jajmani system. Monograph of the Association for Asian Studies, No. 8. Locust Valley, New York: J. J. Augustin.

BENDIX, REINHARD. 1960. Max Weber: an intellectual portrait. New York: Doubleday.

BERREMAN, GERALD. D. 1960a. Caste in India and the United States. American Journal of Sociology 66:120–127.

———. 1960b. Cultural variability and drift in the Himalayan hills. American Anthropologist 62:774–794.

———. 1962a. Behind many masks. Ithaca: The Society for Applied Anthropology.

———. 1962b. Caste and economy in the Himalayas. Economic Development and Cultural Change 10:386–394.

———. 1962c. Pahari polyandry: a comparison. American Anthropologist 64:60–75.

———. 1962d. Village exogamy in northernmost India. Southwestern Journal of Anthropology 18:55–58.

———. 1963. Hindus of the Himalayas. Berkeley and Los Angeles: University of California Press.

———. 1965. The study of caste ranking in India. Southwestern Journal of Anthropology 21:115–129.

———. 1966. Caste in cross-cultural perspective: organizational components. *In* Japan's invisible race, George De Vos and Hiroshi Wagatsuma, editors, pp. 275–324. Berkeley and Los Angeles: University of California Press.

———. 1967a. Stratification, pluralism and interaction: a comparative analysis of caste. *In* Caste and race, comparative approaches, A. de Reuck and J. Knight, editors, pp. 45–73. London: J. and A. Churchill.

———. 1967b. Caste as social process. Southwestern Journal of Anthropology 23:351–370

BÉTEILLE, ANDRÉ. 1962. Sripuram: a village in Tanjore district. The Economic Weekly 14:141–146.

———. 1964. A note on the referents of caste. European Journal of Sociology 5:130–134.

———. 1965. Caste, class and power. Berkeley and Los Angeles: University of California Press.

BHARATI, AGEHANANDA 1961 The ochre robe. London: Allen and Unwin.

———. 1963. Pilgrimage in the Indian tradition. History of Religions 3:135–167.

———. 1966. The decline of teknonymy: changing patterns of husband-wife appellation in India. MS., 12 pp.

BHATT, G. S. 1958. Occupational structure among the Chamars of Dehra Dun. Sociological Annual 1:32–43. Dehra Dun: Sociology Association, D. A. V. College.

BHATTACHARYA, JOGENDRA NATH. 1896. Hindu castes and sects. Calcutta: Thacker, Spink and Co.

BLUNT, E. A. H. 1931. The caste system of northern India. London: Oxford University Press.

BOSE, A. B. AND N. S. JODHA. 1965. The jajmani system in a desert village. Man in India 45:105–126.

BOSE, A. B. AND S. P. MALHOTRA. 1964. Studies in group dynamics (1): factionalism in a desert village. Man in India 44:311–328.

BOSE, NIRMAL KUMAR. 1951. Caste in India. Man in India 31:107–123.

———. 1953a. Cultural anthropology and other essays. Second edition. Calcutta: Indian Associated Publishing Company.

———. 1953b. The Hindu method of tribal absorption. *In his* Cultural anthropology and other essays, pp. 156–170. Calcutta: Indian Associated Publishing Co.

———. 1954. Who are the backward classes? Man in India 34:89–98.

———. 1956. Culture zones of India. Geographical Review of India 18:1–12.

———. 1957. The effect of urbanization on work and leisure. Man in India 37:1–9.

———. 1958a. East and west in Bengal. Man in India 38:157–175.

———. 1958b. Some aspects of caste in Bengal. Man in India 38:73–97.

———. 1958c. Types of villages in West Bengal: a study in social change. The Economic Weekly 10:149–152.

———. 1960. The use of proceedings of caste panchayats. Journal of Social Research (Meerut) 1:98–100.

———. 1964. Change in tribal cultures before and after independence. Man in India 44:1–10.

BOSE, N. K. AND SURAJIT SINHA. 1961. Peasant life in India: a study in unity and diversity. Anthropological Survey of India. Memoir No. 8.

BOSE, SHIB CHUNDER. 1881. The Hindoos as they are. London, Calcutta: Edward Stanford, W. Newman and Co.

BOUGLÉ, CÉLESTIN. 1908. Essais sur le régime des castes. Paris: Felix Alcan.

BRASS, PAUL. 1967. Regions, regionalism, and research in modern Indian society and politics. *In* Regions and regionalism in South Asian studies: an exploratory study, R. I. Crane, editor, pp. 258–270. Duke University Program in Comparative Studies on South Asia. Monograph No. 5.

BRIGHT, WILLIAM. 1960. Linguistic change in some Indian caste dialects. International Journal of American Linguistics 26:19–26.

BROWN, W. NORMAN. 1957. The sanctity of the cow in Hinduism. Journal of the Madras University 28:29–49.

———. 1961 The content of cultural continuity in India. The Journal of Asian Studies 20:427–434.

BUCKLEY, WALTER. 1967. Sociology and modern systems theory. Englewood Cliffs, New Jersey: Prentice Hall.

BURLING, ROBBINS. 1960. An incipient caste organization in the Garo Hills. Man in India 40:283–299.

CARSTAIRS, G. MORRIS. 1953. The case of Thakur Khuman Singh: a culture-conditioned crime. British Journal of Delinquency 4:14–25.

———. 1955. Attitudes to death and suicide in an Indian cultural setting. International Journal of Social Psychiatry 1:33–41.

———. 1957. The twice born: a study of a community of high caste Hindus. London: The Hogarth Press.

———. 1961. Patterns of religious observance in three villages of Rajasthan. Journal of Social Research (Ranchi) 4:59–113.

CASTETS, J. 1931. L'église et le problème de la caste au XVIe siècle. Revue d'Histoire des Missions 8:547–565.

CHANANA, DEV RAJ. 1961a. Caste and mobility. The Economic Weekly 13:1561–1562.

———. 1961b. Sanskritisation, westernisation and India's Northwest. The Economic Weekly 13.409–414.

CHAUHAN, BRIJ RAJ. 1960. An Indian village: some questions. Man in India 40:116–127.

CHHIBBAR, Y. P. 1968. From caste to class, a study of the Indian middle classes. New Delhi: Associated Publishing House.

COHN, BERNARD S. 1955. The changing status of a depressed caste. *In* Village India, M. Marriott, editor, pp. 53–77. Chicago: University of Chicago Press.

———. 1957. India as a racial, linguistic and cultural area. *In* Introducing India in liberal education, Milton Singer, editor, pp. 51–68. Chicago: University of Chicago Press.

COHN, BERNARD S. 1959a. Some notes on law and change in North India. Economic Development and Cultural Change 8:79–93.

———. 1959b. Madhopur revisited. The Economic Weekly 11:963–966.

———. 1960. The initial British impact on India: a case study of the Benares region. The Journal of Asian Studies 19:418–431.

———. 1961a. Chamar family in a North Indian village. The Economic Weekly 13:1051–1055.

———. 1961b. The development and impact of British administration in India. New Delhi: Indian Institute of Public Administration.

———. 1961c. From Indian status to British contract. Journal of Economic History 21:613–628.

———. 1961d. The pasts of an Indian village. Comparative Studies in Society and History 3:241–249.

———. 1962. Review of M. Marriott, caste ranking and community structure in five regions of India and Pakistan. Journal of the American Oriental Society 82:425–430.

———. 1965. Anthropological notes on disputes and law in India. American Anthropologist 67:82–122.

———. 1967. Regions, subjective and objective: their relation to the study of modern Indian history and society. *In* Regions and regionalism in South Asian studies: an exploratory study, R. I. Crane, editor, pp. 5–37. Duke University Program in Comparative Studies in Southern Asia. Monograph No. 5.

COHN, BERNARD S. AND MCKIM MARRIOTT. 1958. Networks and centres in the integration of Indian civilisation. Journal of Social Research (Ranchi) 1:1–9.

COLE, B. L. 1932. The Rajput clans of Rajputana. Census of India, 1931, 27:134–141.

COLLVER, ANDREW. 1963. The family cycle in India and the United States. American Sociological Review 28:86–96.

CORMACK, MARGARET L. 1961. She who rides a peacock. New York: Frederick A. Praeger.

CRONIN, VINCENT. 1959. A pearl to India. New York: E. P. Dutton.

CULSHAW, W. J. 1949. Tribal heritage: a study of the Santals. London: Lutterworth Press.

DAHRENDORF, RALF. 1966. Review of G. Lenski, power and privilege. American Sociological Review 31:714–718.

DAMES, MANSEL LONGWORTH (editor). 1918. The book of Duarte Barbosa, Volume 1 (Volume 2, 1921). London: The Hakluyt Society.

DAMLE, Y. B. 1963. Reference group theory with regard to mobility in caste. Social Action, April 1963.

DANDEKAR, V. M. AND KUMUDINI DANDEKAR. 1953. Survey of fertility and mortality in Poona District. Poona: Gokhale Institute of Politics and Economics.

DARLING, MALCOLM LYALL. 1934. Wisdom and waste in the Punjab village. London: Oxford University Press.

DAS GUPTA, BIWAN KUMAR. 1962. Caste mobility among the Mahato of South Manbhum. Man in India 42:228–236.

DATTA GUPTA, JAYA. 1959. A study on the Paundra Kshatriya of West Bengal. Bulletin of the Department of Anthropology, Government of India 8:109–130.

DATTA-MAJUMDER, NABENDU. 1956. The Santal: a study in culture change. Department of Anthropology, Government of India. Memoir No. 2.

DAVIS, KINGSLEY. 1951. The population of India and Pakistan. Princeton: Princeton University Press.

DE, BARUN. 1967. A historical perspective on theories of regionalism in India. *In* Regions and regionalism in South Asian studies: an exploratory study, R. I. Crane, editor, pp. 48–88. Duke University Program in Comparative Studies in Southern Asia. Monograph No. 5.

DEMING, WILBUR S. 1928. Rāmdās and the Rāmdāsis. London, Calcutta: Oxford University Press.

DERRETT, J. DUNCAN M. 1960. Law and the predicament of the Hindu joint family. The Economic Weekly 12:305–311.

———. 1961. Illegitimates: a test for modern Hindu family law. Journal of the American Oriental Society 81:251–261.

———. 1962. The history of the juridical framework of the joint Hindu family. Contributions to Indian Sociology 6:17–47.

———. 1963. Introduction to modern Hindu law. Bombay: Oxford University Press.

DESAI, I. P. 1955. An analysis. *In* Symposium: caste and joint family. Sociological Bulletin 4:97–117.

———. 1956. The joint family in India: an analysis. Sociological Bulletin 5:144–156.

———. 1964. Some aspects of family in Mahuva. New York: Asia Publishing House.

DESHPANDE, KAMALABAI. 1963. Divorce cases in the court of Poona, an analysis. The Economic Weekly 15:1179–1183.

DEVA, INDRA. 1958. The sociology of Bhojpuri folk-literature. Doctoral thesis, Lucknow University.

DEVONS, ELY AND MAX GLUCKMAN. 1964. Conclusion: modes and consequences of limiting a field of study. *In* Closed systems and open minds: the limits of naïvety in social anthropology, Max Gluckman, editor, pp. 158–261. Chicago: Aldine Publishing Co.

DEVOS, GEORGE. 1967. Discussion. *In* Caste and race: comparative approaches, A. de Reuck and J. Knight, editors, pp. 74–77. London: J. and A. Churchill.

DE VOS, GEORGE AND H. WAGATSUMA. 1966. Japan's invisible race: caste in culture and personality. Berkeley: University of California Press.

DHILLON, HARWANT SINGH. 1955. Leadership and groups in a South Indian village. Planning Commission, Programme Evaluation Organisation. New Delhi: Government of India. P. E. O. Publication No. 9.

DIEHL, CARL GUSTAV. 1956. Instrument and purpose: studies on rites and rituals in South India. Lund: Gleerup.

DREKMEIER, CHARLES. 1962. Kingship and community in early India. Stanford: Stanford University Press.

DRIVER, EDWIN D. 1963. Differential fertility in central India: Princeton: Princeton University Press.

DUBE, S. C. 1955a. A Deccan village. *In* India's villages, pp. 180–192. Calcutta: West Bengal Government Press. (Second edition, 1960, M. N. Srinivas, editor, pp. 202–215. London: Asia Publishing House.)

———. 1955b. Indian village. Ithaca, New York: Cornell University Press.

———. 1955c. Ranking of castes in a Telengana village. The Eastern Anthropologist 8:182–190.

———. 1956. Cultural factors in rural community development. *In* The Indian village: a symposium. The Journal of Asian Studies 16:19–30.

———. 1958. India's changing villages. Ithaca, New York: Cornell University Press.

———. 1960. Approaches to the tribal problem. Journal of Social Research 3:11–15.

DUBOIS, JEAN ANTOIN, ABBÉ. 1928. Hindu manners, customs and ceremonies. (Translated by Henry K. Beauchamp.) Oxford: Clarendon Press.

DUMONT, LOUIS. 1951. Kinship and alliance among the Pramalai Kallar. The Eastern Anthropologist 4:3–26.

———. 1953. The Dravidian kinship terminology as an expression of marriage. Man 54:34–39.

———. 1957a. Hierarchy and marriage alliance in South Indian kinship. Occasional Papers of the Royal Anthropological Institute, No. 12. London: Royal Anthropological Institute.

———. 1957b. Une sous caste de l'Inde du sud. Paris: Mouton.

———. 1959. Dowry in Hindu marriage as a social scientist sees it. The Economic Weekly 11:519–520.

———. 1960. World renunciation in Indian religions. Contributions to Indian Sociology 4:33–62.

———. 1961a. Les marriages Nayar comme faits indiens. L'Homme, Revue Francaise d'Anthropologie 1:11–36.

———. 1961b. Marriage in India: the present state of the question. Contributions to Indian Sociology 5:75–95.

———. 1962. "Tribe" and "caste" in India. Contributions to Indian Sociology 6:120–122.

———. 1963. Le mariage secondaire dans l'Inde du nord. Paris: VIth International Congress of Anthropological and Ethnological Sciences 2:53–55.

———. 1964a. Marriage in India: the present state of the question; postscript to part one. Contributions to Indian Sociology 7:77–98.

———. 1964b. A note on locality in relation to descent. Contributions to Indian Sociology 7:71–76.

———. 1966. Homo hierarchicus. Essai sur le système des castes. Paris: Gallimard.

———. 1967. Caste: a phenomenon of social structure or an aspect of Indian culture? *In* Caste and race, comparative approaches, A. de Reuck and J. Knight, editors, pp. 28–38. London: J. and A. Churchill.

DUMONT, LOUIS AND D. POCOCK. 1957a. For a sociology of India. Contributions to Indian Sociology 1:7–22.

———. 1957b. Village studies. Contributions to Indian Sociology 1:23–42.

———. 1957c. Kinship. Contributions to Indian Sociology 1:43–64.

———. 1960. For a sociology of India: a rejoinder to Dr. Bailey. Contributions to Indian Sociology 4:82–89.

DUTT, NRIPENDRA KUMAR. 1931. Origin and growth of caste in India. London: Kegan Paul, Trench, Trübner.

EDGERTON, FRANKLIN. 1952. The Bhagavad Gītā. Part 2: Interpretation and Arnold's translation. Cambridge: Harvard University Press.

EGLAR, ZEKIYE. 1960. A Punjabi village in Pakistan. New York: Columbia University Press.

ELWIN, VERRIER. 1964. The tribal world of Verrier Elwin. New York and Bombay: Oxford University Press.

EMENEAU, MURRAY. B. 1956. India as a linguistic area. Language 32:3–16.

EPSTEIN, T. SCARLETT. 1959. A sociological analysis of witch beliefs in a Mysore village. The Eastern Anthropologist 12:234–251.

———. 1960. Economic development and peasant marriage in South India. Man in India 40:192–232.

———. 1962. Economic development and social change in South India. Manchester University Press; New York: The Humanities Press.

FARQUHAR, J. N. 1920. An outline of the religious literature of India. London: Oxford University Press.

FERGUSON, FRANCES. N. 1963. The master-disciple relationship in India. Research Reviews (University of North Carolina) 10:22–26.

FERNANDEZ, FRANK. 1965. Indian tribal societies: tribal or peasant? MS., 13 pp. (Mimeo.)

FISCHEL, WALTER J. 1962. Cochin in Jewish history. American Academy for Jewish Research, Proceedings 30:37–59.

———. 1967. The exploration of the Jewish antiquities of Cochin on the Malabar Coast: a historical-critical survey. Journal of the American Oriental Society 87:30–51.

FORTES, MEYER. 1958. Introduction. *In* The developmental cycle in domestic groups, pp. 1–14. Cambridge Papers in Social Anthropology, No. 1. Cambridge: University Press.

FOSTER, GEORGE. M. 1965. Peasant society and the image of limited good. American Anthropologist 67:293–315.

———. 1966. Foster's reply to Kaplan, Saler and Bennett. American Anthropologist 68:210–214.

FOX, RICHARD G. 1967. Resiliency and culture in the Indian caste system: the Umar of U. P. The Journal of Asian Studies 26:575–587.

FREED, STANLEY A. 1963a. Fictive leadership in an Indian village. Ethnology 2:86–103.

———. 1963b. An objective method for determining the collective caste hierarchy of an Indian village. American Anthropologist 65:879–891.

FREED, STANLEY A. AND RUTH S. FREED. 1964. Spirit possession as illness in a North Indian village. Ethnology 3:152–171.

———. 1966. Unity in diversity in the celebration of cattle-curing rites in a North Indian village: a study in the resolution of conflict. American Anthropologist 68:673–692.

FREEDMAN, MAURICE. 1962.The family in China: past and present. Pacific Affairs 34:323–336.

FRYKENBERG, ROBERT ERIC. 1963. Traditional processes of power in South India: an historical analysis of local influence. Indian Economic and Social History Review 1:1–21.

FUCHS, STEPHEN. 1950. The children of Hari: a study of the Nimar Balahis in the Central Provinces of India. Vienna: Verlag Herold.

———. 1960. The Gond and the Bhumia of Eastern Mandla. New York, Bombay: Asia Publishing House.

FUKUTAKE, TADASHI, TSUTOMU OUCHI, AND CHIE NAKANE. 1964. The socio-economic structure of the Indian village. Tokyo: Institute of Asian Economic Affairs.

FÜRER-HAIMENDORF, CHRISTOPH VON. 1943. The Chenchus: jungle folk of the Deccan. London. Macmillan.

———. 1945. The Reddis of the Bison Hills. London: Macmillan.

———. 1967a. Morals and merit: a study of values and social controls in South Asian societies. Chicago: University of Chicago Press.

———. 1967b. The position of tribal populations in modern India. *In* India and Ceylon: unity and diversity, P. Mason, editor, pp. 182–222. New York: Oxford University Press.

GADGIL, D. R. 1965. Women in the working force in India. Bombay: Asia Publishing House.

GAIT, E. A. 1913. Census of India, 1911, Volume 1, part 1. Report. Calcutta: Government Printing Office.

GALANTER, MARC. 1963. Law and caste in modern India. Asian Survey 3:544–559.

———. 1964. Hindu law and the development of the modern Indian legal system. Mimeographed, 32 pp.

———. 1965. Legal materials for the study of Modern India. Appendix: Hindu law and the modern Indian legal system. Mimeographed. The College, University of Chicago.

———. 1966a. The modernization of law. *In* Modernization: the dynamics of growth, M. Weiner, editor, pp. 153–165. New York: Basic Books.

GALANTER, MARC. 1966b. The problem of group membership: some reflections on the judicial view of Indian society. *In* Class, status and power, R. Bendix and S. M. Lipset, editors, pp. 628–640. Second edition. New York: Free Press. (Reprinted from The Journal of the Indian Law Institute, 1962, 4:331–358.)

GANDHI, MOHANDAS K. 1940. An autobiography or the story of my experiments with truth. (Translated from the original in Gujarati by Madadev Desai.) Ahmedabad: Navajivan Publishing House.

GANGARADE, K. D. 1963. Dynamics of a panchayat election. Avard (Journal of the Association of Voluntary Agencies for Rural Development, New Delhi) 5:5–8.

———. 1964. Conflicting value system and social case work. The Journal of Social Work 24:247–256.

GARDNER, PETER M. 1966. Symmetric respect and memorate knowledge: the structure and ecology of individualistic culture. Southwestern Journal of Anthropology 22:389–415.

GEERTZ, CLIFFORD. 1960. The Javanese kikaji: the changing role of a cultural broker. Comparative Studies in Society and History 2:228–249.

———. 1963. Agricultural involution: the process of ecological change in Indonesia. Berkeley and Los Angeles: University of California Press.

GHURYE, G. S. 1953. Indian sadhus. Bombay: The Popular Book Depot.

———. 1959. The scheduled tribes. Second edition. Bombay: The Popular Book Depot.

———. 1960. After a century and a quarter: Lonikand then and now. Bombay: The Popular Book Depot.

———. 1961. Class, caste and occupation. Bombay: The Popular Book Depot.

GIDEON, HELEN. 1962. A baby is born in the Punjab. American Anthropologist 64:1220–1234.

GIST, NOEL P. 1953. Mate selection and mass communication in India. Public Opinion Quarterly 17:481–495.

———. 1954. Occupational differentiation in South India. Social Forces 33:129–138.

———. 1955. Selective migration in South India. Sociological Bulletin 4:147–160.

GNANAMBAL, K. 1960. Ethnography of Gannapur. Cyclostyled, 127 pp.

GOODE, WILLIAM. J. 1963. World revolution and family patterns. New York: The Free Press of Glencoe.

GOPALASWAMI, R. A. 1953. Census of India, 1951, Volume 1, India, part 1–A. Report. New Delhi: Government of India Press.

GORE, M. S. 1961. The husband-wife and the mother-son relationships. Sociological Bulletin 11:91–102.

———. 1965. The traditional Indian family. *In* Comparative family systems, M. F. Nimkoff, editor, pp. 209–231. Boston: Houghton Mifflin.

———. 1968. Urbanization and family change. Bombay: Popular Prakashan.

GOUGH, E. KATHLEEN. 1955. The social structure of a Tanjore village. *In* Village India, M. Marriott, editor, pp. 36–52. Chicago: University of Chicago Press.

———. 1956. Brahmin kinship in a Tamil village. American Anthropologist 58:384–853.

———. 1960. Caste in a Tanjore village. *In* Aspects of caste in South India, Ceylon, and North-West Pakistan, E. R. Leach, editor, pp. 11–60. Cambridge Papers in Social Anthropology, No. 2. Cambridge: Cambridge University Press.

———. 1961a. Mappilla: North Kerala. *In* Matrilineal kinship, David M. Schneider and Kathleen Gough, editors, pp. 415–442. Berkeley and Los Angeles: University of California Press.

———. 1961b. Nayar: Central Kerala. *In* Matrilineal kinship, David M. Schneider and Kathleen Gough, editors, pp. 298–384. Berkeley and Los Angeles: University of California Press.

———. 1963. Indian nationalism and ethnic freedom. *In* The concept of freedom in anthropology, David Bidney, editor, pp. 170–207. The Hague: Mouton.

———. 1965. A note on Nayar marriage. Man 65:8–11.

GOULD, HAROLD A. 1958. The Hindu jajmani system: a case of economic particularism. Southwestern Journal of Anthropology 14:428–437.

———. 1959. The peasant village: centrifugal or centripetal? The Eastern Anthropologist 13:3–16.

———. 1960a. Castes, outcastes and the sociology of stratification. International Journal of Comparative Sociology 1:220–238.

———. 1960b. The micro-demography of marriages in a North Indian area. Southwestern Journal of Anthropology 16:476–491.

GOULD, HAROLD A. 1961a. A further note on village exogamy in North India. Southwestern Journal of Anthropology 17:297–300.

———. 1961b. Sanskritization and westernization: a dynamic view. The Economic Weekly 13:945–950.

———. 1961c. Some preliminary observations concerning the anthropology of industrialization. The Eastern Anthropologist 14:30–47.

———. 1964. The jajmani system of North India: its structure, magnitude and meaning. Ethnology 3:12–41.

———. 1965a. Lucknow rickshawallas: the social organization of an occupational category. International Journal of Comparative Sociology 6:24–47.

———. 1965b. Modern medicine and folk cognition in village India. Human Organization 24:201–208.

———. 1965c. True structural change and the be time dimension in the North Indian kinship system. *In* Studies on Asia, R. K. Sakai, editor, pp. 179–192. Lincoln: University of Nebraska Press.

GRAY, R. M. AND MANILAL C. PAREKH. 1931. Mahatma Gandhi: an essay in appreciation (fourth impression). Calcutta: Association Press.

GRIGSON, W. V. 1949. The Maria Gonds of Bastar. London: Oxford University Press.

GROSS, NEAL, W. S. MASON, AND A. W. MCEACHERN. 1958. Explorations in role analysis: studies of the school superintendency role. New York: John Wiley.

GUHA, UMA. 1965. Caste among rural Bengali Muslims. Man in India 45: 167–169.

GUHA, UMA ANL M. N. KAUL. 1953. A group distance study of the castes of U. P. Bulletin of the Department of Anthropology 2:11–32. Calcutta: Department of Anthropology, Government of India.

GUMPERZ, JOHN J. 1957. Some remarks on regional and social language differences in India. *In* Introducing Indian in liberal education, Milton Singer, editor, pp. 69–79. Chicago: University of Chicago Press.

———. 1958. Dialect differences and social stratification in a North Indian village. American Anthropologist 60: 668–682.

———. 1961. Speech variation and the study of Indian civilization. American Anthropologist 63:976–988.

———. 1964. Religion and social communication in village North India. The Journal of Asian Studies 32:89–98.

GUMPERZ, JOHN J. AND C. M. NAIM. 1960. Formal and informal standards in the Hindi regional language area. International Journal of American Linguistics 26:92–118.

———. 1964. Religion and social communication in village North India. The Journal of Asian Studies 23:89–97.

GUPTA, RAGHURAJ. 1956. Caste ranking and inter-caste relations among the Muslims of a village in North Western U. P. Eastern Anthropologist 10:30–42.

GUPTA, T. R. 1961. Rural family status and migration: study of a Punjab village. The Economic Weekly 13:1597–1603.

GUPTE, B. A. 1919. Hindu holidays and ceremonials. Second edition, revised. Calcutta and Simla: Thacker, Spink and Co.

HARDGRAVE, ROBERT L., JR. 1964. Caste in Kerala: a preface to the elections. The Economic Weekly 16:1841–1847.

———. 1966. Varieties of political behavior among Nadars of Tamilnad. Asian Survey 6:614–621.

HARPER, EDWARD B. 1957a. Hoylu: a belief relating justice and the supernatural. American Anthropologist 59:801–816.

———. 1957b. Shamanism in South India. Southwestern Journal of Anthropology 13:267–287.

———. 1959a. A Hindu village pantheon. Southwestern Journal of Anthropology 15:227–234.

———. 1959b. Two systems of economic exchange in village India. American Anthropologist 61:760–778.

———. 1961. Moneylending in the village economy of the Malnad. The Economic Weekly 13:169–177.

———. 1963. Spirit possession and social structure. *In* Anthropology on the march, Bala Ratnam, editor, pp. 165–197. Madras: The Book Center.

———. 1964. Ritual pollution as an integrator of caste and religion. The Journal of Asian Studies 2:151–197.

———. 1968. Social consequences of an "unsuccessful" low caste movement. *In* Social mobility in the caste system in India, James Silverberg, editor, pp. 36–65. Comparative Studies in society and history. Supplement III. The Hague: Mouton.

HARPER, EDWARD B. AND LOUISE G. HARPER. 1959. Political organization in a Karnataka village. *In* Leadership and political institutions in India, Richard L. Park and Irene Tinker, editors, pp. 453–469. Princeton: Princeton University Press.

HARRISON, SELIG S. 1956a. Caste and the Andhra communists. The American Political Science Review 50:378–404.

———. 1960 India: the most dangerous decades. Princeton: Princeton University Press.

HAYE, CHOWDHRY ABDUL. 1966. The Freedom movement in Mewat and Dr. K. M. Ashraf. *In* Kunwar Mohammed Ashraf: an Indian scholar and revolutionary, 1903–1962, Horst Krüger, editor, pp. 291–336. Berlin: Akademic-Verlag.

HAZLEHURST, LEIGHTON W. 1966. Entrepreneurship and the merchant castes in a Punjab city. Duke University Program in Comparative Studies in Southern Asia. Monograph No. 1.

HEIN, NORVIN. 1958. The Rām Līlā. Journal of American Folklore 71:279–304.

HITCHCOCK, JOHN T. 1958. The idea of the martial Rājpūt. Journal of American Folklore 71: 216–223.

———. 1959. Dominant caste politics in a North Indian village. Mimeographed, 59 pp.

———. 1960. Surat Singh: head judge. *In* In the company of Man, J. B. Casagrande, editor, pp. 234–272. New York: Harper and Brothers.

HOCKINGS, PAUL. 1965. Cultural change among the Badagas: a community of South India. Doctoral dissertation, University of California, Berkeley.

HOMANS, GEORGE C. 1950. The human group. New York: Harcourt, Brace and World.

HONIGMANN, JOHN J. 1960a. South Asian research: a village of renown. Research Previews 7:7–14.

———. 1960b. Education and career specialization in a West Pakistan village of renown. Anthropos 55:825–840.

HOPKINS, EDWARD W. 1884. The ordinances of Manu. London: Trübner and Co.

HSU, FRANCIS L. K. 1963. Clan, caste, club. Princeton: D. Van Nostrand Company.

HUTTON, J. H. 1941. Primitive tribes. *In* Modern India and the West, L. S. S. O'Malley, editor, pp. 417–444. London: Oxford University Press.

———. 1961. Caste in India: its nature, function and origin. Third edition. Bombay: Oxford University Press.

IBBETSON, DENZIL. 1916. Panjab castes. (Reprint of chapter in Census of the Panjab, 1883.) Lahore: Government Printing Press.

INGALLS, DANIEL H. H. 1954. Authority and law in ancient India. Journal of the American Oriental Society, Supplement, No. 17:34–45.

———. 1958. The Brahmin tradition. Journal of American Folklore 71:209–215.

IRSCHIK, EUGENE F. 1969. Politics and social conflict in South India: the non-Brahmin movement, Tamil separatism 1916–1929. Berkeley and Los Angeles: University of California Press.

ISHWARAN, K. 1965. Kinship and distance in rural India. International Journal of Comparative Sociology 6:81–94.

ISAACS, HAROLD R. 1965. India's ex-untouchables. New York: The John Day Company.

IYER, L. K. ANANTHA KRISHNA (ANANTAKRISHNA AYYAR, L. K.). 1909–1912. The Cochin tribes and castes. Madras: Government Printing Press.

IZMIRLIAN, HARRY JR. 1964. Caste, kin and politics in a Punjab village. Doctoral dissertation, University of California, Berkeley.

JACKSON, A. V. WILLIAMS, editor. 1907. History of India. Volume 9. London: The Grolier Society.

JAGALPURE, L. B. AND K. D. KALE. 1938. Sarola Kasar: Study of a Deccan village in the famine zone. Ahmednagar: L. B. Jagalpure.

JAY, EDWARD J. 1959. The anthropologist and tribal warfare. Journal of Social Research (Ranchi) 2:82–89.

———. 1961a. A comparison of tribal and peasant religion with special reference to the Hill Maria Gonds. Mimeographed, 60 pp.

———. 1961b. Social values and economic change: the Hill Marias of Bastar. The Economic Weekly 13:1369–1372.

———. 1964. The concepts of 'field' and 'network' in anthropological research. Man in India 64:137–139.

KALIDASA. 1959. Shakuntala and other writings. (Translated by Arthur W. Ryder.) New York: E. P. Dutton.

KANE, PANDURANG VAMAN. 1941. History of Dharmaśāstra. Volume 2, part 1. Poona: Bhandarkar Oriental Research Institute.

———. 1946. History of Dharmaśāstra. Volume 3. Poona: Bhandarkar Oriental Research Institute.

KANNAN, C. T. 1963. Intercaste and inter-community marriages in India. Bombay: Allied Publishers.

KAPADIA, K. M. 1947. Hindu kinship: an important chapter in Hindu social history. Bombay: The Popular Book Depot.

———. 1956. Rural family patterns. Sociological Bulletin 5:111–126.

———. 1957. A perspective necessary for the study of social change in India. Sociological Bulletin 6:43–60.

———. 1958. Marriage and family in India. Second edition. London: Oxford University Press.

———. 1959. The family in transition. Sociological Bulletin 8:68–99.

———. 1961. The growth of townships in South Gujarat: Maroli Bazar. Sociological Bulletin 10:69–87.

———. 1962. Caste in transition. Sociological Bulletin 12:73–90.

———. 1963. The passing of the traditional society. Fiftieth Indian Science Congress, Delhi.

———. 1966. Marriage and family in India. Third edition. Bombay: Oxford University Press.

KARAKA, DOSABHAI FRAMJI. 1884. History of the Parsis. Volume 1. London: Macmillan.

KARANDIKAR, S. V. 1929. Hindu exogamy. Bombay: Taraporevala.

KARIM, A. K. NAZMUL. 1956. Changing society in India and Pakistan. Dacca: Oxford University Press.

KARVE, IRAWATI. 1953. Kinship organization in India. Poona, Deccan College Monograph Series, No. 11. Poona: Deccan College.

———. 1958a. The Indian village. Bulletin of the Deccan College 18:73–106.

———. 1958b. What is caste? (1) Caste as extended kin. The Economic Weekly 10:125–138.

———. 1961. Hindu society: an interpretation. Poona: Sangam Press.

———. 1962. On the road: a Maharashtrian pilgrimage. Journal of Asian Studies 22:13–30.

———. 1965. Kinship organization in India. Second revised edition. Bombay: Asia Publishing House.

KARVE, IRAWATI AND Y. B. DAMLE. 1963. Group relations in village community. Deccan College Monograph Series. Poona: Deccan College.

KARVE, IRAWATI AND VISHNU MAHADEO DANDEKOR. 1951. Anthropometric measurements of Mahārāshtra. Deccan College Monograph Series, No. 8. Poona: Deccan College.

KAUTILYA. 1961. Kautilya's Arthasāstra. (Translated by R. Shamasastry.) Seventh edition. Mysore: Mysore Printing and Publishing House.

KENNEDY, BETH C. 1954. Rural-urban contrasts in parent-child relations in India. Indian Journal of Social Work 15:162–174. (Reprinted by the Bureau of Research and Publications, Tata Institute of Social Science, Chembur, Bombay.)

KENNEDY, MELVILLE T. 1925. The Chaitanya movement. London and Calcutta: Oxford University Press.

KETKAR, SHRIDHAR VENKATESH. 1909. The history of caste in India. Ithaca: Taylor and Carpenter.

KHADDURI, MAJID AND H. J. LIEBESNY. 1955. Law in the Middle East. Volume 1. Washington: The Middle East Institute.

KHAN, KHAN AHMAD HASAN. 1931. Census of India, 1931, Volume 17. Punjab.

KHARE, R. S. 1960. The Kanya-Kubja Brahmins and their social organization. Southwestern Journal of Anthropology 16:348–367.

KHEDKAR, VITHAN KRISHNAJI. 1959. The divine heritage of the Yadavas. Allahabad: Parmanand.

KLASS, MORTON. 1966. Marriage rules in Bengal. American Anthropologist 68:951–970.

KOCHAR, V. K. 1963. Socio-cultural denominators of domestic life in a Santal village. The Eastern Anthropologist 16:167–180.

KOLENDA, PAULINE MAHAR. 1958. Changing caste ideology in a North Indian village. Journal of Social Issues 14:51–65.

———. 1959. A multiple scaling technique for caste ranking. Man in India 39: 127–147.

———. 1963. Toward a model of the Hindu jajmani system. Human Organization 22:11–31.

———. 1964. Religious anxiety and Hindu fate. The Journal of Asian Studies 23:71–82.

———. 1967. Regional differences in Indian family structure. *In* Regions and regionalism in South Asian Studies: an exploratory study, R. I. Crane, editor, pp. 147–226. Duke University Program in Comparative Studies in Southern Asia. Monograph No. 5.

———. 1968. Region, caste, and family structure: a comparative study of the Indian "joint" family. *In* Structure and change in Indian society, M. Singer and B. S. Cohn, editors. Chicago: Aldine Publishing Company.

KOSAMBI, D. D. 1955. The basis of ancient Indian history (2). Journal of the American Oriental Society 75:226–237.

———. 1965. The culture and civilization of ancient India in historical outline. London: Routledge and Kegan Paul.

KOTHARI, RAJNI AND RUSHIKESH MARU. 1965. Caste and secularism in India: case study of a caste federation. The Journal of Asian Studies 25:33–50.

KRIPALANI, KRISHNA. 1962. Rabindranath Tagore: a biography. New York: Grove Press.

KROEBER, A. L. 1944. Configurations of culture growth. Berkeley and Los Angeles: University of California Press.

———. 1947. Culture groupings in Asia. Southwestern Journal of Anthropology 3:322–330.

KUDRYAVTSEV, M. K. 1964. On the role of Jats in North India's ethnic history. Journal of Social Research (Ranchi) 7:126–135.

———. 1965. Musul'manskie kasty (Muslim castes). *In* Kasty v Indii (Castes in India), G. G. Kotovskii, editor, pp. 214–232. Moscow: Akademiia Nauk SSSR. Institut Narodov Azii.

LACEY, W. G. 1933. Census of India, 1931, Volume 7, part 1. Report, Bihar and Orissa. Patna: Government Printing Press.

LALL, R. MANOHAR. 1933. Among the Hindus: a study of Hindu festivals. Cawnpore: Minerva Press.

LAMBERT, RICHARD D. 1958. Factory workers and the non-factory population in Poona. The Journal of Asian Studies 18:21–42.

———. 1962. The impact of urban society upon village life. *In* India's urban future, Roy Turner, editor, pp. 117–140. Berkeley and Los Angeles: University of California Press.

———. 1963. Workers, factories, and social change in India. Princeton, New Jersey: Princeton University Press.

LEACH, EDMUND R. 1960. Introduction: What should we mean by caste? *In* Aspects of caste in South India, Ceylon and North-West Pakistan, E. R. Leach, editor. Cambridge Papers in Social Anthropology, No. 2. Cambridge: Cambridge University Press.

———. 1967. Caste, class and slavery: the taxonomic problem. *In* Caste and race: comparative approaches, A. de Reuck and J. Knight, editors, pp. 17–27. London: J. and A. Churchill.

LEACOCK, SETH AND DAVID G. MANDELBAUM. 1955. A nineteenth century development project in India: the cotton improvement program. Economic Development and Cultural Change 3:334–351.

LEARMONTH, A. T. A. AND A. M. LEARMONTH. 1958. The regional concept and national development. The Economic Weekly 10:153–156.

LENSKI, GERHARD. 1966. Power and privilege: a theory of social stratification. New York: McGraw-Hill.

LEVINSON, DANIEL J. 1959. Role, personality and social structure in the organizational setting. Journal of Abnormal and Social Psychology 58:170–180.

LEWIS, OSCAR. 1955. Peasant culture in India and Mexico: a comparative analysis. *In* Village India, M. Marriott, editor, pp. 145–170. Chicago: University of Chicago Press.

———. 1958. Village life in Northern India: studies in a Delhi village. Urbana: University of Illinois Press.

LEWIS, OSCAR AND VICTOR BARNOUW. 1956. Caste and the jajmani system in a North Indian village. Scientific Monthly 83:66–81.

LEWIS, OSCAR. (assisted by Victor Barnouw and Harvant Dhillon)

———. 1956. Aspects of land tenure and economics in a North Indian village. Economic Development and Cultural Change 4:279–302.

LOKANATHAN, P. S. 1965a. All India rural household survey. Vol. II. New Delhi: National Council of Applied Economic Research.

———. 1965b. All India rural household survey, 1962. A summary statement on income distribution by rural and All India. Occasional Paper 13. National Council of Applied Economic Research. New Delhi.

LYNCH, OWEN M. 1967. Rural cities in India: continuities and discontinuities. *In* India and Ceylon: unity and diversity, Philip Mason, editor, pp. 142–158. London: Oxford University Press.

MCCLELLAND, DAVID C. 1961. The achieving society. Princeton: D. Van Nostrand.

MCCORMACK, WILLIAM. 1956. Changing leadership of a Mysore village. Mimeographed, 9 pp.

———. 1957. Mysore villager's view of change. Economic Development and Cultural Change 5:257–262.

———. 1958a. The forms of communication in Vīraśaiva religion. Journal of American Folklore 71:325–335.

McCormack, William. 1958b. Sister's daughter marriage in a Mysore village. Man in India 38:34–48.
———. 1959. The development of Hindu law during the British period. Mimeographed, 65 pp.
———. 1960. Social dialects in Dharwar Kannada. International Journal of American Linguistics 26:79–91.
———. 1963. Lingayats as a sect. Journal of the Royal Anthropological Institute 93:59–71.
McCrindle, J. W. 1877. Ancient India as described by Megasthenes and Arrian. London: Trübner.
———. 1901. Ancient India as described in classical literature. London: Constable.
McDonald, Ellen E. 1968. The modernization of communication: vernacular publishing in nineteenth-century Maharashtra. Asian Survey 8:589–606.
MacLachlan, Morgan E. and Alan R. Beals. 1966. The internal and external relationships of a Mysore chiefdom. Journal of Asian and African Studies 1:87–99.
Madan, B. K. 1951. The economics of the Indian village and its implications in social structure. International Social Science Bulletin 3:813–822. Paris: UNESCO.
Madan, T. N. 1962a. The Hindu joint family. Man 62:88–89.
———. 1962b. The joint family: a terminological clarification. International Journal of Comparative Sociology 3:7–16.
———. 1962c. Is the Brahmanic gotra a grouping of kin? Southwestern Journal of Anthropology 18:59–77.
———. 1965. Family and kinship: a study of the Pandits of rural Kashmir. New York: Asia Publishing House.
———. 1968. Caste and development. Economic and Political Weekly 4:285–290.
Mahajan, Mehr Chand. 1963. Looking back. Bombay: Asia Publishing House.
Mahar, Pauline M. (see Kolenda, Pauline Mahar)
Maine, Henry. 1861. Ancient law. London: J. Murray.
———. 1881. Village-communities in the East and West. Fourth edition. London: John Murray.
Majumdar, Dhirendra Nath. 1944. The fortunes of primitive tribes. Lucknow: Universal Publishers.
———. 1958a. Caste and communication in an Indian village. Bombay: Asia Publishing House.
———. 1958b. Races and cultures of India. Bombay: Asia Publishing House.
Majumdar, D. N., M. C. Pradhan, C. Sen, and S. Misra. 1955. Inter-caste relations in Gohanakallan, a village near Lucknow. The Eastern Anthropologist 8:191–214.
Majumdar, R. C. 1960. The classical accounts of India. Calcutta: Firma K. L. Mukhopadhyay.
Malaviya, H. D. 1956. Village panchayats in India. New Delhi: Economic and Political Research Department. All India Congress Committee.
Mandelbaum, David. G. 1938. Polyandry in Kota society. American Anthropologist 40:574–583.
———. 1939. The Jewish way of life in Cochin. Jewish Social Studies 1:423–460.
———. 1941. Social trends and personal pressures. *In* Language, culture and personality, L. Spier, A. I. Hallowell, and S. Newman, editors, pp. 219–238. (Reprinted in Anthropology of folk religion, C. Leslie, editor, 1960, pp. 221–255. New York: Vintage Books.)
———. 1947. Hindu-Moslem conflict in India. The Middle East Journal 1:369–385.
———. 1948. The family in India. Southwestern Journal of Anthropology 4: 123–139.
———. 1949. Population problems in India and Pakistan. Far Eastern Survey 18:283–287.
———. 1954a. Fertility of early years of marriage in India. *In* Professor Ghurye felicitation volume, K. M. Kapadia, editor, pp. 150–168. Bombay: The Popular Book Depot.
———. 1954b. Form, variation and meaning of a ceremony. *In* Method and perspective in anthropology, R. F. Spencer, editor, pp. 60–102. Minneapolis: University of Minnesota Press.
———. 1955. The world and the world view of the Kota. *In* Village India, M. Marriott, editor, pp. 223–254. Chicago: University of Chicago Press.
———. 1956. The Kotas in their social setting. *In* Introduction to the civilization of India, Milton Singer, editor. Chicago: University of Chicago Press.
———. 1959a. Concepts and methods in the study of caste. The Economic Weekly Annual, Volume 2:145–149.
———. 1959b. Social uses of funeral rites. *In* The meaning of death, H. Feifel, editor, pp. 189–217. New York: MacGraw-Hill.

MANDELBAUM, DAVID. G. 1960. A reformer of his people. *In* In the company of man, J. Casagrande, editor, pp. 273–308. New York: Harper.

———. 1962. Review of M. Marriott, caste ranking and community structure in five regions of India and Pakistan. Journal of Asian Studies 21:434–436.

———. 1964. Introduction: process and structure in South Asian religion. *In* Religion in South Asia, Edward B. Harper, editor, pp. 5–20. Seattle: University of Washington Press. (Also published in The Journal of Asian Studies 23:5–20.)

———. 1965. Alcohol and culture. Current Anthropology 6:281–292.

———. 1966. Transcendental and pragmatic aspects of religion. American Anthropologist 68:1174–1191.

MARRIOTT, MCKIM. 1955a. Western medicine in a village of Northern India. *In* Health, culture and community: case studies of public reactions to health programs, Benjamin D. Paul, editor, pp. 239–268. New York: Russell Sage Foundation.

———. 1955b. Little communities in an indigenous civilization. *In* Village India, M. Marriott, editor, pp. 171–222. Chicago: University of Chicago Press.

———. 1959a. Changing channels of cultural transmission in Indian civilization. *In* Intermediate societies, social mobility and communication, Verne Ray, editor, pp. 66–74. Seattle: American Ethnological Society.

———. 1959b. Interactional and attributional theories of caste ranking. Man in India 39:92–107.

———. 1960. Caste ranking and community structure in five regions of India and Pakistan. Poona: G. S. Press.

———. 1962. Communication: rejoinder to Metraux. Journal of Asian Studies 21:263–265.

MARTEN, J. T. 1924. Census of India, 1921, Volume 1, part 1. Report. Calcutta: Government Printing Press.

MARTIN, MONTGOMERY. 1838. The history, antiquities, topography and statistics of Eastern India. London: Allen and Co.

MATHUR, K. S. 1958a. Caste and occupation in a Malwa village. Eastern Anthropologist 12:47–61.

———. 1958b. The Indian village: is it a structural unity? Journal of Social Research (Ranchi) 1:50–53.

———. 1959. Caste and occupation in a Malwa village. Eastern Anthropologist 12:47–61.

———. 1964. Caste and ritual in Malwa village. Bombay: Asia Publishing House.

MAYER, ADRIAN C. 1952. Land and society in Malabar. London: Oxford University Press.

———. 1956. Some hierarchical aspects of caste. Southwestern Journal of Anthropology 12:117–144.

———. 1957. An Indian community development block revisited. Pacific Affairs 30:35–46.

———. 1958a. The dominant caste in a region of Central India. Southwestern Journal of Anthropology 14:407–427.

———. 1958b. Local government elections in a Malwa village. Eastern Anthropologist 9:189–202.

———. 1960. Caste and kinship in Central India: a village and its region. Berkeley and Los Angeles: University of California Press.

———. 1962. System and network: an approach to the study of political process in Dewas. *In* Indian anthropology, T. N. Madan and G. Sarana, editors, pp. 266–278. Bombay: Asia Publishing House.

MAYER, ALBERT AND ASSOCIATES. 1958. Pilot project, India: the story of rural development at Etawah, U. P. Berkeley and Los Angeles: University of California Press.

MAYNARD, H. J. 1917. Influence of the Indian king upon the growth of caste. Journal of the Panjab Historical Society 6:88–100.

MENCHER, JOAN. 1963. Growing up in South Malabar. Human Organization 22:54–65.

———. 1965. The Nayars of South Malabar. *In* Comparative family systems, M. F. Nimkoff, editor, pp. 163–191. Boston: Houghton, Mifflin.

———. 1966. Kerala and Madras: a comparative study of ecology and social structure. Ethnology 5:135–179.

MENCHER, JOAN P. AND HELEN GOLDBERG. 1967. Kinship and marriage regulations among the Namboodiri Brahmins of Kerala. Man n.s. 2:87–106.

METCALFE, CHARLES T. 1833. Appendix 84 to the report of the Select Committee of the House of Commons on the affairs of the East India Company. III-Review, pp. 328–334. Minute on the Upper Provinces. London, 1833. (House of Commons sessional papers 1831–32. XI, superscribed enumeration pp. 692–698.)

MILLER, ERIC J. 1954. Caste and territory in Malabar. American Anthropologist 56:410–420.

MILLER, ERIC J. 1960. Village structure in North Kerala. *In* India's villages, M. N. Srinivas, editor, pp. 42–55. Second revised edition. London: Asia Publishing House.

MINTURN, LEIGH. 1963. The Rājpūts of Khalapur, Part II, child training. *In* Six cultures: studies of child rearing, B. B. Whiting, editor, pp. 301–361. New York and London: John Wiley and Sons.

MINTURN, LEIGH AND JOHN T. HITCHCOCK. 1963. The Rājpūts of Khalapur, India. *In* Six cultures: studies of child rearing, B. B. Whiting, editor, pp. 203–361. New York and London: John Wiley and Sons.

———. 1966. The Rājpūts of Khalapur, India. New York: John Wiley. (Six cultures series, Volume 3.)

MINTURN, LEIGH AND WILLIAM W. LAMBERT. 1964. Mothers of six cultures. New York: John Wiley and Sons.

MISRA, SATISH C. 1964. Muslim communities in Gujarat. New York: Asia Publishing House.

MITRA, A. 1965. Levels of regional development in India, being part 1 of General Report on India. Census of India, 1961, Volume 1, part 1-A (i). Delhi: Government of India Press.

MONGA, VEENA. 1967. Social mobility among the Potters: report of a caste conference. Economic and Political Weekly 2:1047–1055.

MOON, PENDEREL. 1945. Strangers in India. New York: Reynal and Hitchcock.

MORGAN, LEWIS H. 1871. Systems of consanguinity and affinity of the human family. Washington: Smithsonian Institution.

MORRIS, MORRIS DAVID. 1960. Caste and the evolution of the industrial workforce in India. Proceedings of the American Philosophical Society 104:124–133.

———. 1967. Values as an obstacle to economic growth in South Asia, The Journal of Economic History 27:588–607.

MORRIS-JONES, W. H. 1967. The government and politics of India. Anchor Books edition. New York: Doubleday and Co.

MORRISON, WILLIAM A. 1959. Family types in Badlapur: an analysis of a changing institution in a Maharashtrian village. Sociological Bulletin 8:45–67.

MUKERJI, A. B. 1957. The bi-weekly market at Modinagar. The Indian Geographer 2:271–293.

MÜLLER, FREDRICH MAX. 1868. Chips from a German workshop. Volume 2. Second edition. London: Longmans, Green and Co.

MULLICK, BULLORAM (BALARAMA MALLIKA). 1882. Essays on the Hindu family in Bengal. Calcutta: W. Newman and Co.

MURDOCK, GEORGE P. 1949. Social structure. New York: Macmillan.

MYRDAL, GUNNAR. 1968. Asian drama: an inquiry into the poverty of nations. New York: Random House (Pantheon).

NADEL, S. F. 1951. The foundations of social anthropology. London: Cohen and West.

———. 1954. Caste and government in primitive society. Journal of the Anthropological Society of Bombay, pp. 9–22.

NAIR, KUSUM. 1963. Blossoms in the dust. New York: Frederick A. Praeger.

NANDI, PROSHANTA KUMAR. 1965. A study of caste organizations in Kanpur. Man in India 45:84–99.

NANDI, SANTIBHUSHAN AND D. S. TYAGI. 1961. Forms of villages. *In* Peasant Life in India, pp. 1–6. Anthropological Survey of India, Calcutta. Memoir No. 8.

NANDIMATH, S. C. 1942. A handbook of Virasaivism. Bangalore: Basel Mission Press.

NARAIN, DHIRENDRA. 1957. Hindu character (a few glimpses). Bombay: University of Bombay. Sociology Series No. 8.

NARAYAN, JAYAPRAKASH. 1958. Toward a new society. New Delhi: Congress for Cultural Freedom.

NATH, KAMLA. 1965. Women in the new village. The Economic Weekly 17:813–816.

NATH, V. 1961. The village and the community. *In* India's Urban Future, Roy Turner, editor, pp. 139–154. Berkeley and Los Angeles: University of California Press.

———. 1962. Village, caste and community. The Economic Weekly. 14:1877–1882.

NAVALAKHA, SURENDRA KUMAR. 1959. The authority structure among the Bhumij and Bhil: a study in historical causations. The Eastern Anthropologist 13:27–40.

NAYAR, UNNI. 1952. My Malabar. Bombay: Hind Kitabs.

NEALE, WALTER C. 1962. Economic change in rural India: land tenure and reform in Uttar Pradesh, 1800–1955. New Haven and London: Yale University Press.

Neale, Walter C., Harpal Singh and Jai Pal Singh. 1965. Kurali market: a report on the economic geography of marketing in Northern Punjab. Economic Development and Cultural Change 13:129–168.

Nehru, Jawaharlal. 1941. Toward freedom: the autobiography of Jawaharlal Nehru. New York: John Day.

———. 1946. The discovery of India. New York: John Day.

Nehru, S. S. 1932. Caste and credit in the rural area. London:

Neill, Stephen. 1934. Builders of the Indian church. London: Edinburgh House Press.

Newell, W. H. 1963. Inter-caste marriage in Kuzti village. Man 63:55–57.

Nicholas, Ralph W. 1961. Economics of family types in two West Bengal villages. The Economic Weekly 13:1057–1060.

———. 1962. Villages of the Bengal Delta: a study of ecology and peasant society. Doctoral dissertation, University of Chicago.

———. 1963. Ecology and village structure in deltaic West Bengal. The Economic Weekly 15:1185–1196.

———. 1965. Factions: a comparative analysis. *In* Political systems and the distribution of power, Max Gluckman and Fred Eggan, editors, pp. 21–61. London: Tavistock Publications; New York: Frederick A. Praeger. A. S. A. Monograph No. 2.

———. 1966. Segmentary factional political systems. *In* Political anthropology, M. S. Swartz, V. W. Turner, and A. Tinden, editors, pp. 49–59. Chicago: Aldine Publishing Co.

———. 1967. Ritual hierarchy and social relations in rural Bengal. Contributions to Indian Sociology, New Series 1:56–83.

Nicholas, Ralph W. and Tarashish Mukopadhyay. 1962. Politics and law in two West Bengal villages. Bulletin of the Anthropological Survey of India 11:15–39.

Niehoff, Arthur. 1958. A study of matrimonial advertisements in North India. The Eastern Anthropologist 12:73–86.

Nikitin, Afanasy. 1960. Khozhenie za tri moria Afanasiia Nikitina, 1466–1472. (Afanasy Nikitin's voyage beyond three seas, 1466–1472.) B. Kumkes, editor. Moscow. (Text in Russian, Hindi and English.)

O'Malley, L. S. S. 1913. Census of India, 1911, Volume 5, part 1. Report, Bengal, Bihar, Orissa and Sikkim. Calcutta: Bengal Secretariat Book Depot.

———. 1934. India's social heritage. Oxford: Clarendon Press.

———. 1941. Modern India and the West. London: Oxford University Press.

Opler, Morris E. 1956. The extensions of an Indian village. *In* The Indian village: a symposium. The Journal of Asian Studies 16:5–10.

———. 1958. Spirit possession in a rural area of Northern India. *In* Reader in comparative religion, W. A. Lessa and E. Z. Vogt, editors, pp. 553–566. Evanston: Row, Peterson.

———. 1959a. Family, anxiety and religion in a community of North India. *In* Culture and mental health, Marvin K. Opler, editor, pp. 273–289. New York: Macmillan.

———. 1959b. The place of religion in a North Indian village. Southwestern Journal of Anthropology 15:219–226.

———. 1960. Recent changes in family structure in an Indian Village. Anthropological Quarterly 35:93–97.

Opler, Morris E. and Rudra Datt Singh. 1952. Two villages of eastern Uttar Pradesh (U. P.), India: an analysis of similarities and differences. American Anthropologist 54:179–190.

Orans, Martin. 1965. The Santal: a tribe in search of a great tradition. Detroit: Wayne State University Press.

———. 1968. Maximizing in jajmaniland. American Anthropologist 70:875–897.

Orenstein, Henry. 1959. Leadership and caste in a Bombay village. *In* Leadership and political institutions in India, Richard L. Park and Irene Tinker, editors, pp. 415–426. Princeton: Princeton University Press.

———. 1960. Irrigation, settlement pattern and social organization. *In* Selected papers of the fifth international congress of anthropological and ethnological sciences, Philadelphia, Anthony F. C. Wallace, editor, pp. 318–323. Philadelphia: University of Pennsylvania Press.

———. 1961. The recent history of the extended family in India. Social Problems 8:341–350.

———. 1962. Exploitation or function in the interpretation of jajmani. Southwestern Journal of Anthropology 18:302–316.

ORENSTEIN, HENRY. 1963. Caste and the concept "Marātha" in Maharashtra. The Eastern Anthropologist 16:1–9.

———. 1965a. Gaon: conflict and cohesion in an Indian village. Pinceton: Princeton University Press.

———. 1965b. Notes on the ecology of irrigation agriculture in contemporary peasant societies. American Anthropologist 67:1529–1532.

———. 1965c. The structure of Hindu caste values: a preliminary study of hierarchy and ritual defilement. Ethnology 4:1–15.

ORR, W. G. 1947. A sixteenth-century Indian mystic. London and Redhill: Lutterworth Press.

PANIKKAR, K. M. 1956. Hindu society at the cross roads. Second revised edition. Bombay: Asia Publishing House.

———. 1961. Hindu society at the cross roads. Third edition. Bombay: Asia Publishing House.

PARSONS, TALCOTT. 1953. A revised analytical approach to the theory of social stratification. *In* Class, status and power, R. Bendix and S. M. Lipset, editors, pp. 92–128. Glencoe: Free Press.

———. 1961. An outline of the social system. *In* Theories of society, Talcott Parsons *et al*., editors, Volume 1, pp. 30–79. New York: Free Press of Glencoe.

PATNAIK, NITYANANDA. 1953. Study of the weekly market at Barpali. Geographical Review of India 15:19–31.

———. 1960a. Assembly of the Mahanayaka Sudras of Puri District, Orissa. *In* Data on caste: Orissa, pp. 81–118. Anthropological Survey of India, Calcutta. Memoir No. 7.

———. 1960b. Service relationship between barbers and villagers in a small village in Ranpur. The Economic Weekly 12:737–742.

PATNAIK, NITYANANDA AND A. K. RAY. 1960. Oilmen or Teli. *In* Data on caste: Orissa, pp. 9–80. Anthropological Survey of India. Memoir No. 7.

PATTERSON, MAUREEN L. P. 1958. Intercaste marriage in Maharashtra. The Economic Weekly 10:139–142.

PILLAI, N. KUNJAN. 1932. Census of India 1931, Travancore Vol. 28, Part I. Trivandrum: Government Press.

PLANALP, JACK MILAN. 1956. Religious life and values in a North Indian village. Doctoral dissertation, Cornell University.

POCOCK, DAVID F. 1954. The hypergamy of the Patidars. *In* Professor Ghurye felicitation volume, K. M. Kapadia, editor, pp. 195–204. Bombay: The Popular Book Depot.

———. 1955. The movement of castes. Man 55:71–72.

———. 1957a. Bases of faction in Gujerat. British Journal of Sociology 8:295–317.

———. 1957b. Inclusion and exclusion: a process in the caste system of Gujerat. Southwestern Journal of Anthropology 13:19–31.

———. 1962. Notes on jajmani relationships. Contribution to Indian Sociology 6:78–95.

———. 1964. The anthropology of time reckoning. Contributions to Indian Sociology 7:18–29.

POFFENBERGER, THOMAS. 1964. The use of praise. University of Baroda, Department of Child Development. Working papers in Indian personality. MS., 6 pp.

POFFENBERGER, THOMAS AND BIHARI J. PANDYA. n.d. The effect of the dowry system on endogamy among Leva Patidar in a low status village. MS., 8 pp.

PRABHU, PANDHARI NATH. 1954. Hindu social organization. Bombay: The Popular Book Depot.

PRADHAN, M. C. 1965. The Jats of Northern India: their traditional political system. The Economic Weekly 17:1821–1824, 1855–1864.

———. 1966. The political system of the Jats of Northern India. Bombay: Oxford University Press.

PRASAD, RAJENDRA. 1957. Autobiography. Bombay: Asia Publishing House.

PYARELAL (NAIR). 1965. Mahatma Gandhi, Volume 1: the early phase. Ahmedabad: Navajivan Publishing House.

RAGHAVAN, V. 1965. Variety and integration in the pattern of Indian culture. Far Eastern Quarterly 15:33–41.

RAGHUVANSHI, V. P. S. 1966. The institution and working of caste in the latter part of the eighteenth century from European sources. *In* Kunwar Mohammad Ashraf: an Indian scholar and revolutionary 1903–1962, Horst Krüger, editor, pp. 147–175. Berlin: Akademie Verlag.

RAJ, HILDA. 1959. Persistence of caste in South India: an analytic study of the Hindu and Christian Nadar. Doctoral dissertation, American University, Washington, D.C.

RANADE, RAMABAI. 1938. Himself: the autobiography of a Hindu lady. (Translated and adapted by Katherine van Akin Gates from a book wirtten in the Marathi language by Mrs. Ramabai Ranade.) New York, Toronto: Longmans, Green and Co.

RANGACHARI, DIWAN BAHADUR K. 1931. The Sri Vaishnava Brahmans. Bulletin of the Madras Government Museum. Volume 1, part 2. Madras: Government Press.

RAO, C. V. H. 1966. The fifth steel plant: Andhra's case. The Economic and Political Weekly 1:534.

RAO, M. S. A. 1955. Symposium on caste and joint family: in Kerala. Sociological Bulletin 4:122–129.

———. 1957. Social change in Malabar. Bombay: Popular Book Depot.

———. 1961. The jajmani system. The Economic Weekly 13:877–878.

———. 1964. Caste and the Indian army. Economic Weekly 16:1439–1443.

RAO, V. L. S. PRAKASA AND L. S. BHAT. 1960. Planning regions in the Mysore State: the need for readjustment of district boundaries. Calcutta: Indian Statistical Institute. Regional studies No. 1.

RAO, Y. V. LAKSHMANA. 1966. Communication and development: a study of two Indian villages. Minneapolis: University of Minnesota Press.

RATH, R. AND N. C. SIRCAR. 1960a. The cognitive background of six Hindu caste groups regarding the low caste untouchables. Journal of Social Psychology 51:295–306.

———. 1960b. The mental pictures of six Hindu caste groups about each other as reflected in verbal stereotypes. Journal of Social Psychology 51:277–293.

REDDY, N. S. 1952. Transition in caste structure in Andhra Desh with particular reference to depressed castes. Doctoral dissertation. University of Lucknow, Lucknow.

———. 1955. Functional relations of Lohars in a North Indian village. The Eastern Anthropologist 8:129–140.

———. 1963. Spatial variance of custom in Andhra Pradesh. *In* Anthropology on the march, Bala Ratnam, editor, pp. 283–296. Madras: The Book Centre.

REDFIELD, ROBERT. 1955. The little community: viewpoints for the study of a human whole. Chicago: University of Chicago Press.

RENOU, LOUIS. 1953. Religions of ancient India. London: Athlone Press.

RETZLAFF, RALPH H. 1962. Village government in India. London: Asia Publishing House.

REYES-HOCKINGS, AMELIA. 1966. The newspaper as surrogate marriage broker in India. Sociological Bulletin 15:25–39.

RISLEY, H. H. 1892. The tribes and castes of Bengal. Calcutta: Bengal Secretariat Press.

———. 1915. The people of India. Second edition. London: W. Thacker and Co.

RIVERS, W. H. R. 1921. The origin of hypergamy. *In* The Journal of the Bihar and Orissa Research Society 8:9–24.

ROOKSBY, R. L. 1956. Status in a plural society: seminar on social and cultural problems of India, School of Oriental and African Studies, University of London. Mimeographed, 15 pp.

ROSS, AILEEN. D. 1961. The Hindu family in its urban setting. Toronto: University of Toronto Press.

ROSSER, COLIN. 1960. A "hermit" village in Kulu. *In* India's villages, M. N. Srinivas, editor, pp. 77–89. Second revised edition. London: Asia Publishing House.

ROWE, WILLIAM L. 1960. The marriage network and structural change in a North Indian community. Southwestern Journal of Anthropology 16:299–311.

———. 1963. Changing rural class structure and the jajmani system. Human Organization 22:41–44.

———. 1964. Caste, kinship, and association in urban India. MS., 24 pp.

———. 1968. The new Cauhāns: a caste mobility movement in North India. *In* Social mobility in the caste system in India, James Silverberg, editor, pp. 66–67. Comparative Studies in Society and History, Supplement III. The Hague: Mouton.

ROY BURMAN, B. K. 1960. Basic concepts of tribal welfare and tribal integration. Journal of Social Research 3:16–24.

ROY, RAMASHRAY. 1963. Conflict and co-operation in a North Bihar Village. Journal of the Bihar Society 49:297–315.

ROY, SARAT CHANDRA. 1934. Caste, race and religion in India: inadequacies of the current theories of caste. Man in India 14:75–220.

RUDOLPH, LLOYD I. 1965. The modernity of tradition: the democratic incarnation of caste in India. The American Political Science Review 59:975–989.

RUDOLPH, LLOYD I. AND SUSANNE H. RUDOLPH. 1960. The political role of India's caste associations. Pacific Affairs 33:5–22.

———. 1967. The modernity of tradition: political development in India. Chicago: University of Chicago Press.

RUDOLPH, SUSANNE HOEBER. 1965. Self-control and political potency: Gandhi's asceticism. The American Scholar 35:79–97.

RUSSELL, R. V. AND RAI BAHADUR HĪRA LĀL. 1916. The tribes and castes of the Central Provinces of India. Volume 1. London: Macmillan and Co.

SACHCHIDANANDA. 1964. Culture change in tribal Bihar. Calcutta: Bookland Private Limited.

———. 1965 Profiles of tribal culture in Bihar. Calcutta: Firma K. L. Mukhopadhyay.

SANGAVE, VILAS ADINATH. 1959. Jaina community: a social survey. Bombay: Popular Book Depot.

SARMA, JYOTIRMOYEE. 1951. Formal and informal relations in the Hindu joint household of Bengal. Man in India 31:51–71.

———. 1955. A village in West Bengal. *In* India's villages, pp. 161–179. West Bengal Government Press.

———. 1959. The secular status of castes. Eastern Anthropologist 12:87–106.

———. 1960. A village in West Bengal. *In* India's villages, M. N. Srinivas, editor, pp. 180–201. Second revised edition. London: Asia Publishing House.

———. 1964. The nuclearization of joint family households in West Bengal. Man in India 44:193–206.

SCHWARTZBERG, JOSEPH E. 1965. The distribution of selected castes in the North Indian plains. Geographical Review 55:477–495.

———. 1967. Prolegomena to the study of South Asian regions and regionalism. *In* Regions and regionalism in South Asia studies: an exploratory study. R. I. Crane, editor, pp. 85–111. Duke University Program in Comparative Studies in Southern Asia. Mimeograph No. 4.

SEN, LALIT KUMAR. 1965. Family in four Indian villages. Man in India 45:1–16.

SENART, EMILE. 1930. Caste in India. London: Methuen.

SENGUPTA, SUNIL. 1958. Family organization in West Bengal: its nature and dynamics. The Economic Weekly 15:384–389.

SHAH, A. M. 1955a. Caste, economy and territory in the Central Panchmahals. Journal of the Maharaja Sayajirao University of Baroda 4:65–91.

———. 1955b. A dispersed hamlet in the Panchmahals. The Economic Weekly 7:109–116.

———. 1959. Social anthropology and the study of historical societies. The Economic Weekly 11:953–962.

———. 1964a. Basic terms and concepts in the study of family in India. Indian Economic and Social History Review 1:1–36.

———. 1964b. Political systems in eighteenth century Gujarat. Enquiry (Delhi) 1:83–95.

SHAH, A. M. AND R. G. SHROFF. 1958. The Vahāvancā Bārots of Gujarat: a caste of geneologists and mythographers. Journal of American Folklore 71:246–276.

SHAH, B. V. 1960. Joint family system: an opinion survey of Gujarati students. The Economic Weekly 12:1867–1870.

———. 1964. Social change and college students of Gujarāt. Baroda: M.S. University of Baroda.

SHAHANI, SAVITRI. 1961. The joint family: a case study. The Economic Weekly 13:1823–1828.

SHARMA, KAILAS N. 1956a. Urban contacts and cultural change in a little community. Doctoral dissertation, Lucknow University, Lucknow.

———. 1956b. Hypergamy in theory and practice. The Journal of Research 3:18–32.

———. 1961a. Hindu sects and food patterns in North India. Journal of Social Research 4:47–58.

———. 1961b. Occupational mobility of castes in a North Indian village. Southwestern Journal of Anthropology 17:146–164.

———. 1963. Panchayat leadership and resource groups. Sociological Bulletin 12:47–52.

SIEGEL, BERNARD J. AND ALAN R. BEALS. 1960a. Pervasive factionalism. American Anthropologist 62:394–417.

———. 1960b. Conflict and factionalist dispute. The Journal of the Royal Anthropological Institute 90:107–117.

SILVERBERG, JAMES 1959. Caste-ascribed 'status' versus caste-irrelevant roles. Man in India 39:148–162.

SINGER, MILTON. 1956a. Cultural values in India's economic development. Annals of the American Academy of Political and Social Science 305:81–91.

———. 1956b. Introduction. *In* The Indian village: a symposium. The Journal of Asian Studies 16:3–5.

———. 1958. The great tradition in a metropolitan center: Madras. Journal of American Folklore 71:347–388.

———. 1963. The Radha-Krishna bhajans of Madras City. History of Religions 2:183–226.

———. 1964. The social organization of Indian civilization. Diogenes, Winter issue 1964, pp. 84–119.

———. 1966. The modernization of religious beliefs. *In* Modernization, Myron Weiner, editor, pp. 55–67. New York: Basic Books, Inc.

———. 1968. The Indian joint family in modern industry. *In* Structure and change in Indian society, Milton Singer and Bernard S. Cohn, editors, pp. 423–452. Chicago: Aldine Publishing Co.

———. [1969]. Modernization, ritual and belief among industrial leaders in Madras City. *In* Modernization in India: studies in social-cultural aspects, Amar Kumar Singh, editor. Bombay: Asia Publishing House.

SINGH, AMAR KUMAR. 1967. Hindu culture and economic development in India, Conspectus 3:9–32.

SINGH, INDERA P. 1958. A Sikh village. Journal of American Folklore 71:479–503.

———. 1961. Religion in Daleke: a Sikh village. Journal of Social Research (Ranchi) 4:191–219.

SINGH, INDERA P. AND H. L. HARIT. 1960. Effects of urbanization in a Delhi suburban village. Journal of Social Research (Ranchi) 3:38–43.

SINGH, KHUSHWANT. 1953. The Sikhs. London: George Allen and Unwin.

———. 1963–1966. A history of the Sikhs. Two volumes. Princeton: Princeton University Press.

SINGH, RUDRA DATT. 1956. The Unity of an Indian village. *In* The Indian village: a symposium. The Journal of Asian Studies 16:10–19.

SINGH, YOGENDRA. 1959. Group status of factions in rural community. Journal of Social Sciences 2:57–67.

SINHA, D. P. 1963. The role of the Phariya in tribal acculturation in a Central Indian market. Ethnology 2:170–179.

———. 1967. The Phariya in an inter-tribal market. Economic and Political Weekly 2:1373–1378.

SINHA, SURAJIT. 1957a. The media and nature of Hindu-Bhumij interactions. Journal of the Asiatic Society: Letters and Science 23:23–37.

———. 1957b. Tribal cultures of peninsular India as a dimension of little tradition in the study of Indian civilization: a preliminary statement. Man in India 37:93–118.

———. 1958a. Changes in the cycle of festivals in a Bhumij village. Journal of Social Research (Ranchi) 1:24–49.

———. 1958b. Tribal cultures of peninsular India as a dimension of little tradition in the study of Indian civilization: a preliminary statement. Journal of American Folklore 71:504–518.

———. 1959. Bhumij-Kshatriya social movement in South Manbhum. Bulletin of the Department of Anthropology, Government of India 8:9–32.

———. 1962. Status formation and Rajput myth in tribal Central India. Man in India 42:35–80.

———. 1963. Levels of economic initiative and ethnic groups in Pargana Barabhum. The Eastern Anthropologist 16:65–74.

———. 1965. Tribe-caste and tribe-peasant continua in Central India. Man in India 45:57–83.

———. 1967. Caste in India: its essential pattern of socio-cultural integration. *In* Caste and race: comparative approaches, A. de Reuck and J. Knight, editors, pp. 92–105. London: J. and A. Churchill.

SINHA, SURAJIT, BIMAR KUMAR DASGUPTA, AND HEMENDRA NATH BANERGEE. 1961. Agriculture, crafts and weekly markets of South Manbhum. Bulletin of the Anthropological Survey of India. Volume 10, No. 1.

SMITH, DONALD EUGENE. 1963. India as a secular state. Princeton: Princeton University Press.

SMITH, MARIAN W. 1952. The Misal: a structural village group of India and Pakistan. American Anthropologist 54:41–56.

SMITH, WILFRED CANTWELL. 1957. Islam in modern history. Princeton: Princeton University Press.

SOVANI, N. V. 1961. The urban social situation in India. Artha Vijnana 3:85–224.

SOVANI, N. V., D. P. APTE AND R. G. PENDSE. 1956. Poona: a re-survey: the changing pattern of employment and earnings. Poona: Gokhale Institute of Politics and Economics. Publication No. 34.

SPATE, O. H. K. 1954. India and Pakistan: a general and regional geography. New York: E. P. Dutton.

SRINIVAS, M. N. 1942. Marriage and family in Mysore. Bombay: New Book Co.

SRINIVAS, M. N. 1952a. Religion and society among the Coorgs of South India. Oxford: Oxford University Press.
———. 1952b. A joint family dispute in a Mysore village. Journal of the Maharaja Sayarijao University of Baroda 1:7–31.
———. 1954. A caste dispute among washermen of Mysore. Eastern Anthropologist 7:148–168.
———. 1955a. The social structure of a Mysore village. *In* India's villages, pp. 15–32. Calcutta: West Bengal Government Press.
———. 1955b. The social system of Mysore village. *In* Village India, M. Marriott, editor, pp. 1–35. Chicago: University of Chicago Press.
———. 1956a. A note on sanskritization and westernization. Far Eastern Quarterly 15:481–496.
———. 1956b. Regional differences in customs and village institutions. The Economic Weekly 8:215–220.
———. 1959a. The dominant caste in Rampura. American Anthropologist 61:1–16.
———. 1959b. The case of the potter and the priest. Man in India 39:190–209.
———. 1962. Caste in modern India and other essays. Bombay: Asia Publishing House.
———. 1965. Social structure. The National Gazeteer 1:1–77.
———. 1966. Social change in modern India. Berkeley and Los Angeles: University of California Press.
SRINIVAS, M. N. AND ANDRÉ BÉTEILLE. 1964. Networks in Indian social structure. Man 64:165–168.
SRINIVAS, M. N. AND A. M. SHAH. 1960. The myth of the self-sufficiency of the Indian village. The Economic Weekly 12:1375–1378.
SRIVASTAVA, RAM P. 1962. Tribe-caste mobility in India and the case of Kumaon Bhotias. London: Department of Anthropology, School of Oriental and African Studies, University of London. Mimeographed, 80 pp.
SRIVASTAVA, S. K. 1963. The process of desanskritisation in village India. *In* Anthropology on the march, Bala Ratnam, editor, pp. 263–267. Madras: The Book Center.
STAAL, J. F. 1963. Sanskrit and sanskritization. The Journal of Asian Studies 22:261–275.
STEED, GITEL P. 1955. Notes on an approach to a study of personality formation in a Hindu village in Gujarat. *In* Villiage India, M. Marriott, editor, pp. 102–144. Chicago: University of Chicago Press.
STEIN, BURTON. 1960. The economic function of the medieval South Indian temple. Journal of Asian Studies 19:163–176.
———. 1967. Comment on Bernard S. Cohn's paper. *In* Regions and regionalism in South Asian studies, R. I. Crane, editor, pp. 41–47. Duke University Program in Comparative Studies in Southern Asia. Monograph No. 4.
———. 1968. Social mobility and medieval South Indian Hindu sects. *In* Social mobility in the caste system in India, James Silverberg editor, pp. 78–94. Comparative Studies in Society and History, Supplement III. The Hague: Mouton.
STEPHEN, LESLIE. 1921. Henry Sumner Maine. *In* The Dictionary of National Biography, Vol. 12. pp. 787–790. London: Humphrey Milford.
STEVENSON, H. N. L. 1954. Status evaluation in the Hindu caste system. Journal of the Royal Anthropological Institute 84:45–65.
STEVENSON, MRS. SINCLAIR. 1920. The rites of the twice-born. London: Humphrey Milford.
STRIZOWER, SCHIFRA. 1959. Jews as an Indian caste. Jewish Journal of Sociology 1:43–57.
STROOP, MILDRED LUSCHINSKY. 1960. The impact of some recent Indian government legislation on the women of an Indian village. Mimeographed, 9 pp.
TANDON, PRAKASH. 1961. Punjabi century, 1857–1947. London: Chatto and Windus.
THAPAR, ROMILA. 1966. A history of India. Volume 1. Baltimore: Penguin Books.
THOOTHI, N. A. 1935. The Vaishnavas of Gujarat. Bombay, London: Longmans, Green and Co.
THURSTON, EDGAR. 1909. Castes and tribes of Southern India. Seven volumes. Madras: Government Press.
TILAK, LAKSHMIBAI. 1950. I follow after. (Translated by E. Josephine Inster.) Madras: Oxford University Press.
TRIVEDI, R. K. 1965. Fairs and festivals: Gujarat. Census of India, 1961, Volume 5, part 7-B.
TUMIN, MELVIN M. 1967. Social stratification. Englewood Cliffs, New Jersey: Prentice-Hall.
ULLAH, INAYAT. 1958. Caste, patti and faction in the life of a Punjab village. Sociologus n.s. 8:170–186.
UNDERHILL, M. M. 1921. The Hindu religious year. Calcutta: Association Press.

UNNI, K. RAMAN. 1956. Visiting husbands in Malabar. Journal of the Maharaja Sayajirao University of Baroda 5:37–56.

VAN BUITINEN, J. A. B. 1966. On the archaism of the Bhāgavata Purāna. *In* Krishna: myths, rites and attitudes. Honolulu: East-West Center Press.

VIDYARTHI, LALITA P. 1961. The sacred complex in Hindu Gaya. Bombay: Asia Publishing House.

———. 1967. Some preliminary observations on inter-group conflict in India: tribal, rural and industrial. Journal of Social Research 10:1–10.

VOGT, EVON Z. 1960. On the concepts of structure and process in cultural anthropology. American Anthropologist 62:18–33.

VREEDE-DE STUERS, CORA. 1962. Mariage préférential chez les Musalmans de l'Inde du Nord. Revue de Sud-est Asiatique 1962:141–152.

———. 1963. Terminologie de parenté chez les Musalmans Ashrāf de l'Inde Nord. Bijragen tot de taal-, land- en Volkenkunde 119:254–266.

WALLACE, ANTHONY. 1961. The psychic unity of human groups. *In* Studying personality cross-culturally, Bert Kaplan, editor, pp. 129–164. Evanston: Row, Peterson and Co.

WARD, WILLIAM. 1822. A view of the history, literature and mythology of the Hindoos. London: Kingsbury, Parbury and Allen.

WATTERS, THOMAS. 1904. On Yuan Chwang's travels in India, 629–645 A.D., T. W. Rhys Davids and S. W. Bushnell, editors. London: Royal Asiatic Society.

WEBER, MAX. 1958. The religion of India. Glencoe, Illinois: The Free Press.

WEINER, MYRON. 1967. Party building in a new nation. Chicago: University of Chicago Press.

WHEELER, MORTIMER. 1953. The Cambridge history of India. Supplementary volume: the Indus civilization. Cambridge: Cambridge University Press.

WHITING, BEATRICE B. 1963. Introduction. *In* Six cultures: studies of child marriage, B. B. Whiting, editor, pp. 1–13. New York: John Wiley.

———. 1965. Sex identity, conflict and physical violence: a comparative study. *In* The ethnography of law, Laura Nader, editor. American Anthropologist 67 (part 2): 123–140.

WILLIAMS, A. HYATT. 1950. A psychiatric study of Indian soldiers in the Arakan. The British Journal of Medical Psychology 23:130–181.

WINSLOW, J. C. 1923. Narayan Vaman Tilak: the Christian poet of Maharashtra. Calcutta: Association Press.

WISER, WILLIAM H. 1936. The Hindu jajmani system: a socio-economic system inter-relating members of a Hindu village community in service. Lucknow: Lucknow Publishing House.

WISER, WILLIAM H. AND CHARLOTTE VIALL WISER. 1963. Behind mud walls. Berkeley and Los Angeles: University of California Press.

WOLF, ERIC. R. 1966. Kinship, friendship and patron-client relations in complex societies. *In* The social anthropology of complex societies, Michael Banton, editor. London: Tavistock Publications.

WRIGHT, THEODORE P., JR. 1966. The Muslim League in South Indian since independence: a study in minority group political strategies. The American Political Science Review 60:579–599.

YALMAN. NUR. 1962. The structure of Sinhalese kindred: a re-examination of the Dravidian terminology. American Anthropologist 62:548–575.

———. 1967. Under the Bo tree: studies in caste, kinship and marriage in the interior of Ceylon. Berkeley and Los Angeles: University of California Press.

Index